CRITICAL PERSPECTIVES ON CHRISTIAN EDUCATION

a reader on the aims, principles and philosophy of Christian education

CRITICAL PERSPECTIVES ON CHRISTIAN EDUCATION

a reader on the aims, principles and philosophy of Christian education

edited by

Jeff Astley
Director
North of England Institute for Christian Education,
Durham, England

and

Leslie J Francis
D J James Professor of Pastoral Theology,
Trinity College, Carmarthen,
and St David's University College, Lampeter, Wales

Gracewing.

First Published in 1994
Gracewing
Fowler Wright Books
Southern Avenue, Leominster
Herefordshire HR6 0QF

Gracewing Books are distributed

In New Zealand by
Catholic Supplies Ltd
80 Adelaide Rd
Wellington
New Zealand

In Australia by
Charles Paine Pty
8 Ferris Street
North Parramatta
NSW 2151 Australia

In U.S.A. by
Morehouse Publishing
P.O. Box 1321
Harrisburg
PA 17105
U.S.A.

In Canada by
Meakin and Associates
Unit 17, 81 Auriga Drive
Nepean, Ontario, KZE 7Y5
Canada

ISBN 0 85244 254 8

Typesetting by Action Typesetting Limited, Gloucester
Printed by The Cromwell Press, Melksham, Wiltshire

Contents

Preface

Jeff Astley and Leslie J Francis

Critical Perspectives on Christian Education is the first volume of a trilogy of readers designed to explore key issues in Christian education. The other two volumes illustrate *Theological Perspectives on Christian Education* and *Psychological Perspectives on Christian Education*. We believe that these readers will further the theory and practice of Christian education.

Both editors have a long standing interest in and commitment to Christian education. We believe that this debate is best advanced in an interdisciplinary, international and ecumenical context. In particular we have become increasingly aware of the important contribution being made to the field of Christian education during the past two decades through seminal articles published in scholarly journals in the USA, Canada, Australia and Europe, as well as within the UK. Our aim in this trilogy of readers is to re-publish collections of these articles and thereby to make them more readily accessible to a wider readership. In so doing we hope both to advance the quality of scholarly debate about Christian education and to promote good practice and practical application.

The task of editing this reader has been appropriately located within the North of England Institute for Christian Education in Durham, and the Centre for Theology and Education at Trinity College in Carmarthen. Both institutions are church foundations, concerned to undertake research in and promote the development of Christian education.

In this reader and the next we have been assisted in our editorial task by an international group of scholars who have nominated journal articles from the past twenty-five years or so that they regard as being worthy of consideration. Our thanks are due particularly to Brian V Hill (Murdoch, Western Australia), John M Hull (Birmingham, England), T H McLaughlin (Cambridge, England), Charles F Melchert (Lancaster, Pennsylvania, USA), Basil Mitchell (Oxford, England), Allen J Moore (Claremont, California, USA), Mary Elizabeth Moore (Claremont, California, USA), Gabriel Moran (New York, New York, USA), Karl Ernst Nipkow (Tübingen, Germany), Graham Rossiter (Strathfield, New South Wales, Australia), Elmer J Thiessen (Medicine Hat, Alberta, Canada), Michael Warren (Jamaica, New York, USA), Derek Webster (Hull, England) and John H Westerhoff, III (Atlanta, Georgia, USA). We are most grateful to these colleagues for helping us overcome the inevitable limitations of our own interests, sympathies and knowledge, although the final responsibility for the editorial selection remains our own. Select bibliographies of articles on the philosophy and theology of Christian education, drawing on these nominations, are included at the end of the appropriate volume.

We also wish to record our thanks to those who have helped in the processes of collating resources, compiling materials, checking references, copy-editing text, word processing, and seeking permissions, especially Diane Drayson, Dorothy Greenwell, Alma Griffiths, Sue Jones and Anne Rees. Finally, we are truly delighted that so many internationally renowned authors and publishers have wished to join us in making possible the publication and dedication of this reader to mark the retirement of the Right Reverend David Jenkins, Lord Bishop of Durham, as chairman of the North of England Institute for Christian Education.

Jeff Astley
Leslie J Francis
January 1994

Foreword

David Jenkins

This is a remarkably comprehensive volume which should prove to be a veritable 'enquire within' to all who are concerned to think hard, practically and hopefully about Christian education in today's very mixed, pluralistic, and uncertain societies. The range of articles, the authoritative nature of their selection (the editors were assisted by an international panel of students in the field), and the attached bibliographies, mean that experts in the subject (or subjects) can widen their own range and deepen their knowledge. On the other hand, people who have a more 'lay' concern for Christian education − troubled teachers of religion for instance, or church representatives, school heads, and others responsible for a religious element in education, or worried members of curriculum committees who are under pressures from dogmatic believers, dogmatic unbelievers and people of wider religious concerns − all can find much material for information, consultation and reflection.

The expert work of compilation which this volume represents is, in itself, creative. For systematic reflection about Christian education today, drawing on available material, is urgently required. It is particularly required in societies of the Western tradition which claim (or have substantial numbers of people still claiming) that they are basically 'Christian'. What are the appropriate forms of, and role for, Christian education in 'post-Christendom' societies, where the old claims of the obvious importance and dominance of Christianity are clearly socially false, however nostalgically they may be clung to?

How do Christian educators fit into, and live in, clearly secular societies or societies which claim another religious tradition as their basis? And what ought Christian educators to be trying to do in all the societies which seem to have lost their way as to any common religious, cultural or citizenship identity, but are increasingly recognising the vacuum at the heart of society about values, common hopes and sources, or resources, for common citizenship?

Taken-for-granted approaches still linger. ('Of course Christianity should be the major part of the required religious syllabus in our schools; we are a Christian society.') But it is absolutely clear that they can no longer be taken for granted. For more and more citizens deny the premise or simply ignore the issue entirely.

So this is just the time to collect good, reflective, professional and carefully argued material across the whole spectrum of 'Perspectives

on Christian Education'. It must be done in a *critical* way —
especially by those who are concerned that Christian education
should be appropriate for, and relevant to, our confused world and
confused societies — whether they view religion as a member of a
faith community, or whether they dismiss religious approaches, or
cannot come to terms with them.

The editors, therefore, are to be congratulated on the enterprise
and energy of their production. The message to all concerned about
religious and Christian education must be: 'For God's sake, think!'
Otherwise our religious and Christian claims and practices will
become less and less relevant, or more and more liable to be dismissed
as nostalgia, hankering after lost religious influence and power, or a
simple superstitious survival. The challenge is as great as the
opportunity. This book provides an excellent range of material to
assist in positive engagement with both the challenges and the
opportunities.

David Dunelm
Auckland Castle
22 April 1994

PART ONE

Definitions, aims and approaches

Definitions, aims and approaches: an overview
Jeff Astley

This overview offers a general introduction to the debate about the meaning and nature of Christian education. References to articles in the reader are indicated in brackets.

Christian education analysed

Any sort of perspective on the practice of Christian education needs to begin with some attempt to define the meaning, and map the reference, of the term. This is not as easy as it sounds, as the phrase has been used in a variety of different ways.[1] In this reader one major focus of interest is on Christian education understood quite generally as designating those processes by which people learn to become Christian, and to be more Christian (see article 2.4). This is a very broad usage based on a very broad understanding of education.[2] Many authors, however, prefer to restrict Christian education, and cognate terms, to the learning (ordinarily facilitated by some sort of teaching) of Christian beliefs with understanding, often in a critical, reflective way. Such an account of Christian education is usually based on a more restricted, normative account of what counts as ('real') education (see articles 1.1, 1.3, 1.4, 6.1).[3]

This formative, or formative-critical, education into Christianity is often distinguished from education *about* Christianity and other religions, which is seen by many educationalists as a proper subject in public education contexts. In Britain and many other countries this latter subject has traditionally been designated 'religious education' (or 'RE'). In recent decades this has been treated as a 'non-confessional' (that is to say non-evangelistic and non-nurturing) study of the phenomena of Christianity and other world faiths, a study that is mainly concerned with developing understanding (albeit an empathetic understanding) and evaluation, and is not aimed at religious commitment (see especially articles 2.2, 2.4, 3.1).[4] The debate over the justification of this form of teaching about religion in 'secular schooling' has, by comparison and contrast, helped to highlight the distinctive nature of Christian education as the church's task of Christian nurture or formation.

Unfortunately, other countries (notably the USA) have adopted the term 'religious education' (sometimes 'Christian religious education') to designate the more confessional educational activity of inducting people into religion, and many prefer it to the (for them more Protestant) term 'Christian education' or the (traditional Catholic) word 'catechesis'. The reader of this reader, which draws articles from the United States as well as from other English-speaking countries, will need to be alert to these differences of usage.[5]

'Christian education' is a term that is also used to denote a reflective Christian perspective on the practice of general education, including education about religion, usually in the context of school or higher education. Such a 'Christian philosophy of education' may give rise to a Christian approach to, or 'scheme of', general education.[6] (Articles 1.1, 3.3, 6.2, 6.3 and 7.2 in this reader touch on topics relevant to these very different understandings of the phrase Christian education.)

Aims and Approaches

Confessional education into Christianity may be served by a variety of approaches. Some argue that its main thrust should be a process of intentional socialisation, formation or enculturation within the faith community, where people learn not only Christian beliefs but also the attitudes, values and dispositions to act that are appropriate to the Christian (see articles 1.5, 2.4 and section 4).[7] There is also a great deal of Christian learning in the church that is not intentionally engineered by any Christian educator, but flows from the 'hidden curriculum' of the church's worship, social fellowship and other activities.[8]

Others are chary of describing all the above processes as Christian *education*, as we have seen. They would claim not only that education always implies teaching, but also that it should be concerned primarily with cognitive understanding (article 1.4) and, many would add, should include a critical evaluation of Christian belief (article 1.5). Even Christian formation needs to incorporate 'critical openness'; and should precede, allow, or be complemented by critical education that leads to 'Christian criticism' (article 5.3).[9]

This discussion takes up a familiar distinction between:[10]

  a. a formative Christian education, the purpose of which is
      the adoption and deepening of Christian beliefs, values,
      worldview and lifestyle (a Christian 'culture'); and
  b. a critical education into Christianity which stresses
      instead the development in the learner of a critical anal-
      ysis and evaluation of the church's claims in the light of
      her own experience and understanding.

Critical Christian education tends to come in two different
forms, as it may be motivated *either* by a concern for a mor-
al/political/social critique and understanding of Christianity,
particularly as espoused by liberation educators (see articles
5.1, 5.4), *or* by the sort of critical education beloved of liberal
educators, which puts more stress on the learner's rationality
and intellectual autonomy, that is on her 'thinking critically for
herself' (see article 5.3 and the articles in part two.)[11]

Of course the difference between formative and critical
education in Christianity may often be only a difference of
emphasis, and many authors (including those featured in this
volume) acknowledge the importance of both formative and
critical learning outcomes in teaching Christianity. The 'interpretation' or 'dialogue' model for Christian education, which
has become so popular in current theory and practice, is one
attempt to combine at least some aspects of the two approaches
(see section 5).[12]

Learner and Teacher

It is appropriate at this point to offer some analysis of the role
of the Christian educator and the correlative understanding of
the Christian learner. Christian educators tend to operate on
the basis of models (that is systematically applied, extended
metaphors) drawn from other parts of religious or secular life,
often operating with several of these models at the same time.
As many of the models are mutually complementary this is
usually appropriate; but sometimes there is a tension between
the models, and mixing them can have the consequence of
disrupting educational practice.

First, the Christian educator is often viewed as *priest*.
The priest 'is a community person by virtue of his ordi-
nation', and those adopting this model see the Christian education they offer as essentially a community or congregational

affair.[13] They are concerned primarily with the building up of
the church, and this includes the encouraging of the *whole*
church's own educational function as teacher of Christianity
to the world. Although the individual is also an object of
Christian education, this is never in isolation from the body.
The 'priestly-Christian educator' will be most at home with
a Christian education that takes place in the context of the
worship of the whole Christian assembly.[14] (See section 4.)

Second, the *pastor*-model for Christian educators is
somewhat different. Pastoral work is usually much more
of an individual thing: a one-to-one relationship.[15] When
Christian education is practised on this model, the *individual's*
growth in faith, belief or Christian activity becomes the main
target of effort. Of course there are pastors *and* pastors, and
the pastor-model in religious education may operate more
directively (as a spiritual director, 'elder' or confessor) or be
more non-directive (as in pastoral counselling). Pastors may
see themselves as nurturing-gardeners, or as both guides and
exploring-fellow-pilgrims on a mutual journey of search and
discovery, but they will always recognise their responsibility
for the care of their learners.[16] (Again see section 4.)

Third, the above models shade into a view of the Christian
educator as *interpreter*. Such a teacher helps to make the connections between the Christian tradition and the learner's own
experience and, like the uprights of a two-rail fence, provides
the necessary support for both.[17] It is only by thus connecting
the learners 'with the past places of their own and church lives'
that the Christian educator can be called 'a teacher of history'.[18] Such a 'hermeneutical' role for the Christian educator
is now frequently distinguished from the model of the notorious preacher who stands six feet above contradiction, foisting
his or her own interpretation on the listeners' experience (see
p. 7 below). On this account, the Christian educator is, rather,
the 'fellow-pilgrim', 'guide', 'co-enquirer' or 'sponsor' who
shares the experience of the learners and seeks to develop their
skills in making their own connections for themselves. The
logic of this understanding of the model seems to suggest
that the interpreter-Christian educator will work best with individuals and small groups.[19] (See articles 5.1, 5.2 and 5.4.)

Fourth, much attention has been paid recently to the 'liberation approach' to Christian education. This involves the
'conscientisation' of the learner: that is, her critical reflection
leading to critical action-reflection and a changed lifestyle. As

this is a 'collegial and dialogical process of creating reality',[20] exponents of this approach argue that the teacher is to be seen as a 'colleague' or 'fellow freedom fighter' in Christian education's struggle to free the learner and the world. This analysis relates closely to a view of the Christian educator as a *prophet*,[21] raising the consciousness of the hearers and, through her critique of society (and the church), helping to develop their critical faculties. Unlike the pastor-Christian educator or the priest-Christian educator, the iconoclastic and disturbing prophet-Christian educator may be more willing to bring the sword than either to bring peace, or to cry peace where there is no peace.[22]

This may explain the tension often experienced by clergy and ministers who try to combine in their own persons elements of both the (disruptive) prophetic- and the (conservative and conserving) pastoral/priestly-Christian educator; or who attempt to minister to a congregation that has been opened up to more prophetic educational influence from others. (See articles 1.3, 5.1, 5.2 and 5.4.)

Fifth, perhaps one of the most popular models of the Christian educator is that of *preacher*. This blanket term, however, covers a range of activities and it may be argued that many preaching styles and 'philosophies' have already been referred to under the models of priest, pastor, interpreter and prophet. But there are distinctive theories of Christian education that stress the teacher's authenticity and dedication, or his witnessing and proclaiming skills as significant features of the Christian education process.[23] Such accounts are reminiscent of similar views of the vocation and virtues of the good preacher. The primary feature of the preacher-model is the preacher's role as proclaimer of the gospel. Very many writers on Christian education, particulary those influenced by a kerygmatic theology, have understood it in this way.[24] The Christian religious educator here is *keryx*: the herald of the heavenly king, proclaiming the gospel to the learner.[25] This model leads to a very high view of the responsibility and role of the Christian educator as a channel for the voice of God. It should be noted, however, that it also carries with it the danger of ignoring the human contribution of the religious educator's own voice.[26]

Sixth, the other traditionally popular model for the Christian educator has been that of the *school teacher* or *lecturer*. Some have rejected the 'schooling-instructional' paradigm for

Christian education, seeing in it (often unfairly) an undue emphasis on the outer and cognitive aspects of Christianity, a temptation to control and manipulate learners and to predict learning outcomes, or a concentration on the objective of the development of critical thinking at the expense of formation. These activities may be appropriate within Christian education, many claim, but they should not be the *priorities* of the church as they can be in more secular forms of education.[27] Others, as we have seen, have stressed the church's need to pay attention precisely to these elements in its proper religious self-education.[28] All should recognise the danger of confusing 'schooling' (narrowly conceived) and 'education', and of the wrong sort of professionalisation of Christian religious education that limits its domain to where the *real* (schooling-oriented) Christian educators are working. However, when the church engages in what it most easily and explicitly acknowledges as Christian education, whether in Sunday schools, confirmation/church membership classes or adult groups, the dominant model employed is often still that of the school teacher or the (rather formal sort of) lecturer in higher or adult education. This may sometimes result in a style and content of Christian learning that is inappropriately 'academic' and formal.[29]

Taking a more positive view, however, the *teaching model* is entirely appropriate even outside formal academic contexts, provided that it is properly broadened to cover *all* intentional and structured facilitation of learning, and not just cognitive-academic learning.[30] For some, this is the only proper view to take of the Christian educator. James Michael Lee writes:[31]

> According to the teaching theory, the distinctive characteristic of religious instruction is that it is the purposeful and deliberative modification of learner behaviour along religious lines.

For Lee, the teacher ('instructor') is much more than a model for the religious educator drawn from an analogous activity. In his overall theory ('macro-theory') of religious instruction the Christian educator is *literally* a teacher of the Christian religion, but in the wide sense that he or she is a specialist in facilitating the learning of Christian religious behaviours (again in a wide sense). On this broader view, all the above models and approaches to Christian education may be subsumed under some aspect or another of the category of Christian teaching. Other Christian educationalists have recently sought to articulate, in their own different ways, the role of the teacher in Christian education.[32]

Notes

1. See John M Hull, *Studies in Religion and Education*, Lewes, Falmer, 1984, pp. 39, 206; Jeff Astley and David Day, 'The contours of Christian education,' in J Astley and D Day (eds), *The Contours of Christian Education*, Great Wakering, McCrimmons, 1992, chapter 1; Fred Hughes, *What Do You Mean: Christian Education?*, Carlisle, Paternoster, 1992.

2. Compare Jeff Astley, *The Philosophy of Christian Religious Education*, Birmingham, Alabama, Religious Education Press; London, SPCK, 1994, chapters 1 and 3; but contrast, for example, Kevin Nichols, 'The logical geography of catechesis,' in J Astley and D Day, *op. cit.*, chapter 4.

3. See P H Hirst and R S Peters, *The Logic of Education*, London, Routledge and Kegan Paul, 1970, chapter 2; and various papers in the following collections: R S Peters (ed.), *The Concept of Education*, London, Routledge and Kegan Paul, 1967; R S Peters (ed.), *The Philosophy of Education*, Oxford, Oxford University Press, 1973; R F Dearden *et al.* (eds), *Education and the Development of Reason*, London, Routledge and Kegan Paul, 1972; Glen Langford and D J O'Connor (eds), *New Essays in the Philosophy of Education*, London, Routledge and Kegan Paul, 1973; S C Brown (ed.), *Philosophers Discuss Education*, London, Macmillan, 1975; Roger Straughan and John Wilson (eds), *Philosophers on Education*, London, Macmillan, 1987. This normative concept of education has been questioned. See, for example, James E McClellan, *Philosophy of Education*, Englewood Cliffs, New Jersey, Prentice-Hall, 1976; Anthony O'Hear, *Education, Society and Human Nature*, London, Routledge and Kegan Paul, 1981; John White, *The Aims of Education Restated*, London, Routledge and Kegan Paul, 1982. R S Peters has himself admitted that his concept of education is 'too specific'. See his comments in P H Hirst (ed.), *Educational Theory and its Foundation Disciplines*, London, Routledge and Kegan Paul, 1983, pp. 37, 41–43. Philosophers of education have, in a similar way, often restricted the term 'learning' to those situations that (i) fulfil certain cognitive conditions (for example attending to evidence or knowledge-with-understanding) and (ii) imply a certain freedom and self-directedness in the learner. Psychologists of education, on the other hand, accept a much broader definition of learning in terms of a change in beliefs, attitudes, values, skills or dispositions brought about by experience.

4. See also Ninian Smart, *Secular Education and the Logic of Religion*, London, Faber and Faber, 1968; Schools Council, *Religious Education in Secondary Schools*, London, Evans/Methuen, 1971; *A Groundplan for the Study of Religion*, London, Schools Council, 1977; Michael Grimmitt, *What Can I Do in RE?*, Great Wakering, McCrimmons, 1978. On 'confessional', see Robin H Shepherd, 'Confessionalism,' in John M Sutcliffe (ed.), *A Dictionary of Religious Education*, London, SCM, 1984, pp. 93–94. Some authors

argue for the possibility of 'education in' religion even in secular schools: see articles 1.2 and 2.3 below.

5.   Compare Gabriel Moran, 'Religious education,' in Mircea Eliade (ed.), *Encyclopedia of Religion*, volume 12, London, Collier Macmillan, 1987, pp. 318–323. The US usage is related to the fact that public education in the United States eschews religious observance and confessional religious education. That debate has recently been re-opened, see Stanley Hauerwas and John H Westerhoff (eds), *Schooling Christians*, Grand Rapids, Michigan, Eerdmans, 1992.

6.   See J Astley and D Day, *op. cit.*, pp. 15-16 and references; and various essays in Leslie J Francis and Adrian Thatcher (eds), *Christian Perspectives for Education: a reader in the theology of education*, Leominster, Fowler Wright, 1990.

7.   See also Charles R Foster, 'The faith community as a guiding image for Christian education,' in Jack L Seymour and Donald E Miller (eds), *Contemporary Approaches to Christian Education*, Nashville, Tennessee, Abingdon, 1982, chapter 3; C Ellis Nelson, *Where Faith Begins*, Atlanta, John Knox Press, 1976; and the following works by John H Westerhoff: *Will Our Children have Faith?*, New York, Seabury, 1976; *Building God's People in a Materialistic Society*, New York, Seabury, 1983; *Living the Faith Community*, San Francisco, Harper and Row, 1985; and with Gwen Kennedy Neville, *Generation to Generation*, New York, Pilgrim Press, 1979.

8.   See Jeff Astley, 'Christian worship and the hidden curriculum of Christian learning,' in J Astley and D Day (eds), *op. cit.*, chapter 10.

9.   See also John Hull, *What Prevents Christian Adults from Learning?*, London, SCM, 1985; Leon McKenzie, 'The purposes and scope of adult religious education,' in Nancy Foltz (ed.), *Handbook of Adult Religious Education*, Birmingham, Alabama, Religious Education Press, 1986, chapter 1; Thomas H Groome, *Christian Religious Education*, San Francisco, Harper and Row, 1980, chapters 2 and 6.

10.   See Leon McKenzie, *The Religious Education of Adults*, Birmingham, Alabama, Religious Education Press, 1982, pp. 36–37, 63–67; J Astley, *The Philosophy of Christian Religious Education, op. cit.*, chapter 5.

11.   See also J Astley, *The Philosophy of Christian Religious Education, op. cit.*, pp. 84–91.

12.   See also T Groome, *Christian Religious Education, op. cit.*, pp.121–127 and *passim*; and Jeff Astley, 'Tradition and experience: conservative and liberal models for Christian education,' in J Astley and D Day (eds), *op. cit.*, chapter 3.

13.   William H Willimon, *Worship as Pastoral Care*, Nashville, Tennessee, Abingdon, 1979, p. 205.

14.   Such a priestly-communitarian model is capable of both a Protestant and a Catholic redaction. There is a considerable literature on the theme of worship and Christian education, particularly from Roman Catholic and Anglican sources. See, for example, Gwen Kennedy Neville and John Westerhoff, *Learning Through Liturgy*, New York, Seabury, 1978; Robert L Browning and Roy A Reed, *The Sacraments in Religious Education and Liturgy*, Birmingham, Alabama,

Religious Education Press, 1985; Michael Warren, 'Catechesis: an enriching category for religious education,' in M Warren (ed.), *Sourcebook for Modern Catechetics*, Winona, Minnesota, St Mary's Press, 1983, chapter 28. See also article 4.2.

15. Yet the priest-model and community emphasis may also be relevant here, if we agree with Willimon that 'the liturgy itself and a congregation's experience of divine worship already functions, even if in a secondary way, as pastoral care' (Willimon, *op. cit.*, p. 48).

16. Compare James W Fowler, *Stages of Faith*, San Francisco, Harper and Row, 1981, chapter 24; James Michael Lee, *The Shape of Religious Instruction*, Birmingham, Alabama, Religious Education Press, 1971, pp. 251–253 and his 'Catechesis sometimes, religious instruction always,' in Marlene Mayr (ed.), *Does the Church Really Want Religious Education?*, Birmingham, Alabama, Religious Education Press, 1988, pp. 37, 47; John H Westerhoff III, 'The Challenge,' in J H Westerhoff and O C Edwards (eds), *A Faithful Church*, Wilton, Connecticut, Morehouse-Barlow, 1981, pp. 5–6; Thomas H Groome, 'The spirituality of the religious educator,' *Religious Education*, 83, 1988, pp. 15–16.

17. David P Killen, 'Indigenous theological education and Christian formation,' *Insight*, 11, 1984, pp. 3–13. A similar view argues that the Christian educator should be a 'translator' rather than a 'transmitter' of the tradition, aiding communication between the church's tradition and the learner's experience through her familiarity with both of their 'languages'.

18. David S Steward and Margaret S Steward, 'Action-reflection-action,' in Maria Harris (ed.), *Parish Religious Education*, New York, Paulist, 1978, p. 91.

19. See Jack L Seymour and Carol A Wehrheim, 'Faith seeking understanding: interpretation as a task of Christian education,' in J L Seymour and D E Miller (eds), *op. cit.*, chapter 6.

20. Jack L Seymour, in J L Seymour and D E Miller, *op. cit.*, p. 26. For Paulo Freire, 'no one conscientises anyone else. The educator and the people together conscientise themselves' (Paulo Freire, 'Education, liberation and the church,' *Religious Education*, 79, 1984, p. 528).

21. J L Seymour, *op. cit.*, p. 27; cf. Allen J Moore, 'Liberation and the future of Christian education,' in J L Seymour and D E Miller (eds), *op. cit.*, chapter 5.

22. See T Groome, *Christian Religious Education, op. cit.*, pp. 270-273.

23. Compare the critical account of such theories in James Michael Lee, *The Flow of Religious Instruction*, Birmingham, Alabama, Religious Education Press, 1973, chapter 7.

24. See A McBride, *Catechetics: A Theology of Proclamation*, Milwaukee, Bruce, 1966, p.150; compare Howard Burgess, *An Invitation to Religious Education*, Birmingham, Alabama, Religious Education Press, 1975, chapter 3 and Mary C Boys, *Biblical Interpretation in Religious Education*, Birmingham, Alabama, Religious Education Press, 1980, chapter 2.

25. See Johannes Hofinger, *The Art of Teaching Christian Doctrine*, London, Sands, 1962, p. 20, cf. p. 197; and Joseph Andreas

Jungmann, *The Good News Yesterday and Today*, translated by William A Huesman, New York, Sadlier, 1962, *passim*. Compare also Karl Barth's *Church Dogmatics, I*, 1, translated by G W Bromiley, Edinburgh, T and T Clark, 1975, p. 52; and *Church Dogmatics, I*, 2, translated by G T Thomson and Harold Knight, Edinburgh, T and T Clark, 1956, pp. 802-812.

26.   It must be stressed that we are speaking here, as in the above cases, of preaching as a *model* for all or most of Christian education; and not of the activity of *actual preaching* as being all or most of what Christian education should be.

27   Compare John H Westerhoff, *Will Our Children have Faith?*, New York, Seabury, 1976, chapter 1; see also J H Westerhoff's response to C F Melchert (article 1.4) in *Living Light*, 14, 1977, pp. 354–356.

28.   See, for example, Gabriel Moran, 'Where now, what next?' in Padraic O'Hare (ed.), *Foundations of Religious Education*, New York, Paulist, 1978, pp. 105–106. Moran does recognise, however, that in religion 'teaching means to show someone a way of life' and that 'the religious form of teaching stands in marked contrast to modern concepts of teaching' as rational explanation, dispassionate before the evidence. He adds that 'no religion could survive on classroom teaching alone' ('Religious education,' in Mircea Eliade [ed.], *op. cit.*, p. 322).

29   Nevertheless, the church is still in need of *some* Christian education designed along these lines. Very many Christians have the potential to achieve a fuller understanding of Christianity, and this has often been denied them by the church's lack of formal academic educational provision. Cf: 'In many respects the doctrines of the church are much more sophisticated than average thinking and the problem is too little education and not too much' (David Martin, *A Sociology of English Religion*, London, SCM, 1967, p. 114).

30.   For a very wide understanding of the subject-matter content of Christian education, see James M Lee, *The Content of Religious Instruction,* Birmingham, Alabama, Religious Education Press, 1985, *passim*.

31.   J M Lee, *The Flow of Religious Instruction, op. cit.,* p. 196; cf. also his *The Shape of Religious Instruction, op. cit.*, p. 8 and chapter 3.

32.   See, for example, Richard Osmer, *A Teachable Spirit: recovering the teaching office in the church*, Louisville, Kentucky, Westminster/John Knox Press, 1990; Maria Harris, *Teaching and Religious Imagination: an essay in the theology of teaching,* San Francisco, Harper, 1991; Clark M Williamson and Ronald L Allen, *The Teaching Minister*, Louisville, Kentucky, Westminster/John Knox Press, 1991. For a range of other models of Christian education, see Timothy Arthur Lines, *Functional Images of the Religious Educator,* Birmingham, Alabama, Religious Education Press, 1992.

1. Definitions and clarification

In this first section we bring together five articles that analyse the ways in which the term 'education' functions in such phrases as 'religious education' and 'Christian education'.

Evelina Orteza y Miranda's article, first published in the *British Journal of Religious Education*, 8, 1986, pp. 94–102, discusses 'Some problems with the expression "Christian education"'. She distinguishes two senses of the phrase: education or knowledge that a Christian ought to have as a Christian, and education that is (distinctively) Christian. The author argues that this second sense is problematic, at least on a particular, restrictive understanding of education, and proposes 'Christian perspective' as a more appropriate term.

John Wilson is well known for his contributions to the philosophy of religious and, particularly, moral education.[1] His early article, 'Taking religious education seriously' was published in *Learning for Living*, 16, 1976, pp. 18–24 and is essentially an analysis of the concept of educating people *in* religion. His conceptual analysis focuses first on religion, distinguished as being closely tied up with notions of awe and worship, and then moves on to discuss the competences that are required for a person to be properly educated in religion, so as to be able to avoid making mistakes in religion. These competences include being 'open to, or able actually to feel' certain emotions and attitudes and being 'able to identify, refine and criticise these feelings, in relation to their objects or targets.' This process of bringing certain feelings to consciousness and inspecting them critically, is distinguished from other activities of inducting into or educating learners about religion.

Gabriel Moran's contributions to the understanding of religious education span many years.[2] In his article 'Two languages of religious education,' first published in *Living Light*, 14, 1977, pp. 7–15, he distinguishes the ecclesiastical language of religious education ('governed by the relation of theology ... to catechetics/Christian education', in which theology is the dominant partner) from its educational language (in the sense of 'the systematic planning of experience

13

for growth in human understanding', in which religion and education are like a bickering couple who do not get on together 'but who are worse when apart'). While the entire educational setting is capable of having religious significance, Moran concentrates on the three elements of studying religion 'from within', studying it 'from a distance', and the (indirect) teaching of the practice of a religious life, specifically the contemplative, sacramental and moral-protest practices. Here catechetics/Christian education returns in a broader context which is less subservient to theology.

Charles Melchert's 'What is religious education?' is another classic of the late 1970s, having been published in *Living Light*, 14, 1977 pp. 339–352. Melchert analyses the concept of education, adopting the value and cognitive conditions as defining characteristics of the practice, together with four other criteria. He goes on to explore the role of education in terms of helping others to know and understand, and of religious education's doing this 'in the ways appropriate to religion'. These include not only traditional academic study, but also 'more experiential, ineffable and self-transcending ways'.

John Westerhoff has been another major influence on Christian education theory and practice, especially in the United States, over very many years.[3] His article 'Formation, education, instruction', first published in *Religious Education,* 82, 1987, pp. 578–591, traces his own use of such terms as 'intentional enculturation' and 'catechesis', and his opposition to the 'schooling-instructional paradigm' for the church's task of Christian education. He then distinguishes three processes that make up catechesis: formation, defined as 'intentional, relational, experiential activities within the life of a story-formed faith community'; education, defined as 'critical reflective activities related to these communal activities'; and instruction, defined as 'the means by which knowledge and skills useful to communal life are transmitted, acquired and understood'. He relates these to the educational reflections of Paul Tillich and Michael Polanyi, and concludes with some questions for further study.

Professor Evelina Orteza y Miranda is Professor of Education in the Department of Educational Policy and Administrative Studies of the University of Calgary, Alberta, Canada. John Wilson lectures in the Department of Educational Studies of the University of Oxford, England. Professor Gabriel Moran is Professor of Religion and Education in the Department of

Cultural Foundations at New York University, New York City, USA. Dr Charles F Melchert was formerly Dean and Professor of Education and Religion at the Presbyterian School of Christian Education, Richmond, Virginia, USA. He now resides at Lancaster, Pennsylvania. The Revd Dr John H Westerhoff III is currently Warden of the Institute of Pastoral Studies, St Bartholomew's Episcopal Church, Atlanta, Georgia. He was formerly Professor of Theology and Christian Nurture at Duke University Divinity School, Durham, North Carolina, USA.

Notes

1. See, for example, John Wilson, *Education in Religion and the Emotions*, London, Heinemann, 1971; John Wilson, 'First steps in religious education,' in Brenda Watson (ed.), *Priorities in Religious Education*, London, Falmer, 1992, chapter 1; John Wilson, Norman Williams and Barry Sugarman, *Introduction to Moral Education*, Harmondsworth, Penguin, 1967; John Wilson, *A New Introduction to Moral Education*, London, Cassell, 1990.
2. See, for example, Gabriel Moran, *Catechesis of Revelation*, New York, Herder and Herder, 1966; *Design for Religion*, New York, Herder and Herder, 1970; *Interplay: a theory of religion and education*, Winona, Minnesota, St Mary's Press, 1981; *Religious Education as a Second Language*, Birmingham, Alabama, Religious Education Press, 1989.
3. See, for example, John H Westerhoff III, *Will Our Children Have Faith?*, New York, Seabury, 1976; *Building God's People in a Materialistic Society*, New York, Seabury, 1983; *Living the Faith Community*, San Francisco, Harper and Row, 1985; also John H Westerhoff and Gwen Kennedy Neville, *Generation to Generation*, New York, Pilgrim Press, 1979.

1.1 Some problems with the expression 'Christian education'

Evelina Orteza y Miranda

The recent revival of interest in religion and religious matters seem to have inspired and encouraged support for the development of Christian schools within the public school system as alternative public schools. As part of the public school system, Christian schools are supported by public funds. The acceptance of this idea has been the subject of debate recently in Calgary, Alberta, Canada.[1] There is also a beginning of a lively discussion on whether or not there is a Christian sociology, Christian psychology, etc.[2] The latter could be suggestive of the Christian Reformed view that 'distinctive Christian theories are obtainable in all disciplines, if we work from biblical presuppositions about man and nature.'[3]

These questions are not necessarily new and recent for Christian educators/academicians or for any one who has taken the implications of one's Christian beliefs seriously. These questions derive from the meaning of being a Christian. To be a Christian is not to specialise in Christianity in the same way that being a scientist is to specialise in an aspect of science. To be a Christian is to embrace a distinctive way of life, viewing the whole world and all that is taking place and is in it from the Christian perspective. If the creaturely activities of Christians, for example, business, schooling, politics, industry, etc., are parts of total life, they, as internal parts of the whole, necessarily partake of the qualities of total life.

Even if they are not new and recent questions, nonetheless, there seems to be a renewed vigour and rigour in discussions about them. These developments may be taken as positive signs of awakening within the entire Christian community, hence, calling for celebration. But before we do this we need, first, to be clear of what it is that we are talking about when we talk of Christian schools, Christian sociology, Christian psychology, etc. And if these are instances of a broader concept, namely, 'Christian education', then its clarification is the prior task. To paraphrase St Paul's admonition, zeal without enlightenment is not necessarily indicative of a Christian manner of thinking.[4] In 1 Corinthians 14:9, St Paul reminds us of the importance of knowing clearly the meaning of words we employ: 'Unless you speak intelligible words with your tongue, how will anyone know what you are saying? You will just be speaking into the air.' The motive of clarity of our talk is love for the communicants of the church.

When 'Christian education' is clarified, that is, its central and necessary features are identified, it could judge whether or not Christian psychology, Christian sociology, or Christian schools are, indeed, cases of education. If they are, then our second task is to discuss possibilities for their development and to identify logical difficulties in the development, if there are any.

This article limits its task to clarifying 'Christian education'. It will show that there are two senses of 'Christian education'. Between them, the second sense is problematic and it is the focus of analysis in this article. In particular it enquires into the question of what exactly is Christian about Christian education/knowledge, for example Christian literature, Christian art, etc. The article shows some of the difficulties raised by this question and suggests that 'Christian education' does not mean that there is something exactly and definitely Christian about education but that there is a Christian perspective on it or a Christian manner of viewing it. Discussion on Christian perspective and its implications is not intended in this article.

Before I proceed to deal with the tasks of this article, allow me to say that I am aware that some of these problems on Christian education and on the related topic of education and religion have been discussed in papers too many to mention. To readers of this journal who have by now come to some conclusions about these problems, I beg of their charity and patience to deal with these difficulties again with me.

The terms 'education' and 'knowledge'

First, a word about the term education. There are many and diverse uses of 'education'. This is due to its ambiguous and vague characteristics. While all of them could be acceptable, given their specific uses, not all of them may be said to be central to its meaning. Consider the common expression 'Education is life.' This does not mean that education is equated with life, using 'is' in the sense of equivalence, hence also defining education. Rather, the expression means that education is like life. It is, indeed, a lifelong activity. Since life is suggestive of process, that is, when one has life one is said to be living, so also is education a process. It goes on and on, from the cradle to the grave. But life is not central to the meaning of education because the expression 'education is life' can be negated and no illogicality occurs, thus, 'Life is not just education.' Life does not solely consist of academic/cognitive problems and it is not confined to classrooms and class schedules. 'Life', in its comprehensive sense, embraces anything and everything that goes on in the world, including 'education', meaning formal, classroom education or schooling. One's life may include formal, classroom education but one's life is not equated with it. However, as the brief analysis shows, education and life are related because they share the feature of process.

The term 'education' is also used in connection with the teaching profession. When one plans to become a teacher, one enrolls in a College/Faculty of Education. To say 'I am taking courses in education' is also to say 'I am taking courses that prepare me for the teaching profession.' The common practice of associating these terms together has led, in turn, to the practice of treating them as though they were synonymous with each other. This, of course, is not so. Nonetheless, it is acceptable to use them interchangeably and specify that they are so used. Sometimes 'education' is also used to mean 'instruction', as in the statement 'There should be religious education in schools.'

Given the many uses/meanings of 'education', which one of them could be shown to be central, or perhaps even necessary, to it? Consider the fact that what we consider the nature of knowledge to be often influences our concept of education or our manners of educating. To hold on to a speculative view of knowledge, for example, is also to prefer educational institutions that give top priority to speculative manners of thinking, thus concentrating on works of scholars like Hans-Georg Gadamer or Paul Ricoeur, for example. Our changing and different views of knowledge usually lead to different ways of educative teaching and of structuring different educational institutions and experiences. This shows the close connection between 'education' and 'knowledge'. It does not, however, conclude that 'knowledge' is a central or necessary meaning of 'education'. For more direct evidence regarding their necessary connection, consider the following statements: (1) 'We believe in the power of education to help solve the personal problems of individuals, as well as the social dilemmas of our changing society.'[5] (2) Education is going on and no knowledge claims are being taught. (3) Education has nothing to do with acquiring knowledge.

In (1) 'education' is used to mean 'knowledge', more specifically, knowledge of psychology, of sociology, of politics and of economics. It can be used interchangeably with knowledge with no change or loss of meaning. Statements (2) and (3), however, are nonsensical because contradictory: education is both asserted and denied at the same time. Indeed, it is common to say that the main task of education, in the sense of formalised state institution, is the transmission of knowledge. To speak of an educational institution is also to speak of that institution as engaged, along with other activities, necessarily in the activity of transmitting knowledge of some things. As well, an educated person is, among other things, a person who has some knowledge about some things. To say that an educated person is one who is ignorant of everything is, surely, odd. It is clear that 'education' and 'knowledge' are not only closely associated with each other, in the sense that 'education' and the 'teaching profession' are, but that 'knowledge' is central to the meaning of 'education'. Whenever 'education' is used, 'knowledge' is necessarily taken into account. To focus on the centrality of knowledge in the meaning of 'education', or, perhaps, even to equate one with the other, does not however suggest that both terms are reducible one to the other. Obviously, 'education' is more encompassing than 'knowledge', involving among others such concepts as schooling, teaching, learning, moral development, and nurturing. This is the wider sense of 'education' and will be so used in this article. 'Education' to mean 'knowledge' is referred to as its narrow sense and also labelled its second sense.

The term knowledge, as employed in this article, seeks to observe the epistemological conditions of truth, evidence, and beliefs. This means, among other things, that there are standards external to knowledge claims that are employed to assess their acceptability. To say that I know that X is true, it must be the case that X is true. But X is not true simply because I hold it to be true or say that it is so. There are evidential grounds supporting the claim that X is true. And acceptability of these grounds, in turn, requires the employment of certain procedures in assessing them. In other words, one knows how to go about assessing the truth or falsity of the claim and acceptability of the supporting evidences. Indeed, any claim to knowledge that is worth considering is, in principle, open to public enquiry and assessment and subject to validation, verification, and justification. Belief, of course, is a necessary condition of knowledge in the sense that when one knows that X is true one also believes that X is true. Belief, however, by itself and on its own, does not establish the existence of its object; neither does it establish itself to be true. What is true is that someone holds on to a belief that X is true but not necessarily that X is true. In sum, 'knowledge' is used in this paper to mean either logical or evidential truth.

To those who may object to the use of knowledge in this article as restrictive and, from the start, prejudicial against Christian education or religious knowledge, two reasons may be offered to counter the objection. First, to subject religious claims to knowledge to the severest test is to find out how far they can stand up to such a test. For the point is not merely to uphold them on any ground, even on grounds of personal conviction, the easiest, but to uphold them on grounds currently acceptable to and respected by the main stream of scholarship. To subject them to a weak test for the sole purpose of *ensuring*, right from the start, that religious claims can be shown to be acceptable epistemologically is to prejudice the enquiry for it. Indeed, it is to misunderstand the purpose of enquiry and to fall short of academic integrity. Second, for those who uphold religious claims and claims to knowledge there is no need to be timid and distant from the ongoing epistemological debate on truth, meaning, and justification. On the contrary, it is necessary to participate in the scholarly debate on issues that presently confront the disciplines and, indirectly, the times and our lives. The need is to be heard and such a need can only be given hearing if the treatment of religion and its epistemological problems is not defensive and polemical but intends to serve matters of truth. The need is to present one's case in as scholarly and academically respectable a manner as possible.

If, in the end, our efforts to establish credibility of religious knowledge are woefully short of all public grounds, the response is not to despair and give up. Rather, it is to carry on and continue our reflection on the meaning of religion, of Christianity, and on whether or not its intent and implications have been correctly understood. It is possible that Christians have made too many claims on many consequential matters without necessarily knowing and understanding them and their cosmic implications. Now, to address the question on ambiguities of 'Christian education'.

The first sense of 'Christian education'

The concept of Christian education is ambiguous. In one sense, it means the education or knowledge a Christian ought to have as a Christian. It is knowledge for the Christian. If one is a Christian, then, one ought to know something about one's Christian beliefs and understand them. If one claims to be a Christian and also claims to know nothing about one's Christianity or Christian beliefs, the claim may be seriously questioned. How could one say 'I am a Christian' and at the same time say 'I know nothing about being a Christian or what it means'? If I know nothing about X, how would I know how and to whom to apply it? Christians who do not take time to study and know their beliefs suggest that they are not serious about their being Christians. It does not matter whether or not they are aware of implicitly making this claim. It is, of course, possible that someone knows what Christians ought to know but the individual is not a Christian. The individual is a student of but not a believer in Christianity. This means that 'Christian education' could also be expanded to read 'Christian education for anyone who is interested in knowing something about it'.

'Christian education', meaning knowledge a Christian ought to have as a Christian, and the wider sense of education are commonly employed by churches. Thus a Director of Christian Education in a church is one who is in charge of its educational programme, usually consisting of Sunday School curriculum and activities designed to enhance one's understanding of what is being studied in Sunday schools, now also variously given such labels as Christian education, family bible hour, or bible study. It involves the teaching of biblical truths and, more importantly, the nurturing of one's faith and encouraging its practice in one's total life. Its aim is discipleship. The terms 'medical education' meaning knowledge which medical doctors as doctors ought to have, and 'legal education', knowledge which lawyers as lawyers ought to have, function in the same way as 'Christian education', knowledge a Christian ought to have as a Christian. They are not, however encompassing of total life as 'Christian education' is in the sense that churches employ it.

The second sense of 'Christian education'

'Christian education' could also mean education that is Christian. To identify it as such is to distinguish it from other kinds of education. And its being Christian is what is distinctive about it. But what exactly is Christian about this education? Taking into account the narrow sense of 'education', this is a most difficult question to answer.

Suppose it is said that given the meaning of 'Christian', it follows that education that is distinctively Christian is one that is characterised by its metaphysical, revelatory claims, for example, God is the creator of all things, the sustainer of the world, etc. Now, how do these Christian claims fit education in its narrow sense? If education is constituted of knowledge, as it is understood in this article, and if the truths of the Christian claims are presupposed, therefore not subject to any enquiry for purposes of either accepting or rejecting them, then 'education' and 'Christian' do not logically fit. The conditions for accepting Christian claims are not identical to those of education. Christian claims are, ultimately, accepted by faith by Christians. Even in principle, they are not verifiable or falsifiable. Education, on the other hand, is always open to public critical inquiry, subject to the questioning of human reason. Indeed, education presupposes the development of critical mindedness. So, 'Christian' and 'education' may be said to be independent of each other. To force their relatedness is wrong. It is on this point of each one enjoying a different logical status that Professor Paul H Hirst argued that 'Christian education' could be a contradiction in terms.[6]

Perhaps, contradict is too strong a term to use. For if knowledge and the Christian claims belong to a different logical status, then one cannot rule out or contradict the other. But not to rule out, contradict, or deny the other, is also not to give support to each other. It is to disregard their relevancy to each other. Even without the possibility of a contradiction, the above conclusion does not advance the case of Christian education.

Moreover, to say that such an education is characterised by Christian claims is still in need of further elaboration. For example, what does 'characterisation' mean? Is it central to 'education' such that there is a substantial change in the meaning of 'education' or does it mean emphasis? But whatever its meaning, the logical distinction that obtains between 'Christian' and 'education' defies talk of any kind of relatedness.

Suppose there is a ship afloat on the sea. Science, as a clear case of a body of knowledge, explains that it floats because it has displaced water equal to its own weight. The explanation is true of, relevant to, and adequate to a certain state of affairs in the world that is being explained. It is a statement of physics; a scientific statement. As an explanation, an exemplification of a law, it explains all cases of floating objects everywhere. The state of affairs being explained, why the object is afloat, is judged correctly to be a problem of physics. And a corresponding appropriate explanation is given. Both the state of affairs and the explanation have the same logical status. This means that if a state of affairs is a scientific problem, then it needs (logical sense) a scientific answer/explanation. A scientific problem is not only viewed from the scientific perspective but it ought to be so viewed because the scientific perspective is central to it.

How would Christian education (second sense) respond to the above situation? The scientific explanation is accepted because it is scientific and, more importantly, it is one of God's truths. If all the other necessary explanations pertinent to the floating of the ship could be organised and systematised, the ultimate explanation for the ship floating is that God sustains it at that particular point, even as God sustains the whole universe. The latter statement is of Christian education. How does it differ from the previous explanation?

Observe that the Christian explanation about the floating of a ship is not necessarily based on the problem itself, which is buoyancy, although matters of observation are not disregarded. But accepting them, along with scientific explanations, does not constitute the ultimate explanation of what one is seeing, which explanation Christian education provides. Seemingly, it has nothing to do with the ship floating on the sea, for it could be rejected and the scientific explanation would still hold. To accept the latter, it is not necessary, indeed some would say it is not relevant, to accept the ultimate explanation of God's sustaining power. Whether or not one accepts Christianity is irrelevant to accepting scientific explanations. The latter has its own set of criteria for judging its acceptability and appropriateness as explanations independent of Christian beliefs.

Moreover, the Christian explanation does not seem to change the nature of the problem, or add another explanation to it so that it may be said the explanation is now more adequate and comprehensive than before. It cannot do this because, as previously stated, its logical status is distinct from that of science. Moreover, there is no way of showing publicly whether or not the ultimate explanation is true. True or false, correct or incorrect, no one knows how to go about enquiring into it. It is unassailable because now beyond human assessment. To argue that it is so because it is drawn from the Christian belief of creator-creation dependency relationship is to conclude its public discussion and to put it beyond the realm of education.

To say that a scientific problem must be explained from a scientific point is redundant. To give it a Christian explanation, however, although not redundant, is not to explain it at all! To insist on its acceptance as part of education, however it is incorporated into or said to characterise education, is to insist on accepting an extravagant claim the usefulness of which to education is not clear, or perhaps to others is clearly dubious.

Perhaps science, as a case of knowledge, is too restrictive and demanding, making it impossible for 'Christian education' (second sense) to come near to fulfilling its standards. Could other areas of knowledge which partly consist of subjective preferences, private values, insights, and interpretations and which are not strictly objective provide a case for Christian education? That is, could a claim to a legitimate case for Christian education be reasonably made in these areas?

Consider, for example, literature. It is common to hear of Christian poets, novelists and writers. Suppose it is said that their creations qualify as Christian literature, what exactly is Christian about their literature? At once it is clear that literature is literature, with its own standards of truth, validation and assessment procedures, or literary criticisms, rules of interpretation, and a set of concepts central to it, regardless of whether writers are Christians or not. Literature is an autonomous undertaking. This does not necessarily imply that there is no Christian literature.

Suppose it is said that literature is Christian when it treats common Christian themes, such as, for example, the presence of evil in the world, God's justification of actions to humanity, the impending end of the world, hints of redemptive history, and treats them with a clear Christian perspective. Of course, even non-Christian writers deal with these topics, considering that they have a universal appeal. Their treatment of them, however, may not show a Christian basis. Evil could be dealt with independent of sin. Evil as one's inhumanity to another is an observable historical fact. But whether Christian or not, the writer's work on these topics/themes, etc., is judged good, poor, inadequate, etc., not on the basis of one's religious commitment but on grounds of literary requirements and standards. (To deliberately disregard them, aiming solely to employ literature as an instrument for promoting one's religious beliefs is, perhaps, not to understand the seriousness of the literary activity. If and when a Christian writer does this then one's academic integrity and honesty may be called to question.) There are Christian writers who may deal with so-called Christian themes of the scriptures and treat them in accord with the truth of the scriptures. In this limited sense the expression 'Christian literature' may be allowed but not in the sense that Christianity determines the answer to the question of what constitutes literature, so that all its requirements, central concepts, standards of criticism, etc., are derived from Christianity and it is now substantially distinguished from other non-Christian literature so as to merit another name.

The same comments may be made about Christian visual art. It is not that there is Christian art distinguished from and auton-omous from non-Christian art by its distinctive characteristics derived from Christianity. If this were so, then judgment on it is not based on aesthetic grounds alone but, more importantly, on whether or not it is Christian. If it is insisted that there is a distinctive Christian art, autonomous of non-Christian art, this means that an entirely new set of criteria has been developed to judge pieces of art as Christian or not Christian art. This is not so now. What is clear, however, is that there is Christian art in the sense that there are artists who deal with timeless Christian themes, such as God's love and search for humanity, conflict of evil and good in the world, humanity's attempt to usurp God's place, etc., and treat them in a way that shows clearly presupposed Christian values and truths. As in literature, one's Christianity does not define or constitute art. Art remains an independent serious activity with requirements and standards internal to itself. Anyone, regardless of religious affiliation, may engage in and be good at it.

It appears that what is problematic is our understanding of what 'Christian education', 'Christian art', 'Christian literature', etc., mean. In the above discussion, specifically on Christian art/Christian literature, the meaning which is arguable is that there are distinctive Christian elements/themes/topics, etc., in art and literature. Aside from the abstract topics of evil, good, etc., Christian themes have been portrayed visibly in such varied works of art as those of Van Gogh's *The Good Samaritan* (1890), Stanley Spencer's *The Last Supper* (1920), Graham Sutherland's *The Crucifixion* (1946), and Marc Chagall's *The Jerusalem Windows* (1962). These portrayals or themes, topics, etc., distinguish Christian art from other kinds of art which may not be or are never concerned with such themes. In this sense Christian art or Christian literature is not different from abstract art or primitive art, and from Classical literature or Romantic literature. They are distinguished from each other by their themes, topics, etc., and manners of portraying them. They are accepted as pieces of art or literature not because they are identified as Christian, abstract, primitive, classical or romantic but because they meet the standards of art and literature, whatever they are. So from the distinction established regarding Christian art or

Christian literature, it does not follow that for art or literature to be Christian both must be *defined* and *determined* by Christian beliefs.

The point so far established is that the meaning of 'education' in its narrow sense, and the meaning of 'Christian' suggest irreconcilable differences or non-relatedness between them. Science, which is a clear case of knowledge/education, in the discussion shows this to be particularly so. On the other hand, the discussion showed that in some instances of education/knowledge, for example in art and literature, there is a limited sense of Christian literature and Christian art that is acceptable. Accommodating Christian concerns in these activities, however, does not necessitate redefining art and literature to accord with Christianity.

Suppose the same reasoning applied to matters of science. Would there be a sense of 'Christian science' that could be acceptable? For example, could some Christian concerns, say the origin of life, its theistic significance, etc., be accommodated by science? Yes, of course, but they would be treated in a scientific way and Christian truths would not be presupposed. There would be no need to judge the problem Christian. Indeed, science would not know how to deal with problems, whatever they are, except in a scientific way.

Consider another approach. Suppose it is said that what is Christian in the expression 'Christian science' are the comments about science which are motivated by Christian beliefs. The comments, however, cannot be part of or incorporated in science in the same manner that Christian themes/concerns could be incorporated in literature and art and in this sense could be significant characteristics of art and literature or distinctive of them as art. Science and its activities, having to do with natural and physical matters of the observable realm, are not affected by Christian comments or concerns. Its criteria for assessment of truth, evidence, its verification methodology, etc., remain intact. To insist on using the expression 'Christian science' in this sense is trivial if not ridiculous. However, the attempt here may be salvaged if it is said that what exactly is Christian about Christian science are those aspects of science which are judged acceptable to and by Christianity because they are supportive of or in harmony with Christian beliefs. To the extent that science is in harmony with Christian beliefs, to that extent it is judged Christian. It could be said that judging science in this way is considering science instrumentally and not as an activity with its own intrinsic goods. A scientific activity must be judged acceptable because it meets the criteria of science. Moreover, the answer prefaced by 'to the extent' is vague raising the question of its specific extent. The answer is not precise enough to be convincing. The attempt is not altogether successful even if the use of 'Christian science' in this sense seems acceptable.

Before concluding this section, consider the expression 'Christian education' (second sense) again in the light of the above discussion. Suppose it is said that education is Christian when it emphasises Christian concerns or problems or considers them central to its concern. But if these Christian concerns are not necessarily dealt with in a Christian way, emphasising the acceptance of a commitment to Christian truths, then this is not necessarily 'Christian education' (second sense). For example, on problems of obedience to authority or sanctity of marriage, with its corresponding question of the necessity of sex education, the concern of education/knowledge is the establishment of a correct understanding of these problems as informed by pertinent knowledge about them and creation of appropriate solutions to them. Although they may be judged Christian concerns, treatment of them is limited only to those aspects of the problem that corresponds to education/knowledge. In short, they are treated like any ordinary problem, within the grasp of human reason and intelligence. There is no appeal to God, to God's truths, or matters of faith. There is nothing distinctively Christian about it. In this way, the aspect of the problems that essentially defines them as Christian is not taken into account. What is dealt with are not necessarily and distinctively Christian problems but problems of education/knowledge. To emphasise Christian problems, concerns, etc., in education is not necessarily to deal with them in a Christian way, with the values and truths of Christianity presupposed in the manner of clarifying and solving them. But, of course, to deal with them in this Christian way may not be acceptable to education, either. The use of 'Christian education' in the second sense is not warranted.

One final attempt to argue for the acceptance of the expression 'Christian education'. Suppose 'Christian education', in both senses, is Christian in the sense that the intents, purposes, and aims of education are all derived from and based on Christian beliefs. To achieve them, the means or subjects taught and manners of teaching all subscribe to Christian doctrines. It is not simply that there are Christian elements, characteristics, or emphases in this kind of education but that it presupposes Christianity. So, if it is Christian, it must be education/educational; if education/educational, it must be Christian. It is to redefine the concept 'education' to accord with the concept 'Christian'. This eliminates the irreconcilable problems between them noted earlier.

In other words, the basic presuppositions of Christianity now also condition the employment of 'education'/'knowledge'. But if the term 'knowledge' is working well, that is, able to discriminate between cases that are clearly cases of knowledge and those which are not and those which are peripheral or doubtful ones, then there are no reasons for modifying its use. Moreover, what of the meaning of some of its related terms, for example, verifiability, testability, evidence, publicity, etc.? It could be answered, of course, that their meaning, along with 'knowledge'/'education', would be altered, modified, or broadened, securing coherence and relatedness between and among them. This could be an enormous undertaking, considering that the stipulated meanings could easily run counter to the ordinary use of these terms.

Suppose, however, that such a change is allowed. What happens? To change the conditions of knowledge/education by giving them a special meaning, which meaning is private and meaningful only to Christians, brings us back to the first sense of 'Christian education'. If it is this sense of 'Christian education' that is intended, there is no need to redefine 'education' but rather to employ a more appropriate expression, namely 'Christian schools' or 'Christian schooling'. In this way the Christian intentions are clear, which are to promote and nurture the Christian faith, to encourage commitment to it, even indoctrinate it, not necessarily in its pejorative sense but in the sense of holding on to it and deepening one's faith in it in the presence of temporal evidences contrary to it. It is not only that students are taught to understand this faith but that they are brought up and reared in it. There is no need to be apologetic about the school being an arm of the church and about its aims, namely to socialise students into the *milieu* of Christianity in the school setting.

If the above conclusion is not acceptable and insistence on the use of 'Christian education' continues, this means that much work has to be done in explicating its meaning and arguing for its acceptance in the light of current understanding about education and transmission of knowledge. Or it could be said, along with Professor Paul H Hirst, that the use of 'education' in this instance is in its primitive sense:[7]

> Whatever is held by the group to be true or valuable, simply because it is held to be true or valuable, is what is passed on so that it comes to be held as true and valuable by others in turn. On this view, clearly there can be a Christian concept of education, one based on what Christians hold to be true and valuable in education, in which they seek that the next generation shall think likewise.

Given the difficulties of the expression 'Christian education', this article suggests that 'Christian perspective' is the more appropriate term to use. It is less pretentious in its claims to achieving strict conditions of knowledge, and thus avoids the difficulties discussed in this paper and encourages dialogue between and among different religious perspectives. To discuss the concept 'Christian perspective', however, requires another article.

Notes

1. See Ralph M Miller, 'Is the religious alternative school useful in the public school system?' *Journal of Educational Thought,* 16, 1982, pp. 113–115.
2. See, for example, David Lyon, *Christians and Sociology: towards a Christian perspective,* London, Intervarsity Press, 1975; *Journal of American Scientific Affiliation,* 43, 2, 1982: George W Garger, 'A Christian sociology?' pp. 100-104; T L Frisby, 'Descriptive and ideal psychological theory,' pp. 97-99; Timothy Sherratt, 'By what authority: verification of theories in the social sciences: a Christian perspective,' pp. 77–83.
3. 'Christian higher education in Australia,' *Journal of Christian Education,* 72, 1981, p. 54.
4. Romans 10:2.
5. William H Young, 'Education,' in Robert W Smith (ed.), *Christ and the Modern Mind,* Downers Grove, Illinois, Inter-Varsity Press, 1972, p. 157.
6. See Paul H Hirst, 'Christian education: a contradiction in terms,' *Learning for Living,* 11, 4, 1972, pp. 6–11.
7. *Ibid.,* p. 8.

1.2 Taking religious education seriously
John Wilson

In this article I have two quite different things to say. The first concerns the requirements of *any serious* attempt to think about (or indeed to practise) anything that could reasonably be called 'religious education' or 'education in religion'. The second concerns a few basic points which, in my opinion, seem to follow fairly obviously from any such serious attempt.

Of these, the former is both more important and (as I see it) less disputable than the latter. It is also the one thing which is least attended to in the constant flow of literature, debates, working parties and so forth which flock around religious education like Homeric ghosts seeking blood; and because it is not attended to, most of what is said and written on the subject appears shadowy and bloodless.

Religious education

It seems incontestable that we educate people *in* various subjects, spheres of thought or activity, departments of life, or whatever terms we use to distinguish one area from another; also that the notion of education carries with it the ideas of success and failure, progress and mistakes, learning more or less, being more or less well-informed, understanding, perceptive, etc. In most subjects (areas) this is entirely clear: under such headings as history, English, science and so on we have some idea both about what we are doing, and about whether we succeed or fail, in this or that case, in doing it. Not just anything counts as education in science or learning history, and not just anything counts as being good at (well-educated in) science or having learned a lot of history.

Without some such idea of what we are doing, we could hardly educate at all, for we would not know what would count as educating. Thus without some established tradition or understanding of what science is and how to do it well, we should not know (1) what to count as science (as opposed to alchemy, or magic), or (2) what to count as success and failure, mistakes and correctness, progress or backsliding, on the part of our pupils. To put this generally, without (1) a clear definition of the subject or area, and (2) clear criteria of success, we should not know whether we were educating pupils at all — as against merely giving them a good time, keeping them amused, telling them a few interesting facts, and so on.

Sometimes (1) and (2) are comparatively easy to state. It is not too hard to give some account both of what mathematics, science, history or Latin grammar are, and of what counts as doing them well, making a mistake in them, and so on. But sometimes they are harder. We might argue, for instance, about what is to count as literature (and hence education in literature), and about just what it is to be good at (perceptive, understanding, well-informed, etc., about) literature. But even here, if we did not have some idea of what we were doing, we could hardly do it at all. We know, at least, that certain things do not count as literature, that it is one thing to discuss the Norman Conquest, or the cases of *mensa*, or magnetism, or the square root of 144, and another thing to try to appreciate Shakespeare or Chaucer. In fact, there is a wide measure of what one might call unconscious agreement amongst English teachers: they may find it hard to put down clearly on paper just what counts as a good appreciation of literature, but they may well be able to recognise cases of it in practice.

However, if there is serious dispute about (1) and (2), it is clearly essential to reach agreement about these before we can proceed, for the simple reason that otherwise we do not know, in a quite literal sense, what we are doing. With religious education the situation is, in my judgment, about as bad as it can be. It would not even be quite true to say that there is serious dispute about (1) what is to count as religion (and hence education in religion), and (2) what is to count as progress, success, being better-educated, etc., in this area – not, at least, in many educational circles. My impression is that these questions have not been squarely faced at all. There are disputes, but not about these questions. Most of such disputes appear to arise from certain very general ideas or movements which go on under the heading of religious education. Most of these I find unintelligible, since those who engage in them rarely or never give a clear account of (1) and (2). Hence, since I know neither what they count as religion nor what they could as being educated in it, I am unable to know whether their remarks are sensible or not.

Suppose a Martian were to appear and say, 'My goodness, you chaps on earth are missing out on one terribly important area of education – you just don't educate your pupils in squmpery at all, yet it's a most important subject (topic, department of life, etc.).' It would be difficult even for the least serious of us not to reply, 'Well, that's interesting, but tell us (1) what 'squmpery' is as a subject or topic – what does the term include and what does it exclude? Perhaps we already deal with it under another name, or perhaps it overlaps with one of our existing subjects. Then we want to know (2) what counts as being good at squmpery, what makes a good or competent or perceptive squmper. After that, perhaps we can do business.'

With religion and religious education we do not adopt this procedure, or not wholeheartedly. There are a variety of reasons for this. One is that we think we know already − yet, since people give (or at least tacitly imply) such widely different accounts, we cannot all be right. Another is that we have an emotional vested interest in influencing children in certain ways (transmitting, inculcating, teaching, indoctrinating, etc., certain things), and we pursue and defend this interest without worrying much about whether it can properly be entitled religion or religious education. A third reason, if possible more pernicious than the previous two, is the vague idea that we cannot or ought not to get clear at all; perhaps we should not try to reach the truth − perhaps there is no truth to reach − and had better settle for what is politically acceptable, or for a general consensus, or for the current fashion. These and other tendencies, too numerous to mention here, are standing temptations for all of us. They are marks of not being serious about what we are doing.

Fortunately (though there is a temptation to deny this too) words do not mean just anything. If somebody taught his or her pupils algebra and claimed to be engaging in religious education, we should say that this is an insecure grasp of English. We might want to examine the teacher's dictionary, if not his or her head. However imprecise or plastic the term religion, it has some limits; so too with education. So we have a starting-point, surely the only starting point for a serious person; that is, we just have to do the work of finding out what these limits are. Partly in doing this, we shall also be working at finding out the ways in which a person can be good or bad, competent or incompetent, sane or barmy, correct or incorrect in this area. To be clear about what the area is involves some clarity, as it were *en passant*, about what it is to perform well or badly in it.

It is unfortunate that contemporary philosophers of education tend to put these (very obvious) points in too restrictive a form, thereby offering many of us a (feeble) excuse for dodging them. Hirst, for instance, writes of religion as a 'form of thought' or 'form of knowledge', and seems to imply that 'religion' refers only to a particular kind of religion.[1] I want to stress that whatever deficiencies there may be in this (or any other) account, the basic points of methodology or procedure that I have made above still stand. Exactly how we are to describe religion, and to describe what counts as performing well or being educated in it, is precisely our problem. My point is simply that it is a problem which has to be solved before we can go any farther.

The only possible way out of this, so far as I can see, would be to give some account of religion to which the whole notion of criteria of success did not apply. One might, I suppose, regard religion as something which simply overtook one, like lightning or lumbago, and about which nothing could profitably be done. There would then be no sense to be made of words like right, wrong, sensible, prejudiced, perceptive, understanding, correct, progress, wise and so on in reference to this sphere – either as predicated of particular beliefs and attitudes, or of people with these beliefs and attitudes. Some religious believers occasionally talk as if they took this view, but I doubt whether anyone seriously does. We believe, surely, that religion is within the scope of reason and under-standing in some way – that it is not wholly arbitrary, a matter of taste, or a matter of indifference. In any case, if it is wholly outside the scope of understanding, and if no criteria of success apply, then education in this sphere is impossible. We could only note that various people and societies were overtaken by various beliefs and attitudes, without having anything to say (because, on this view, there could be nothing to say) about whether some of them were more sensible, or wiser, or truer, or more perceptive, than others.[2]

I have read with interest, and often with admiration, the writings of various *doyens* in religious education – in particular those of Goldman, Loukes and Smart; but I am bound to say that I have not found these points properly catered for. Goldman seems to interpret 'religion' along grotesquely specific lines, and takes it as equivalent to one version of Christianity. Loukes, with whose more specifically practical and educational view on religious education I have the most sympathy, interprets it on much more modern (one might say, post-Quaker) lines, and regards it as roughly coextensive with almost *any* 'outlook on life', 'ultimate commitment', 'meaning we give to the world', 'infinite dimension of experience', and so on. This hardly caters for worshippers of Baal or Poseidon, who would have found most of such talk unintelligible. One would like from him a clearer account of what attitudes, outlooks, beliefs, or psy-chological states did not count as 'religious'. Even Smart, despite his philosophical ability, seems more interested in what is found in actual religions than in trying to define a *sui generis* form,[3] mode or area of thought and activity which may fairly be entitled religious. This might lead, in practical education, to something more like a shop-window tour of various faiths than a determined attempt to educate pupils in relation to whatever criteria of success fit this *sui generis* form.

It is necessary to add with some haste that these cavalier remarks do not of course begin to do justice to the contribution which these thinkers have made to both the theory and the practice of religious education. But the difficulty of assessing these contributions brings us straight back to the basic questions I have been talking about. With lesser writers one has the distinct suspicion that what they really want is to get something, of which they have a fairly clear idea, done in schools, and the theoretical or philosophical backing for this is then added more or less *ad hoc*. There is perhaps a touch of this even in Goldman, who is plainly not very interested in the questions but hurries on to the applications of Piagetian psychology as quickly as possible. But this is no way for serious educationalists to do business. We must know what we are talking about first.

As a final, if disconnected, point in this section I should like to stress that these questions are intellectual, not political. By this I mean that any attempt to reach a general consensus, or something which will embrace as many people and offend as few people as possible, is doomed to failure. For one may get a consensus but still be wrong. It is not a matter of determining what is acceptable to Christians of various persuasions, immigrant Sikhs, the Humanist Society and so forth, but of determining what is reasonable. This, I suspect, is why the constant round of conferences, agreed syllabuses, helpful remarks by religious advisers, teacher-inspired working-papers and so on are not of much use; they tend to politics, not to truth. The fact is that we are not as yet clear about what we are trying to do but we can at least be clear about our own ignorance, and bend our efforts in the right direction.

Religion

How do we identify beliefs, attitudes, activities and so on as religious? To give the term any clear sense at all we have to exclude beliefs, etc., which we already categorise under some other heading – for instance, historical, moral, scientific or aesthetic in the case of beliefs; or in the case of ideals or outlooks on life, those we might call political or moral or aesthetic ideals. On what grounds do we classify at least some of the things people do in churches and temples under religion, rather than (say) mental health, moral uplift, music or even gymnastics?

I should like to cut a long story of conceptual analysis short here, and simply say without further argument that religion is tied pretty tightly to the notions of awe and worship. These notions themselves no doubt require further explication, which I have tried to give elsewhere, but as at least a sighting shot they seem clear enough. One may, for instance, apply the standard test of the border-line case: asking at what point (say) a man's attitude towards women could be called religious, we should naturally look to see at what point he ceased merely to admire, desire, respect or even wonder at them, and began to revere, be in awe of, and worship them – ending perhaps in the full-blown case in which he seriously sees and describes them as goddesses, gives them names, sacrifices to them and so forth.

Similarly we should be more inclined to describe Communism or Marxism as a religion the more that Communists and Marxists saw and described Lenin (or Marx, or whoever) not just as in a high degree important or admirable or outstanding, but as some kind of god – and 'god' implies something to be worshipped.

Whether or not particular enterprises which we call religions always meet this criterion hardly matters, nor does it matter that religion obviously has many connections with other types of activity – notoriously, with morality. What matters is to get some tolerably clear account of a *sui generis* activity which does the maximum justice to the word 'religion' (so that it is fair to describe it under that title) as we actually use it in normal speech, and which distinguishes it from other activities, in a way which is generally intelligible to anybody. This process has nothing to do with

a. the historical origins of religion;
b. the particular beliefs, attitudes, etc., of particular religions;
c. any questions about whether religion itself is desirable; or
d. the place religion may have in various societies or cultures.

On this criterion, the account given (far too briefly) above seems to me in general satisfactory.

Educated in religion

On this account, the crucial question is, 'What sort of mistakes or failures (good moves or successes) are possible in this area?' Plainly this question has answers. Most obviously, one can be in awe of or worship the wrong things (gods, people). Somebody who worships, say, Hitler must have made some kind of mistake, or failed in some kind of understanding – at least, that is our view, and even if we are wrong there is something to discuss here. What sort of characteristics would a person properly educated in religion have, that would enable him to avoid failures of this kind?

Some answers are fairly easy. Such a person would, presumably, be well-informed about Hitlerism (or whatever religion being considered). He or she would perhaps need to know something about its history, or literature, or cultural background, and about its professed beliefs. He or she might with profit consider its moral code and its social consequences. But, useful though all this might be, it hardly seems central to the religion *qua* religion. Such a person might become well-educated in the history (literature, sociology, etc.) of religion, but would still have to face a central question, roughly of the form, 'Some people believe X to be worth worshipping. Are they right?'

In other words, the person would still have to make some judgment about the attitude or emotional investment which necessarily lies at the core of all religion. Only such an attitude can make sense of religious beliefs. Indeed, the beliefs are largely a linguistic expression of the attitude. To see and feel Christ (Hitler, Poseidon, Nature, or whatever) as god − this element is central. That somebody called Jesus (or whoever it may be) was born on a certain date, acted in a certain way, said certain things and so on is, so far, a matter of historical, not religious, education. It turns into religion when we are told that he is divine, worshipful, to be adored, regarded with awe, the destined leader, etc. As soon as any specifically religious term is used − god, supernatural, divine and many others − we have to face the question of whether the attitude which these words incorporate is appropriate.

There seem to be two general types of competence here. The first, which I now feel to have underplayed in what I have written elsewhere, is that the person must be open to, or able actually to feel, the emotions and attitudes which he might then want to invest or adopt. Whether or not this kind of openness and ability to feel is sufficiently cognitive to count as education is an arguable point which we can perhaps leave on one side. A parallel here is with aesthetics. Learning to appreciate works of art is only possible at all if the pupil is capable of actually having certain feelings which can then be directed and sophisticated (educated, if you like). If they are, as it were, emotionally blind − if they do not allow themselves to feel or to be conscious of their feelings − we cannot even start. A person who cannot feel the pull of various religions or objects or worship, perhaps because he dare not, is not well placed to be educated.

The second general type of competence is to be able to identify, refine, and criticise these feelings, in relation to their objects or targets. If I feel in some general way drawn towards Hitler, or Jesus, or Buddhism, or whatever, I have to ask myself, just what do I feel? What, more precisely, are my emotions in relation to this person or other object of worship? In particular, do I see the person (object) straight? Am I projecting things onto him, deceiving myself, inventing? What is he really like? Do my feelings fit their target? Am I just seeking an authority, or unconsciously rebelling against my parents, or trying to furnish the world to fit my own desires? What *am* I doing exactly?

Another parallel (besides aesthetics) which displays both these types is the case of falling or being in love. Certainly the educated person here will need to know some facts about the other person. I meet Flossie and find myself strangely drawn towards her. No doubt I ought to know about her family background, her past history, and so forth. But in order to make right decisions and adopt appropriate attitudes, I must (1) be able to feel love, and (2) scrutinise my feelings and their object in order to determine their appropriateness. As we all know, this is an immensely difficult task – so difficult, indeed, that we may give it up as a bad job. There will be the temptation to say that 'It's just a matter of taste', 'You can't do anything about it anyway, it's a sort of compulsion', and so on. Yet we know both that we can make mistakes here, and that – with difficulty because we know very little about how to do it – we can improve ourselves. So too with religion.

The central practical question for religious educators, then, is of the form, 'Under what conditions (with what teachers, using what materials, in what social contexts or relationships) does it happen that pupils can become more able to bring their feelings to consciousness and to inspect them critically, in the area roughly bounded by awe, worship, and cognate terms?' If there is a discipline or enterprise which seems more nearly relevant to this than any other, I suppose it is some kind of clinical psychology or psychotherapy, and we should expect to learn a great deal from those in this field. My guess is that it happens best in non-directive relationships of trust, and that any practical advances will be made by exploring further how to set up or induce such relationships, also that we shall not get far unless we take seriously into account what various pupils actually do worship (revere, stand in awe of, etc.), and in general begin with the existing state of their emotions.

This is not to dismiss other types of work in religious education as useless; but almost everything depends on how it is used. To get pupils to feel, or strongly imagine, what it is like to worship (say) Jehovah would obviously be impossible without using the bible, but this is a very different thing from simply using it as factual information, or as literature, or as part of our cultural heritage. Similarly a text-book on Greek polytheism may be no more than academic, whereas to be able to feel the pull, the power, of those psychic forces encapsulated in Aphrodite, Apollo, Zeus and so on is likely to be much more effective. What sort of feelings about purity must the authors of the food taboos in Leviticus have had? Do the pupils recognise any such feelings in themselves? What is it about pop stars, or football heroes, which attracts such strong emotions? Why did the Germans fall for Hitler? These are the sort of starting-points for developing the required emotional insight. I do not say questions to be discussed because that is liable to turn into an unreal and well-defended set of opinions or beliefs which conceal (even as they unconsciously contain) the real feelings lying below the surface.

It seem to me entirely clear that this subject is in its infancy and that there are many theoretical and practical problems to be solved. This should not deter practising teachers from doing all that they can along these lines. What it should do, surely, is to distinguish this from other things which are not properly described as religious education or education in religion at all. We may want to inculcate Christianity; to give pupils some familiarity with the facts and background of world religions; to make sure that, as members of a Christian or post-Christian culture, they are aware of the part that faith has played; to discuss moral or political problems, social welfare, or contemporary society; to talk generally about life, ultimate reality, commitment. Any or all of these may be justifiable enterprises but they are not, or certainly not centrally, education in religion.

I hope that two points will emerge quite clearly in regard to these other enterprises:

First, I am not denying that some enterprises, at least, may in practice be coextensive with what should be done in the enterprise of religious education. To take the most obvious case, suppose a parent's or a school's aim is conceived in some such terms as transmitting the Christian faith, or bringing up their children as good Muslims. Much of what they did might be a useful, perhaps even an essential, basis or background for the children being educated in religion. They would at least know what a religious tradition and environment was like – something which seems necessary if they are to accept or reject it with any degree of rationality or understanding, just as some kind of clear-cut moral tradition and environment seems necessary at least as a background for moral education. So too with transmitting a cultural heritage; obviously it is desirable, from the strictly educational point of view, that children should be familiar with the bible (Koran, etc.). But there is, clearly, a great difference in ultimate aims, even if some of the methods – what the child is taught, and the tradition in which the child is placed – overlap.

Second, I do not deny that these other aims may be in themselves desirable, and may sometimes be reasonably thought to take precedence over strictly educational aims. The important thing is that they should be distinguished. If parents, rightly or wrongly, insist that some aims be pursued for some of the time, for instance that their children should receive an hour's instruction every day from a strictly Roman Catholic (Marxist, Buddhist, etc.) viewpoint, we must at least distinguish this from whatever time should be spent in more open forms of religious education. That hour's teaching followed by a genuinely 'open' hour would be infinitely better than two hours of general muddle.

An extremist might, I suppose, hold that no time should be spent in doing what I have called education in religion, on the grounds that certain beliefs or traditions or institutions are so important and desirable that children should be brought up wholly within them, without running any risk of contamination (as such a person might call it) from an enterprise which would necessarily involve doubt, enquiry, comparison with other beliefs, and mixing with adherents of other traditions. I think it is fair to describe such a person as an extremist because it is hard to see how the enterprise of education could not be regarded as some sort of good, at least for some people for some part of their time. One might think that it should be restricted to pupils above a certain age, level of intelligence, or level of psychological maturity. But as long as we wish people to hold (or not to hold) religious beliefs of any kind for good reasons, we must provide some contexts in which these reasons are examined.

It is, in any case, very difficult to see how this sort of separatism could be viable under modern conditions of communication, and especially in a pluralist society. This is, of course, an empirical rather than a conceptual argument; but if we attempt to resist the empirical facts we shall find ourselves having to resist communication in general. We, that is, any separatist partisan group, will need special schools, effective censorship of radio, television, literature, etc., and some way of preventing our children from meeting and arguing with other children or adults of a different persuasion. This is not a logical impossibility, but something which might well bring more loss than gain, for 'contamination' spreads not just by the existence of different religious persuasions, but rather by the existence of more general norms and ideas that inhere in communication – the idea that one ought to have reasons for what one believes, that evidence must be produced in argument, that one should try to understand another's point of view, and so forth. Even if this were thought, as it might in specific instances reasonably be thought, to be undesirable, the process is not easily reversible.

But be that as it may, I address myself primarily to those many people who do, in fact, feel that some more open (educational) enterprise needs to be undertaken. I think this climate of opinion has been increasingly prevalent for some decades but what has happened, as in the case of moral education, suggests chiefly something like a failure of nerve and clear-headedness. We feel uncertain about accepting past or present authorities, about indoctrination, about the narrowness of sticking to Christianity: well and good. But we then find a vacuum, just because we have no clear idea of what to do instead, and so we mess about, filling in the time in ways which we hope are at least interesting, stimulating, relevant and so forth. I make so bold as to say that as soon as we adopt a serious posture towards what we are doing, it does not take very long to establish (roughly) what religion is and what it is to be educated in it. Our problem is not an intellectual one, requiring the endless labour of philosophers of religion, but the emotional problem of adopting the right posture. Whether or not the particular account I have given is substantially correct does not so much matter.

Notes

1. See, for example, P H Hirst and R S Peters, *The Logic of Education,* London, Routledge and Kegan Paul, 1970, p. 64.
2. Cf. my *Education in Religion and the Emotion,* London, Heinemann, 1971, p. 4 ff.
3. *Op. cit.,* pp. 21 ff.

1.3 Two languages of religious education

Gabriel Moran

The contemporary religious scene presents a paradox. I think it could be said that religious education has become one of the most urgent, practical and universal problems confronting our society. At the same time, religious education in the Christian churches seems relegated to secondary importance. Despite some progress during the last decade, religious educators often experience a lack of institutional support for their work. Their day-to-day efforts at improvement have to continue; for example, getting a few more dollars in the budget for adult education. What is also necessary is to examine the context in which the term religious education derives its meaning.

This article looks at two different ways that religious education can be spoken about. None of us can suddenly change institutional patterns but each of us can make changes in the way he or she speaks. Change of language is at the centre of institutional change.

The languages of religious education I examine can be called ecclesiastical and educational. The first has the value of concreteness but the danger of parochialism. The second exists only in inchoate form and needs the concreteness which church, synagogue and other religious organisations can bring to it. I do not advocate abandoning the first for the second but I am opposing the reduction of religious education to the language of the church. In Catholic circles this reduction occurs through equating religious education and catechetics; the parallel in Protestant writing happens with the use of the term Christian education.

A common procedure is to acknowledge in an early footnote that there is some debate over the terms catechetics and religious education. Not being able to resolve the problem, the author tries to leave the issue open and not choose between the two terms. That attitude may appear liberal but its effect is to restrict enquiry to a field defined by church language. From an educational perspective that field of enquiry may not be adequate for many church people. Toward people who are not in the church this restriction of language is intolerant.

I think that there is no debate on the fact that 'religious education' is etymologically, historically and operationally wider in meaning than catechetics or Christian education. It is that very breadth which some people fear because it suggests abstraction or generality. Their concern is well placed. People are not religious in general; they are concretely and specifically religious with their words and their bodies. An education that only looked at religion in general would not be adequate as religious education. But neither is it educationally adequate today to use the particular language of a church without relating it to a broader context. Theodore Roszak states the problem succinctly: 'We must learn to be loyal to our choices without being parochial in our study or appreciation.'[1]

Ecclesiastical language

The ecclesiastical language of religious education is governed by the relation of theology (including the Christian scriptures) to catechetics/Christian education. Nothing is allowed into the content of catechetics/Christian education unless approved by theology. The main thing to be studied about the ecclesiastical form of religious education is the meaning of theology.

The first and obvious question for theology is the appropriateness of the word theology. The word has pretentious connotations of speaking for God or about God. For the purpose of articulating a Christian position it is not obvious that the word theology is either necessary or helpful. At the least, anyone using the word theology ought to be sensitive to the fact that many people are immediately suspicious of the claim inherent to the word. A religious statement clearly has a place in education; a theological statement already carries a judgment whose legitimacy has to be educationally questioned.

The trouble begins when theology assumes control of religious discourse. In Christian writing, theological is often used interchangeably with religious. In discussions of religious language the examples are regularly taken from the Christian bible. Religious conflicts are assumed to spring from opposing theologies when what might be in question is the Christian bible-theology as an adequate religious language.

Undoubtedly the word theology could designate one model for understanding religion. The word model refers here to a consistent pattern of language with the implication that there are alternate models. Recent discussion about 'models of theology' is somewhat misleading. The models turn out to be historical periods in the development of theology or variations on the themes within theology.[2] Theology does not have models because theology is a model. To speak of alternative models one would have to turn, for example, to Jewish religious studies.

When theology does not see itself as one model it tends to absorb Judaism into itself. It refers to Judeo-Christian tradition as if the Jewish and Christian were not in considerable conflict of interpretation. Christian and Jewish people use many of the same words (God, covenant, messiah, salvation, etc.) but they speak different languages. The word theology is used by a few Jewish writers today but it has little strength within the whole Jewish tradition. If enough of Judaism became comfortable with the word theology, then there would be at least two models of theology, namely, a Jewish model and a Christian model. Until that happens, which is not likely, there remain Jewish study and (Christian) theology.

It is difficult to make the above point in the Christian churches without seeming to attack certain persons and their profession. Nothing I have said disparages the study of the Christian scriptures, church history and doctrine. Not just the churches but the rest of the world needs scholarly examination of that material which is so much a part of our lives. People within the churches who neglect that study do themselves a disservice. People outside the churches who think they can simply eliminate Christianity from western society are extremely naive.

Even less would I wish to minimise the work of people called catechists or Christian educators. As a group of people they are as intelligent, dedicated and hard working as any group I know. Their work enables people to participate in the rich tradition of the Christian churches. Nonetheless, it must be said that their effectiveness is limited by the language and institutional patterns which define catechetics/Christian education. One part of that pattern, for example, is a division along sexual lines: theologians are nearly all men (and theology is a bastion of sexist writing) while catechists/Christian educators are typically women.

In summary, the ecclesiastical form of religious education has two components: theology and catechetics/Christian education. In practice, however, theology stands outside the discussion of religious education and merely dictates the content to be used. To the extent that rich religious material is present in theology (especially material from Jewish and Christian bibles) the educational content can be very effective. But there is more to education than a body of material called content. The institutional structure is itself educative or miseducative. Church divisions, sexual and otherwise, cannot be effectively criticised from within those divisions. Catechetics cannot dialogue with theology because theology controls the language. The way to open dialogue within churches is to place the study of religion into an educational rather than ecclesiastical context.

Education in religion

In this section I would like to describe the components of a full context for education in religion. It should be immediately acknowledged that there is no ideal educational world ready for church people to step into. Educational establishments can be every bit as narrow and rigid as religious organisations. By using the word educational for this way of speaking I am weighing the choice in this direction. But this usage also allows that much of the religious material spoken of ecclesiastically can reappear in an educational language.

Education tends to get taken over by school in a way similar to the church's control of religion. Education is not simply larger than school, it is a different kind of thing. By education I mean the systematic planning of experience for growth in human understanding. Schools are one way to promote education and in our world probably a necessary one. But schools should not be over-estimated as they were by the Dewey enthusiasts of the 1920's and the passionate opponents of schools in the 1960's. While it is true, Dewey said, that church, family, work, etc. were not established for educational purposes, they have been and they remain educationally important.[3]

Within education, religious issues might surface anywhere: in the questions of a small child at home, in the discussions at a factory or on the evening TV programme. By religion I refer to what pertains to the origin, destiny or deepest meaning of our world and finds expression in social gestures. The religious is something out of the ordinary that calls the ordinary into question. Religion exists not simply as mental construct but as personal attitude, communal symbol and bodily behaviour.

It should be noted that religion and education are at some odds. Religion breaks out of the ordinary, that is, what is ordered, controlled and fixed as 'the world'. Education is concerned with bringing experience under control; quite naturally it concentrates upon the ordinary. Especially as institutionalised in the modern world, education tends to heighten the rational or controlling element of experience. Education distrusts religion and yet needs its impulse lest educational institutions close in on themselves. Religion refuses any final constraints but for its own good religion needs some guidance and temporal forms. Religion and education are like a bickering couple who don't get along well together but who are worse off when apart. The near impossibility of religious education might be a consolation for those in the work. The closer one gets to a real religious education, the greater becomes the tension between the two words.

The entire educational setting is capable of having religious significance. But there should be three places where religion is formal and evident. These three parts of education in religion are:

a.   the study of a specific religion from within;
b.   the study of religion from a position of some distance;
c.   the practice of a religious life.

The first and the third are obviously related and should be in constant interchange. The first and the second are also related and should be mutually corrective.

The study of religion from 'within'

The word 'within' is necessarily ambiguous. It doesn't necessarily mean being a member of an organisation but generally that is part of getting the feel from within. Religious institutions need appreciation on their own terms. For example, if a person has not lived in Asia and got inside a world that is both political and religious, it is difficult to understand Buddhism. A Jew who has been surrounded since childhood with stories from the Talmud knows Judaism in a way that is probably impossible for a Christian person to duplicate. In Christian circles it is said that one cannot be a theologian without having (Christian) faith.

The 'within' is nonetheless a word that admits of degrees. A supposition of education is that one can see the world with new eyes, either one's own corrected vision or the eyes of another person. The correction of vision is a hard discipline and one that is never fully successful. But we really have no other choice other than working to understand the within of things, the hidden recesses of our own lives and the strange within of other peoples. The word 'within' does not imply introversion or defensiveness but rather the appreciation of things for their own unique selves.

There is no apology needed, therefore, for a course on the synoptic gospels or the history of church councils. In fact, there is a need for patient, detailed and scholarly study of Christian documents. This academic field could be called theology but at the least the word should be temporarily suspended for further questioning.

There are writers today who say that we need a theology that instead of being ideological should be 'critical-emancipative'.[4] I share their concern but I suggest that they ask whether the word theology can be almost reversed in meaning. Many people are justifiably suspicious of sudden conversions. A drastic change of meaning can occur only as a different group of people in a different social context engage in the activity. The class of people (sexual, racial, economic) who write books trying to change the meaning of theology cannot bring off the job alone. To find help they might direct more of their attention to theology's role (any theology) in the establishing and perpetuating of a class structured church. Instead of assuming that there is a theology that liberates they might better describe their interest as a liberating education that has reference to both church and non-church worlds.

The study of religion 'from a distance'

The second element of a full religious education is study of religion 'from a distance'. I could use the image of 'without' as a parallel to 'within' but to speak of being without or outside religion is already a big assumption. It would suggest that someone can get to a point of detached objectivity from which to examine religion. This kind of study is more appropriately called intersubjective than objective. It is a stepping back from involvement in one religion to consider its relation to other religious and nonreligious choices.

I use the word distance as a psychological image as well as an institutional reference. As the word within could admit of degrees so one can distance oneself in various ways and degrees to get another perspective on one's own or another's religious life. Taken in isolation this approach to religion would be inadequate and perhaps destructive. As one component of a religious education the study with distancing is crucial to the whole project.

The obvious place to engage in this form of religious education is the public sector of education. The study of religion in the public schools of the United States is legally possible and educationally desirable. State and private colleges are making considerable progress here but progress is very slow at elementary and secondary levels. The biggest problem is the absence of a language to discuss religion as a normal part of public education. Since the language of religious education has been under the control of churches, religious education in the public sector is left to speak a peculiarly artificial jargon.

The two phrases which run throughout literature on religion and public education are: 'teach about religion' (as opposed to teaching religion) and 'the objective teaching of religion'. Neither phrase is very helpful. The first is taken from a court ruling but it is not the Supreme Court's job to create educational language. The court is rightfully opposed to government imposition of prayers and proselytisation by any religious group in the public schools. But the way to get rid of mindlessness, sentimentalism and proselytisation in religion is to teach religion, that is, to examine the issues of religion in a critical and unbiased way. The phrase 'teach about religion' creates an artificial notion of objectivity and gives over the language of teaching religion to many people who indoctrinate rather than teach.

The same can be said of the phrase 'the objective teaching of religion'. The several meanings of the word objective do nothing but confuse the issue. Insofar as one simply refers to the characteristics of an object, then all study and teaching are objective and the phrase is a redundancy. If one means by objective the positive value of unbiased, then objective is a demand in all teaching and study. If objective means not being involved at all in a subject, then the phrase expresses something that is probably not possible and certainly not desirable. One cannot understand religion without involving one's subjectivity.

When teaching and education are attempted, religious questions become volatile. Nonetheless, if we cannot examine religion in institutions set aside for education, where are we to look? The great majority of school children (including Roman Catholics) go to public schools. Religion ought to be part of that education in school if only to make those schools be more public. It would be to the churches' advantage to let go of the words by which they try to hegemonise religious education, starting with the phrase 'teach religion'. It will be a slow journey, in any case, but we cannot begin without a clear and firm conviction that religious education and public education are not separate sectors.

The practice of religious life

There is last but not least the practice of a religious life. The briefest summary of this practice is prayer and social action. One could use other terms to describe religious practice but there is a long tradition (especially within Roman Catholicism) that puts a contemplative pole at one end of religious practice and action for social justice at the other end.

This part of religious education is neither studied nor taught, at least directly. The education in this area is more indirect than in the previous two elements. For example, I cannot teach someone how to pray. I can teach a person how to breathe better (a crucial factor in most traditions) or how to say a formula for prayer. There is an element of privacy or intimacy that has to be respected here. I referred to theology as including the Christian scriptures; there are other uses of the Christian bible, particularly in the liturgy. There is a study of the eucharist and there is a practice of eucharist; the two should be carefully distinguished. There is a time for criticising the sexism of traditional prayers; there is another time to pray with ancient formulas.

This area of religious education could be called catechetics/Christian education but I would not do it too quickly. Just as with theology, the changed context and restricted purpose of catechetics has to be fully grasped. Certainly the ancient meaning of catechetical and its close relation to sacramental life make it a desirable word to retain. (Christian education does not have that specific historical association but obviously the term can be acceptable.) Practice belongs at the centre of education. Practices which the Christian churches can bring to education include the contemplative, the sacramental and the protest against injustice.

For its own health catechetics cannot claim to be more than a part of religious education. Far from lessening the importance of this work the context would finally allow the biblical, liturgical and ethical concerns to speak back to what has been called theology. For example, if we experience God's presence in contemplative or liturgical prayer, this experience is not something whose meaning is to be undercut by theology's premises. If a child calls God she as well as he, perhaps this is not a mistake to be corrected by theology but a challenge to the existence of what has been called theology. If the biographies of contemporary saints speak a very different language from theology, then it might be theology which needs a religious education.

The test which I offer for this meaning of religious education is that it would save what we most value from our past but would open new doors for the future. A good distinction does not destroy any of the past though it may chasten our claims about past and present. In the past we may have spoken as if we alone had the truth. The challenge now of religious education is to help us speak and live the truth we know while also removing the intolerance which is embedded in our language. To any other person or group we can then say: Here is our way. Show us your way.

Notes
1. Theodore Roszak, *Unfinished Animal,* New York, Harper and Row, 1975, p. 203.
2. David Tracy, *Blessed Rage for Order,* New York, Seabury, 1975.
3. Lawrence Cremin, *Public Education,* New York, Basic Books, 1976.
4. Edward Schillebeeckx, *The Understanding of Faith,* New York, Seabury, 1974, pp. 131–154.

1.4 What is religious education?
Charles F Melchert

The fact that there is some question about what constitutes religious education needs no documenting to anyone who reads journals or travels to professional meetings. The same concern for what is religious education recurs not only in the United States, but also in Canada, Britain, Scandinavia, Australia, and elsewhere.

As I see this question, 'What is religious education?' it is essentially a quest for some way of distinguishing what a religious educator does from what everyone else does. Is there anything unique or distinctive about the task and responsibility of the religious educator? What makes us different from the social studies teacher, or the preacher, or the counsellor? If there is something unique about our functioning, what is it?

One way of beginning to get a handle on this concern is to take the language seriously as we use it. What does it mean to call something 'education' and 'religious' and 'religious education'?

Education: six criteria

First, let us note that education is not the same as schooling, and secondly, that we are speaking here about the *process* of education, and not the product or label. That means that we are examining the concept education as it designates a way of doing something with people, and not as it refers to a school, or something one 'gets'. Thirdly, let us not examine education in its broadest sense, as everything that happens to anyone, for a concept so broadly taken offers no help in clarifying distinctive or unique features.

I contend that an examination of education shows that there are six elements or criteria which are necessary to the structure of the concept.[1]

1. To call something education implies that it is an *intentional activity* and that the result is not entirely accidental. We would think it most strange if someone were to say, 'I am educated, but I didn't mean for it to happen.' This is one way in which education differs conceptually from learning, which can be quite accidental. Education implies intentionally directed learning.
2. To call something education implies that it is of *value*. It is

48

logically contradictory to say that one has been educated, and yet has in no way changed for the better.[2] This value criterion applies both to the product and to the process of education. This suggests that simply adding teaching to learning does not automatically produce education, if either the product or the process is valueless or detrimental.

3. To call something education implies that it *involves knowing and understanding in depth and breadth*. Thus education is more than simply accumulating know-how, training or facts. Education implies that the learner is gaining an ability to see connections or relationships within a field and among different fields, what Beck calls 'a working understanding of the world and of life.'[3]

4. Calling something education implies reference to a rather long period of *time*. Education seems not to be comfortably used of an afternoon's experience, but rather suggests a period of years. When we ask if a particular activity is education, one of the concerns implied is whether that activity will open up to the future, whether it will be likely to lead beyond itself. Some types of experiences seem to be dead-end events that dampen curiosity and decrease interest in further learning, thus foreshortening the time and inhibiting education.

5. To speak of education implies the necessity of *interpersonal interactions*. More important, this relationship is of a particular kind. It is a helping relationship. A teacher's primary function with a learner is to help the pupil learn. Stating this so baldly makes me embarrassed about even calling attention to such an obvious fact. Yet if one takes this fact seriously and examines all the activities of one's own teaching from this view, it soon becomes plain how seldom we think of the effect of the quality of our relationships on the learning processes of students.

   The necessity of this helping dimension in the educational process becomes more apparent when we consider the variety of types of understandings appropriate to the human being in the educational endeavour. Many kinds of understandings can only be attained in close relationships with other human beings – and we shall later see that these types of understandings are not peripheral to the educational process at the most basic level.[4]

6. Speaking of education implies the presence of something we can only call *wholeness*. Education involves the entire person, the totality of his or her life, and it affects all of that person's relationships – with self, with others, with things and with ideas. To be educated means more than being an expert in one area of specialisation. It means more than having gone to four years of college or having a graduate degree. As one becomes educated, one finds oneself acquiring

certain inclinations which significantly influence one's style of life and experience.[5] One becomes more inclined not only to have knowledge but to use it to inform one's actions. One finds oneself being curious about all sorts of things — there seems to be increasingly a desire to know and understand even beyond the superficial level. It is quite appropriate, conceptually speaking, that recent developments in psychology and educational theory have combined to stress not only the traditional intellectual aspects of education, but also its emotional, behavioural, political, social and spiritual dimensions.

These six criteria, I am claiming, are not simply my own or someone else's personal preference or opinion. Rather they are public, non-arbitrary, even necessary component parts of that concept we call education, and they are implicit in our use of the language. Conceptual analysis helps us make explicit what usually remains implicit even though present. But analysis does not tell us that we should continue to use the language as we have and do. One sometimes meets characters on a golf course who do strange things like throw clubs high in the air, or curse vehemently at inanimate bodies of water and sand. Are they playing golf when doing such things? Analysis helps make clear what constitutes the game in question in its more rudimentary dimensions, and thus allows us to choose our games more precisely. One can legitimately conclude, 'If that is what education is, then we mean to be doing something else.' Just because golf or education are valuable activities does not mean that everyone ought always to play that game, nor need they feel less worthy should they choose to play ping-pong or counselling instead.

But let us return to our basic question. Does this analysis help us understand what is unique or distinctive about religious education? Yes, insofar as it helps us clarify what is educational about religious education. One thing which is unique about education is that it has this unique combination of elements. But to move beyond analysis for a moment, let me suggest that one of the ways of clarifying the unique and distinctive tasks of religious education, insofar as it is education, is seeing the primary importance of the combination of two of the criteria — understanding and helping.

Helping

Many other disciplines, such as philosophy, are concerned with understanding and knowing, but as disciplines they are not fundamentally concerned with *helping* others to know and understand. That happens as these disciplines become aligned with educational purposes. But those educational purposes remain ancillary to the discipline's basic function, namely, to increase knowledge and understanding themselves, for their own sake. On the other hand there are a variety of helping relationships, a variety of ways of dealing with people, and it is education's focus on gaining knowledge and understanding that helps distinguish it from other ways of helping people. Let us amplify how these two dimensions of the educational process clarify our distinctive responsibilities.

Helping, as a way of viewing the educational process, helps focus clearly the relational nature of the educational task. Helping implies the presence of and the interaction between at least two people, even if that help is mediated through a book or some piece of educational technology. The subject matter and one's experience is important, but the only way to know if one is being helpful is by reference to the one being helped.

Since the helping entails a social relationship, moral considerations are automatically intrinsic to the process. Not only must the subject be valuable, but also the manner of the learning and the quality of the relationship must meet moral standards. Most fundamentally it must demonstrate respect for the persons involved. Any plan or programme which reduces persons on either side of the educational interaction to something less than human, falls short of a fully moral relationship. Thus when the learner is regarded as an object to be manipulated into end-states predetermined in advance without his or her consent, as is often the case in behaviourist or behaviourialist schemas, there is a constant temptation to a less than fully moral relationship with persons.[6] This can be compensated for if the teacher consciously keeps clearly in mind the goal of this learning manipulation, and works continuously to bring the learner into a conscious adoption and participation in the task-setting and means-determination.

How a teacher or anyone who exercises a teaching function views himself or herself relates significantly to the effectiveness of the teaching-learning relationship.[7] This means that one's effectiveness as a teacher will likely be enhanced by the attainment of increased knowledge and understanding of four types:

a. knowledge and understanding of the subject matter, and especially as it is translated to the cognitive and experiential levels appropriate to this age group or this individual;
b. knowledge and understanding of oneself – one's own personal makeup, needs, motives, values, effect on others, tendencies to distort, and one's own teaching strengths and weaknesses;
c. knowledge and understanding of others, including cognitive, emotional, religious, and moral developmental characteristics, and an awareness of where a certain characteristic leads in future development; in addition to some sense of

the strength of particular abilities or age-level characteristics in people of various ages or personalities. Often it is the case that some attributes vital to education are not strong or are derided by some groups (for example, peers) at some stages, and thus will call for support and strengthening;

d. knowledge and understanding of the likely cause and effect relationships in teaching methods and strategies and resources.

It must not be assumed that the helping relationship is a one-way process. Any teacher knows better than that. Indeed, as the complexity of what is being taught increases (for example, in areas such as religion, or with goals such as understanding) the assurance of success decreases, and greater is the need for a mutuality which increasingly approaches equality between teacher and learner. This means there will be increased learner involvement, initiative and choice in directing the learning. When this observation is coupled with the recognition of the time needed for an educational process to achieve anything like fulfilment and wholeness, it becomes a moral as well as an educational expectation that the learner assume increasing responsibility for his or her own education.

Insofar as the helping relationship being described here is an educational process, it is shaped particularly by the intention to help increase the knowledge and understanding of the participants. Let us now turn to the understanding dimension.

Understanding

Knowledge, the conditions of knowledge in both its strong and weak senses, has been explored by philosophers for centuries and seems relatively well known. Understanding, on the other hand, has been less well mapped out and perhaps is even more complex. Let us begin with the educational concern in focus — What does one do when one understands?

First, note that to understand something is not completely equivalent to being understanding. One can be an understanding person or be understanding toward another without, at the same time, having an understanding of that person's behaviour. Conversely, one can understand another's behaviour without, at the same time, being understanding toward him or his behaviour.

We can describe six elements of the act of understanding, though they will not necessarily occur in the same sequence, nor will they all be present in every act of understanding.[8]

1. We attend, notice, see, image, hear, think, smell, touch or sense something. Gestalt psychology has shown that we can attend to an object directly, focally, or we can see it as part of the context

of another object. How we attend is influenced by many factors. I may see a bowl of bananas when I am hungry and be aware of the bananas as something to consume, and ignore the bowl completely. If I am not hungry, and have just heard a discussion of aesthetic form, I may be more attentive to the bowl and fruit as form and grace and less conscious of it as a source of stomach stuffing.

2. Sometimes as we attend we become aware of a deficiency or perplexity in our understanding of that object. Something doesn't make sense, or there is felt a need to 'get hold' of this more fully. This awareness of a lack of understanding may come either intentionally or quite by chance, and thus it may occur because I search for areas in which I do not fully understand, or because awareness of my deficiency either just seems to happen to me or someone brings it to my attention.

3. Such a recognition can either awaken or build upon a desire to understand or comprehend. If Piaget is correct, every infant comes into this world with a desire to know and understand the world and self. The intensity of this desire varies and it seems it can even be lost or stamped out. As one grows, values shape this understanding process too. One finds oneself paying more attention to and desiring to understand more fully, things and areas which one comes to value.

4. Attending to the perplexity or deficiency and wanting to understand more fully, a pattern emerges or is constructed. We see connections, relationships, which we did not see before − either within the object itself (thus increasing the depth of our understanding of that object) or in its relations with other objects (thus increasing the breadth of our understanding). This seeing of connections cannot always be produced on demand. Sometimes it happens quickly; at other times it may take years of struggling with a problem. It happens in as many ways as there are objects or subjects to understand and ways to understand them. It can happen consciously by making one thing which is known a pattern or model of another which is less well known,[9] or it can happen less consciously as an image occurs to me, or presents itself, thus fusing the disparate parts into a whole meaning.[10] In this aspect of the act of understanding we have perhaps the essence of the act − the fundamentally unitive nature of understanding − making things connected or whole which are not seen as such before understanding occurs. .

5. Thus I say 'I understand.' Whether it happens suddenly, with the well-known flash of insight or outsight and the shout of 'Eureka!' or whether it dawns slowly and cumulatively, almost unnoticed, its presence usually has a stimulating effect on the one who understands. There is a feeling of having put something

together. There is a sense of accomplishment, of competence, sometimes of relief, sometimes of gratefulness or peace.

6. However, that is not the end. Having achieved understanding does not guarantee that the understanding is correct. As Lonergan has convincingly shown, one can have the experience described above and still be mistaken. One can always ask legitimately, 'But is it so?' The answer to that question, no matter how difficult to attain, is either yes or no.[11] If one answers no, that does not mean it was all a hoax. Indeed, misunderstanding or mistaken or partial understanding is itself an important part of the process of understanding even more fully in depth and breadth.

Now to return to our basic question. We are not interested in understanding understanding simply because it is interesting, but especially as it helps us understand the educational process in religion as a process of helping others understand in religion. We need now to turn to religion and ask what contribution the 'religious' makes to the religious education. Then we shall be in a better position to ask about helping and understanding specifically in religion and religious education.

What is religion?

It has been difficult to clarify what constitutes education, helping and understanding, but that is nothing compared to the difficulties of answering the question, 'What is religion?' As Johnson asks so tellingly, 'What has not been done in the name of religion?' The complexity of the issues and the diversity of the responses to the question have led some to despair of an answer at all. Others find their way by adopting patently reductionistic schemes, as do Durkheim, Marx and Freud. Still others remain on the sidelines by adopting the permanently detached and neutral stance of the phenomenologist. Others jump into the fray with both feet and insist that some particular religion is right or superior. It would seem the height of absurdity to claim to be able to use conceptual analysis in religion, when one of the persistent claims of religionists is that the heart of the matter is ineffable. If religion has fundamentally to do with a non-linguistic, non-conceptual ultimate, then conceptual analysis begins with something of a handicap.

First, note the three terms most used: religion, religions, and religious. The first two are terms which refer either to one religion in particular or to many differing religions. Perhaps the first question we must face in this exploration is 'Is religion one or many?' Religious, on the other hand, denotes something more of a quality, something that modifies or qualifies something else. We say that someone belongs to a religion, but when we affirm that one is a religious person, we usually imply something qualitatively different from or more than being an adherent of some religion. So our second concern shall be, can we identify the nature of the 'religious' dimension or quality of human experience?

It should be noted that I approach these questions with an educator's interests. While I do not try to shape religion to fit the Procrustean bed of education, neither do I explore religion solely for its own sake, but with a view to understanding how religion and the religious influence the educational process.

Is religion one or many? Ninian Smart rejects the search for a common core or a 'unity' among the religions on the grounds that once a principle of unity is stated, many participants in each religion will not agree that such a unifying principle is central to their religion or their perception of their religion. Smart rather turns to 'formal characteristics' of the various religions as a way of specifying what constitutes religion. He describes six dimensions which every religion has in common: a religion has doctrines or beliefs; it has myths or narratives; it has ethics; and on the more practical and existential side, a religion has a ritual; it has an experiential dimension; and a social or institutional dimension.[12] These six dimensions permit us to identify what various religions have in common, as well as how they differ. The dimensions also permit us to see how such ideologies as humanism or Marxism have religious meanings. This approach rightly recognises the complexity and richness of religion, and rejects reductionism. The dimensions recognise that a religion has external as well as internal concerns. Yet is it true that all that religions have in common is the existence of these six formal categories? Can we reject a normative search for unity simply because some will not agree with the results of that search? Taking a vote is hardly a viable procedure for settling a normative issue.

John Wilson, on the other hand, takes the opposite tack. He argues that before we can get around to being clear about religious education we have to have a clear idea of what counts as religion and what would count as being good at it.[13] Otherwise we have no way of knowing what we work toward educationally. To know this, Wilson argues, we need to seek what is *sui generis* about religion, and one need not be sure that everyone agrees. Wilson assumes that the uniqueness of religion can be found by finding the one category which marks religion off from other forms of human activity. Wilson argues that the only category which distinguishes religion falls within what Smart calls the experiential dimension. Awe is the one thing that 'religion is uniquely concerned with'.[14] Awe, when combined with a belief that the object is worthy of that awe, expresses itself in worship, and that is distinctively religion's concern. This awe is fundamentally an emotion, and thus Wilson goes on to speak of the need for the education of the emotions in religious education. In the process Wilson seems to reduce religion to this individual emotional dimension and suggests that all other religious expressions are rooted in it.[15]

Both approaches are useful, and yet both need expanding if we are to be true to the full nature of religion and also be fully adequate to the needs of the religious educator.

Apprehending the ineffable

Wilson correctly identifies awe and its expression in worship as being fundamental to religious experience, though Smart more adequately describes the complex multi-dimensionality of religion. I think it presumptuous, at best, to claim that religion can be reduced not only to the private individual, but to only one emotion within that individual. What bothers me with both approaches, either the reductionistic or the purely descriptive, is that though both affirm the existence of claims to ineffability and transcendence in most, if not all, religions, neither takes those claims seriously enough in their treatment of religion. I should like to suggest that taking such claims seriously gives us better grounds for understanding both the complex ideological and social nature of religion, which Smart describes, as well as the basic awe experience to which Wilson points. Perhaps more important, for our immediate purposes, attention to these is extremely illuminating for the kinds of understanding which are especially appropriate in religion.

Robert Ornstein has summarised a great deal of research into the specialisation of function within the two hemispheres of the human brain. Studies have shown that the left hemisphere of the brain (which controls the right side of the body) is responsible for verbal, mathematical, logical and analytical functioning, while the right hemisphere of the brain (which controls the left side of the body) is responsible for the moral, gestural, spatial, artistic, synthetic, wholistic and even mystical modes of consciousness.[16] What is particularly intriguing about this specialisation in the human brain is that despite healthy and normal functioning of the corpus callosum, which is the instrument of communication between the two hemispheres, there seems to be a fundamental inability of each area of specialisation to adequately express in its own terms the cognising or structuring of experiential data from other areas. Thus logical operations cannot be adequately expressed verbally. Thus the ineffable has a very specific meaning, although it perhaps ought not be limited to inability to express in words, but the inability to express across modes of consciousness. Polanyi describes the same phenomenon, although he calls it tacit knowing, in our ability to infallibly recognise another's face, and yet our inability to describe that same face to another who doesn't know it, so they can recognise it.

What is important to note here is not only the ineffability of these modes of consciousness, but also the direct apprehension of the reality which they embody. Drawing a picture, using a gesture, apprehending a mystical oneness, are not simply ways of communicating with others, but are more fundamentally ways of structuring experience just as valid as verbal and logical ways of structuring experience. But they are qualitatively different, and they thus permit kinds of structuring different from the sequential and analytic modes of structuring characteristic of logical and verbal processes.

To return to the explicit religions, then, we recognise a similar directness of apprehension and ineffability operating in these religions, and yet adherents insist that these ineffable apprehensions help structure meaning in their lives and experience. As with the communication between hemispheres of the brain, use of more than one mode of consciousness permits greater articulation and understanding of any phenomenon than does only one mode alone. So the direct apprehension of a vision of God may well be better understood by attempts to structure that apprehension (retrospectively) by exploring the doctrinal implications of it, the ethical implications, by picturing it, by putting it to music, and so on. Similarly with communication of such experiences. We can often tell a story or paint a word picture which will help evoke a similar feeling in others, if they have had some experience akin to the one we are trying to communicate. In other words, when attempting to translate across modes of consciousness and areas of specialisation in the brain, as we necessarily do in such areas as religion and aesthetics, we must use what Kierkegaard called indirection.

Religious education

As a religious educator, then, I find that Smart's six dimensions and Wilson's description of awe are not only differing descriptions of religion. Rather the very nature of awe, and of the understanding appropriate to it, suggests an organising principle for the six dimensions. The dimensions are not unrelated, but each leads to the others, although the experiential dimension seems to be the force which grounds and gives vitality to the others. Each of the other dimensions can be seen as arising from attempts of peoples to reason about, describe and spell out the implications of the experience which is essentially ineffable. That would suggest that giving learners an understanding of doctrines, myths, ethics, rituals, and social forms of religions *requires* some understanding, perhaps even some direct apprehension, of the awe which is capable of impelling worship, or of the mystical apprehension of the relatedness of all things in the ground of being. Without that it is very hard to understand some of the force and ineluctibility of religion for most peoples.

Similarly with the notion of transcendence. Here it helps to pay attention to the language we use, especially when we call someone religious. When we say 'She is a religious', we mean little more than that she is a member of an order or religious community. But when we say, 'She is a religious person', we imply something qualitatively different about her as a person, by implication, that she is somehow different from one whom we might call 'non-religious'. Sometimes that means little more than 'She goes to church faithfully.' But generally it tends to mean something more qualitative. What is that something more? When we say something like 'He did that job religiously for thirty years', we imply a conscientiousness about duties, or a style of work which can only be called devoted, or committed. This kind of speaking can be used in a thoroughly secular manner, so there is no necessary reference to the person's participation in any particular religion. We speak this way to indicate a certain quality to their life. Very often the people referred to as having this quality speak of their life or work with a sense that they see it in terms far larger than a task to be done daily. Often they speak in terms of their sense of their place in a social scheme, or in a universal plan, or their sense of duty to some ideal or cause, or of their job or life as an expression of their devotion to a god, their commitment to an ideal.

It is at points like these that reductionistic strategies most clearly betray their inadequacy. This is true of Wilson, Freud, Marx, or even, more close to home, Goldman.[17] Do we turn to children to discover the essence of pure science? It seems rather, to me, that to recognise most clearly, for the use of the educator especially, the sensitivities appropriate to religious people, we need to turn not to those who have it in its most minimal fashion, but to the most proficient practitioners, the religious geniuses, if you will. We need to ask how one gets that way, beginning with childhood, and then ask what one needs, either in skills, attitudes or understandings, to comprehend the essence of that religious quality. For example, what distinguishes people like Gandhi, Hammarskjold, or Martin Luther King is not simply their able political leadership during difficult periods, but their religious or spiritual quality, their ability to see the political dimensions of their activities in the far broader frame of reference, to see them not only as political but also as profoundly religious or spiritual events. Such persons have a vision, as do those we mentioned above, and because of that are not only dedicated and conscientious to their tasks, but are sensitive to the direction of events, and to self-transcending significance of those events and their place in them. Often such people appear quite humble, and though they feel unequal to the tasks, they rise to the occasion, and they help peoples, even whole cultures rise and transcend themselves and their times. Each of us has had at least small glimmers of that sense of being called to be something more than we are at the moment.

To return again to the description of the domain of the religious educator, we see again the complexity and the variety of the types of understanding appropriate to the arena we call religion and the religious. To help another come to fuller understandings of such matters demands a style of helping relationship which is perhaps more appropriately called ministry. For it implies, as does the concept ministry, an ability to help in such a way that you put yourself at the service of others and their attempts to know and understand. But it perhaps also means a willingness to engage in this endeavour not only with the immature. Indeed full exploration of even some of the dimensions suggested here would seem to call for longer-term relationships, at considerably greater depth than is usually advocated in most popular religious education texts.[18] It would also seem to suggest a more disciplined approach to teaching and learning and the fullest possible use of one's intellectual, emotional, moral, relational and spiritual resources well into maturity.

This analysis suggests, in conclusion, that religious education, insofar as it is true both to education and to religion, will entail helping others to understand in the ways appropriate to religion, and that such ways include not only the traditional academic and intellectual pursuits, but also the more experiential, ineffable and self-transcending ways of understanding appropriate to and characteristic of religions and the religious. I feel compelled to stress, so as to avoid misunderstanding, that helping others to understand the experiential dimensions of religion is not necessarily the same as giving them those experiences or expecting them to be or become committed to that experience or a religion. Educationally what is being sought is understanding.[19]

Whether the conceptualisation offered here as a possible answer to the question 'What is religious education?' ultimately proves to be the so-called right answer is insignificant beside the necessity of stimulating thorough discussion of such issues. My concern remains to arrive at a clear understanding of the nature and task of religious education, so that our thinking as well as our practice will have integrity both in its educational dimensions and its religious dimensions.

Notes

1. For fuller treatment of the following points see my 'Does the church really want religious education?' *Religious Education,* 69, 1974, pp. 12–22. See also P H Hirst and R S Peters, *The Logic of Education,* London, Routledge and Kegan Paul, 1970, chapter 2, and R S Downie, E M Loudfoot and E Telfer, *Education and Personal Relationships,* London, Methuen, 1974, chapter 2.
2. R S Peters, *Ethics and Education,* London, Allen and Unwin, 1966, p. 20.

3. Clive Beck, *Educational Philosophy and Theory,* Boston, Little, Brown, 1974, p. 50.
4. This point is stressed in Bruner's description of 'pre-emptive metaphors' which inhibit learning in his *Toward a Theory of Instruction,* Cambridge, Massachusetts, Belknap, 1966, chapter 7, or in Jones' sensitive descriptions of how children's feelings about death and family relationships affect not only the vitality and quality of their learning but also the content and style of their dancing! See Richard Jones, *Fantasy and Feeling in Education,* New York, New York University Press, 1968, pp. 28–46.
5. R S Downie, E M Loudfoot and E Telfer, *Education and Personal Relationships,* London, Methuen, 1974, p. 20.
6. This is ultimately Freire's point about the inadequacy of certain conceptualisations of the human being implicit in the literary programmes; see Freire's 'The adult literacy process as cultural action for freedom,' *Harvard Educational Review,* 40, 1970, pp. 205–212.
7. A W Combs, D L Avila and W W Purkey, *Helping Relationships,* Boston, Allyn and Bacon, 1971.
8. The framework for the description of understanding presented here was greatly informed by an excellent discussion by David Pole, 'Understanding: a psychical process,' in the *Proceedings of the Aristotelian Society,* 60, 1960, pp. 253–268. Also see my more extended treatment of this issue, especially its educational implications, in the forthcoming festschrift for Randolph C Miller by the Religious Education Press, edited by the Cullys, in my chapter entitled, 'Understanding in religious education.'
9. Excellent discussions of this process can be found in Max Black, *Models and Metaphors,* Ithica, New York, Cornell University Press, 1962, and its religious application in Ian Ramsey, *Models and Mystery,* London, Oxford University Press, 1964, and in its educational application in Marc Belth, *Education as a Discipline,* Boston, Allyn and Bacon, 1965, and *New World of Education,* Boston, Allyn and Bacon, 1970, and in its religious education application in my own 'The significance of Marc Belth for religious education,' *Religious Education,* 64, 1969, pp. 261–265.
10. A thorough and provocative description of this process can be found in James Loder, *Religious Pathology and Christian Faith,* Philadelphia, Westminster Press, 1966.
11. Bernard Lonergan, SJ, *Insight: a study of human understanding,* New York, Philosophical Library, 1970, especially pp. 82–83 and chapter 9.
12. Ninian Smart and D Horder, *New Movements in Religious Education,* London, Temple Smith, 1975, chapter 1, by Smart, 'What is Religion?'
13. John Wilson, *Education in Religion and the Emotions,* London, Heineman, 1971, chapter 2.
14. *Ibid.,* p. 34.
15. *Ibid.,* chapter 3.
16. Robert Ornstein, *The Psychology of Consciousness,* San Francisco, Freeman, 1972, pp. 51ff.
17. Ronald Goldman, *Religious Thinking From Childhood to Adolescence,* London, Routledge and Kegan Paul, 1964, pp. 10–14.
18. See my 1974 paper for the Association of Professors and Researchers in Religious Education, 'Wisdom: old paradigm for education,' for further suggestions along this line.
19. See my chapter, 'Commitment in religion and education,' in G Durka and J M Smith, *Emerging Issues in Religious Education,* New York, Paulist Press, 1976, pp. 88–89.

1.5 Formation, education, instruction
John Westerhoff

There is much that we learn only over time from the judgments of our critics, the wisdom of our colleagues, and our own critical reflections. This article is a consequence of such learning. In it I will review briefly fifteen years of hunches, suggest summarily some present convictions, and explain some issues I hope to address in the next few years.

For better or worse, I think as I write, or perhaps I write so I will know that I am thinking. All of which makes sense, unless you are a reader who reads all present hunches as reasoned conclusions. Timothy Lines in *Systemic Religious Education*[1] comments correctly that I have not yet constructed a careful, reasoned, systemic framework for religious education. Perhaps it is, as he suggests, my personality, but I would prefer to explain it in terms of my age. Theory construction like philosophy and theology is work best done in the wisdom of old age. When we are young, then imaginative, eclectic, undeveloped hunches to be explored and reflected upon are more reasonable and yet can make a contribution to the present and become the foundation for later more systematic work. Nevertheless, at fifty-four I'm near a point of transition, which explains this short essay.

Past hunches

Fifteen years ago, in *Generation to Generation*,[2] I introduced the concept 'intentional religious socialisation or enculturation', defined as 'a process consisting of lifelong, intentional and unintentional, formal and informal mechanisms through which persons and communities sustain and transmit their faith (world view and value system) and lifestyles'. Religious education I defined as 'deliberate systematic and sustained efforts within a community of faith which aim at enabling persons and groups to evolve particular ways of thinking, feeling, and acting'. I suggested that socialisation was the more inclusive understanding of learning, for it included both the covert or hidden curriculum of communal life and the overt curriculum of the educator. I went on to suggest that education is best understood as one aspect of religious socialisation and that socialisation join education as being understood as intentional activities.

As I reread that article I am aware of its lack of clarity and its numerous contradictions. As I reflect on its historic significance,

I believe I was trying to find a way out of what appeared to me to be a serious flaw in the Protestant understanding of the church's educational ministry. For the most part, I found that Protestants, functionally if not theoretically, envisioned education as instruction in a schooling context. While I acknowledged the historic role of what I called the schooling-instructional paradigm, I advocated that the church establish an alternative paradigm, one that not only expanded our understanding of education but included insights from socialisation and enculturation theory. In *Will Our Children Have Faith?*[3] I named this alternative, the community of faith-enculturation paradigm. Soon there were those who were talking about a socialisation model of Christian education; and even I got caught up in their enthusiasm and perhaps gave the impression that I was opposed to all schooling and instruction. Then to complicate my attempts to develop an alternative paradigm for intentional learning in the church as an educative community, I became increasingly dissatisfied with twentieth century Protestant use of terms such as 'religious', 'Christian', and/or 'church education'. I therefore reverted to the early church's use of the word 'catechesis' and connected it to both my understanding of intentional religious enculturation and religious education, though I never adequately defined what I meant by education as contrasted with intentional enculturation.

In retrospect, I had not thought through my hunches or attempted to articulate them adequately. I was clearer on what I found inadequate, than I was about what might replace it. I was advocating more than explaining or defending. The results could have been anticipated. Some Protestants disliked the term catechesis because they saw it as a Roman Catholic term; some Roman Catholics disliked it because they are unhappy with their experience of its use. Some of my critics correctly understood my use of catechesis as referring to the whole process of Christian becoming, but they believed that this was asking the word to carry more meaning than was possible. To complicate the situation, because my personal interest was in enculturation, it appeared as if my understanding of catechesis denied or neglected education. Therefore some concluded that I had turned education into enculturation. Others were critical because they believed educators should properly focus on education and not enculturation. Having connected enculturation with indoctrination, they believed educators needed to be concerned primarily with those educational processes which free and enable. Still others feared that catechesis was a church word and would therefore draw upon the 'sacred sciences' (scripture and tradition) to the neglect or detriment of the social sciences.

All of these criticisms I have attempted to take seriously. Many, I believe, were a direct result of my own weak thinking and unclear writing. In any case, in this article I intend to be more precise and clear. I suspect there will still be disagreement, but I hope that this article will help clarify my thoughts and focus the conversation.

Present convictions

Tertullian wrote, 'Christians are made, not born', and the process by which Christians are made was identified as 'catechesis'. I admit I like it precisely because it is a church word. I think it is wrongheaded to permit the secular world or the social sciences to establish the agenda, control the vocabulary, or determine the nature and character of theology, the church, or intentional learning within the church. Of course, the church needs to be in conversation with the secular world and open to the insights of the social sciences, but the authority of the church remains scripture, tradition and reason. And I remain committed to theology as the 'queen of the sciences'. I am, therefore, committed to the word catechesis to indicate all intentional learning within a community of Christian faith and life. We are made *a* Christian at our baptism. We spend the rest of our lives involved in a process of becoming more Christian. That life long process is one of catechesis.

Having said that, I am aware that I need to be more precise in naming the various distinctive, deliberate (intentional), systematic (related), sustained (life-long) processes which comprise catechesis. Let me suggest three: formation, education, and instruction.

Formation implies 'shaping' and refers to intentional, relational, experiential activities within the life of a story-formed faith community. *Education* implies 'reshaping' and refers to critical reflective activities related to these communal experiences. And *instruction* implies 'building' and refers to the means by which knowledge and skills useful to communal life are transmitted, acquired and understood. Formation forms the body of Christ, education reforms it, and instruction builds it up.

There are, of course, other useful ways to name and describe these three distinct, interrelated processes. Paul Tillich, the theologian, in his *Theology of Culture*,[4] wrote of three educational aims: inducting education, humanistic education, and technical education. For Tillich, inducting education focused upon the incorporation of persons into the actuality of the body Christian, the life and spirit of the Christian faith community and its tradition, through the participation of the persons in the life of the community. The aim of this formational process is to conserve the church's catholic substance (tradition), to maintain its identity as the body of Christ, and to initiate persons over time into its faith and life. This process I have called formation or nurture.

Humanistic education, on the other hand, aims to develop and actualise human potential, personal and social. As such, humanistic education emphasises the protestant principle of prophetic judgment on the tradition, frees persons from the stifling power of inducting education and makes possible both individuation and the reformation of communal expressions and manifestations of faith and life. This process is what I have called simply education.

Technical education, namely the transmission and acquisition of knowledge and skills through instructional means, also serves the needs of the church. Christians need to know the content of scripture, history and tradition. They need to be able to interpret scripture, reflect theologically, think morally, and act with historical consciousness (memory and vision). Further, they need to be knowledgeable of the nature and character of the spiritual life as well as to have acquired the skills necessary for a personal and corporate spiritual discipline. The list goes on; instruction is the means by which such are acquired.

In our day one of the most important contributors to instruction (technical education) is James Michael Lee. His three books, *The Shape of Religious Instruction*, *The Flow of Religious Instruction*, and *The Content of Religious Instruction*,[5] have made an important contribution to the field. Humanistic education (what I call Christian education) has one of its most creative advocates in Thomas Groome. His book, *Christian Religious Education*,[6] is of immense significance. However, formation (inducting education) has been generally ignored or neglected. There are of course important exceptions, but the trend today appears to emphasise education and/or instruction. Unless formation, education and instruction are distinguished from each other, even as they are all affirmed as interrelated processes necessary for Christian becoming, the vitality of the Christian faith and life will be diminished.

Parenthetically, other contemporary thinkers have identified the importance of these interdependent processes. For example, Michael Polanyi, the philosopher of science, identifies two essential processes in the scientific enterprise. The first he calls apprenticeship and the second, discovery. Polanyi's apprenticeship is very much like formation or intentional enculturation in that it ensures that the next generation will be assimilated into the established insights and behaviours of living master scientists. His second process, discovery, is similar to education or enquiry and critical reflection in that it ensures that these apprenticeships will not deteriorate into a benevolent brainwashing, but will free new masters to reveal as yet undiscovered truth. Apprenticeship ensures a faithful binding to the tradition; discovery ensures that the tradition will be kept alive through renewal and reform. In the first process, the master shapes or moulds the apprentice into the mind, heart and behaviour of the master; in the second, the master frees the apprentice from captivity to him or herself so that the apprentice can become a master. Further, it needs to be acknowledged that this same dual process is well known in the arts. Before young artists are set free to create, they apprentice themselves to a master.

Catechesis

The three deliberate (intentional), systematic (related) and sustained (life-long) processes that comprise catechesis are Christian formation, Christian education and Christian instruction. These elements within the community of Christian faith and life establish, build up, equip, and enable it to be Christ's body or presence in the world to the end that all people are restored to unity with God and each other.

I. *Christian Formation*
   A. Definition of the formational process:
      to experience Christian faith and life.
   B. Outcomes of the formational process:
      1. to incorporate − to induct persons into the life and spirit of a Christian faith community and to establish their identity as members of Christ's body, the church;
      2. to enculturate − to shape persons into an historic community's present understandings of Christian faith, character, and consciousness;
      3. to apprentice − to provide a context in which new members can observe and imitate ways of Christian living foundational to later judgments and ownership.
   C. Components of the formational process:
      1. participation in its rite (rituals and ceremonials);
      2. environment (what persons see, touch, taste, smell and hear);
      3. interrelational experiences;
      4. behaviour observed, supported, and encouraged;
      5. role models presented (past and present);
      6. organisations (how time is structured, what programmes offered);
      7. naming (how language is used, what things are called).

II. *Christian Education*
   A. Definition of the educational process:
      to reflect on experience in the light of Christian faith and life.
   B. Outcomes of the educational process:
      1. to humanise − to aid individuation and the development of the human potential for wilful life as autonomous persons in relationship;
      2. to criticise − to engage in a careful analysis, synthesis, and judgment on traditional understandings and ways of life;

      3. to discover − to encourage the freedom to create the new and to produce change.
- C. Steps in the educational process:
  1. name and describe experience and related feelings;
  2. explore intuitively alternative interpretations, meanings and possibilities until clear understandings of the inner nature of the experience is achieved;
  3. express these initial insights, compare and contrast them with corresponding insights in scripture and tradition and through rational processes arrive at summary convictions;
  4. express initial implications of these convictions, compare and contrast them with ethical principles and norms of Christian faith and through rational processes arrive at summary commitments to action(s);
  5. manifest these commitments in willing action(s) and evaluating their consequences.

III. *Christian Instruction*
- A. Definition of the instructional process:
  to acquire knowledge and skills considered necessary and useful to Christian life.
- B. Outcomes of the instructional process:
  1. to know − to be knowledgeable of the scriptures, the tradition, (fundamental, constructive and practical theology) and the community's social and intellectual history;
  2. to use − to be able to interpret scripture, think historically and theologically and reflect morally;
  3. to do − to be able to relate to God in ever deepening and loving ways and to others, personally and socially, in caring and liberating ways.
- C. Steps in the instructional process:
  1. establish participants and context;
  2. establish aims or goals;
  3. establish behavioural and/or process objectives;
  4. establish instructional activities and resources;
  5. conduct these activities;
  6. evaluate.

Future work

In the next years I plan to devote my studies to unlocking some of the secrets of formation. My next major project, after I complete a book with Caroline Hughes[7] on ministry as character traits and a book with John Eusden[8] on the human spirit and the visual arts, is a major work on Christian formation. And then, God willing, I hope in my later years to write a systematic work on Catechetics: Formation, Education and Instruction. What follows is a beginning list of questions which I hope to explore in the not too distant future.

First, what ends might formation appropriately address? My hunch is that there are particular ends which can best be formed through education or instruction, but there are some which can only be achieved fully through the processes of formation. My present list includes *faith*, that is, our perceptions of life and our lives, our world view or social construction of reality; *character*, that is, our sense of identity as a communal person in the image of God and our disposition to behave in ways appropriate to that identity, namely the virtues and our terminal/instrumental values; and *consciousness*, that is, that personal-social awareness necessary for wilful autonomous life and our attitudes toward life.

Second, what is the relationship between what we know about enculturation and Christian formation? Enculturation is a natural process of formal and informal, intentional and unintentional means by which persons are integrated into a social group and acquire its culture, that is, its learned, shared understandings and ways of life. *Enculturation* can be distinguished from *acculturation* or the learning of appropriate behaviour in a second culture without losing the basic characteristics of one's own; from *assimilation* or the learning of a new culture and thereby losing or leaving behind one's original culture; and from *biculturalisation* or the blending of two cultures, keeping some characteristics of each and in time giving birth to a new cultural expression.

Christian formation is an intentional process of initiation and incorporation into a Christian faith community with distinctive understandings and ways of life which differentiate it from the general culture. I contend that the church needs to be an intentional community which attempts to shape the subjectivity of persons so that they might be able to feel, think, and behave within the context of the Christian tradition which is embodied in symbols, myths and rituals and who are thereby enabled to interact meaningfully with others who do not share their interpretative world view and value system. (I call this a catholic sectarianism.) To put it in other words, Christians need to be intentionally formed into the faith and life of the Christian community, even as they are acculturated for life in North American society. (This is necessary if the church is to be in-but-not-of the world.) An ever present concern must be the realisation that if the formation process is not done well, persons may be assimilated into the society, which implies losing their sense of self-identity as believers in Jesus Christ and members of his church, or they may be biculturised which means becoming a secularised Christian who cannot differentiate between being *a* Christian, a member of the institutional church, and being Christian, one who manifests a way of life informed by peculiar and particular perceptions of life and our lives.

Third, what is the proper context for formation? My hunch is that formation requires an intentional faith community. This implies, I believe, a common sacred narrative which both informs and is manifested in its common life; a common authority established and used by the community to govern its life and to discern how it should live; a common set of personal and communal rites by which the community is bound together over time and enabled to reconstitute itself as a distinctive community of faith, character and consciousness; and a common life together that is more like a family than an institution and with a distinct character as well as an agreed upon place and role in society.

Fourth, what help can scripture and tradition give us in understanding formation? Vernon Robbins in his book *Jesus the Teacher*[9] claims that Jesus was a unique teacher. Instead of waiting for potential students to seek him out, sit at his feet and take notes as in the school tradition, Jesus sought and summoned students to become companion-apprentices as in the itinerant tradition, promising to make them into people who are able to seek, summon, and commission others through a similar process of identification and observation and imitation.

Aaron Milavec, in his book *To Empower as Jesus Did*,[10] makes the interesting observation that typically we translate the Greek word *didasko* as 'teacher' and *didaskein* as 'to teach'. He points out that as a result of this translation, Pasolini in his film of St Matthew's Gospel represents Jesus as a teacher without a classroom travelling about delivering lectures in the form of homilies, that is, as story/conversations, to convey beliefs and ethical principles. He goes on to point out that the same Greek words for teacher and to teach can be translated as 'master' and 'to apprentice', that is to live with or accompany, to be guided and shaped by life shared with a master.

So it is that James, the first bishop of the church in Jerusalem, in a homily delivered to the elect before their baptism (The Letter of James) lays stress on the moral life expected of those who follow the way of Jesus and therefore warns that not many of them should be catechists, for more will be expected of them. Why? Because catechising implies apprenticing and the catechist is called to be a master to apprentices, which further implies that the catechist will focus her or his attention on an ever deepening and loving relationship to God.

Similarly, the understanding of the catechumenate in the early church was founded on apprenticeship, that is a formation process in which persons apprenticed themselves to the community and participated in its life accompanied by a sponsor who represented the community. Through this process the catechumen, the enquiring

Christian, travelled through the community's yearly cycle so as to make its story their story; shared in a ministry of reconciliation, healing, and service by caring for the sick, hurt, prisoner, orphan and lonely, and developed an intimate relationship to God by practising the disciplines of prayer and discernment. It was only after a lengthy three year period of formation or apprenticeship to the community that during Lent the elect reflected on their experience of the Christian way and using the Lord's prayer and the Apostles Creed were instructed in the knowledge of the faith and its implications for their lives. My hunch is that this total process, but especially the formation dimension, needs to be more carefully examined and explored.

Fifth, what are the formation processes? My hunch is that they are the following:

a. ritual life, that is, participation in the repetitive symbolic actions expressive of the community's sacred narrative;
b. role models, that is, those whose lives are celebrated and/or whose understandings and ways of life are witnessed and affirmed;
c. human interpersonal relations and interactions with members of the community which prescribe and reinforce appropriate identity and behaviour;
d. the environment (what persons see, touch, taste, smell, hear) and artifacts which support a particular view of life and 'habits of the heart';
e. the social organisation (hierarchy and bases for discussion) and common life (roles and status) of the various social units which comprise church;
f. the behaviours observed, affirmed and encouraged through life in the community; and
g. naming, that is, how the community uses language.

My further hunch is that ritual participation remains the key to formation.

Sixth, what is the nature of the human being who is to be formed? Behind this question are some important theological issues, for example, original sin. Historically, there have been two points of view, a biological view which asserts that sin is in our genes and a sociological view which understands sin as being present in the world into which we are born and socialised. Both, I believe, need to be held in tension. At birth, I contend, the human heart has a longing for relationship with God, self and others; the human soul is implanted with the image of God and the human mind with the possibility of discerning the will of God, but with a propensity expressing a different dimension of the same historical process. On the one hand, the self is aware of having grown out of the past, of being formed and shaped by our own and others' past decisions and actions; and on the other hand, the self knows that it is always moving into an open future which will be shaped and influenced by the decisions and actions we make in the present. We are never victims, but always relational beings in process.

My hunch is that the church needs to take this interactive process more seriously and assume greater responsibility for how it lives and thereby potentially influences others. My hunch is that it also needs to provide the possibility for persons to reflect upon and respond to their formation experience so as to prevent formation from becoming a repressive force of influence, as well as to make possible individuation and autonomous faith and life.

Seventh, what is the relationship between formation, education and instruction? Formation has been criticised unjustly for being solely a domesticating process supportive of the status quo. In so far as no social unit can exist over time unless it comprises both continuity and changes, formation is necessarily concerned with both. This combined focus of the formation process is especially important for Christianity, which as an historical religion has its roots in the past, a past which is comprised of a vision of the future. Christian faith proclaims that God's reign established in the past, is present in the present and to be abided in so that it might be actualised or fulfilled in the future. To be formed into such a perception of life is to be formed as persons who strive to maintain continuity with the past, bring a critical perspective to its understanding; and present expression and a willingness to acquire the knowledge and skills necessary for its reform and survival.

My hunch is that we will discover that formation is necessary if human beings are to be motivated to use their capacity for critical reflection and learning in positive ways. The capacity for the use of reason in critical reflection (to be educated) is not in and of itself good; it can be used for positive or negative ends, just as formation and instruction can. Further, without its formation or nurture, the capacity for critical reflection will remain dormant. More serious, formation determines the purposes to which this capacity will be used. My hunch is that the key to understanding the development and use of critical reflection will be found in formation. Indeed, it seems more than likely that formation will provide the key to both education and instruction, especially education and instruction that can rightfully claim to be Christian.

Eighth, how then do we plan for Christian formation? To begin with the formation process is highly complex and all encompassing. It is difficult fully to grasp it, let alone evaluate and plan. For example, formation is affected by the sociological character of a parish, by the parish's organisation and programme, by its leadership, by its facilities and their use, by its worship, by the nature and character of its common life, by its social, historical and cultural context and denominational ethos. A thorough analysis of enculturation within a congregation would be difficult. Such an analysis is complicated by the realisation that formation places experience before reflection and therefore requires an understanding of the experiences persons have within the life of the church, or better, how they perceive their experiences. Formation emphasises process over content; in fact, it reminds us that the way we learn is what we learn. Formation also focuses its attention on the community and its life rather than on an individual, all of which makes understanding and being mindful about enculturation in the church difficult.

Further, formation requires intentional communal life. There is a lot of talking among people about community, but few want to give the effort necessary for true community. It is complicated when we realise that intentionality requires time and effort. While the quality of time spent in the church is more important than the quantity, quality is difficult to achieve. Many persons are not willing to support with their lives and resources a small close-knit cohesive community of faith that is sharply distinguished from the society at large, a community fully committed to developing and preserving their distinctive identity and way of life while still participating in a somewhat alien culture.

My hunch, therefore, is that if Christian formation is to be possible, the church needs also to engage in an educational action, namely: to reflect critically on the church as we know it, the experiences we have within it. Further, Christian faith cannot be inherited or simply passed on. My hunch is that it is first made present for us through the processes of formation, but at some point education needs to provide a context for persons to make a decision for or against it. There is no way we can guarantee that a person will grow up Christian. We can shape persons in the faith and life of the church, but then we must provide them with the opportunity of a free decision. The issue can never be: how can we communicate the Gospel so that it will always be accepted? We can only make possible a genuine decision. We all know the pain of meeting those who reject the Gospel or accept a distortion of it, but it is just as painful to meet those who have never made a decision one way or the other. A genuine decision necessitates first being shaped or formed by experience within a community of Christian faith and life, followed by a period of critical reflection, doubt and searching, and finally an act of decision, followed by instruction in the knowledge and skills necessary for faithful life.

But even as I write, I seem to make it sound too much like a linear process when it is in fact fundamentally circular with moments of dominance. Formation shapes our disposition critically to reflect and to desire knowledge and skills. Education forms an open, critical consciousness and stimulates our need to know and do. Instruction aids us to acquire the skill of critical reflection and to name and understand our experiences. And so the three unite in a deliberate, systematic, and sustained process within a faith community called catechesis.

Conclusion

Other issues surely need to be addressed. This list is just a beginning and what I have said about them only preliminary and incomplete. While I have been exploring such questions for fifteen years, I feel like I have only begun. With the help of colleagues, critics and friends, I hope I may make some small contribution to what I believe is one of the pressing concerns facing the church in our day, namely the relationship between formation, education, and instruction, but especially the nature and character of Christian formation.

Notes
1. Timothy Lines, *Systemic Religious Education,* Birmingham, Alabama, Religious Education Press, 1987.
2. John H Westerhoff and Gwen K Neville, *Generation to Generation,* Philadelphia, United Church Press, 1974.
3. John H Westerhoff, *Will Our Children Have Faith?* New York, Seabury Press, 1976.
4. Paul Tillich, *Theology of Culture,* New York, Oxford University Press, 1959.
5. See James Michael Lee's trilogy: *The Shape of Religious Instruction: a social science approach,* Birmingham, Alabama, Religious Education Press, 1971; *The Flow of Religious Instruction: a social science approach,* Birmingham, Alabama, Religious Education Press, 1973; *The Content of Religious Instruction: a social science approach,* Birmingham, Alabama, Religious Education Press, 1985.
6. Thomas H Groome, *Christian Religious Education: sharing our story and vision,* San Francisco, Harper and Row, 1980.
7. John H Westerhoff and Caroline Hughes, *On the Threshold of God's Future,* San Francisco, Harper and Row, 1986.
8. John H Westerhoff and John Eusden, *The Spiritual Life: learning East and West,* San Francisco, Harper and Row, 1984.
9. Vernon K Robbins, *Jesus the Teacher: a socio-rhetorical interpretation of Mark,* Philadelphia, Fortress Press, 1984.
10. Aaron Milavec, *To Empower as Jesus Did: acquiring spiritual power through apprenticeship,* Lewiston, New York, Edwin Mellen Press, 1982.

2. Christian education and education about Christianity

In those countries which permit some form of religious education in the curriculum of publicly-funded schooling, the distinction between a Christian education which aims at teaching people to be (more) Christian and a religious education that teaches people about Christianity, along with other religions, is often well defined. The following four articles contribute to the debate on the strengths and weaknesses of this distinction.

Raymond Holley's early article 'Learning religion' was first published in *Learning for Living*, 10, 1971, pp. 14–19. It clarifies the distinction between teaching Christianity (religion) and teaching about Christianity (religion), and the limited area of overlap between the learning outcomes of these two processes. 'Learning Christianity' is said to cover five distinct types of learning of which only two, namely 'retaining information' and 'understanding Christian discourse', are pertinent to religious education about Christianity. The other three (acquiring religious skills, adopting religious attitudes, and learning to know God in a personal relationship) are outcomes peculiar to teaching Christianity.[1]

'Education as a second-order form of experience and its relation to religion,' first published in *Journal of Philosophy of Education*, 13, 1979, pp. 83–90, is an article that takes as its starting point the claim that the aim of education 'is to encapsulate experience in symbolic forms' so as to enable learners to understand it better. The author, John Sealey, draws a distinction between first-order forms of experience and the ('one step removed') second-order forms with which education is concerned. 'Reflection on the nature of history, that is to say, coming to understand what a historian is doing ..., is not itself to do history.' Similarly, in a school educational context, religious education is about understanding the concepts and principles of that experience that is designated religious. It does not involve getting the student to become a religious person, in the sense of one who follows the religious life.[2]

Donald Hudson, however, seems to question the sharp distinction made by earlier contributors to this section, in a discussion that brings us back to the notion of education *in* a religion, particularly through an analysis of what it means to *think* religiously (or at least theistically). Hudson is a professional philosopher who has been willing to extend his interests to educational issues. His article 'The loneliness of the religious educator' was first published in *Perspectives*, 9, 1982, pp. 23–36. Here, and elsewhere,[3] Hudson criticises the view that religious education is necessarily different from education in other disciplines, such as science. He argues, rather, that all disciplines have their 'principles of procedure' or governing assumptions that determine what is to count as a proper explanation or experience within the discipline. For science this is the uniformity of nature. For (the Christian) religion it is the existence of God: 'it seeks to explain things in terms of God's existence'. Education in religion (not just 'about' it)[4] involves people in learning to think religiously, including their applying theories of God's nature and purpose to their own circumstances.

Jeff Astley's 'The place of understanding in Christian education and education about Christianity' was first published in *British Journal of Religious Education*, 16, 1994, pp. 90–101. This article adopts a broader understanding of Christian education than some others we have surveyed, and underlines particularly the significance of affective states as outcomes of Christian religious education and education about Christianity.[4] The author highlights the role of empathy in this latter process, and proceeds to argue that the distinction between Christian education and education about Christianity is more a difference of degree than a distinction of kind. He concludes with some suggestions as to the practical implications of this claim.

Raymond Holley was Senior Lecturer in Religious Studies at the West London Institute of Higher Education. Dr John Sealey has taught philosophy of education in England, the West Indies and Sweden. He is currently Professor in the University of Botswana. Dr W Donald Hudson was sometime Reader in Moral Philosophy in the Department of Philosophy of the University of Exeter, England. The Revd Dr Jeff Astley is Director of the North of England Institute for Christian Education, and Honorary Lecturer in Theology and Education in the University of Durham, England.

Notes

1. See also Raymond Holley, *Religious Education and Religious Understanding: an introduction to the philosophy of religious education*, London, Routledge and Kegan Paul, 1978.
2. The distinction is underlined in John Sealey, 'Teaching "about" and teaching "what is" in religion,' *British Journal of Religious Education*, 2, 1979, pp. 56–60; *Religious Education: philosophical perspectives,* London, George Allen and Unwin, 1985.
3. In addition to the works cited in his article, see also W D Hudson, 'Two questions about religious education,' in Roger Straughan and John Wilson (eds), *Philosophers on Education*, Basingstoke and London, Macmillan, 1987, chapter 7. In this paper he more clearly distinguishes the twin tasks of religious education as initiation into theological thinking and initiation into religious devotion.
4. See also Jeff Astley, *The Philosophy of Christian Religious Education*, Birmingham, Alabama, Religious Education Press; London, SPCK, 1994, chapters 1, 6, 7 and 9.

2.1 Learning religion
Raymond Holley

During the past few years both certain supporters and certain opponents of religious education in state schools have advocated teaching about religion rather than teaching religion. This article is not concerned with whether or not religion should be taught in schools but rather with what could be meant by the distinction which is being drawn here. The primary question to be faced is, 'What is meant by teaching religion?' for unless this is clear the advocation of teaching about religion in contradistinction to teaching religion only confounds confusion. Of course, even *if* one becomes clear about the meanings of these contending phrases there nevertheless remain the practical questions of the justification of religious education in the curriculum, and of the advocacy of teaching about religion, for practical questions are not answered simply and automatically through clarificatory analysis.

The initial problem in determining the meaning of teaching religion is to know what substance to give to the notoriously difficult concept of religion. This deserves an article, or series of articles, to itself and therefore, at the risk of being accused of being narrow, stipulative or dogmatic, I shall confine myself to considering 'teaching Christianity'.

The notion of 'teaching'

Teaching, it is often said, is a polymorphous concept (using Ryle's terminology) for it can take many forms, and whether one conceives these forms as activities and thus necessarily gives due weight to the implicit intention of the teacher, or whether one understands these forms in primarily interpersonal terms and concentrates attention upon resultant development of the pupil, it seems true to say that the notion teaching always implies that there shall be some substance, some content, for a person to learn. In central cases (where professional teachers are at work) learning is most certainly implicit, and even in peripheral cases where one remarks (for example of garage mechanics) 'That will teach him not to remove starting-dogs with cold chisels' or 'She taught herself Greek' such remarks are meaningless unless it is being implied that there is some content to be learned. Teaching always implies learning, even if learning does not necessarily imply teaching.

The difficulty is that learning is not monolithic. Learning to chop wood is very different from learning that the sum of the angles of a rectilinear triangle are equal to two right angles, and learning to be punctual is again different from learning to appreciate Beethoven's *Pastoral Symphony*. There are different kinds, types or forms of learning and inasmuch as teaching is to be fundamentally unpacked in terms of learning so there are different kinds of teaching. And the thesis is that *within Christianity there are different kinds of learning* and that therefore teaching Christianity must be understood strictly as a shorthand phrase. There are numerous teachings of Christianity to be undertaken. This might be best illustrated by laying out five distinct types of learning within the Christian religion.

Learning Christianity means retaining information

The first type of learning may be termed retention of information about Christianity. This must be the bedrock of any higher or deeper study of the Christian religion for the rather simple and obvious reason that without it no understanding or critical thinking about Christianity can get off the ground. One needs to be informed that Christians believe that God is a triune person to be worshipped, not a blind force to be deflected and harnessed; that man's sin destroys the possibility of friendship at its deepest and best both with God and fellow-man and that through a gracious act God has effected an atonement through the Lord Jesus Christ; that the church is an everlasting communion of saints and not just the biggest landlord of slum property in England. Some of this information may be couched in purely religious terminology but much of it will be of an historical and moral nature for both these forms of knowledge are vibrant in the warp and woof of the Christian cloth and without information about the church's history, and the church in history, together with facts about Christian ethics there can be no real understanding of Christianity. So information about the Roman occupation of Palestine at the time of Jesus; about Peter and Paul, Bede and Boniface, Anselm and Aquinas; about evangelism and ecumenism, priests and piscinas must be given. Furthermore such information will reflect that Christians believe that one ought not simply to respect other people but that one ought to love others; not simply that one ought to care for others as centres of consciousness and value but as if they were Christ himself. Some of this information may well have to be regarded strictly as sociological rather than religious and as such can never logically be regarded as central and fundamental to the Christian way of life but it (or a certain amount of it) is nevertheless fundamental to learning anything of Christianity.

Learning Christianity means understanding Christian discourse

Such information could be acquired entirely by rote, however, so that pupils become walking encyclopaedia of inert data having neither understanding of the concepts involved and their interrelatedness nor their purchase upon life together with this purchase being rooted in particular circumstances. It seems to me that this is what Professor Hirst[1] draws attention to in his examination of liberal education and his theory of 'the forms of knowledge' (and I feel it is not without significance that although R F Dearden[2] adopts Hirst's structure of knowledge as the basis of his curriculum he talks of 'forms of understanding'). Hirst argues that 'by a form of knowledge is meant a distinct way in which our experience becomes structured round the use of accepted public symbols' and that 'each involve certain central concepts peculiar in character to the form' and that these concepts 'form a network of possible relationships in which experience can be understood'. Furthermore 'each form has distinctive expressions that are testable against experience in accordance with particular criteria that are particular to the form' and 'the forms have developed particular techniques and skills for exploring experience and testing these distinctive expressions'.

Whether or not one agrees with Hirst that there is an autonomous form of knowledge termed religion, and whether or not one would wish to ascribe to any religious statement the title of knowledge, it seems difficult to ignore his characterisation of theoretical knowledge if one is to exemplify what is involved in understanding particular (for example scientific, aesthetic, religious) statements. There is a need to get inside the concepts and to be able to use them in a logical, coherent, criteria-ridden manner. There is a need to be able to see situations and states of affairs in accordance with autonomous mental structures; to interpret and make sense of this life by facing and answering critical questions having due regard for the logic of the discourse employed in posing the questions. And this implies commitment to the norms and standards inherent in the discourse. This, of course, does not imply conversion to a particular way of life but rather the hypothetical situation that should it be said of a person that he understands the Christian religion then what is meant is that he is able to use Christian concepts logically and that he respects the rules written into the very structure of the discourse. *Learning to understand Christianity does not necessarily imply being a Christian, but it does entail submitting oneself to the logic of the dimension* and not attempting to bend the rules to suit one's own conveniences and prejudices.

Against this it might be argued that learning to understand the Christian religion is not possible until faith has been established. Did not Anselm say, '*Credo ut intelligam*' and is it not true that throughout history those men and woman who have been regarded as authorities on the Christian religion have been first and foremost believers? This seems to be most certainly true and yet the point to be grasped is that there are degrees of understanding. One's understanding of a matter may be shallow or deep or even non-existent.

If it is non-existent (and this is the second point) then there can be no belief. Until a person has learned some facts about Christ and has some understanding of the Christian religion it is logically impossible for him to be a believer in Christ. One cannot believe in that which one does not know and understand to some degree. Therefore in order that faith may be established (if that is one's aim) some information must be acquired and some understanding launched first. But there can be little doubt that *without belief in Christ understanding of the Christian religion will remain comparatively shallow* for the rules, criteria and concepts which constitute the public discourse have their ultimate grounds in personal involvement with Christ.

Learning Christianity means acquiring skills

Such understanding of the Christian religion will necessarily be built upon the first type of learning set out but insofar as Christianity is a way of life and not simply a theoretical mapping of a particular aspect of experience so understanding will involve, and only be furthered by the acquisition of certain esoteric religious skills. Pre-eminent among such skills is knowing how to worship for in the worship of God in Christ the great doctrines of the faith take on new (and full) dimensions. Concepts such as sin, confession, repentance, prayer, adoration, humility etc. come alive in having purchase upon life in worship, and man's relation to God and his correct attitude to him is expressed and epitomised.

Knowing how to worship God is not something innate in humanity. It involves skills which have to be learned, and such learning is brought about not through instruction by word of mouth alone but by being in the presence of people practising such arts and by trying them out for oneself. Analogous situations exist throughout the education of the child – in the learning of games and handicraft, of science and writing essays, of mathematics and morals. To learn how to worship is as fundamental to learning Christianity as to learn how to experiment and observe and assess results is to learning science, if not more so.

The skills to be learned in religion are not solely associated with worship and there are many skills which carry over from one discipline to another and which are common to any study. To mention them all here would be tedious if not banal but one is reminded of the words of William Cory (1823–92) the lyric poet and master of Eton:

You go to a great school not so much for knowledge as for arts and habits;
For the habit of attention, for the art of expression;
For the art of entering quickly into another person's thoughts;

For the art of indicating assent or dissent in graduated terms;
For the art of working out what is possible in a given time;
For taste, for discrimination, for mental courage and soberness.

Reference to words such as these, however, must not be understood as denial of the earlier contention that pre-eminent amongst the skills to be learned in the Christian religion are those associated with worship.

Learning Christianity means adopting attitudes

Worship, however, is not simply a matter of skills. It implies attitudes, dispositions and a particular orientation of the whole person. Implied in that statement is a fourth type of learning which, unlike those already indicated, is not epistemic in essence. In the passage quoted above Cory refers to 'the habit of attention' and whilst it would make sense to talk of teaching children to know that they ought to attend to their studies, and even to teaching them how to attend to such work, the habit of attention surely refers to that kind of learning which can be expressed as learning to attend. Such learning is not essentially either the acquisition of propositional or procedural knowledge, although it may involve one or both types of knowledge. But such involvement must not be misconstrued as identification. A person may know that such and such a way is the way to bath, and that he or she ought to keep clean, and also how to keep clean, but may not possess the habit of cleanliness of body and thus is found, as the advertisements indicate, in an invidious position. He or she has not learned to be clean.

Learning to be is part and parcel of the Christian religion. Involved in that way of life is learning to be humble, loving, charitable, thoughtful, critical and above all Christ-like and reverential towards God. Indeed many would wish to argue from inside the faith that such learning is far more central than the propositional statements of religion with which philosophers (naturally) concern themselves, and many critics outside the faith rightly condemn Christians for not behaving in accordance with their own precepts and doctrines – for *being* hypocritical. The beatitudes are concerned with this kind of learning and chapter 5 of Matthew's Gospel ends with the somewhat alarming and challenging command, 'You therefore must be perfect, as your heavenly father is perfect.'

Learning Christianity means learning to know God

This learning to be is closely associated with, and often fed by a fifth kind of learning inherent in the Christian religion. What I have in mind here is the acquisition of that kind of knowledge sometimes referred to as 'knowledge of direct object'. There seem to be many philosophers who either dismiss this as not being knowledge in any way akin to proposition and procedural knowledge or regard it as better understood when reduced to talk about feelings, awareness or acquaintance. That its kinship with the public forms of knowledge mentioned is minimal I would accept, but I am not able to accept the reductionists' dismissal of such knowledge *qua* knowledge. To know the beauty of a sunset, the cogency of an argument, or the thrill of walking across the Downs on a windy starlit night is not the same as knowing *that* a sunset can be beautiful, that Anselm's ontological arguments for the existence of God are erudite, or that there is fun in midnight hiking. Neither is it the same as saying one feels the beauty of the sunset, or one is aware of the cogency of the arguments, or one is acquainted with the joys of hiking. Such feelings, awareness, acquaintance are often *implicit* in such knowledge statements but to *identify* them with knowledge of the direct object is false. If this were not so then statements of the form, 'A is acquainted with X but does not know X' (where X is a direct object) would be contradictory. But they are not necessarily contradictory. It is quite in order to say, 'John is acquainted with Jane but does not know Jane.' In similar fashion it would be true to say that Pontius Pilate was acquainted with Jesus, aware of his presence and possessed certain feelings about him (presumably) but to say that Pilate knew Jesus would be to overstep the mark.

This use of the word know implies a depth of association and involvement which is often beyond articulation in terse, succinct terminology and is greater than awareness and acquaintance. It is very much a matter of the individual person's own experience and this necessarily so if it involves acquaintance with and confrontation by the object. It certainly is not something that is available second-hand. Such knowledge in the Christian religion is pre-eminently exemplified in knowledge of God in the life of the believer and derivatively knowledge of other persons in the communion of saints — derivatively insofar as the individual person's knowledge of God structures and illuminates his apperception of others so that he recognises them as God's children. And such knowledge has to be learned, and like learning to be it is not so much a matter of acquisition of fact and theoretical cognition (if these two can be separated) but rather the conscious entering into and fostering of relationships with the necessary willingness to be open to the establishment of appropriate relationships.

The argument is, then, that *there are at least five distinct types of learning encompassed by the Christian religion* which must be given due regard whenever there is any talk about learning the Christian religion. By way of summary, and for ease of reference, they are:

a.   retention of information (of historical, ethical, sociological
     nature) about Christianity;
b.   commitment to rules and standards inherent in the dis-
     course enabling logical use of Christian concepts (that is,
     understanding);
c.   acquisition of skills (especially those of worship);
d.   adoption of Christian attitudes, habits, dispositions;
e.   entrance into personal relationships.

Are there ways of learning Christianity which cannot be taught?

With these five distinct types of learning encompassed by the
Christian religion in mind, and giving due regard to the earlier
contention that learning does not necessarily imply teaching, it
might be profitable to face the question, 'Are there any types of
learning among these five which cannot be taught?' for if there are
then they are not being referred to either in talk about teaching
Christianity or teaching about Christianity.

The type of learning outstanding among the five as a candidate for the category learning-without-teaching is the fifth. Such
learning understood in terms of entrance into personal relationships
culminating in knowing other persons and pre-eminently knowing
God seems to be beyond the manipulations and engineerings of
a third party. With regard to knowing other persons a teacher
may well facilitate the setting up of personal relationships through
group dynamics, through social organisation, through discussion
and through making himself open to such relationships but he
can never insist on a personal relationship which will lead to
knowledge of persons. In particular I fail to see what apparatus
is available to him whereby he can engineer a confrontation of God
with individual persons. To know God is something ultimately of
an incredibly private nature and such learning as is involved here
is in its final nature God-given not teacher-given.

At a first glance the fourth type of learning appears to be a candidate for this category of learning-without-teacher insofar as while
it is fairly easy to comprehend ways in which one may draw the
attention of pupils to the central importance of such virtues to the
Christian religion, the establishment of such virtues in human lives
has to overcome the logical difficulty enunciated long ago by Aristotle (cf *Ethics* Book 2, Chapter 4). Being charitable, for example,
involves not just doing particular works but doing them with a
particular mental/spiritual disposition. Nevertheless the acquisition
of the latter seems intimately connected with the doing of charitable works. This is a paradox. However, there does seem to be a
time-honoured way out of this logical conundrum and that is that
children can be taught to be virtuous not simply through exhor-

tation but also by being brought up in the presence of those who exhibit such virtues in their own lives.

Of the other three types of learning little needs to be said. One can give information; one can develop understanding; and one can train in skills. Thus *there are at least four distinct types of learning in the Christian religion which can be taught* and which one may justifiably infer are being spoken of if the phrase teaching Christianity is used as a blanket term without qualification.

The notion of teaching about

Over against teaching religion (Christianity), however, is held teaching about religion (Christianity) and in order to get clearer about the latter one might consider, by way of analogy, what is being implied when one speaks of teaching about other possible subjects of the curriculum. Consider teaching about French. Certainly learning of one type or another is being implied. One could get the children to learn that French is the mother-tongue of that nation living across the English Channel from ourselves; that it is an Indo-European language derived in large part from Latin; that it has great importance as an international language of diplomacy and so on. In a similar fashion one might consider what it would mean to teach about mathematics or science. The important points to be grasped are:

a.   there is no contradiction in saying, 'I have been teaching about X without teaching X';
b.   the status of the propositions comprising the teaching about X is that they need not belong to the X discourse;
c.   teaching about X need not necessarily imply anything more than a meagre, shallow understanding of X.

The first point above is merely a summary of common experience. Some readers of this article will have been taught something about Sanskrit and may know and understand a great deal about that language but in fact have never been taught this holy tongue and do not know it and cannot use it intelligibly. This leads to the second point, that whilst it is quite possible to do a great deal of teaching about, say, mathematics the resultant knowledge will be historical, sociological and technical and need not be mathematical. Of course it will be argued that unless children have some idea of what language or mathematics (or cachalot, or nutrino, or God) is then such teaching about can never get off the ground. But whilst this argument may be granted, nevertheless the third point above needs to be stated firmly, and that is that only a *minimum* understanding of the central topic needs to be acquired to enable one to teach about it.

Teaching about Christianity

To return to the analysis of types of learning within Christinity outlined earlier, it would seem to follow from what has been said there
that teaching about Christianity certainly implies the first type of
learning (that is, retention of information about Christianity) and
also the second (that is, learning to understand Christian discourse)
but this latter *only to a limited degree*. Furthermore that alone is a
sufficient characterisation of teaching about Christianity in terms of
learning types. Certainly teaching about Christianity need not necessarily imply either acquiring esoteric Christian skills or virtues.
Therefore one is entitled to conclude that teaching about Christianity
involves, and is, less than teaching Christianity, whereas teaching
Christianity will necessarily include teaching about Christianity.

The questions which stem from this analysis (assuming it is
correct!) seem to be of great practical importance. Is teaching
about Christianity/any religion sufficient to achieve religious *education?* Is there any type of learning in Christianity (religion) implied
in teaching Christianity which ought *not* to be made available in
state schools? Can one *teach* all the major religions of the world
or only *teach about* some, and *teach* one? And presumably whilst it
is possible to *teach about* religion might it not be true that believers
only can *teach* their faith?

Notes
1.   Cf. 'Liberal education and the nature of knowledge,' in R D Archambault
     (ed.), *Philosophical Analysis and Education,* London, Routledge and Kegan
     Paul, 1965.
2.   Cf. R F Dearden, *The Philosophy of Primary Education*, London, Routledge
     and Kegan Paul, 1968.

2.2 Education as a second-order form of experience and its relation to religion
John Sealey

The thesis

I shall assume that whatever else goes on in the structured schooling situation, education centrally exists to promote a knowledge and understanding of experience in terms of its conceptual nature. Put another way, the aim of education is to encapsulate experience in symbolic forms enabling students the better to focus upon, and understand, experience. None of this is to deny that there may be different ways in which a knowledge of experience in terms of concepts may be taught in the educational process, but that is a problem for methodology, not philosophy. What I have to say negates nothing of what is said, for example, by D W Hamlyn about 'the delicate balance between principles and cases ... between an understanding of principles in general terms and an understanding of their relevance to particular cases'.[1]

In using the term second-order I perhaps raise the question in the reader's mind: is that not a term we use of the activity of philosophy? Of course there is a connection and I make the comparison advisedly. The second-order nature of philosophy consists in philosophy's examination of established forms of experience. With mathematics established, philosophy reflects upon the nature of mathematics; given history, philosophy reflects upon the nature of historical thinking, and so on. In this sense it is said that philosophy is a reflective activity. But is a reflective, second-order activity always philosophy? I do not know the answer to this. Hirst and Peters seem sure that a reflective activity is not always philosophy: 'A teacher, for instance, can reflect about what prompts people to paint pictures.' This, they say, is a reflective activity but not a philosophical activity. It is a problem within the first-order activity of psychology.[2] Accepting that this particular point is a psychological one, what might be said about the questions 'What was the relationship between Charles the First and the Long Parliament?' or 'How could it be said that the disciples thought of Jesus as the Messiah?' Could it not be cogently argued that these are second-order questions in that they deal with reflective thought concerning concepts not only in history and religion but also in established areas of psychology, politics, biblical exegesis and so on? If this be admitted, what do we make of the summary of the nature of philosophy by Hirst and Peters: 'Philosophy, in brief, is concerned with questions about the analysis of concepts and with questions about the grounds of knowledge, belief, actions and activities'?[3] After all education, too, is concerned with the analysis of concepts; even, perhaps, concerned to give good reasons for supposing that something is knowledge; to distinguish one area from another. Also like philosophy, education, as Scheffler reminds us 'fosters criticism' of knowledge, 'striving for a systematic and penetrating comprehension of' the human environment.[4] It is a nice point as to where a study of, say, history ends and philosophy begins. It is an important issue which, however, I do not think much affects my immediate thesis which is that education is a second-order form of experience. It is also the case, of course, that education, involving a wide range of activities as it does, includes activities which are neither philosophical nor reflective or second-order, such as the passing on of information; teaching the multiplication tables by rote; practising the high-jump, etc. Like the teaching of reading and writing these activities may help enormously to facilitate the formation of concepts, but as isolated activities they do not provide the kind of inter-relatedness of human experience characteristic of conceptual knowledge and the wider enterprise of education. They are not what might be called the *raison d'être* of education.

Whatever may be said about the second-order nature of philosophy, my claim that education, in the structured schooling situation, is a second-order form of experience is based upon the thinking that the process of education involves teaching with the intention of getting students to come to know and understand a variety of experiences by means of the concepts thought to be central to those experiences; furthermore (and more significantly), that coming to know and understand these concepts is not to engage in the experiences themselves. This is what I would call the reflective nature of education. It is the thesis I shall attempt to elaborate. But with regard to concepts, one might example the concepts central to his forms of knowledge mentioned by Paul Hirst, in this connection. Whatever one thinks of Hirst's analysis as a whole it seems clearly the case that there are concepts central to any given area of knowledge. My argument assumes this and, furthermore, that not to know what these concepts are, what they mean, how they are distinctive, etc., is to lack a knowledge and understanding of all experience in any but the vaguest of ways. To teach students more than the central concepts of the various forms of experience (where these can be thought to be generally agreed upon) − for example, to teach students special skills in essay-writing, to teach them to play a musical instrument, archaeological digging, computer programming and so on − is all grist to the mill, time and resources permitting. Not only will this further practice be in addition to other school work such as an appreciation of literature, an appreciation of music, geography, mathematics and so on, it will also serve the function of deepening, imparting more meaning to, making more precise, strengthening, the learning of those concepts which comprise our understanding of experience.

To teach students more than the central concepts (whatever they may be thought to be) of a given form of experience is to add important icing to the educational cake. To teach less than the central concepts of the particular human experience we may be currently teaching is not merely to give students no cake at all; it is to get them to mistake the icing for the cake.

What do I mean by form of experience? A person's life consists of many different experiences. In any given day, year or lifetime these experiences may be seen to overlap; most often they are interconnected to make up the warp and woof of life. Many experiences can be distinguished and given distinctive characteristics. Although in certain cases it may not be possible to show precise boundaries for any but the simplest experience, I think it may be said that the attempt to make distinctions between experiences, and to categorise them, is a pre-requisite of the development of human knowledge. The point need not be elaborated. I simply use form of experience as a generic term to denote distinguishable human experiences.

There are, then, many different forms of experience. I shall pick out a number of them sufficient to illustrate the sort of distinctions that are in fact made and, more importantly, to illustrate that while education is itself a form of experience it is different from most other forms of experience in that it is a second-order form of experience. Education differs from philosophy not necessarily in virtue of its second-order nature but in certain other respects which I have indicated but which do not affect the present argument.

In summary, education's second-order nature consists in teaching students with the intention that they shall come to know and understand the concepts thought to be central to certain distinctive experiences; that this process is not itself part of those experiences; that education, in this sense, is a reflective process.

First-order forms of experience contrasted with education

Forms of experience may be distinguished from one another. Riding a horse is different from driving a bus; being a mathematician is different from being a psychologist; being an office-clerk is different from being a bricklayer or painter; being an archaeologist is different from being a priest; all of them are different from practising medicine and so on. These are first-order experiences in that, in engaging in them we are not engaged in reflecting about them. They may therefore be distinguished from the process of education, for education is precisely the activity in which we do engage in reflecting on the other forms of experience.

A person working within a first-order experience such as brick-layer, lawyer or office-clerk who continues with his education is normally considered to be doing so in addition to his daily work. We might say of the professional historian and the professor of physics in a university department that they are educated but not that they are continuing their education, although like the brick-layer, they might be doing that in addition to their professional work. One might reasonably suppose that they already know the concepts central to their work — they have been educated. Indeed, we would not normally confuse education with first-order forms of experience. It is true that a chemist in his laboratory is learning something; presumably she intends to learn something; but few would want to say that thereby she is undergoing a process of edu-cation. They would say, rather, she is doing research, diagnosing a virus or making up a new kind of foot-powder and so on. The bus driver, in the course of his duties, may learn a great deal of human psychology but we would not normally say, because of that, that he is being educated — except, perhaps, in an extended sense, as when we say of an ill-mannered person 'He or she has no education.' (Of course a case could be argued for a person's being educated without being conscious of it. But is it not somewhat odd to speak of unconscious reflection on matters of experience?) The historian writing a third book on the legislation of Imperial Rome is not, by this fact, said to be undergoing a process of education.

But confusion can arise if a teacher believes he has a group of chemists when what he has in fact is a group of students who are studying the kind of work a chemist does, and who forgets that his intention is to get them to learn chemistry and not how to be a chemist. If the teacher thinks he has a group of bus drivers rather than students studying social psychology there will be confusion. When a history teacher takes a first-year secondary school group for their first lesson and tells them about transport in the stone-age, does this mean she is talking to historians? Being a chemist, a bus driver or a historian is not the same kind of thing as being a student of experiences. What the student (in or out of school) is doing (or at least what the teacher intends him to be doing — we are not especially concerned with the achievement sense, here) is learning the techniques, understanding the concepts, coming to grips with the principles involved in the work of all chemists, all bus drivers (or, rather, in the education context, the work of the social psychologist) and all historians. Any practical work (in or outside the school) involved in coming to an understanding of these first-order experiences is a simulated first-order experience; if the outside visit or practical work is part and parcel of the educational process then by definition it cannot be the first-order experience itself. However, since simulated activity is one of the best teaching methods it is understandable that some people come to think that it is the experience or activity that is the objective rather than the understanding of the concepts and being able to relate them to other fields of first-order experiences which will, together, form the notion of what may be called the educated person. But methods of teaching and learning are part of the process of education, not part of the first-order experience itself. Hence, the student who simulates some of the activities of a chemist in the school laboratory is not in fact a chemist and cannot be regarded as working within a first-order activity.

A short while ago I saw an old film with Spencer Tracy playing the part of Jekyll and Hyde. When Jekyll mixed his liquids, in the laboratory, he was not reflecting about chemistry, or coming to grips with the concepts of chemical change in general. He was thinking about Hyde. The school student may seem to be mixing chemicals in exactly the same way as Jekyll is learning certain chemical facts already known to all chemists; he is, by learning these facts, trying to come to grips with the concepts of chemistry; he is reflecting only on the nature of chemistry and the concepts of scientific work – not something beyond. This is not to deny, of course, that there can be learning by experience, for that is precisely what the teacher intends. But this is not enough; one can learn a skill and remain uneducated; one can learn facts and remain uneducated; one can gather information and remain uneducated. The grasp of concepts within the various forms of knowledge requires reflection upon those skills, facts and information, and it is this characteristic which marks education off from a first-order experience. Reflection upon the nature of bus driving is not itself to drive a bus, although driving a bus will probably help towards an understanding of the activity.[5] Reflecting on the nature of history, that is to say, coming to understand what a historian is doing; looking at examples of her work, analysing it, and so on, is not itself to do history. A historian *qua* historian does not reflect on the nature of the work of a historian. This is why I describe certain activities as simulated first-order experiences. Learning by experience is simply one of the (many) ways by which we may come to know and understand something.

Education as a preparation for first-order experience

Characterised as a second-order form of experience, education is, so to speak, one step removed from other forms of experience. However unrealistic this may seem at first sight, there is a logical gap between a first-order experience and education defined as a second-order experience. As a matter of contingent fact the distinction is not as unrealistic as it seems because, while there is a conceptual difference there is considerable *de facto* interaction.

Education, in the structured and formal sense, is and is intended to be a preparation for other forms of experience. To be more precise, it is intended to be a preparation for all other forms of experience; and the use of the universal 'all' is significant. I do not want to consider other major aspects of the concept of education in this article, but I would suggest that to suppose that education is and ought to be limited to a preparation for some, but not other, forms of experience would mean narrowing the scope of rational enquiry and the training of the enquiring mind which, I would further stipulate, is a necessary part of the process of education. Thus the idea of students being brought to the threshold of first-order activities may not be a bad way of describing the educational process. The threshold is also the objective of education since, as a second-order form of experience and different in kind from first-order forms of experience, it cannot have an objective of a logically disparate kind. It is, I think, at this point that Scheffler is led to disagree with Gilbert Ryle (at least on the matter of moral norms) who thought of teaching, within the concept of education, as the passing on of skills.

Scheffler says, against Ryle:[6]

> What is at issue is thus, it seems to me, not whether inculcation of norms shall take place, but rather what norms shall be inculcated and in what manner, whether, for example, our norms shall be restrictive or generous, authoritarian or democratic, whether they shall be dogmatically instilled by our educational institutions or whether they shall be taught — explained and submitted to the independent judgment of pupils.

Scheffler therefore makes the point that the inculcation of norms shall take place, his main argument being: 'The inculcation of habits, norms, and propensities pervades all known educational practice, and such practice is not therefore merely a matter of skills.'[7] Of course Scheffler has already decided that 'our educational aim is, in fact, not merely to teach pupils *how* to be good citizens but, in particular, to *be* good citizens, not merely *how* to go about voting, but *to* vote.'[8] He thereby refutes Ryle's idea of education as the acquisition of skills (which would enable a student to choose whether certain norms are to be accepted or rejected) and replaces it with the idea of making the teacher directly responsible both for what norms shall be inculcated and the manner of inculcation. Scheffler is not merely saying that teachers cannot avoid inculcation of norms (a manifest truth) but that they ought to inculcate specific norms. To give pupils the skills with which to choose, says Schleffer, is not enough. However, the fact that such 'propensities pervade all known educational practice' is not an argument for saying either that they ought to, or that they ought to be this rather than that. The point that teachers ought to inculcate moral norms (however enlightened the method may be) is a tough and unsolved value problem. Are we sure, for example (as Scheffler asserts) that we are 'concerned that (pupils) acquire democratic habits'? The argument for giving the skills of discrimination to pupils, for bringing them to the threshold, is one which gives priority to the freedom of choice within first-order forms of experience. It applies as much to other first-order forms of experience as it does to moral norms. This, I think, is an eminently reasonable position. But there is a logical point to be made which gives more power to Ryle than to Scheffler on this issue. It is that, on the view of education as a second-order activity, the teacher may (logically) only aim at getting students to understand (by reflecting upon etc.) the concepts of being a voter, being democratic and so on, because being democratic etc. is a first-order form of experience.

Religious education

The special problem that confronts religious education is that teaching religion is thought by many to be the same as teaching students to be religious. But that this is a confusion is now, perhaps, clear in that, if my view is correct, teaching religion (or religious education) is a second-order activity, whereas being religious (like being a priest) is a first-order form of experience. Being religious, or even being taught to be religious (which has an objective beyond the threshold − to use that metaphor again) logically cannot be a second-order activity because teaching within the educational process means that the teacher shall have the intention of bringing about the learning of the concepts of religion and the religious life rather than being religious. To recognise the experiences, to understand the concepts, of a chemist or historian or, in this case, the religious person is not itself to be or become a chemist, historian or religious person (all first-order experiences). It seems clear to me that in order for one to be or become a chemist, historian or a religious person, rather more specific training together with some kind of commitment or choice to go beyond the threshold is required; or, in the case of the religious person, one might say personal religious experiences are required. But neither the specific training of the chemist nor the provision of specific religious experiences seem to be a requirement of, or even necessary to, the educational process which is, rather, to bring to students an understanding of the chemist's work and the religious person's life. The more precise distinction between education and training is the subject for a somewhat different (although related) discussion. Sufficient to say here that even if we were to reduce education to training there would still be, perhaps, a conceptual difference between education/training on the one hand and the first-order experience of the educated/trained person on the other. It would depend on how we defined training of course.

What is necessary to the educational enterprise is the learning outcome in terms of knowledge and understanding as opposed to being; or at least it is the teacher's intention that the student will learn. In the achievement sense of teaching what is learnt might be better described as an appreciation of the subjects studied in much the same way as music education involves an appreciation, at least, of music. After all, it is not at all incongruous to describe as musically educated a person who can play no instrument and does not sing. It seems to me that to suppose otherwise, that is, to suppose that education is a first-order experience in which the student must be regarded as a budding artist, mathematician, historian, scientist, writer etc., all at once, is to recognise that education has most often failed.

As I have argued, education in the formal, schooling sense, is intended to underpin all first-order forms of experience; doing or being something within a first-order experience does not seem appropriate to the conceptual nature of the educational process. To use Oakeshott's phrasing, education is a process of becoming human; for, while it is possible that first-order experiences (for example learning some kind of psychology while being a bus driver) will add to the process of becoming human, it is not this intention or objective that the bus driver (or his company) has in mind. The second-order nature of education does not presuppose that any particular outcome shall necessarily follow. The process of education as a second-order form of experience is the condition of becoming rather than being or doing anything of the first-order kind.

It might be argued that in the case of music, mathematics, literature, art and so on, a pupil can (and does) do them but not very well. Is it appropriate to say this of religion? Can we say 'He believes in God – but not very well'? No. But to believe in God equals, in the mathematical form of experience, to be a mathematician – he is not that either. In the first there is a lack of conviction etc., in the second a lack of skill, commitment and so on. Both are beyond the threshold of education. Yet we need not pose the problem like this at all. Education is never a question merely of skill or conviction – or even commitment, except, perhaps, to education (and that is doubtful!); it is a question of understanding the concepts, grasping the principles etc., of various forms of experience. Thus a student may grasp the concept of God as well as he may grasp the concept or concepts of mathematics.

It is not even always necessary or appropriate for students to learn by doing (for example, touching a flame to find it hot; sex, etc.). We are here in the realm of different methods of learning different concepts. It seems to be appropriate to learn mathematics or cooking by utilising certain forms of practical work; but it is not necessarily appropriate to come to an understanding of literature by writing literature; nor in coming to recognise masterwork in painting is it necessary to paint or be a painter. Similarly in religion one does not have to be religious in order to understand religion. The tests for what has come to be known by a student will vary also. It may be appropriate in mathematics for students to work out equations to indicate their grasp of principles, but it is not appropriate in religion to test a student's understanding by requiring him or her to become religious for half-an-hour. To test whether a student has come to understand the appropriate religious concepts he or she may be required, rather, to give a written or oral account of, for example, the concept of transcendence, or the Christian concept of sin. (One surely does not have to sin to be able to know what sin is.) The tests in different forms of knowledge will therefore differ according to the form. In a sense the tests for both mathematics, say, and religion may be termed analysis of the relevant form of thinking. We may call a person mathematically educated if, and only if, that person can give a correct account of a required number of mathematical concepts; we may call a person religiously educated if, and only if, that person can give an appropriate account of the required number of religious concepts. Similarly in music or literature and, I believe, in morals, too.

Paul Hirst has commented on what cannot be taught, as part of public education, in religious education:[9]

> What cannot be part of education, however, would be seeking to develop, say, a disposition to worship in that faith, or certain emotions such as love of God, when that very disposition, or these emotions, are only a justifiable development if the religion is accepted by the individual. That acceptance I have argued is a personal, private judgment which education, committed to reason alone as it is, has no right to foreclose.

Now, if I understand this properly, what Hirst is objecting to here is the first-order experience being religious, or the teacher's objective to teach to be religious and, if my analysis be accepted, there is a logical reason for not being able to teach the sort of disposition Hirst mentions. It is simply that such dispositions are not educational by nature. It cannot be true to say, therefore, that religious education is not possible.[10] Neither can it be said that religious beliefs cannot be taught in public education, as Hirst would argue. Religious beliefs are no less susceptible to educational treatment than beliefs in music, art, historical judgment or literature. The crucial point is that teachers cannot (logically) teach students to believe in matters which are not susceptible to the rational teaching-learning process. It is perfectly possible (that is, logically and educationally possible) to teach the belief that Jesus was the son of God as long as it is understood that the elements involved in the teaching are a rational appraisal of the relevant concepts, the objective of which is the understanding (learning) of the belief. Indeed, I would argue that this is precisely the kind of subject-matter that ought (logically) to be taught in religious education, for example (in Christianity) Jesus as son of God; sin; redemption; baptism and so on, rather than the historical, psychological and sociological connections with religious belief that are more often taught, and which too often masquerade as religious education. Neither student nor teacher need be committed to the concepts since to be committed in this way would be to cross the threshold into a first-order experience. But to teach the belief that Jesus was the son of God is no different in terms of education from teaching the historical belief that Napoleon and Churchill were charlatans. Whether the student comes to believe either statement is not the concern of the teacher *qua* educator. The teacher's concern is that the student shall come to understand the beliefs and the concepts involved. There is a world of difference between teaching the belief that Jesus was the son of God, and teaching students to believe that Jesus was the son of God. The first is an educational enterprise; the second is not.

The fact that there is a distinction between the existential nature of human knowledge and an appreciation of that knowledge (a reflective experience), between being religious, being a writer, being a musician or painter, on the one hand, and attempting to grasp the distinctive, conceptual nature of these areas on the other, seems hardly deniable. It seems inevitable that compulsory public education should be characterised by the latter while the former may be left to specific training institutions, or, in the case of religion, to the individual's private interpretation of experience which, by definition, is not itself part of the educational enterprise.

Notes

1. D W Hamlyn, 'The logical and psychological aspects of learning,' in R S Peters (ed.), *The Concept of Education,* London, Routledge and Kegan Paul, 1967, p. 27.
2. P H Hirst and R S Peters, *The Logic of Education,* London, Routledge and Kegan Paul, 1970, p. 2.
3. *Ibid.,* p. 3.
4. I Scheffler, *Reason and Teaching,* London, Routledge and Kegan Paul, 1973, p. 129.
5. M Oakeshott shrewdly, although somewhat elusively, comments: 'The distinction between a driver and a learner-driver is not insignificant,' in his chapter 'Learning and teaching,' in R S Peters (ed.), *The Concept of Education,* London, Routledge and Kegan Paul, 1973, p. 156.
6. I Scheffler, *The Language of Education,* Illinois, Charles C Thomas, 1960, p. 99, note 39.
7. *Ibid.,* p. 99.
8. *Ibid.,* p. 98 (Scheffler's italics).
9. P H Hirst, *Moral Education in a Secular Society,* London, University of London Press, 1974, p. 84.
10. See, for example, R Marples, 'Is religious education possible?' *Journal of Philosophy of Education,* 12, 1978, in which Marples argues that 'religious

education is not possible' because religion cannot be taught with 'full understanding' without at the same time indoctrinating pupils. In arguing that
religious education is possible, W D Hudson, in his article 'Is religious education possible?' in G Langford and D J O'Connor (eds), *New Essays in the
Philosophy of Education,* London, Routledge and Kegan Paul, 1973, makes
a number of relevant points but tends to incite the spectre of indoctrination
into malevolent activity when he speaks of pupils being 'initiated into religious
belief' and 'devotion'. I believe he is on far safer ground when, in his postscript,
Hudson 'hazards the view' that religious education is *logically* necessary within
the framework of general education.

2.3 The loneliness of the religious educator
W D Hudson

Education 'about' and education 'in'

There is an obvious difference between education *about* a subject and education *in* it. A school teacher could, for example, pass on a great deal of information about mathematics — such as who have been its most distinguished practitioners, what sort of problems it can solve, how important to industry those trained in it are nowadays, and so on — without giving the pupils any instruction in the subject itself. But if that were all the teacher did, it would be absurd to call him a mathematics teacher. Teaching about mathematics, such as I have just supposed, is education in subjects other than mathematics — in history, logic, economics, or whatever, rather than in how to do arithmetic, algebra and the rest. When we call someone a teacher of mathematics or any other subject, what we normally mean and are taken to mean is, quite clearly, that he educates the pupils in the subject concerned, not simply gives them information about it which belongs to other subjects.

There appears, however, to be one exception to what I have just been saying, namely teachers of religion, by which I mean of religious instruction, religious education, religious studies, or whatever the latest name for the subject is in schools. It has become fashionable to regard such teachers as educators about, rather than in, their subject. Although everyone would consider it absurd to say of a history or chemistry teacher, for example, that she exists, not to produce novice historians or chemists, but simply to give her pupils information about history or chemistry in case they should ever wish to take up these subjects for themselves, it is not now considered at all absurd to say this *mutatis mutandis* about those who teach religion. The opinion is widely held that their proper function is not to make their pupils religious but simply to give them such knowledge of the literature or history of religion as will enable them to head in the right direction, should they ever decide to explore that region of human experience for themselves. This conception of religious education has commended itself not least to those who actually do the job. One gets the impression from many of the more articulate teachers of religion that they now consider it the only intellectually and morally respectable view to take of their function in schools.

It is one which sets them apart from all other kinds of teacher and constitutes what I call in my title their loneliness. This conception of their job demands of them a degree of detachment from their subject and an avoidance of initiation in their method, such as are required from teachers of no other sort. On the contrary, teachers of other sorts are the more esteemed, the more attached they are to their subject and the greater the enthusiasm with which they plunge their pupils into its definitive ways of thought or practice. A good history teacher makes no bones about getting her pupils to think historically; a good sports teacher offers no apology for urging them to train athletically. But not so the teacher of religion! According to the conception of his job which we are considering, he must not take his pupils into his subject but rather point it out to them from afar. He is, if you like, a travel agent handing out brochures about that distant country, but not a guide or conductor whose job it is actually to take anybody there.

Now, I can see that teachers of religion who are not themselves believers — and we are told there are many of them about — will find it easy to accommodate themselves to this conception of their job. From their point of view, religion is simply a set of illusions which they feel no urge or obligation to propagate. They will be quite content to think of themselves as members of the history, literature or current affairs departments, employed to teach these subjects with particular reference to the influence of the said illusions. Now and then they may wonder why anyone is foolish enough to pay them to do so; but if that is a form of loneliness, it is not the one of which I am thinking in this paper.

But how can teachers of religion who are themselves believers rest content with the idea that they are educators about, but not in, their subject? From their point of view religion is anything but a set of illusions. It is a body of truth at least as real as natural science, a realm of experience at least as significant as art, and a form of activity at least as important as sport or any craft. How then can they feel other than isolated by the conception of religious education to which I have been referring? No other kind of teacher who feels about her subject as they do about theirs is required to hold off it, or to refrain from initiating her pupils into it, as they are by this conception of their job. And their loneliness, be it noted, is not simply the feeling of being different from other teachers. It is of a deeper kind than that, the kind called alienation — that is, a feeling of isolation not so much from others as from oneself. To be an educator who has to stand back from his subject and his pupils — as this fashionable conception requires religious educators to do — is like not being an educator at all. Small wonder that teachers of religion often strike one as out on a limb, lacking in confidence, apologetic. Is it surprising if some of them, in unbuttoned moments, confess to doubts about whether they should be in schools at all?

Is religion different?

The reason usually given for this alienating conception of the religious educator's job is that religion has certain features which make it different from all other school subjects and impose on those who teach it a moral obligation to educate their pupils about, but not in, their subject. I want to consider in the remainder of this short article whether these isolating features really do characterise religion and whether the moral obligation which they are supposed to entail really does exist.

But first I ought to make a little clearer just what I mean by education *in* a subject. Science serves as the obvious example. What constitutes education in it? I think the most comprehensive answer is something like this: initiation into the principle of procedure on which that whole discipline depends. It is the principle that there are (to put it simply) certain observable uniformities of cause and effect in nature. Pure science is concerned to discover what these uniformities are; applied science, to show how we can act in accordance with them. Learning to think scientifically means learning to explain things theoretically and to tackle things practically, in the light which pure or applied science can shed. Educating one's pupils in the subject means sharing with them such theoretical knowledge of nature's uniformities as they can comprehend, and showing them how to use this knowledge for their own practical purposes.

Now, why should not an account of education in religion be given which runs parallel to this all the way through? Just as science rests on the principle that nature is uniform, religion may be said to rest on the principle that God exists. Pure religion (to retain this form of expression) is concerned to discover what God's nature and will are; applied religion, to show how we can act in accordance with them. Learning to think religiously is learning to explain what goes on, and to tackle what needs to be done, in the light which pure or applied religion may shed. Teaching religion means sharing with one's pupils such theories of God's nature and purpose as they are capable of comprehending, and showing them how to apply these doctrines to their own circumstances. This comparison between religion and science is, as I pointed out just now, thought to be vitiated by certain features of religion which make it different from science or any other school subject. So let us consider what these features are supposed to be.

To begin with, we are sometimes told that, whereas all other subjects are based on knowledge, religion is based only on belief. The uniformity of nature on which science is based is said to be an indisputable fact, the reality of the past which history takes for granted a matter beyond all doubt, and so on, but the existence of God at best a mere conjecture. The thing to notice is that this line of thought takes each subject to be based in the last analysis upon an empirically testable hypothesis of one kind or another, and it differentiates religion from the rest on the putative ground that, whilst all other such hypotheses have been proved to be true, that on which religion is based has not.

This account of the matter is, I feel sure, mistaken. It has a superficial plausibility and there are still some philosophers, notably Quine, who would wish to defend it, though even so empirically-minded a thinker as A J Ayer, the last of the logical positivists, finds Quine's opinions unconvincing.[1] The truth appears to be that propositions such as 'Nature is uniform', 'The past is real', 'God exists', etc., are none of them hypotheses. Expressly to make that point, a number of philosophers have variously described them as 'fundamental propositions' (Wittgenstein), 'absolute presuppositions' (Collingwood), 'end statements' (van Buren) and so on.[2]

It is obvious that *within* their respective disciplines, these propositions are not hypotheses because nothing counts against them (or even for them). Within science nothing counts against the uniformity of nature; within history, against the reality of the past; within religion, against God's existence. Does anything, then, count for or against them *without* their respective disciplines? We may feel tempted to insist that there must be some way of deciding whether they are true or false. But when we try to discover it, do we not find ourselves dragging these propositions by the scruff of the neck, so to speak, into universes of discourse where they obviously do not belong? A case in point would be treating the existence of God as if it were a scientific hypothesis which is patently not what it is supposed to be. There is no point in thinking of anything as a hypothesis unless you can form some conception of what would count for or against it; but it is just this which we do not seem able to do where the kind of proposition under discussion is concerned.

To recall an expression I used a moment ago, these propositions are 'principles of procedure'. They function logically as methodological rules, determining what counts as an explanation — and less obviously as an experience — within their respective subjects. A scientist, for example, proceeds on the assumption that nature is uniform in the sense that for her explaining anything means showing it to be an instance of certain observed regularities of occurrence called natural laws. If she cannot explain it in this way, she does not conclude that nature is not uniform but only that her own knowledge of its uniformity must be defective. True, some scientists would say that what goes on in the depths of matter is no longer explicable in terms of causal laws; that in the last analysis, sub-atomic particles appear to be, as I heard a physicist put it recently, 'self-organising in ways reminiscent of consciousness'. But, whatever this may mean, it does not impugn what I have been saying. The point which the physicist to whom I have just referred was making was that what has happened in his subject seems to have brought it to a close. Where there are no uniformities to look for in nature, there is nothing more left for a physicist to do.

My aim in all this has simply been to make it clear that religion is similar to other subjects in its logical structure. Like them, it is based on a principle of procedure; it seeks to explain things in terms of God's existence. I hope I have said enough about this similarity to discredit the facile contention that whilst other subjects are based on knowledge, religion is based on something inferior called belief.

But if that contention is abandoned, there are other features which have also been said to make religion different from all other subjects. For instance, we are sometimes told that it does not (for want of a better expression) 'deliver the goods' as other subjects do. Again, the obvious contrast is with science. The latter has immeasurably extended the human understanding of nature and thereby the power to control it to one's own advantage. The remark 'what use is science?' would be an absurd one to make. Our lives are full of its use. But 'what use is religion?' would strike many as a perfectly legitimate thing to say in pejorative tones. When your car breaks down, there is certainly far more chance that you will be able to get it to go, if you have been taught how to fix cars rather than how to pray. But if that is the kind of thing which is meant by a subject 'delivering the goods', it rests on a pretty narrow interpretation of that expression, does it not? It takes 'the goods' to consist exclusively in the power to control things. But there are surely other sorts of 'goods' besides that.

G E Moore contended that of all the goods known to humanity, the two chief are aesthetic enjoyments and personal affections.[3] And who would not place them high on a list? But neither of them can be conceived as ways of controlling one's environment. Aesthetic enjoyment is not a way of mastering the things around you but of responding to them; personal affection is not a way of dominating people but of opening your heart to them. Martin Buber and his followers, it may be recalled, contrasted 'I-thou' with 'I-it' relationships. 'I-thou' ones are the kind in which that to which you are related is conceived to lay a kind of claim upon you and to offer a kind of succour to you. In 'I-it' relationships, by contrast, that to which you are related is simply conceived as there for you to exploit. It is possible to regard things or people in either of these ways, as 'thous' or 'its'. But Moore's highest goods — the enjoyment of art in all its forms and the love of persons in all their variety — are only delivered when things or people are conceived of as 'thous' not 'its'. Therefore, it does not in any way downgrade a subject which is designed to increase a pupil's appreciation of art or understanding of people, if we point out that its use is not to enable us to control our environment but rather to receive more fully all that environment has to give us.

What then of religion? There is no doubt that it establishes a kind of 'I-thou' relationship. Even if the 'thou' in this case is an imaginary, not a real, object, that remains true. The least we are entitled to say, therefore, is that it is inept to criticise religion adversely for not 'delivering the goods' in the sense of enabling us to control environment advantageously. It is not that kind of good.

But some would say that religion does not 'deliver the goods' in any other sense either. Whereas aesthetic enjoyments and personal affections are indisputably enriching relationships, that which religion established is, in their opinion, pernicious. It entangles us in a tissue of illusions or an incubus of obsessions. It is a kind of opium or a form of neurosis. But I do not find much force in such strictures. They rest on ideological prejudices of the Marxist, Freudian, or whatever, kind, which have long been exposed as pseudo-scientific. It is, I think, simply an empirical fact, quite apart from whether religious beliefs are illusions or not, that for every example which might be given to support the contention that religion impoverishes (in the ordinary senses of that word) human life, a plausible counter-example can be given to support the view that it enriches (in the ordinary senses of that word) the existence of those who embrace it. So my conclusion on this alleged difference is simply this: there is no compelling ground for the view that, whilst other subjects 'deliver the goods', religion does not.

A third feature of religion which is said to make it different from all other school subjects is the wide variety of the opinions held within it. There is certainly no denying this variety. Between the religions now prevalent in the world − and even within each of them − there are countless differences of belief or practice. But I wonder if this really makes religion so very different from other subjects.

Variety of opinion within religion is of two main kinds. In part, it is variation between opinions which are logically incompatible with one another and, in part, between ones which are not. On the one hand religious believers hold certain views which are contrary or contradictory and in such case they cannot all be correct; but on the other hand they hold other views which are not necessarily inconsistent with one another, and may even be complementary, and in such case these views could conceivably all be correct. It is worth noticing, in passing, that in these ecumenical days religious believers seem to be, if anything, more interested in differences of belief which are conceivably complementary than in those which are clearly contradictory. I shall come back to this in a moment or two.

Here I am only concerned with whether or not the variety of

opinion within religion really does make it different from all other subjects. The difference is certainly not absolute. In science, history, and even such precise subjects as mathematics, variations of opinion undoubtedly occur, some of which turn out to be compatible with one another, others not. Is the difference then relative? Is it simply the extent of the diversity of opinion in religion which sets it apart from other subjects? All sorts of factors – temperamental, historical, cultural, sociological, etc. – play a part in determining people's religious beliefs, both collectively and individually. It is not surprising therefore that opinions should differ. But is the extent of this variation really so much greater than in other subjects? Scientists are interested in widely different branches of their subject. Historians offer exceedingly varied interpretations of the past. And the last thing you could say of literary or art critics is that they all think the same. Yet no one suggests that this variety of opinion as to what is significant or satisfying in such disciplines is a good reason for not educating pupils in, but only about, them. Why then in the case of religion?

There is a fourth difference between religion and other subjects which certainly does seem to set it apart from them much more radically than any of the three differences we have considered so far. It is this: in religion there is no generally accepted method of resolving differences of opinion as there is in other subjects. Mathematicians, scientists, historians, even literary or art critics, in their respective disciplines are more or less agreed about the conditions which an opinion has to fulfil in order to be true or false, reasonable or unreasonable. They are often divided about whether or not a particular opinion passes the relevant tests, but there is a broad consensus about what would falsify a hypothesis in science, render plausible a reconstruction of events in history, or make a judgment intelligent in criticism. By contrast any such generally accepted method of resolving differences of opinion seems to be notoriously lacking in religion. There is some agreement, of course, within sectional groups – the tradition of the church, the word of scripture, the inner light, and so on are severally considered to be authoritative determinants of what should be believed, and what not, in various branches of the Christian church. But there does not appear to be any agreed methodology within the world's major religions, taken one by one, let alone in all of them taken together. This fact certainly gives some reason to doubt whether education *in* religion can be the same kind of thing as education *in* science, history, or whatever; and even to suspect that, once allowed, it will necessarily take the form of initiation into prejudice and bigotry rather than into anything which resembles a rational way of arriving at opinions. Such doubts and suspicions are deepened by the extent to which religion has made a virtue of conviction. Simply having opinions and holding on to them come hell or high water is sometimes presented as a paradigm of religious faith whereas it would be given, to say the most, only qualified approval in any other discipline.

I readily concede therefore that this fourth difference between religion and other subjects raises in an acute form the question whether religion should be in the school curriculum at all. But I do not think the answer is irredeemably in the negative. There are at least two considerations which give one pause.

First, the emergence of an agreed methodology in any subject takes time, and in one as complex as religion is bound to be, if there is any truth in it at all, the mere fact that those who profess it still have a long way to go in arriving at agreed ways of resolving their disagreements does not in itself disqualify that subject altogether from a place in the school curriculum.

Then again there are, as I suggested just now in my reference to the ecumenical movement, some signs that the quest for an agreed methodology is being pursued more actively and successfully in these latter days than it has been hitherto. It is not perhaps too much to hope that in the foreseeable future open-mindedness will supplant conviction in the hierarchy of religious virtues. Open-mindedness is, of course, only desirable in religion or anywhere else if it is an expression of rationality rather than indifference. I do not commend, any more than St Paul did, being blown about by every wind of doctrine; but I do commend the rationalist ideal of holding even one's most cherished convictions open to revision if what appears to be good reason for revising them becomes evident. I have written at length elsewhere on the possibility as well as the desirability of such an attitude in religion.[4]

Conclusion

My conclusion, then, is that there are no differences between religion and all other subjects which impose a moral obligation on teachers of religion to educate their pupils about, but not in, their subject. If any religious educators feel isolated from other teachers by such an obligation, their loneliness is delusional. They are in schools to do the same kind of job as any other kind of teacher and they should make no bones about, and offer no apology for, doing it in as committed and methodical a way as they can. They are educators in the ordinary and not any alienated, sense of the word. Their job is to initiate their pupils into a kind of explanation and a form of experience, constituted by the principle of procedure which makes religion what it is.

Two things remain to be said, not by the way of qualification but only of comment, upon the view I have just expressed. One is that any given society has the right to decide whether or not it wants religion to be taught in its schools. I have not been saying that it ought to want this, only that, if it does, those who teach the subject have precisely the same kind of job to do as teachers of any other subject. It is only the society as a whole, not teachers, who have the moral right to decide whether there shall be religion in schools or not. If the idea that pupils should be educated about, but not in, religion is canvassed because it enables teachers of religion to keep their jobs in a society which does not really want them, then it is a contemptible conception. But I do not think that is how things are in our society. A majority of people would, I think, exercise their moral right by voting for religious education in schools rather than against it, if called upon to decide. And they would mean education in religion, not just about it.

That brings me to the second thing which remains to be said. All educators as such have certain moral obligations: to find out all they can about their subject, to be tolerant of opinions within it other than their own, to encourage pupils to think for themselves, and so on. Whatever constitutes reasonableness in a teacher of any sort should characterise teachers of religion, no less than what constitutes devotion. And so, when it comes to moral obligations, it is not any which set him apart from other teachers that the religious educator is under, but only such as he shares with them in a common enterprise of the highest worth.

Notes

1. W V Quine, 'On Carnap's view of ontology,' in his *Ways of Paradox,* New York, 1966; and A J Ayer, 'Metaphysics and common sense,' in his collection of papers with the same title, London, 1969.
2. See L Wittgenstein, *On Certainty,* Oxford, Blackwell, 1974; R G Collingwood, *Essay on Metaphysics,* Oxford, Oxford University Press, 1940; P Van Buren, *The Secular Meaning of the Gospel,* Harmondsworth, Penguin, 1965.
3. See his *Principia Ethica,* Cambridge, Cambridge University Press, 1903, chapter 6.
4. See my 'Is religious education possible?' in G Langford and D J O'Connor (eds), *New Essays in the Philosophy of Education*, London, Routledge and Kegan Paul, 1973; *A Philosophical Approach to Religion,* London, Macmillan, 1974, chapter 6; 'Learning to be rational,' *Proceedings of the Philosophy of Education Society of Great Britain,* 11, 1977; 'The rational system of beliefs,' in David Martin (ed.), *Sociology and Theology*, London, Harvester, 1980; 'Trusting to reason,' *New Universities Quarterly,* 34, 1980, pp. 241–57.

2.4 The place of understanding in Christian education and education about Christianity

Jeff Astley

Terminology

Much discussion of the nature of religious education has distinguished a non-confessional secular religious education about religions, from educational processes that aim to create, and sometimes succeed in creating, religious commitment. The former is said to be appropriate in publicly-funded educational institutions, the latter in religious communities. Christian education, on one definition,[1] labels those formative educational processes that result in Christian learning, usually by the intentional facilitation of teaching. Christian learning is understood here to connote the learning of Christianity, in the sense of the learner's adoption or deepening of Christian beliefs, attitudes and values, as well as dispositions to act in Christian ways through love, prayer and worship, and other moral and cultic overt behaviour. All such cognitive, affective and lifestyle components of Christianity may be regarded as capable of being learned; they may well be learned in the same way as other attitudes, beliefs and behaviour dispositions are learned.[2]

Christian education is often regarded as synonymous with teaching Christianity and distinguished from teaching about Christianity. Unfortunately the language of teaching Christianity, and teaching religion generally, suffers from some ambiguity and I shall not employ that particular phrase here.[3] The meaning of teaching about Christianity − as a non-confessional, non-nurturing and non-evangelistic study of the Christian religion (Christian studies) − is clearer; and it is usually clearly distinguished from Christian education that teaches people to *be* Christian.

Christian learning

(Much of what follows may be applied, *mutatis mutandis*, to other religions, to the extent that those religions may be analysed in a way similar to the one adopted below with regard to Christianity.)

The range of Christian attributes

In order to discuss our distinction further it is necessary to make some attempt to analyse what it means for a person to be Christian.

This is always likely to be a contentious matter. My own list of Christian attributes would read as follows.[4] Most of these may be learned directly. Others may be learned indirectly as we learn the continuing states and dispositions that predispose us to, for example, religious experience and overt religious behaviour.

a. *Christian beliefs-that, understanding and knowledge*: including beliefs about God, Jesus, the church, human nature and the world;

b. *Christian beliefs-in*: including faith and trust in God, Jesus etc., or in salvation, baptism etc.;

c. *Christian attitudes and values*: covering the attitudes and dispositions of Christian spirituality and the Christian virtues;

d. *Christian emotions and feelings*: including awe, pity, joy etc.;

e. *Christian experiences*: in the sense of objective religious experiences of God, Christ, the Spirit etc. and their activities;

f. *Christian moral actions*: for example active love, forgiveness, trust and obedience;

g. *Christian religious actions*: for example prayer, profession of faith, evangelism, worship and church membership or involvement;

h. *Christian/theological reflection and criticism*: including those interpretative and evaluative cognitive skills and processes that lead to active critical Christian reflection and theological thinking. Some would argue that Christian education is not truly 'education' if the formation of this learning outcome is neglected.

The centrality of Christian affect

I would contend, following the classic arguments of Jonathan Edwards,[5] that the place of feelings within Christianity is paramount. Not only are they a crucial element within the affective states that fall under categories (b), (c) and (d) above, but they are also powerful contributory causes of Christian moral and religious activity and accompany all authentic Christian experience, knowledge and understanding. Much Christian education, it has been said, is therefore primarily a matter of 'the shaping of religious emotions and affections in the context of teaching doctrine'.[6] This will be seen to be an important claim when we come to discuss further the distinction between Christian education and education about Christianity.

Explicit/implicit and distinctive/characteristic Christianity

Only some of this range of Christian beliefs, attitudes and actions may be said to be explicitly and distinctively Christian: in particular those beliefs associated with the figure of Jesus and those actions that are peculiar to the Christian church, for example in baptism and the eucharist. Many of the Christian attributes, unless they are linked by definition with that which is explicitly and distinctively Christian, may be described as merely characteristic of Christianity and as implicitly Christian attributes. These include many Christian religious beliefs about God, creation, providence, life after death, the world etc.; many Christian actions, such as prayer and some forms of worship, fellowship, acts of charity etc.; and most Christian spirituality and religious and moral attitudes and values, including the traditional lists of Christian virtues and 'fruits of the Spirit'. Most of the Christian feelings that underlie, or operate as components of, the categories of Christian attitude and action also fall under the implicit and characteristic description. Many of them, indeed, are only implicitly and characteristically *religious*. What makes them distinctively and explicitly Christian is the articulation of their distinctive targets (Jesus, the eucharist, etc.).

Christian education and secular religious education

The distinction

We are now in a position to take up the distinction between Christian education (seen primarily as Christian nurture or formation) as a proper activity of the church, and school religious education as a justifiable part of secular education outside the church. The latter activity is usually interpreted as teaching very few, or even none, of the Christian learning outcomes enumerated above. Thus phenomenological religious education about Christianity is often said to be concerned solely with understanding. The beliefs-that which the religious education teacher aims to develop are beliefs about Christianity, rather than beliefs about God, Jesus, the church etc. They are therefore beliefs about Christian beliefs, as well as beliefs about Christian attitudes, emotions, experiences, evaluations, and actions. To be religiously educated about Christianity, on this view, is to acquire some knowledge and understanding of the complex of attributes that make up being a Christian.

We must not be misled by the fact that understanding a proposition is a component part of believing it, into thinking that the understanding of religious beliefs-that that secular religious education encourages is necessarily in every respect the same understanding that is a component of such religious beliefs. As we shall see later, understanding is in one sense not an all-or-nothing commodity. It comes in degrees, and the religious understanding of the religionist is usually of a fuller, deeper and more complex quality than is possible for the student who is not 'inside' that religion.[7] In another sense, however, there appears to be a difference in kind between a participant's religious understanding, where this is construed as using religious language and being religious (with understanding), and an observer's understanding of these activities (this understanding).[8] But even this distinction is difficult to preserve as a hard and fast one where the religious affections are concerned.

The role of empathy

Some proponents of phenomenological religious education claim that the study of religion can produce an understanding of it from the point of view of a religious adherent.[9] This is to make a claim that can all too easily be overdone. It is based on the argument that the student's understanding should be an empathetic understanding, appropriate to affect-related beliefs and actions, and to the feeling dimension of attitudes, experiences, and emotions. What is empathetic understanding? It is a form of imaginative comprehension that involves projecting oneself into another person's standpoint, including (in this case) the feeling-states of a Christian believer, so that we may properly understand him or her. This activity ('feeling in') is commonly said to be different from sympathy, which is a matter of 'feeling with' the believer, that is sharing these feeling states.

But to understand anything is to know what it is like, at least to some degree. To have an articulated, descriptive understanding of, and therefore also a belief about, a proposition is to know what it would be like for the proposition to be true. Now it is possible to adopt a behaviourist account of religious adherents and claim that a descriptive knowledge of their overt behaviour fully fulfils this condition. To know about religious feelings, therefore, we would only need to know about publicly observable actions such as kneeling and speaking. However, most people would view this as an inadequate understanding of what it is to feel. It may be that feelings are often, perhaps always, accompanied by overt behaviour, and that we can only know who has which feelings on the basis of their behaviour. It may be that we can only understand and talk about how we feel because we have been brought up − as embodied beings − in a social context where such behaviour is observable and correlates with language about feelings. But in the end we are forced to admit that our introspection tells us that there is more to our feelings than our overt behaviour. We may go further: we can only understand feeling-states in so far as we have them, or something very like them, ourselves. Empathy is often presented as being no more than a sort of vicarious experience of other people's feelings, attitudes etc.; but in order to be this it needs to be, or at least to presuppose, an experience in oneself.

Mariasusai Dhavamony argues that 'imitative or reproductive experiencing is not even a condition of understanding another's experience', but he means by this only that we do not need to be having the same experience at the time. He goes on: 'one should have previously experienced oneself sadness to really understand another person's sadness' and 'empathy denotes the understanding of the behaviour of another on the basis of one's own experiences and behaviour'. Here we have a form of the argument from analogy to other minds, which is dependent on our having access 'to our own inner religious experiences, emotions, thoughts and ideas'.[10]

Bracketing and mimicking

Ninian Smart is more philosophically acute in his account of empathy. He notes that the 'bracketing' that is such an important part of the phenomenological approach to the study of religion is 'not solely concerned with matters of truth, but also of value, feeling, ritual etc. . . . The bracketing must also be a bracketing of expressions of value, feeling, etc.'[11] In studying religion, of course, we are seeking to understand religious beliefs, emotions, experiences and so on, and not to express them; but 'an important part of description is what may be called "bracketed expression"'.[12] Because of this emotional bracketing, empathy does not amount to full sympathy.

Here Smart introduces the analogy of play-acting or novel-reading, as similarly 'making use of empathetic imagination':[13]

> The actor . . . succeeds in a quite practical manner in bracketing the emotions, dispositions, etc., which he presents on the stage. There can be no *a priori* reason why the phenomenologist should not imaginatively rehearse the feelings and beliefs of those he aims evocatively to describe.

Elsewhere Smart calls this a kind of mimicking, involving bracketed make-belief, and makes two significant admissions. The first is that 'it is certainly a bit easier to go in for make-belief if you half-believe and think that considerable insight is to be derived from the tradition you mimic'. The second is that 'the flavour of the bracketing is likely to be sweet − that is, the mimicking of feelings may be such that the describer not only empathises but also sympathises'.[14]

An actor can, of course, just feign tears by producing the overt behaviour usually associated with inner grief. This sort of purely behaviourist acting must be exceedingly difficult. Smart's analogy better fits the case where an actor (a method actor?) is feeling something for herself. The actor's felt emotion may not be quite the same as that of her character. It may be a self-induced, secular spookiness for example, rather than religious awe evoked by the Other. It can certainly be described as having a different target, often an imaginary person or event. Yet it must be somewhat similar. And if the actor herself is asked, as is the student of religion, properly to understand, and then in the more usual sense to describe these emotions to us, that similarity must be even closer.[15]

Observers and participants

To understand and properly describe another's emotion, it is surely necessary at some time to have felt that emotion, or something very like it, for oneself. The alternative would be like a four-year-old trying to understand what it is like for an adult to fall in love, or a person born deaf attempting to describe adequately a musical performance.

An empathetic understanding of religion, therefore, does seem to depend in part on the learner having had some religious, quasi-religious or semi-religious experiences of her or his own. It is said that this empathetic understanding is different from a sympathetic understanding in which the learner shares the religionist's religious affections; but the difference now appears to be one of degree, rather than a difference in kind. In order for observers to understand religious emotions, attitudes, evaluations and spirituality properly, they need some taste of them. Admittedly they need much more than a taste in order to *be* religious.[16] A full understanding, that is participant-understanding, of the religious affections is not available to the observer unless and until the observer becomes more of a participant and empathy completely turns into sympathy. However, the observer's understanding does not need to be as full and complete as is the participant's understanding. It is not to be expected that the student of any human phenomenon should have the same quality of understanding possessed by those he or she is studying. Nevertheless, the taste is from the same cooking pot as the full meal.

We may further observe that although the belief elements and cognitive implicates of religious emotions and attitudes are often distinctively religious, and distinctive of particular religions such as Christianity, the feeling-elements themselves on the whole are not. Numinous feelings or mystical affections may be peculiar to religious contexts, even particular religious contexts, but most other religious feelings, for example of affection, concern, trust or devotion, are also to be found outside the religions, and certainly outside the Christian religion. They are to be placed among the implicitly, though characteristically, religious attributes of Christianity. These are not quasi-religious or semi-religious feelings, to be regarded as merely analogous to real religious feeling. They are implicitly religious, and implicitly Christian, feelings.

Degrees of understanding

Let us return to the issue of degrees of understanding.[17] I am claiming that a full understanding (participant-understanding) of all the appropriate religious attributes in the affective domain is only possible for those who possess them all to the full themselves. An understanding adequate for the needs of the student of religion − and therefore of school religious education about Christianity − is possible, however, for those who have only a second-hand (observer's) experience of the expression of many of these attributes, together with some first-hand experience of emotions similar to religious awe or mystical union, as well as their own feelings of joy, wonder, gratitude, shame, etc.

The distinction between the two types of understanding now looks very much like the distinction between two ends of a continuous spectrum of understanding. We may speak then, whenever we come across affective learning outcomes, of a spectrum stretching from empathetic educational understanding of a religion (observer-understanding[18]) at one end, to sympathetic religious understanding (participant-understanding) at the other. To put it differently, the scale extends from partial understanding (which may be solely based on characteristically religious feelings, and on those that are only analogous to distinctively religious feeling) at the one extreme, to full understanding (based on having distinctively, as well as characteristically, religious feeling) at the other. The spectrum will be further modified when we use it to chart the understanding of a particular religion such as Christianity and consider the rather different distinction between what is distinctive of Christianity and what is (only) characteristically Christian.

Others have acknowledged the importance of the fact that we can sensibly speak of degrees of religious understanding and of religious consciousness.[19] Michael Grimmitt acknowledges that being 'conscious of religion' and having 'religious consciousness' are 'different points on a continuum', adding that 'it is extremely difficult to identify when and how the former passes into the latter'. He continues, in writing of school religious education:[20]

> In seeking to enable pupils to become conscious of religion, religious beliefs and values and a religious interpretation of life, religious education may be seen as contributing to a process which enhances the religious consciousness of pupils even though it is not its intention to bring it to a form which is indistinguishable from religious faith.

Does this suggest that, when measured in terms of their actual educational outcomes (the teacher's intention notwithstanding), both secular religious education about Christianity and Christian education lead to results that can be plotted on the same scale, and may well be found to overlap on that scale? In which case a hard and fast distinction between the two approaches to the teaching of religion cannot plausibly be maintained.

The blurring of the distinction

It is the element of feeling that particularly prevents us from drawing a sharp distinction between secular religious education about Christianity and Christian formative education (or nurture). Such a distinction might appear to be possible in the areas of cognition and overt behaviour, but only if we can sharply distinguish between understanding a belief-that or an action, and the different process of believing or acting religiously for ourselves. The understanding of feelings, however, seems to be dependent on having these attributes, or something very like them, in a way that understanding pure (non-affective) cognition or pure (non-affective) overt behaviour would not. The nature of feeling, then, and of the way in which it is known – which includes a partly private, introspective element – should give us pause before drawing too sharply the lines of demarcation between secular religious education and religious nurture, in the case of those religions where feeling is a central component. I have argued that Christianity is such a religion. When measured in terms of learning outcomes, therefore, these two types of religious education occupy two overlapping bands on a continuous scale. They do not label two separate and completely distinct activities.

This conclusion, which results from a consideration of the understanding of religious feeling, can be widened to some extent. Feeling is central to Christianity not only in the area of attitude, evaluation, emotion and experience, but also in relation to Christian belief and action. In any integrated, holistic view of what it is to be Christian, belief and overt behaviour are closely related to affect, so that a proper understanding of either of them must also involve some understanding of Christian religious feeling. Non-affective cognitions or volitions do not in fact exist in the real world. A scale ranging from full to partial, that is participant to observer, understanding may therefore also be created for the cognitive domain of religious attributes, in so far as religious beliefs etc. are intimately related to religious affections and a proper understanding of the former requires an understanding of the feelings that accompany them, are contained within them, or arise from them. A similar point may be made about overt religious behaviour.

To summarise: the aims of secular religious education and Christian nurture are here being assessed in terms of learning outcome objectives. My point is that the learning outcome objectives of secular religious education, in particular the understanding of Christianity when fully unpacked, includes some element of development of those feelings (with of course, reflection on them) that are also components of Christian attitudes, emotions, experiences and evaluations, and concomitants of Christian belief and action. The fuller the understanding of Christianity being aimed at, the wider and deeper these feelings need to be. Phenomenological teaching about religion may in principle be said to overlap with religious formation in the sense that it too produces religious attributes, that is, implicitly and characteristically religious feelings.

This is the hole in the dyke that prevents the complete separation of the sea water of Christian nurture from the reclaimed land of secular religious education. Yet dykes with holes will still hold back a lot of water. Christian education and secular religious education remain very different sorts of activities with regard to the broad scope of their outcomes and objectives. But that difference may now be seen as a difference in (marked) degree, but not as a difference in kind.

Some criticisms

A theological criticism

Whether my list of Christian attributes represents the fully Christian, or fully Christianly educated, person is an issue to be decided by Christian theology, as is the question as to what the minimum requirements are for those who are to be designated Christian. However complete one strives to make a taxonomy of Christian attributes or Christian learning outcomes, some theologians will raise the charge of reductionism. They will contend that the list represents only contingent expressions or even conditions of something else that is far more fundamental, in particular some metaphysical change in a person's inner being or in her or his relationship with God. This, it is often claimed, is the essential element in becoming and being a Christian.

I do not wish to deny such claims, but would emphasise here that education is a practical matter. There may indeed be supernatural changes in a Christian that lie beneath the human beliefs, attitudes, and activities listed above, changes which do not necessarily correlate with these attributes and cannot in the same way be known by observation.[21] Nevertheless, I would contend that the practice of Christian education needs a definition of being Christian that is of some use to it. Many theological definitions fail this test.

An educational criticism

Theologians may not be the only ones who wish to take issue with this account of learning Christianity, for we touch here on the debate about evaluation of educational programmes and assessment of learners. Some educationalists might argue that what is being presented here collapses into a behavioural objectives model of Christian learning, and is therefore open to the criticisms often made of all such models. The behavioural objectives model has been dismissed as 'an extremely narrow view of the teaching and learning process'.

Its critics claim that it is a view that is appropriate to training but not to education (adopting a more normative account of education than I have used), that it is impracticable (because it is impossible to specify all the objectives even in one area of learning), and that it implies some form of positivism.[22] I would argue in response that most of the educationalists' criticisms are irrelevant to my account of Christian learning for two reasons. First, I have specified these learning outcomes as a description of what it means to be a Christian and they therefore provide an appropriate account of formative Christian education. Secondly, I do not claim that they may all be reduced to observable overt behaviour. I do recognise that some critics have a point when they object to the application of the objectives model to a curriculum with highly specific, short-term behavioural objectives. I would agree with these critics that all learning cannot be immediately tested, and that the testing of overt behaviour can never exhaustively evaluate a changed disposition or capability.

We should note that what lies at the heart of the behavioural objectives model is an attempt to clarify the activities of teaching and learning by a specification of observable changes as intended learning outcomes. At the very least this provides educational evaluation with something to evaluate, and on those grounds alone it should be viewed more sympathetically by practical Christian educators.[23]

Others may criticise the implied application of the model to religious education about Christianity, arguing that a proper induction into a subject leads to unpredictable learning outcomes as students who are engaged in individual thinking explore that area of knowledge creatively.[24] Nevertheless, if empathetic understanding is regarded as an important component of knowledge about religion this particular learning outcome is being specified in a fairly determinate manner.

Some practical implications

Secular religious education

It may be thought that the argument in this article is merely of logical interest, without any significant practical implications. Against this one might contend that the blurring of the nurture/education distinction could significantly affect debate about the role of religious education in the secular school. This is perhaps particularly the case at the political level, where the demand for religious education of a particular nature seems to be partly determined by a particular view of the nature of what I have designated implicit/characteristic Christianity, together with a desire to see schools engaged in formative education directed to this goal. Those who wish to 'see more Christianity taught in schools' very often have in mind the learning of such implicitly Christian attributes as compassion, responsibility, trust, care and awe, all of which are attributes with strong affective components that will need to be developed to some extent in pupils as we teach them *about* these aspects of Christianity.

The argument may have a further practical outcome in that it might encourage Christian teachers and other Christians to be more positive towards education about Christianity, and all religious education teachers to be more willing to consider curricular materials and methods devised in overtly nurturing Christian contexts. On the other hand, the argument might also convince the more secular-minded teachers that they have further reasons to be wary of these processes, methods and materials.

Such consequences are not peculiar to this discussion, of course. As has often been noted, the distinction between secular religious education and Christian education is already blurred by the fact that much school religious education teaching includes as an element within its syllabus, or as a component of the whole educational enterprise of which it forms a part, one or more of the following objectives:

a. the encouragement and enabling of the pupil's 'personal quest' for her or his own religion;
b. the education of the emotions; and
c. moral education.

These activities are usually taken to include not only the development of the pupil's powers critically to appraise religions, emotions and moral claims, but also some development in the pupil of those personal attributes that are also central to religions, emotions and morality – in particular those elements of feeling discussed above. Thus Kevin Nichols argues that elements in school education such as the education of feeling and moral education (and, he adds, pastoral care) already broaden the scope of education 'so that at least some elements of catechesis can find a place in it'.[25]

Church schools

It may be argued further that the breakdown of a hard and fast nurture/education distinction with regard to the understanding of Christianity enables us to argue for a church school as something of a half-way house, at least in those contexts – for example Britain – where its support, funding and control is provided by a partnership between the church and the secular state. We have seen that at least some learning outcomes may be arranged to occupy a continuous spectrum between being fully Christian oneself and understanding someone else's Christianity, because understanding Christianity includes having some implicitly religious (Christian) feelings. A person who possesses these feelings will be regarded by some as already being partly (even if only implicitly or characteristically) Christian, at least in the domain of feelings. The church school could quite appropriately see itself as encouraging the development of. learning outcomes that lie somewhere between these outcomes of the secular school (at the extreme − only implicitly, characteristically Christian − end of the spectrum) and those of the seminary or church (at the other extreme − the fully and explicitly, distinctively Christian end). Such a school might well attempt to provide its pupils with a fuller understanding of Christianity than does the secular school, by trying to make them in this way somewhat more Christian than the secular school's pupils. In particular it might seek to produce more by way of Christian affect by developing more of the implicit and characteristic Christian attitudes, emotions and experiences, and perhaps even a few of the explicit and distinctive ones. This should strengthen the pupils' understanding of Christianity, without necessarily developing the full range of Christian attributes, especially those beliefs and actions that are more properly the objective of the church's Christian education practice.

I believe that many church schools might welcome an account of what it is to be Christian, and to be Christianly educated, that allows them to distinguish in this way their own educational endeavours both from those of the secular school and from those of a fully-fledged nurturing church community.

Notes

1. For other definitions see J M Hull, *Studies in Religion and Education,* Lewes, Falmer, 1984, p. 39; J Astley and D Day (eds), *The Contours of Christian Education,* Great Wakering, McCrimmons, 1992, chapter 1.
2. J M Lee, *The Flow of Religious Instruction,* Birmingham, Alabama, Religious Education Press, 1973, and *The Content of Religious Instruction,* Birmingham, Alabama, Religious Education Press, 1982.
3. See the literature cited in J Astley, 'Will the real Christianity please stand up?' *British Journal of Religious Education,* 15, 1992, p. 11, note 3.
4. For lists of the range of Christian attributes or objectives of Christian education see R C Miller, 'The objective of Christian education,' in M J Taylor (ed.), *An Introduction to Christian Education,* Nashville, Tennessee, Abingdon, 1966; J H Westerhoff, 'Religious education and catechesis: appendix II,' in M C Felderhof (ed.), *Religious Education in a Pluralistic Society,* London, Hodder and Stoughton, 1985, pp. 71−74; D S Amalorpavadass, 'Catechesis as a pastoral task of the church,' in M Warren (ed.), *A Sourcebook for Modern Catechetics,* Winona, Minnesota, St Mary's Press, 1983, pp. 342−343, 353−355. These accounts fit closely with the social scientist's list of dimensions of religion or religious variables.
5. Jonathan Edwards, *Select Works, Volume III: treatise concerning the religious affections,* London, Banner of Truth, 1961, pp. 27−32.
6. J A Bernsten, 'Christian affections and the catechumenate,' *Worship,* 52, 1978, p. 194; see also P L Holmer, *Making Christian Sense,* Philadelphia, Westminster Press, 1985, pp. 55−60 and I S Caldwell, 'Communicating the gospel,' *Religious Education,* 60, 1965, p. 350.
7. This is not to say that, in the cognitive domain, a social scientist might not 'claim to understand what goes on in a culture more explicitly than members of the culture themselves,' for example by seeing the functional role of their

religious beliefs. This is argued by M A Arbib, *In Search of the Person,* Amherst, University of Massachusetts Press, 1985, p. 96.

8. This distinction is developed by D Z Phillips. See his *Faith and Philosophical Enquiry,* London, Routledge and Kegan Paul, 1965, pp. 166–167, 230 and *Belief, Change and Forms of Life,* London, Macmillan, 1986, pp. 11–12.

9. *A Groundplan for the Study of Religion,* London, Schools Council, 1977, pp. 22–23.

10. M Dhavamony, *Phenomenology of Religion,* Rome, Gregorian University Press, 1973, pp. 18–19, 20.

11. N Smart, *The Phenomenon of Religion,* London and Basingstoke, Macmillan, 1973, p. 32.

12. *Ibid.,* p. 33. Smart writes that the 'expression' of a religious tradition is a sort of preaching or re-presentation of its faith: it is 'positional' rather than 'descriptive-scientific' (cf. *ibid.,* pp. 12–13).

13. *Ibid.,* p. 75.

14. N Smart, *The Science of Religion and the Sociology of Knowledge,* Princeton, New Jersey, Princeton University Press, 1973, p. 37. Elsewhere Smart writes more ambiguously of the student's need 'to get something of the feel of it (a religious event)'; see, for example, 'Phenomenology of religion,' in J M Sutcliffe (ed.), *A Dictionary of Religious Education,* London, SCM, 1984, p. 258.

15. If we are to understand what the student understands, the same qualification applies to us. This is a development of the analogy of acting, where the audience's own understanding of emotion is a precondition of proper communication.

16. Compare K Surin, 'Can the experiential and the phenomenological approaches be reconciled?' *British Journal of Religious Education,* 2, 1980, p. 103.

17. Compare N Smart, *Concept and Empathy,* London and Basingstoke, Macmillan, 1986, pp. 197–198. Smart notes that 'the concept of understanding has to do with degree: there are more or less profound, more or less superficial understandings ...it is not an all-or-nothing-at-all matter, whereas the argument about commitment to a tradition is posed in this way' (p. 224).

18. The empathetic student of religion has been described as a 'participant observer', or 'watcher', who enters the world of the religious believer and yet remains detached (A J H Leech, 'Another look at phenomenology and religious education,' *British Journal of Religious Education,* 11, 1989, pp. 70–75). The 'observer-understanding' referred to here is of this nature: that is, more than the (non-empathetic) understanding of a total outsider.

19. Compare Gabriel Moran in N H Thompson (ed.), *Religious Pluralism and Religious Education,* Birmingham, Alabama, Religious Education Press, 1988, p. 54.

20. M Grimmitt, *Religious Education and Human Development,* Great Wakering, McCrimmons, 1987, p. 137.

21. My point is not that 'only the observable is real.' It is that only realities that are directly observable (I would include the introspectively observable), or whose existence can be inferred from what is directly observable, or can be known as necessary conditions of observation and knowledge as such, can be *known* to be real.

22. Thus D Lawton, *An Introduction to Teaching and Learning,* London, Hodder and Stoughton, 1981, quotation from p. 116; L Stenhouse, *An Introduction to Curriculum Research and Development,* London, Heinemann, 1975, chapter 6; M MacDonald-Ross, 'Behavioural objectives: a critical review,' *Instructional Science,* 2, 1973. Compare also the criticisms surveyed, with attempted answers, by W J Popham in his paper 'Probing the validity of arguments against behavioural goals,' in R J Kibler *et al.* (eds), *Behavioural Objectives and Instruction,* Boston, Allyn and Bacon, 1970.

23. Compare R W Tyler, *Basic Principles of Curriculum and Instruction,* Chicago, University of Chicago Press, 1949, pp. 46–60; H Taba, *Curriculum Development: theory and practice,* New York, Harcourt, Brace and World, 1962, p. 199.

24. Compare Elliot Eisner's analysis of 'expressive objectives/outcomes' in his *The Educational Imagination,* New York, Macmillan, 1979, chapter 6. See also H A Alexander, 'Elliot Eisner's artistic model of education,' *Religious Education,* 81, 1986, pp. 45–59,

25. K Nichols, *Orientations,* Slough, St Paul Publications, 1979, p. 20.

3. Professionalism and confessionalism

In this section the school context of religious education is explored further. We have brought together these articles not only to illustrate the on-going debate about the justification of religious education in 'secular education', which itself sheds light on the nature of Christian education as a confessional activity leading to religious commitment; but also as a contribution to Christian reflection on general educational practice.

Peter Gardner's article, 'Religious education: in defence of non-commitment,' was first published in the *Journal of Philosophy of Education*, 14, 1980, pp. 157–168. He articulates the now broadly adopted ('secularist') account of the nature of religious education in public education, which views it as oriented towards the *elucidation* of religion rather than its *advocacy* (see article 9.1), but here this is largely on the grounds that 'genuine doubts exist and can reasonably exist about the epistemic status' of religious assertions. He defends, against a range of criticisms, the claim that religion should be treated as a special case in public education.

Brian Hill's question 'Will and should the religious studies appropriate to schools in a pluralistic society foster religious relativism?' raises the issue of relativism, a topic that will be considered in greater depth in section 10 of this reader. We include the article here as a good example of a defence of a model of 'multi-faith' religious education which 'should be equally acceptable to both the state school and the religiously sponsored school'. Hill criticises various teaching strategies that promote 'religious emotivism', 'religious universalism' or 'religious relativism', and details by contrast a particular educational stance that 'endorses the view that truth-claims
... *are* intrinsic to religious discourse' while conceding the need to teach about more than one religion. This article was first published in *British Journal of Religious Education*, 12, 1990, pp. 126–136.

Trevor Cooling also distinguishes 'secular' religious education in public education from confessional ('faith-based') approaches that promote and nurture faith. In the context of a discussion of professionalism and the concept of fairness, however, Cooling challenges both the assumption that confessionalism is neither objective nor rational, and the assumption that educational goals are innocent of all confessional presuppositions. He argues that 'secular religious education is not ... value neutral', not least because it is founded on the belief that harmonious relations between faith communities should be promoted by state education. Unrestricted confessional approaches are 'quite appropriate' in contexts where the constraints of secularity do not apply, but restraint ought to be shown in state-maintained secular institutions. 'Professionalism, confessionalism and religious education: an exploration from the British context' was first published simultaneously in *Spectrum*, 25, 1993, pp. 129–145 and *Panorama*, 1993.[1]

Peter Gardner teaches in the Department of Education of the University of Warwick, Coventry, England. Professor Brian V Hill is Professor of Education in the School of Education of Murdoch University, Murdoch, Western Australia. Dr Trevor Cooling is Projects Officer for the Association of Christian Teachers of England, based at Stapleford House Education Centre, Nottingham, England.

Notes
1.   See also Trevor Cooling, *A Christian Vision for State Education,* London, SPCK, 1994.

3.1 Religious education: in defence of non-commitment

Peter Gardner

Introduction

According to John Stuart Mill,[1] the

> diversity of opinion among men of equal ability, and who have taken equal pains to arrive at the truth ... should of itself be a warning to a conscientious teacher that he has no right to impose his opinion authoritatively upon a youthful mind.... The pupil should not be addressed as if his religion had been chosen for him, but as one who will have to choose it for himself.

Mill's remarks were made with university teachers in mind. A century and more later Mill's prescription is being repeated as guidance for teachers in schools. The result, or so we are told, 'is that religious education teachers are learning to think more as educators, and less as catechists or evangelists.'[2] As educators, they are being encouraged away from the enshrined religious particularity and commitment of the 1944 Education Act by various new agreed syllabuses and by influential reports which advocate diversity and recommend the serious consideration of non-theistic perspectives.[3]

To some thinkers this recent movement in religious education, a movement often called 'the new religious education', has little to commend it. E R Norman, for example, in the 1977 *Black Paper*, having surveyed the scepticism, pluralism and what he regards as the undesirable social consequences of the new religious education concludes: 'Doubtless it would be preferable to dispense with religious education altogether, rather than see it transformed in the present manner.'[4] Furthermore, although recent philosophical literature contains little assessment of the supposed dire consequences of the new movement, there is a not inconsiderable amount of contemporary philosophical writing which, either explicitly or implicitly, is opposed to the underpinnings of the new religious education. If such attacks are successful, then regardless of how it stands up to the rhetoric of its opponents, the new movement will not be able to withstand the test of reason. What I propose to do in this paper is to examine several of the various strands of this philosophical opposition, although I will begin by describing a certain attitude, an attitude which embodies many of the positions that underpin the new religious education and which, as we shall see, had a variety of philosophical opponents. For want of a better term I will call this attitude 'secularist'.[5] It is an attitude towards religion, or possibly I should say religions, as well as religious statements and religious education. It can be outlined as follows: Religions involve unique ways of looking at the world, and unique claims, such claims being irreducible to those that are non-religious, such as those of ethics or sociology. However, as genuine doubts exist and can reasonably exist about the epistemic status of such claims, then if the teaching of religion is to be part of the educational process, these claims should not be taught as true, as statements to be believed; rather if religion is to be taught, a distinction must be drawn between elucidation and advocacy,[6] and the former should be the appropriate method of teaching. Now even if we were to accept that there are what have been called 'forms of knowledge' and that these should be catered for in a curriculum, since religion is not a form of knowledge, such an acceptance would provide no basis for finding a place in the curriculum for religion. Nevertheless, religions do afford unique perspectives, and many features of our world would remain unilluminated and unappreciated were people incapable of approaching them from a religious standpoint,[7] and these are reasons for teaching religion in the way described above. In addition for many people a religious life-style is part of the good life, and this is another argument for bringing about an awareness of religious issues.

This attitude embodies proposals about the epistemic status and uniqueness of religious claims, about why a religious perspective is important and, hence, why religion should be taught. It also involves recommendations about the nature or manner of the teaching appropriate in this area, recommendations that are in keeping with Mill's advice. Several features of these proposals and recommendations have been attacked in recent philosophical writings on religion and religious education, and what I want to do now is to turn to those attacks, beginning with those which are directed against the scepticism which is an essential part of the secularist attitude.

Arguments for religious knowledge

Those who would claim, against the secularist, that religious statements are objects of knowledge and not merely objects of belief, must have been encouraged by Professor Hirst's essay 'Liberal education and the nature of knowledge', where religion is classified as a form of knowledge,[8] one of the reasons for this classification being that religion 'has distinctive expressions that are testable against experience in accordance with particular criteria that are peculiar to the form.'[9] Over the years these remarks have precipitated various questions and objections[10] but then, strange as it may seem, Hirst himself appears to have been one of the least committed to there being a domain of religious knowledge. Indeed in the same year as the publication of 'Liberal education and the nature of knowledge', Hirst wrote that because of doubts about tests in religion, 'we can hardly maintain that we have a domain of religious knowledge and truth. All we can claim there is, is a domain of beliefs and the acceptance of any one set of these must be recognised as a matter of personal decision',[11] a view which was not only echoed by some of those opposed to religion being categorised as a form of knowledge, but which Hirst has continued to express in some of his later writings on this subject.[12] Yet, whatever Hirst's retractions, his original suggestion has been influential, and one of the latest writers to reveal this influence is Allen Brent. In this recent book *Philosophical Foundations for the Curriculum* Brent defends what he takes to be Hirst's view that an area such as religion is a form of knowledge against 'those who would claim ... that only science can give us knowledge and that everything else is belief and opinion. The later-Wittgenstein', Brent continues:[13]

> would argue that Hirst's opponents in this matter are committing the essentialist fallacy.... The later-Wittgenstein insists that what gives the various claims to truth the ability to be verified, and thereby described as 'knowledge', is not some exhaustive definition or paradigm ... it is that ... they possess with each other a 'family resemblance'. Hirst's forms do possess this family resemblance in their comparable but distinguishable networks of categorical and substantive concepts, with truth procedures related to the former, their testability against experience that is not necessarily empirical experience, etc.

One's first response to this argument might be that the opponents whom Brent is challenging have such a restricted epistemology that a rejection of their case does little to strengthen his own. Secondly, one can observe that what Hirst presents is, implicitly, an essentialist account of knowledge and, explicitly, an essentialist account of what is to rate as a form of knowledge; what permeates this thinking is a craving for generality which Brent, following the later-Wittgenstein, apparently opposes. Thirdly, Brent's argument meets none of the objections raised by Hirst and others about the proposals advanced in 'Liberal education and the nature of knowledge'. Operating with Brent's paradigm we might ask: how are we to verify religious knowledge claims? How are we to test them against experience? How are we to cope with logical problems, such as the problem of evil, which would have us reject some of the networks in some religions? In brief, the kernel of Brent's case is a restatement of a much questioned position; it is by no means a response to believers and non-believers who would maintain that religion is not a domain of knowledge.

Still, although we may defend secularism against this argument from Brent, we must not conclude from the foregoing that Hirst is sympathetic to the secularist stance. The fact is that while in several of his writings he has opposed the cognitivist position expressed in 'Liberal education and the nature of knowledge', and reasoned in favour of the secularist proposal that religion is a unique domain of beliefs, and not of knowledge,[14] in some of his latest essays we find Hirst arguing that such a proposal is incoherent.[15] The success of such an argument would clearly deal an important blow against secularism, which is why it is deserving of attention. In this most recent presentation of this argument in his essay 'The forms of knowledge revisited', Hirst begins by suggesting that attempts to reduce religious propositions to those of other areas such as morals, history and aesthetics, will be unsuccessful. However, if religious propositions are irreducible then, he suggests, it would be incoherent to claim that they can only be objects of belief. 'The reason for this', he writes,[16]

> is just that the meaning of religious propositions, as any others, rests on a grasp of the truth criteria for such propositions. If these propositions belong to a logically unique form, then their truth criteria must be unique. Religious propositions are then only intelligible to those who know these unique truth criteria. But can such unique truth conditions be known without our actually being able to judge any propositions of this kind true or false? ... If meaning is tied to knowing a unique set of truth criteria, is not meaning tied to our actually satisfying these in judging some propositions true or false? ... The claim to an irreducible, unique form of propositional meaning, thus seems to necessitate that at last (*sic*) some proposition of this kind be known to be true ... and the claim that religion involves a unique form of belief only, is incoherent.

According to Martin Simons[17] this argument is a variation of St Anselm's ontological argument. Following this suggestion we might interpret Hirst as simply attempting to argue from the premise that we, like the fool, find religious propositions meaningful, to the conclusion that we have religious knowledge. Such a simple interpretation however, might be questioned on the grounds, first, that at least in the past Hirst had held out little hope for ontological auguments[18] and, secondly, of which more later, this interpretation pays no attention to Hirst's concern for the irreducibility of religious propositions. Still, were we to pursue this simple interpretation, we would see Hirst arguing that understanding religious propositions requires knowledge of their truth criteria, which entails knowledge of some of the propositions in question. Now whatever the merits or otherwise of Hirst's theory of meaning, the last stage of this argument is invalid. By knowledge of truth criteria Hirst means knowledge of the kind of tests one would need to employ to establish the truth of a proposition,[19] and obviously we can know the truth criteria for a set of propositions without knowing any of those propositions. For example, A J Ayer knew the truth criteria of 'There are mountains on the other side of the moon' at the time of writing *Language, Truth and Logic*, but he did not know that there were such mountains at that time. Of course, were Hirst to accept the mistaken thesis that knowledge of truth criteria entails knowledge of the propositions for which we have the criteria, he would not be the only contemporary educational philosopher to do so. James Gribble, for instance, maintains: 'There is no valid distinction between "knowing facts" and 'knowing how to make judgments about what is the case"',[20] a claim which is false since it overlooks the distinction between the possession of an ability and its employment. Looked at from this position we can observe that to know the truth criteria for a set of propositions is to have certain abilities, but this in no way entails that one has actually employed those abilities under the appropriate circumstances and so come to know: as I M Crombie remarks: 'For the Christian the operation of getting into a position to decide (upon the truth of religious propositions) is called dying.'[21]

To accept a simple ontological interpretation of Hirst's argument is, then, to attribute to Hirst a mistaken thesis of the kind just considered. Such an attribution may seem unfair, not just because we may have difficulty in reconciling such a thesis with views that Hirst has advanced elsewhere[22] but, more importantly, because our interpretation pays no attention to Hirst's concern for irreducibility, even though the claim for irreducibility occupies a central position in his reasoning. In an attempt to rectify this omission we may advance the following interpretation of Hirst's argument: understanding religious propositions or, indeed, understanding any set of irreducible propositions, involves knowing truth criteria which, in view of the irreducibility of the propositions in question, will be unique, and this entails knowledge of some of the propositions in question.

Here again one can suggest that the conclusion does not follow. If, as we have just seen, knowledge of truth criteria does not entail knowledge of some of the propositions concerned, then surely the same holds even when we are concerned with unique truth criteria. The fact that a set of truth criteria happens to be distinctive or peculiar is clearly no guarantee that they have given rise to unique propositional knowledge, so why should someone claim otherwise? Such a claim, I suspect, might be founded on the view that while, in general, knowledge of the truth criteria for some set of propositions does not entail knowledge of any of those propositions, where we are concerned with a unique domain, some of the criteria must have been employed in practice or else everything would be chaos within that domain for nothing could count as the correct application of a term − and, it will be pointed out, we do not find chaos within the domain of religion. In reply we might say that were all religions to be lumped together there could be considerable chaos, although rather than pursue that line of inquiry what we can do here is to utilise a response that Hirst himself once made in dealing with an objection raised by D Z Phillips[23] which was very similar to the objection just presented. Hirst observed that since 'people do use religious terms according to well established rules, religious discourse ... is not a chaos',[24] but the fact that people abide by such rules and conventions does not imply that they have established a truth of what they are saying.[25] Thus within Christianity, or at least within certain forms of Christianity, rules exist which determine what it is permissible to say about hell, heaven and purgatory. However, this is not to say that the existence of these states has been established. Consequently, the absence of chaos within the religious domain, if there is such an absence, can be explicated by indicating the existence of rules and conventions, rather than assuming that the truth criteria in that domain have been employed and truths established.

In the light of the preceding enquiries, therefore, it seems that even under our new interpretation Hirst's attempt to show that the secularist stance is incoherent is unsuccessful. Yet it might be possible to do more than indicate that Hirst's conclusion does not follow. As we have seen, Hirst seeks to argue that understanding a unique set of propositions involves knowing a unique set of truth criteria because the meaning of a proposition is tied to its particular truth criterion. In addition Hirst wants to argue that knowledge of a unique set of criteria entails knowledge of some of the propositions for which we have the criteria. Now I take it that we can argue that each proposition is unique. Suppose, for instance, we assumed that one proposition was reducible to another. If this were the case, then the statement which would express the first would express the second. In which case, it seems, we are not concerned with two propositions but only with one − but, then, if all propositions are unique, and we are to follow Hirst's reasoning, the truth criteria for each proposition form a unique set. Moreover, since we have to know these unique truth criteria in order to understand each proposition, it would seem that by Hirst's reasoning we must know a unique set of truth criteria for each proposition we understand. Furthermore, since knowledge of a unique set of truth criteria does, as far as Hirst is concerned, entail knowledge of some of the propositions for which they are the criteria, it would appear that he would have us accept that we know every proposition we understand. This, needless to say, is unacceptable, although it would seem to follow from Hirst's premises. So I suggest we sum up our enquiry into Hirst's argument by saying that not only does he fail to establish his conclusion, his argument might also be rejected because of its untenable consequence.

Arguments from understanding

Secularism, as we have seen, is concerned with more than views about the epistemic status of religious propositions. It also includes recommendations about how religious material should be handled, prescribing elucidation rather than advocacy, teaching about rather than teaching to be religious. Now this is another aspect of secularism which can and has come under attack, particularly by those who subscribe to what we might call the argument from religious understanding. According to this argument the distinction between teaching about and teaching to be cannot be drawn, because if pupils or anyone are to hold beliefs about religion or have some religious understanding, they must believe in, they must have a religious commitment.[26]

One may suspect that when pressed this particular piece of reasoning will turn out to involve a variation of what Flew has called 'the no-true-Scotsman move'.[27] Suppose, for instance, a subscriber to the view that religious understanding involves religious commitment were to be faced with the example of the person who once believed but who no longer believes. The subscriber might say that such a person no longer *really* understands if he ever *really* understood in the first place. Such a remark would reveal the employment of what, following Flew, we might call an 'arbitrarily made-to-measure necessary truth',[28] whereby religious commitment is being *made* a logically necessary condition of so-called *real* religious understanding. The appropriate response to such a move is to say that one is not concerned with idiosyncratic definitions of '*real* understanding', but that one is concerned with understanding.[29]

It would, however, be unfair to accuse all subscribers to the argument from understanding of being guilty of such trivial arbitrariness. The fact is that a case, which might be thought to owe a great deal to the later-Wittgenstein, can be advanced in support of this argument, and such a case has recently been presented by R Marples in his essay 'Is religious education possible?'[30] In some respects Marples' proposals about religion are reminiscent of Beardsmore's about morality. In his book *Moral Reasoning* Beardsmore advanced the thesis that to be part of a form of life is to recognise the moral import of certain statements.[31] For Marples to belong to a certain form of life, or to participate in certain language games, is to recognise some statements as expressing conceptual truths.[32] Of course, Marples does not want to maintain that we must believe or recognise as a conceptual truth everything we understand; his thesis is that relative to certain language games, such as the religious language game, understanding certain fundamental propositions and recognising them to be true 'are one and the same thing',[33] for these will be conceptual truths.

One problem with this thesis is that it may lead one to conclude that either the atheist does not understand, hence does not believe what he purports to believe or, in so far as he has beliefs about religion, which is the more acceptable of the possibilities, the concepts he has differ from those employed by the theist, in which case, surprisingly, there is no disagreement between the atheist and the theist. To his credit Beardsmore recognised that tying meaning to forms of life could render disagreement impossible, and he tried to avoid such an unacceptable conclusion,[34] although whether he was successful is a matter of some dispute.[35] Unfortunately, as far as I can tell, Marples does not seem to be aware of such a consequence.[36] Yet if religious meanings are rooted in forms of life in such a way that fundamental religious propositions are analytic within a certain form of life, then, if atheists understand what they believe on religious matters, they must be employing different religious concepts from those employed by members of the religious form of life. Moreover, presumably the atheistic form of life will also have its conceptual truths. What then about the agnostics? Is their scepticism necessarily true relative to their language game? And what about those theists who fail to recognise that the bases of their faith are trivialities? Should they do some conceptual analysis, or do they belong to a unique religious form of life with unique concepts where, contrary to the 'normal' rules, the basic propositions are not analytic? I am not sure how Marples would answer these questions, but given that thesis under consideration, communication about religion becomes one of the wonders of the world.

The way out of such problems is not to erect a theory of meaning or understanding which can so readily lead to the unacceptable consequences of conceptual relativism; rather, it might be to see how we test for understanding and how the word 'understanding' is employed. Usually a person is said to have grasped a concept if he can identify things to which the concept applies, which is often taken as indicating concrete understanding, or if he can give us an account of the things to which the concept applies, and this is often taken as indicating formal understanding.[37] Clearly tests for concrete understanding are difficult when we are dealing with religious concepts, although we can and do test for formal understanding, and such tests can be passed by both believers and non-believers. Thus an atheist can give an account of what it would be for something properly to be called sin, or a miracle, or a divine command, etc. This, I am aware, may not be a very exciting approach to understanding, but it does have the benefits of being in accord with normal usage, of allowing for disagreement and of not making a mystery out of communication.

Here it would be claimed that my proposals are concerned with the descriptive use of religious language, and pay no attention to the performative nature of many religious utterances, although this is an important feature of religious language and, hence, of religious meaning and understanding. Such an observation would have the support of W D Hudson who maintains: 'the language in which religious belief is expressed is performative. In saying, for instance, "God is our Father", a Christian as such is not simply stating what he (*sic*) takes to be a fact; he is reposing his trust in God, acknowledging his duty to God, or whatever.'[38] Now this can be used as a base for the following argument: in order to appreciate these performative aspects of religious language, the learner must participate in worship or, to use Hudson's phrase, be 'initiated into devotion'; if the secularist is not prepared to countenance these activities, then he or she will be denying the learner access to an important feature of religious meaning; if the secularist is prepared to foster such an appreciation of religious meaning, he or she will have to accept the need for initiation into devotion, and this will conflict with the espousal of non-advocacy.

In response I would suggest that the conflict envisaged in this objection would constitute a genuine problem if it were the case that the only way to appreciate the performative nature of certain religious utterances was through devotional activities – but I reject the antecedent. Participation is not the only route to the appreciation of illocutionary acts and forces. Bachelors and spinsters can understand what the bride and groom are doing in a marriage ceremony, the calm and shy can recognise the speech acts of the politician without ever having stood on the hustings, and you do not have to be a fast bowler to know that an appeal can be much more than a question. What is more, reposing trust, acknowledging one's duty, and so on, are not unique to religious devotion; these could be appreciated by analogy. In brief, this addition to the argument from understanding is at least as weak as its predecessor.

A reductio of the secularist stance

Even if the secularist position about the teaching of religion can withstand the argument from understanding, such a position may still face a powerful attack which can be seen as an attempted *reductio ad absurdum* of the secularist's insistence on openness and elucidation rather then advocacy and evangelism. Variations of this argument are to be found in several sources. Raymond Holley, for example, presents a species of this argument in his criticism of Dearden's suggestion about omitting religion from the primary school curriculum. 'Why', asks Holley, 'single out religion for omission from the primary school curriculum on these grounds, that is on grounds of *truth*?'[39] In other words, if we should exclude religious education on the ground that we cannot establish what is true in religion, should we not also exclude areas such as aesthetics and ethics? Another species of this argument can be advanced in terms of indoctrination. The following extract is an instance of this type of variation and it is taken from Raymond Holley's recent book *Religious Education and Religious Understanding*.[40]

> What tends to be forgotten is ... that a good many moral, aesthetic and historical judgments ... present similar logical difficulties. To isolate religious education, and to label it alone as indoctrinatory on the grounds that spiritual insights are logically complex and difficult to verify, is to exhibit a fanatical form of ideological selectivity unworthy of anyone who preaches objective rationality.

Of course, the secularist is not proposing to banish religious education, although he is advocating that one avoids teaching religion in a certain way, and this is sufficient to generate an argument of the kind just considered. For instance, it might be asked: if problems relating to establishing the truth of religious claims constitute grounds for an open, non-evangelical non-committed approach to religion, should not this approach be adopted in areas such as aesthetics and ethics for precisely similar reasons? This, it could be said, is an unacceptable conclusion which makes nonsense of the secularist's position. Alternatively, if this unpalatable consequence is rejected, does this not mean that the secularist is being fanatical and is guilty of a kind of irrationalism?

Faced with such questioning the secularist could say that the epistemological problems encountered in religion do not arise in ethics or aesthetics, or could argue that there are reasons for treating religion as a special case. Now there may be ethical naturalists, intuitionists and even emotivists who would insist that ethics, unlike religion, generates no outstanding epistemological difficulty. However, rather than pursue that defence, I will consider the second, namely that religion is a special case. Here one can argue initially that a significant difference between aesthetics and religion is that aesthetics is lacking in practical import; which is to say that as a general rule a person's aesthetic beliefs do not determine much of his life. In this light aesthetic education may not seem all that important. This is not to deny that there might be instances where aesthetic education, although some might prefer to call it aesthetic training, would be extremely influential, as in Plato's *Republic*, but in such cases aesthetics is closely bound up with ethics and moral education, and I will discuss these in a moment. So, in brief, the first part of this defence is that an individual's aesthetic beliefs do not determine his life in the way that a theist's religious beliefs determine his. In this respect it can be claimed that we should be much more careful about how we teach religion than how we teach aesthetics.[41]

What then of moral education? Here one can begin by suggesting that in dealing with children some form of moral education, whether caught or taught, will be unavoidable,[42] but one can deal with children without teaching them religious beliefs. There again, suppose one were to argue against moral education, or teaching in morals, on the basis of difficulties of establishing moral truths. Such an argument could stem from the meta-ethical base that, to use Atkinson's familiar terms,[43] in morals one cannot establish what is true, cogent or correct, and the conclusion would be that people should refrain from moral education. With such reasoning one is treading on extremely paradoxical territory; in so far as the conclusion is advanced as true, cogent and correct it contradicts its meta-ethical base, while the meta-ethical base itself denies that the conclusion can be treated seriously. Yet to deny that we can establish what is true, cogent or correct in religion and to con-clude that we should refrain from advocacy and evangelism in this area is to encounter nothing resembling a paradox. Consequently, we may summarise the second part of this defence as follows: some form of moral education seems unavoidable in education, although this is not true of religious education; furthermore, although it may be paradoxical to argue against moral education on the basis of problems about establishing what is true, no such paradox arises when we consider similar objections to the teaching of religious beliefs.

On the strength of these considerations it appears that the secu-larist can say that while it may look as though he or she should be equally concerned with aesthetics and ethics, there are significant reasons for treating religion as a special case, and doing so need not exhibit a fanatical form of selectivity, or be unworthy of someone committed to rationality. Instead it can be based on due concern for the influence of religious beliefs, and a recognition of the fact that the inculcation of such beliefs is avoidable. Admittedly such concern, such recognition, and the unwillingness to inculcate in the face of such diversity and disagreement may involve a price. W D Hudson, for example, would say that secularism is not concerned with religious education, since such a title should be preserved for education *in* religious belief, rather than *about* such beliefs[44] and that the process deserving this title should include initiation into religious devotion and worship.[45] Obviously the secularist is not going to advocate initiation into activities which presuppose the truth of claims about which there is such disagreement.[46] Still, if the cost of taking this stance is the loss of a title, that will be no great price to pay.

An argument from the need for criteria of evaluation

The final argument I want to explore can be seen as an attempt to show that the educational proposals of secularism will be either inadequate or inconsistent.

It might be claimed that if we are to present religious information and theories to pupils, then we should endeavour to equip pupils to evaluate and assess this material. Such a claim would have the support of David G Kibble, who has recently argued 'that a quest for truth within religious studies is both a desirable and a necessary aim'.[47] Kibble quotes with approval a School's Council working paper which warns: 'It is not sufficient to parade the alternatives before the eyes of the imagination and leave it at that, as if there were no objective ways of judging the relative truth or adequacy.'[48] Unfortunately, as far as Kibble is concerned, this warning has not been heeded, with the result that 'students ... are given permission to collect pieces from a plethora of religions and to construct their own individual eclectic religion, with the assumption that the student himself (*sic*) is the sole judge of truth'.[49]

Now if secularism does nothing to equip the learner for assessment and evaluation, it might be said to be unconcerned with preparing the learner to make an informed choice for him or her self. Hence, its educational proposals could be said to be inadequate. Additionally it might be seen as involving the unacceptable view that in this area the student is the sole arbiter of truth. I say unacceptable because even in domains where evidence can gain least purchase, others might still detect inconsistencies in an individual's thought, and show that the individual is wrong. However, if the secularist were to try to avoid these criticisms and to satisfy the recommendations of someone like Kibble, would the secularist not come into conflict with his commitment to elucidation and the avoidance of advocacy? By way of tackling this question let us consider Kibble's criteria for assessing the correctness of different religious theories or systems.

Following F Ferré, Kibble presents internal and external criteria.[50] The internal criteria cover consistency and coherence. Consistency is the requirement that 'the facts contained in it (that is, a system) must "fit in" with one another, rather as an individual piece fits in a jig-saw'[51] (*sic*), while coherence is the requirement that 'the facts must form a particular pattern ... like a pattern or picture in a jigsaw'.[52] Here one may feel that Kibble is being somewhat incautious in his use of 'facts', and wonder what precisely the demand for coherence involves. Presumably the proposal that the so-called facts form a particular pattern is not the demand that they conform to a particular creed, but that the various claims should form a kind of complete thesis, and explain the things that the system purports to explain and account for the occurrence of what are significant events according to the system. Kibble's external criteria are that the system 'must be applicable to experience; it must fit in with the student's experience, it must "ring true"'.[53]

Clearly religious systems are applicable to experience in the sense that they provide frameworks in terms of which events are interpreted and feelings and emotions are seen as significant. Equally, of course, for some people events and experiences do not fit in with a particular system. Watching a loved one suffer from a terminal illness may be an experience that conflicts with some people's view of a theory which presents God as an all-loving, all-powerful father. Similarly a person's experience or realisation of the grandeur and wealth of Rome may conflict with this view of a system whose secular norms are concerned with humility and charity.

As these criteria stand I do not believe that concern for them need in any way compromise the secularist's position. The secularist could emphasise the need for consistency and coherence in evaluating systems, and direct attention to the fact that these are systems within which people 'see' and appreciate the world, its existence and its events. In accordance with such direction the secularist could encourage the learner to look for fittingness and conflicts. Such encouragement is not evangelism; it is not concerned with the advocacy of one creed in particular, or of religious systems in general. Indeed, if the secularist follows Kibble's advice he or she will realise that the kind of enquiry being encouraged 'will ... involve an element of personal judgment, even of "intuition"; as a result (he or she) will not expect to find ... students all believing the same'.[54] But then, one would expect the secularist to emphasise the personal, possibly intuitive, and non-demonstrable nature of the beliefs that one finds in this area; in pointing this out, the secularist would be merely articulating what is a feature of secularism.

Incidentally, you may be wondering why an emphasis on consistency, coherence and personal judgment should be thought of as furnishing an antidote to the religious eclecticism that so worries Kibble. Apart from the obvious issue that such an emphasis may reduce the number of inconsistent and incoherent religious stances, I can see no reason for thinking that such an approach will yield an ecumenical base.

An argument for the need for criteria of evaluation does not, then, provide opposition for secularism. In fact such an argument would have the support of the secularist, for while possibly regarding religion as unknown territory, he or she does not regard it as forbidden, or as being an area where everything is equally sound. Where a secularist would have to withdraw this support for this type of argument would be when the criteria for assessment become more restrictive than those presented by Kibble as, for instance, if they took on a particular religious or denominational bias. However, providing they remain at the level of generality considered above, concern for them is in no way inconsistent with secularism.

Conclusion

It is time to draw some threads together. I began by outlining a particular attitude towards religions and what I called religious education, an attitude which might be seen as underpinning many of the new developments and recommendations in the teaching of religion. I called that attitude secularism, and in the arguments that have followed I have endeavoured to defend such an attitude against various recent claims and attacks. I have attempted to defend secularism from those who would maintain that we have religious knowledge and from those who would claim that uniqueness plus understanding entail knowledge. Subsequently I tried to oppose not only those who would argue that religious understanding involves religious commitment or requires religious worship, but also those who would maintain that the secularist attitude involves an irrational bias. Finally I have attempted to show that the importance of the place of criteria of evaluation in the teaching of religion neither reveals an inadequacy nor leads to an inconsistency in secularism.

Such defences, needless to say, do not demonstrate the tenability of secularism, and indeed numerous problems, particularly, I suspect, of a practical nature, remain to be explored and tackled — but the defences I have presented do, I hope, indicate that secularism is a much sturdier creature than some would have us believe. There are, of course, more opponents of secularism available at present and, no doubt, even more on the way. All I have been able to do in this article is to explore and, I trust, rebuff certain and prominent features of the opposition. Given new opponents, new defences will be called for. Looked at from this point of view one might say that the price of secularism is vigilance. I nearly said 'eternal vigilance' but that, I suspect, would be a paradoxical price to pay.

Notes

1. J S Mill, 'Inaugural address,' in J B Schneewind (ed.), *Mill's Essays on Literature and Society,* New York, Collier-Macmillan, 1965, p. 399.
2. N Smart, and D Horder, 'Editors' preface,' in N Smart and D Horder (eds), *New Movements in Religious Education,* London, Temple Smith, 1975, p. i.
3. See for example, J M Hull, 'Agreed syllabuses, past, present and future,' in N Smart and D Horder (eds), *New Movements in Religious Education,* London, Temple Smith, 1975, pp. 114-117.
4. E R Norman, 'The threat to religion,' in C B Cox and R Boyson (eds), *Black Paper 1977,* London, Temple Smith, 1977, p. 103.
5. I feel I should point out that I have not chosen this term because of some commitment on my part to any established body of beliefs that might be known as secularist. In fact nothing hangs on my use of 'secularist' or 'secularism', since I use these terms merely as labels for a certain attitude and theory which I have attempted to explain quite fully.
6. As far as I am aware D Z Phillips was the first to express the distinction between instructing about and instructing in terms of 'elucidation' and 'advocacy'. See D Z Phillips, 'Philosophy and religious education,' *British Journal of Educational Studies,* 18, 1970, pp. 13-14.
7. For what appear to be similar arguments see P H Hirst, 'Morals, religion and the maintained school,' *British Journal of Educational Studies,* 14, 1965, p.

13 and T Devlin and M Warnock, *What Must We Teach?*, London, Temple Smith, 1977, pp. 88–91.

8. P H Hirst, 'Liberal education and the nature of knowledge,' in R D Archambault, (ed.), *Philosophical Analysis and Education,* London, Routledge and Kegan Paul, 1965, p. 131.

9. P H Hirst, *op. cit,* p. 129.

10. See, for example, J Gribble, 'Forms of knowledge,' *Educational Philosophy and Theory,* 2, 1970; D C Phillips, 'The distinguishing features of forms of knowledge,' *Educational Philosophy and Theory,* 3, 1971, pp. 27–36; A J Watt, 'Forms of knowledge and norms of rationality,' *Educational Philosophy and Theory,* 6, 1974, pp. 1–11; R G Woods and R St C Barrow, *An Introduction to the Philosophy of Education,* chapter 2, London, Methuen, 1975.

11. P H Hirst, 'Morals, religion and the maintained school,' *op. cit.,* p. 12.

12. See, for example, P H Hirst, 'Religion: a form of knowledge? A reply,' *Learning for Living,* 12, 1973, pp. 9–10; P H Hirst, *Moral Education in a Secular Society,* London, Hodder and Stoughton, 1974, pp. 80-81; P H Hirst, *Knowledge and the Curriculum,* London, Routledge and Kegan Paul, 1974, pp. 187-188.

13. A Brent, *Philosophical Foundations for the Curriculum,* London, Allen and Unwin, 1978, pp. 156–157.

14. See, for example, P H Hirst, 'Philosophy and religious education: a reply to D Z Phillips,' *British Journal of Educational Studies,* 18, 1970, pp. 213-215; P H Hirst, 'Morals, religion and the maintained school,' *op. cit.;* P H Hirst, 'Religion: a form of knowledge? A reply,' *op. cit.*

15. See, P H Hirst, 'Forms of knowledge: a reply to Elizabeth Hindness,' *Proceedings of the Philosophy of Education Society of Great Britain,* 7, 1973, pp. 265–266; P H Hirst, 'The forms of knowledge re-visited,' in *Knowledge and the Curriculum, op. cit.,* pp. 88-89.

16. P H Hirst, 'The forms of knowledge re-visited,' *op. cit.,* pp. 88–89.

17. M Simons, 'The forms of knowledge again,' *Educational Philosophy and Theory,* 7, 1975, p. 43.

18. See P H Hirst, 'Morals, religion and the maintained school,' *op. cit.,* p. 15.

19. See, for example, P H Hirst, 'Forms of knowledge: a reply to Elizabeth Hindness,' *op. cit.,* p. 264; P H Hirst, 'The forms of knowledge re-visited,' *op. cit.,* p. 88.

20. J Gribble, *Introduction to Philosophy of Education,* Boston, Allyn and Bacon, 1969, p. 69. It may be of interest to observe that Gribble presents this reductionist account of propositional knowledge after arguing that 'knowing that' cannot be reduced to 'knowing how'!

21. I M Crombie, 'Theology and falsification,' in A G N Flew and A MacIntyre (eds), *New Essays in Philosophical Theology,* London, SCM Press, 1955, p. 126.

22. See, for example, P H Hirst, 'Morals, religion and the maintained school,' *op. cit.;* and P H Hirst, *Knowledge and the Curriculum, op. cit.,* p. 187, where Hirst says 'pupils can only understand any religious position if they begin to grasp its concepts. . . . But such understanding does not imply belief in or acceptance of, what is understood.' It is clear from this that Hirst is not accepting that understanding religious propositions entails knowledge of some of those propositions.

23. See D Z Phillips, 'Philosophy and religious education,' *op. cit.,* pp. 7-10.

24. P H Hirst, 'Philosophy and religious education: a reply to D Z Phillips,' *op. cit.,* p. 214.

25. Cf. *Ibid.*

26. Cf. R Holley, 'Raymond Holley examines Dearden's arguments on religious education,' *Learning for Living,* 9, 1970, p. 20.

27. A G N Flew, *Thinking About Thinking,* London, Fontana, 1975, chapter 3.

28. A G N Flew, *op. cit.,* p. 49.

29. Here it may prove illuminating to recall that C L Stevenson in his examination of persuasive definitions directed our attention to Aldous Huxley's *Eyeless in Gaza* where true temperance is described as a bottle of claret with each meal and three double whiskies after dinner. See C L Stevenson, 'Persuasive definitions,' *Mind,* 47, 1938, p. 335.

30. R Marples, 'Is religious education possible?' *Journal of Philosophy of Education,* 12, 1978, pp. 81–91.

31. See R W Beardsmore, *Moral Reasoning,* London, Routledge and Kegan Paul, 1969, chapter 8.
32. See R Marples, *op. cit.,* p. 87.
33. *Ibid.*
34. See R W Beardsmore, *op. cit.,* p. 94.
35. See R Trigg, *Reason and Commitment,* London, Cambridge University Press, 1973, p. 66f.
36. I say 'as far as I can tell' here because although Marples argues that religious understanding involves religious beliefs (see, for instance, *op. cit.,* pp. 86-87), he also seeks to distinguish between what he calls 'partial understanding of religious concepts' and 'full understanding' (*op. cit.,* p. 90), and appears willing to accept that full, but not partial, understanding requires religious belief, since full understanding involves the recognition of the relevant 'conceptual truths'. Thus, it may seem unfair to accuse Marples of suggesting that the atheist does not understand what he purports to believe, or that the atheist and the theist do not disagree, because Marple's view might be that the atheist has only a partial understanding of religious concepts. This will no doubt be offensive to atheists, who will claim that there is nothing partial about their understanding. Yet, if full understanding requires certain relevant beliefs, then either the atheist does not fully understand what he purports to believe, since if he fully understood, he would recognise his beliefs necessarily to be false, *or* he does fully understand, but employs different concepts to, and hence does not disagree with, the theist. In which case it may seem that Marples is not fully aware of the consequences of his position. I should add, lest I leave the wrong impression, that Marples is not in favour of developing full understanding because it would involve the inculcation of religious beliefs.
37. Cf. J P White, *Towards a Compulsory Curriculum,* London, Routledge and Kegan Paul, 1973, pp. 26–27.
38. W D Hudson, 'Is religious education possible?' in G Langford and D J O'Connor (eds), *New Essays in the Philosophy of Education,* London, Routledge and Kegan Paul, 1973, p. 183.
39. R Holley, *op. cit.,* p. 18.
40. R Holley, *Religious Education and Religious Understanding,* London, Routledge and Kegan Paul, 1978, p. 164.
41. Another argument that could be presented here is that, at least when compared with aesthetics, there is a reason for treating religion differently, and this reason is that while no one doubts the existence of beauty, some people do have doubts about the existence of a God, or about the existence of a divine purpose, etc. When I presented a version of this paper at the University of Birmingham this argument was advanced by Professor Dearden, and it is one which seems worthy of attention in this context. The fact of the matter is that, except in the sceptical atmosphere of philosophy seminars, we do not doubt whether beautiful things exist. We may disagree about whether something is beautiful, but we do not disagree about whether there are things of beauty. The same cannot be said about the fundamental ontological assertions of religion. Obviously this difference is worth bearing in mind, particularly with regard to arguments that are based on supposed similarities between religious and aesthetic education.
42. In this connection I am at least *partly* in agreement with the Newsom Report when it says: 'Teachers can only escape from their influence over the moral and spiritual development of their pupils by closing their schools' (Central Advisory Council for Education, *Half Our Future,* London, Her Majesty's Stationery Office, 1963, p. 53). Where I might disagree is over the word 'spiritual', my point being that we can deal with children without being instrumental in their coming to believe or disbelieve in a religion or religions.
43. See R F Atkinson, 'Instruction and indoctrination,' in R D Archambault (ed.), *Philosophical Analysis and Education,* London, Routledge and Kegan Paul, 1965, p. 176.
44. See W D Hudson, *op. cit.,* pp. 188–189.
45. See W D Hudson, *op. cit.,* p. 183.
46. Cf. P H Hirst, *Knowledge and the Curriculum, op. cit.,* p. 188.
47. D G Kibble, 'Religious studies and the quest for truth,' *British Journal of Educational Studies,* 24, 1976, p. 153.

48. School's Council Working Paper 36, *Religious Education in Secondary Schools,* London, Evans/Methuen Educational, 1971, p. 26, quoted by Kibble, *op. cit.,* p. 153.
49. D G Kibble, *op. cit.,* p. 153.
50. Kibble refers to F Ferre, *Language, Logic and God,* London, Fontana, 1970. See D G Kibble, *op. cit.,* pp. 152, 154.
51. D G Kibble, *op. cit.,* p. 152.
52. *Ibid.*
53. *Ibid.*
54. *Ibid.*

3.2 Will and should the religious studies appropriate to schools in a pluralistic society foster religious relativism?
Brian V Hill

'There is only one religion', said George Bernard Shaw, 'though there are a hundred versions of it.'[1] He was referring to the crusading fervour which he found that he, as a Socialist, had in common with earnest clergy of many stripes, even though their gospels were so different from his. The turn of the century must have been a heady period. Shaw testifies that he found religion to be 'alive again, coming back upon men, even upon clergymen, with such power that not the Church of England itself could keep it out'.

He was, no doubt, referring to a similarity in *emotional fervour* between himself and the clergy rather than any beliefs held in common, but for precisely this reason his comment epitomises a viewpoint widespread among academics. This is the view that the seat of religion resides in the emotions. Religions develop powerful mental pictures which help their adherents to stay sane in a crazy world. It is unfortunate that these pictures are usually represented as truth-claims. If only the leaders of faith communities would concede that their common property was sincerity and basic goodwill, and minimise differences of belief, then we could all work together to reduce prejudice and ignorance, enabling pluralistic societies to function more smoothly.

This is a form of relativism. It may be termed 'religious emotivism'. As we shall see later, there is an inherent logical flaw in it. There is, however, another relativistic viewpoint which gives more status to belief-claims, and which I shall call 'religious universalism'. This stance regards all religions as providing partial glimpses of the truth, so that the task ahead is to find and foster their areas of agreement, again minimising the differences.

Interestingly, those who have contributed most to the development of multi-faith policies for religious studies in schools have, on the whole, also tended to be religious emotivists or universalists. This has had a polarising effect on the debate. Other people, of the kind who believe that religious truth-claims have to be taken seriously and literally, are then driven to defend the traditional view that in school religious studies we should promote our own faith alone. They are deterred from bringing that view itself under scrutiny by the suspicion that the only alternative is some form of relativism.

If relativism is the inevitable result of trying to accommodate the sensibilities of people of different traditions in a pluralistic society, they say, then we shall hang on to whatever cultural advantage our faith has gained and promote it in as many schools as we can, on a mono-faith model. This understandable backlash effect was clearly apparent in the debate preceding the 1988 Education Reform Act which gave rise to the current provisions in it for religious education.[2]

The result, in terms of educational theory, is a stalemate, with minimum dialogue between the two approaches. This is not a healthy state to be in, especially in societies where, for good or ill, people of diverse convictions must find some way of living together without bloodshed.

In this article I will begin by explaining the meaning I attach to the term *religious relativism*. Then I will examine the *epistemologies* that underlie some common approaches to religious studies, asking whether multi-faith approaches are logically bound to presuppose a relativistic attitude to religion. Thirdly, I will examine possible *teaching strategies* for multi-faith studies, asking whether multi-faith approaches are bound in practice to foster a relativistic attitude to religion. I will argue that neither is inevitable, and that guidelines can be formulated for an approach to multi-faith studies which does not pre-emptively imply religious relativism – or religious absolutism, for that matter. My last step will be to ask whether this approach, developed with the state school in mind, may not also serve in *the religiously sponsored school*.

Religious relativism

First, then, let us tease out the term 'relativism' a little more. The general notion denies the possibility of absolute truth. The term arises in several kinds of discourse. *Epistemologically*, for instance, we are reminded that humans are fallible creatures, incapable of knowing everything, therefore whatever we claim to know is open to challenge. There can be nothing which is known to be absolutely true. This is epistemological relativism.

On the *conceptual level*, we are reminded that humans themselves are the creators of the language and concepts they use, and there is ample anthropological evidence that people in different cultures and language groups describe the world differently from each other. In such situations, 'truth' is relative to the discourse being employed. This is conceptual relativism.

In regard to *religious* discourse, the notion of relativism is given a further twist. Religious relativists regard revelation as either speculative opinion, often triggered by private mystical experience and therefore subjective, or as illustrative myth which intelligent

believers know they are not supposed to take literally. The appropriate reaction, then, when one encounters religions which purport
to make truth-claims, is to turn the epistemological question into
a psychological one. One does not ask 'Does this correspond to
reality?' but 'Does acceptance of this claim help the individual to
cope with life?' This is the move recommended by William James,
when he urges us to treat a belief as true 'if it works for you'.

Epistemological relativism

Let us look more carefully at these three kinds of relativism. Epistemological relativists claim that it is impossible to know anything
for certain. This claim is incoherent, for it purports to know at
least one thing for certain — its own absolute claim. This is a
logical absurdity of the same kind as saying that all generalisations
are false. But in practice, few proponents of this view accept that
the case for epistemological relativism can be vanquished by this
simple criticism alone.

John Dewey, for example, spoke for a great body of scientific
relativists or Fictionalists[3] when he said that 'the true means the
verified and means nothing else'.[4] His disciples allege that one can
pursue the scientific quest without presuming, as Realists do, that
scientific advance brings us progressively closer to describing what
is really there. Since Thomas Kuhn,[5] it has been fashionable to
emphasise that scientists inevitably work within paradigms whose
survival depends not on their truth value but on their heuristic fer-
tility in generating useful hypotheses and models.

I suspect that Fictionalism is really only a conceptual fancy which
in practice is constantly refuted by the attitudes of actual scientists
as they seek to strengthen the fit between their theories and an
external world which they know very well is not just part of their
imagination but stands over against them. The Realist echoes this
attitude by insisting that we cannot even have a concept of truth
unless we also have a prior concept of an objective reality which
can, at least to some extent, be known. Dewey's attempt to redefine
truth as 'the verified' does not negate this, since one must still ask
'verified with reference to what?'

It is probably obvious that my sympathies in this protracted
debate are with the Realist. The essential point for our *present*
purpose, however, is that the adoption of either a Fictionalist or
a Realist position is an activity at the presuppositional level. It is
not something which can be resolved by empirical test, because our
very understanding of what 'testing' means will be determined by
the presuppositions we embrace. This makes the adoption of either
position *an act of reasonable faith*. Any curriculum which does not
at some stage make this clear to students is potentially misleading
and indoctrinative.

Conceptual relativism

Conceptual relativism is more subtle. Not only does it deny the possibility of knowing the truth, but it relativises the concept of truth itself by relating it to the particular linguistic 'form of life' in which it is employed. This position draws strength both from Wittgenstein's argument that human beings develop a number of conceptual schemes by which they make sense of the world, and from Benjamin Whorf's theories about the incommensurability of the linguistic maps which people living in different cultures create for themselves. On this view, 'truth' boils down to two things: internal consistency within the particular realm of discourse, and agreement between those using it as to what shall count as true. To the person outside that form of discourse, its truth claims may simply appear meaningless or false.

If conceptual relativism were true (whatever that now means), then communication between users of different discourses would not be possible. Clearly it is. Confusions are frequently resolved, and this must be because the discussants meet in a common world, and can work towards mutual comprehension by teaching each other – often, in the beginning, ostensively – how they refer to that common world.

Whorf's celebrated example of the Eskimo's several words for 'snow', making distinctions that the English language does not make, is taken by some to demonstrate the incommensurability of different conceptual frameworks. But the very example itself is an exercise in bridging the gap because it *explains* in English the differentiations which Eskimoes make when referring to snow. Inter-communication *is* possible. And just as inhabitants of different forms of life meet in the same external reality, so they entertain some concepts in common – universal concepts – by virtue of their encounter with that reality.[6] One of these universal concepts is truth itself.

Once again, it is clear from this brief summary of an on-going philosophical debate that my own sympathies do not lie with *conceptual* relativism either. For our *present* purpose, however, it is enough to point out that it is a position which can be disputed. Therefore it should not be adopted presumptively in a teaching strategy.

Religious relativism

We come then to the case of religious relativism. For those who espouse either of the two previous kinds of relativism, of course, religious truth-claims become just another special case of the general argument. Religious beliefs are simply inter-subjective agreements. It does not necessarily follow, however, that if one is a religious relativist one will also be either an epistemological or a conceptual relativist, or both.

There are, for example, many people who embrace Realist theories of truth when it comes to the natural and social sciences, but who view religion in the way I described at the beginning, as a thing primarily of the emotions. Thus, one may be prepared to say that the concept of truth *is* applicable in discourse about the natural world, where recognised verification procedures can be employed, but that it is inapplicable to talk about God or religious experience where, it is claimed, they cannot be employed.

This argument may seem to have some plausibility in relation to those religions which depend heavily on a philosophical framework in which historical elements, such as the alleged manifestations of Vishnu in certain mortals, may be put in the category of devout myths without affecting the inner logic of the system. But it most certainly will not wash in the case of religions such as Judaism and Christianity whose belief-structures *hinge* on the interpretations given to certain historical events. Take away the Exodus miracles or the Resurrection, and the residual frameworks of Judaism and Christianity, far from being a filtration of the essence, constitute quite different religions.[7]

But the relativist argument does not even represent adequately religions with a more abstract centre. For they too are making truth-claims. A belief that the reality we experience is best described in terms of the Tao, or as an illusion self-imposed by the Atman or universal consciousness,[8] has important implications both for scientific investigation and for personal life-style. Such beliefs generate distinct life-legitimations no less significant for thought and action than the Christian story of a personal God who literally intervenes in human history.

In this respect, I have quoted before[9] the case of the sociologist Karl Mannheim. Driven from Germany by the Nazi take-over, Mannheim was initially critical of the muddle he perceived British democracy to be in. In later years, however, he came to admire it and to attribute many of its features to the influence of Christianity. In the book *Diagnosis of Our Time*, he advocated that steps be taken to nurture the 'democratic personality type', and he called on Christian leaders to take the lead in this task.[10]

Mannheim saw a problem, however, in the absolutist claims inherent in Christian belief, and so he urged his Christian friends to relinquish them in the interests of getting general agreement. A friendly critic commented at the time: 'Mannheim's point of view is that of an external observer who had never really understood the essential nature of the Christian religion.'[11]

The point applies more generally. Religious emotivism mistakes cause for effect. The emotional appeal of most religions depends heavily on the confidence which their *truth-claims* inspire. If they did purport to be saying something true and reliable about the cosmos and the ground of the individual's significance within it, then they would attract far fewer adherents. Religious emotivism is a lame-duck theoretical construct.

I said earlier that another variety of relativism in the religious sphere is universalism. Epistemologically, this stance is more robust. It appears to take seriously the fact that religions involve an appeal to rationality, which makes them something more than just emotional security blankets. Nevertheless, denying the possibility of propositional revelation, religious universalism puts all religions on the same footing, as human attempts to conceptualise a cosmos which is too mysterious to be contained in any one explanatory system. Hence our intellectual obligation is to acknowledge that there are many paths up the mountain, so we must be as eclectic as possible in our openness to this kind of truth.

Some efforts have been made in recent times to build religious communities around the universalist approach, notably in theosophy and the B'hai faith. To the extent that they have attracted adherents, especially from the educated middle classes, they have proved that they have to be taken seriously, but intellectual and scriptural[12] objections to religious universalism are numerous. We are therefore obliged to insist yet again that it would be an inadmissibly preemptive move to presuppose religious relativism in formulating approaches to the teaching of religion in schools.

But maybe we cannot help doing so. If, for epistemological or practical reasons, it is impossible to present multi-faith studies without presupposing religious relativism, then no hope remains for a unified educational theory of religious studies in schools. I must therefore meet this challenge, in the first instance at the epistemological level.

Does the multi-faith approach presuppose a particular epistemology?

We may distinguish between four normative epistemologies which could, in theory, underlie the teaching of religion. The first I will call the *literal-exclusive* stance. This epistemology agrees that we should look to religion for important truth about the nature of reality, asserts that only one religious system can ultimately be right about the essentials, believes that it has access to that one, and assumes that it therefore only makes sense to teach that one.

The second stance I will call *literal-persuasive*. This stance endorses the view that truth-claims in sentence-form *are* intrinsic to religious discourse, and that in the end only one religion can ultimately be right about the minimum core description of the world, but it recognises that many religions claim to have that answer, and it therefore concedes the need to teach about more than one religion, encouraging a personal choice on the most reasonable grounds available.

The third stance may be clumsily described as *quasi-literal-inclusive*. This stance, like the previous two, accepts the premise that it is appropriate to seek truth in religious belief-claims, but it draws back from the assumption that any one religion has the ultimate key to the minimum core, believing that all have something to contribute, and that it is safest to include the study of as many of the major religions as is feasible. Since, however, the truth thus obtained must be disentangled from any historical claims that other faiths would dispute, I say that it is only *quasi*-propositional. Such propositions as survive this test will tend to be at such a high level of generality as to prohibit many of the analytic operations we customarily apply to propositions.

The remaining stance is *mythical-persuasive*, that is, it sees the function of religion to be the dissemination of general ideas and heroic stories which reduce anxiety and foster purposeful living, while taking it for granted that there are many paths to peace. Individuals are therefore encouraged to make a personal choice on psychological grounds.

Literal-exclusive

In evaluating these four contenders, it is clear that the first — the literal-exclusive epistemology — is inherently antagonistic to the concept of multi-faith studies. It typifies the traditional classroom approach to Christianity, Islam and other major religions — and the current policy behind the Iron Curtain of propagating Marxist Leninism exclusively as an ultimate philosophy of life.

Secondly, this epistemology is at odds with accepted views of what schooling should contribute to a person's education. If one thing has emerged from the forays of recent philosophers of education into conceptual analysis, it is that nothing less will do in the pluralistic society than the development of individuals with critical rationality and the willingness to take responsibility for their choices. Something *more* than this may be needed — the rationalists of the London school, for instance, provide thin gruel for people with a positive vision of the caring, familial community — but nothing *less* will do.

Indoctrination is something less. It involves the blinkering of the student's awareness by the propagation of partisan views without the opportunity to study related evidences and objections, let alone alternative views. The case against indoctrination has been made convincingly by many recent writers. While some Christian writers and school systems are apparently willing to endorse indoctrination, provided the faith to be taught is their own,[13] the practice is inconsistent with the way Jesus dealt with learners,[14] and it seems that the general body of Christian opinion in western industrial countries is against it, even in the interests of the faith one cherishes.

There are, of course, major religions and other world views which do not share these scruples, and which indoctrinate where they can, especially in countries where they enjoy ideological monopoly. Since the task I undertook in this paper was to see what prospects exist for a coherent policy of multi-faith studies, it is clear that adoption of a literal-exclusive epistemology would rule it out. That leaves the other three possibilities, which I would like to deal with in reverse order.

Mythical-persuasive

The fourth epistemological stance, which I called mythical-persuasive, is clearly twin to the position of religious emotivism which I spelled out earlier. And equally obviously, the stance is compatible with multi-faith studies.

On this view, the quest for inner peace is to be pursued in as many quarters as possible. But the reasons are all psychological. The stance denies that there are any epistemological justifications for studying religion. And because this solution is inherently relativistic, it does not solve the problem which is the nub of this paper. Multi-faith studies could be approached in this fashion, and they sometimes are, in the context, for example, of courses in 'personal and moral development', but they are open to the criticisms expressed earlier and lack a dimension essential to the understanding of religion, namely, the study of truth-claims.

Quasi-literal-inclusive

The third stance, which I called quasi-literal-inclusive, is also clearly compatible with the notion of multi-faith studies, and there are several exemplars to choose from in current curriculum development. Most well-known amongst these are the English world-faiths approaches represented, for example, by the Birmingham syllabus[15] and the book on world faiths edited by Cole.[16] What turns an apparent respect for the propositional truth-claims of religions into a *quasi*-respect is the tendency for these approaches to rely on the so-called 'phenomenological' method which calls for the 'bracketing out' of questions of truth and falsity in the studies undertaken.[17]

It need not follow that a phenomenological approach rules out the study of truth claims *per se*, but observation suggests that in practice it cohabits with religious universalism. Many modern religious educators, for example, are attracted to the model of 'faith-development' constructed by James Fowler.[18] Fowler is uncomfortable with the notion that faith is assent to certain beliefs, preferring to emphasise the religious responsiveness of the individual. In the furthest reaches of his model, particularism in belief has been transcended, and the faith held is universalistic. Its exemplars are such people, he says, as Mahatma Gandhi, Mother

Teresa and Martin Luther King. Truth is in the living, rather than the believing.

This judgment on the quasi-literal-inclusive stance may seem rather harsh and sweeping. But if we recall the comment made earlier about the part that claims to historical revelation play in some religions, then this approach prevents the study of them in their own terms. This can be brought out by asking to what degree particular courses in religious studies encourage students to question what they are being taught; to examine the truth-claims advanced by religious and secularist faith-communities as propositions appealing to evidence; to appreciate the motivational strength of strongly held, absolutist beliefs; and to strive towards the moment when students individually take stands on the best evidence available. Such objectives are, no doubt, controversial and will need to be handled with great care in the classroom, but without them an epistemological relativism will be pre-emptively commended.

Literal-persuasive

We are left then with the second stance, which I called literal-persuasive. This stance does not devalue particular religions by playing down the fact that they make exclusive truth-claims. That fact is recognised; and recognised not as peripheral to the religious phenomenon, but as central to it. Religions purport to be life-orienting explanations of the reality in which we exist. They make specific claims about beliefs and values which are inadequately represented if studied in isolation, rather than as building blocks in a total explanatory belief structure.

It will therefore be important, if it can be done, to help students to proceed beyond a merely descriptive knowledge of the diversity of religious faiths and practices. We need to help them to grasp the centrality and embeddedness of truth-claims in religious and secularist life-stances. We also need to develop their ability to weigh up such claims critically and encourage the disposition to make an informed decision about the part, if any, which religion will play in their own lives.

The literal-persuasive stance leaves it to the religions themselves to persuade the student, though the evidences it will be appropriate to present will include not only the inherent truth-claims of the respective religions but the available historical evidence of what are the experiential and social consequences of embracing them. It would be dishonest, for example, to pretend that all religions are equally multi-racial and egalitarian in their messages, equally comprehensive and consistent in their intellectual systematisations, or equally ameliorative in their concern for temporal social justice. They are not. It is educationally necessary to encourage critical comparisons in this area, without necessarily supplying a set of official answers.[19]

If, notwithstanding our adopting this epistemological stance, the students themselves reach a relativistic conclusion about religions, that will be entirely their business. Whether we ourselves agree with them on this point, *we* will have discharged our duty not to pre-empt their commitment.

The logical conditions I have spelled out add up to a tall order; but without them it is unlikely that we will be able to avert an inherent religious relativism in our presentation of religious materials. If it can be done, then the literal-persuasive stance is the one we are looking for. But the question now becomes an empirical one – *can* it be done?

Will appropriate teaching strategies tend to promote relativism?

The question we are now addressing is: Of the teaching approaches one might adopt in presenting multi-faith studies, are there any which will not carry an implicit or even explicit bias towards religious relativism? As we mentioned at the beginning, those on the other side of the pedagogic chasm in religious education see the very act of teaching about more than one religion as inevitably relativistic in effect. Several possible approaches come to mind, and I will mention only four. These are not intended to correlate directly with the four normative epistemologies I discussed earlier.

Segregated instruction

The first is a policy of segregated instruction. This requires that the multi-faith nature of our society be recognised by leaving it to the religious groups themselves to carry out their own instruction, whilst the state school excludes religious studies from its range. Several countries endorse this policy in one way or another.

In my own country of Australia, one State allows representatives of religious groups to enter the school to take adherents of their respective groups in segregated classes, whilst debarring the general study of religion from the secular curriculum for which the regular teaching staff are responsible. Public schools in the United States generally steer clear of religious studies in any guise because of the current interpretation of the First Amendment to the Constitution. In Singapore, each school is required to nominate one of six religions and base its religious instruction on that one alone.[20]

Whatever else they are, such policies can hardly be considered educational. In the schools where religion *is* taught, there is a strong likelihood that indoctrination and intolerance will be promoted, as we saw in discussing the first epistemological stance. In the schools where it is not taught in the general curriculum, its exclusion conveys two messages. The first is that religion is not considered to have epistemic relevance. That is an implicit vote for religious emotivism. The second is that it is not considered to have sufficient social importance to warrant inclusion. In any education worthy of the name, the first message should not be allowed to escape inspection, and the second should be promptly refuted on empirical grounds.

Descriptive presentation

The second possible teaching strategy is to provide studies of religions through descriptive presentation. The emphasis here is on the pervasiveness of the religious phenomenon in human affairs. Religious traditions exist, they are taken seriously by many people, and in the interests of communal harmony we should remove mutual ignorance and encourage tolerant co-existence.

At the same time, and for the same reasons, we should not invite critical evaluation or urge any questioning of the status quo, either in the student's own personal commitment, or on a wider level. The procedure is 'phenomenological'. Alternatively, practice in what some call 'value clarification'[21] is encouraged, but only in the interests of enabling the individual to reach a satisfactory *personal* equilibrium independent of asking whether the values embraced are true.

The implicit value judgment in this case is either religious emotivism or religious universalism, depending on how much weight is given to the making of truth-claims by the different religions. Either way, religious relativism is tacitly endorsed by the method. To say this is not to deny the value of impartial descriptive presentation, and even values clarification, as a means of laying down a data-base on which the student may build the higher outcomes of comparative evaluation and commitment. But in terms of the requirements of our analysis, it is insufficient by itself.

Impartial analysis

The third possibility is impartial analysis. Here the rubric is that the teacher shall encourage students to develop the skills necessary to compare and evaluate the truth-claims and social effects of more than one religion. Consistent with this goal, the teacher shall foster a classroom climate of impartial skill development, taking the role of a neutral moderator of discussion. I analysed this teaching model some years ago,[22] and will simply summarise its implications here. It is an approach which could, in the right hands, make students aware of the nature and force of the absolutist truth claims of religious traditions, and foster their powers of analysis and evaluation.

Yet this model has one crucial flaw. The neutral posture of the teacher is likely to subvert two aspects of the lesson: the appeal to rationality and the fostering of personal commitment.

In the first case, the attempt to encourage rational discussion and evaluation founders at the point where students ask, as they frequently do, 'But what do you think?' The teacher who replies that this question is either not allowable or not relevant thereby denies the efficacy of open enquiry.

In the second case, the fostering of a well-founded personal commitment is likely to ring hollow if teachers are not authorised and encouraged to bear willing testimony to their own committedness. One conclusion students might reasonably draw from the teacher's neutrality, in the absence of explanations to the contrary, is that religious commitment is at worst a recreational option, and at best a logically arbitrary[23] personal choice. Either way, religious relativism is again pre-emptively endorsed. This is the very bogey we have been trying to dispel.

Impartial-exemplary study

What, then, if anything, will suffice as an appropriate teaching strategy? A fourth possibility is to capitalise on the most attractive features of the second and third approaches described above, whilst authorising the school and the teacher to exemplify in themselves commitment to values believed to be true. I will call this the Impartial-Exemplary approach. Features of this approach would include the following points.

1. The knowledge base of religious studies would include systematic attention to more than one religion; preferably, a sampling related to the backgrounds of most of the students attending that school.
2. The religious tradition most dominant in the particular culture would receive the most attention, and its influence on social and political developments in that culture would be teased out.
3. Students would be made aware of the intellectual and motivational influence of religious truth-claims on believers in the particular traditions.
4. Students would be encouraged to develop skills of critical examination and evaluation, particularly with respect to religious belief-claims and derivative moral values.
5. At the same time, students would be helped to develop powers of empathy and sensitivity towards other persons, especially with respect to the ways in which they respond to their religious beliefs and see the world.
6. The teacher would.be authorised to reveal his or her personal beliefs if the lesson warranted it, subject to the proviso that students would bè encouraged to include this information in their data base without being pressured to agree with the teacher's stance.
7. Similarly, assessment of students would be on the basis of dem-

onstrated capacities — cognitive and affective — not professed commitments.

I submit that this set of specifications provides a teaching approach which resolves the problem raised at the beginning of this paper. It allows the teaching of religion to proceed in an atmosphere which leaves the student free to exercise a reasoned choice as to whether to take a relativist or an absolutist position vis-a-vis religious belief and commitment.

Implications for the religiously-sponsored school

My last task is to ask whether the model we have developed has anything to offer those whose main concern is with the teaching of religion within the context of a religiously sponsored school. A first reaction might be to say that since a particular religion undergirds the school, there is no need to engage in any such debate, because one is under no obligation to concede that a relativist position is possible in regard to religion.

Politically speaking, such a school is at liberty to adopt such a position. It could then adopt a teaching strategy of the kind described above as segregated religious instruction, based on a literal-exclusive epistemology.

But if there has been any general cogency in the arguments examined in this paper, then they must also have some bearing on what the religiously sponsored school is trying to do. On moral grounds, for example, such a school must surely be concerned about the possibility of lapsing into indoctrination, through a failure to help students develop a critical consciousness towards the religious pluralism of their society.

Such a failure would invoke the opposite error from that detected in many current approaches. In this case, there would not be a pre-emptive bias towards religious relativism, but a pre-emptive bias towards religious absolutism. We owe it to our students to avoid either kind of pre-emption, so that they will be able to make that decision for themselves.

I now submit that the specifications set out for multi-faith studies in the previous section are, in fact, appropriate to the teaching of religion in a religiously sponsored school. What religion does not wish its adherents to make an informed choice which will weather the challenges of life in the pluralistic society?

Furthermore, the school classroom is a learning environment characterised by compulsory curriculum and assessment. As I have sought to emphasise elsewhere,[24] this lays upon the teacher an obligation to enhance the understanding, skills and affective capacities of learners without placing them under any kind of duress with respect to personal attitudes and commitments; hence guidelines 1, 3, 4 and 5 apply.

It is possible that the religiously sponsored school could be better placed than many state schools to complement its formal curriculum with efforts in *voluntary* settings to evangelise and encourage commitment but, in both kinds of schools, the ethical parameters within the compulsory classroom are surely similar; hence the applicability, in particular, of guidelines 6 and 7.

At the same time, the religiously sponsored school will wish to feature, possibly more prominently than the state school, the teachings of its own faith. It will also hope to exemplify that faith in practice, both as a dynamic community and through the examples of its staff. Guidelines 2 and 6 provide ample opportunity for such expressions.

Conclusion

In conclusion, I have sought in this article to bridge a great divide between theorists of religious education by developing a set of guidelines which avoid a pre-emptive bias towards either religious relativism or religious absolutism in one's approach. If my arguments hold, then we have here an adequate, and educationally defensible method of teaching religion in the classroom which is equally applicable, and should be equally acceptable, to both the state school and the religiously sponsored school.

What I have not discussed is the relative weightings to be attached to the various guidelines, depending on the age levels of the students. I have been speaking for the curriculum of compulsory schooling as a whole, not for particular stages in that process. Given the general validity of the guidelines, it is then appropriate to apply developmental considerations to their implementation.

I have not attempted that task, but I would want to say that whatever the age level, it is surely desirable to impart some measure of multi-faith awareness to the child. In today's world, we cannot afford the luxury of turning a blind eye to our neighbour's differences. This may mean that in the lower primary school the fifth guideline is strongly represented and the fourth hardly at all, but in the long haul all must play their part in an adequate religious education.

Notes
1. George Bernard Shaw, *Plays Pleasant,* Harmondsworth, Penguin Books, 1946, p. vi.
2. I have discussed these provisions elsewhere, in Brian V Hill, 'Spiritual values in the Education Reform Act: a source of acrimony, apathy or accord?' *British Journal of Educational Studies,* 37, 1989, pp. 169–182.
3. This, and its opposite, 'Realism', are the terms used in R Harre, *The Philosophies of Science,* London, Oxford University Press, 1972, pp. 80–95.
4. John Dewey, *Reconstruction in Philosophy,* New York, Mentor, 1950, p. 131. One discussant of this paper suggested that Dewey was more hospitable to absolute values than this represents him to be, but I have argued elsewhere that in logical terms he is firmly relativist. See Brian V Hill, *Education and the Endangered Individual,* New York, Teachers College Press, pp. 131–150.
5. Thomas Kuhn, *The Structure of Scientific Revolutions,* Chicago, University of Chicago Press, 1962.

6. See Roger Trigg's argument against conceptual relativism in *Reason and Commitment,* Cambridge, Cambridge University Press, 1973.

7. The Bultmann project of 'demythologisation' is precisely of this character, and has in fact the reverse effect of 'mythologising' those elements which contribute most centrally to the truth claims of these religions. Bultmann's method does not purify Christianity but alters it at the core.

8. R Puligandla, *Fundamentals of Indian Philosophy,* Nashville, New York, Abingdon Press, 1975, pp. 201f.

9. Brian V Hill, *op. cit.,* p. 110.

10. Karl Mannheim, *Diagnosis of Our Time,* London, Kegan Paul, 1943, p. 100.

11. S J Curtis, *An Introduction to the Philosophy of Education,* London, University Tutorial Press, 1958, p. 207.

12. I use the term generically for the inspired writings of major religions, but particularly those which appeal for their verification to historical evidences.

13. It should be remembered that what is sauce for the goose is sauce for the gander. Such Christians must not be surprised or indignant if proponents of other religions and humanisms demand the right to do the same in their own special purpose schools.

14. I have addressed this point in *The Greening of Christian Education,* Sydney, Lancer Books, 1985, pp. 30−31 and 72−75.

15. Birmingham City Education Committee, *Agreed Syllabus of Religious Instruction,* 1975.

16. Owen Cole, *World Faiths in Education,* London, George Allen and Unwin, 1981.

17. See Michael Grimmitt's critique of the phenomenological approach in *Religious Education and Human Development,* Great Wakering, Essex, McCrimmons, 1987, pp. 209−212.

18. James Fowler, *Stages of Faith,* Melbourne, Dove Communications, 1981. I am indebted to colleague Cynthia Dixon for drawing my attention to this aspect of Fowler's definitions.

19. See Brian V Hill, 'Values education in a secular democracy,' *Journal of the Indian Council for Philosophical Research,* 3, 1985, pp. 65−79.

20. In more detail, in 1980 the Minister of Education ruled that the school was to nominate Bible Knowledge, Islamic Studies, Hindu Studies, Buddhist Studies or World Religions. Later, Confucianism was added. The reason given was to provide an underpinning for the moral education curriculum which was being developed at the time. Clearly, it was possible to adopt a multi-faith approach by nominating World Religions, and this was the commonest option taken up in state schools, but on the face of it the strategy implied a religious emotivist epistemology, in that it did not matter which religion one taught so long as some religious base was laid down. Given this overall policy, even the World Religions course would appear to be a gesture towards religious universalism, rather than the sort of enquiry we have been commending above.

21. The reference is particularly to the approach of L E Raths, M Harmin and S B Simon, *Values and Teaching,* Columbus, Ohio, Merrill, 2nd ed., 1978.

22. See 'The teacher's faith: dare I let my students know where I stand personally?' in Brian V Hill, *Faith at the Blackboard,* Grand Rapids, Michigan, Eerdmans, 1982, pp. 105−121. An earlier version appeared as 'Teacher commitment and the ethics of teaching for commitment,' *Religious Education,* 76, 1981, pp. 322−336. Some similar points are made by Mary Warnock in 'The neutral teacher,' in Monica J Taylor (ed.), *Progress and Problems in Moral Education,* Slough, NFER, 1975, pp. 103−112.

23. Which is not to say that the teacher may not have good reasons for holding the position, but that in the sense developed by R M Hare, they are justifications deriving from an ultimately primitive set of value preferences for which no further justification can be provided.

24. For example 'Compulsory education: should I be in favour of compulsory strategies in education?' in Brian V Hill, *Faith at the Blackboard,* Grand Rapids, Michigan, Eerdmans, 1982, chapter 1.

3.3 Professionalism, confessionalism and religious education: an exploration from the British context
Trevor Cooling

Introduction

Firstly a word of explanation for those unfamiliar with the British situation. Schools in England and Wales which are maintained by the state independently of any church involvement are legally required to provide religious education for *all* pupils. This must be non-denominational and not designed to convert pupils. The challenge these schools face is to make religious education appropriate for all their pupils irrespective of personal religious convictions or background. This type of religious education is usually described as *secular*, because it does not promote any particular religious faith, to distinguish it from a faith-based approach which emphasises the transmission of particular beliefs within a community. Although the details of legislation in Scotland are different, the distinction between the two approaches still applies. Recent debates surrounding the new Core Syllabus in Northern Ireland, where religious education in state schools is still largely faith-based, suggest that it will increasingly be invoked there in the future.

An important point to grasp is that discussions of professionalism have been largely based on this secular model. For example, in promotional literature for the Professional Council for Religious Education, the largest association of religious education teachers in the UK, it is stated that 'PCfRE is a purely professional body independent of any particular faith'. Professionalism is, therefore, distinguished from the so-called confessional, faith-based approach, usually described as nurture, which seeks to further the religious goal of promoting faith. In this paper my purpose is to explore exactly what the notion of professionalism, defined as independence of any particular faith, might mean.

Description or value judgment

The distinction between professionalism and confessionalism is, of itself, unproblematic if its purpose is to make a non-evaluative differentiation between contextually determined, although equally legitimate, approaches to the educational treatment of religion. To be described either as a confessional or as a professional teacher would not, then, represent a particular value judgment on the worth of one's work. Rather it would serve to specify the context one was working in and the goals one was pursuing. It should then be perfectly possible for any one teacher to be both professional and confessional, depending on whether she or he was working in a secular or a faith community context. In theory there should be no inherent contradiction. The problem comes, however, if an over-riding value is ascribed to either of these two processes in such a way that the other activity is deemed to be in some sense inferior, immoral or perhaps even anti-Christian. My argument will be that, although the non-evaluative distinction is widely supported in the British literature, there has been an increasingly influential tendency to treat the confessional model as inherently inferior. To demonstrate this it is necessary for me to unpack in more detail the notion of professionalism as applied to secular religious education.

The goal of secular education

Of fundamental importance for our study is the way in which the concept of fairness has been seen as one crucially important feature of secular, state-maintained religious education[1] (for example Jackson, 1984; McLaughlin, 1992). By this is meant that in a democracy which embraces a plurality of religious traditions amongst its citizens, as Britain does, the state should neither promote any one set of religious beliefs nor allow any one particular religious group to have domination in any of its activities. It is therefore widely accepted that, to use Brian Hill's terminology, the role of the secular state in a plural society is to create a 'middle ground' where 'peoples from various faith communities and cultures can transact their business and engage in dialogue' (1985, p. 68) without being compromised by the imposition of a religious ideology they do not share. Brian Crittenden describes the underlying educational principle as 'respect for diversity in areas of belief where people may reasonably differ' (1988, p. 126).

The concept of fairness as applied to secular education particularly demands that the controversial nature of religion is recognised. Usually this is interpreted in terms of three principles.

Principle 1: The integrity of the pupils and teachers must be respected. By this it is meant that pupils and teachers should be free from any pressurising to accept particular religious beliefs or to engage in practices which are offensive to them. Neither the hidden nor the overt religious curriculum of publicly funded schools should treat any particular religious belief as normative.

Principle 2: The integrity of the religions should also be respected. By this it is meant that in using religious material in an educational context outside that of the 'owning' faith community, teachers should take great care not to abuse the material by misrepresenting its significance for that faith community. In state maintained schools any teaching of a religion should be true to the adherent's perspective.[2]

Principle 3: Teachers working in the secular context should not discriminate between faith communities on religious grounds alone. By this it is meant that members of faith communities should be entitled to expect that their children, and their religious aspirations for those children, will be treated with due respect. Furthermore they should also be entitled to expect that, within the constraints of a crowded curriculum, their tradition will receive appropriate attention.[3]

These principles suggest that a key element in the idea of professionalism is the acceptance that, in the secular context, there are clear restrictions on the goals that religious educators may legitimately seek to pursue. This is because a professional teacher is bound by the norms of fairness appropriate to the secular context. He of she will therefore be, to use a term coined by John Hull, 'divergent' in the sense that his (*sic*) 'personal religious faith may not be the same as the content of his teaching and his hopes and expectations for his pupils' (Hull, 1980, p. 1). There is however no inherent reason why professionals may not also, in good conscience, engage in the confessional activity of nurture when they are working as teachers in a faith community context. Here their personal religious faith can converge with their teaching commitments, because there are no restrictions on pursuing faith-based goals.[4]

The commitment to fairness in the secular domain and to the pursuit of religious goals in the faith community context need not then conflict. A good case can therefore be made for regarding nurture and secular education as complementary, although distinct, processes. The difficulties arise with those teachers who wish to engage in contextually inappropriate behaviour such that, to quote Michael Grimmitt from his important article on this subject, 'the roles of the religious nurturer and the religious educator are confused' (1981, p. 50).

The drift from fairness in secular education

The attack on the principle of fairness by those who want to treat secular education as an opportunity for nurture and thereby universalise confessional goals is well-documented (for example Hull, 1991; Cooling, 1992; Jackson, 1992). My concern in this paper is to deal with what I regard as the less widely recognised attack, which arises out of a desire to both reinterpret and universalise the professional standards appropriate to secular education.

A particular evidence of this is the unease that is expressed with the concept of nurture or religious upbringing in the writings of some religious educators (for example Attfield, 1991). Probably the most influential expression comes in the work of Paul Hirst,[5] who wants to distinguish between what he calls 'sophisticated' and 'primitive' approaches to education. For Hirst the former is concerned with the promotion of rational autonomy. The latter however is concerned with the transmission of the beliefs and customs of a particular group irrespective of their public, disputable rational status. Although in places he accepts the validity of both these processes,[6] the use of the term 'primitive' implies that faith transmission is, in his opinion, a dubious activity. Indeed he sees the sophisticated view of education as one every intelligent Christian should accept (1974, p. 85) and he goes as far as to claim that the best way to be a Christian is to be thoroughly secular (1974, p. 53). The secular model of education not only conflicts with a confessional approach to education according to Hirst (indeed he calls the notion of confessional education a 'contradiction in terms'), but is also superior to it. Others have developed Hirst's arguments further, maintaining that confessional approaches threatened the success of secular education with its goal of promoting rational autonomy and are, therefore, illegitimate (for example Kazepides, 1982; Blake, 1983; Callan, 1985; Gardner, 1988; Wilson, 1992).

One important reason for this shift from viewing secular education and nurture as complementary to viewing them as in conflict arises from the concern that a confessional activity like nurture is basically irrational and entails indoctrination. The objection is two-fold (Callan, 1985; Lloyd, 1986). The first is that 'the right of self-determination which the child will acquire as an adult is threatened by a religious upbringing and therefore parents have no right to provide such an upbringing' (Callan, 1985, p. 111). The argument is that in matters where rational standards can provide no clear criteria for choosing between beliefs, the principle of autonomy demands that people are enabled to choose for themselves. Intervention in such cases is unjustifiable (White, 1973). This is especially true of religious beliefs which can have such a shaping influence on a person's life and where those acquired in early life tend to persist. The educationalist's fear is that children will simply be victims of their own backgrounds. The second argument against the rationality of nurture is that it results in individuals holding beliefs in an unshakeable fashion which does not take account of their contestable status. Both these objections rest on an assessment of religious belief as radically contestable in the sense of having a dubious rational status when compared with other types of 'knowledge' (Callan, 1989). Many confessional processes are not considered to recognise this important fact, whereas the professional approach appropriate to secular education does.[7]

A second important factor in the development of this opposition between the two activities is the idea that secular education has a justification that is independent of theology, derived from the principles of rationality alone, whereas nurture is dependent on theological justifications which are inherently controversial and specific to particular communities of faith (Hirst, 1974 chapter 5; Hull, 1984, chapter 20 and p. 222). Education is, then, objective, because it is based on the universal norms of rational thought, in a way that nurture is not.[8] John Wilson (1992, p. 22) has expressed this view succinctly:

> The aims of anything that can respectably be called religious education, as we have seen, are common ground to any rational person. These aims, then, can and must be shared by Catholics, atheists, humanists and all other such groups. To talk about Jewish or Protestant education in religion must be seen as silly as talking about Jewish or Protestant education in science or literature.

Religious arguments cannot, therefore, legitimately challenge educational principles. They are always private matters. By contrast, educational principles are public in a sense which makes them universally normative and gives them a higher authority than any religious belief. It is therefore argued that theology can never adjudicate on educational principles, its only role is to provide illumination or religious support for them.

The importance of this discussion for our purposes is that a secular educational approach is now identified with the notion of rationality. Nurture, and other faith-community-specific transmission activities like evangelism, are, however, seen at best as only justified insofar as they cohere with educational principles. At worst they are viewed as being in opposition to rationality. The net result is that professional behaviour is seen to embody rational standards, whereas confessional behaviour is very suspect by those same standards. To put this another way, the professional model is deemed to embody standards of objectivity which can legitimately be insisted upon in the public or secular realm because they are rational. In contrast, the confessional model is not objective since it entails transmitting beliefs that are rationally contestable and is therefore only appropriate, if at all, to the private domain. Professionalism is rational, confessionalism is not. In a modern western framework such ideas can lead to only one conclusion. Secular education is superior to confessional activities.

It is these distinctions which account for another prominent feature in discussions of this subject, namely the argument that the prior commitment of religious education teachers working in the secular context should be to educational principles rather than to their personal religious beliefs. This widely disseminated doctrine embodies the notion that educational principles are public and authoritative, whereas personal religious beliefs are merely private matters. So the demand is made (Cox, 1983, p. 57) that:

> If a teacher becomes conscious that his (*sic*) religious commitments are conflicting with his educational obligations the latter should determine what he does in the classroom.

Recognising the spiritually destructive nature for teachers of such a conflict of loyalties, John Hull has suggested that they should find a personal theology which enables them to be committed to rational and secular educational principles on religious grounds. The public and the private are thereby in harmonious relationship. To be professional is then defined in terms of a form of confessionalism, that is, the pursuit of religious goals, but ones which are educational (Hull, 1980, p. 1). Professional teachers are therefore those that have a more rational personal theology.

This assertion of course raises the question of exactly what constitutes a rational theology or, put another way, what sort of theology can respect the secularity of education (Hull, 1984, p. 263). This is a complex epistemological question[9] which is well beyond the scope of this short article. However it is sufficient here to point out that, in a number of influential writings, it is generally seen to be associated with the more radical or liberal end of theological thought. Thus the acceptance of pluralist theology[10] as the appropriate response to religious diversity, of relativism as the appropriate attitude to religious truth claims, of free personal choice of religious belief and of a degree of scepticism as the appropriate personal response to the controversial nature of religious belief and, finally, of a subjectivist view of the status of religious propositions are characteristics of this educational theology. Some writers even equate a professional stance with the adoption of agnosticism as the appropriate foundation for religious education (for example Cox, 1983, p. 57; Gardner, 1991, p. 79). Such an epistemology brings education into conflict with more traditional forms of religious belief which value absolute commitment, adopt a realist understanding of religious propositions, are inclusivist or exclusivist in their attitude to other religions and encourage the passing on of the faith from one generation to the next.

From our point of view the important issue is not whether or not one form of theology can be established as being more rational than another, but whether attempting to define a rational theology in this way is going to generate an approach to religious education which is fair. Since the question of what is, or what is not, a rational form of religious belief is itself an issue on which people may reasonably differ,[11] it would appear that seeking to do this can only result in the imposition of a particular religious perspective on the school population in general. Such a strategy is clearly a denial of the concept of fairness. The charge that religious education is propagating a form of secular humanism, more popularly referred to as the 'multi-faith mish-mash',[12] is to a large degree based on this sense that the subject discriminates against and privatises more traditional forms of religious belief.

I therefore suggest that, if the standards appropriate to secular religious education are to be based on the concept of fairness, we will have to find a different way of distinguishing professionalism from a confessional approach. It is simply not adequate to declare certain forms of confessionalism as professional and therefore acceptable, whilst forbidding other forms, on the basis of the (controversial) claim that some theologies are more rational or more education-ally compatible than others. It is to the suggestion of a positive way forward that I now turn.

Towards reinstituting the concept of fairness in secular religious education

Probably the single most important step is to challenge the notion that educational principles can be established independently of ref-erence to confessional goals.[13] In the planning of a curriculum, religious educators will inevitably find themselves dealing with fun-damental questions of purpose and significance, including what it means to be human and the nature of knowledge. It is very dif-ficult to see how theological reflection can be treated as *inherently* irrelevant to these or, to put the point another way, how it can be maintained that a logical error has been committed by introducing theological language into consideration of them (as is required by the thesis of the independent rationality of education). Furthermore Jeff Astley has made the important point that it is impossible to avoid theological criteria in selecting suitable content to include in a religious education programme (Astley, 1988). Jack Priestley's assessment (1992, p. 27) of the independence thesis is that it is based on:

> the false assumption that somewhere there exists a set of discrete criteria for an activity called education. The totally false premise is that at root that activity can somehow be value-free

or, we might qualify, controversy-free.

What must, of course, be accepted is that non-theological, albeit still confessional, values, for example from humanist or atheist perspectives, are as relevant as theological values in discussions of education. What, however, must be rejected is the notion that there are some rational, objective answers to educational questions which define a professional stance and are universally authoritative and logically prior to the particular confessional answers of 'faith' communities. To deny this point amounts to making 'public' (in the sense of normative for all) the 'private' (in the sense of being specific to a particular faith community) humanist position that religion is irrelevant in the 'public' (in the sense of what is common to humans) domain.

The conclusion that follows from this is that educational goals are inescapably confessional, in the sense that they will reflect the presuppositional beliefs of those framing them and therefore reflect faith-based goals. The challenge for secular religious education in its quest for fairness is not, then, to pursue some alchemist's quest for an objective, non-confessional rationale, but is rather to develop strategies for dealing with the inevitably confessional aspirations of teachers. To be a professional teacher is, I suggest, to handle one's confessional, and incidentally quite legitimate, aspirations in a manner that is appropriate in the context of state-maintained, secular education.

It is therefore necessary to define goals that are appropriate to this context. In faith communities it is quite legitimate to pursue specifically faith-based goals (but see note 4). The requirement for fairness makes this illegitimate in the secular context. However, although the State cannot seek to prescribe particular religious beliefs for its citizens, it is a legitimate concern for it to seek to ensure that the competing belief systems present in the plural society do not become a source of danger either to individual citizens or to society as a whole. Put another way, a proper concern for secular religious education is to promote attitudes which will enable adherents of different faiths to work together towards achieving the common good and towards creating community in the context of plurality (Palmer, 1991; Browning, 1990; Jones, 1987). The Chairman of the English National Curriculum Council, in an important speech, (Pascall, 1992, paragraph 26) expressed this as follows:

> Learning about religions has more than an intellectual and practical application. For the stability of our society, and the maintaining of good personal relationships and behaviour towards others, it is vital that, through the increased understanding of beliefs and practices, our children come to respect the rights of others to hold beliefs different from their own, and both accept and value the many cultures, religions and traditions evident around them while remaining secure in their own.

Secular religious education is not therefore value-neutral. It certainly is founded on the principle of fairness, which means it cannot take sides in controversial religious matters. However it is also founded on the belief that it is legitimate for the state to promote, through education, the attitudes that will make harmonious relations possible between the competing faith communities which exist amongst its citizens. Its role as an arbitrator is, therefore, non-negotiable.

One important component of such an approach will be to teach pupils the art of conversation (Aspin, 1988; Jackson, 1992). The aim will be to empower them so that they can both explain their beliefs to others and listen to and learn from the explanations of those they disagree with. The goal will be to create a climate where pupils will come to understand each other as committed adherents of different ways of life.

Education and coalition

These civic concerns for harmony and respect in the plural society are accepted by many faith communities as legitimate goals for state-maintained education. They represent an area where a number of belief systems overlap. The view I am advancing represents what we can therefore call a coalition approach to defining educational goals, where a group of people work together to achieve a common goal but for what may be individually very different reasons. The *Shorter Oxford Dictionary* defines a coalition as 'a temporary alliance of distinct parties for limited purposes'. In the case of secular education the purposes are limited because they do not represent the full scale pursuit of the confessional, faith-based goals which believers would naturally pursue given a less restricted situation. The crucial point is that to participate in the coalition of secular education, teachers have to be able to accept restraints on their otherwise quite legitimate confessional desire to pursue goals particular to their own faith position. They do this in recognition of the ethical limits that exist for government in promoting particular religious beliefs and out of a recognition of the importance of promoting community harmony. At the same time they will continue to be committed to their specific confessional convictions as of first order importance. Being able to embrace these restraints and live with the tensions they create is the mark of the professional. For the Christian they are part of the calling to be in, but not of, the world.

A specific example may help. There are what might be called more traditional Christians who believe that what they perceive as the polytheism of Hinduism is nothing less than the worship of idols. On the basis of their own belief that idolatry is forbidden they are therefore committed to the position that Hinduism is, in this respect, wrong. Within the confessional context it would be quite legitimate for them to maintain this as part of the normative framework. They should of course, as a Christian responsibility, seek to ensure they have represented the Hindu position accurately in doing this and never allow such differences over questions of religious truth to degenerate into racist or sectarian attitude.

However, as teachers in the secular educational context, it would be quite illegitimate for such Christians to use their power as employees of the state to insist on the correctness of their position. They have to recognise that this is a controversial matter on which people may reasonably differ and on which the secular state has no right to adjudicate. Secular schools can therefore never declare Hindu polytheism to be wrong in the sense that particular Christian faith communities might do. Neither can they declare it to be right. Individual teachers may of course offer an opinion on this matter as long as it is clear that it is controversial and specific to their own beliefs. This should not however be done in any way that is likely to negate their responsibility to promote respect and harmony.

Furthermore, the secular school should respect the integrity of individual pupils and teachers. For example, no child or teacher should be required to either eat or refrain from eating food offered to a god on a visit to a Hindu temple. Or again, no pupil or teacher should be required to subscribe to the view that Hindu polytheism is as valid as Christian monotheism on the basis of educational principles.[14]

A second important feature of a coalition approach is that it presupposes a situation where no one set of faith-based presuppositions can be treated as providing the only legitimate underpinning for secular education. Rather, participants in the coalition will each need to generate a rationale, be that theological or non-theological, which will enable them to embrace the limited goals of secular education. To do this each person will have to draw upon the resources of his or her own faith. There will therefore be as many confessional underpinnings to secular education as there are participating faith communities. An important consequence of this argument is that professional training should give attention to helping teachers relate their personal theology to secular educational goals. It is quite erroneous to treat personal theology as irrelevant in defining professionalism.

Of course there will be certain religious communities which are unable to provide this theological endorsement and will therefore reject fairness between faiths and the promotion of harmony as the appropriate governing principles for the educational policy of the state. It then follows that they cannot expect sympathetic treatment from secular education.[15] A priority in the dialogue between secular educators and these communities should be to help them discover those theological resources latent within their own traditions, but which may have previously been little noticed, which will enable them to endorse secular educational goals without compromise to their integrity. However the fact that many faith communities do appeal to the principle of fairness, for example as in the demand for state-funded Muslim schools, suggests that it is a principle which attracts wide support. It can therefore form a viable basis for a consensus-based secular education which is theologically non-discriminatory in the sense that it demands no more than assent to a limited role for the state in matters of religious belief.

A third important characteristic of a successful coalition is that a clear understanding is established as to how the fundamental differences of belief that exist between its members are to be handled. In other words, there has to be a clearly defined code of conduct.[16] Two currently influential examples will suffice to illustrate this point.

Firstly, it is now widely accepted that responsible secular religious educators will employ 'owning' and 'grounding' language (Read *et al.*, 1986, pp. 60–61). By this it is meant that all truth claims are to be presented as owned by a particular individual, for example the vicar, or as grounded in particular faith communities. So a phrase such as 'Christians believe ...' is preferred to one like 'thinking people no longer believe ...'. The purpose of utilising this style is to avoid compromising both pupil and teacher by assuming, or seeking to coerce, their assent to certain propositions through the use of inclusive language.

A second example comes from the 'Religion in the Service of the Child Project' based at Birmingham University. Here it is suggested that in using religious material with young children there should come a point at which a 'distancing device' is introduced into the lesson (Grimmitt *et al.*, 1991, pp. 10–11). The purpose of this is to create a boundary which most of the children may not cross, so that they can clearly distinguish religious material that does not belong to them from that which does. So, for example, the only children allowed to share food dedicated to Ganesh are those who actually belong to the Hindu community. To achieve the same effect, the project also employs a series of books comprising photographs of a child belonging to a faith community involved in the practices of that community. This enables particular religious material to be spoken of in the third person as belonging to, for example, the Sikh boy Sabjit (Grimmitt *et al.*, 1991, p. 51) and avoids giving the impression that all the class are expected to enter a faith relationship with it.

The important point to note about any educational code of conduct developed under this model is that it cannot be treated as a statement of a rational or global or publicly approved theology, a basis of faith to which all are expected to subscribe. It is rather a pragmatic agreement which makes partnership possible in the achievement of limited goals and supports the promotion of community harmony. Instead of seeking to reduce differences between religious believers by aspiring to consensus of belief, this approach celebrates them by affirming the fact that they exist and by not treating that as problematic. It also acknowledges these differences by providing opportunities for co-operative action in a way that affirms the theological integrity of the believer, including those many whose beliefs are representative of more traditional forms of religious commitment. Furthermore, it ascribes value and dignity to those processes of education that take place within faith communities, because it is no longer necessary to insist that a model of education appropriate to the 'public' domain is in some way superior to that appropriate to the 'private' domain.[17]

Conclusion

In this article I have sought to clarify the concept of professional behaviour as applied to secular education by proposing that a commitment to fairness is the appropriate value base for religious education in that particular context. Approaches which distinguish professionalism from confessional behaviour in terms of the adoption of a rational objectivity which is considered to be independent of theological commitment, have been rejected on the grounds that they are a denial of this concept of fairness. Following from this the notion that certain theologies can be more professional, in the sense of being more objective or rational because they accord more closely with educational principles, has been challenged.

In contrast, I have argued that all religious educators are confessional because no one can escape defining religious education in terms of faith-based goals. Given this insight, I have proposed that professional behaviour is defined in terms of adherence to a code of conduct which is derived from the limited goals appropriate to the secular educational context and which is acceptable to most faith communities. To be professional is then to restrain the full application of one's perfectly legitimate confessional aspirations out of respect for the constraints that apply in state-maintained educational institutions. Unrestrained confessional approaches are, however, quite appropriate in contexts where the constraints of secularity do not apply. Professionalism and confessionalism are therefore not mutually exclusive, but reflect the norms of the context specific activities of secular education and faith transmission.[18]

Notes

1. I am aware that the concept of fairness needs both considerable unpacking and further justification. I do attempt this to a degree here (see Cooling, 1992, for a more detailed treatment), but this is not the main purpose of this paper. Here I am concerned with the limited task of evaluating whether the claim that fairness is currently the value base for secular education can be substantiated. It is also important to note that fairness is only one defining feature of secular religious education. This can be described as representing the political dimension of this particular activity. There is also an important epistemological dimension which grapples with distinguishing reasonable from unreasonable forms of religious belief. This paper only touches on that issue (see also note 4), but I have developed the discussion at greater length elsewhere (see Cooling, 1992). Suffice it to point out here that any development of a religious epistemology that can underpin secular education must be constrained by the demand for fairness in the sense that it cannot make normative a particular, controversial view of what it is to be rational in the religious domain.

2. At the same time this does not mean that the use made of religious material in the faith community and secular contexts will be the same. See Cooling (1993) for a further discussion of this point.

3. Decisions as to the local, national and international importance of communities and their numbers in a local community will, for example, be relevant criteria in deciding the degree to which a religion will figure in a curriculum.

4. It is important that a distinction is maintained between indoctrination and legitimate confessional activities. I would wish to agree with the argument that nurture should be compatible with notions of 'critical openness' (Hull, 1984) or 'normal rational autonomy' (Thiessen, 1991). An important challenge will be to develop an adequate epistemological interpretation of these notions, which I have attempted in Cooling, 1992, chapter 5. An acceptance of the validity of confessionalism does not therefore imply that anything goes in the transmission of religious belief.

5. Hirst's view of the relationship between education and faith-based processes like nurture is easily presented as a crude distinction between the rational and the irrational with religion having no role to play in education. However Hirst did not espouse such a crude secularism (see Hirst, 1981, 1985; McLaughlin, 1992a). My criticisms are directed at two, currently influential, legacies of his treatment of these themes. First at his concern to divorce the concept of education from any faith transmission process (which relates to his concern to separate the notion of rationality or public, objective knowledge from faith) and second at his desire to make faith-based approaches answerable to the standards of secular education.

6. See 1974, p. 90 for comments on religious family life, and 1981 where he seeks to legitimate catechesis in church schools.

7. This epistemological view has come under extensive criticism of late. See, for example, Thiessen (1985), Gunton (1991), and Cooling (1992).

8. Secular education then becomes the only form of education worthy of the name. Any attempt to give faith-based definitions of education are deemed to be contradictions in terms.

9. I develop the points made in this paragraph at length in Cooling (1992) chapters 1 and 2.

10. I here use pluralist as describing a normative approach to the theology of religions. John Hick has developed such a position in great detail. See, for example Hick (1989).

11. See, for example, Gunton (1991) and Netland (1991) for a different view from what I describe as the radical position. See also the comments by the Lord Bishop of Ripon during a debate in the House of Lords on religious education on 17th June 1992 (House of Lords, 1991, p. 256).

12. I therefore disagree with John Hull (1991) where he does not seem to take seriously the theological objections to some multifaith approaches, preferring to represent such objections as arising from a fear of contamination by other religions. The works of Lesslie Newbigin (for example 1989) and the Gospel and Our Culture Movement (for example Montefiore, 1991) are examples of such concerns.

13. This is a major point which needs more detailed challenging than I can attempt within the confines of this brief paper. Readers are referred to Cooling (1992), chapter 3, for a detailed critique of the independence thesis.

14. See McLaughlin (1992b) for another example in his discussion of the treatment of homosexuality. He argues that the fact that homosexuality should be accepted as a legitimate lifestyle in the public realm does not prejudge the question of whether it is a morally acceptable lifestyle *per se*. So-called private beliefs will need to be drawn on in answering this question.

15. At this point it may be objected that I am smuggling in a theological criterion since the objectors are raising theological arguments against my view of education. I am, it is claimed, therefore defeating my claim to be adhering to the principle of fairness. My reply is that since my argument is that no educational rationale can escape a confessional underpinning, it is inevitable that secular education built upon the principle of fairness will discriminate against those theological positions that cannot endorse fairness. Such discrimination is however justified on the grounds that it is not contradictory to refuse to extend the protection offered by the concept of fairness to those faith groups that will not extend it to others. Furthermore the future health of society entails that groups that do not value harmony, cooperation and justice for others are not given undue influence in the public realm. Public, secular education will therefore always demand that its constituent faith communities jump a theological fence. My fence is however lower than that erected by the positions

that I have criticised in this paper, because it can be cleared by those holding more traditional beliefs, and does not contradict its own claim to fairness.

16. I count Edward Hulmes (1979) as a significant example of a work seeking to grapple with defining such a code of conduct.

17. I therefore agree with clearly distinguishing the limited educational function of schooling (the activity secular educational institutions can legitimately engage in) from the more comprehensive, and in my opinion more important, educational function of nurture.

18. The author wishes to thank Dr Robert Jackson and Dr T H McLaughlin for their comments on an earlier draft of this paper.

References

Aspin, D (1988) 'Critical openness as a platform for diversity: towards an ethic of belonging,' in B O'Keeffe (ed.), *Schools for Tomorrow: building walls or building bridges,* Lewes, Falmer Press.

Astley, J (1988) 'Theology and curriculum selection,' *British Journal of Religious Education,* 10, pp. 86-91.

Attfield, D (1991) 'The challenge of the Education Reform Act to church schools,' *British Journal of Religious Education,* 13, pp. 136–142.

Blake, N (1983) 'Church schools, RE and the multi-ethnic community: a reply to D Aspin,' *Journal of Philosophy of Education,* 17, pp. 241–250.

Browning, R (1990) 'Befriending the world: beyond inter-faith dialogue to action,' *Religious Education,* 85, pp. 331–345.

Callan, E (1985) 'McLaughlin on parental rights,' *Journal of Philosophy of Education,* 19, pp. 111–118.

Callan, E (1989) 'Godless moral education and liberal tolerance,' *Journal of Philosophy of Education,* 23, pp. 267–281.

Cooling, T (1992) 'The epistemological foundations of contemporary religious education: an exploration with special reference to the evangelical Christian traditions,' unpublished PhD dissertation, University of Birmingham.

Cooling, T (1993) 'The use of Christianity in the primary school curriculum,' *British Journal of Religious Education,* 15, 3, pp. 14–22.

Cox, E (1983) *Problems and Possibilities For Religious Education,* London, Hodder and Stoughton.

Crittenden, B (1988) *Parents, the State and the Right to Educate,* Melbourne, Australia, Melbourne University Press.

Gardner, P (1988) 'Religious upbringing and the ideal of autonomy,' *Journal of Philosophy of Education,* 22, pp. 89–105.

Gardner, P (1991) 'Personal autonomy and religious upbringing: the problem,' *Journal of Philosophy of Education,* 25, pp. 69–81.

Grimmitt, M (1981) 'When is commitment a problem in religious education?' *British Journal of Educational Studies,* 29, pp. 42–53.

Grimmitt, M *et al.* (1991) *A Gift to the Child: religious education in the primary school,* London, Simon and Schuster.

Gunton, C (1992) 'Knowledge and culture: towards an epistomology of the concrete,' in H Montefiore (ed.), *The Gospel and Contemporary Culture,* London, Mowbray, pp. 84–102.

Hick, J (1989) *An Interpretation of Religion,* Basingstoke, Macmillan Press.

Hill, B (1985) 'Values education in a secular democracy,' *Journal of the Indian Council for Philosophical Research,* 3, pp. 65–79.

Hirst, P (1972) 'Christian education: a contradiction in terms?' *Learning For Living,* 11, 4, pp. 6–11.

Hirst, P (1974) *Moral Education in a Secular Society,* London, University of London Press.

Hirst, P (1981) 'Education, catechesis and the church school,' *British Journal of Religious Education,* 3, pp. 85–93.

Hirst, P (1985) 'Education and diversity of belief,' in M C Felderhof (ed.), *Religious Education in a Pluralistic Society,* London, Hodder and Stoughton, pp. 5–17.

House of Lords (1992) *Official Report 17 June,* London, HMSO.

Hull, J (1980) 'Editorial,' *British Journal of Religious Education,* 3, pp. 1–2.

Hull, J (1984) *Studies in Religion and Education,* Lewes, Falmer Press.

Hull, J (1991) *Mishmash: religious education in a multi-cultural Britain,* Derby, Christian Education Movement.

Hulmes, E (1979) *Commitment and Neutrality in Religious Education,* London, Geoffrey Chapman.

Jackson, R (1984) 'The concerns of religious education and the characterization of Hinduism,' *British Journal of Religious Education,* 6, pp. 141–146.

Jackson, R (1992) 'The misrepresentations of religious education,' in M Leicester and M Taylor (eds), *Ethics, Ethnicity and Education,* London, Kogan Page.

Jones, M (1987) 'Prejudice,' in G Haydon (ed.), *Education For a Pluralist Society: Bedford Way Papers 30,* London, University of London Institute of Education.

Kazepides, T (1982) 'Educating, socialising and indoctrinating,' *Journal of Philosophy of Education,* 16, pp. 155–165.

Lloyd, I (1986) 'Confession and reason,' *British Journal of Religious Education,* 8, pp. 140–145.

McLaughlin, T H (1992a) 'Christian education and schooling: a liberal perspective,' unpublished paper read at Stapleford House Education Centre on 4th January.

McLaughlin, T H (1992b) 'Fairness, controversiality and the common school,' *Spectrum,* 24, pp. 105–118.

Montefiore, H (1992) *The Gospel and Contemporary Culture,* London, Mowbray.

Netland, H (1991) *Dissonant Voices: religious pluralism and the question of truth,* Leicester, Apollos.

Newbigin, L (1989) *The Gospel in a Pluralist Society,* London, SPCK.

Palmer, M (1991) *What Should We Teach?: Christians and education in a pluralist world,* Geneva, Switzerland, World Council of Churches.

Pascall, D (1992) Speech to Association of Religious Education Advisers and Inspectors, Keele University 10th July.

Priestley, J (1992) 'Whitehead revisited. Religion and education: an organic whole,' in B Watson (ed.), *Priorities in Religious Education,* London, Falmer Press, pp. 26–37.

Read, G *et al.* (1986) *How Do I Teach RE?,* London, Mary Glasgow Publications.

Thiessen, E (1985) 'A defense of a distinctively Christian curriculum,' *Religious Education,* 80, pp. 37–50.

Thiessen, E (1991) 'Christian nurture, indoctrination and liberal education,' *Spectrum,* 23, pp. 105–124.

White, J (1973) *Towards A Compulsory Curriculum,* London, Routledge and Kegan Paul.

Wilson, J (1992) 'First steps in religious education,' in B Watson (ed.), *Priorities in Religious Education,* London, Falmer Press, pp. 10–25.

4. Formation and nurture

In this section and the next we move much deeper into the territory of the church's task of education for Christian commitment, and explore a range of approaches to such a 'confessional' Christian religious education. The three articles collected in section 4 reflect on the approach that is often described by the metaphors of forming (giving a determinate form to) and nurturing ('suckling' or 'nourishing') faith.

T H McLaughlin argues that liberal parents may provide a religious upbringing for their children that is neither indoctrinatory nor an enemy to the child's personal and moral autonomy. He contends that there are good reasons for holding that parents have a right to introduce their children to a 'coherent primary culture' that the parents have substantially determined for themselves, and that this primary culture may properly contain religious elements. Further, 'far from hindering the child's capacity for autonomy in this field, the provision of an appropriate form of religious upbringing is in fact facilitating it'. 'Parental rights and the religious upbringing of children' first appeared in *Journal of Philosophy of Education*, 18, 1984, pp. 75–83.

Dean M Martin's article, 'Learning to become a Christian,' was first published in *Religious Education*, 82, 1987, pp. 94–114. Like many contemporary philosophical commentators on religion, Martin's approach is deeply indebted to the later writings of Ludwig Wittgenstein. Wittgenstein's insights are applied here to the formal and informal ways in which people learn the Christian concepts (especially the concept of God) by acquiring and exercising linguistic capacities. These concepts 'are learned within the Christian community where they have instituted ruled uses', often in the affective context of worship. Martin proceeds to analyse the role of 'unshakeable beliefs' (fundamental convictions that 'need not be forfeited no matter how things go in the world') within Christianity and Christian education.[1] He concludes that their adoption and appropriation (or, rather, passionate seizing) involves a learning of the means of salvation, 'via the exigencies of life', that is more than just a learning of the Christian belief-system.[2]

Michael Warren's article, 'Religious formation in the context of social formation,' was first published in *Religious Education*, 82, 1987, pp. 515–528. This contribution widens the discussion to consider formation as 'a central and inevitable process in all of human life'. Warren notes that the importance of formation in religion is to be recognised in the face of the powerful formative influences of the wider culture. He reviews three significant areas of general formation (the formation of perception, the formation of language and thought, and the formation of consciousness) before moving on to reflect on religious formation in the believing community. 'Communities are formative in the stances they take,' he claims; and in our consumerist culture this will involve the religious educator in a 'struggle with (such) conflicting ideas and values'.

Dr T H McLaughlin teaches in the Department of Education of the University of Cambridge, England. Dr Dean M Martin is Professor in the Department of Religion and Philosophy at Campbell University, USA. Professor Michael Warren is Professor of Religious Education in the Department of Theology and Religious Studies of St John's University, Jamaica, New York, USA.

Notes

1. See article 4.1 and section 8. Donald Hudson's essay 'The rational system of beliefs,' in David Martin *et al.*, *Sociology and Theology: alliance and conflict*, Brighton, Harvester, 1980, chapter 5, is particularly relevant here.
2. See also article 9.1, and the literature cited in notes 5 and 20 on pp. 300–301.

4.1 Parental rights and the religious upbringing of children

T H McLaughlin

Do parents have a right to bring up their children in their own, particular, religious faith? The right of parents to give their children a religious upbringing (or, for that matter, an anti-religious upbringing) is often merely taken for granted in liberal democratic states and is seen as a right of a particularly important and fundamental kind. But can such a basic parental right be defended?

This important question has been neglected. Within the liberal tradition in Philosophy of Education, for example, much has been written about the illegitimacy of developing in children an unjustifiably determinate conception of 'the good life', but discussion has tended to focus almost exclusively on teachers and schools, rather than on parents, as indoctrinators.

The rights of parents are now being subjected to increasing scrutiny by philosophers and philosophers of education. One of the most controversial areas of debate is the extent to which parents can claim the right to choose and control the formal education and schooling of their children on religious grounds. It is clear, however, that little progress can be made in this debate without clarification of the underlying, more fundamental, claim of parents to the right to determine religious upbringing. In this article, I shall attempt a preliminary examination of this fundamental claim. Although I shall not draw out the implications of the discussion for parental rights over formal education and schooling, the potential significance of these implications will be apparent.

I am interested in how this fundamental question might be approached from a liberal point of view. Can a liberal state concede the right of parents to bring up their children in a given religion, and can a liberal parent – one committed to a range of liberal values – consistently and in good conscience claim such a right? To bring out the issues clearly, I shall therefore conduct my argument within the framework of a fairly strong form of liberalism, involving the following assumptions:

a. that the development of personal and moral autonomy is a fundamental value and parents should have this as a major aim in the upbringing of their children;

b. the most justifiable form of society is an open, pluralist, democratic one where there is maximum toleration of diversity and a commitment to free critical debate as the most rational means of advancing the pursuit of truth in all its forms;

c.   that no one set of religious beliefs can be *shown* to be objectively true.

These assumptions are, of course, widely challenged, especially by religious believers seeking to justify their rights over the religious upbringing of their children. (There is, however, no reason in my view why a religious believer *must* reject these assumptions. They are not only compatible with but also demanded by many forms of religious faith.) The assumptions face challenges from other directions too. But in this article I shall be leaving to one side the adequacy of the liberal position and shall argue within a framework provided by its central assumptions. The article, therefore, has a narrow focus, and does not seek to address some fundamental questions about the justification of liberal values which could not be ignored in a fuller account.

Commitment to (a), (b) and (c) rules out, or severely limits the scope of, a range of arguments that might be deployed to defend the fundamental parental right in question. Assumption (a), the importance of developing the personal and moral autonomy of the child, calls into question, for example, two arguments used by David Bridges in his article 'Non-paternalistic arguments in support of parents' rights over their children's education'.[1] First Bridges quotes approvingly Coons and Sugarman's question: 'How can the best interest of the child be pursued by society when there is no collective perception of that interest?'[2] and claims that 'the division of opinion among the adult community as to what is in fact good for children undermines their claims to paternalistic intervention in children's liberty in the name of such good'.[3] This stress on the indeterminacy of the child's interest provides a starting point not only for arguments claiming that, in the midst of perplexity, parents are in the best position to perceive and determine any paternalistic intervention that may be justified on behalf of their children.[4] Commitment to (a), however, involves the claim that, whilst there may be some indeterminacy as to what is in the detailed interest of particular children, there *is* something that can be shown to be in the general interest of all of them: the development of their personal and moral autonomy. Coons and Sugarman themselves seem to recognise this when they claim that the development of autonomy is 'an indispensable intellectual and ethical ideal'[5] and that they 'know no worthier objective'.[6] Their commitment to autonomy is equivocal however, in that they describe their position as merely a 'personal view'[7] and one that has no generally binding force. Thus, whilst they try to show that their proposals for family choice in education are consistent with the development of the child's personal and moral autonomy,[8] they see no grounds for insisting that *all* parents must value that development.[9] Their position is therefore in conflict with (a), which sees parents' rights as limited by, or defined in relation to, their duty to ensure their child's eventual autonomy.[10] The second argument used by Bridges is that parents have a right to give their children a religious upbringing as an extension of their right to practise their own religion.[11] But a commitment to (a) introduces a restriction on this right. Bridges makes the criterion of restriction here to be whether the child actually rebels against the religious upbringing being provided. Thus he claims that, if the child does not rebel:[12]

> people standing outside a parent-child relationship which allows both parties to lead a life which satisfies their value preferences, are put in a position of interfering in both lives in order to impose on them a set of values which the observers prefer.

Bridges considers that this is an interference which 'it is in practice very difficult to justify'.[13] Although the *practical* problems are very difficult here, from the perspective of (a) the issues of *principle* are clearer. Just because the child does not complain it does not mean that all is well; the child's docility may well be the result of indoctrination or the manipulation of natural affections and loyalties. As Steven Lukes points out, a person may exercise power over another not only by getting the other to do what he or she does not want to do, but also by 'influencing, shaping or determining' those very wants.[14] Indeed, Lukes argues, the securing of compliance by controlling thoughts and desires is the 'supreme exercise' of power. Failure to recognise this, he claims, leads to the false assumption that 'if people feel no grievances, then they have no interests that are harmed by the use of power'.[15] Against this, Lukes insists on a distinction between wants and 'real interests'. On the liberal view, an important aspect of what is in the 'real interests' of children is their development into personal and moral autonomy. Since this development can be clearly frustrated by the use of power in the manipulation of wants, parents, at the very least, must balance their right to exercise their religious freedom against the right of their children to become autonomous individuals.

A commitment to (a), therefore, introduces a crucial factor into the determination of parental rights. In itself, of course, it does not indicate clearly what these rights should be, since there are problems in determining exactly what is *meant* by personal and moral autonomy in relation to religion, and how it is developed. But (a) asserts that the questions must be taken into account when discussing parents' rights over their children's religious upbringing.

The kinds of defence of basic parental rights over religious upbringing excluded by (b) and (c) can be quite easily brought out. Assumption (b) clearly excludes arguments of the form that a given religious upbringing is necessary for the child to become an acceptable member of society or to avoid disadvantage or discrimination. Assumption (c) excludes arguments based on a parental claim that their religious faith is demonstrably true and that therefore they are justified in transmitting this faith to their children at all costs. This infringes the liberal principle that nobody can claim power by asserting a privileged insight into the good of others

Having outlined some of the implications of arguing from a liberal perspective, we can now turn directly to the question: from this perspective, do parents have a right to bring up their children in their own, particular, religious faith ?

A Negative Answer

One answer which has emerged concerning this question is an apparently negative one. Thus John White argues in *The Aims of Education Re-stated* that:[16]

> if the parent has an obligation to bring up his (*sic*) child as a morally autonomous person, he cannot at the same time have the right to indoctrinate him with any beliefs whatsoever, since some beliefs may contradict those on which educational endeavour should be based. It is hard to see, for instance, how a desire for one's child's moral autonomy is compatible with the attempt to make him into a good Christian, Muslim or orthodox Jew ... The unavoidable implication seems to be that parents should not be left with this freedom to indoctrinate. Ways must be found, by compulsion, persuasion or enlightened public opinion, to prevent them from hindering the proper education of their children.... The freedom of the parent to bring up his own children according to his own lights has long seemed sacrosanct. But I would urge objectors to reflect on the rational basis of this belief. *Has* it a rational basis, in fact ? Or is it just prejudice?

In this way, White challenges 'the parent's alleged right to bring a child up in his own religion, political persuasion or *weltanschauung*'.[17]

There is an important distinction which is blurred here between 'bringing up' and 'indoctrinating'. At times White seems to be referring to the former, as in phrases such as 'to bring a child up in his own religion' and 'to bring up his own children according to his own lights'. But in other places there is a more direct reference to indoctrination. White's view of indoctrination is that it involves an intention on the part of the indoctrinator to bring about belief that a proposition (or series of propositions) is true in such a way that nothing will subsequently shake that belief.[18] Clearly a liberal will object to religious upbringing in this sense, since it constitutes an attempt to restrict in a substantial way the child's eventual ability to function autonomously.

But must a religious upbringing be of this indoctrinatory kind? Is there not a less stringent form of upbringing where a definite world view is presented to the child as part of a 'coherent primary culture', but where the parent abides by the liberal principles calling for him or her to allow the child to develop and exercise the freedom to eventually challenge that culture and form his or her own life ideals? Can a religious upbringing in this sense be acceptable to a liberal, where it is seen as one of a range of acceptable 'primary cultures' that might be provided for a child?

Towards a Positive Answer

The notion of a 'primary culture' is one which is developed by Bruce Ackerman in *Social Justice in the Liberal State*.[19] Ackerman acknowledges the dilemma arising for a liberal from the fact that children are not born fully fledged and autonomous participants in the liberal form of life. In their earliest years they are necessarily dependent both physically and culturally upon adults and their development towards autonomy is a slow and gradual one. Parents are therefore justified in giving their children a stable and coherent 'primary culture' since this is the precondition of the child's subsequent development into an autonomous liberal citizen.

Thus, in Ackerman's view, the need for stability gives parents the right to determine the character of this 'primary culture' themselves, without undue interference from other individuals or agencies. A parent, for example, has a right to shield the child from a group of adults 'ringing the door simultaneously, each demanding the right to provide different moral vocabularies and environments within which the child may understand his (*sic*) resistance to his primary culture'.[20] The need for coherence gives parents the right to introduce their children to a substantive set of practices, beliefs and values since:[21]

> while an infant may learn English or Urdu or both, there are limits to the cultural diversity he can confront without losing a sense of the meanings that the noises and motions might ultimately signify. Exposing the child to an endless and changing Babel of talk and behaviour will only prevent the development of the abilities he requires if he is ever to take his place among the citizenry.

For Ackerman, the argument for the need for cultural stability and coherence gradually loses force as the child develops 'dialogic competence' and the ability to face challenges to his primary culture without being disorientated. Indeed Ackerman argues that parents have an obligation not only to take the developing questioning of their children but also to provide them with 'a *liberal* education – with cultural equipment that permits the child to criticise, as well as affirm, parental ideals'.[22]

Ackerman is unclear about the possible restrictions that might be placed on the notion of an acceptable 'primary culture'. He argues that:[23]

> No single method of child-rearing can pretend to provide the unique path to liberal citizenship. While different parents will present vastly different dialogic and behavioural models to their children, the outcome so far as liberal theory is concerned, will typically be very much the same.

This seems to be because of the basic point that whatever the initial culture provided, conflict will arise between the parent and the child (that is, the child will have desires frustrated by parental attempts to constrain them), and as a result of this conflict the child will be able to obtain the beginnings of dialogic competence. 'At this point, they will not only cry when their desires are frustrated; they will sometimes challenge the legitimacy of their constraints by manipulating the symbolic forms placed at their disposal by their primary culture'.[24] Presumably, this basic requirement excludes some forms of child-rearing (those that fail to develop the child's language of self-control for example). But given the satisfaction of these basic requirements, are all 'dialogic and behavioural models' equally valuable as far as an outcome acceptable to a liberal is concerned ? Are stability and coherence the only criteria for a primary culture acceptable to a liberal? Granted Ackerman's commitment to the principle of autonomy and the obligations he lays on parents in relation to the realisation of this ideal, it seems that he needs to say more about restrictions on forms of 'primary culture'. For example, an indoctrinatory form is inconsistent with basic principles.

Is it possible for a non-indoctrinatory form of religious upbringing to constitute a 'primary culture' that is acceptable to a liberal ? This might be denied in several ways.

First, is it possible to give a child a religious upbringing which preserves autonomy? One way in which a decisively negative answer could be given to this question is if it could be shown that the notions of reasoning, evaluation and truth are inappropriate or impossible in religion, since this effectively destroys any possibility of autonomous judgment at all in this sphere. On this view religious belief becomes a matter of non-rational faith or cultural conditioning. Without pursuing this complex issue at this point, we can note that most liberals are prepared to keep an open mind on these aspects of the status of religious belief. We can therefore, I think, legitimately expand the last of the liberal assumptions outlined at the beginning of the article as follows:

c.   that no one set of religious beliefs can be *shown* to be objectively true, but that reasoning, evaluation, truth and therefore rationally autonomous faith are not in principle impossible in the sphere of religion.

If the possibility of a religious upbringing which preserves autonomy is admitted in principle, what other considerations are relevant to the notion? Peter Hobson, in his article 'Some reflections on parents' rights in the upbringing of their children',[25] seems to present this issue as a matter of avoiding certain methods of religious upbringing and certain kinds of religious content. But this leaves out the important question of the appropriate intention to be adopted by the parent. Clearly this is crucial. To fall within the liberal framework of our discussion, this intention must incorporate the central aim of developing the child's autonomy. But can this intention be coherently characterised in the case of a religious upbringing? The problems here arise from the questions: are parents providing such an upbringing aiming at *faith* on the part of their children or *autonomy*?

My argument seems to imply that both faith *and* autonomy are being aimed at here, but is an intention of this kind a coherent one? Incoherence can be avoided if a distinction is made between the long-term and short-term aims of the parents. Their long-term, or ultimate, aim is to place their children in a position where they can autonomously choose to accept or reject their religious faith — or religious faith in general. Since, however, these parents have decided to approach the development of their child's autonomy in religion through exposing them to their own particular religious faith, their short-term aim is the development of faith; albeit a faith which is not closed off from future revision or rejection. So a coherent way of characterising the intention of the parents is that they are aiming at *autonomy via faith*.

Two worries arise concerning this notion, one from the side of religious faith, and the other from the side of liberal values. First, must not parents who are religious believers value *faith* rather than *autonomy* in their children? The answer is that the conflict between faith and autonomy in the religious faith of a liberal is a false one. From such a position, what is demanded is autonomous religious faith based on appropriate reasoning and evaluation, not mere lip-service or conditioning. The essential freedom of the act of faith must be preserved. Religious liberal parents may well hope that their child's eventual autonomy will be exercised in favour of faith; but in the logic of their own religious, as well as liberal, position, this must remain a hope rather than a requirement. The second worry is that the parent here might not be committed to autonomy in a sufficiently strong sense to satisfy liberal demands. For example autonomy might be seen as limited in scope (its exercise being confined to details within a religious faith rather than its fundamental basis) or it might be conceived in a restrictive way (as merely a device for securing a more adequate religious faith on the part of the child). Commitment to a sufficiently strong sense of autonomy is therefore necessary if the 'autonomy via faith' intention is to be acceptable to a liberal.

A general problem which arises concerning this intention can be brought out in the following way. Despite the liberal character of the intention, it is not difficult to imagine that, given the pervasiveness and significance of the child's early experiences and in particular the powerful unintentional emotional and psychological pressures and influences that parents may exercise on their children, that the child will end its primary culture with a set of fixed religious beliefs that are very difficult to shake later. Two connected questions arise from this observation. First, will not the parent who aims at autonomy in the long run have to take steps during the period of primary culture to see that this development of fixed religious beliefs in the child does not occur? Second, if this is so, is this compatible with the parents' other aims of instilling a particular set of beliefs? With regard to the first it seems clear that liberal parents *do* have a responsibility to ensure that their children do not emerge from their primary culture with a set of fixed beliefs, in one sense of this term. For there is an ambiguity in the notion of 'fixed beliefs'. In the strong sense, 'fixed beliefs' are so pervasively and thoroughly established that nothing can shake them. A child with a set of beliefs 'fixed' in this sense possesses the kind of 'indoctrinated state of mind' deplored by liberals. It is perfectly true that this state of mind can be developed in a child despite the explicit intention of the parents, and it is important for parents to be alert to this. Parents, therefore, have the responsibility not merely to formulate their intentions accurately but also to monitor both the methods, content and consequences of their upbringing, and to avoid and remedy anything likely to produce 'fixed beliefs' in this strong sense. There is, however, a second, weaker, sense of 'fixed beliefs' where such beliefs are not seen as 'fixed' in the sense of 'unshakeable' but 'fixed' in the sense of 'stable'. Whilst a parent has a responsibility to ensure that the child emerges from his or her primary culture without fixed beliefs in the strong sense, it seems to me that it is part of the parent's responsibility to ensure that the child emerges with fixed beliefs in the weak or 'stable' sense since such a set of stable beliefs of various kinds is necessary to the provision of a coherent primary culture for the child. This distinction between a weak and strong sense of 'fixed belief' enables us to offer an answer to the second question, namely that there is a compatibility between the aim of developing autonomy and the presentation of a particular set of beliefs provided that the beliefs developed are fixed in the weak sense (that is, stable, but open to subsequent challenge and development) and not in the strong (that is, unchangeable) sense. It is true that the nature of the beliefs actually developed is not merely a question of the intention of the parent, though the intention is important: there is a need for vigilance on his or her part of the kind outlined above. But it is not the case that such vigilance demands the avoidance by the parent of the presentation of any particular set of beliefs.

I have acknowledged the important point that, although it is necessary to attend to the explicit intentions of parents, these intentions are not the only factor influencing the nature of the beliefs eventually developed in the child. What must a parent providing a liberal religious upbringing actually *do* in order to 'avoid and remedy' the development of unshakeable religious beliefs? Little research of either a philosophical or an empirical kind has been done on this question, and treatments of religious upbringing in literature and drama tend overwhelmingly to illustrate its indoctrinatory forms. In the absence of a detailed account, however, I claim that the general features of a liberal religious upbringing can be discerned and the notion itself plausibly defended.

Such an upbringing provides the child with a definite religious framework of beliefs, practices and dispositions, but parents must be committed to a range of attitudes and procedures which lay the foundations for autonomy and guard against indoctrination. Some of these can be briefly sketched. At an appropriate point, parents should encourage the child to ask questions and be willing to respond to the questioning honestly and in a way which respects the child's developing cognitive and emotional maturity;[26] make the child aware that religion is a matter of faith rather than universally publicly agreed belief, and that there is much disagreement in this area; encourage attitudes of tolerance and understanding in relation to religious disagreement; indicate that morality is not exclusively dependent upon religion; be alert to even subtle forms of psychological or emotional blackmail; ensure that the affective, emotional and dispositional aspects of their child's religious development takes place in appropriate relationship with the cognitive aspect of that development, so that irrational, compulsive or neurotic forms of religious behaviour or response are guarded against; respect the eventual freedom of the child to refuse to participate in religious practices, and so on. Such an upbringing calls for complex and sensitive judgments on the part of the parents concerning the balance to be struck between the presentation and inculcation of their own religious views and the need to respect and facilitate their child's developing autonomy. These judgments can never be made in an ideal or abstract way and are necessarily influenced by facts of human nature which bear upon family life. Nevertheless I maintain that the general parental attitudes and procedures implied in liberal religious upbringing can be broadly outlined. These do not have the form of unrealisable ideals, but can be translated into quite concrete terms. It is true, of course, that the ideals involved here are not *wholly* realisable. In the nature of things no guarantee could ever be given that any form of child upbringing will lead to fully autonomous judgment on the part of the child. Indeed, the aim of 'fully autonomous judgment' is itself unrealistic; autonomy is always a matter of degree.

Religion and Primary Culture

Can it therefore be claimed that a non-indoctrinatory form of religious upbringing can be regarded as an acceptable form of 'primary culture' with which to equip a child?

This claim might be rejected on the grounds that whilst the arguments advanced hold true for the presentation of certain kinds of 'sets of beliefs', the presentation of particular sets of *religious* beliefs cannot be justified in the same manner. The attack might be developed in the following way: the criterion of an acceptable 'primary culture' is that it should be 'the least restrictive environment consistent with (the child's) dialogic and behavioural development'.[27] But the provision of a religious element goes beyond this necessary minimum. The child unquestionably needs in a very fundamental sense at this stage things such as language, consistency and coherence of parental behaviour and expectations, love, moral training and so on. But is religion *necessary* or *fundamental* in quite the same way? Should it not be left out of a child's primary upbringing and introduced at a point when the child is begining to think for him or herself? In my view there are a range of arguments which can be developed against this attack:

1. Religion is not merely a set of propositions about a range of rather abstract questions such that it can be left for treatment until the child is able to tackle questions of this kind for him or herself. Religion involves a range of social practices, attitudes, rituals, etc. and is very much more closely linked to *culture* (as claimed by, for example, Durkheim) than is realised by the proponents of religiously neutral child upbringing. In many cases, to ask a family to excise the religious elements from its culture for the purpose of child upbringing is in effect to ask it to change its culture completely. This would clearly seem to infringe the liberal principle of freedom of religion. As we saw earlier, whilst this principle does not extend to the right to frustrate the eventual autonomy of the child, it cannot be restricted so much that the family is forced to stop practising its religion altogether.

2. It is impossible for a parent who practises a religious faith to insulate his or her children from that faith. This is because it will colour the child's view of life, his or her substantive moral commitments and values, the patterns of behaviour in the family and so on. So it will inevitably be 'caught' by the child brought up in the family as part of the 'subtle and continuous reinforcement of cultural norms'[28] to which Ackerman draws attention. But far from constituting an argument *against* removing religion at the primary stage, does not this lend substance to the worries mentioned earlier about picking up fixed beliefs? These worries are eased by the argument developed above that it is possible to harmonise the presentation of a particular set of religious beliefs with a concern for the development of the autonomy of the child. What seems clear is that if the right of a parent to exercise religious freedom is conceded, then it will be impossible for that parent to isolate the children from being influenced by his or her faith, despite the concern that ultimately they should make up their own minds about it. Since 'ought' implies 'can' is it possible to claim that a parent enjoying an appropriate degree of religious freedom has an obligation to excise all religious elements from the upbringing of children?

3. If an account of the nature of the religious domain can be given which stresses the significance of *practice* to religious meaning and understanding and the importance for autonomous choice of being 'on the inside' of a given religion then a liberal parent could argue that giving a religious upbringing is in fact giving the child an experience which will enable the child to evaluate religion for him or herself in a significant way. This could be linked to the point that it is impossible to develop an adequate understanding of religion *in abstracto*, but that this can only be achieved through a particular religion. So, it might be argued, far from hindering the child's capacity for autonomy in this field, the provision of an appropriate form of religious upbringing is in fact facilitating it.

4. It is not possible to separate out moral from religious discourse and values in quite the way envisaged by the proponent of 'religiously neutral' upbringing.

Conclusion

In conclusion, I argue that there is a non-indoctrinatory form of religious upbringing which a liberal can in good conscience claim a right to offer to his or her child. This is because:

a. there are good reasons for holding that a parent has a right to introduce the child to a 'primary culture' that the parent

      — rather than the child or other adults — has substantially determined;

b.   in the light of the arguments (1) to (4) outlined above it can be claimed that this 'primary culture' can contain religious elements;

c.   if the parent avoids indoctrination and takes other steps to safeguard autonomy, such as accepting the eventual exposure of the child to other influences which might help him or her to form life ideals, there is little need to be concerned that (a) and (b) will hinder the development of the child's personal and moral autonomy — an aim which, as a liberal, the parent must hold as fundamental.

The commitments on the part of the parents implied in (c) have important implications for the kind of rights they can legitimately claim over the subsequent formal education and schooling of their children.[29]

Notes

1.   D Bridges, 'Non-paternalistic arguments in support of parents' rights over their children's education,' *Journal of Philosophy of Education,* 18, 1984, pp. 55–61.

2.   J E Coons and S D Sugarman, *Education by Choice: the case for family control,* Berkeley, University of California Press, 1978, p. 45.

3.   D Bridges, *op. cit.,* p. 56.

4.   See J E Coons and S D Sugarman, *op. cit.,* chapter 4.

5.   J E Coons and S D Sugarman, *op. cit.,* p. 72.

6.   J E Coons and S D Sugarman, *op. cit.,* p. 72.

7.   J E Coons and S D Sugarman, *op. cit.,* p. 71.

8.   J E Coons and S D Sugarman, *op. cit.,* especially chapter 5.

9.   J E Coons and S D Sugarman, *op. cit.,* p. 85.

10.   For an account of parents' educational rights and duties from this perspective see P White, *Beyond Domination,* London, Routledge and Kegan Paul, 1983, especially chapter 5.

11.   D Bridges, *op. cit.,* pp. 58–9.

12.   D Bridges, *op. cit.,* p. 58.

13.   D Bridges, *op. cit.,* p. 58.

14.   S Lukes, *Power: a radical view,* London, Macmillan, 1974, p. 23.

15.   S Lukes, *op. cit.,* p. 24. For an interesting discussion of Lukes' argument see P White, *op. cit.,* pp. 19–30.

16.   J P White, *The Aims of Education Re-stated,* London, Routledge and Kegan Paul, 1982, pp. 166-167.

17.   J P White, *op. cit.,* p. 166.

18.   J P White, 'Indoctrination and intentions' and 'Indoctrination without doctrines?' in I Snook (ed.), *Concepts of Indoctrination: philosophical essays,* London, Routledge and Kegan Paul, 1972.

19.   B A Ackerman, *Social Justice in the Liberal State,* New Haven, Yale University Press, 1980.

20.   B A Ackerman, *op. cit.,* p. 155.

21.   B A Ackerman, *op. cit.,* p. 141.

22.   B A Ackerman, *op. cit.,* p. 117 (author's emphasis).

23.   B A Ackerman, *op. cit.,* pp. 140–141.

24.   B A Ackerman, *op. cit.,* p. 141.

25.   P Hobson, 'Some reflections on parents' rights in the upbringing of their children,' *Journal of Philosophy of Education,* 18, 1984, pp. 63–74.

26.   See G B Matthews, *Philosophy and the Young Child,* Cambridge, Massachusetts, Harvard University Press, 1980, for an account of the philosophical significance

of the questioning of young children and the importance of adult encouragement of this embryonic philosophising for the enhancement of the spirit of independent intellectual enquiry in children.

27. B A Ackerman, *op. cit.,* p. 152.
28. B A Ackerman, *op. cit.,* p. 147.
29. I would like to thank John White for his very helpful critical comments on the ideas developed here, and members of the Cambridge and West Midlands branches of the Philosophy of Education Society of Great Britain for their discussion of earlier versions of this paper.

4.2 Learning to become a Christian
Dean M Martin

Learning to become a Christian is a rich and multi-faceted matter. Likewise, teaching others in Christian ways places serious and many-sided demands upon those who would undertake the task. Much to the chagrin of religious teachers within the church setting, learning does not always transpire, even given the appropriate instructional activities and the teacher's best efforts. On the other hand, it is consoling to note that a very considerable amount of learning in young and old alike takes place when no explicit teaching is performed. Such observations as these not only mark a logical distinction between teaching and learning, but they also call attention to the highly ramified non-instructional settings and ways in which one comes to learn the manifold components of the Christian faith and life. In a discussion of such learning, therefore, completeness becomes a receding goal and one must chasten any lofty expectations. What is offered instead is a sketch of some of the salient features and movements in the learning and, where relevant, the teaching as well. It is important to point out that the interests in the following pages are philosophical rather than psychological. The latter, if present at all, are quite incidental. By the same token, the essay shows a continuing indebtedness to Ludwig Wittgenstein[1] and those influenced by his philosophical writings.

The two major segments, in turn, are given over to a treatment of how the learner gains the ability to use the concepts of the faith and how he or she begins to assimilate the beliefs of Christianity. It is explicitly acknowledged that these concerns are inextricably bound together. Nonetheless, there are important distinctions between them and, thus, pertinent things that deserve noting about the one that are inappropriate to the other. The concepts, for example, are likened to capacities which one acquires and therewith exercises in verbal and non-verbal ways. Special consideration is given to the learning of the concept of God. The fundamental beliefs of the church, by comparison, are truths that Christians live by. In this context, it is pointed out from various angles that the Christian teaching takes the form of a kind of enculturation rather than indoctrination with all its pejorative overtones. It will be argued withal that the learning which transpires within the church is preparatory for the actual embracing of the Christian faith by the learners and the gradual reduplicating of it in their own lives. By so doing, the initiates are to become marked by all the changes in their affections and actions that are already integrally tied up with and required by the concepts and beliefs of Christianity. Indeed, only when the affections and behaviour are appropriately transformed do the words of faith fit the mouth of the believer.

The words of faith

In order to achieve clarity about the meaning of a word, Wittgenstein often admonishes his reader to look at the actual uses to which it is put. An investigation of the established uses will lay everything open to view, including the meaning.[2] By offering such a reminder, Wittgenstein is fighting a very common, but not stupid, prejudice of regarding the meaning as an object for which a word stands (like a name or label) or as an accompanying mental process. An alternative approach sometimes taken by Wittgenstein in order to get an unclouded view of its meaning is to ask how a particular word is learned or taught. There is a close link between the proceedings that therein transpire and the determination of what a word means.[3] Whether dealing with number or colour words, the sensation of pain, or the concept of good in ethics, Wittgenstein is repeatedly preoccupied with how people, typically the young, come to master the use of this or that word. As a result, it has been said that in his philosophical work, Wittgenstein makes a 'pedagogical turn'.[4] Even the learning of religious concepts such as 'God' does not escape his occasional investigation (for example, *Lectures and Conversations*, p. 59 and *Culture and Value*, p. 82). His remarks in this regard, though brief, are sufficiently provocative and fetching to warrant extension. It is with this interest that focus is fixed on the multitude of ways in which the words germane to the religious life come to be acquired by one who is a potential candidate for the Christian faith.

It is worth being reminded at the outset that children (or any other aspirant to the faith) are taught to use Christian concepts by those who already share the words of faith – parsons and priests, teachers and elders, mothers and fathers, to name a few. That is, the concepts are learned within the Christian community where they have instituted ruled uses. To note that the uses of concepts like 'God', 'creation', 'grace', 'sin', etc. are rule-governed is simply to say that those uses are public rather than private or esoteric, regulated rather than random or contrived. Indeed, what counts as the correct use of a particular word is already embedded in the language of believers and determined by longstanding consensus. As a matter of course, therefore, the learner of things religious must be trained to employ the words in accord with established practice as clearly exemplified in the pages of scripture and other paradigmatic instances of the language of faith. The pupils are not merely brought thereby to speak as others around them speak who are believers; they are taught to use the concepts in ruled ways. In keeping with this fact, there is a massive array of ways in which the religious teacher will question, chide, prompt, guide and encourage the learners in the correct wielding of this or that concept. With all such teaching efforts, there just is a proper compulsion imposed upon the pupils in the learning of the religious (or any other) concepts which is akin to the necessity found in logic. For this reason, the rules arbitrating the appropriate exercise of Christian words may be referred to as comprising a logic or grammar of faith.[5]

Though the uses to which one can put the concepts are regulated via rules, the proceedings that take place in the teaching and learning are as variegated as the kinds of concepts within the Christian faith.[6] Most of the instruction, however, involves utilising a discernible range of teaching devices, some more fundamental than others. None of them is technical. All of them, in fact, turn out to be readily accessible in the home as well as the church. Thus, the young students are directed to biblical stories, the words and deeds of Jesus, commands and beliefs, parables and allegories, proverbs and psalms. In addition, they are asked to memorise scripture verses, repeat the creeds, sing songs and say prayers. Then, too, there is the even more informal and improvised use of other aids of instruction such as pictures, illustrations (real or imagined), probing questions, lively anecdotes, serious admonitions, etc. In the course of these manifold procedures of teaching and over time, the pupils will begin to discern the ways in which such concepts as 'God', 'sin', 'final judgment' and 'salvation' are put to work. By means of the bible and associated materials, the teacher sees to it that the words of faith are placed in such sequences and appropriate contexts that the ruled uses become apparent. There will, indeed, be occasions on which the teacher will make more direct appeal to the rules of use. In correcting a misguided use of a word, the teacher might interject: 'You cannot say ...' or 'There is no such thing as ... here.' However, the instruction only infrequently takes such a turn, for the pupils are not so much learning to rehearse the rules as acquiring the ability to speak.

Sunday school, catechism class and the home as well provide the stages for straightforward instruction in the faith and its ingredient language. Herein the teacher's efforts constitute the primary focus. What must be remembered, however, is that the learners are elsewhere exposed to the concepts as they are exercised in a wide spectrum of circumstances and for any number of purposes where no intentional act of teaching is undertaken. The fact is that it is typically by means of such exposure, rather than instruction as such, that religious language (or any other) is acquired. Within the church, the setting of worship in its numerous forms is of special interest. For herein the role of the words of faith is quite pronounced. Further, and related, the surroundings of worship (like the pages of scripture) bring into rather bold relief the component of pathos — awe, reverence, gratitude, etc. — that is so closely tied to the language. Too, although the aspirants remain, as it were, one step removed from the faith, they do become participants in the activities of worship. In the singing of hymns, in prayers of praise and penitence, in credal affirmations of faith, in sermonic reflections and biblical readings — in these and other activities[7] the concepts are employed by those gathered. The ruled uses of the relevant words can be gleaned by the learners by means of the observing, the following along, and the involvement in the practices which provide the original home for the words. Through the repeated association of certain themes — God and grace, sin and guilt — coupled with the human responsiveness in worship, the language of faith takes on life and meaning.

Even in isolation from worship and the deliberate instructional efforts of the faithful, a wealth of learning transpires quite inadvertently. That is, the language of religion (like other language) is mainly learned by long exposure to the spontaneous and unrehearsed fashion in which adult believers — often, though not only, one's parents — speak to one another and with those outside the faith. In such cases, the learners' attention will be fixed on the ways in which certain words are employed, how various remarks bear on one another and how the believers fit their behaviour (linguistic and non-linguistic) into this or that set of surroundings.[8] In short, the learners will give heed to the words used, surely, but also to the tissue of linguistic exchange, the ebb and flow of action and reaction. The learners will be impressed to see how the concepts of the faith are caught up and put to work by others in very compelling ways and over a gamut of circumstances — in mourning with those who mourn, in loving one's neighbour, in bearing testimony to the Gospel, in extending a Christian greeting, in forgiving one another, in hoping, giving, feeding, correcting, etc. Within these and a host of other activities, the words get ordered such that the attentive aspirants can hardly fail to notice. Such instances begin to show, besides, how the concepts are tightly woven into the fabric of the Christian form of life and exercised in non-verbal as well as verbal ways. Equally evident is the fact that the concepts are most powerfully wielded in the stream of life itself. Disengaged from those ordinary contexts in life (and worship too) the words of faith hang in the air. The occasions for their application are lacking.

In the light of the foregoing, it comes as no surprise that the learning of the language of faith is gradual and piecemeal — as it is with the rest of our concepts. There is no short route to an understanding of that language, no immediate and intuitive grasp. The learnings, like the teaching, takes place over a protracted stretch of time. The students are thereby steeped in the words of faith. They are, as it were, enculturated to and by them in a second-hand, or third person, fashion.[9] That is, the language is a language that belongs in the mouths of others but is imparted, bit by bit, to the aspirants. As the learners listen to the others as they speak, participate in sabbath worship, are imbibed with biblical story and verse, answer difficult questions about beliefs in catechism class, come to pray at appropriate times, etc. – as these instances accumulate, there begin to emerge some abilities, predominantly verbal in character. As the pupils exhibit their ability in speech not once and by chance but regularly, then they may be said, in that respect, to possess the concepts. Part of having or understanding the concepts is shown in the fact that they know the revelant circumstances, the time and the place and the way to speak. All of this is simply to provide notice that the acquisition of the concepts consists in developing particular capacities or skills.[10] Concepts *are* capacities belonging first to others and, with training, to the prospective candidate. The pupils manifest their powers with the language not by thinking a correlative object (called the meaning) or by way of a peculiar mental process, but by flexing the words in ruled ways – in praying, singing, praising God, stating beliefs and a host of others.

Nonetheless, conceptual powers are not exhausted by putting the words on one's lips in an ordered and coherent manner. The competencies which the concepts authorise are more far-reaching and involve the reordering and redirecting of one's affections. The capacities, in short, are not only linguistic but non-linguistic as well. If the concepts enable the learners to speak, they must also be capacitated by them to fear and love God, hate that which is evil, be joyous in tribulation, take little thought about tomorrow, and be hopeful, forgiving, kind and humble. This is part of their meaning and the concepts are not fully understood unless those affective and behavioural alterations eventually issue. Understanding the words of religion is not just a matter of words alone.[11] Indeed, the demands imposed upon the learners by the language of faith are so arduous and deep that it is no wonder at all that the language must become genuinely their own, in the first-person mode of expression rather than the third-person, if one is to be changed in the requisite ways. If, instead, the words of faith belong to the pupils only by way of enculturation, by virtue of others and through exposure, this is not enough. The learners, in a more deliberate and self-conscious mode, must embrace the faith and reduplicate it in their own lives. The pupils must, so to speak, fit their lives to the language and allow the governing concepts to alter their wishes, aims, desires, emotions and loves. When the transformation occurs, then even the linguistic uses of the concepts become an actual performance of their own faith, not just a demonstration of important verbal skills. The language is both the expression of such a change as well as the cause of it.

Central and deep as it is in the faith, the concept 'God' provides a fitting example of some of the themes already addressed. In religious instruction, that concept is among the earliest learned.[12] Moreover, the term is taught and learned in ordinary ways and in settings that include the home, church classrooms and sanctuaries of worship. Children begin to acquire the concept largely through stories, for example, the stories of creation, Adam and Eve, perhaps Noah and the flood. Other biblical narratives also fill out the concept, such as Moses and the law, stories of God's judgment upon Israel and, ultimately, the news that Jesus is God's son. In time, the learner begins to be able to use certain expressions such as 'creator', 'judge', 'God's will', 'disobedience to God', 'the love of God', and many more. In short, the pupils come to learn many of the ruled ways of using the word 'God'; they discern what can and cannot be said of God. Naturally, along the way, there will be training and correction if the students go wrong. For instance, they will need to be helped to see that, despite some superficial similarities, the term 'God' is not used in the same way as is a proper name. It has a very different role from that given to the names of biblical figures (like Moses) or one's own kindred and acquaintances. (Cf. *Lectures and Conversations*, p. 59.) The child, after all, does not learn the meaning of 'God' by having someone point and say: 'That's God'. The term 'God', that is, is not a name in any ordinary sense, but a concept. (Cf. *Culture and Value*, p. 50.) Some pictorial ways of speaking of God can be misleading in this connection, for example, that God walks through the garden, sees, hears, etc. The pupil must learn the techniques for using such expressions. For example, there will be no talk of ankles, eyebrows or earlobes; nor of a body or even a person with a name! God is a spirit and invisible rather than a person. In sometimes fledgling ways, thereby, the students are learning the grammar of the concept 'God' – how to use it in ways that make sense. They find that, at the behest of teachers and parents, scripture and sermon, they must forfeit some ways of speaking in favour of other ways.

It should already be apparent that the language linked to 'God' is not a technical jargon, requiring specialised tools for teaching. There is an ordinary range of words – 'creator', 'just', 'power', and many others. But these are used in very particular ways when referring to God. In the religious context, talk of 'God's law' or 'eternal love' and speaking of God as 'final judge' or 'saviour of the world' – these remain at a logical distance from the primary, that is ordinary, uses of the ingredient terms of 'law', 'love', 'judge', and 'saviour'.[13] The ramifications these words receive in reference to 'God' constitute a part of the grammar of that concept. By way of good teachers, the bible, hymns, liturgy and the rest, the student is exposed to the guarded ways of exercising these vivid and graphic means of speaking about God. Metaphor, parable, stories, allegories are the necessary and enriching means of instruction. With a little imagination on the part of the pupil, the extended, or secondary, uses of the relevant descriptive phrases regarding God can thus be learned. But the distance, the differences, which separate the secondary sense from the customary employment can only be given the right effect for those who are already familiar with those ordinary uses. 'Could you explain the concept of ... God's goodness?', Wittgenstein asks, 'without using the concept of goodness?' He replies: 'If you want to get the right *effect* with your words, certainly not.' (*Culture and Value*, p. 80.) The point being made is a logical one, not a psychological one.[14] The learners will be unable to see the force of the extended ways various terms apply to God if they are bereft of those daily modes of language to which the religious uses stand in a somewhat dissonant relation.

Christian worship is one pivotal setting in which the God-concept is exercised in ways that provide it with appropriate distinctiveness and depth. For, among other things, worship calls into the foreground the affective elements so closely bound to the linguistic uses of the concept 'God'. In hymns and the bible, in sacrament and sermon, in liturgy and prayer, it becomes evident to an aspirant that the logic of 'God' is such that before God one acknowledges guilt and gratitude; one lays before God one's loves and life; one worships God in fear and in faith. These connections are not fortuitous. Though the young learner may be only partially prepared for such deep pathos, it constitutes part of the formation of the concept 'God'. That is, without such things as fear, contrition, and increasing love for God, the concept has not been fully understood. The concept and the affections emerge together. The pupil, in short, does not know the true God or know God truly by a simple use of the word 'God'. God is genuinely known only when God's identity is established in a manner that includes one's passions.[15]

A closely related but rather different point should be emphasised in this connection, *viz.* that worship is not cut off from occasions of deep passional significance in daily life such as guilt and sin, birth and death, joy and suffering. In these and many other natural daily matrices (and not just in worship) the word 'God' is also employed in vigorous ways. It is the gravity and poignancy of the surroundings that make such an appeal to God fitting. But the point is that these events of life get caught up in communal worship as well — in prayer, praise, and confession, for instance. The religious practices, along with the ingredient concepts, would not be what they are without the inextricable link with the wrenching circumstances of life.[16] Although younger learners may have little or no exposure to such circumstances, the force of the concept 'God' depends in part on what is outside of religion, in life itself as it were. (Cf. *Culture and Value*, p. 86.)

Unshakeable beliefs

The rules governing religious concepts — 'God', 'Holy Spirit', 'sin', 'love', 'last judgment', etc. — have binding power within the

Christian community. That is, if the learners are capacitated to use them in linguistic and non-linguistic ways, they must exercise them like *this* and the manner is given in and with the teaching. Closely interlaced with them, however, are a number of explicit teachings, or doctrines, of the church. That God created the heavens and the earth, that humankind is fallen, that Christ died to save the ungodly, that he was resurrected from the dead, that God will be the final judge of all humanity − these and other graphic beliefs are taught as fundamental convictions that stand at the bedrock of the Christian faith. There is an intimate relation between the foundational beliefs and the grammatical rules because the former, like the latter, authoritatively determine what can and cannot be said within the context of the faith. In that respect at least, those tenets of Christianity also comprise a part of the grammar of faith. They stand at a comparably deep logical level with the rules governing the concepts.[17] The fact that these two components are inseparable also becomes conspicuous in the teaching and learning of how to become a Christian. They emerge together in the training just as they are found together in the literature and worship of the Christian fellowship. More precisely, in learning the requisite concepts, one of the capacities which the learner acquires is doctrinal ability, that is, the ability to state and tie together certain beliefs. On the other hand, in learning the central beliefs, the student is given ready access to some pivotal uses of the concepts. In treating the instruction and learning associated with the fundamentals of faith, attention is given, in turn, to the content, method and aim of the teaching.

Because they are so tightly knit together, it is a bit artificial to isolate the fundamental beliefs from the concepts as though now the former alone comprise the *content* of the teaching. Moreover, the beliefs, like the words of faith, are taught and learned from within much broader surroundings that include multiple religious practices (prayers, hymns, etc.), affections and, indeed, the way or form of life of those who have made the faith their own. Thus, as noted earlier and amplified subsequently, 'enculturation' is the more accurately descriptive term to use (rather than, say, 'indoctrination') in reference to these proceedings.[18] Yet there are the teachings, the basic truths, of faith which form an essential part of the pedagogical content. In informal and gentle ways, they are presented as matters of certainty. Meanwhile, the pupils imbibe the teachings (like the concepts and other practices) in a second-hand manner and primarily on the authority of the adults who teach them. Obviously, not all of the church's teachings stand at the logically fundamental level. For the most part, they are the sorts of beliefs that are gathered up and conveniently summarised in Christian credal affirmations. A belief which does merit this status, however, would not rightly be described as an opinion; still less would one speak of an hypothesis or theory. All of these sound queer. For this reason, words like 'doctrine' or even 'dogma' are used. (*Lectures and Conversations*, p. 57.) Not only do the fundamental beliefs give expression to the positive and irreducible substance of faith, but also they would serve as brakes, intended to halt the young prospect − like those who already heartily embrace the faith − from being blown about by the winds of numerous alien doctrines. (Cf. *Culture and Value*, p. 29.)

In this light, it is appropriate to notice that when the central doctrines of Christianity are imparted to the learner, the *method* is such that no appeal is made by the teacher to empirical reasoning or evidence. But this is not a defect in the teaching procedures as some might think who regard the methods of science as the final tribunal for adjudicating questions of truth. Indeed, the beliefs that God is maker of all things, that God judges the wickedness of humanity, that Christ is God incarnate, that his life, death and resurrection bring redemption from sin, that the church is the body of Christ − these articles of faith and others are empirically groundless. They do not pretend to be otherwise. That is the *character* of religious beliefs as contrasted with scientific hypotheses. Alternatively, if there were evidence upon which the tenets of faith were grounded, then this would undermine their role in the religious life. (*Lectures and Conversations*, p. 56.) Believers simply do not treat these convictions as matters of reasonability. (*Lectures and Conversations*, p. 58.) Although religion urges this teaching or that, Wittgenstein (*Culture and Value*, p. 29) points out:

> it cannot justify this and once it even tries to, it becomes repellent; because for every reason it offers there is a valid counter-reason. It is more convincing to say 'Think like this! however strangely it may strike you' or 'Won't you do this? − however repugnant you find it.'

That is to say, those who impart such a belief without apology, but with care and tenderness, are more correct than those who try to offer evidential grounds. (*Lectures and Conversations*, p. 63.) The primary point then is: this non-evidential method of instruction is not taken up in the temporary absence of a superior one. In their own lives and as they instruct others, believers do not make use of reason here. (*Lectures and Conversations*, p. 59.)

Naturally, there will be generous use of sacred writ and church tradition in tutoring young learners in the faith. But even the bible, still less tradition, is not so much used as grounds in consequence of which the pupil is to accept the beliefs since, strictly speaking, an appeal to biblical warrant can only serve as a viable reason for those who already share the faith. Or, stated directly − and this is the important element, the rudimentary beliefs are as foundational as any grounds that might be given in support of them within religion! Therefore, it would be more accurate to say that children, in an innocent and unselfconscious way, believe what is taught them seriously by adults within the church. Once more, they are simply being acculturated to Christian ways. In the instructional setting, then, the text is used to provide rich and indispensable access to those central convictions which, though groundless, need to be sketched out by the teacher for the aspirants. The latter are steeped in the stories of creation and fall, prophetic diatribes, Jesus' teachings, the drama of the Passion narrative and the words of Peter and Paul. When these are joined with the teacher's own inventive devices and with regular participation in the activities of worship, the beliefs (like the concepts) commence to loom large for the young learners. After a while, they begin to see that the miscellany of fundamental teachings meshes together in important ways. Light begins to dawn gradually over the landscape of the doctrines so that their general contours and relations take shape. The sweep from creation to final judgment, the fall of humanity coupled with God's unchanging grace in Christ — these connections and more become apparent to the pupils. It could even be said that the inculcated beliefs combine to constitute a loose system, one which bespeaks a certain picture of the world, the self and God. *Within* that framework of underived foundational tenets shared by the faithful, there are even certain distinctive lines of reasoning that are granted legitimacy and to which appeal can be made by believers on specifiable occasions.[19]

Interestingly enough, there is a fairly striking parallel here with Wittgenstein's description of how a child forms a picture of the world when brought up in a culture in which education and science are the prevailing influences.[20] Of special significance is the observation that, while prescribing the ordinary course of reasoning, the scientific view of the world has at its foundations a veritable nest of fundamental propositions that are themselves imparted to the child in an ungrounded manner. Not even experience, the mainstay of science itself, can accurately be said to provide grounds on the basis of which the learner inherits them. Rather, as the instruction proceeds, the child learns to believe a wide, but not disconnected, array of things, most of it on human authority and in an unquestioning way. Some judgments, though not all, are so deeply embedded in the rest that is learned that they stay fixed in place as a foundation. That physical objects (for example, trees, books, etc.) are real, that the future will be like the past, that one has a body, two hands, a brain, that others are not automata, etc. — these and other common sense truisms which interested Wittgenstein are gulped down, so to speak, simply as a matter of course in the learning. No grounds are ever given; no ratiocination is involved in the instruction.[21] Instead of requiring grounds, the elemental judgments of common sense constitute the riverbed of all scientific enquiry. In all their breadth, they determine the kinds of reasons and evidence that are to be acknowledged, the doubts that may be sensibly entertained, etc. The groundless propositions that are at the foundations, moreover, do form a network of beliefs — a kind of mythology, as Wittgenstein calls it — which issues in a particular picture of the world. In due season, then, the individual learns to judge in conformity with others — *viz.*, scientifically,

Despite the obvious similarities, there are differences between the proceedings just described and the non-empirical way in which the religious teachings are inculcated via enculturation.[22] The differences in the teaching and learning further point to a far-reaching characteristic of religious beliefs themselves. For the moment, it can be noted that the judgments associated with the commonly shared scientific view of the world are *tacitly* learned without even being formulated or stated in the various pedagogical activities or elsewhere. Foundational religious beliefs, on the other hand, must be explicitly called to the attention of the learners (via bible or other device) for their assimilation. Hand in hand with this goes the fact that in the learning, the aspirants in religion are exposed (for instance, in a service of worship) to serious occasions on which these religious convictions are gathered up in Christian creeds and openly avowed and recited. The recitation of common sense truisms, by comparison, would usually be regarded as nothing more than idle chatter at best. Moreover, the aspirant will eventually need to appropriate the church's teachings in a fully passionate and self-conscious way that is utterly unnecessary and unsolicited with foundational judgments of common sense. These features encountered in the learning are rooted in a further difference that has even broader proportions. That is, religious beliefs do not command the same kind of massive human consensus so characteristic of the normal scientific way of judging the world. On the contrary, Christian teachings typically run against the grain of any culture, including one geared toward scientific activity. So they must be expressly taught, heartily embraced and repeatedly rehearsed by the faithful. But the opposition arises not merely because the religious convictions will not be submitted to empirical investigation. Primarily it can be traced back to the reverberations which those religious teachings would introduce into an individual's life.

In view of the inherent struggle which the faith would entail, it is sometimes said that the *aim* of Christian training is to instil the beliefs in the learners such that they will cleave to them unshakeably, come what may. There is something misleading about stating the matter in just this fashion. Nevertheless, it is unobjectionable insofar as it is intended to deny that the aim is merely to get the pupil to learn the beliefs by rote and parrot them back. Moreover, it is unquestionably true that, from the start of religious instruction, the teachers, parents, deacons, and pastors, indeed, the entire congregation, seek to nurture the young in the faith. They do so with the bold hope that sooner or later the learners will passionately seize the faith and become unshakeable in it. (*Lectures and Conversations*, p. 54.) After all, adult believers, those who provide the teaching, are all too aware of the onslaughts in the face of which one must cleave to the faith. There is, for example, the compelling pull of temptation; there will be personal trial in the midst of frustration, loss, defeat; then there is the ridicule of others. Other perturbations can be imagined. Therefore, in being taught the beliefs, the aspirants are also instructed that through the ages Christians have found their beliefs to be a veritable refuge in precisely these kinds of trouble. Stated differently, no matter how powerful these occurrences may be, they are not related to religious beliefs in any way analogous to the manner in which contrary evidence disconfirms a theory or hypothesis in science. This is partly what is meant when it is said that the beliefs which are imparted are fundamental in nature; they need not be forfeited no matter how things go in the world. It is not the world with its ebb and flow which undermines faith; it is the believer's steadfastness in faith that overcomes the world.

There is yet another and related aspect to the need for unswerving faith. For it is also recognised by those who provide Christian training that the fundamental teachings of the church (like the concepts) are inseparably joined with a strenuous way of living and behaving. Thus, the beliefs are so taught that, singly and together, they hold forth a picture which, if embraced, would regulate the entire direction of one's life. (Cf. *Lectures and Conversations*, pp. 54, 56.) For instance, the learners are shown that, with these governing beliefs, they would be required to take certain risks, spend themselves in self-forgetful ways, hold earthly treasures at arm's length and receive each day and meal as a gift. They would need to learn patience, humility, love, hope and all kinds of other odd dispositions and affections that go with the beliefs. With the help of good teachers and others who care, then, the aspirants come to discern how the teachings are to be accompanied by strange passional and behavioural differences which would place a radical strain on their lives.[23] When adult believers indeed carry themselves in these ways, it becomes evident that theirs must be the most unshakeable of all beliefs for they do things here that they would not do on the basis of judgments that are far better established scientifically. (*Lectures and Conversations*, p. 54.) Taken from a different angle, it could be said that the doctrines or dogmas of the faith are finally useless unless and until they somehow take hold of individuals and are held fast by them so that they turn their lives around – unyieldingly stay turned around. (*Culture and Value*, p. 53.)

What, it should be asked, is sufficient to prompt such a radical breach in an individual's life and produce such unshakeable beliefs? Well, not the religious instruction by itself! That is why it is misleading to say that the aim of the teaching is to get the learners to hold firmly to the received beliefs – as though, along with the learning of the beliefs, how they hang together as a framework, etc., one more result could be passed on, *viz.*, the passion with which they are to be seized. It needs to be remembered that in the tutoring, the pupil gathers in the beliefs (and concepts) in a third person, or second-hand, fashion, much as one is enculturated into a set of traditions which is transmitted from one generation to another. Yet that is not sufficient. The beliefs are initially the expression of somebody else's faith − a teacher, parent, or biblical author. But the beliefs must become the first person expression of the learner's own faith.[24] What is required here is a heartfelt commitment to, an embracing of, the faith in one's own life. The conditions that placed those beliefs in others' mouths must be realised and redone by each aspirant in turn. The teaching how to become a Christian, then, in all its myriad forms and variations, is necessary but only preparatory, much like planting a seed. Wittgenstein (*Culture and Value*, p. 64) summarises the situation thus:

> It strikes me that a religious belief could only be something like a passionate commitment to a system of reference .... Instruction in a religious faith, therefore, would have to take the form of a portrayal, a description, of that system of reference, while at the same time being an appeal to conscience. And this combination would have to result in the pupil himself (*sic*), of his own accord, passionately taking hold of the system of reference. It would be as though someone were first to let me see the hopelessness of my situation and then show me the means of rescue until, of my own accord, or not at any rate led to it by my instructor, I ran to it and grasped it.

The passion, the running to it and grasping hold − all of this is absolutely ingredient. Coming to learn the framework of central beliefs (and concepts), the grammar of faith, may bring one to the brink; but no one or no instruction alone can bestow the requisite pathos upon another. In short, if no such conversion is forthcoming, it cannot be said that the teaching failed in its purpose.

By virtue of what, then, does an individual, young or old, come to seize hold of the Christian faith? One should be reluctant to pontificate here. But it could be said that life itself, that is experiences of various kinds of suffering, can educate one to such belief. (Cf. *Culture and Value*, p. 85.) The Christian religion, after all, is specifically for those who need infinite help, those in torment, the lost ones of the world. (Cf. *Culture and Value*, p. 46.) The Christian scriptures, the teachings of the church and the witness of saints and reformers, give prominent place, for instance, to the experience of guilt which is a torture to a person, causing storms within one's soul.[25] The flood of despair over one's own wretchedness can be such that it engulfs and utterly immobilises one. Though such an experience is one which comes with years, the church's teachings can provide a welcomed beacon light for such a one who has hopelessly lost the way. This, it might be said, is how Christianity fits human life. That is, while Christianity includes doctrines in its grammar, it does not offer theories. Rather, it provides (*Culture and Value*, p. 28):

a description of something that actually takes place in human life. For 'consciousness of sin' is a real event and so are despair and salvation through faith. Those who speak of such things ... are simply describing what has happened to them, whatever gloss anyone may want to put on it.

So the belief that Jesus is God incarnate or that his death and resurrection are for the sake of sinful people — these are not so much doctrines about which one speculates or gesticulates. Properly appropriated, they can turn out to be the means of one's salvation from sin. The beliefs, therefore, like the concepts, are intricately and necessarily bound up with experiences which, one might say, lie outside of religion, in life itself.[26] The learners of Christian truths may come to demonstrate deftness in stating, relating and debating the doctrines. But their learning will be mostly in vain unless they also learn, via the exigencies of life, that they must open rather than contract their hearts with respect to the means of salvation. (Cf. *Culture and Value*, p. 46.)

Concluding remarks

As the foregoing suggests, learners (really of all ages) can be and are taught so that, in time and one at a time, they may become Christians. Surely, however, even this is not the terminal point of the training; it is more like a new beginning. The personal appropriation of the words and beliefs of Christianity is not a task for a single hour; nor is it a pastime. So if the pupils have been converted *to* Christianity, it should also be noted that they are now to be continually built up, instructed, challenged and chastened *by* Christianity.[27] With this, the spotlight shifts from a context in which instruction is initiated by and dependent upon the efforts of others while the pupils learn from a position that is one step removed. Rather, now the interest, even the happy compulsion, for deeper and more heartfelt faith stems from the new initiates themselves. Of course, the progress comes slowly by means of small achievements with each passing day and one still does need the bible, worship, caring Christian brothers and sisters and, yes, even teachers. But the gains begin to add up over the course of years and even one's lifetime. Dispositions are made more malleable to the rules of faith; beliefs come to be held with increasing steadfastness; witness becomes more gladhearted and true; the world's interests fade in significance; temptation is overcome one day at a time. The list could be extended. In sum, there is progress, if also perhaps retrogression. With the passing of the years, everything in the believers' lives — the world, other persons, their possessions, etc. — becomes different and they find that they are doing things of which they never thought themselves capable. (Cf. *Culture and Value*, p. 33.)

The story is related that one of Wittgenstein's pupils wrote him, indicating that he had become a Christian. The pupil further intimated in the letter that he, Wittgenstein, was partly responsible for this conversion because, on his advice, the student had begun a reading of Soren Kierkegaard's pages. Wittgenstein, it is said, wrote back to say: 'If someone tells me that he has bought the outfit of a tightrope-walker I am not impressed until I see what is done with it.'[28] The pedagogy of Christianity fits one with the outfit, but getting one's balance, as it were, in mid-air, and *keeping* it, is the demand and the promise of faith. Sustaining the analogy, Wittgenstein says elsewhere that the serious religious person 'is like a tightrope walker. He almost looks as though he were walking on nothing but air. His support is the slenderest imaginable. And yet it is really possible to walk on it.' (*Culture and Value*, p. 73.) If, therefore, the initiates find themselves one day thinking and willing and doing things that they once thought impossible, then they may remember with great gratitude some of their teachers, their parents, Christian friends who nurtured them, etc. But finally they likely will acknowledge that it was a miracle that faith became implanted in their hearts. They probably will confess that it was not so much themselves or even quite their teachers that brought this about, but God in Christ Jesus drawing them unto himself. For this, too, is part of the grammar of faith.

Notes

1. References to Wittgenstein's works which treat religious themes directly and in a more sustained way will be highlighted by inclusion (in abbreviated form) in the body of the essay. These include: *Lectures and Conversations on Aesthetics, Psychology and Religious Belief* (edited by Cyril Barrett, Oxford, Basil Blackwell, 1966) and *Culture and Value* (edited by G H von Wright in collaboration with Heikki Nyman and translated by Peter Winch, Oxford, Basil Blackwell, 1980). Throughout the following notes references to the former will be abbreviated as LC, followed by page number; the latter is abbreviated as CV, followed by page number. References to other writings of Wittgenstein will be made (also in abbreviated form) in notes. These include: *Philosophical Investigations* (translated by G E M Anscombe, New York, Macmillan, 1953); *Zettel* (edited by G E M Anscombe and G H von Wright and translated by G E M Anscombe, Berkeley and Los Angeles, University of California Press, 1967); and *On Certainty* (edited by G E M Anscombe and G H von Wright and translated by Denis Paul and G E M Anscombe, New York and Evanston, Harper and Row, 1969). These works are abbreviated, respectively, as follows: PI, Z, and OC. Except where noted, the numbers following these abbreviations will designate the relevant sections into which the works are divided.

2. On the connection between meaning and use, cf. especially PI, 43, 116, 340, 432, p. 212, p. 220.

3. On this topic cf. especially PI, 5, 77, p. 226; also Z, 387, 412. Cf. also an early remark by Wittgenstein concerning the importance of considering how a word is learned or taught in D A T Gasking and A C Jackson, 'Wittgenstein as a teacher,' in K T Fann (ed.), *Ludwig Wittgenstein: the man and his philosophy,* New York, Dell Publishing Company, 1967, p. 54.

4. The phrase is taken from C J B Macmillan, 'Wittgenstein and the problems of teaching and learning,' *Proceedings of the Sixth International Wittgenstein Symposium, Volume 8: Language and Ontology*, Hingham, Massachusetts, D Reidel Publishing Company, 1982, p. 483 and the same author's 'On certainty and indoctrination,' *Synthese*, 56, 1983, p. 363. It is highly probable that the prominence given to how children are taught and learn language and its practices stems, in

no small part, from Wittgenstein's years as a school teacher in remote Austrian villages between 1920-26. That period would certainly have provided him with a wealth of first-hand observations from which to draw in reminding his readers of the ordinary proceedings involved as a child masters one or another concept. W W Bartley makes a more specific and daring claim. He proposes that the themes of the Austrian, or Glockel, School Reform Movement (in which, he claims, Wittgenstein took an active part) were directly influential in the development of the views represented in the PI. Cf W W Bartley, *Wittgenstein,* London, Quartet Books, 1974, pp. 103 – 04. This assessment has been seriously questioned by Eugene C Hargrove in his 'Wittgenstein, Bartley, and the Glockel School Reform,' *Journal of the History of Philosophy,* 18, 1980, pp. 453 – 61.

5.   Thus Paul Holmer's penetrating work entitled *The Grammar of Faith,* San Francisco, Harper and Row, 1978, in which the author wrestles with some very taxing religious and philosophical issues. Cf. especially his essay entitled 'What theology is and does: again,' pp. 17 – 36. At the same time, the reader is referred to various passages in Wittgenstein's works which treat the notion of rules, grammar and other related topics. For example, cf. PI, 31, 54, 198, 202, 206, 224, 225, 371, 373, 496, 497; also Z, 55, 318, 320. In PI, 373, Wittgenstein likens theology to grammar.

6.   In assembling the remarks in this paragraph and the next, I have been helped considerably by the work of Paul Holmer, especially his 'Religion from an existential standpoint,' in J Clayton Feaver and William Horosz (eds), *Religion in Philosophical and Cultural Perspective,* Princeton, New Jersey, D Van Nostrand, 1967, pp. 147 – 73.

7.   The term 'language-games' is often used by Wittgenstein to refer to such activities as these and many others quite removed from religion – for example telling jokes, giving orders and obeying them, reporting an event, forming and testing a hypothesis, cursing, greeting, etc. This term was coined by Wittgenstein with a specific purpose in view, *viz.,* to bring into prominence the fact that speaking is interwoven into the activities of life. On this topic, cf. for instance, PI, 7, 23, 31, 116, 563, 564, p. 200.

8.   Some of these thoughts have been prompted by Rush Rhees' important article 'Wittgenstein's builders,' *Proceedings of the Aristotelian Society,* 60, 1959 – 60, especially pp. 180, 184.

9.   Cf. Paul Holmer, 'Religion from an existential standpoint,' *op. cit.,* pp. 149 – 50, 168 – 69.

10. This is a topic that gets very careful treatment in several of Paul Holmer's works. But cf. especially the essay, 'Theology and concepts,' *The Grammar of Faith, op. cit.,* pp. 136 – 158.

11. In Z, 144, Wittgenstein says: 'How words are understood is not told by words alone.' Then, in parenthesis, he adds the word 'Theology'.

12. Interestingly enough, Wittgenstein asks: 'How are we taught the word "God" (its use, that is)? I cannot give a full grammatical description of it. But I can, as it were, make some contributions to such a description; I can say a good deal about it and perhaps in time assemble a sort of collection of examples.' (CV, p. 83.) On the theme of this paragraph in my essay, cf. also Paul Holmer's 'Theology and knowing God,' *The Grammar of Faith, op. cit.,* especially pp. 200 – 12 and Rush Rhees' essay 'Religion and language,' in his book *Without Answers,* New York, Schocken Books, 1969, especially pp. 125 – 32. Cf. also D Z Phillips 'Philosophy, theology and the reality of God,' in his book *Faith and Philosophical Enquiry,* New York, Schocken Books, 1971, pp. 5 – 6.

13. Cf. Cora Diamond, 'Secondary sense,' *Proceedings of the Aristotelian Society,* 67, 1966-67, pp. 203 – 04. This essay ties together a theme in PI, especially p. 226 *(viz.* the distinction between a primary and secondary sense of a word) with remarks that Wittgenstein made about ethics and religion in his 'Lecture on ethics,' *Philosophical Review,* 74, 1965, pp. 3 – 12.

14. Again, Cora Diamond makes the point in speaking of the distinction Wittgenstein once made between a relative (primary) and absolute (secondary) use of the ethical notion of 'ought'. She says: 'That this relation holds is not an empirical claim. . . . Thus it would be confused to object to the view I have been expounding that the question which use of "ought" a child learns first, the absolute or the relative, is to be settled empirically. No use of "ought" is the absolute use if it is the only

use a person grasps.' ('Secondary sense,' *op. cit.,* pp. 201–02) The issue addressed here has a peripheral relation to the question raised by Stephen Toulmin concerning whether there are *logical* strata in our language which would display themselves in the actual acquisition of concepts. Cf. especially his 'Concepts and the explanation of human behavior,' in T Mischel (ed.), *Human Action: conceptual and empirical issues,* New York, Academic Press, 1969, pp. 79ff.

15. Cf. especially Paul Holmer, *Making Christian Sense* (Spirituality and the Christian Life Series, edited by Richard H Bell), Philadelphia, Westminster Press, 1984, pp. 54–56.

16. D Z Phillips, 'Religious beliefs and language-games,' in his book *Faith and Philosophical Enquiry, op. cit.,* pp. 96-97; also his 'Wittgenstein's full stop,' in Irving Block (ed.), *Perspectives on the Philosophy of Wittgenstein,* Oxford, Basil Blackwell, 1981, pp. 186–87.

17. Although these remarks can probably stand on their own, the reader's attention is called to my article *'On Certainty* and religious belief,' *Religious Studies,* 20, 1984, especially pp. 595–96 and 606, note 1, where this issue is addressed. The text of OC also figures heavily, albeit indirectly, in the pages which follow in the present article.

18. Though with very different interests, Richard H Gatchel argues that the term 'enculturation' is to be preferred over 'indoctrination' in his 'The evolution of the concept,' in I A Snook (ed.), *Concepts of Indoctrination,* London, Routledge and Kegan Paul, 1972, pp. 9–16.

19. Such reasons would include appeal to biblical authority (whether Moses, Jesus' teachings, Paul's letters, etc.), conciliar decisions, religious experience, the entailment of certain beliefs already placed beyond question. These types of reasons do have force, though only within the community of those who already share the faith. One kind of occasion on which appeal to such reasons, or others, would be appropriate is the case of resolving a dispute between believers over a finer point of doctrine. In such a dispute there would already be tacit agreement on the fundamental elements of the faith and therewith the sorts of grounds/reasons that would carry weight in adjudicating the disagreement. On this, cf. also my 'On certainty and religious belief,' pp. 603–05 and Norman Malcolm, 'Is it a religious belief that God exists?' in John Hick (ed.), *Faith and the Philosophers,* London, Macmillan, 1964, p. 109.

20. Norman Malcolm explores this analogy in some detail. Cf. 'The groundlessness of belief,' in his book *Thought and Knowledge,* New York, Cornell University Press, 1977, pp. 199–216. Note also my *'On Certainty* and religious belief,' *op cit.,* pp. 593–608 for an extensive treatment of the similarities. The themes summarised in this paragraph form the thrust of much of Wittgenstein's book, OC, which among other things is a discussion of G E Moore's truisms of common sense. Some of the seminal passages which would further acquaint the reader with Wittgenstein's general line of thought are as follows: OC, 95, 96, 97, 103, 105, 128, 129, 136, 137, 141, 144, 146, 147, 150, 152, 159, 162, 166, 167, 235, 273, 281, 308, 309, 358, 378, 449, 494, 510, 608, 609, 670.

21. Because the fundamental judgments are taught without rational weighing of grounds, C J B Macmillan has some concern that the mode of teaching here envisioned in Wittgenstein's OC comes very close to what recent commentators consider indoctrination. Cf. his *'On Certainty* and indoctrination,' especially pp. 365–71. As already noted, the term to be preferred in this context and with reference to religious instruction as well is 'enculturation'.

22. These differences are given more extensive treatment in my *'On Certainty* and religious belief,' *op. cit.,* pp. 608–13.

23. In emphasising this point, Norman Malcolm forcefully illustrates: 'It might be worth remarking that one could not expect a religious man to be well-adjusted to the world, if it is a teaching of his religion that he must cast off worldly considerations. A man who desired to be perfect was enjoined by Jesus to sell his possessions and give to the poor (Matthew 19:21). If any one of us were to believe in his heart that this is necessary and had the courage to act on it, he would thereby begin to live an abnormal life. This would have no tendency to prove that he had a neuropathic temperament, but rather that he was a doer of the word and not a hearer only.' ('Is it a religious belief that God exists,' *op. cit.,* p. 103.)

24. The same distinction is made by Paul Holmer in a slightly different way by suggesting that one learns in what he calls an 'about' mood – like an account that we can get from others who have travelled that way before. But this language 'about' the faith must be transformed, in the mouth of the learner, into the language 'of' faith. Cf. *The Grammar of Faith, op. cit.,* pp. 24–25.
25. On the phenomenon of guilt and its connection with religious belief, cf. Norman Malcolm's discussion of 'Anselm's arguments,' in D Z Phillips (ed.), *Religion and Understanding,* New York, Macmillan, 1967, pp. 60–61 and Malcolm's 'Is it a religious belief that God exists,' *op. cit.,* p. 110. In the former article, he cites an appropriate passage from Soren Kierkegaard's *Journals* which reads: 'There is only one proof of the truth of Christianity and that, quite rightly, is from the emotions, when the dread of sin and a heavy conscience torture a man into crossing the narrow line between despair bordering upon madness – and Christendom.'
26. Cf. this article, above.
27. Paul Holmer makes this important point in *Making Christian Sense, op. cit.,* p. 103.
28. M O'C Drury, 'Some notes on conversations with Wittgenstein,' in Rush Rhees (ed.), *Recollections of Wittgenstein,* New York, Oxford University Press, 1984, p. 88.

4.3 Religious formation in the context of social formation
Michael Warren

The underlying thesis of this article is that formation, far from being a process used mainly by religious groups to reproduce among adherents beliefs and lifestyle considered appropriate, is a central and inevitable process in all of human life. Understanding how 'formative' all aspects of social and cultural life are will lay a groundwork for understanding the importance and even urgency of formation within religious groups. Actually, as we shall see, formation assumes its inevitable importance in religious groups precisely in the face of the powerful formative structures found in wider social and cultural life. Overlooking the relationship between formation as a social and cultural fact of life and religious formation leaves one open to misconstruing religious formation as a kind of structure of manipulative control, which brings about compliance without full awareness or consent. Though distortions are possible in religious formation and they need examination and critique, categorical dismissals of religious formations' values and importance will not stand up under critical scrutiny. Here I wish to give three examples of 'formations' that affect us all but of which we tend to be marginally aware and then examine religious formation, using formation in Christian churches as my main example.

Formation of perception

At the beginning of *The Long Revolution*, Raymond Williams explores the ways in which all persons from their earliest moments must learn how to see. Though many assume their senses provide them with an accurate means of understanding the world, our senses alone cannot teach us unless the data the senses offer us are interpreted for us within some system. Williams reminds us that the information received through the senses has to be interpreted according to certain schemas before what we call 'reality' forms.[1]

> One's version of the world one inhabits has a central biological function: it is a form of interaction with one's environment which allows a person to maintain life and to achieve greater control over the environment ... We 'see' in certain ways, that is, we interpret sensory information according to certain rules, as a way of living. But these ways, these rules and interpretations, are, as a whole, neither

fixed nor constant. We can learn new rules and new interpretations, as a result of which we shall literally see in new ways.

These rules of interpretation, then, according to which we see and name reality are handed on to us from others. At least in the beginning, these rules are 'givens' we are not capable of questioning. We are formed to see in the way we do. Those familiar with Berger and Luckmann's *The Social Construction of Reality* or with the thought of philosophers of science such as Abraham Kaplan and Michael Polanyi find little new in my account of Williams' point. However, Williams moves into and strives to map territory never adequately explored by Berger and Luckmann: culture.

Culture is human formation at its widest angle:[2]

> the particular interpretations carried by particular cultures give us certain 'rules' or 'models', without which no human being can 'see' in the ordinary sense, at all. In each individual, the learning of these rules, through inheritance and culture, is kind of creation, in that the distinctively human world, the ordinary 'reality' that culture defines, forms only as the rules are learned. Particular cultures carry particular versions of reality, which can be said to create, in the sense that cultures carrying different rules ... create their own worlds which their bearers ordinarily experience.

In helping us see how our seeing is shaped by culture's ultimate sort of formation, Williams' interest is toward being able to critique and question culture as a human product. Understanding culture and its rules of interpretation as human products is a first step to questioning and talking back to these human constructs. We shall see later the significance of this matter for religious formation.

Language and the formation of thought

Another person who helps us understand how thoroughly formed our lives are is Peggy Rosenthal, in her study of the patterns that exist in language.[3] As the subtitle of her book, 'Some leading words and where they lead us', suggests, her interest is not so much with the syntactical patterns of language, even though these are themselves a kind of mould into which our thought is poured and by which it is formed. She explores another dimension of the formative power of language: the way in which the meanings of words shift over time and take on colourations and nuance that predate our thought and form it as a kind of mould within a mould. 'Words ... act as receptacles into which different disciplines and ideologies and traditions of thought pour their particular meanings, their favourite value-laden concepts.'[4] Rosenthal conceives of her 'leading words' as those which assume positions of power in a particular language and which then direct us to think and act in particular ways. Admitting that her view of our relation to these words might be alarming, she further admits that in her approach:[5]

> We are not seen as leading our own language anywhere at all, but as being led by it. Our words, even our common everyday ones, are seen as an active force in our lives; our own position with respect to them is seen as passive. This is indeed a disturbing position to find ourselves in, but ... the normal operations of language do put us in this passive position: language works to give us much less control over 'what we mean' than we generally assume we have. Even when we think we are choosing our words with care and giving them precise meanings, they can mean much more (or less) than we think; and when we use them carelessly, without thinking, they can still carry thoughts. These thoughts we are not aware of, these meanings we do no intend, can then carry us into certain beliefs and behaviour — whether or not we notice where we are going.

Rosenthal's position is similar to Williams',[6] since she is pointing out how thoroughly formed is the linguistic world we come to inhabit. We like to think of our choice of language as under our conscious control so that we say what we mean, while in fact 'words say what *they* mean more than what *we* mean'.[7] Certain words attract us and so we select them, but dimensions of that attraction and selection lie outside our conscious intentions. Rosenthal examines our culturally-conditioned predilection for the word self and for word clusters like growth, development, and potential; our preference for these words has a history, which can be examined and interpreted. Like Williams, Rosenthal's interest is in helping us become conscious of the connotative meaning already structured into words and word clusters, so we can expand our awareness and control of our own meaning. As she puts it:[8]

> We can indeed increase the extent of our consciousness of (language's) operations, as we are doing here, and thereby give ourselves more control over our language than we usually have. But unless we make this deliberate effort to watch how our words are working, we will be worked on by them and manipulated by their meanings unawares.

Basically her book is an exercise in cultural analysis, bringing into close examination the way culture puts forth leading words which are formative of meaning apart from ordinary consciousness.

This matter is of central importance in modern thought, so much so that I do not even attempt to compile a bibliography of related works.[9] Instead, I cite briefly a single book providing important questions for religious persons in the US: *The Habits of the Heart*. If Rosenthal's book extends Williams' *Keywords*, Bellah *et al.*'s

Habits of the Heart extends hers, by examining how moral confusion is masked by, at the same time it is helped along by, one's use of language, including some of the same leading words she analyses.[10] In many ways, *Habits* is an examination of language, in the sense of the choice of word and word patterns used by the persons under study. As examples, the following passages:[11]

> We are not saying that the people to whom we talked have empty selves. Most of them are serious, engaged, deeply involved in the world. But insofar as they are limited to a language of radical and individual autonomy, as many of them are, they cannot think about themselves or others as arbitrary centres of volition. They cannot express the fullness of being that is actually there.

> We found ... people often on the defensive, struggling for the biblical and republican language that could express their aspirations, often expressing themselves in the very therapeutic rhetoric that they consciously reject. *It is a rhetoric that educated middle-class Americans, and through the medium of television and other mass communications, increasingly all Americans, cannot avoid.* (Emphasis added.) And yet even those most trapped in the language of the isolated self are troubled by the nihilism they sense there and eager to find a way of overcoming the emptiness of purely arbitrary 'values'.

Bellah and his associates here seem to suggest not only that we are formed by the language available to us but also that we can be trapped within that language, locked into a mindset that an alternative language must unlock. To extend Rosenthal's metaphor, the formative mould is an iron one.

Hegemony and the formation of consciousness

Pierre Bourdieu, in his social critique of the production of taste, notes that every economic system produces among the people in it the dispositions needed for that economy to succeed.[12] If we accepted that the production of religious dispositions and frames of reference is religious formation, then, at least in part, we must also accept that the production of dispositions by an economic system is also a kind of formation, though perhaps far less conscious. This second kind of formation needs more attention if we are to understand the efficiency with which it forms.

The Italian thinker, Antonio Gramsci, in his theory of hegemony, has provided a helpful theoretical base for understanding how this social process of formation can succeed outside of our awareness. Basically hegemony is a process by which the consent of the dominated classes is obtained for programmes not in their best interests. The dominant classes shape the issues in such a way that these issues seem to embrace the needs and interests of the subordinate groups, at the same time that they mask and hide the deeper, controlling and directing interests of the dominant. For those who insist on ignoring the significance of class structures, hegemony is irreversible. Hegemony then is not raw coercion; it is one group's orchestration of compliance in another group through structuring the consciousness of the second group. Hegemony is by its nature covert, and because it shapes consciousness and action, religious persons need to understand how it works. An effective translator of Gramsci's idea for English-speakers is Raymond Williams.

Williams explains that hegemony makes use of a total way of looking at reality that saturates society to such an extent and is lived at such a depth that it becomes, for those immersed in it, simple commonsense.[13] Perhaps the best current example of hegemony is the network of commonsense, accepted 'truths' that emerge from an economic order of consumption. Persons are defined as consumers, and readily accept that definition as an appropriate *self-definition*, which as it is lived out takes on an even more stubborn taken-for-grantedness. As Williams put it,[14] hegemony:

> is the central, effective and dominant system of meanings and values, which are not merely abstract but which are organised and lived. That is why hegemony is not to be understood at the level of mere opinion or mere manipulation. It is whole body of practices and expectations; our assignments of energy, our ordinary understanding of the nature of man and of his world. It is a set of meanings and values which as (because) they are experienced as practices appear as reciprocally confirming. It thus constitutes a sense of reality for most people in society, a sense of absolute, because experienced, reality beyond which it is very difficult for most members of the society to move, in most areas of their lives.

If hegemony is more than consciousness but an entire way of being in the world, it is not a static system but is actively being reproduced in the rising generations, especially by what Williams calls 'the systems of incorporation into a society'. He names the modes of incorporation into a society as having great social significance', citing educational institutions as key agencies for the transmission of hegemony.[15]

Not only is hegemony an active process in the sense it is lived; it is also highly adaptive, ever ready to co-opt even critiques within its wider definitions of reality. Hegemony:[16]

> is not just the past, the dry husks of ideology which we can more easily discard ... It is something more substantial and more flexible than any abstract imposed ideology. *Thus we have to recognise the alternative meanings and values, the alternative opinions and attitudes, even some alternative senses of the world, which can be accom-*

> *modated and tolerated within a particular effective and dominant culture.* (Emphasis added here and below.) This has been much under-emphasised in our notions ... of hegemony. And the under-emphasis opens the way for retreat to an indifferent complexity. In the practice of politics, for example, there are certain truly incorporated modes of what are nevertheless, within those terms, real opposition, that are felt and fought out ... Whatever the degree of internal conflict or internal variation, *they do not in practice go beyond the limits of the central effective and dominant definitions.* This is true, for example, of the practice of parliamentary politics, though its internal oppositions are real. It is true about a whole range of practices and arguments ... Whatever the degree of internal controversy and variation, they do not exceed the limits of the central corporate definitions.

Williams' description of hegemony is so laid out that he seems to be saying almost that there is no hope of countering it. Yet Williams' life-work, if I be permitted to interpret it, has been to point out the stubborn-because-unseen structures that tend to determine our lives, so they can be contested and, if need be, shifted. As a cultural critic, he brings out of hiding procedures and processes that have a human face and a human form, which he then fingerprints.

Williams explicitly states that in religious groups he finds what he calls residual cultural forms, that is, experiences, meanings, and values, that do not fit and are not able to be expressed in terms of the dominant culture but which continue to be lived and practised. These experiences and meanings are of course in contrast to the majority of religious meanings which are subsumed under the umbrella of the dominant system,[17] and they provide an important wedge in the seemingly impenetrable facade of hegemony.

At this point, I have noted that the proper avenue for approaching religious formation is by the route of understanding how formative social and cultural systems are for all persons. I illustrated my point with somewhat brief descriptions of how culture forms our perceptive system, how language moulds our thought, and finally, how hegemony, a notion that embraces entire social and cultural systems, permits us to think and act only within limits set by dominant elites. These examples were selected from a number of possible ones because they are of personal interest to me, having been of help in my own study of how things work. Now there remains the task of showing the significance of religious formation precisely in the face of the power of the wider social and cultural forces.

I hope that the above descriptions, especially of hegemony, clarify that the question is not one of whether or not there will be formation in human life. The question is rather: How does formation work in the wider culture and how must religious persons undertake a counter-formation in order to ensure the viability of their communal religious meaning systems. This question appears to be easily overlooked by many persons today. I met a woman recently, a former Roman Catholic, who told me of the pains she had endured at the hand of functionaries in the church and of her decision, long-held at this point, not to give any religious formation to her children but let them decide for themselves the entire question of their religious orientation. I told her that while she would be silent about her faith, the marketeers and panderers to consumer lust would not be silent or inactive. They are not going to let her children decide for themselves. They would be at her children, selling them a very clear vision of the world and a vision that in fact functions as a religion, meaning it proposes its values as the ultimate ones worth living one's life for and even worth dying for. A religion imagines the possibilities of human life for us; and the marketeers imagine existence, so I told her, at its least. As I reflected on the matter later, I saw the question was not whether or not the children would receive formation; formation was inevitable. The question was which kind of formation would help them imagine a human life.

Behind my words to this woman was a conviction that both religion and the wider culture claim the meanings they propose are the ultimate ones. The wider culture, as Williams hints in describing hegemony, makes its claims to ultimacy *covertly*; a religious system makes its claims overtly. The problem is that the covert claims can be more powerful because, never explicitly made, they are harder to identify and resist. When cast in the hegemonic form, the wider culture forms us, creates in us habits of the heart and dispositions needed by the economic system, and we tend, not just to overlook what is happening, but to be unable to notice.

Religious formation

Religious educators understand the importance of the processes by which religious groups help new members participate in their understandings and way of life. Among religions, these processes vary widely, with some relying on carefully structured steps of initiation and subsequent reality maintenance, while others expect ordinary life lived with the believing group to be the most usual and sufficient means of taking on their religious way. Within religions, these processes have varied over time, as can be seen in the development of the catechumenate in the early Christian churches, a lengthy period of preparation that gradually fell into disuse starting about the year 300 AD only to be revived in the last twenty-five years. The importance of these processes, either informal or carefully structured, has been highlighted by modern sociology,[18] particularly by the theoretical framework offered by Berger and Luckmann in *The Social Construction of Reality*.

Religious formation today is an issue of special significance among religious groups in areas of the world where electronic communications technology has been made widely available at the local level. My reasons for making this claim are as follows. Any particular religious tradition is itself a culture, that is a 'signifying system through which a social order is communicated, reproduced, experienced and explored.'[19] It is a zone of signification, and one, as pointed out above, that explicitly claims its meanings to be the ultimate ones. But a religious zone of signification exists within a wider culture which, especially in pluralistic societies, does not espouse a particular religious vision. However, even if it did, its vision would not be identical to or as focused as the explicit religious culture. In either case, the religious tradition has to maintain its own meanings in the face of the wider culture.

In modern industrial and post-industrial societies, however, the wider culture is based on understandings and values that run counter to a religious vision. These values run toward unfettered capitalism, strategies of domination to protect financial privilege, and an ethic of consumerism. Taken together such values represent a zone of ultimacy, which becomes a kind of secular religion. As I have already explained, these claims to ultimacy are covert, possessing the special power of the non-explicit: that it is more difficult to name and resist. However in a world that has developed the technology for electronic communications media and made that technology widely available, the communication of meaning has taken on a new power unprecedented in the history of the race. Not the technology and its accessibility only, but the techniques of communication within the various forms of communication empower the consumer culture in a decisive way, to convince, to 'reproduce the dispositions needed by the economy', and to enforce its covert claims to ultimacy.

The force and plausibility of the electronic imagination of the self as consumer works to undercut, decisively I would say, a person's commitment to a religious vision and a local group's commitment to a religious way.[20] Such an angle on US culture might alarm some as an attack of modernity. It certainly critiques culture from the point of the Christian sacred writings but is not so much *against* what is current, which should not be allowed to hide behind a label of modernity, but rather it is an affirmation of *the particularity and uniqueness of a religious vision*.

What I have described here is more than a crisis of conflicting claims; it is rather a crisis of conflicting imaginations of the nature of human life. Claims are verbal and, regardless of commitments, one can spar over verbal claims. However, an imagination of life has gone beyond the verbal, deep into the psyche. When a person *lives* one imagination, which is a consumerist one, but continues to *talk* another but religious one, the illusion of the spoken commitment tends to mask the fact of the lived commitment. According to US philosopher Charles Peirce, the definition of a belief is that it orients the behaviour of those who hold it:[21]

> Belief consists mainly in being able and deliberately prepared to adopt the formula believed in as the guide to action; the essence of belief is the establishment of a habit; and different beliefs are distinguished by the different modes of action to which they give rise.

The lived commitment is the one that is actually formative. Jacques Ellul reminds us of this fact in a telling comparison:[22]

> In one respect there is ... an obvious point of similarity between what takes place in Marxism and in Christianity. Both have made practice the touchstone of truth or authenticity. In other words, it is by practice that we have to appreciate or not the intentions or purity of the doctrine, of the truth of the origin or source.

If practice defines doctrine, Ellul also notes that false practice inevitably engenders false doctrine and false theory, and, I would add, a false life among the community. Dorothee Soelle points out that even prayer becomes subverted and it becomes impossible to pray words like, Create a pure heart in me, O God, and give me a new and steadfast spirit (Psalm 51:10). 'A prayer like this presupposed certain needs for renewal and change that have been destroyed. In the time of hedonism ... all the needs that once had reference to being have now been exchanged for new ones which have reference to more having.'[23] Her view is echoed by the claims of another religious thinker that 'religion is tending to degenerate into a decent formula wherewith to embellish a comfortable life'.[24]

A good model of how a religious tradition in its local communities can deal with the rival imaginations of the human can be found in the catechumenal process of the early church and its emphasis on the way one lived one's life. Here I do not intend to lay out the catechumenal process, so readily accessible now in multiple sources, but rather to emphasise how the restructuring of lived commitments was central to the whole ethos of the catechumenate.

The catechumenate was a method of formation, not just in doctrinal purity, but in the re-imagined self, with a re-directed affect and restructured patterns of life. This theme of shifts in primary commitments comes up again and again in the writings of early Christian writers. Origen writes (C. Cels. 3, 59):

> When it becomes evident that the disciples are purified by the word and have begun, as far as possible, to live better, only then are they invited to know our mysteries

adding in another place (Hom. V, 6 in Iud):[25]

> The profound and secret mysteries must not be given, at first, to disciples, but they must be first instructed in the correction of their life style.

For Origen, re-structuring of life was prior to being given the secrets of the Christian way. Tertullian makes the same point:[26]

> It (penitence and change of one's ways) presses most urgently ... upon those recruits who have just begun to give ear to the flow of divine discourse, and who, like puppies newly born, creep about uncertainly, with eyes as yet unopened .... We are not baptised so that we may cease committing sin but because we have ceased.

Regis Duffy maintains that the early communities demanded reorientation commitments and life styles as prior conditions for admission to full membership for those who would join their fellowship. He points out that the reason the usual length of the catechumenate was three years was that it took that long for the re-direction of one's life structure.[27]

Conclusion

I am aware that I have not laid out here any specific proposal for religious formation, such as developmental steps that could be followed. In a sense the ancient catechumenate provides a fine model. What I have done has been rather to lay out the problem, one that cannot be solved by strategies designed for children alone. When not integral to the lived life of actual communities, religious education, Christian education and catechesis are puny endeavours. The main formative agent is the believing community[28] and, its verbal declarations notwithstanding, its communal or corporate commitments and way of viewing reality are, for better or worse, the key formative factors. The reason John Westerhoff's tract, *Will Our Children Have Faith?*[29] has had such an influence in the Christian churches is that he brought to new awareness this very truth. Communities are formative in the stances they take. I believe that certain stances are so out of tune with the dominant culture that once they are taken, they seriously disrupt the hegemonic meaning patterns as well as the hegemonic living patterns. In the face of a consumerist culture, one such stance is solidarity with victims, especially with those judged to be non productive and useless. In a culture like ours, no community will espouse solidarity with victims without going through a struggle with conflicting ideas and values, but the dialogue such a struggle would involve could be important, even salvific.[30]

The assembly of believers is one of the few places in current US society where a group of persons assembles publicly in the name of a vision that counters so many of the assumptions of the consumer culture, a fact that gives such an assembly a special political potential. In such assemblies, the process of maintaining within a community a reality that contradicts the wider hegemonic culture always involves intense dialogue, as sociologist Peter Berger reminds us:[31]

It is possible to sum up the dialectic formation of identity by saying that the individual becomes that which he (*sic*) is addressed as by others. One may add that the individual appropriates the world in conversation with others and, furthermore, that both identity and world remain real to himself only as long as he can continue the conversation.

The last point is very important, for it implies that socialisation can never be completed, that it must be an ongoing process throughout the lifetime of the individual ... The difficulty of keeping a world going expresses itself psychologically in the difficulty of keeping this world subjectively plausible. The world is built up in the consciousness of the individual by conversation with significant others (such as parents, teachers, peers). The world is maintained as subjective reality by the same sort of conversation, be it with the same or with new significant others (such as spouses, friends, or associates). If such conversation is disrupted (the spouse dies, the friends disappear, or one comes to leave one's original social milieu), the world begins to totter, to lose its subjective plausibility. In other words, the subjective reality of the world hangs on the thin thread of conversation ... The maintenance of such continuity is one of the most important imperatives of the social order.

I would add to Berger's analysis of the *conversational* aspect of reality maintenance an emphasis on the key role that patterns of behaviour, that is, life structure, have in keeping a counter-cultural vision plausible.

Still, the specific process by which a community moves towards such a commitment is not charitable in a blueprint sense, but somewhere in the process there will be a radical kind of religious education − or Christian education − or catechesis.[32]

Notes

1.   Raymond Williams, *The Long Revolution,* New York, Columbia University Press, 1961, p. 18.
2.   *Ibid.*
3.   Peggy Rosenthal, *Words and Values: some leading words and where they lead us,* New York, Oxford University Press, 1984.
4.   *Ibid.,* p. 42.
5.   *Ibid.,* p. viii.
6.   One of the first books Rosenthal cites in grounding her own study is Williams' *Keywords,* Oxford, Oxford University Press, 1976: her own book is in some senses an extension of Williams.
7.   *Ibid.,* p. 42.
8.   *Ibid.,* p. 42.
9.   One I have found very helpful and used recently in *Youth, Gospel, Liberation,* New York, Harper and Row, 1987, is George Steiner, *Language and Silence,* New York, Atheneum, 1967.
10.   Though I find correlations between the two books, such as in their examination of the use of the word 'self,' Bellah *et al.* do not refer to Rosenthal's work. See Robert N Bellah, Richard Madsen, William M Sullivan, Ann Swidler and Steven M Tipton, *Habits of the Heart: individualism and commitment in American life,* Berkeley, University of California Press, 1985.
11.   *Ibid.,* pp. 81, 83. See also pp. 306 and 336, though the entire book is, I claim, an examination of language.

12. Pierre Bourdieu, *Distinction: a social critique of the judgement of taste,* Cambridge, Massachusetts, Harvard University Press, 1984, pp. 100–101. I find a very graphic working out of Bourdieu's thesis in Raymond Williams' earlier book, *The Country and the City,* New York, Oxford University Press, 1973. See especially his survey and analysis of how vagrancy came to be redefined in England, so as to serve the labour needs of the new industrialism, chapter 8, 'Nature's threads,' pp. 68–86. Also, Bourdieu's notion of the creation of disposition is similar to Williams' own notion, repeated often in his writings, of the creation of 'a structure of feeling.' See *Country and City,* where the idea is not indexed, pp. 73, 79, 87, 96, 112, 178, 195, 209, 236, 252, 270, 297.

13. Raymond Williams, 'Base in superstructure in Marxist cultural theory,' in *Problems in Materialism and Culture,* New York, Schocken Books, 1980, pp. 31–49. Also in Roger Dale, *et al., Schooling and Capitalism: a sociological reader,* London, Routledge and Kegan Paul, 1976, pp. 202–210.

14. *Ibid.,* p. 38.

15. I have found a helpful survey of some Marxist critiques of education, including some valuable material on hegemony from an educational perspective, to be, Henry Giroux, 'Theories of reproduction and resistance in the new sociology of education: a critical analysis,' *Harvard Educational Review,* 53, 1983, pp. 257–293.

16. *Ibid.,* pp. 39–40.

17. *Ibid.,* pp. 40–42.

18. Here I would call attention to studies of the ways the Jewish people maintained their identity in the face of cultural forces that might have fully undermined it. For example, Norman K Gottwald, *The Tribes of Yahweh,* New York, Orbis, 1979.

19. Raymond Williams, *The Sociology of Culture,* New York, Schocken Books, 1982, p. 13.

20. For an overview of some efforts to face this problem, see Paul Giurlanda, 'The challenge of post-liberal theology,' *Commonweal,* 30 January, 1987, pp. 40–42. Giurlanda pays special attention to the work of Stanley Hauerwas. For a current Jewish example of a religious group resisting the wider culture, see Lis Harris' three-part essay on the Lubovitch Hasidim, written from the point of view of a secular Jew originally in searching out her religious roots but who came to write her account in relation to the key liturgical celebrations of this sect. Lis Harris, 'The holy days: parts I, II, III,' *The New Yorker,* September 16, 23, 30, 1985.

21. Cited in Thomas McCarthy, *The Critical Theory of Jurgen Habermas,* Massachusetts, Cambridge, MIT Press, 1978, p. 63.

22. Jacques Ellul, *The Subversion of Christianity,* Grand Rapids, Michigan, Eerdmans, 1986, p. 4.

23. Dorothee Soelle, '"Thou shalt have no other jeans before me": the need for liberation in a consumerist society,' in B Mahan and D Richesin (eds), *The Challenge of Liberation Theology,* New York, Orbis, 1981, pp. 4–16, at 6.

24. Matthew Fox, *Original Blessing,* California, Bear and Company, 1980, p. 10.

25. Both quotes appear in D Capelle, 'L'Introduction du catechumenat a Rome,' *Recherches de Theologie Ancienne et Medievale, 5,* 1933, p. 151, notes 38 and 39.

26. Tertullian, 'On penitence,' *Treatises on Penance,* translated by W Le Saint, Westminster, Newman, 1959, pp. 24, 25–26.

27. Regis Duffy, 'Liturgical catechesis: catechumenal models,' unpublished paper, given as The Mary Charles Bryce Lecture, Catholic University, Washington, DC, April 1983.

28. Here I agree with C Ellis Nelson's assertion in *Where Faith Begins* that the family is a necessary formative element in Christian faith but not sufficient. Two key quotes from Nelson on this matter: 'What is the natural agency for communicating that reality (faith)? ... the natural agency of communication is the community of believers,' p. 30. 'A family is not a society, although it has some of the qualities of a society, such as different work assignments to the individuals in the family and rewards and punishments given to individuals according to the way they behave. A family is not a society because as a unity it does not have continuity: new families are formed, but particular families die out. Also, the relationship within families is highly personal, whereas in a society relation-

ships are impersonal. If a political leader is killed he is replaced, for that role in a society must be played: but if an individual in a family is killed, he [*sic*] as a person cannot be replaced. This distinction is an important one. On the one hand, the family is one of the most important units for communicating faith and the meaning of faith. On the other hand, we cannot work out a system of Christian nurture based on the family alone because the family is more an agent of culture and society than it is an independent unit. We cannot assume that society can be "family-like, only bigger." The difference between the family and society is a difference in kind rather than in degree or size. We must watch this point carefully. There is always a tendency to assume that the problems of society would be solved if we could just expand the virtues of the family to the society,' pp. 37–38. See, C Ellis Nelson, *Where Faith Begins,* Atlanta, John Knox Press, 1967.

29. John H Westerhoff III, *Will Our Children Have Faith?* New York, Seabury-Crossroad, 1976. Those who examine Westerhoff's career to date will find that his life-long preoccupation has been with contexts, with culture, and with the possibilities of the local church.

30. C Ellis Nelson brings out the inescapability and importance of conflict at various places in *Where Faith Begins.* See pp. 87–94 and 182–211, *passim.*

31. Peter Berger, *The Sacred Canopy: elements of a sociological theory of religion,* New York, Doubleday Anchor Books, 1969, pp. 16–17.

32. The ideas in this article are carried forward in Michael Warren, *Communication and Cultural Analysis: a religious view,* Westport, Connecticut, Bergin and Garvey, 1992.

5. Interpretation and criticism

The formative education discussed in section 4 may be contrasted with, or complemented by, a more critical or dialogical form of Christian education that rearranges the cultural furniture rather than simply inheriting it, or views the Christian educator as an interpreter or translator rather than primarily as a transmitter of traditional beliefs and values or an enabler of socialisation or enculturation.[1]

Thomas Groome's work on the theory and practice of Christian education is well-known.[2] In 'Shared Christian praxis: a possible theory/method of religious education,' first published in *Lumen Vitae*, 31, 1976, pp. 186–208, he proposes a praxis method for Christian education. The article traces interpretations of praxis ('action reflectively done') in Aristotle, Marx, Habermas and the Frankfurt School, before discussing its role in theology and Christian education. Groome's proposal for a 'shared Christian praxis' involves critical reflection on present action, together with dialogue/encounter between individuals who share their reflections and visions with one another. The five steps of this process are discussed, including the crucial 'dialectical hermeneutic' between the learners' stories and visions and those of the Christian tradition.

A similar interpretation model of Christian education is adopted by Douglas Wingeier. 'Faith translation' is defined as the rational interpretation of our experience in the light of the root sources of faith in scripture and tradition. This is Christian education as theologising from below up: 'the process ... begins with experience and attempts to discover meanings therein and relate them to religious beliefs which have been found meaningful to previous generations'. In this way, the Christian educator translates the word of God into contemporary forms and enables a dialogue between human experience and Christian tradition from which new insights (contemporary revelations) flow. The contribution of faith translation to responsible doctrinal pluralism is discussed. Wingeier's article, 'Christian education as faith translation,' was first published in *Living Light*, 14, 1977, pp. 393 – 406.

Article 5.3 is reprinted from the British Council of Churches' report *Understanding Christian Nurture*, edited by John Hull and first published in 1981. We have reprinted selections from the introduction and the first chapter. Here, and elsewhere,[3] the concept of 'critical openness' (as a critical, testing attitude) is explored, with particular reference to the contribution it makes to a defence of Christian nurture as a non-indoctrinatory activity. Critical openness and autonomy are first compared and contrasted. Later the openness of Christian criticism, and its role within a wider view of Christian nurture (which distinguishes it from 'Christian training' etc.), is defended on both educational and theological grounds.

Kieran Scott's article, 'Three traditions of religious education,' first appeared in *Religious Education,* 79, 1984, pp. 323 – 339. It offers a survey of approaches to Christian educational based on a three-fold typology of traditions, each with its own conceptual framework and its own understanding of educational process and purpose. The 'ecclesiastical encultural' tradition (see section 4) covers catechesis, nurture and religious socialisation; it is closely tied to practical outcomes of deepening faith and Christian practice. The 'revisionist' tradition (see articles 5.1, 5.2 and 5.3) involves critical hermeneutics and educational emancipation and leads to reflective understanding of the tradition, re-creation of personal beliefs, values and actions, and transformation of our social world. The 'reconceptionalist' tradition involves being religious 'in an educationally appropriate way', in the context of a variety of cultures and worldviews, so as to understand one's own tradition and live by it as well as understanding the religious traditions of others (Gabriel Moran is one exponent, see article 1.3). The strengths and weaknesses of each approach are noted.

Professor Thomas H Groome is Professor of Theology and Religious Education in the Institute of Religious Education and Pastoral Ministry at Boston College, Chestnut Hill, Massachusetts, USA. Professor Douglas E Wingeier is Professor of Practical Theology at Garrett-Evangelical Theological Seminary, Evanston, Illinois, USA. Professor John M Hull is Professor of Religious Education in the Faculty of Education and Continuing Studies of the University of Birmingham, England. Professor Kieran Scott is Professor of Theology and Religious Education in the Departmemt of Theology at St Bonaventure University, New York, USA.

Notes

1. See Leon McKenzie, *The Religious Education of Adults*, Birmingham, Alabama, Religious Education Press, 1982, pp. 36–37, 63-64, and the overview to part one. Warren's article (4.3), with some others in section 4, already notes the role of dialogue and criticism in a radical or liberal Christian education. Others have denied that formative religious education need be conservative, arguing that the gospel that Christian education passes on is itself catalytic of a new learning that can be self-critical of much of the received Christian tradition, resulting in Christian liberation. See John H Westerhoff, 'Christian education: kerygma v. didache,' in John Ferguson (ed.), *Christianity, Society and Education*, London, SPCK, 1981, pp. 188–195, and article 1.5.
2. See especially Thomas H Groome, *Christian Religious Education*, San Francisco, Harper and Row, 1980; and his articles in the select bibliography.
3. See also *The Child in the Church,* London, British Council of Churches, 1976, *passim;* John M Hull, *Studies in Religion and Education*, Lewes, Falmer, 1984, pp. 190, 193, 205, 209, 211, 220; John M Hull, *What Prevents Christian Adults from Learning?*, London, SCM, 1985.

5.1 Shared Christian praxis: a possible theory/ method of religious education

Thomas Groome

Introduction

The word and concept of praxis has been emerging with increasing frequency of late in our Christian religious talk.[1] Theologians of the liberation motif, who bring a praxis methodology to the doing of theology, have spearheaded its return to our consciousness, along with a rediscovered awareness that the word and work of Christ are events of freedom for us.

I am proposing here that we do our Christian education[2] by a method of praxis. However, the rationale for so proposing is not a jumping on the latest theological bandwagon – liberation theology. In fact, as I mention later, I am critical of how many of the liberationists use the term praxis. I believe they often misuse it, or use too narrow an understanding of it. The epistemological method of praxis is certainly not their exclusive domain. Also, I would hope that at this point in time we, in the field of Christian education, have ceased to think of our educational ministry as the delivery system of any theology. (Such an idea is a poor understanding of both theology and education.) Theology is one of the variables in what we are about but there is a uniqueness to our task that establishes Christian education as an independent discipline. The uniqueness of our concern lies in the interest we bring to the process. Our interest is to enable ourselves with other people to encounter Christ, through him and in the Spirit to enter into communion with the Father and with each other (to become *ecclesia*) and to interpret and live our lives in the light of his word. It is a making present of God's word and an enabling of people, including ourselves, to come to speak our own word in a response that is seen in the lives we live. I believe that this interest can best be served and promoted by a praxis method of doing Christian education. First, however, we must be clear on what we mean by praxis. For such clarification I turn, not to liberation theology, but to the thinking of the Critical Theorists of the Frankfurt School and especially to the reflection of Jürgen Habermas.[3]

Some interpretations of praxis

Ancient philosophy

The Greeks of old posed the question: What life should a person live?

They saw him or her as having three options from which to choose: the life of enjoyment, political life and the life of contemplation.[4] Aristotle talked about these three life possibilities more concretely as three kinds of human activity and more specifically as three ways of knowing. He called them *theoria, praxis* and *poiesis*. He probably borrowed the terms from Pythagoras, who did not invent them either.

For Aristotle, *theoria* 'signifies those sciences and activities that are concerned with knowing for its own sake'.[5] This amounts to a spiritual type of contemplation of ideas, objects and events. This notion is consistent with the religious origins of *theoria*. Habermas says, 'The *theoros* was the representative sent by Greek cities to public celebrations. Through *theoria*, that is through looking on, he abandoned himself to the sacred events.'[6]

Knowing by praxis, for Aristotle, was not a matter of intellectual looking on, but involved the twin moments of reflection and participation. Praxis was action that was reflectively done or was reflection upon the action that was being done. It was only in being reflectively done that it was known. This led Aristotle to equate praxis knowledge with the *living* of an ethical life.

The third activity or way of knowing was *poiesis*. This referred to the activity of making artifacts and the knowledge, or perhaps more accurately the skill, upon which such activity was based. Lobkowicz, talking about the difference between praxis and poiesis in Aristotle, says 'The distinction is not easily rendered in English: what comes closest to it is the difference between 'doing' and 'making'. We do sports or business or politics, and we make ships or houses or statutes.'[7]

Oversimplifying in a sense, it is still accurate to say that praxis is a combination of the theoria dimension (reflection) and the poiesis dimension (action). Thus praxis is a reflective action. As a way of knowing, knowledge is that which is possessed by reflection on what is being done which in turn leads to further action in an ongoing process. Praxis knowledge must involve the twin moments of doing and reflecting.

Karl Marx

Praxis as a way of knowing was greatly overshadowed by theoria in Western philosophy from Aristotle to the recent past. Theory/knowing was seen as something that was to be applied to praxis/doing. This set up a dichotomy between theoria and praxis and the gap between the two has proved to be a difficult one to bridge. It was Karl Marx, in a dialectical relationship with Hegel's concept of Geist, that reunited theory and praxis and reintroduced praxis as the primary way of knowing. Instead of taking theory as something to be formulated and then applied to practice, Marx reestablished the dialectical relationship between theoria and praxis and claimed that knowledge is primarily something that is done and is not knowledge until it is done. For Marx, theory emerges from what is being reflectively done and in turn leads to further action, which in turn is reflected upon and so on, in an ongoing dialectic.

However, there was a problem in Marx's concept of the reflective moment in praxis. The problem was amplified in his followers. While he was no crude materialist, yet because he saw that which mediates between the subject knowing and the object known exclusively as human labour, and saw the dialectical process as the objectification of that labour, Marx reduced the reflective moment to the level of 'production feedback'.[8] For Marx, the synthesis that is knowledge, 'no longer appears as an activity of thought but as one of material production'.[9] Habermas says 'Marx deludes himself about the nature of reflection when he reduces it to labour',[10] and adds 'By reducing the self-positing of the absolute ego to the more tangible productive activity of the species, he eliminates reflection as such as a motive force of history, even though he retains the framework of the philosophy of reflection.'[11]

This bequeathed two problems to later Marxists and to people who would attempt a praxis epistemology. First, it gave too limited a concept of praxis as if all life could be talked of as economic praxis. Secondly, since production feedback was seen to be inevitable, it led later Marxists to 'reify' (George Lukacs) the evolutionary process and to see it as happening inevitably, regardless of human cooperation.

The Critical Theorists and especially Jürgen Habermas make a valuable corrective to the concept of praxis that broadens and reaffirms the importance of both its reflective and active moments.

The Frankfurt School of Critical Theory

The Frankfurt Institute is an amazing school of thinkers, who for more than fifty years now have dedicated themselves to theoretical innovation and unrestrained social research. A very diverse group of scholars, their numbers have included such major thinkers as Marx Horkheimer, Theodore Adorno, Eric Fromm, Herbert Marcuse, Friedrich Pollock and Karl Wittfogel. In many ways their work can be seen as a relentless attempt to take seriously Marx's slogan, 'We wish to find the new world through criticism of the old.' They are a reaction to the fetishised and reified concept of the evolutionary process of party Marxism that was unable to explain the reluctance of the proletariat to fulfil their historical role.

Basically, their concern was to reunite the object of knowledge with the constitutive activity of the knowing subject, within a historical process. The relationship between the two had been severed by the 'objectivist illusion' of both the capitalist and socialist systems. In the opinion of the Critical Theorists the relationship is mediated by communication and reflection. The reflection is on the genesis of one's present consciousness. This requires a reclaiming of one's individual and collective pasts. This is done by critical reason. Reflective reason is a means by which reality is mediated to the knowing subject.

A critical reasoning is essential to a coming to consciousness which in turn is essential for emancipation. The Frankfurt school's reestablishing of the importance of reflective reason also stressed the active element in cognition. The historical process is not out of human control. On the contrary, by critical reflection people can choose and guide the process. Because of this no system of philosophy can be accepted as a body of received truth. That would be to fall into the positivist illusion.

Attention to psychoanalysis (the influence of Fromm, among others) led to the Critical Theorists emphasising the role of memory in the critical process. All reification is a forgetting, and thus remembering is necessary if reification is to be overcome and replaced by conscious decisions based on reflective reason.

As the immediate context out of which Habermas has emerged, the contribution of the Frankfurt school, by way of epistemology, is the reestablishing of the subjective element in the process. Knowledge is by doing, but essential to this is the reason, reflection and memory of the knowing subject.[12]

Jürgen Habermas

Habermas is a leading spokesman of the Frankfurt school today, but he is also in a dialectical relationship with the leading critical thinkers of the school before him.

Basically, Habermas's contribution is to broaden Marx's concept of both action and reflection and to pose a new basis for the unity of theory and praxis. The basis he proposes for their unity is that of cognitive interests. Rejecting the 'objectivist illusion' Habermas claims that all the sciences of knowing/modes of action (he names three) have an interest and their interest shape what is known. He says, 'Of course the expression "interest" is intended to indicate the unity of the life context in which cognition is embedded; expressions capable of truth have reference to a reality which is objectified (that is, simultaneously, disclosed and constituted) as such in two different contexts of action and expression. The underlying "interests" establishes the unity between this constitutive context in which knowledge is rooted and the structure of the possible application which this knowledge can have.'[13] In other words, the connection between the knowledge that one knows (theory) and the use to which that knowledge is put (practice) lies in the basic interests of the knowing subject. We know what we want to know in order that we may do.

Thus, it is only in doing that knowledge is known, and the connection between the doing and the knowing is the interest which the knowing subject brings to the process. However, if all the sciences of knowing are not critically aware of their constitutive interests, then the consequence is control rather than freedom and the praxis will be incapable of causing the freedom Marx envisaged.

I will briefly outline his explanation of this position. He divided the sciences of knowing into three categories: the empirical analytical sciences, the historical hermeneutic sciences and the critical sciences.

Empirical analytical sciences: The action of the empirical analytical sciences is 'purposive rational', aimed at identifying, utilising and maintaining predictability and reliability in the world. Habermas argues that these sciences are rooted in an interest in control. 'By virtue of its structure, purposive rational action is the exercise of control.'[14] The control he refers to is a technical one. Such sciences lead to a rationalisation of the system of production by a suspension of critical reflection. This amounts to domination but the domination is legitimated by productivity.[15] In this way of knowing the synthesis that is knowledge is mediated by labour-production. But in this lies the controlling interest of such sciences. Thus, Marx's posing of labour as the mediator between the object known and the subject knowing is not capable on its own of leading to the emancipation he envisaged.

Historical hermeneutic sciences: These are the second group of sciences in Habermas's division. He explains them by saying, 'Hermeneutic is the scientific form of the interpretative activities of everyday life.'[16] But these sciences also have an interest in control — here a practical control. They are aimed at 'the maintenance of the inter-subjectivity of mutual understanding, within whose horizon reality can first appear as something.'[17] The interest of the hermeneutic sciences is a practical one aimed at maintaining mutual understanding in the social context. Put simply, the outcome of the hermeneutical act is determined by the interest the interpreters bring to the act, namely, a practical interest of maintaining a mutual understanding within a common tradition. It is this interest which mediates between what is known and the subject knowing.

For Habermas, in so far as persons are unaware of the interest in their knowing process, knowledge will maintain things as they appear to be rather than liberate consciousness to see things as they really are and to create them as they might be. There is a third group of sciences, however, which, Habermas argues, arise when such an emancipating interest is foremost.

The critical sciences: Habermas uses psychoanalysis as his central example of a critical science but also makes it clear that the critical sciences include 'the sciences of social action — economics, sociology and political science'.[18] The key ingredient of the critical sciences is self-reflection. Critical self-reflection is essential if the genesis of one's attitude is to be remembered and its interest made apparent.

Both are necessary if emancipation is to occur. 'A state defined by both cognitive performances and fixed attitudes can be overcome only if its genesis is analytically remembered. A past state, if put off and merely repressed, would retain its power over the present.'[19]

The interest of these sciences is an emancipatory one because self-reflection can cause perception of the genesis of one's attitudes and thus free the present of the control of a past state. Here, what in effect happens is that by reflection the knower becomes aware of the genesis of his/her attitude, comes to see the interest in that attitude, and thus is emancipated to create a present independent of a controlling past. As a result, a person is now capable of acting freely rather than being determined by a positivistic ideology. In Habermas's own words, 'Self-reflection is at once intuition and emancipation, comprehension and liberation from dogmatic dependence.'[20] This is so because, 'By becoming transparent to itself in its self-producing, the ego frees itself from dogmatism.'[21] Thus this process of self-critical reflection that returns to the genesis of present action to unmask its interests, ideologies and assumptions can be emancipatory.

What has Habermas done here? In effect, he has established the inner bond between praxis and theory in all these sciences and bases their unity in each science on their constitutive interests. But the problem is that the empirical analytical and hermeneutic sciences dictate a system of norms, laws and values which, if they remain uncritiqued in their interest, become an ideology that will be controlling rather than emancipatory. The critical sciences contain elements of the first two but, by reflecting critically on the genesis of present action and on the laws and norms generated by the other two interests, the process is capable of leading to emancipation.

From the point of view of our interest in this, Habermas has broadened the concept of praxis to include the technical and hermeneutical praxis but has also gone beyond these to a critical praxis. In this he has recovered and deepened the concept of self-reflection as a moment of praxis. He seeks a deeper self-reflective subjectivity that is understood in a more wholistic manner and which uncovers the interest that lies at the genesis of present action. Secondly, in addition to broadening the concept of reflection, Habermas has also broadened the concept of action beyond what Marx conceived it to be (objectified labour). In addition to Marx, he stresses the action of hermeneutics and of the emancipatory sciences. Thus the whole concept of praxis is extended in a way that is capable of leading to emancipation. By proposing a self-reflective critical praxis that is far broader than reflection on the economic system, he requires critique of the whole spectrum of the symbols, attitudes, norms, laws and ideologies that suspend doubt and control people by distorting and repressing dialogue.

In summary, for Habermas knowledge is by praxis. But the action and self-reflection of praxis is broadened and the interest that unites theory and practice specified as that which must become transparent to the knower if emancipation is to ensue. If this is done then a praxis way of knowing can be emancipatory.

Praxis in theology

A praxis epistemology and approach to doing theology is emerging as what may prove to be a new paradigm in theological method. There are various expressions of praxis theology (usually called liberation theologies)[22] – feminist theology, third world theology, black and minority theology, some strands of political theology, etc.[23] When a praxis method is used, Schillebeeckx says, 'Theology is the critical self-consciousness of Christian praxis in the world and church.'[24] In Christian theology, however, the critical reflection on action is done in the light of the word of God. This is what differentiates Christian theology from philosophy. Thus, Gutierrez says, 'theology is a critical reflection . . . in the light of the word accepted in faith . . . on historical praxis'.[25] The key point here is that theology is primarily something that is done. It is Christian praxis first and then the articulation of the consciousness that arises from this praxis is theology. But the articulation is the second step and arises from one's praxis (in contradistinction to the typical scholastic method). Gutierrez says, 'Theology follows; it is the second step. What Hegel used to say about philosophy can be likewise applied to theology: It rises only at sundown.'[26]

However, I have found that none of the liberation theologians understand praxis, and especially the critical reflection moment of praxis, as Habermas uses it. While I greatly admire the work of Gustavo Gutierrez, it seems to me he has a too narrow economic concept of praxis and thus fails to attend to racist and sexist oppression. Habermas' thinking has a valuable corrective to offer to the liberation theologians on this point.[27]

Praxis in Christian education

At the bedrock of our Christian education task there is an epistemological question – what does to know mean? – and in this case, to know Christ. The pedagogical question is how should we go about enabling others with ourselves to know him. If our epistemology is one of theoria, that is, seeing knowledge as an intellectual attainment of the mind that is gained by reflection, then Christianity will be seen as a list of truths to be comprehended by the intellect. Then the Christian educator will be drawn inevitably to use what Paulo Freire calls a 'banking concept' of education to deposit divine truths in the minds of people.[28] I believe that much of our traditional Christian education has been based on such an epistemology and as a consequence has used such an approach. Instead I opt for a praxis epistemology. However, the praxis cannot be a technical praxis, that is, arranging the variables in a learning situation to produce desired behavioural outcomes à la James Michael Lee. Such a catechesis has the interest of technical control and is legitimated by productivity, that is, producing Christian behaviour according to our criteria. Nor can it be based on an hermeneutical praxis alone, for example, the process of enculturation or socialisation recommended by many current theorists of Christian education. Such a Christian education has the interest of practical control and will result in a maintaining of the present status quo and a conditioning of our students into our taken for granted religious culture. Then the dialectic between the radical values of the Gospel and our present culture will be lost as will be the dialectic between our present and the values of the kingdom toward which we must be moving. But if the Christian education is done by a critical praxis as outlined above in Habermas's third cateogy of sciences, then I believe our educating can be truly liberating and our future will be built on our past and present but not on a reproduction of it. However, this assumes that our task should have the interest of liberation in the first place.

Primary to critical praxis is to be aware of one's assumptions and interests. Thus it is time that I made mine transparent.

My experience of praxis

I come to talk about a theory/method of Christian education with two assumptions about Christianity. The first is that we are 'people of the way'. Christianity is primarily a way of life to be lived, a lifestyle, a way of being and doing in the world. The second is that the word and work of Christ are a call to and the wherewithal by which we can come to the 'glorious freedom' of the sons and daughters of God (Romans 8:21). Christ made liberation from the slavery of sin and the freedom to enter into communion with God and each other possible.

These assumptions give rise to two interests I bring to the task. Since they are the interests I want to see fulfilled they can also be talked of as two criteria by which any attempt to make the story of the Christ event present to people must be judged. Firstly, our Christian education should lessen the gap between a person's articulated faith and his/her action, that is, his/her knowing of Christ ought to be a doing of Christlike actions. Secondly, our Christian education should help people to personally appropriate the meaning of their faith in a way which enables them to go on reinterpreting and doing its meaning in later life situations. In other words, our Christian education must enable people to become decision-makers who exercise their freedom as God's children in creating with God and each other their future.

Given these assumptions and interests, there are a number of serious considerations that might decide us to use a praxis approach to doing Christian education. I offer the following reflections.

First, a praxis doing of Christian education seems more likely to narrow the gap between a person's professed faith and action. This is so because in a praxis approach what is professed is the articulation of something that is being done and not of what has been deposited. This is a response to the first criterion of Christian education posed above.

Second, the critical reflective moment in praxis insists on the importance of the free choosing of the knowing subject. Thus, a praxis approach is more likely than other epistemologies to enable people to be decision-makers who exercise their freedom as God's children in creating with God their future. This is a response to the second criterion.

Third, I believe a strong case can be made, though space does not permit here, for claiming that the biblical concept of knowing is closer to a praxis epistemology than to a theoria one. It is not enough to profess 'Lord, Lord' – we must also 'do the will of the Father'. Truly to *know* God in the biblical sense is to do God's will. A praxis epistemology seems more likely to facilitate such a 'knowing'.

Fourth, Gabriel Moran's argument (*The Present Revelation*) that one's concept of revelation determines how one does theology has much truth to it. He says, 'Revelation is not a theological concept similar to others, but instead a premise for theological construction as a whole.'[29] I believe one's concept of revelation has an equally determining effect on how we do Christian education. If we have a static concept of revelation and understand it is something given only in the past, then the theologian's and the educator's job is simply to explain and teach, respectively, how that revelation applies to our present life. This is a theoria approach to knowing in that it begins with the theory and attempts to apply it to practice. A static concept of revelation gives rise to a theoria approach to knowing, in this case, to knowing God's will for us. If, however, revelation is seen as an ongoing process, then Christian education ought to begin with critical reflection on the present events where God is actively revealing self. The critical reflection must be done in the light of the story of God's self-revelation in the events of the lives of our forebears but it should begin in our present. I believe this is what Vatican II was calling us to do when it spoke of the duty of 'scrutinising the signs of the times and interpreting them in the light of the Gospel'.[30] If one accepts a process concept of revelation, as I do (and as Vatican II tended toward), then I believe this points us to a praxis epistemology for our Christian education task.

Fifth, if the word and work of Christ are taken to be affairs of freedom for us (and how else can we take them?) then, given the emancipatory possibility of a praxis epistemology, a praxis method of doing Christian education is more likely to respond to the liberating interests of Christianity than other epistemologies.

Christian education: a shared Christian praxis

I propose that Christian education should be done by a sharing in dialogue of critical reflection on Christian action. The sources of critique for the critical reflection are the memory of how God has revealed himself in the events of the lives of our people in the past and the vision of God's kingdom toward which we are called. I write of this method as dialogue/critical reflection/action. However, it may be more pronounceably called 'shared praxis'. I will describe each of the components of this proposal.

Critical reflection: My description of both critical reflection and action draws heavily on Habermas. Critical reflection is an evaluative analysis[31] of something, in and of itself, that attempts to unmask the assumptions of social conditioning. It is a coming to an awareness of something in its immediacy, instead of as it is socially mediated. In other words, it is a comprehending of the issue being critiqued as it is itself and not as the norms and traditions of society tell one that it is. To unmask such assumptions it is necessary to return to the genesis of one's consciousness. This is done by remembering.[32] The purpose of this returning to the genesis is to come to see the interest that underlies present consciousness. This interest is uncovered by critical reason. Thus there is an interplay of reason and memory in the process of critical reflection. The remembering of the genesis can release repressed dialogue. The seeing of the interest unmasks ideology. As a result the process can be emancipatory, that is, help to free the person from that which holds him/her bound.

This critical looking back is done as a means toward looking forward. In this sense there is a future interest in the reflection in that the looking back makes way for future action. It is a deliberative and critical asking of − in light of how and why I am acting − how will I act in the future? Thus the looking back at the genesis and interest is not a contemplative stance toward the past. It is not done out of curiosity. It is a critical looking at the past so that future action may be freely chosen and be given direction, rather than allowing the future to be shaped by the ideologies, norms, traditions etc. of the society that mediates us.

Action: Here the term action is used to refer to that which is reflected upon. It has a much broader meaning than is usually given the word action in everyday usage. The primary object of reflection is the subject who is reflecting. Thus all reflection is primarily self-reflection.[33] The subject reflects upon his or her present state, be that intellectual, emotional or physical. As seen above, the process of critical reflection on action is to take one back to past experiences and doings that are the genesis of present action. Thus the self that is reflected upon is the historical self in that the present is the consequence of the past. Thus, to speak of reflection on *present* action is not to imply that it is on an ahistorical action that only pertains to the present isolated moment. On the contrary, it is the present as the embodiment of the past and the possibility of the future on which the subject reflects. In reflecting on our present we must attend to the past so that we can intend the future.

I said above that critical reflection is primarily on the self. But the self is socially mediated. Therefore the reflection is ultimately on the society. No one comes to be in isolation. All of us have come to be what we are in a dialectical relationship with our social influences. Thus the reflection is on the laws, norms, mores, traditions, symbols, ideologies, etc. of society that have mediated our present action. The reflection must be done in this broader social context if the assumptions of social conditioning are to be unmasked and if emancipation is to ensue.

Dialogue: Dialogue is always necessary in any process of humanisation because we come to be human in encounter with other people. But remembering that I am proposing dialogue/critical reflection/action as a theory/method of Christian education, there is an added reason why dialogue is necessary in such a context. It is only when praxis is done in the light of the Christian story and the vision that calls us forward, and the reflection is shared in dialogue, that it can become a religious educating by the Christian community with each other. The *content* of the Christian education, to call it that, is the shared Christian praxis. Thus dialogue is necessary in Christian religious education, or, in other words, our educating always requires a Christian community (*ecclesia*) if it is to be Christian.

What is shared in the dialogue is the articulation of the people's critical reflection on their action. Therefore, by dialogue I mean an encounter between two or more people where they share their reflective stories and visions with each other. Perhaps the kind of encounter I intend here has been best described by Buber's I/Thou relationship.

But it is not only the personal stories and visions that are reflected upon and shared in Christian education. The critical reflection must be done in the light of the story and the vision of the total Christian community.

The story and the vision as the sources of critique

By story here I mean the memory of how God has revealed himself to our people in the events of our past. In more traditional language it could even be called scripture and tradition. By vision I mean the vision of the Kingdom of God, the Kingdom of Shalom toward which the story points. It is given as a gift in Christ, but the gift comes to us as a grace that enables us to be cocreators of that Kingdom with God.

In a Christian context, the sources of critique which the critical reflector brings to evaluate his or her action are the story and the vision. What I am saying is that in Christian practice there is an ultimate overall genesis of the Christian story and an all-encompassing vision of the Kingdom of Shalom in light of which the genesis and the vision of present action is to be critiqued. Our present action, if it is to be a Christian praxis, must always be critiqued in the light of our Christian story and the vision to which that story points and draws us. In the shared praxis that is Christian education, we look at the genesis of present action to see if it is the genesis of the story, and we look at the vision embodied in present action to see if it is the vision of the Kingdom. Thus there is a remembering of the story to see if present action is faithful to it and a looking toward the vision to see if present action is creative of it.

Here, however, we must be careful. I am not posing the story and the vision as two positivistic ideologies that control our present. Remembering that the story has often been distorted and the vision foreclosed, they themselves must be critically reflected upon as they are made present. There must be maintained a constant dialectic between the story and the present. Thus, while the present is judged by the story, what has often been a distorted version of the story is judged by the present. Instead of merely asking, 'What does the story say to my life?', there is also an asking of 'What does my life say to and ask of the story?' If this is not done, the story is as likely to be used for oppression as it is for liberation. We have surely learned this from our history. The story must be critically remembered so we can transform it in our present and in freedom create the vision. If our story is simply recalled as the criterion of the present and the future, then the future will be no more than a repetition of our past. That will be stagnation rather than a moving forward toward the Kingdom. And there is a similar dialectic to be maintained between the present and that vision.

In the Christian educational process all the participants, educators included, make present their reflective stories and the visions they give rise to. But it is particularly the responsibility of the educator to make present the Christian story and the vision toward which it points. This is the specifically catechetical activity within the task of Christian education. It is the 'echoing', the 'handing down' of the story that is remembered, of God's self-revelation to our people in the events of our past.[34] This is especially true if the other participants have not heard the story before, for example, in early childhood Christian education. The catechist must be the embodiment of the collective memory.

In summary, then, Christian education by shared praxis is a way of being together in which there is a sharing in dialogue of a praxis that is done in faithfulness to the story and in creation of the vision.

A story of praxis Christian education

Looking to Christ, the incarnate story of God's self-revelation to us, we find in him a model of a praxis catechist. No one knew the Father better than he because no one more perfectly did God's Will and embodied God's Word. (Perhaps if the Word had not become flesh we could continue with our theoria approach to telling people about him.) But let us look specifically at the incident on the road to Emmaus, an obviously Christian educational situation, and see what we can find there now.

The story is told in chapter 24 of St Luke's Gospel, verses 13–35. On Easter Sunday two disciples were making their way to Emmaus, a little village 'seven miles distant from Jerusalem' (verse 13). They were greatly distressed and despondent because of 'the things that went on ... these past few days' (verse 18) 'that had to do with Jesus of Nazareth' (verse 20). (Present action.) Jesus met them on the road and entered into their company. However, they did not recognise that it was he. He entered into dialogue with them, heard their stories and sensed their pain and confusion. But he did not tell them who he was. Instead, calling attention to the present interest they had, 'we are hoping that he was the one who would set Israel free' (verse 21), he said 'what little sense you have!' (verse 25). Then he recalled to their minds the past story of their people and reminded them of 'every passage of scripture which referred to him' (verse 27). (Critical reflection on their present action in light of the community story.) They still did not recognise him but he continued to wait on them and refused to tell them. Since it was 'nearly evening' and the day was 'practically over' (verse 29) they invited him to spend the night with them as a guest. He agreed. Then, at the table, seated with them, 'He took bread, pronounced the blessing, then broke the bread and began to distribute it to them. With that their eyes were opened and they recognised him' (verses 30–31). As they told the story later, they 'had come to know him in the breaking of bread' (verse 35).

This story of the Lord encountering, entering into dialogue with them, pointing out present interests which prevented them from recognising him, reminding them of and reinterpreting a past story, refusing to tell them but gently waiting for them to come to see (what Freire would call conscientisation) is the memory that we must attempt to be faithful to as we do our Christian education in our own time.

An example from my own praxis

I have been struggling for some time now to do and to articulate the doing of a Christian education by praxis. Whether they know it or not, or use the same language to talk about it, I believe many other Christian educators have been doing something similar. The following example comes out of my own attempts. Perhaps recounting it here may help to clarify what I intend by a Christian education by shared praxis. This example is of a one day retreat I conducted recently with about 40 senior high school boys. It is not a perfect example. In fact, when I do such a retreat again, I will do it differently. I see this as being consistent with a praxis approach. The doing of it can only be worked out in a praxis and then we must reflect critically on the very process we have used to inform our further action.

The theme for the one day retreat, chosen by the boys themselves, was the Eucharist. We began the day with a discussion with the whole group. I asked questions about why they had chosen this topic as the theme for the day, asked them to recall their past experiences with the Eucharist, how they felt about the Sunday liturgies in their own parishes, and how they were handling what has been traditionally presented to them as 'the obligation of Sunday mass'. They tried in vain to cast me in a traditional role of 'priest with all the answers'. They asked questions like 'Do we still have to go?' 'Is it a mortal sin if we miss?' etc. I did not answer these questions but instead asked 'What do you think?' or 'Why do you ask me?' I asked them to reflect on the basis of their present attitudes toward the mass.

After about thirty minutes of dialogue I showed a film. The film portrayed life as a journey, a journey which can be lonely and on which we need the strength and support of other people. This was an attempt to focus attention on a dimension of human action to which the Eucharist responds. The film was followed by another period of general discussion. In this dialogue there emerged an awareness of a felt sense of loneliness and the need for support. Many of the boys spoke about the need for friends and said that without their friends 'they could never make it'. There was evidence of a good deal of anxiety about their future journey and the possibility of failure, especially from the point of view of what they would do after high school.

After this discussion we divided into six groups. I told them that since they had chosen the theme of the Eucharist for the day, in light of the dialogue that had already taken place I wanted them to look at some of the scripture passages that refer either directly or indirectly to the Eucharist. Each of the groups took one of the following six passages: the accounts of the last supper (Matthew, Mark, Luke and I Corinthians), the multiplication of the loaves and fishes (Matthew 14: 13–21), and the bread of life discourse (John 6:25–70). On reflection now my action seems unduly directive. But I saw that it was a recalling to their minds of the obvious scripture passages that refer to the Eucharist — after the fashion of the Lord on the road to Emmaus. I suggested the basic question to each group — 'What does this passage say to me in my life and what does my life ask of this passage right now?'

After the small group discussion I told the story of the Eucharist to the general group. I talked about it briefly within our Roman Catholic tradition. I said something of the way we have understood it in the past and of the present attitudes toward it. I spoke of it as an action that embodies Christ's presence with us as a community, an event, in which we can encounter the saving Christ in a special way and thus receive nourishment and sustenance for our journey that empowers us to reach out to each other in love and support. I saw this telling of the story as an opening of the avenues of dialogue for the participants who heretofore had most often heard the Eucharist spoken of as 'the obligation of Sunday mass'. I also made it clear that within the Catholic tradition there are a number of theological interpretations of the meaning of the Eucharist.

Then we moved again to general group participation and to a sharing of what had happened in the small groups participative hermeneutics. Now there was a noticeable difference in the way of talking about the Eucharist in contrast to the talk in the opening session of the morning. There were such remarks as 'Why did the church ever talk about the Eucharist as an obligation?' 'The Eucharist is really a way of getting in touch with people.' 'It's difficult to ever think of it (the mass) as anything but something I have to do ... that is how they taught us.' Out of this discussion the request was made that we might celebrate a Eucharist together at the end of the day. The boys spent about 45 minutes selecting a theme, choosing the scripture readings, practising songs, assigning liturgical functions etc. The mass lasted about 90 minutes, and for me at least, was a most joyful celebration.

Reflecting now on that story, there are a number of things I will do differently the next time. It is not a perfect example of shared praxis as I have described it. According to the steps as I now outline them below, it would have been better perhaps not to begin by talking about the Eucharist and their present attitudes toward it. It might have been better, I think, to begin with a sharing of present needs and a focusing on loneliness and the need for support. Also in my dialogue I did not bring them back sufficiently to the genesis of their own attitudes – though this was partly because of a lack of time, one day. However, because of this the critical reflection dimension of the process was weak and also there was not enough talk of the vision nor of what the Eucharist can be for the Christian community. As a result the futuring dimension of the day was not clearly articulated. Yet, there was a reconceptualising activity that occurred and the Eucharist that was 'done' at the end of the day was a future action rather than a repetition of what they were accustomed to. With all its flaws, (and can a praxis Christian education ever be done perfectly in the sense that we cannot improve upon it?) it is an example of an attempt at the sharing of critical reflection on present action in the light of the community story and vision.

Steps in a religious education by shared praxis

I know that I have attempted to cover too much ground here in a short article. My attempt, I am sure, is as beclouding as it is clarifying. Knowing this I conclude by outlining the practical steps to be followed in using a praxis approach in a formal Christian education situation. This may help to demonstrate in a practical manner what I intend.

This is only one possible way to organise a Christian education by praxis. The steps I outline here arise from my own attempts, such as the example above, to do a catechesis by praxis. (This must be the basis of my steps if I am to be consistent with my own framework.) However, I have found that every time I approach a group to do Christian education by praxis with them, I come away and reflect that I will do it a little differently next time. The steps must be worked out in an actual praxis and, as we do it, we will come to greater clarity about how to approach different situations. Anyhow, reflecting on my own praxis, I tentatively offer the following possible steps.[35]

Step 1: The process begins by attending to the present action of the participants. I intend 'action' here as I have defined it. Thus it includes the activities, aspirations, feelings, needs, hopes, beliefs, anxieties, etc. of the participants. However, in a formal pedagogical situation the attention to action obviously must have some focus. This focusing is more particularly the responsibility of the educator. I say more particularly in that, if a focus does not emerge from the group, then it is his/her responsibility to suggest a focus. However, the action of the participants must be verbalised personally by all the group. It cannot be a case of the educator saying 'this is what your needs, emotions, interests, beliefs, etc. are' and then responding to that assumed action.

Step 2: This is a making present by each participant of their reflective stories and visions as they relate to the focus of the group. Thus for example, if the focus of attention is the Eucharist, then there must be time for the participants to recount their own experiences and understanding of the Eucharist and their vision of what the Eucharist can be in their lives. I see this step as the beginning of the critical reflection as it is a remembering of the genesis of present action. In the retreat example above, this step was represented by the opening discussion on their present attitude to the Eucharist and the questioning of those attitudes.

Step 3: This is an encounter by the participants with the Christian community story and vision. Here the Christian educator is the one more particularly responsible for making present the story and vision and the dimension of them that responds to the present focus of the group. Strictly speaking, this is the act of catechesis within the process. In the examples cited, this step 3 was done especially by my telling of the story of the Eucharist and by the participants' encounter with the eucharistic texts.

Step 4: This is an articulation and sharing of critical reflection on the community story and vision and a reflection by the participants on their own stories and visions in the light of the critiqued community memory and visions. Here the participants share their answer to the question − 'What does the story and the vision say to my present action and what does my present action say to and ask of the story and vision?' What I am referring to here is what Walter Wink calls a dialectical hermeneutic.[36] In the retreat example, this step 4 was represented by the sharing in groups of the boys' reflections on the scripture texts.

Step 5: This is a decision-making process by the group concerning future action that is to be done, that is what is to be consciously done in the light of the story that will be creative of the vision. The critical reflection on action must lead to further action that is reflected upon, etc. Simply to stop at step 4 would be to miss the point of the whole process. If the educational process does not lead to Christian reflective action, then in this context there is no knowledge or certainly it is not the Lord that is 'known', for to *know* him is to *do* his will. In the example cited, the new Eucharist which arose from the boys out of their day's process together was one possible form of a visible future action in that context. However, the reconceptualising of the Eucharist which seemed to take place could also be seen as future action. I should also add here that in an actual process these steps overlap each other. I separate them here for the sake of some clarity of description.

Conclusion

In such a short article, I have left vast areas and huge questions untouched. Though it may sound otherwise, I am not naively proposing a praxis way of doing Christian education as the panacea for which we have been waiting, to solve our problems in every situation. From my own attempts I am aware of some of its limitations, though that is not made evident here. Also, I see a praxis Christian education as being in a dialectical relationship with the present 'experiential catechesis' or 'intentional socialisation' that now seems to hold centre stage. Praxis Christian education goes beyond both of these in its method of critical reflection. That has not been demonstrated here either and it is important. Again, the kind of language we use to talk of what we are about as Christian educators is crucial to our task. So much of our present language is likely to maintain us in an oppressive monological banking approach to religious education. I can only mention this as an issue in passing. Also, I believe the very role of the educator must itself be reenvisioned if a praxis Christian education is to be done. Further, while methodologically a praxis Christian education is a going beyond the document from our American bishops, *To Teach as Jesus Did*, it is also faithful to the threefold dimension of catechesis outlined there: *Kerygma* (the story and the vision), *Koinonia* (the Christian communities' way of being together in reflective dialogue), *Diakonia* (leading to further Christian praxis in the world). In America we still await our National Catechetical Directory. But for now we can at least rejoice at the method of approach that has been used. Never before has such a large scale consultation of the reflection of the people on their Christian praxis been undertaken. Rather than some 'experts' telling the American church how to do Christian education (which would be a theoria approach) the procedure has been to begin with the reflection of the whole community on their Christian educating action. I am excited at the hope that the final document will be an articulation of that community reflection on our Christian education praxis that is capable of moving us forward.

My intention here was simply to introduce the notion of praxis Christian education, clarify the concept of praxis, to attempt to describe how it might be done and the rationale upon which it is based. Of course, we will only truly 'know' praxis Christian education as we do it. I say, let us move forward with it.

Notes

1. This concept is developed further in Thomas H Groome, *Christian Religious Education*, San Francisco, Harper and Row, 1980.
2. I am aware of the present debate and attempt to clarify the meaning of the terms religious education, Christian education, catechesis, church education, etc. As the debate continues I want to leave my own position open to development and change. However, for now I settle for the following understanding and usage of Christian education and catechesis. By education I mean the attending to the future possibility of the total person. See Dwayne Huebner, 'Curriculum as concern for man's temporality,' in William Pinar (ed.), *Curriculum Theorizing,* Berkeley, California, McCutchen Publishing Co., 1975. It is the leading out of the person *(educere)* to become the human being that is his/her potential. The word Christian refers to the specificity of our particular educational task in that it is an enabling of people to mature in their potential to enter into a communion with God and each other through Christ. I see it as more than coincidental that the word education at its root *(educere* − to lead out) is so close in meaning to the root of the word church/*ecclesia (ek-kletoi* − those who are called out). I believe our Christian education task can be named as the enabling of our people to become Church. I understand catechesis (being faithful to the etymology of the word and to its scriptural use) as the 'echoing', the 'handing down' of the Good News. In this article I refer to it as 'the telling of the story'. Because of this I understand it as one activity within the ministry of Christian education. As a word I am hesitant to think that we can redefine it away from its etymological roots to make it describe the totality of what we are about as Christian educators. This Christian education can be either formal or informal. In an informal sense the church's whole way of being in the world is educational both for its members and for its non-members. However, in this paper I am using Christian education to refer to any deliberate and formal attempt that has as its intention that of fulfilling the task of Christian education as described above. Stating the obvious, but perhaps necessary because of our past conditioning, this is not to equate our education with schooling. In my use of the terms Christian education and catechesis here I am indebted to Richard McBrien's paper, 'Toward an American catechesis,' delivered at the East Coast Conference for Religious Education, Washington, February 27, 1976.
3. I trust it will be clear that my turning to Habermas is not a naive attempt to 'apply' him to Christian education. Instead, I use his insights to clarify what I mean by praxis and also to substantiate the rationale for claiming that the critically reflective moment of praxis can be emancipatory.
4. Nicholas Lobkowicz, *Theory and Practice: history of a concept from Aristotle to Marx,* Notre Dame, Indiana, University of Notre Dame Press, 1967, p. 3.
5. Richard J Bernstein, *Praxis and Action,* Philadelphia, University of Pennsylvania Press, 1971, p. IX.
6. Jürgen Habermas, *Knowledge and Human Interests,* Boston, Beacon Press, 1971, p. 301.

7. Lobkowicz, *Theory and Practice, op. cit.,* p. 9.
8. Trent Schroyer, *The Critique of Domination,* New York, George Brazille, 1973, p. 141.
9. Habermas, *Knowledge and Human Interests, op. cit.,* p. 31.
10. *Ibid.,* p. 43.
11. *Ibid.,* p. 44.
12. See Martin Jay, *The Dialectical Imagination,* London, Heinemann Educational, 1973; Trent Schroyer, *The Critique of Domination,* New York, Braziller, 1973; Anthony Quinton, 'Critical theory: on the Frankfurt school,' *Encounter,* 43, 1974; Edward Schillebeeckx, *The Understanding of Faith,* New York, Seabury Press, 1974.
13. Jürgen Habermas, *Theory and Practice,* Boston, Beacon Press, 1973, p. 9.
14. Jürgen Habermas, *Toward a Rational Society,* Boston, Beacon Press, 1968, p. 82.
15. *Ibid.,* p. 83.
16. Habermas, *Knowledge and Human Interests, op. cit.,* p. 175.
17. *Ibid.,* p. 176.
18. *Ibid.,* p. 310.
19. *Ibid.,* pp. 18–19.
20. *Ibid.,* p. 208.
21. *Ibid.,* p. 205.
22. I personally wish we could settle for the term 'praxis theology' rather than liberation theology. While 'liberation' is an empowering and clarifying word for us as we speak about the meaning of the Christ event, in our culture it has probably been discredited for now, just by association of ideas, for example when I mention liberation to a general audience some of them immediately think of the Symbionese Liberation Army.
23. Francis P Fiorenza, 'Latin American liberation theology,' *Interpretation,* 28, 1974, p. 441.
24. Edward Schillebeeckx, *The Understanding of Faith,* New York, Seabury Press, 1974, p. 154.
25. Gustabo Gutiérrez, *A Theology of Liberation,* Maryknoll, New York, Orbis Books, 1973, p. 145.
26. *Ibid.,* p. 11.
27. In this regard I believe the valuable exploratory work of Charles Davis on praxis as a theological method holds much promise for the development of a full scale praxis theology. See Charles Davis, *Theology and Praxis: Cross Currents,* Summer, 1973 and *Toward a Critical Theology in Philosophy of Religion and Theology,* 1975, American Academy of Religion Annual Meeting, 1975, compiled by James W McClendon Jr, Printing Department, University of Montana, Missoula, Montana, 1975.
28. Paulo Freire, *Pedagogy of the Oppressed,* New York, Herder and Herder, 1970, p. 58.
29. Gabriel Moran, *The Present Revelation,* New York, Seabury Press, 1972, p. 21.
30. Walter M Abbott (ed.), *The Documents of Vatican II,* New York, Guild Press, 1966, pp. 201–202.
31. I intend a Freudian meaning for 'evaluative analysis'. The analysis is not simply an intuitive looking at the situation in question, which would be contemplative, but rather a critical analysis of it that bares the social influences that were formative of the present attitude.
32. Remembering here, like analysis, is not a facile calling to mind. This would still maintain past influences in a reified way. Rather, it is a critical remembering that undoes the reification of the past, thus releasing repressed dialogue, so that the present can transform the past memory rather than be controlled by it. The meaning I intend for both 'analysis' and 'remembering' are similar to what Habermas means when he speaks about 'analytically remembering'. See Habermas, *Knowledge and Human Interests, op. cit.,* p. 301.
33. Paul Ricoeur, *Freud and Philosophy,* New Haven, Connecticut, Yale University Press, 1970, p. 219.
34. To say how this might be done would be the subject of another article. However, let me say in passing that if the story is to be experienced as an event, then the

sacramental symbols that are the expressions of our story and of our hope are powerful possibilities.

35. I should note that in their genesis these steps were informed by the steps outlined by Freire in *Pedagogy of the Oppressed, op. cit.,* pp. 102 ff.

36. Walter Wink, *The Bible in Human Transformation,* Philadelphia, Fortress Press, 1973, p. 19.

5.2 Christian education as faith translation
Douglas E Wingeier

The extreme individualism, cultural pluralism, and knowledge explosion which characterise today's society have created a climate in which persons are forced to do their own thinking and decision-making. The alternatives to making meaning out of one's own experience are often intellectual confusion on the one hand and submission to authoritarianism on the other. This is no less a challenge to Christians than to others in our culture. The winds of scepticism and relativism have made it virtually impossible to rely on an authoritative book, creed, or hierarchy to provide intellectual or moral certainty.

To those for whom theology had once provided a sure avenue to truth and reliable guidelines for decision-making, this wholesale questioning of the 'tried and true' has caused consternation and disillusionment. Persons have been forced to recognise that their faith is not so much a set of propositions 'once and for all delivered to the saints' (Jude 3) as it is a commitment to certain values and persons which is both informed and tested by a growing, changing perspective on life.

For Christians, this belief system is shaped by scripture and tradition, and interpreted through the filters of personal experience and rational faculties. This process of rational interpretation of our experience in the light of the root sources of faith in scripture and tradition is what is meant by faith translation. It is a two-way process, involving the development of a belief system, and the assigning of meaning to experience in terms of this growing understanding.

Unless these two aspects are kept closely connected, the groundwork is laid for the separation between religion and life. Conceptual learning and making meaning of experience are two sides of the same coin, and must be integrated in the process of faith translation, and in the programme of Christian education which makes it possible. One of the essential functions of Christian education is to provide the resources, guidelines, and skills for faith translation, and to give opportunity to practise it within a caring and intentional community.

Educational factors

Faith translation, to be meaningful and effective, must take account of several factors in the educational process, notably human development, enculturation, and historical consciousness.

Human development: Of course, the process of faith translation is one which culminates only in adulthood, when the needed cognitive abilities, experiential background, and physical and emotional capacities are available in fully-developed form. But persons of all ages experience life and require a perceptive system, a set of values, an understanding of self, and a network of relationships within which to assimilate and make sense of it. Hence, faith translation is an appropriate and necessary activity at every age, and assistance and training for it must be provided in keeping with what is understood about the developmental needs, tasks, and capabilities of persons at each stage of development. The insights of Erikson, Piaget, Kohlberg, Fowler, and others therefore provide valuable guidance for Christian educators in designing procedures to enable persons to engage in faith translation.

Enculturation: Both religious concepts and experience of necessity grow out of the world view, value systems and network of communities in which persons are educated. Persons tend to assume the values, belief system and self-identity which are transmitted to them through the group in which they find security and belonging. A community with a story, tradition, and climate of caring and support will communicate its values to its members, and instil a sense of commitment and loyalty. A church which is also a community will be an effective matrix for socialisation and growth. Through its agency, both the 'faith delivered to the saints' and the daily experience of individuals must be translated into thoughtforms relevant to and understandable by the community. Faith translation makes use of this enculturation process in enabling persons to develop categories of meaning for interpreting their experience which are relevant to life in their setting and at the same time establish the ties of a common story with their faith community.

Historical consciousness: Christians are people with a history, affirming a continuity with the whole people of God and claiming origins in the biblical story of the people of Israel and the followers of Jesus. Throughout their history, God had raised interpreters of the divine message. God's gift of steadfast, reconciling love is timeless, but has been embodied and translated by God's people in each new situation.

Hence, at each stage of history, the forms of worship and congregational life and the symbolic actions and words which have best communicated the divine message have been quite different. Where for one age David's dance before the ark was appropriate, for another only sombre songs rendered in whole notes seemed fitting. At one time the image of God as king spoke relevantly of sovereignty, whereas at another 'the family of God' concept more adequately expressed God's nature. At one point in history temporal and spiritual powers were wedded in a union of church and state, while at others Christians linked arms to defy civil authorities − in the Coliseum at Rome or on the streets of Selma. This re-translation of a timeless message is first evident in the bible, as when Jesus upset previous notions by giving human need priority over ritualistic rules in his attitude toward the sabbath, or when New Testament writers interpreted the Messianic passages to apply to Jesus.

It is from this perspective that we view the task of Christian education. Faith is not just a set of propositions or a body of knowledge to be preserved and transmitted from one generation to the next. Rather, faith is a vital relationship with God, the expressions of which must change to be relevant to the life circumstances of different ages. We expect the image of a living God to change as God is self-manifest in different times and places. The task of Christian education then, is not to freeze past conceptions and extract from them ideas and forms which make us secure in the present, but rather to discover how and where God is expressing himself to bring persons into encounter with these fresh, dynamic manifestations. These experiences then need to be understood and communicated in meaningful thought forms which may be evaluated in light of time-tested guidelines.

Historical consciousness thus involves a sensitivity to the historically conditioned nature of past formulations of truth, an openness to dynamic new expressions, and commitment to the continuous translation of God's timeless revelation into forms relevant to contemporary culture. Historical documents are thus understood in light of the cultural conditions out of which they are produced. One may thereby distinguish between the dated elements of these writings and those which are still meaningful today. According to this understanding, all particular formulations of religious truth — whether contained in the bible or developed by later generations — are relative to the culture and thought forms out of which they grew. No book, creed or form of polity can possibly contain or convey the fullness of the divine revelation to persons in all times and places.

Christian education must help persons develop this historical consciousness — to accept the limits of the human mind to comprehend the nature and will of God, to become aware that scripture and tradition are culturally-conditioned and thus historically-limited interpretations of God's word, to understand that these formulations do not limit but rather point to truth, and to bring the essential meaning of past heritage into the present without imposing the cultural framework in which it was originally set.

Doing faith translation

Theology traditionally has been defined as the knowledge or science of God. The term has usually referred to the systematic discipline of discovering, expounding and defending religious truths. It has been largely a deductive endeavour, starting with the revelation of God through the bible and attempting to incorporate all the experience of the community of faith into one logical, comprehensive, and internally consistent system of thought. Because this task has required special skills, training, and vocabulary, it for the most part has been confined to a small, elite group of professional theologians.

Faith translation takes an opposite approach. It is inductive, reflective, and all-inclusive. Every Christian − in fact, every human being who thinks seriously about experience in relation to ultimate concerns − is considered a theologian. The process of theologising begins with experience and attempts to discover meanings therein and relate them to religious beliefs which have been found meaningful by previous generations. Theology from this perspective is not a system but a process. It is not primarily an abstract theoretical exercise, but a concrete reflection on experience. It discovers the concepts of redemption, grace, koinonia, covenant, and resurrection through identifying them in the ongoingness of life.

Thus, to leave theology to the professional theologians is to deprive the ordinary person of the necessary and growth-producing task of utilising reliable guidelines to make meaning out of experience. In this sense it is difficult to conceive of a growing Christian who does not reflect theologically on experience as a regular practice. Therefore, it is essential that Christian education equip persons with the skills and procedures to do it adequately

To do this, an awareness of the factors involved in the learning process is essential. Persons have a natural *potential* for learning and growth. One is motivated to learn when one sees the *relevance* of the experience at hand to one's needs, interests, or goals. Learning proceeds in continuity from the known to the unknown. What is learned is influenced by one's *perceptual screen* which is composed of individual biases, meanings, images, concerns and poses. Learning involves active *dialogue* with a task, idea, person, or group. When self-perceptions are challenged, or new ideas and experiences encountered, real *pain* is felt as a condition of significant learning.

Learning occurs through *doing* and problem-solving. At the same time, *knowing*, or the acquisition and comprehension of data, is also essential. Learning is also facilitated by responsible participation in the educational process − *choosing* directions, and deciding actions. The confluent learning of the whole person involves *feeling* as well as thinking. Because learning is *change*, persons must learn how to learn, thus remaining open to new experience. An important goal of education is the *empowerment* of persons to act responsibly. Learning takes place through interpersonal relationships and through *identification* with the life style and commitments of the teacher and community.

In some religious communions, the guidelines developed for faith translation are scripture, tradition, reason, and experience. Taken together, these four are interdependent and both set boundaries to, and encourage freedom, flexibility, and variety in, the theologising process. In the process of faith translation, each of the four both informs and tests the other three, so that in the 'forcefield' thus created, the growing person and his or her faith are engaged in a continuous sequence of experience-reflection-action. Let us examine these guidelines more closely.

Scripture: The bible is viewed by some persons as being the infallible word of God. Others see it as containing God's word, as a human record in which persons express the way God's revelation has come to them. Still others describe it as a source book containing guidelines for faith and life, rooted in the past but still relevant today.

Another view is that the bible is the history of God's people. God is self-revealed in the events from creation through the cross to the founding of the church. Through understanding this story, we can come to know God and God's word and will for today. In this historical record is a frequent witness to the intense interaction between God and God's people, both individual and collective. And in the reading of it one is encountered by the spirit of the living God who invites the reader to enter a growing and confronting relationship with God in the here and now. Each of these views is an expression of the meaning the bible has for some persons.[1]

In interpreting scripture as a basis for faith translation, several principles have been developed by biblical scholars.

1. We must try to understand the life world out of which the passage comes and to which it is addressed. The more we know of the thought forms and daily life of the people of the bible, the better we can understand the meaning behind the words of the bible.
2. Likewise, we must be aware of the life world out of which we come as we interact with the bible. The interpretation we give to what we read is coloured by our preconceptions of what the world is like, which in turn are strongly influenced by our world view, value system, and communication patterns.
3. We are to search for the intentionality of the text. As we try to discover what the writer was intending to communicate, we are better able to avoid proof-texting and private interpretation, and to get behind a literal reading to the major emphasis which is consistent with the total biblical message.
4. Parts must be related to the whole. By determining the primary elements in the biblical revelation as a whole, as well as examining the context of a specific passage, we can better discover the value and validity of particular emphases or verses.
5. Similarly, while not expecting complete consistency and uniformity, we are to look for common themes. As a tapestry of divine-human encounter woven together by many unifying threads, the bible is itself an expression of theological pluralism.

6. If we remain open, we can expect an event to happen in us as we read the bible, for the word of God will address us at our point of need and vulnerability. We are to ask, what is God wanting to say to me through the scripture?

7. A related principle is to make interpretation situational and concrete. Even as God revealed himself through the historical events recorded in scripture, so God is calling us to repond in terms of specific situations in the here and now.

8. Finally, we are reminded that interpretation takes place within the Christian community. Hearing and responding to God's word is not a private matter, but must be tested in dialogue and life together with other members of the body. Written interpretations and helps prepared by committed Christians who have devoted their lives to the study of scripture must be utilised. Group bible study and corporate sharing of insights engender a climate of mutual teaching and learning out of which may emerge a growing consensus of what God is saying to God's people in a particular time and place.

When these eight principles are followed, the meaning of God's message in scripture becomes clearer, and Christian educators become more effective in engaging persons in faith translation in dialogue with and response to the word.

Tradition: Tradition is the dynamic, ongoing process by which the past becomes present and is carried into the future. It is not primarily a body of knowledge or belief which is to be preserved and transmitted from one generation to the next. Rather, it is the living process by which a culture or religious group understands itself and the events which shape its identity and lifestyle. In the words of 'Fiddler on the Roof', 'because of our traditions everyone here knows who he is and what God expects him to do'.

The word 'tradition' is used in three senses – the normative, the historical, and the dynamic. In the *normative* sense, tradition is the living, self-renewing word of God revealing himself anew to each age and setting. As revealed to and through the people of Israel and Jesus and his followers, it is recorded in but not confined to the bible. The tradition is the spring out of which flows a never-ending succession of traditions. In the Old Testament, the law, the prophets, and the writings represent three successive stages of tradition or interpretation – each created in response to the life-giving word. The New Testament, the early creeds and countless efforts at faith translation in the long centuries since, are all similarly efforts of God's people to respond to the tradition by developing traditions. In this historical sense, each religious body has a tradition by which it is identified. This is made up of its distinctive doctrinal emphases, worship forms, organisational patterns, and styles of interaction. All of these are strongly influenced by the historical circumstances and cultural origins out of which the group developed.

Tradition in the dynamic sense is the traditioning process — the ongoing ineraction of God's word with God's people — through which the tradition is translated into traditions relevant to particular times and places. It is through this process that the grace and power of God are continually made known in new forms of expression, patterns of common life, and doctrinal formulations.

From one perspective the traditioning process is the activity of God's spirit judging the incompleteness of particular traditions, creating vital new expressions of the tradition, and calling people to respond in ways which are both faithful and innovative, both responsible and liberating.

From another perspective the traditioning process is known as intentional religious socialisation.[2] By this means a community of faith initiates individuals into its world view, values, and lifestyle, and leads them gradually to make these their own. In this process persons develop a sense of identity through commitment and belonging to the community, and at the same time the community renews its understanding and way of life while remaining faithful to its origins. Christian educators concerned that this enculturation process be effective and vital will give attention not only to formal classroom teaching but also to all aspects of the congregation's life together which have potential impact on the young. These include the forms of architecture and room arrangement, styles of relating and decision-making, patterns of worship and fellowship, and activities of stewardship and service.

There are several important implications of tradition for Christian education.

1.   Christian faith has a content. Members of the Christian community must know this content. The story of the bible and the theological meanings derived from it must be taught and learned. To help persons learn their own tradition does not mean a mere recitation of historical facts or memorisation of doctrinal affirmations, however. A more constructive approach is to help persons develop appreciation for the struggles of their forebears in the faith out of which their particular expressions of the tradition were formed. These understandings then become the conceptual framework for making meaning out of experience. The antennae for perceiving the activity of God in everyday events, and the values which orient one toward a Christian lifestyle, are developed through engagement with scripture and tradition in the lifelong process of faith translation.

2.   The function of Christian education is not simply to conserve and pass on woodenly a set doctrinal formulation. Rather, it must recognise that each traditional statement is only an imperfect

and culturally-conditioned expression of the living tradition, and hence subject to interpretation in light of new experience through which God reveals God's will to contemporary persons. Hence, the task of Christian education is not only to enable persons to become aware of the living tradition and its expressions in a variety of traditions, but also to participate with God in the traditioning process – translating the word into vital, contemporary forms. New patterns of worship, art forms, ways of ordering the common life, and mission endeavours are all avenues for faith translation.

3. Christian education can make a vital contribution to overcoming the barriers of doctrine, polity, and worship pattern which have divided the Christian community. Through learning that faithful and creative response to the tradition is a more basic responsibility than rigid adherence to a particular tradition, Christians will be better able to accept and respect one another as being together within the larger context of grace.

4. This approach to tradition also makes the climate of doctrinal pluralism both acceptable and desirable. The traditions are understood as culturally-conditioned interpretations of God's self-revelation at different points in history. As such they all are affirmed as evidences of the faithfulness of God's people, and as sources of learning about what God has revealed in the past. At the same time, they are not to be venerated in ways which lead to intolerance or primary loyalty. To give one's loyalty primarily to the tradition of one denomination or school of thought, while perhaps orthodox in the sense of remaining within a particular doctrinal stance, may actually become quite heretical by blinding one to the activity of God in the traditioning process of the present.

5. Christian education takes seriously the experience of the person and community in the here and now, for it is here that God is actively revealing himself. The learning process consists of a dialogue between event and reflection on event – between experience and tradition. Each throws light on the other, and in this dialogical process new insights come into being. A young fellowship expresses and experiences God's redemptive love through welcoming an unattractive teenager. The discouragement of an abortive social action project, when understood in the light of the Hebrew exile, makes possible a deeper grasp of the eschatological hope. An experience of alienation in family relationships, set alongside the story of Hosea and Gomer, grounds one in the assurance of God's mercy and steadfast love.

As Christian educators engage in the traditioning process in these ways, they combine the transmissive and creative functions of education. Thus they are both faithful to the identity of the church as a people of history and responsive to the dynamic, revelatory activity of God in the experience of the present.

Reason: Reason is the power of the human intellect. Its role is to order, categorise and make sense out of human experience. The human person is meaning-maker. She or he utilises the categories of thought and value and the mental functions of sensation, perception, association, imagination, analysis, conceptualisation, logic, and memory, in the process of making meaning out of the events of life. These mental processes are the gifts of God to all persons regardless of religious persuasion.

Reason is a test of the interpretations developed out of scripture, tradition, and experience. Faith expressed cognitively must take adequate account of science and empirical knowledge, and the principles of coherence and consistency. At the same time what seems rational must be measured against the standards of scripture, tradition, and experience, for it must be recognised that religious truth may transcend the limits of human rationality. The primary tools available to human beings to apprehend and interpret scripture, tradition, and experience, however, are the rational faculties. All faith translation of necessity involves reason.

If our formulations of faith are to be clear, cogent, credible, and communicable, it is important to examine the correlation between revelation and reason, faith and science, grace and nature. For Christian education, this means that insight from general education and the behavioural sciences are valid and necessary resources. Persons are whole and respond in like ways in all kinds of settings. Christian educators need a thorough understanding of how learning takes place, how personality develops, how communication occurs, how groups function, how knowledge is acquired, how behaviour is modified, how concepts are formed, how a society may be organised with justice and equity, and how values become operative in individual and social living. The task of Christian education is to enable persons to utilise this knowledge and skill in apprehending the message of God, interpreting their experience in its light, and communicating it in ways relevant to contemporary thought forms and life styles.

What is needed is a creative integration between these tools and insights and the wisdom about the human experience made known through God's interaction with people past and present. This may be accomplished through a method of correlation[3] which is based on four affirmations:

a. the primary aim of Christian education is so to transform society and shape human experience that persons may actualise the image of God in which they are created;

b. the world is one and it is God's and the church exists within it, so that experiences of the learner in

both church and society partake of the same characteristics;
c.   truth is one and it is God's, which means that insights into
the learning process, personality development, and group
dynamics come ultimately from God and apply with equal
validity to both general and Christian education;
d.   the learner is one and she or he is God's and thus has a
common set of responses and core of experiences to bring
to the education enterprise in either a secular or a religious
setting.

Operating from these assumptions, the method of correlation will be
sensitive to crossing points between meanings from the biblical story
and living tradition on the one hand, and insights from the realm of
human experience as interpreted by reason on the other. These points
of intersection between faith and experience remain unrecognised to
the person who is totally immersed either in the here and now or in
the historical language of faith. A dialogical stance is required —
an openness to the revelation of God through all four sources of
religious truth (scripture, tradition, reason, and experience), and a
searching attitude to discover the crossing points among them.

The role of educational ministry is to help persons adopt the
attitude of expectancy expressed by Samuel — 'Speak, Lord, for your
servant is listening' — as they enter life's experiences. The method of
correlation depends on both elements in the dialogical process — *listening* to what experience has to teach and *speaking* the word of faith
in making religious meaning out of experience. Christian education
can enable persons to develop both of these abilities.

Experience: God is active in and reveals himself through all experience. Some religious traditions place heavy emphasis on 'religious
experience', describing it in terms of personal faith and assurance of
God's pardoning love, abiding presence, and sure guidance. But
in reality there is no event which takes place outside the sphere of
God's creative and redemptive care, and no experience in which a
person who has eyes to see and ears to hear may not encounter God
and learn from God.

Of course, the meaning attached to experience is largely conditioned by the way one has been socialised by the culture. The set
of categories through which one views an event is mainly acquired
from parents and others who mediate the world to young children.

When one's perceptive system, set of values, and self-image are
specifically Christian, one then begins to interpret experience in self-
consciously theological terms. Everyday events all involve interaction
with God. Thus, not only the experiences traditionally referred to
as religious — salvation, prayer, worship, fellowship, etc. — but
all experience is to be understood as 'religious experience'. God's
creative, reconciling, and judging love intersects with all of life. Our

response is to be aware of God's activity, to correlate our understanding of the biblical story with the events in our own story, and to be faithful in living out of this understanding.

Thus, grace is found in both a conversion experience during a church service and the acceptance of an unlovely or mischievous child by a dedicated teacher. Redemption is seen in both the life-changing encounter of an alcoholic with the 'power beyond oneself' introduced by Alcoholics Anonymous and the inclusion of a young person from a broken home in a caring youth fellowship. The work of God's spirit is perceived in both the inspiration of a mountain-top worship experience and the deep fellowship of an encounter group. The activity of God is identified in both the rapid church growth of a country like Indonesia and the feeding of the hungry, redistribution of land, and empowerment of women in mainland China. The healing power of God is experienced in both prayer and surgery.

One example of how faith grows out of experience occurred on an overnight campout of junior children during vacation church school. After all were supposedly asleep, the boys crept out and staged a raid on the girls. The girls were frightened, and one became so hysterical that she had to be taken home. The boys regretted their escapade, but could not find a way to apologise. The next day the leaders told the story of the prodigal son and opened up a discussion on the theme of reconciliation. This enabled the boys to say they were sorry and the girls to express their forgiveness. The group experienced a real healing of relationships. During the closing moments of worship, they became profoundly aware that the God of grace and reconciliation was present among them. They knew what these concepts meant because they had encountered the realities of separation and forgiveness in a concrete experience. They were theologising about their experience, and internalising the meanings as elements in a growing belief system. This was faith translation!

Christian education must provide individuals with opportunities like this to encounter God in their experience. Experiences of acceptance, belonging, confrontation, conflict, service, witness, and sharing can serve as aspects of the curriculum of Christian education and as data for the process of faith translation. For God is working in all events and experiences to accomplish the divine purpose.

The task of Christian education in relation to experience is thus seen to be several-fold:

a. to take human experience seriously as the arena of God's activity of creation, redemption, and revelation, and to develop the programme of Chrisian nurture around the experience of the learner;
b. to make persons aware that God is present in all the events of their lives, and to enable them to respond to God there in faith and mission;

c. to help persons develop a perceptive system, set of values, self image, and network of relationships, which are self-consciously Christian, so that they may apprehend and respond to their experience out of this perspective;

d. to enable persons to develop the sensitivity and skill to reflect on and comprehend their experience in terms of the images of the biblical story;

e. to help persons discover the crossing points between the categories of biblical faith and the events of everyday life. It is at these points that life-transforming insights may penetrate to the core of the consciousness through the agency of the Holy Spirit, and personal identity may be shaped in the image of God. It is at these points that faith translation takes place.

To call to each person to theologise by correlating faith with experience and making meaning out of everyday events makes theological pluralism both desirable and inevitable. Since the experience of each individual or sub-culture is unique, and each one's perception of events is coloured by a distinctive set of understandings and values, each person's theology will be different. Christian faith is too rich and dynamic to be captured in any one set of worship forms or credal statements.

As the word is made flesh in different settings, it will be expressed in a variety of ways. But each will be valid for its interpreters, because each will be a product of serious, rational reflection upon their experience of life, based on a study of scripture and an awareness of their faith tradition. This is the basis of responsible pluralism, in which persons love and respect one another and value what they can learn from each other's experience to inform and nurture their respective pilgrimages of faith.

Responsible doctrinal pluralism is to be clearly distinguished from a 'theological indifferentism' which holds that all beliefs are equally valid and that a person need only be sincere in his or her faith. Responsible pluralism rejects this *laissez faire* stance, while at the same time realising that it is not enough simply to attempt to recover an old credal orthodoxy or establish a new one. Instead it affirms that truth transcends any human effort to capture and convey it. It therefore encourages freedom and respect for a variety of expressions of religious truth, as shaped by and addressed to the needs and conditions of various cultural groups and historical settings. Responsible theological pluralism is grounded in the common core of biblical teaching, and expects to find some aspects of the word of God expressed in the distinctive emphases of various denominations, as well as in current and developing theological positions such as the theology of liberation and process theology.

Christian education will assist persons in developing this attitude of responsible pluralism, as a basis for determining their own theological position and for engaging in dialogue with those of other persuasions. This will involve both the nurture of a mature self-acceptance, sense of security and recognition of one's human limitations, and the exposure to a wide spectrum of theological thought.

Faith translation is thus seen to be an essential function of Christian education. It not only undergirds a much-needed stance of responsible doctrinal pluralism, but also contributes significantly to the growth in faith and understanding of Christians.

Notes

1. See Dorothy Jean Furnish, *Exploring the Bible with Children,* New York, Abingdon Press, 1975, pp. 28–39, for a more complete description of these and other ways of viewing the bible.
2. The concept of intentional religious socialisation is developed by John H Westerhoff III and Gwen Kennedy Neville in *Generation to Generation,* Philadelphia, United Church Press, 1974.
3. The method of correlation was first developed by Paul Tillich. It is applied to religious education in a helpful way in Joseph D Ban, *Education for Change,* Valley Forge, Judson Press, 1968, pp. 59–68.

5.3 Critical openness in Christian nurture
John M Hull et al

Christian nurture

The British Council of Churches' report *The Child in the Church*[1] distinguished Christian nurture from secular education, instruction and indoctrination. 'Instruction may be to do with learning the skills which will get you a job; secular education is to do with becoming a reflective person; Christian nurture is to do with becoming a Christian person.' In that report we found Christian nurture to be compatible with secular education but incompatible with indoctrination. It has a difference in aim from secular education since it is concerned to further enquiry and personal development in accordance with a Christian understanding of personhood. Indoctrination, however, seeks to deprive a person of personhood. It is concerned with conformity to correct ideas, not open to rational argument and persuasion, and must override individual judgment. However, this position poses a number of questions. Believing Christian nurture is about nurturing children into a received tradition (a Christian past) how can this be effected while avoiding the dangers of indoctination? Is it possible to nurture into a tradition with a dogmatic basis and yet be open? What is the rationale in theology for a Christian nurture which would be non-authoritarian and open to other views? These were the kinds of questions posed by our previous work and which led us to make the recommendation: 'We recommend that the renewal of the churches' ministry in nurturing both children and adults requires for its support a theology which sees critical openness as springing from Christian commitment.' In other words we saw 'critical openness' as the central idea in the resolution of these problems. It is the main feature which distinguishes the faith-fostering activities of the mainstream churches from those of the sects. Without an understanding of this there is no satisfactory way in which Christian upbringing in open, plural societies can be defended against the charge that it is indoctrinatory, and without the practice of critical openness there is no way whereby Christian adults can be formed so as to live freely and creatively in plural societies.

Armed with the idea of critical openness let us return to the situation in which Christian nurture exists side by side with secular education. We see that critical openness is a central feature of western education. The education of the young child emphasises discovery, exploration, stimulating and directing the child's curiosity. The older pupil is to become critically aware of his or her own beliefs and values. He or she is encouraged to look at evidence, to give reasons and to think for him or her self. Secular education and Christian nurture share the same spirit of critical openness but they differ in their goals, the latter seeking to deepen Christian life and faith whilst the former is compatible with a wide range of religious and non-religious attitudes. In educational discussion critical openness is usually called autonomy.

Christian nurture, as the process of learning and growing which intends to deepen Christian faith, once had a dominant position, if not a virtual monopoly of the learning situations in Britain. Christian learning was the main model of learning, and this situation continued even after the state entered education in its own right in 1870. For most of the century which followed, the church, the church school and the county or state school were in partnership as offering Christian nurture. Today all that is changed. Secular education has come of age. The study of education, through its branches such as educational psychology, philosophy and sociology, has now generated a wide range of theories of education and models of schooling, and the process of Christian nurture, once taken for granted, is now exposed as but one amongst many processes and types of learning. How does Christian nurture relate to the processes of secular education and secular schooling? In what ways is it similar? In what ways is it different? Christian nurture can appear to be rather parochial, rather narrow, offering only constricted horizons to young people, while secular education presents itself as open, all-embracing, allied with scientific discovery, able, through a multitude of techniques and aids, to offer the widest opportunities to all. Will not Christian nurture seem to be concerned with its own survival rather than with the genuine wellbeing of the young? May it not even appear to be a process of indoctrination?

Not only is our society marked by various patterns of learning, most of which are secular, but it is increasingly varied religiously. Most religious groups seem to have found the relativity and the comparisons which are implied by their living side by side an embarrassment. Various ways of dealing with this may be seen, ranging from the attempt to establish dominance over the society, to a virtual withdrawal from society. In the plural cities of the Middle East (and of Belfast) communities are geographically divided along religious lines. This certainly simplifies the problem of transmission of an undiluted religious heritage. In most western countries we find a proliferation of religious sects, marked by their vigorous proselytism, removing the young convert from the family or secluding him or her from society entirely for a time. The sectarian patterns of instruction tend to be very authoritarian, with an emphasis on obedient acceptance of the doctrines of the movement, teaching certain standard replies to objections, and training in how to ward off criticisms. One can see the advantages of these methods. They seem likely to prevent the movement from suffering from competition, and to increase the coherence of the movement and its hold over its young people.

But what should be the policy of the main Christian churches in these matters? Generally speaking, particularly in recent years, the ecumenical churches have been uneasy about closed authoritarian instruction, and have often adopted a policy of deliberate openness towards each other and the various surrounding religious and educational movements. But is there not some risk that the open approach will mean that our young people and children will be lost to less scrupulous bodies? And do not young people develop with greater confidence when protected? Does not the very word 'nurture' suggest a degree of secluded protection? And what is the rationale in theology itself for a Christian nurture which would be non-authoritarian and open to other views?

Critical openness and autonomy

The expressions 'critical openness' and 'autonomy' are similar but not identical. Both describe the one who thinks for him or her self, and both agree that this is not to be confused with thinking what one likes. A person who thinks for himself in mathematics has freedom with the concepts he is using and may even be creative with them. He is their master because he understands them. But they have also mastered him. He is under their discipline, and he cannot just think what he likes about them. It is because the ideas of autonomy and critical openness emphasise the importance of understanding reasons that this distinction is made between thinking for oneself and thinking what someone (whether yourself or someone else) happens to like to think.

Another similarity between critical openness and autonomy is that the two ideas each imply a process of growth, or are states achieved during or after growth. Educational philosophers and psychologists have often discussed the obstacles to autonomy, and the means of fostering its early appearance. Growth is necessary not only to attain autonomy but also to maintain it. Autonomy may be lost not only to others but also to my own past self. If my past self so directs my thinking as to stop me from responding with suitable creativity to the problems of today, I have become heteronomous – ruled by another self, my own past self.

Although, as we have seen, being autonomous requires one to be open to the call of reason, and in that sense to stand under the discipline of reason, this aspect of the idea is more obvious in the expression 'critical openness'. To be open is to listen, to be ready to receive other persons, to hear new ideas, to re-examine one's own past, whereas autonomy could perhaps suggest a certain isolation, even a self-enclosed independence, or it might suggest individualism, whereas critical openness is intended to suggest that one is in a community, a learning community, in which one both speaks and listens, being both critical and receptive. A pre-requisite of learning is humility. You must recognise that there is something to be learned and that it may be worth learning. The term 'critical openness' suggests better than the term 'autonomy' this humility and this probing towards the unknown.

The expression 'critical openness' has another advantage. The things which exist to be known are more important than the satisfactions they give us in knowing them. The objects of knowledge have what we might call a primacy of value over the various values which knowing selves derive from their knowledge, like a feeling of fulfilment. This view of knowledge is not confined to Christians and it can be defended on purely philosophical grounds, but it is consistent with Christian faith, and indeed, seems to be required by it. God is glorified because of being God, not because praising God gives the believer a sense of wellbeing. God is trusted because God is worthy of trust, not because such trust secures salvation. Just so, if we take this view, the world itself is to be investigated not mainly because such investigation is useful, or satisfying, or tending to produce certain ethical qualities, but because it is marvellous. In the end, it is that which makes the investigation satisfying and gives it its ethical qualities. Again, history is to be studied not primarily because of its contemporary relevance, or its character-building effects but because humanity itself is worthy of study, and the study of history is a love of the human past, not seen merely as a curiosity, but as a critical and self-critical brotherly interest and respect for the people of the past. Now, the idea of autonomy usually takes the form of announcing conditional regulations for the living of the rational life: 'In as much as one believes, feels and acts, one should do so truthfully, reasonably.' We may contrast this view, which states how one should live *to the extent* that one decides to live that way, with the view which declares that we *ought* to actively pursue new knowledge, ought to seek truth, ought to follow hard after beauty, because they demand this of us. The latter view could be called 'open rationality'. It is clearly close to Christian faith, and has affinities with the Christian virtues of faith, hope and love. While the word autonomy could express these emphases, the term 'critical openness' is a more effective way of highlighting them.

Theological roots

Critical openness is also related to the New Testament image of the Christian life. 'The prophets who prophesied of the grace that was to be yours searched and enquired about this salvation. They enquired what person or time was indicated by the Spirit of Christ within them' (1 Peter 1: 10–11).[2] The prophets are certainly not thought of here as examining the evidence of their prophecies to see if it was credible or not. Rather, they made a spiritual and perhaps mystical search into the inner meaning to discover what was discoverable, the truth hidden there. The sense is similar to John 5:39, where the Jews are spoken of as searching the scriptures. The Beroean Jews (Acts 17:11) displayed a spirit of enquiry which was possibly closer to that which we meet today, when they 'received the word with all eagerness, examining the scriptures daily to see if these things were so'. When the Spirit of God or Christ is described as 'searching', the reference is to a searching out and bringing to light of what is already known, a probing or testing, as when Christ searches the minds and hearts of men and women (Revelation 2:23), or 'The Spirit searches everything, even the depths of God' (1 Corinthians 2:10), but when this searching Spirit indwells in the hearts of believers, they are enabled to search out what they did *not* know before, giving them spiritual insight and discerning power. So 'The spiritual man judges all things, but is himself to be judged by no one' (1 Corinthians 2:15). The penetrating power of the Spirit is spoken of in Romans 8:26–27), where human ignorance of what to pray for is overcome by the searching knowledge of the Spirit, too deep for words. This power of penetrating enquiry is to be turned outwards, as when Christians are advised to 'test the spirits, to see whether they are of God' (1 John 4:1) and inwards, as when the Corinthian Christians were told 'Examine yourselves, to see whether you are holding to your faith. Test yourselves' (2 Corinthians 13:5). The gift of discrimination is impelled by the knowledge of God's discrimination (judgment) between people. 'If we judged ourselves truly, we should not be judged. When we are judged by the Lord we are chastened, so that we may not be condemned along with the world' (1 Corinthians 11:31f). It is because the judgment of the Lord is expressed through his giving of himself in the bread and the wine (1 Corinthians 11:27) that Christians are not only to examine themselves before they partake but also to discern the body of the Lord (vv. 28f). We can see that the critical and discriminating spirit of the early church sprang thus not only from the Old Testament doctrine of the all-searching eye of God but also from the peculiar tension of the early Christian community, caught between a given salvation and a not yet given vindication. It is this situation of being poised on the brink of a great crisis, of being granted complete certainty, yet enjoying it in uncertainty, which gave the Christian critical spirit its essential flavour. On the one hand, 'there is no condemnation' (Romans 8:1) and on the other hand, 'the time has come for judgment to begin with the household of God' (1 Peter 4:17). Certainly, there are times when this critical spirit of testing is to be suspended. When the Corinthian Christians sit down to dinner, they are not to ask questions about the food set before them, just for conscience sake, but to eat it up in the name of faith (1 Corinthians 10:25, 27), and Paul acknowledges the limits of self-knowledge and self-criticism. 'It is a very small thing that I should be judged by you or by any human court. I do not even judge myself' (1 Corinthians 4:3). The key thought is that it is ultimately God who is the supreme tester and validator of hearts. 'It is the Lord who judges me' (1 Corinthians 4:4).

This enquiring spirit of the early church may be called 'eschatological criticism'. It springs from a knowledge that the goal has not yet been grasped (Philippians 3:12), the future not yet known (1 John 3:2), the true and the false grow side by side (Matthew 13:30). Everything therefore was to be tested, and that which survived the test was to be held fast.

'You judge according to the flesh. I judge no one. Yet even if I do judge, my judgment is true, for it is not I alone that judge, but I and he who sent me' (John 8:15 – 16). The opposing poles of human error and divine insight are brought together in the church, which is in the world, and therefore cannot assess, and it is in the Spirit, and therefore assesses everything. The criticism which we have seen to be so marked a feature of the early Christian existence sprang from the ambiguities which this situation posed. Were the prophets true or false (1 John 4:5)? Were the miracles those of Christ or anti-Christ (2 Thessalonians 2:9 – 12)? Satan himself appears as an angel of light. One must be always vigilant, always watchful, ready for constant examination (Luke 12:35 – 40). The stress on this was part of the 'instruction of the Lord' (Ephesians 6:4), part of his chastening, by means of which suffering itself was part of the lesson which disclosed the truth (Hebrews 12:3 – 11), and made the whole Christian life one of discipleship in the school of Christ (Matthew 11:29; 13:52). In some senses, there were limits to this spirit of criticism. The question was which was the wheat and which the tares, not whether there was any wheat. It was a matter of when and where the Christ would come, not whether. And yet, in another sense, there were no limits, for the situation was one from which only the 'end' would bring any escape (1 Thessalonians 5:1 – 11). Until the day when the perfect came, the believer just had to go on, peering into the dark mirror (1 Corinthians 13:12). It was radical in that the tension between the old age and the new age was absolute. It was the doubt and the criticism which belonged to the Kingdom, the seed growing secretly (Mark 4:26 – 29). The critical doubt was itself an expression of life in the Kingdom (Luke 12:54 – 59), since it sprang out of the perception that the Kingdom was, and yet was not yet. The critical testing of all things was a demand of Christian obedience (Mark 13:5 – 6). It was directed to the uncertainties, but it sprang from the certainties (Mark 13:32 – 36). Any child growing up into the Kingdom would have to grow up through that testing, being examined and learning to examine. But this was easy, because of the nature of the child and the nature of the Kingdom. For unless the Kingdom was received as a little child, it could not be entered (Mark 10:15). For the child such learning is natural, and it is also the nature of the Kingdom to consist of such learners.

Christian nurture and general education

Christian nurture is offered by Christians to Christians in order to strengthen Christian faith and to develop Christian character. Christian nurture is easily distinguished from general education, including religious education as carried on in state schools, since the latter does not *intend* to build up Christian faith (although like any other worthwhile activity it may have this effect) nor *must* the teachers of general education, including religious education, be Christians, although they *may* be. Moreover, general education is offered to all. It is possible but not necessary to base general education on Christian faith but it is necessary that Christian nurture should spring from and be defined by Christian faith. The distinction is important but the words which express it may vary. It is quite possible to call 'Christian nurture' 'Christian education' and to mean by the latter term the whole of the Christian upbringing process, but the disadvantage of this terminology is that it may carry the implication that general education is positively or even necessarily non-Christian, whereas, as has just been pointed out, general education *may* spring from Christian presuppositions, and when that is actually the case, such general education is also in a sense, properly described as a Christian education. It is to avoid this confusion that the expression 'Christian nurture' is used.

Grasping the point of the distinction depends to some extent on acknowledging that there is an 'outside' with respect to the church, a realm of human culture and expertise, which pursues its own goals. These goals are to be distinguished from the obvious or immediate goals of church life but they are not necessarily hostile to the church, and may be 'outside' only in the sense that they are ruled by their own logic. So we have such human enterprises as science, medicine, the fine arts and education. Whatever the relation between such pursuits and the institutionalised church as well as the Christian gospel (and these relations are of many kinds, often intimate and subtle) nevertheless they cannot be reduced to ecclesiastical or theological pursuits simply and without remainder. So in order to see the point of the Christian nurture/secular education distinction it is necessary to recognise that Christian faith exists in a plural world, plural not only culturally but intellectually and conceptually. Thus it becomes one thing to seek or intend to bring up one's children as Christians within the church and another thing (not better or worse but different) to seek to educate them vocationally, culturally and intellectually for life in the world. These two activities will of course be related in all sorts of ways; the point is simply that they can be distinguished as well as related and that to some degree the formation of the church's policy in Christian nurture will be shaped by the recognition of the difference.

It may also be that perception of the Christian nurture/secular education distinction is coloured by traditional Christian background. The Catholic Church, for instance, has never relinquished to the state its own prerogative as educator of the people, and possesses an integrated parish and day school system combining both Christian nurture and general education. For many Catholics therefore the distinction may seem unreal, or inapplicable to their own situation, or even misleading and dangerous. For the Free Churches, the right of the state to educate has long been granted, but individuals and churches may differ in the degree to which it is realised that secular education is a more or less independent sphere of activity, and they may also differ about the degree to which the distinction is a good thing or a bad thing. For many Free Church people the perception of the Christian nurture/secular education difference is a matter of how to construe the presence of Christian faith in the world, and so a matter of how to understand mission, especially mission in a secularised and highly specialised society. The Anglican Church occupies an intermediate position and exhibits both kinds of response.

Christian nurture, especially of children, is made more problematic by the fact that it is, in Britain, taking place in a society in which the models of learning are controlled by secular education. It is probably true that the reaction of most religious groups to the relativising pressures of pluralism has been to create special, segregated residential areas. No doubt the Christian, Jewish and Muslim quarters of cities in the Middle East are not only culturally and linguistically convenient but also simplify the passing on of religious belief. But such religious apartheid is ill at ease with the mobility, the mass communications and the common schools of the western democracies. In a society in which education at its best insists that everything is to be examined, how can a process in which some things are not to be examined (if this is indeed the situation of Christian nurture) escape inferior status and moral reproach? Is it then the case that Christian nurture does have affinities with anti-autonomous and conformist processes? If Christians were content, as some seem to be, to let education have a monopoly of critical openness and to allow Christian nurture to be assimilated into Christian instruction or even Christian (*sic*) indoctrination, the problem of the relation of critical openness to Christian nurture would be solved simply by denying that critical openness has any place in Christian nurture.

But then *either* Christian parents think that critical openness is bad for everyone's children, *or* they think it good for other people's children but bad for their own,

or they think it good for other people's children and good for their own except in the area of their religious development.

The first position would mean the breakdown of the Christian enterprise within modern secular education and the triumph, within the churches, of authoritarian instruction. The second position is not much better; indeed, it seems less consistent, and would lead to Christians continuing to support enquiring education in the public sector but withdrawing their own children. But in some ways, the last position is the worst of all, since the young Christian is now given to understand that he or she may think for him or her self in every area except that which is expected to be his or her deepest commitment. Such a policy will not attract worthwhile young people for more than a few years, nor will it deserve to.

If Christian nurture were to be collapsed into Christian instruction the idea of being a Christian person would also have changed. Just as education, instruction, socialisation, indoctrination and so on imply different views of humanity, so Christian nurture, Christian instruction, Christian training and so on imply different views of Christian humanity. Are Christians to be conformist, passive acceptors of authority, unable to adapt to crises, too set in the received ways to think creatively? Only a Christian nurtured in critical openness can have characteristics other than these. For those who think that this *other* Christian life is essential for the continued vitality and relevance of Christian faith, the problem of how Christian nurture is deliberately to promote Christian life and faith while possessing critical openness is a central concern.

The Christian tradition

In our earlier discussion of the New Testament elements in the concept of critical openness, it was pointed out that testing, careful investigation, diligent enquiry and the other New Testament ideas which are similar to our idea of critical openness sprang not accidentally but inevitably from the early Church's understanding of its position between two ages. It would be natural to suppose that the fusion of the Greek spirit of intellectual enquiry with the Hebrew-Christian traditions which took place during the development of patristic theology would have heightened this aspect of Christian living still more, and made self-criticism and open scrutiny of others a strong element in the Christian tradition. This does not seem to have happened in quite this simple manner. Such passages as 1 Timothy 1:3−8; 6:3−4; 2 Timothy 2:2−9; Titus 1:9−11 and 2 Peter 2 suggest that even before the end of the Apostolic Age an authoritarian conservatism was beginning to harden the arteries of the church. Such wide-ranging minds as those of Clement of Alexandria and Origen are to be found, but often the history of Christian thought shows that a period of creative criticism is followed by a time of sterile scholasticism, and this phenomenon is not confined to theology. The European church in the sixteenth century presents a remarkable example of Christian self-criticism, but often one gets the impression that in spite of a profound reappraisal of the foundations of Christian faith the resulting doctrinal systems were taught with majestic authority, as if they themselves were immune to the searching criticism which they devoted to other Christian systems. Not until the late eighteenth and nineteenth centuries, with the rise of biblical criticism and the appearance of such self-critical theologies of culture as that of Friedrich Schleiermacher, does the glory of the Christian critical spirit emerge again. But by then, it was almost too late. Certain assumptions about the nature of Christian faith had gathered such strength that they had become almost instinctive to the ordinary Christian mind. In the many works written in Britain during the first thirty years of the twentieth century which dealt with the problem of introducing the criticism of the bible to schoolchildren, we can see some of the first attempts to reintroduce the critical spirit into the programmes of Christian instruction and nurture which the churches were providing in the schools. The problem-centred method of teaching religious education and the experimental approaches of the 1960s also represented adaptations of Christian nurture to the demands of a critical and exploratory secular education, but during the 1970s there was something of a relapse, many churches returning to more authoritarian kinds of teaching emphasising passivity, acceptance and obedience. The early Christian vision of examination has been splendidly restored in contemporary theology, but it is vital for the faith nurturing programmes of the churches today that it be restored to the Christian nurture and upbringing of children and especially to lay education within the churches.

Several areas of Christian faith and life now seem at first sight to be ill at ease with the spirit of Christian critical openness. These include the idea of the finality of Christian faith, the nature of authority and of revelation, the conception of God, and certain aspects of Christian spirituality. But is it true that these areas are really hostile to critical openness? Might not an examination show that in fact they impel the Christian towards autonomy and criticism?

Christian faith and self criticism

If the Christian faith is final and perfect, how can it require or be amenable to self-criticism? Sometimes an attempt is made to make room for criticism by distinguishing between finality in principle and the actual state of the faith, which is still in progress. In Catholicism, this sometimes takes the form of belief in a gradual unfolding, such that the essentials are present from the start, their implications being consistently unpacked with the passage of time. In its Protestant form, the usual idea is that the actual life and faith of the church is criticised in the light of the bible, which is idealised as the pure deposit of revealed faith, the final truth to which the actual church is always being summoned and by which it is judged.

Whether in its Catholic or Protestant form, this approach does make some room for Christian criticism. The actual church, for example, can be judged by the ideal of the essential church, the church as it most truly is. Or (to take another example) if the true faith is gradually being developed, or gradually being realised, then we need to have in our minds some of the norms or marks of the true faith, so that we can see whether they are present in any situation of the actual church which claims to be a fuller realisation of the Gospel. But then these norms or marks will have to be disussed and given their relative weight, and the criteria for selecting them rather than others will have to be set out. All this will demand a critical approach towards the faith itself, not only in its actual but in its ideal or essential form.

But problems remain. Does the kind of approach we have outlined give the Christian sufficient ground for criticising the essentials themselves? Is there not some risk that the very distinction between the real faith and the actual faith, the former being used as a standard by which to assess the latter, will tend to leave the true faith unpurged? Surely the distinction between the real and the actual will itself tend to break down. If we investigate the 'marks' of the true faith, some may be found to be less eternal, and so might be moved from the 'real' class into the 'actual' class. And indeed the history of theology presents us with many cases of shifts of this kind. In the last resort, in spite of its frequent usefulness, this approach to the problem of reconciling finality and criticism seems likely to become a device for restraining criticism of the central features and confining it to criticism of peripheral matters. The idea then becomes to hold fast to the bible and criticise everything else, or to hold fast to Christ, or the church and to criticise everything else. But the Christian principle of self-criticism must flow from the whole of the Christian faith and not be exercised against some aspect on the initiative of some other aspect. Christian criticism cannot rest content with a sort of content division within Christian faith. It must flow from the whole and react against the whole.

A second possible approach would be to distinguish the finality of experience from the finality of thought. The idea of the finality of the work of Christ can refer to its experienced religious adequacy. I may find that tomorrow I am even more deeply satisfied. That would not carry the implication that yesterday my satisfaction was less than complete for me as I was then. I may grow in my capacity for experiencing the profound beauty of the cross of Christ, without ever being conscious of dissatisfaction. In this sense, finality and development are compatible. The last coach on the train is always final, regardless of the speed of the train. But if I articulate my experience in propositions, that is if I theologise about it, then my cognitions of today may be in tension with those of yesterday and I may have to choose. Perhaps this distinction between experienced finality (the lack of any experience of religious dissatisfaction) and reflective infinality (the knowledge that sharper and clearer expression may show me that I was at least partly wrong in *speaking* about it the way I did yesterday) may help to define the nature of critical openness in relation to the finality and perfection of the Christian faith.

The distinction between experienced and articulated finality does however have its limits. Can experience and reflection be so neatly distinguished? Does not the distinction lead me to be critically open towards the thoughts of others but self-enclosed as far as my experience goes? Does it not fail to open me to the *experience* of others? And may I not delude myself about my experience, thinking I was satisfied when I was not, or attributing my satisfaction to this when later I realise it was that which was the true source of my satisfaction? Is there not some danger of absolutising experience, so that while I may criticise yesterday's theology, I may never theologically criticise yesterday's religious experience, or today's? It is not easy to see how this approach can be defended any better than the last one from the suspicion that in the end it can become a way for limiting the operation of critical openness.

In discussing the problem of critical openness towards the future of the child, *The Child in the Church* (1976) remarks that the Christian nurturer knows what he or she is nurturing children out of, but not what he or she is nurturing them into. 'They know the resources but not the use which will be made of them'. This conception could be compatible with either of the two views discussed above. But whereas the 1976 report suggests the metaphor of the paintbox, the metaphor of the hidden time capsule might attract some. Christian faith may be misleadingly regarded as a capsule full of items hidden by Christ and the early church two thousand years ago. We are learning how to unlock the compartments, and to draw out new items, not knowing what impact they will have upon us or our Christian future. But the truth is more complex. The past of Christian faith is not protected from its environment in a time capsule, to be opened by us, to find each thing as it was when first stored away. The past of Christian faith is available to us only in language and ritual. Both are inescapably embedded in culture, and demand constant re-interpretation. No doubt the past is just exactly whatever it was. But we do not know what it was, and as we make it *our* past, our perceptions of it also change. Not only do we not know for what future we are nurturing our young Christians; we do not fully know from what past we are nurturing them. Their perceptions of the Christian past may be as different from ours as ours are from the generation of Christians who lived before form criticism. And just as individuals may have false experience, self-deluding experience, only recognised and corrected in the light of a later wholeness, so whole communities and traditions may pass through periods of mistaken experience. What else are prophets for but to awaken people to this?

Another and perhaps more promising alternative is that we should seek to apply and extend the early Christian idea of the eschatological ambiguity of the church's life as an impulse to examine everything carefully. Christian faith has finality and completeness within it but this is perceived according to the promise, by faith and hope. The perfect future, as and when it is realised, can be seen, looking back, to be the product of the past. But to one looking forward, the future shape cannot be easily extrapolated from the present or the past. We strain our minds and eyes with eager expectation, looking, wondering, trying to discern the signs, trying to discriminate between the false and the true, looking for the emerging reality (Romans 8:19; Philippians 3:13) which is Christ. Christ is the centre of critical openness for the Christian, not only in so far as he is the model which we imitate in his earthly ministry but in so far as he is the one who is still to come. This form of teleological or eschatological finality is also connected with the doctrine of justification by faith. It does express an experienced reality, for living with the criticism which is a mark of the ambiguous in-between age affects the way life is experienced, seen and felt, but it must be emphasised that fundamentally one must describe this finality in theological terms not psychological. But the eschatological ambiguity leads us straight into the problem of authority.

Critical openness and divine authority

Let us begin our examination of the relation between authority and critical openness by distinguishing the authoritative from the authoritarian. An authoritative view carries authority for certain reasons. Perhaps the knowledge, advice or instruction comes from one who is wise, experienced or loved. Perhaps the counsel is presented with good arguments. But an authoritarian position is so merely by decree. The authoritarian person admits of no criteria for the assessing of his authority; he offers no reasons beyond the command itself. But if there are criteria then they must be examined, compared, ascertained, and the pronouncement itself must also be examined to see whether it meets the requirements of the criteria. So if religious authority is authoritative, then it demands scrutiny by its very nature. But if it is authoritarian, it will brook no criticism, and indeed, criticism could find no starting place. Criteria-referenced authority summons the co-operative effort of the one who stands beneath the authority. But the authoritarian decree is right because of its power alone. The authoritarian person is right because he says so. The authoritarian book is true because it claims to be. Here openness becomes disobedience and criticism is impudence. Of what kind is the authority of God – authoritative or authoritarian?

Sometimes an attempt is made to avoid the force of this distinction, and the implications for Christian life which flow from it, by introducing such euphemisms as 'innate authority' or 'self-authenticating authority'. Innate authority is one which acknowledges no criteria. It remains mysterious, baffling, frustrating. 'Why don't you want to go to London?' 'I just don't want to.' 'But *why*?' There is no *reason* why the friend should not change his or her mind. 'Oh, all right, I will go after all.' 'What made you change your mind?' 'I don't know. I just decided to go after all.' You are pleased with the decision, but as mystified as ever. It is not possible to enter into understanding and sympathetic relations with someone whose decisions are arbitrary. This remains true even if, as in the case of God, the danger of unpredictable ethical changes is removed. Such a God could not be the Thou of man; such a God could not be the counsellor and guide, for to accept such guidance would be to renounce the status of person and to accept the status of slave. You may trust God in the dark, but you cannot trust a dark God.

The mystery of God is not the mystery of the arbitrary. In front of the merely arbitrary, one can only shrug one's shoulders or resign oneself. The arbitrary repels; it resists attempts to enter it. It is whimsical, even if the whims are matters of life and death. But the mystery of God is wondrous. It draws one into its depths. One wonders not that there is so little to know but that there is so much to know. It is when the mysterious ways of the Lord have been penetrated to some extent (Romans 9–11) that one cries out in worship, 'O the depth of the riches and wisdom and knowledge of God! How unsearchable are the judgments and how inscrutable his ways!' (Romans 11:33). Here one is walking in the light which penetrates further and further back, into eternity. But a dark God, one whose commands are authoritarian, plunges one into confusion and credulity, whilst remaining unrevealed. It is true that not everything in God is discoverable by human reason, but it is equally true that nothing in God plunges reason into dismay.

When problems of authority are being discussed, distinctions are sometimes made between autonomy, heteronomy and theonomy. Autonomy is obeying a self-imposed or responsibly recognised rule or standard. Heteronomy is submitting to a law or standard imposed by another, Theonomy is submitting to the law of God. Theonomy, it is sometimes said, differs from heteronomy because it is a voluntary submission to the divine rule which summons but does not compel our submission. But the same questions which we ask of the distinction between heteronomy and autonomy need to be asked of the concept 'theonomy'. Theonomy can take either an autonomous or a heteronomous form. In its heteronomous form, theonomy is submitting, of my own free will, to a law to which I am invited. But when I submit voluntarily, do I do so for reasons or not? If there are no reasons, how does my submission differ from an arbitrary whim of mine? The attempt to save the Christian doctrine of humanity by emphasising the voluntary nature of the submission is only partly successful, if it be the case that I voluntarily yield myself by an arbitrary whim. But perhaps it was not a whim. Perhaps I felt constrained. But did I perceive, in the constraint, something which made me believe that it came from God? If so, would not the recognising of that have involved me in the criteria for what comes from God and what does not? And would I not then be on the edge of experiencing the constraint of reasons? On the other hand, if there were no reasons to believe the constraint came from God, then surely the constraint was merely a blind force to which I gave in. It is easy to see that the notion of theonomy can be interpreted in such a way that it becomes merely another name for heteronomy, all the more dangerous because it involves me in submitting to a dark God. But if theonomy is interpreted as autonomy, then it becomes rather like our idea of critical openness, since it emphasises the virtues of humility and loving listening to God in an alert, thoughtful way. Autonomous theonomy would seek out the nature of God, not God's whims, and would seek to distinguish this nature by certain non-subjective norms, whether drawn from history or philosophy or theology or from ethics, and seek to draw up criteria for knowing when the voice was indeed the voice of the Master. We can see therefore that the idea of theonomy, although a valuable idea, cannot be used to avoid the challenge of the distinction between heteronomy and autonomy, but must itself be examined to see to which of these it may be closest.

The alternatives are clear. Either we have a dictator God, or we are called to the life of critical openness. But God, in self-declaration as a God for humanity, in becoming available to us in personal relation, invites us to accept a reasonable service. Critical openness is the pedagogical technique adopted by a God who is personal and desires us to be persons. Without it, faith in God could not be purged; nor could it be anything other than the confidence of the gambler.

Critical openness and divine revelation

At first sight, the Christian idea of revelation might look ill at ease with the Christian idea of critical openness, for it might seem to exalt the reason of humanity against the revelation of God. But the calling to critical openness *flows from* the nature of the Christian revelation of God as being one in self-offering to humanity. It is *part* of the revelation and should not be thought of as being hostile to it. Only when

God is thought of as being authoritarian and God's self-revealing is thought of as being outside the context of personal life, an imposition external to the person, can critical openness be thought of as exalting the reason of humanity against the divine revelation. For if God is not authoritarian, then it must be that through God's self-revelation as being not authoritarian, God is summoning us to critical openness. God, in willing to bring us to personhood, may adopt only such means as are compatible with personhood and which tend to the creation of persons. But autonomy or critical openness is an essential attribute of personhood. Authoritarianism and autonomy are incompatible. According to the criteria of personhood and what it entails, God is wise, wise in selecting this goal from the lesser goals which might have been selected, and wise in selecting the kinds of relation with God's creatures which are best suited to the accomplishment of this goal. It is God's wise decree that God's creatures should be critically open. God has called us into fellowship with himself, having made us mind as well as spirit. The fellowship of spirit is love and the fellowship of mind with mind is critical openness. The criteria for this situation are drawn from the nature of mind itself. Theism without critical openness (a dictatorial God) would empty the Christian view of humanity of its dignity, the rational soul, the image of God, and it would empty God of the role as the creator and saviour of persons.

The revelation of God is received supremely through Jesus Christ. He is described as the logos of God (John 1:1) without whom nothing was made. The logos is the light of humanity and becomes man. The life of critical openness which the believer lives is a fellowship with this one who is himself the expression of the universal coherence and harmony of God. But this life is a fellowship of like with like ('conformed to the image of his Son' [Romans 8:29]) not a substitution of the logos for our human minds. The heteronomous believer follows an Apollinarian Christ, one whose mind is replaced by the logos of God. Some Christians misinterpreting such texts as 2 Corinthians 10:5 and Galatians 2:20, seek to give up their minds, to have them replaced by the mind of God. But the mystery of Christian fellowship 'in Christ' is a mystery of 'walking with the Lord', being 'in communion' with him, not a situation where our human minds are invaded and expelled by God's mind. The same reasoning which led the church to reject the Apollinarian heresy leads to the life of critical openness, both in its response to Christ as the logos of God and in its imitation of Jesus, true man and true God.

Was Jesus critically open? His teaching about the incoming Kingdom indicates his openness towards the end of Judaism as he knew it. Jesus' secure love and faith enabled him to be critically open in ethics, towards the law and so on. It is however a form of critical openness which leads to the courage to do rather than to what we would call autonomous speculation. Jesus operated beneath an umbrella of Jewish faith; he was not a critical theist of the Greek kind. Nevertheless, Jesus did raise and react to radical questions of his society, limited as all societies are by the prevailing world view. For our part, we must be as critical of our western culture (including its Greek inheritance) as Jesus was of the history and institutions of Israel. So even although our context is wider than that of Jesus he has certainly manifested the ideal of Christian critical openness.

Critical openness and the nature of God

The idea of finality led us to consider authority and that in turn led us into a consideration of the nature of Christian revelation. But what of the God who is so revealed? We have spoken of God as seeking to promote personal life, as autonomy is a feature of personhood, seeking to advance autonomy. But God is person. Can God be thought of then as critically open? God is clearly autonomous. God thinks for himself, seeing that God is supreme intelligence and knows everything. But can God be thought of as possessing those special features which made us prefer the expression 'critical openness' to 'autonomy'? *We* must be open because we know that our knowledge is only a fraction of the total sum of knowledge, and we must be critical because we so easily mistake falsehood for knowledge. But the divine knowledge is perfect in its quality and in its extent. God knows all there is to be known, and God knows it infallibly and in perfect accuracy of detail. Indeed God knows it as its creator rather than, or as well as, its observer. Add to all this the traditional assertion that God's knowledge, like God's being, is eternal and 'eternally simultaneous', that the past and the future are as totally present to God as is the present. It seems then that in God there can be no learning, no surprise at the novelties which are thrown up in our expanding universe, even those novelties that come from the free decisions of other centres of consciousness and will, and so God can have no critical openness!

On the other hand, scripture licenses a different vocabulary for speaking of God. God remembers our sins no more, relents in punishments, awaits us with loving-kindness, enters into resolutions befitting the turn of events, is involved in the progress of God's people and delights in creations. In fact it might be said that the God of scripture is critically open in all the ways in which we are − towards the future, towards the actions and needs of others, in selecting from present possibilities, in discriminating between values, but without the weaknesses in our criticism imposed upon us by the fact that we are never acquainted with all the facts, and the limitations upon our openness imposed by the fact that we build barriers between ourselves and other creatures.

It will be said that this language is anthropomorphic. But the most 'metaphysical' of religious language itself retains anthropomorphic elements. (Language is not less anthropomorphic simply by being more abstract.) And it is surely wise, in moving from scriptural imagery of God to philosophical conceptualisation, to beware of straining too much in the quest for an unattainable purity. God's being is fuller, not thinner, than anything we can properly conceive and articulate. And if there are aspects or components of critical openness, as we have described it, that are attractive in themselves and not merely as means to further ends, that belong to the perfection of spirit and not only to its process, then must we not attribute them also to God, indeed as to their apotheosis? Are there such aspects or components of critical openness? There would seem to be two (related) essential ingredients of critical openness as an ideal, namely an attentive (loving) receptivity to the wondrous world that is in principle without limits (that puts no *a priori* limits on itself) on the one hand, and on the other the will and the skill to distinguish the true from the merely plausible. But these would seem each to belong to the ideal perfection of the life of the spirit. If this is so, then they may be attributed to God. And, indeed, is it not enough to state them in this way to see that they do belong to God, and in supereminent manner? God is the one who is open and attentive, so lovingly attentive as never to be deceived, not fitfully and to but some creatures as we are, but eternally and to all creatures. We can even say of God's critical openness (as of God's knowledge and love – of which in the end critical openness is an essential aspect) that it *sustains* all being and all developments in being, that it therefore sustains also *our* critical openness, our aspiration to be perfect like God, in this respect also.

Humanity therefore in being critically open is, however imperfectly, in the image of God. The thought is perhaps a strange one, because the vocabulary is not the traditional religious vocabulary. But the appeal to be 'perfect as your Father in heaven is perfect' (Matthew 5:48) if it means that we should be perfect in this respect and in that respect – whatever these may be which are appropriate perfections for creatures to aspire towards – may be construed as including amongst these many respects this one: to be critically open (within the limits of finitude) as God is critically open (within the limits of infinitude). How are we to live before such a God? This brings us to the question of spirituality.

Critical openness and Christian commitment

People sometimes ask whether we are to be critically open at the expense of our loyalty to Christ. The question arises because critical openness is not one of the traditional Christian virtues, but is preconceived as being in potential hostility to Christian commitment. Christians seldom ask whether we should be loving at the expense of our loyalty to Christ. To be loving is to be Christian. But, in a less important but still significant way, to be critically open is also to be Christian. Christians have no monopoly of love just as they have no monopoly of critical openness, but the logic of their faith drives them in these directions and gives a distinctive meaning to their love and their criticism. But traditional Christian spirituality with its emphasis on such virtues as obedience and submissiveness might seem ill at ease with a spirituality of critical openness. This feeling (for it is no more) arises simply because the implications of critical openness for spirituality are not thought through. So the following comments are offered.

Critical openness is sometimes thought of as if it exhibited a proud spirit instead of a mood of self-repudiating acceptance. This is usually a mistake. The critically open person cannot but be humble, because in openness to others he or she acknowledges the need for help, and in criticism he or she acknowledges fallibility. Inasmuch as critical openness is certainly not thinking what appeals to you or believing what you like or accepting what makes you comfortable, it is a repudiation of self-centredness. The critically open person is the one who knows he or she has much to learn.

The critically open Christian is far removed from the one who has the 'spirit of fear' (Romans 8:15). Instead such a person exercises Christian responsibility, as a son not a slave, and seeks to test everything, in order to hold fast that which is good.

It is true that there is some New Testament imagery which might seem to emphasise the passivity and the dependence of discipleship. We are sheep, a little flock, branches of the vine, we are to leave all and to follow him without question or delay. But other strands emphasise Christian responsibility – we are to count the cost like the king setting out to war, we are to take risks with our talents, we are to be wise as serpents. Moreover, critical openness is part of the abandoning of the old securities which is part of discipleship. How could Jewish men who were not critically open have responded to the question of Jesus about who he was? It should also be pointed out that to belong to the school of Christ cannot be similar to belonging to the school of (say) Aristotle. The follower of Aristotle seeks to elaborate the system of Aristotle. But Jesus founded no system, wrote no book.

The criticism which flows from faith is not the only kind of questioning which the Christian may experience. There is also the problem of sinful doubt. In the New Testament we read not only of the testing which is required of the alert, expectant eschatological church but also of those who deliberately or in blindness turn from the light, falling even deeper into their sin (Mark 3:28f; John 3:19–21; 8:43). How are we to distinguish between the scepticism to which faith is called by faith itself and the doubt which is the product of sin and leads to further sin?

The Christian must examine his or her own motives carefully. Is it the case that after years of calm confidence, I am now beginning to question Christian faith? Then could this be because I have become too comfortable? Is it because I am falling a prey to intellectual arrogance? Is it through my laziness in allowing my faith to remain puerile while the rest of my thinking becomes more sophisticated? Is it because I am chafing under the sacrificial implications of Christian faith? Or is it, on the other hand, because my complacency is at last being shattered by the realisation that the Lord has yet more light and truth to show forth from his word? Is it that I am growing out of shallow and defensive dogmatism? Is it that my faith has until now been heteronomous but at last I am beginning to struggle with my personal vocation to become mature in Christ? The thoughtful Christian will acknowledge that such criticism is itself part of his or her life which must be tested by the same enquiring spirit. The false prophets and the true are not only found in the world outside. They are also in our own hearts. But clearly it can be no answer to play safe, to refuse the calling of mature criticism because of a fear of falling into sinful doubt. The servant who did not dare take any risks, but hid his talent in the ground, was condemned by his master for being too scrupulous, when he knew all the time that his master was very demanding. And, although the reality of sinful doubt must never be minimised, the doctrine of justification by faith may give us some encouragement and release us from the inhibiting fears of doubt, which might otherwise paralyse Christian criticism.

It may be that critical openness cannot be made compatible with the Presbyterian doctrine of the covenant, as it developed in seventeenth century Protestant scholasticism, in which the idea that the covenant is bestowed conditionally creates a series of limits, which, if transgressed, place one outside the covenant. But if the older reformed principle of justification by faith is taken seriously, and extended into the intellectual realm as well as the moral realm, then the Christian, being accepted regardless of conditions, is set free from intellectually inhibiting religious fears. There are no degrees of justification. The justified Christian is thus set free from fear in order to pursue God's path to personhood. Just as in ethics, justification by faith sets the Christian free to respond to new situations, so critical openness is the life of the Christian mind, flowing from the same principle – which itself is open to critical reflection, and so on for ever. We can see therefore that critical openness is *not* a basic Christian concept (such as the grace of God is) but a derived or consequential attribute of Christian living. It is derived from ideas such as the personhood of God, the nature of the divine image, the Christian hope in the future, the character of discipleship towards Jesus and so on, and we are emboldened to walk this way because of justification by faith. The old Christian symbol of this is not the maze, which presents one with many hazardous choices, but the single-track labyrinth. This is an incredibly convoluted path, with innumerable doublings back, apparent lack of progress, a sudden coming near the goal only to be thrust out to the perimeter, and yet a way in which, at the last, there is no being lost.

Is lack of critical openness culpable for the modern Christian? The pluralistic situation of modern western society is without precedent. Whether this will be a lasting condition of the west we do not know. But clearly in this situation, as long as it lasts, it is most important for the future of Christian faith that it should be critically open both towards itself and towards its fellow (or rival) world views. If we are in a melting-pot stage, in which the outlines of a new synthesis are being forged (that is, when pluralism will be overcome in some new kind of society) then it is even more vital for Christians, by exercising critical openness, to play an active part in the shaping of this. We conclude that it would be culpable for the church to neglect this, and that, to some extent, in ways appropriate to his or her other gifts and callings, each Christian should endeavour to make some contribution to Christian critical openness.

Critical openness as method

But are there limits to Christian critical openness? To limit criticism would be to resist learning and so to declare that development was complete. But what if criticism were to indicate that all the sacred relics were forgeries, the Gospels without historical foundation and the concept of God incoherent? What if criticism explodes the Christian faith? This possibility expresses the ambiguity of faith and it cannot be removed, either by criticism itself or by naive assertion. To restrain criticism because it seemed to be going in the wrong direction would be such an act of intellectual dishonesty that the ethics of Christian intellectual life would be destroyed in any case. After all, if criticism were justified in dissolving faith one would be left with something more closely approaching the truth than one had before, whereas if criticism were restrained because of fear of unwelcome conclusions, one would be left with neither the best truth available nor the Christian faith (since its intellectual calling would have been betrayed).

It should be understood that the idea of there being no limits to Christian critical openness is a methodological principle. It tells us *how* to live the intellectual calling of the Christian. It is because it is to do with method that Christian critical openness can recoil upon the axioms out of which it springs (for example, it springs from faith in a certain kind of God, yet it can also ask if there is such a God). The *content* of Christian faith pushes us towards the *method* of critical openness, and the content cannot be immune from the method it dictates, even although we do not know what method might be dictated by any content of faith which might follow the present content if that were to be destroyed by criticism. In emphasising that this is a method, we mean that the Christian must act *as if* it were *possibly* the case that his or her beliefs were false. An alarmist reaction would be quite inappropriate – we do not actually think that Christian faith is anywhere near the point of collapse, but we must accept the possibility if our intellectual quest is to have integrity. The paradigm under which the Christian quest is conducted must itself be questioned, and indeed, it invites us to question it. This can be seen in Jesus' questions, 'Why do you call me good?' 'Whom do men say that I am?' 'Having ears, do you hear?' Note that a similar methodological readiness for doubt is required from the atheist. This is a method of enquiry, to which the Christian is prompted by individual special reasons, but which is also mandatory for all thinking and testing of hypotheses.

The other side of methodological scepticism is methodological dogmatism. Without dogmatism there could be no critical openness, for rigorous and searching enquiry would be impossible if beliefs were abandoned at the first breath of doubt. It is only the beliefs which are cared about enough to struggle over, to commit oneself to, to defend to the end, which can receive the deepest criticism. This is as true in the case of scientific research as it is of theology. But this element of dogmatism is important because it creates the conditions for critical openness, not because it limits its scope. Dogmatism without criticism is sterile, and criticism without dogmatism is empty.

The distinctiveness of Christian nurture

We have seen that Christian nurture is similar to secular education in that both are committed to enquiry, both are concerned with learning in order to make yet further learning possible. By virtue of this characteristic, Christian faith may provide a rationale for both kinds of processes, since Christian faith is driven towards this position by its own internal logic. We can therefore speak of 'Christian education' in the sense of a Christian rationale for the processes of learning, and of 'Christian nurture' in the sense of a Christian rationale (and in this case there could be no other kind of rationale) for a Christian learning about Christian faith leading to deeper Christian faith. Christian nurture can thus be defended against the charge that it is closed authoritarian instruction, and its humane and ethical status are assured.

But does our discussion prove too much? We began with the problem of how Christian nurture could possess critical openness and yet intend the deepening of Christian faith. We saw that education and Christian nurture each share in the spirit of enquiry. Have we now reached a point where the similarity between Christian nurture and general education is so close that anything a child might gain from Christian nurture could in any case have been gained from education, that is a county school religious education including Christian studies? Is there any particular benefit to be gained from Christian nurture?

First we should remember the differing hopes or intentions of the Christian nurturer and the educator teaching Christian studies. Christian nurture, through its critical openness, can contemplate the possibility of the collapse of Christian faith, but what it expects, hopes for and intends is the strengthening of Christian faith. Critical openness tests, expands and fulfils Christian faith. Christian nurture is based upon the hypothesis that Christianity is true and can be seen to be yet more true. There is nothing odd or illogical about the combination of this commitment with this critical openness. Scientific commitment and enquiry have similar features. We have already noted the place of dogmatism in science, pointing out that only if the adherents of theories defend them vigorously, try by every scientific means to secure them against attack, try to adapt them to meet objections, and set high standards for their overthrow, can science be protected from the situation where theories were lightly advanced and easily given up. The commitment ensures the depth of probing without which the advance of truth would be difficult because the discussion would be superficial. In religion, although the word 'dogmatism' is best avoided because of its pejorative history, the same is true. It is only sensible that there should be a *strong* commitment to rational religious beliefs provided they are held in the spirit of critical openness and with the contemplation of the possibility (although not the expectation of the likelihood) that they may be false. In the case of the Christian religion, where the commitment and the criticism flow from the same central ideas, the connection is still more evident and coherent.

Secondly, we should remember the relation between Christian theology and education and nurture respectively. It has already been pointed out that there can be no other rationale for Christian nurture than that provided by Christian theology, which is therefore in a necessary and sufficient relationship to the practice of Christian nurture. But Christian theology has but a partial and a possible relation to the practice of education.

Combining these two distinctions, we may say that Christian nurture is a servant of faith, and it is this faithful service which impels it to be critically open towards faith itself, as faith in the Christian sense requires, but education, although also *capable* of being justified by faith, is an independent activity of secular humanity. Reversing the servant metaphor, we may say that theology is lord of Christian nurture. Christian nurture is captive to theology but theology is servant to education. Theology appraises education, tries to illumine, but cannot prescribe, except in circumstances when education becomes itself captive to ideologies hostile to Christian faith, and then education is no longer open to being compatible with Christian education, and Christian theology must denounce it.

But as long as a Christian rationale for secular education is *possible*, that interpretation remains as a service. There can be necessary attack (where education has become anti-Christian) but there can be no *necessary* support, because non-Christians can be educators. This question has to do with the circumstances when the saying 'He that is not against us is for us' (Mark 9:40) must be exchanged for the saying 'He who is not with me is against me, and he who does not gather with me scatters' (Luke 11:23). The critical openness of Christian nurture is a Christian critical openness; the critical openness of education is merely compatible with Christian faith.

The third reason for maintaining the education/Christian nurture distinction has to do with the spheres in which the two activities take place, or their social agencies. Christian nurture is a domestic activity of the church; education is a public activity of the state, assuming that in certain circumstances the state has the right to educate, although like all other rights of the state, there are limits to its operation.

The fourth reason why Christian nurture is different from education has to do with the pedagogical character of the two processes, but is also connected with the nature of the agencies or spheres. In principle (for example, in certain countries of Asia) a satisfactory religious education need make but minor reference to Christianity. And even in western countries, pupils can become educated concerning several or any religions. But because it is a prolongation of the conditions of infancy, a prolongation which seeks to bring the infant to maturity and not keep him or her in infancy, and yet begins from the conditions of infancy and takes them seriously as the inheritance of the child, a child can *only* be nurtured in his or her own religion. You can indoctrinate a child into anything, and in the case of Christianity, that would mean alienating him or her from the Christian family tradition, and you can educate a child into anything worthwhile, and in the case of Christianity, that would mean respecting but not necessarily promoting the Christian family tradition.

The fifth mark of Christian nurture as against education is that Christian nurture proceeds from an assumption that teacher and learner are *inside* the Christian faith, whereas education only invites the pupil to *imagine* what it would be like to be inside a faith, or (in the situation where a pupil is being educated in his or her own faith) education invites the pupil to imagine what it would be like to be *outside* that faith. The whole environment of the secular school, the plurality present in the classroom, the range of teacher commitments, the nature and style of the public examinations — all contribute to this ethos. Suspension of belief or disbelief is an important part of educational method in the religious area, but has a smaller and different role to play in Christian nurture.

The sixth distinction is that education in religion is appropriate for all, but Christian nurture is appropriate only for Christians. Christian nurture is based upon the belief that there are Christian children.

Finally, Christian nurture takes place in the context of worship (and not merely the study or exploration of worship), in a specialised faith community, where the child, as a Christian, learns from the word of God. These factors give Christian nurture an ethos, an emotional context, which are quite different from that provided by education in county schools.

Of course it may be the case that these distinctions make little practical difference in some situations, especially with adolescent pupils. It may be that even young people within the churches are so deeply secularised that with them as with the general pupils in the state schools all that the teacher, whether Christian nurturer or religious educator, can offer is a fundamental pre-catechesis or introduction which will begin to make learning possible in these areas. But even where this were the case, and the starting point was thus similar, the ending point would be different. As the processes got under way, the differences would emerge, or, if they did not, the teacher might have succeeded as educator whilst a colleague in the church might have failed as Christian nurturer.

Notes

1. *The Child in the Church,* London, British Council of Churches, 1976, chapter 4.
2. All biblical quotations in this article are from the Revised Standard Version, copyright 1946 and 1952, Division of Christian Education, National Council of Churches in the USA.

5.4 Three traditions of religious education
Kieran Scott

This article is a proposal to satisfy a 'blessed rage for order' in the current field of religious education. This order is necessary on the following accounts:

1. No clearly defined field of religious education exists today. As a logical consequence, there is no consensus on the foundational underpinnings, scope, methodology and operating principles.[1] The root problem is one of conceptualisation.

2. No consensus exists on the usage of key terminology in religious education today. Our conceptual confusion is tied to a linguistic cluttering of terms. The terms catechesis, Christian nurture/education, Christian religious education, religious education, continue to be utilised interchangeable.[2] Seldom is there consistent awareness that each term 'reflects a distinctive variance in our understanding of who we are and what we are about'.[3]
   Are the terms simply different manifestations (aspects, subsets) of the broader field of religious education?[4] Currently, the terms run together or are juxtaposed without adequate attention to the conceptual gap between them.

3. Consequently, no clearly defined purpose exists for religious education today. Is our work maintenance or/and emancipation, traditioning or/and transformation, conversion or/and critique, socialisation or/and social reconstruction? Religious educators in the 1970s and 1980s, notes Norma Thompson, feel much like the King of Siam in *The King and I*: 'Sometimes I think I am not sure of what I absolutely know.'[5]

4. Finally, in spite of some recent promising efforts, adequate attention to the theory of religious education has been found wanting. The results have been: foundational principles go unquestioned, philosophical options blurred and professional identity confused.[6] In effect, religious education as a field and profession remains notably undeveloped.

The work of this article is to create a clearing for consistent conversation in the field. The task is to distinguish and clarify the terms we use − with their different languages and lenses on reality. I propose a three-pronged typology of traditions as a scheme for ordering the field and a device for systematic reflection on it. The traditions can be named as:

a. the ecclesial enculturation tradition (inner border model) represented by catechesis, Christian nurture and socialisation theories;
b. the revisionist tradition (dialectical border model) portrayed by Christian religious education; and
c. the reconceptualist tradition (border crossing model) noted for its attempt to retrieve and reconstruct the root meaning of the term religious education

Each of these traditions has its own conceptual framework, educational process and purposes. Each structures our thinking and gives form to our lives in diverse and, sometimes, divergent ways. They are not conceived according to the same rationale or carry the same priorities and principles. Developmentally, each tradition could be conceived as a deeper stage in religious education development.[7] My thesis is: the ecclesial enculturation and revisionist traditions can embody part of the meaning of religious education. However, neither can constitute a full reconceptualised theory of religious education. In this article, I will explicate the conceptual framework, process and purpose of each of the traditions, indicate their strength and weakness, and conclude with some implications for parish religious education.

The ecclesial enculturation tradition

In the ecclesial encultural tradition, I identify religious educators engaged in catechesis, Christian nurture/education and religious socialisation.[8] (Much of what goes on under the heading of Jewish education could also be included here.) I name the tradition ecclesial enculturation as an apt and accurate description of its conceptual framework, process and purpose. It is an inner border model in terms of its enclosed ecclesial interests and external focus.

Conceptual Framework: Catechesis, Christian nurture and religious socialisation theories take as their frame of reference service in and on behalf of the church. It is educative work carried on in the name of, with the approbation of, and under the guidance of the church. I recognise that there are minor differences between these terms. Yet, I believe they are substantially united in their attempt to situate church religious education within an enculturation model. Here I will focus on the catechetical expression of this tradition.

Catechesis is unabashedly confessional. Its constitutive interest is to awaken, nourish and develop one's personal belief, to hand on the tradition, solidify one's religious identity and build up the ecclesial body.[9] It is 'enculturation in a transforming community'.[10]

The identity of catechesis is currently tied to denominational

(Roman Catholic) religion. It is 'the nursery of the church'.[11] Its tasks are defined as acquiring and transmitting a religion: to become rooted and identified with a body of people and moulded into the character and meaning system of its communal life. It could be called the tribal phase of religious education.

Catechesis is set in the framework of church ministry. This self-understanding (educational ministry) is its guiding vision – directing it to focus on conservation of tradition and deepening of religious affiliation. These concerns are an indigenous part of the church's mission.

In its conceptual stance, this model sticks to its own tradition. It claims to respect the territorial rights of others, but its prevailing concern is to be vigilant about its own borders. Here Catholic, Protestant and Jew pursue their own way, but this inner border model does not provide an adequate comprehensive context for meaningful dialogues in the contemporary religious world.

Process: Religious educators in the catechetical tradition view their work as initiation, adaptation, transmission, translation, church-maintenance. It is a life-long process and the work of the entire Christian community. Its process is one of enculturation, nurture, evangelisation and conversion. Its main educational effort is to provide people with experience of belonging to a community. In general, the catechetical enterprise understands itself as the total church process whereby the faithful deepen their fidelity and mature in their commitment to the ecclesial community.

Purpose: Catechetical objectives have always been closely related to practical outcomes: practising church membership, transmission of the heritage, handing on the symbols of the tradition and deepening of loyalty to one's beliefs, meanings and values. The *National Catechetical Directory* concisely notes its four major tasks:

a. to proclaim the Christian gospel;
b. to participate in efforts to develop and maintain the Christian community;
c. to lead people to worship and prayer; and
d. to motivate them to serve others.

This delineation of tasks broadens the scope of catechesis from the almost-exclusive cognitive confinement associated with it from the sixteenth century down to the early twentieth century. Padraic O'Hare captures well its current spirit and aim: 'The most invariant intention of catechetical ministers,' he writes, 'is to induct persons into what Tillich called "the present actuality of the group". This catechetical effort is an inducement to accept and to make their own, the faith, loyalty, piety and cognitive perspective of the mainstream of the church as presently understood and practised'.[12] In a word, it is denominational 'education in the faith'.

Gifts: There is a fundamental truth in the catechetical form of religious education. It functions as a vital reminder that there is a place for passing on the past in religious education. Its focus is conditioned by the awareness that 'when the ancients become inaccessible the modern becomes unintelligible'.[13]

The catechist's role of guardian of tradition, retriever of ancient wisdom and sustainer of religious sensibilities is of critical educational importance to people's lives today. 'It seems to me,' writes Henry C Simmons, 'that in the normal course of events we all, at least as young children, need that kind of religious education. We need to learn to live with the language, symbols, and culture of a community which is safe, which is secure, and which presents itself as the only possible way of conceptualising the world.'[14] Catechesis, then, shows a deep devotion to cumulative tradition, ritual, and the sacramental, contemplation, life-long development, and the particularity of one's people. These can be vital resources in education today. They can help transform the meaning of education, resist its rationalistic bias and its exclusive housing in schools.

At its best, catechesis affirms rootedness in one's own religious tradition, fosters denominational identity and nurtures religious development. It holds the possibility of being an enriching category[15] and *one* genuine manifestation of religious education.

Limits: Paradoxically, some of the strengths of catechesis are also its weakness. The strength of particularity can become enclosed in the parochial. Its language reveals and represents an inner world of Roman Catholicism. This semantic world tends to conceal awareness of a larger world of religious diversity and to lack a public character to build bridges of communication with it. It is an intimate, self-isolating language that fosters conventional religious identity,[16] and its stress on institutional self-identity may not be sufficient to sustain Roman Catholics in the world in which we now live.

There also remains a lingering suspicion with regard to the principles, process and purposes of catechesis. Do they honour and are they compatible with openness, enquiry, freedom and the critical spirit? In other words, can catechesis confront modernity? Or is it an example of the way new rhetoric can camouflage old attitudes? Kenneth Barker writes, 'Catechesis can become simply the preservation of a taken-for-granted culture. It can degenerate into a delivery system which channels established beliefs and values without stimulating critical thinking with regard to their validity. It can lull the members of the community into a sense of false security, assuring them of safety and not challenging them to change. It can hand on a received heritage without questioning its authority.'[17]

There can be a provincialism, then, in the catechetical tradition. It can nurture a hothouse flower of a culture, existing in its own hermetically sealed environment. This setting can foster an unreflective attitude toward church form, an undialectical hermeneutic of one's tradition, a naivety with regard to its enculturation and a blindness to the larger public context of the tradition. It can turn the mind of a denomination upon itself as a standard for itself.

Finally, this ecclesial enculturation tradition ignores the educational connection. It has deliberately severed itself from an educational framework and influence. Education, however, could be an invaluable asset to catechesis/Christian nurture/religious socialisation. It could offer first a context in which to examine itself – with a hermeneutic of suspicion, and second a framework to see itself as only *one* possible tradition of religious education.

The revisionist tradition

In the revisionist tradition, I identify religious educators engaged in the work of critical hermeneutics, traditioning and transformation, and educational emancipation. This tradition tends to gather under the cumbersome term 'Christian religious education' and represents a deeper (and distancing) stage in religious education development. The term indicates the search for a new model – beyond ecclesial enculturation. Current representative examples include Thomas Groome and Mary C Boys (on the Catholic side) and Mary Elizabeth Moore and Jack L Seymour (on the Protestant side). I recognise that there are some significant differences within this group. Yet I believe they share the same 'family resemblance'.[18]

I name this tradition revisionist because of its conceptual framework, process and purpose. It is a dialectical border model in terms of its internal critical enquiry of tradition(s) and its external reflectiveness on the public world.

Conceptual Framework: Christian religious education takes as its frame of reference the intersection of religious tradition and contemporary human experience. It is an interdisciplinary venture foundationally informed by both theology and educational theory. Its proponents claim theology and education enter a reciprocal relationship – both informing and transforming each other. This claim, however, may not stand up as Christian religious education becomes, in effect, a practical theology.

In the revisionist tradition, Christian religious educators navigate within and between the broader contexts of the Christian community and the current social environment. Conceptually, a critically correlational method structures the framework for this tradition and sets forth the outlines for its educational process.[19]

Christian religious education is the work of the church, that is, educational ministry. However, it flies in the face of a purely confessional mentality. Its starting point is 'right in the middle, at the intersection' [20] of church and culture. So, while the enterprise functions at the centre of the ecclesial community, it does so with a hermeneutic of suspicion.

Process: Christian religious educators dare to be Christian and modern. They believe in the life of the mind in connection with the life of the spirit. The educational process involves the application of modern critical reason to the beliefs, symbols, values, texts and lived-life of the Christian tradition. In effect, Christian religious education is the Christian tradition become self-conscious.

Religious educators in the revisionist tradition view their work with a double emphasis. They attempt to hold on to two educational poles: conservation and liberation,[21] continuity and change,[22] tradition and transformation,[23] devotion and enquiry.[24] They refuse to settle fully on an enculturation model, but rather promote a critical, dialectical and intentional response to the historical and conditioning forces in the church community and its cultural environment. As Mary Elizabeth Moore notes, 'Education functions in the community to transmit tradition ... to enable people to interpret the meaning of their experience and to open the possibility of transforming the individual, the faith community and the world.' The functions, then, are both to conserve and to transform.[25]

This dialectical method embodied in the revisionist tradition engages persons in dialogue with the Christian tradition (past, present and future).[26] This, in turn, opens possibilities both for the recreation of the tradition and the persons within the tradition. The Christian heritage is enlarged and the lived-life of the community reconstructed. What is significant here is that the reconstruction of the heritage takes place in and through an educational process.

Purpose: Christian religious education seeks to lead people out to personally, critically and freely appropriate their heritage by unmasking its assumptions and historical condition. It aims to engage persons in intelligent participation in the living Christian community and 'to make accessible tradition and transformation'.[27] Among its primary goals are:

a. reflective knowledge and understanding of the tradition;
b. the recreation of personal beliefs, values and actions; and
c. the transformation of our social and public world.

Its constitutive interests, therefore, are emancipatory.[28]

Gifts: There is a fundamental truth in the Christian religious education form of religious education. It functions as a vital reminder that there is a place for the best of critical reason in religious education in the Christian tradition. Religious traditions need critique to stay in grace. This Protestant principle saves us from dogmatism, fanaticism, traditionalism and idolatry. George

Albert Coe wrote, 'Nothing, in fact, could be more religious than finding and putting into operation a method for the continuous self-criticism (which means self-testing and judging) of religion and of religious institutions.'[29]

Christian religious educators hold in tension conservation (of tradition) and liberation (of the world). This work is of critical educational importance to our lives. It creates an opening for the reinterpretation and reappropriation of the Christian story and symbols. The tradition itself is enriched; and its guiding metaphors direct it toward the work of freedom.

At its best, then, Christian religious education weds tradition and modernity, continuity and change, community and critique. It re-roots us in the Christian tradition – but with a critical distance.

Limits: The revisionist tradition ushers in a new posture toward religious affiliation – critical affirmation. This new stance, however, does not shift the conceptual framework or content. Substantially, the ecclesial enculturation paradigm remains, but in a revised form.

Is Christian religious education not a (critical) educational method designed to pass on a (critical) theology? Is it not simply an experiential educational strategy to transmit contemporary theologies? While this approach deepens the reflective process, religious education is confined to being a delivery system for the prevailing theology. Theology holds a place of primacy over curriculum content, criteria and concepts. In effect, Christian religious education becomes a form of practical theology or theological praxis, and education becomes a critical tool or method to make its content accessible to the ecclesial community.[30]

I hasten to stress that Christians do need the solid substance and best of contemporary theology to acquire a perspective on the length, breadth, and depth of their religious tradition. They need teaching and study in their own tradition that is intellectually stimulating and critically reconstructive. Theology is a rich source and offers access to the wealth of the Christian heritage. It ought, therefore, to be a vital part of the content of our religious education curriculum.

If religious education, however, is to emerge as an academically respectable field and profession in its own right, it needs to be more than a subdivision of theology or confined to its framework or content. Two reasons could be offered. The first is that a vast treasure of religious material and experience lies beyond the realm of theology. This content could be of inestimable value to the development of our religious lives. In other words, there ought to be room for *more* religious content (beyond the specifically theological) in our education curriculum. The second reason is that in the contemporary religious context, the theological enterprise itself needs a broad ecumenical, educational and developmental framework. This would allow Christian religious educators to explore their own tradition, challenge its claims vis-a-vis other traditions and, thereby, evoke a free response. Christian religious educators cannot assume that religious questions and commitments are already resolved in the lives of their people. They need an open and pluralistic context to explore with tolerance the vital religious issues confronting them in the modern world.

Finally, Christian religious education fails to push the critical process to some of its logical conclusions. The critique loses much of its bite as fundamental Christian assumptions on revelation are not put at risk, current ecclesial patterns of power go unchallenged and many of its sacred images have lost their power to shape the imagination of contemporary Christians. In a word, tension, if not conflict, seems to exist between the purpose, process and pattern of the enterprise.

Christian religious education, then, needs an educational framework to be true to itself and its emancipatory interests. This would allow it to discover itself as one genuine expression of religious education within a rich and complex field.

The reconceptualist tradition

The reconceptualist tradition represents an attempt to retrieve and reconstruct the richest meaning of the term religious education. This emerging tradition is a paradigmatic shift, a conceptual reordering that integrates the religious and educational in life. The task here is to get back to the true and surplus meaning of the words, and to name and recognise the multiple forms of religious education in our midst.

The reconceptualist tradition is a border crossing model. Its vision transcends the local ecclesial community – without negating it. It opens up or crosses over into a large public context with new content and a redesigned curriculum. Gabriel Moran and Maria Harris are among its leading proponents today.[31]

Conceptual Framework: A reconceptualised religious education takes education as its overarching frame of reference. It self-consciously works out of an educational rather than ministerial framework. Imaginally, there is 'a passing over'[32] beyond the parish and the parochial into the larger social and public context of education. Education becomes the arena for dealing with the critical religious issues and concerns of life. It is the setting in which diverse religious traditions (Catholic, Protestant, Jew, etc.) can converse on educational matters. Religion and education intersect in this interactive framework of critical and appreciative intelligence.

Conceptually, this field of religious education houses the many forms of religion as they interplay (or intersect) with the various forms of education in multiple settings. We can hardly yet imagine the richness and complexity of this emerging paradigm. Education provides a clearing or a point at which to begin conversation across all religious lines — between individuals and institutions, different religious traditions and the religious and nonreligious in life. Education also supplies the metaphors and models of action for the enterprise. If this reconceptualist tradition is to come of age, a sense of history and a sense of imagination will be required to do justice to this merger of the religious and educational in the contemporary world.

Process: A reconceptualised religious education is a way of being religious in 'a new key', that is in a context of education. We are challenged to face up to religious issues in an educationally appropriate way. This entails exploring 'the meaning of one's own religious life in relation to both those who share that life and those who do not'.[33] The process is not a cold exercise in comparative religions stressing objectivity, hard facts, further knowledge or interesting comparisons. Neither is it merely a phenomenology or a philosophy of religion. Genuine intra- and inter-religious dialogue is sought through a process of self-reflection, sympathetic understanding, open encounter and mutual exchange.[34] An analogical[35] and educational imagination[36] plays a central role in a re-claiming and transcending of one's own religious standpoint.[37] The process is one of 'disciplined intersubjectivity'.[38] It does not start with prior confessional assumptions nor is it tied to denominational self-interests. Proselytising, evangelising and dogmatising are contrary to its spirit and purpose. Rather, the commitment is to uninhibited interaction and enquiry in which understanding is sought.

Religious education in a reconceptualised mode is the way we go about understanding our own religious tradition, convictions and our God over against the religious identity of 'the other', the stranger.[39] John Dunne's method of 'passing over' to other persons, cultures and religions and 'coming back' is an invaluable educational technique at our service here. 'What one does in passing over,' claims Dunne, 'is try to enter sympathetically into the feelings of another person, become receptive to the images which give expression to his feelings, attain insight into those images, and then come back enriched by this insight to an understanding of one's own life which can guide one into the future.'[40] This educational process:

a. allows aspects of our own standpoint and story to surface;
b. is the means by which we gain access to a universal religious experience and the different worlds of other religions;
c. makes available space for authentic dialogue with them; and
d. leads to the shifting and enrichment of our own standpoint and story.

The educational stance, then, is one of rootedness and openness, that is, critical appreciation of one's own tradition and empathetic understanding of the religious ways of others.

As we set out on this educational adventure, we need a vehicle or a way of speaking that allows for *public* conversation and convergence. A reconceptualised religious education advocates a mediating educational language.[41] It seeks to create categories that will allow for beginning conversation across barriers. This public discourse attempts to be precise and comprehensive and works toward reducing intolerance in our own speech patterns. In other words, it offers the possibility for communicative competence on religious and educational matters.[42]

Purpose: Religious education wants to make us at home in this world but discontented with its limits. It is a way of learning to live intelligently and religiously in the modern world. This world of religious diversity is an intellectual and spiritual fact for contemporary life.[43] The aim of religious education is to allow a tradition to become self-conscious and cosmopolitan. It seeks to foster greater appreciation of one's own religious life and less misunderstanding of other people's. Gabriel Moran states it succinctly and perceptively: 'Religious education has, or ought to have, a two-fold goal: first, understanding one's own religious tradition, so that one can live by the richest resources of that tradition; and second, understanding to whatever degree possible the religious life of other people.'[44] Its purpose, then, is to explore religious expressions, religious structures and traditions so that we might understand ourselves and others. This posture may put our own standpoint at risk. It offers, however, the possibility of reconstructing our heritage and contributing to its development.

In the final analysis, a reconceptualised religious education seeks educational space where public dialogue can ensue between religious traditions and between the religious and non-religious on the pressing religious questions of our time. Its ultimate goal is to assist people to think, feel, imagine, act and grow religiously in an intelligent manner.

Gifts. A reconceptualised religious education refuses to allow religious education to be reduced to church matters and maintenance. It represents a fundamental conceptual break with current educational trends and traditions in the Christian church. It seeks to retrieve two of the key words in human speech, and disclose their pervasive implications for our lives. Developmentally, we can consider it the most mature form of religious education.

There is a fundamental truth in the reconceptualised form of religious education. It functions as a vital reminder that 'there is no way to know who we are except in some kind of contrast with things we are not'.[45] We need others − persons, cultures, religions − to aid us to know and be ourselves. This educational process enables us to step out of our own parochial mindset, ideology and identity and pass over to the other standpoints, values and truths. This journey sets us on a corporate search for truth, value and identity.[46] It will lead to the reconstruction of our religious imagination[47] and the expansion of the horizon of our tradition.[48]

Education provides the context for this crossfertilisation. It offers a starting point to begin conversation across religious and non-religious lines and a foundation for authentic dialogue. It demonstrates, firstly the *need* for a disciplined study and understanding of one's own tradition; and secondly the *necessity* for interreligious dialogue with other religious groups. This form of religious education can transform religious traditions, increase tolerance and nurture mutual understanding. This makes it of inestimable value in a world of religious conflicts and global strife.

At its best, then, a reconceptualised religious education provides a meaning of religious education in which the Christian church and other religious bodies can participate. It resists the domestication of the religious to church-talk or the educational to school-talk. From the side of education, it challenges the reduction and rationalisation of education in schooling. From the side of the religious, it challenges religious traditions with the power of educational critique. Its creative contribution, therefore, is to offer a context that opens public discourse on religious questions and makes accessible religious encounter.

Limits: Critics of the reconceptualistic tradition raise questions and pose as problematic the following elements in its position: First, the reconceptualist tradition, for the most part, remains on the drawing board. It is largely undeveloped in practice and no consensus has yet emerged for it to acquire the allegiance of professional religious educators. Second, the reconceptualist position is in danger of remaining ideational and lacking historical grounding. It has yet to be embodied in a fully developed curriculum or programmatic form. Questions remain as to the structure and nature of an accredited degree in religious education in light of its new scope, form and purpose. And third, catechists and Christian religious educators find it difficult to identify with the reconceptualist tradition. Their convictional knowing and commitments foster loyalty to the particularity of their own traditions. The paradigmatic shift required seems unnecessary or, at least, to risk too much. It could lead to the deconstruction of firmly held tenets in their religious traditions.

The reconceptualist tradition, however, is in its infancy stage. Its advent has signalled the dawning of a new stage in religious education development. It is a tradition born out of the roots of our historical past and emerging out of fresh images for a future. The current deficiencies in educational theory and our narrow concept of the religious, however, are obstacles to the emergence and maturation of this tradition. Only a return to the sources will overcome these obstacles. The task, in fact, is twofold: to retrieve the root meaning of the religious and education in life, and to rediscover their mutliple forms in our midst.

Implications for church religious education

Randolph Crump Miller writes, 'No church ever teaches in a completely open-minded manner, and its educational theory has been mixed with indoctrination so that the desired result is predetermined.'[49] Miller's observations are accurate of the past and much of the present. However, a reconstructed religious education calls for a reversal of this form of church education in every respect.

In light of the foregoing discussions, then, I will briefly conclude with some implications of a reconceptualist religious education for education in church:

1. A reconceptulalised religious education offers the church an educational context to examine its life and its work. Its role is to bring educational critique to the existing church – its programmes, pattern of power, linguistic forms and operating assumptions. A reformational process ensues.
2. A reconceptualised religious education prevents closure in the life of the church. Its process provokes thinking, examines forms and challenges all claims to finality. This may result in a methodological reversal in the manner of transmission of the Christian tradition.
3. A reconceptualised religious education sets the church and its educational work in the context of encounter with diverse religious and non-religious worlds. Wilfred Cantwell Smith argues that the cognitive claims of the Christian tradition must also be true for those of other religions if they are genuinely to be true for Christians. 'No statement about Christian faith,' he claims, 'is valid to which in principle a non-Christian could not agree.'[50] This epistemological principle challenges the churches to structure their educational work on more universal foundations and to legitimate their claims *vis-à-vis* other religious groups. This process of education may result in taming some of our cherished claims and abandoning others. It could lead to a reconstruction of our religious identity and re-creation of our religious imagination.
4. In a reconceptualist form of religious education, old issues take on new life in an ecumenical context. Religious groups are directed to explore, challenge and develop their belief and

doctrines. The educational posture calls for critical appreciation, that is, the affirmation, reconstruction and transcending of the Christian tradition. This educational process increases tolerance, lessens arrogance and fosters mutual understanding. It also provides a setting where doctrinal conflicts can be transformed into creative tensions.

5.   A reconceptualised religious education builds a suspension bridge between the work of the church and the great public issues of our day. Questions of justice and peace, equality and ecology, public policy and interpersonal relations are critical issues for both church and society. Nothing from ordinary experience, then, is beyond consideration in its curriculum. It offers a mediating language to link the rich wisdom and prophetic vision of the church to these pressing social and public concerns in the modern world.

6.   Finally, a reconceptualised religious education sees the total life of the church community as the only adequate educator. Each parish not only has an educational programme but ought to be an educational programme. That is, it ought to develop the reflective consciousness of the total community, be an environment for life-long growth in learning and keep open the search for truth within a critical and pluralistic milieu.

In the short run, this form of religious education may be a threat to the church. In the long run, however, it will give the church credibility and legitimacy before the public world.

Notes

1.   See Berard Marthaler, 'A discipline in quest of an identity: religious education,' *Horizons,* 3, 1976, pp. 203−215; Padraic O'Hare (ed.), *Foundation of Religious Education,* New York, Paulist Press, 1978; John H Westerhoff (ed.), *Who Are We? the quest for a religious education,* Birmingham, Alabama, Religious Education Press, 1978, and 'A discipline in crisis,' *Religious Education,* 74, 1979, pp. 7−15.

2.   See Kieran Scott, 'Communicative competence and religious education,' *Lumen Vitae,* 35, 1980, pp. 75−96; and 'Catechesis and religious education: uncovering the nature of our work,' *PACE,* 12, April 1981−82, Issue F, 1−4.

3.   John H Westerhoff, *Who Are We?, op. cit.,* pp. 12−13.

4.   John Elias, 'The three publics of religious educators,' *Religious Education,* 77, 1982, pp. 615−627.

5.   See Norma H Thompson, 'What's going on in religious education?' *Intellect,* December 1976, p. 163.

6.   I attempt to deal with some of the historical origins and identity of the field and profession in 'Religious education and professional religious: a conflict of interest?' *Religious Education,* 77, 1982, pp. 587−603.

7.   See Gabriel Moran, 'A theory of religious education development,' in his book *Religious Education Development,* Minneapolis, Winston, 1983, pp. 183−207. Henry C Simmons reaffirmed this interpretation in a personal correspondence (August 9, 1983).

8.   Some representative examples include *Sharing the Light of Faith: National Catechetical Directory for Catholics of the United States,* Washington, DC, USCC, 1979; *Catechesi Tradendae,* Washington, DC, USCC, 1980; C Ellis Nelson, *Where Faith Begins,* Atlanta, John Knox Press, 1967; Charles Foster,

'The faith community as a guiding image for Christian education,' in Jack L Seymour and Donald E Miller (eds), *Contemporary Approaches to Christian Education,* Nashville, Abingdon, 1982, pp. 53–71; John H Westerhoff, *Generation to Generation,* Philadelphia, United Church Press, 1974, and *Will Our Children Have Faith?* New York, Seabury, 1976, chapter 3; Berard Marthaler, 'Socialization as a model for catechesis,' in Padraic O'Hare, *op. cit.,* pp. 64–92. In Kenneth Barker's typology this tradition is named 'The cultural type': See *Religious Education, Catechesis and Freedom,* Birmingham, Alabama, Religious Education Press, 1981, chapter 5.

9. See D S Amalorpavadas, 'Catechesis as a pastoral task of the church,' *Lumen Vitae,* 27, 1972, pp. 259–280; Berard Marthaler, 'Handing on the symbols of faith,' *Chicago Studies,* 19, 1980, pp. 21–33; and Michael Warren (ed.), *Sourcebook for Modern Catechetics,* Winona, St Mary's Press, 1983. Warren's edited collection contains 31 articles charting the history of catechetics and analysing some of its current seminal issues.

10. Henry C Simmons.

11. See Jack L Seymour, *From Sunday School to Church School: continuities in Protestant church education in the United States, 1860-1929,* Washington, DC, University Press of America, 1982. Seymour's scholarly revisionist history of the Sunday school uncovers the enduring assumptions undergirding Protestant church education. A parallel case, I believe, could be made for some similar continuities and change in the Roman Catholic catechetical tradition.

12. Padraic O'Hare, 'Ministry and education: an interim impression of US Catholic Patterns,' *PACE,* 13, April 1983, p. 5. See also Mary Charles Bryce, 'Sharing the light of faith: catechetical threshold for the US Church,' *Lumen Vitae,* 34, 1979, pp. 393–407.

13. Eva Braun, *Paradoxes of Education in a Republic,* Chicago, University of Chicago Press, 1979, p. 88.

14. Henry C Simmons.

15. See Michael Warren, 'Catechesis as an enriching category for religious education,' *Religious Education,* 76, 1981, pp. 115–127.

16. On the distinction between conventional and post-conventional religious identity, see Charles Davis, 'Our new religious identity,' *Studies in Religion/Sciences Religiouses,* 9, 1, 1980, pp. 25–39.

17. Kenneth Barker, *op. cit.,* p. 227.

18. Representative literature in this revisionist tradition include Thomas Groome, 'Shared Christian praxis: a possible theory/method of religious education,' *Lumen Vitae,* 31, 1976, pp. 186–208; 'The critical principle in Christian education and the task of prophecy,' *Religious Education,* 72, 1977, pp. 262–272; 'Christian education: a task of present dialectical hermeneutics,' *The Living Light,* 14, 1977, pp. 408–423; *Christian Religious Education,* San Francisco, Harper and Row, 1980; Mary C Boys, 'Religious education: access to traditions and transformation,' in Padraic O'Hare (ed.), *Tradition and Transformation,* Birmingham, Alabama, Religious Education Press, 1979, pp. 9–34; 'The standpoint of religious education,' *Religious Education,* 76, 1981, pp. 128–141; Mary Elizabeth Moore, *Education for Continuity and Change: a new model for Christian religious education,* Nashville, Abingdon, 1982; Jack L Seymour and Carol A Wehrheim, 'Faith seeking understanding: interpretation as a task of Christian education,' in Jack L Seymour and Donald E Miller, *op. cit.,* pp. 123–143; Malcolm Warford, *The Necessary Illusion: church culture and educational change,* Philadelphia, United Church Press, 1976; Gloria Durka, 'Christian nurture and critical openness,' *Lumen Vitae,* 36, 1981, pp. 263–286; 'Toward a critical theory of teaching,' *Religious Education,* 74, 1979, pp. 39–48; and Berard Marthaler, 'Towards a revisionist model of catechetics (reflections on David Tracy's *Blessed Rage for Order),'* *Living Light,* 13, 1976, pp. 458, 468–469.

19. This is particularly true of the educational methodologies employed by Thomas Groome and Mary Elizabeth Moore.

20. Mary Elizabeth Moore, *Education for Continuity and Change, op. cit.,* p. 110.

21. Thomas Groome, *Christian Religious Education, op. cit.*

22. Mary Elizabeth Moore, *Education for Continuity and Change, op. cit.*

23. Mary C Boys, 'Religious education: access to tradition and transformation,' *op. cit.*

24. Padraic O'Hare, 'Education for devotion and inquiry: reflections on a questionable assumption,' *Religious Education,* 75, 1981, pp. 505–516.

25. Mary Elizabeth Moore, *Education for Continuity and Change, op. cit.,* p. 134.

26. Thomas Groome names this method 'shared praxis' and Mary Elizabeth Moore 'traditioning'.

27. The terms are Mary C Boys'.

28. See, for example, Thomas Groome, 'Christian education for freedom: a "shared praxis" approach,' in Padraic O'Hare (ed.), *Foundations of Religious Education,* New York, Paulist Press, 1978, pp. 8–39, and Allen J Moore, 'Liberation and the future of Christian education,' in Jack L Seymour and Donald E Miller (eds), *Contemporary Approaches to Christian Education,* Nashville, Abingdon, 1982, pp. 103–122.

29. George Albert Coe, *What Is Christian Education?* New York, Scribner's, 1929, p. 241.

30. On the relationship of theology to religious education, see John Gilbert, 'Theological pluralism and religious education,' *Religious Education,* 70, 1975, pp. 579–585; Thomas Groome, *Christian Religious Education, op. cit.,* pp. 227–230; Ian Knox, *Above or Within? the supernatural in religious education,* Birmingham, Alabama, Religious Education Press, 1975, pp. 245-257; James Michael Lee, *The Shape of Religious Instruction,* Birmingham, Alabama, Religious Education Press, 1971, pp. 245–257; Gabriel Moran, 'From obstacle to modest contributor: theology in religious education,' in Norma H Thompson (ed.), *Religious Education and Theology,* Birmingham, Alabama, Religious Education Press, 1982, pp. 42–70; Norma H Thompson, 'Current issues in religious education,' *Religious Education,* 73, 1978, pp. 611–626.

31. See Maria Harris, 'Education: the overall framework,' *The DRE Book,* New York, Paulist Press, 1976, pp. 114–134; Gabriel Moran, 'The intersection of religion and education,' *Religious Education,* 69, 1974, pp. 531–541; 'Two languages of religious education,' *The Living Light,* 14, 1977, pp. 7–15; 'Where now, what next?' in Padraic O'Hare (ed.), *Foundations of Religious Education,* New York, Paulist Press, 1978, pp. 93–110 and *Interplay: a theology of religion and education,* Winona, St Mary's Press, 1981, 'A theory of religious education development,' in *Religious Education Development, op. cit.,* pp. 183–207.

32. The phraseology is John Dunne's. See *A Search for God in Time and Memory,* New York, Macmillan, 1967, and *The Way of All the Earth,* New York, Macmillan, 1972.

33. Gabriel Moran, 'From obstacle to modest contributor: theology in religious education,' *op. cit.,* pp. 51–52.

34. See Raimundo Panikkar, *The Intrareligious Dialogue,* New York, Paulist Press, 1978, and 'Toward an ecumenical ecumenism,' *Journal of Ecumenical Studies,* 19, 1982, pp. 781–786.

35. See David Tracy, *The Analogical Imagination,* New York, Crossroad, 1981. Tracy's methodology for conversing with a person or classic is a striking example of what is needed here.

36. See Elliott Eisner, *The Educational Imagination,* New York, Paulist Press, 1979.

37. On the technique for interreligious dialogue and the role of the religious imagination in the process see Paul Knitter, 'Religious imagination and interreligious dialogue,' in Robert Masson (ed.), *The Pedagogy of God's Image: essays on symbol and the religious imagination,* Chico, California, Scholars Press, 1982, pp. 97–112.

38. Philip Phenix, 'Religion in public education: principles and issues,' in David E Engel (ed.), *Religion in Public Education,* New York, Paulist Press, 1974, pp. 57–74.

39. Paul Knitter, 'Religious imagination and interreligious dialogue,' *op cit.*

40. John Dunne, *The Way of All the Earth, op. cit.,* p. 53.

41. Gabriel Moran, 'Two languages of religious education,' *op. cit.*

42. Kieren Scott, 'Communicative competence and religious education,' *op. cit.*

43. See Wilfred Cantwell Smith, *Religious Diversity,* edited by Willard G Oxtoby, New York, Harper and Row, 1976.
44. Gabriel Moran, *Interplay, op. cit.,* p. 37.
45. Robert Bellah, 'Commentary and proposed agenda: the normative framework for pluralism in America,' *Soundings,* 61, 1978, p. 362.
46. Charles Davis, 'Our new religious identity,' *op. cit.*
47. Paul Knitter, 'Religious imagination and interreligious dialogues,' *op. cit.*
48. John Dunne, *The Way of All the Earth, op. cit.*
49. Randolph Crump Miller, *The Theory of Christian Education Practice,* Birmingham, Alabama, Religious Education Press, 1980, p. 279.
50. Wilfred Cantwell Smith, *Toward a World Theology*, Philadelphia, Westminster, 1981, p. 126.

PART TWO

Reason, religion and education

Reason, religion and education: an overview

Jeff Astley

In part two of this reader we focus more clearly on philosophical topics, and in particular on the role of reason in Christian religious education. Again references to articles in the reader are contained in brackets.[1]

In Britain at least much of the debate about Christian education has been informed by the analytic tradition in philosophy of education which has often seen education as a matter of developing rational autonomy (independent thinking) and 'trusting to reason'. From this standpoint, Paul Hirst has famously criticised Christian education as a contradiction in terms on the grounds that open-ended education is dominated by a concern for knowledge, truth and autonomous, universal reason, whereas religions are matters of disputable beliefs and particular faith commitments (article 6.1, see also section 6 in general and the introduction to that section). This chimes in with criticisms of Christian education as being indoctrinatory, in that its intention or method or result is to teach people something that they cannot then 'unlearn' even when they find good evidence against it.

The place of reason in Christianity is, of course, highly controversial. Many theologians recognise that reason has a critical, clarifying and systematising function in religion; but deny that it is to be found among the sources of religion.[2] But most of them would say that Christianity is rational or reasonable in that it accords with reason but that, like sensory knowledge, moral knowledge and so on, its foundations lie elsewhere. Those who employ a rather restricted concept of reason have been most negative in their view of the enterprise of Christian education, whereas those who take a broader view of reason, or one that is more complex and less abstract, appear to be most successful in defending the activity.

A number of points may be made in the context of a discussion about the role of reason in religion and religious education.

First, appeals to reason often sound as though they are referring to a single, unitary, neutral tool. But, as John Kleinig reminds us:[3]

> The reification of concepts so characteristic of Western phi-
> losophers should not blind us to the fact that there is no
> such thing as Reason. There are simply people who think
> (that is, reason), and who do this well or badly. Behind
> their thinking activity there lurks no parent animal 'Reason',
> intuitively observed and self-evidently sovereign, but a set
> of culturally acquired and alterable standards by which that
> thinking activity can be evaluated. The so-called 'laws of logic',
> perhaps the most permanent standards of rational assessment,
> comprise only a small part of the critical apparatus to which
> we appeal when making rational appraisals. Other parts are
> highly controversial.

Certainly the elementary laws of logical thinking will not get us very far in assessing the rationality of a religious belief, or any other belief for that matter.

Second, many definitions of indoctrination are too simple-minded, for what counts to a person as good evidence against her belief is dependent on the belief-system that she holds. 'Good evidence' is not a neutral term with a reference that is independent of the context in which it is used. Further, metaphysical claims (whether they be about the existence of God or an 'outside world'), and basic or fundamental propositions that serve either as the foundations or the presuppositions of knowledge, are inevitably (and properly) less easy to dislodge by apparently conflicting evidence. The debate about indoctrination needs to take account of the range of types of beliefs within both religion and other disciplines (especially science), for beliefs are not all falsifiable to the same degree within any discipline of thought. (On indoctrination see particularly section 8 below.)[4]

Third, there is no Olympian or Archimedean point outside all belief-systems from which they can be evaluated in a non-partisan manner. All evaluations take place from some particular standpoint: one cannot view anything without standing somewhere to do the viewing. Some educational rhetoric about 'trusting to reason' and being 'impartial' seems to imply that such a general, abstract, presuppositionless and value-free position is possible, and that is surely a chimera (see articles 3.2, 3.3, 6.3).

Fourth, reason operates in different ways in different contexts, or different 'forms of life'. Being reasonable or rational in religion is by no means necessarily the same as being reasonable or rational in scientific, ethical or aesthetic judgments. Further, what counts as our 'rational system of beliefs' may well change because of factors that are broadly sociological and psychological, rather than purely 'rational'.[5]

Fifth, Christian theology, like other world-views, has developed a complex system of reasoning to enable it to cope with the complexity and multi-faceted nature of the reality to which it refers. Thus, for example, it often speaks in paradoxes: holding together apparently contradictory beliefs so as to bear witness to important, disparate insights into reality. A too pedantic and clear-cut use of simplistic reason might collapse such paradoxes, and thus jettison significant illumination for the sake of a clarity achieved too early in the exploration.[6]

Sixth, the broad definition of Christian education noted in the overview to part one of this reader includes both 'formative education' and 'critical education' under its umbrella. Much discussion in the philosophy of education focuses on the importance of critical education, the analysis and evaluation of knowledge-claims, within a 'liberal education'. But education in general, and Christian education in particular, should recognise that the formation of a person's identity and world-view must happen before such criticism can develop. Education also makes persons, and Christian education makes Christian persons, in that we learn to be someone-with-a-viewpoint before we can assess other people and their viewpoints, and certainly before we can be critical about, and rationally change, ourselves and our beliefs (see article 4.1).[7]

Seventh, the importance of 'critical openness' in Christian nurture has received much attention through the work of John M Hull and others (as in article 5.3).[8] Most Christians of a broadly liberal theological persuasion would expect some 'openness' to be the mark of any education into Christianity. To affirm this is like being in favour of virtue. The question still remains as to the nature (and limits) of such openness in any given Christian education experience. Critical openness should be discussed as much under a psychological, as under a philosophical (or theological) heading, if it is accepted that it can never result in anything more than a clearer view of the foundations on which a person stands. Critical reason alone cannot lay, or re-lay, such foundations. Indeed the foundations of religion, many would claim, are essentially psychological foundations with philosophical implications, rather than *vice-versa*.[9]

In any case, there are profound psychological, as well as philosophical, issues involved in any discussion as to whether, and how far, Christian education should be an 'open ended', 'tentative' and exploratory searching for meaning within the Christian tradition,[10] and how far it might include a more radical 'testing to destruction' of Christian affirmations.[11]

Eighth, discussions about the place of reason have their setting in life in the area of teaching about beliefs rather than the teaching of attitudes, values or skills. It may be that behaviourist accounts of education (including Christian education) founder by not including the element of understanding/appreciation in their definition of learning.[12] However, a number of philosophers of education would be willing to recognise among the aims of general, publicly-funded education the importance and appropriateness of forming attitudes, dispositions and moral virtues: that is, the inculcation or moulding of character.[13] Moral education is not just the education of moral thinking.[14] Similarly Christian education seeks to educate people not just to know the truth, but to do the truth, and indeed to 'be the truth'. Such a person-making aim can only be defended on the basis of judgments about what are the intrinsically valuable states of the human personality and the components of human fulfilment. Christian theology and Christian ethics have much to say on these subjects.

Ninth, in so far as reason is developed so as to operate effectively in the cognitive (intellectual) domain, its limitations are patent when we move to the area of human affections (feelings) and volitions. There reason, when simplistically understood, is often transcended, despite the cognitive appraisals that must be recognised as integral to a proper analysis of emotions.[15] For all love, and most commitments, go 'beyond the evidence' in some way or another; not 'unreasonably beyond', perhaps, but life does not get started until we act 'despite the appearances'. The logic of certain key terms in both personal relationships and the Christian tradition is such that extreme open-mindedness, tentativeness and critical rationality are inimical to their development. Examples would include 'trust', 'love', 'commitment', 'hope' and 'faith' (see article 7.1). It is a mark of true personal commitments that they are tenaciously held. Certainly, 'she loves me' and 'God loves me' are propositions that are not appropriately given up at the first sign of falsifying evidence, from flying crockery or disappointed prayer.[16]

Tenth, such tenacity of belief is an important feature of the way scientists view their own very general theories or research programmes,[17] and our trust in the intelligibility of the universe and our own ability to understand it plays an important heuristic role in the furtherance of all our knowledge. Christian education may have insights to offer here which a more secular education needs to receive. The role of 'self-fulfilling beliefs' in personal relationships and religion is also worthy of reflection. If I bring up my children to believe that people love them, often despite the evidence, they will take the step of risk and form relationships with them, and love may be engendered. If I bring them up to trust people, some of them at least will become trustworthy by thus being trusted. There are great dangers here, of course. But are there not also some parallels with learning to love and trust 'Reality'?[18]

Eleventh, a naïve relativism of the 'it doesn't matter what you believe because everything is relative' kind is easily overthrown, and should be resisted. But a more sophisticated (because qualified) form of relativism is less open to criticism, and has found many supporters among contemporary philosophers. It is also less of a threat to the religionist and the religious educator, while demanding a deeper understanding of the proper balance between formative and critical education within a religious tradition, and perhaps a more risky form of the latter (see articles 10.1 and 10.2).[19]

Twelfth, non-cognitive (non-factual) understandings of the Christian religion, which understand language about God and life after death as expressing a commitment to a way of life and a set of spiritual values, rather than as assertions about the existence of supernatural entities or states, have been adopted by a number of philosophers of religion.[20] Inevitably this leads to a very different interpretation of Christian education from that demanded by more traditional, cognitive understandings. Such 'expressivist' interpretations of religion tend to play down its cognitive dimension and the teaching and learning of religious beliefs as doctrinal claims, and to lay the stress instead on the affective and volitional ('lifestyle') outcomes of Christian education.

Notes

1. Some of the material here is amended from Jeff Astley, 'On learning religion,' *The Modern Churchman*, 29, 1987, pp. 26–34, with permission. See also Jeff Astley, *The Philosophy of Christian Religious Education*, Birmingham, Alabama, Religious Education Press; London, SPCK, 1994, parts 2, 3 and 4.

2. Cf. John Macquarrie, *Principles of Christian Theology*, London, SCM, 1966, chapters 1 and 2; Patrick Burke, *The Fragile Universe*, London and Basingstoke, Macmillan, 1979, chapter 4.

3. John Kleinig, *Philosophical Issues in Education*, London and Canberra, Croom Helm, 1982, p. 265.

4. On indoctrination in general, see I A Snook (ed.), *Concepts of Indoctrination*, London, Routledge and Kegan Paul, 1972; I A Snook, *Indoctrination and Education*, London, Routledge and Kegan Paul, 1972; Ben Spiecker and Roger Straughan (eds), *Freedom and Indoctrination in Education: international perspectives*, London, Cassell, 1991. On indoctrination in religious education, see also Basil Mitchell, 'Appendix B,' in *The Fourth R*, London, SPCK, 1970; and the discussion and literature cited in Elmer J Thiessen, *Teaching for Commitment: liberal education, indoctrination and Christian nurture*, Leominster, Gracewing; Montreal, McGill-Queen's University Press, 1993.

5. On religion as (or contained within) a form of life, see especially the writings of D Z Phillips, particularly: *Faith and Philosophical Inquiry*, London, Routledge and Kegan Paul, 1970; *Religion without Explanation*, Oxford, Blackwell, 1976; *Belief, Change and Forms of Life*, London, Macmillan, 1986; *Faith after Foundationalism*, London and New York, Routledge, 1988. Compare also W Donald Hudson, *A Philosophical Approach to Religion*, London, Macmillan, 1974; Norman Malcolm, 'The Groundlessness of Belief,' in Stuart C Brown (ed.), *Reason and Religion*, Ithaca, New York, Cornell University Press, 1977, chapter 7. On 'the rational system of beliefs,' see W Donald Hudson's article with that title in David Martin *et al.*, *Sociology and Theology: alliance and conflict*, Brighton, Harvester, 1980, chapter 5.

6. Compare John Wisdom, *Paradox and Discovery*, Oxford, Blackwell, 1965, chapter 11; I T Ramsey and N Smart, 'Paradox in Religion,' *Proceedings of the Aristotelian Society*, supplementary volume 33, 1959, pp. 195–218.

7. Compare also Elmer J Thiessen, 'Christian nurture, indoctrination and liberal education,' in Jeff Astley and David Day (eds), *The Contours of Christian Education*, Great Wakering, McCrimmons, 1992, chapter 5.

8. See also John M Hull, *Studies in Religion and Education*, Lewes, Falmer, 1984, parts 4 and 5.

9. See Donald Evans, *Struggle and Fulfillment*, Cleveland, Collins, 1979.
10. See Kevin Nichols, 'Commitment, search and dialogue,' in his *Voice of the Hidden Waterfall*, London, Paulist, 1980, chapter 7.
11. This is regarded by Donald MacKinnon as essential to the task of theology in a 'secular' university context: see his article in T Shanin (ed.), *The Rules of the Game*, London, Tavistock, 1972, p. 168.
12. Compare Kleinig, *op. cit.*, p. 37.
13. Compare John White, *The Aims of Education Restated*, London, Routledge and Kegan Paul, 1982.
14. See Stanley Hauerwas, 'Character, narrative, and growth in the Christian life,' in James Fowler and Antoine Vergote (eds), *Toward Moral and Religious Maturity,* Morristown, New Jersey, Silver Burdett, 1980, pp. 441–484; Craig Dykstra, *Vision and Character*, New York, Paulist, 1981; David Cooper, *Authenticity and Learning*, London, Routledge and Kegan Paul, 1983.
15. See, for example, William Lyons, *Emotion*, Cambridge, Cambridge University Press, 1980.
16. See Basil Mitchell's response to Anthony Flew in Basil Mitchell (ed.), *Philosophy of Religion*, Oxford, Oxford University Press, 1971, pp. 18–20; also I T Ramsey, 'History and the gospels: some philosophical reflections,' *Studia Evangelica*, 3, 1964, pp. 201–217 and R S Heimbeck, *Theology and Meaning*, London, George Allen and Unwin, 1969.
17. For a general discussion see Imre Lakatos and Alan Musgrave (eds), *Criticism and the Growth of Knowledge,* Cambridge, Cambridge University Press, 1970; Ian Barbour, *Myths, Models and Paradigms*, London, SCM, 1974; Michael C Banner, *The Justification of Science and the Rationality of Religious Belief,* Oxford, Oxford University Press, 1990
18. Cf. Peter L Berger, *A Rumour of Angels*, Harmondsworth, Penguin, 1970, chapter 3; Erik Erikson, *Childhood and Society*, New York, W W Norton, 1963, chapter 7; Hans Küng, *Does God Exist?*, New York, Random House, 1981.
19. For a defence of a qualified form of relativism and an account of its relevance for religion, see Joseph Runzo, *Reason, Relativism and God*, Basingstoke, Macmillan, 1986. The two sides of the relativism debate in philosophy are presented in Joseph Margolis, *The Truth about Relativism*, Oxford, Blackwell, 1991 and Harvey Siegel, *Relativism Refuted*, Dordrecht, Holland, Reidel, 1987. A useful reader is Kenneth Baynes *et al.*, *After Philosophy*, Cambridge, Massachusetts, MIT Press, 1987.
20. See D Z Phillips, *Religion without Explanation, op. cit.*, chapters 10 and 11; Don Cupitt, *Taking Leave of God*, London, SCM, 1980, chapters 4 and 5, *Creation out of Nothing*, London, SCM, 1990, chapter 4 and *The Time Being*, London, SCM, 1992, *passim*; Gareth Moore, *Believing in God*, Edinburgh, T and T Clark, 1988.

6. Liberal education and belief

A number of responses to Paul Hirst's rejection of the combination of the terms 'Christian' and 'education' have already been noted (see, for example, articles 1.1, 2.2, 3.1 and 3.3).[1]

Hirst's classic article, 'Christian education: a contradiction in terms?' was published in *Learning for Living*, 11, 1972, pp. 6–11.[2] It distinguished 'two quite different views of education': the broad, 'primitive concept' of passing on to children what we believe, and a more specific, 'sophisticated' view of 'passing on knowledge, understanding and reason', identified here as being determined 'by what on publicly acknowledged rational grounds we can claim to know and understand'. Education in this latter sense is concerned with objectivity and reason, in that knowledge claims are judged by 'clearly recognisable objective grounds'. Such considerations should not allow the teaching of any set of religious beliefs, only 'the radically controversial character' of all religious claims. In so far as any form of religious education goes beyond this concern for objectivity and reason, Hirst declares himself 'against it'.

John Hull's article in response to some of the elements of Hirst's position was first published in *British Journal of Educational Studies,* 24, 1976, pp. 127–143. It is entitled 'Christian theology and educational theory: can there be connections?' Drawing on a number of Hirst's publications, Hull rehearses the sociological, logical, and methodological arguments against such a relationship and offers his own critique of them. Hull concludes that these arguments 'are unconvincing in themselves and inconsistent with (Hirst's) arguments elsewhere ... about the relation between Christian theology and other spheres such as ethics'.

A recent contribution to the continuing debate is provided by T H McLaughlin's article, 'Fairness, controversiality and the common school,' first published in *Spectrum*, 24, 1992, pp. 105–118. Here the notion of liberal education, with the development of 'critical reflective judgment' and the learner's autonomy at its heart, is discussed in the context of public schooling. McLaughlin suggests that many Christians would applaud such 'public' values, but notes both the dangers of freighting the concepts of autonomy and critical reason with illicit assumptions that are antagonistic to religious belief, and the extent to which scope exists within a liberal education 'for religious believers ... to make significant demands of the common school with regard to its fair handling of controversial questions'.

Professor Paul H Hirst was formerly Professor of Education in the University of Cambridge Department of Education, England. Professor John M Hull is Professor of Religious Education in the Faculty of Education and Continuing Studies of the University of Birmingham, England. Dr T H McLaughlin teaches in the Department of Education of the University of Cambridge, England.

Notes

1. For other responses to Paul Hirst, see Bernard Curtis, 'Religious education: a pleonasm,' *Learning for Living*, 11, 1972, 11–14; Leslie J Francis, 'The logic of education, theology, and the church school,' *Oxford Review of Education*, 9, 1983, pp. 147–162; Elmer J Thiessen, 'A defense of a distinctively Christian curriculum,' *Religious Education*, 80, 1985, pp. 37–50; and article 9.1.

2. See also Paul H Hirst, 'Morals, religion and the maintained school,' *British Journal of Educational Studies*, 14, 1965, pp. 5–18; 'Education, catechesis and the church school,' *British Journal of Religious Education*, 3, 1981, pp. 85–93, 101. A more qualified critique is offered by Hirst in his paper 'Education and diversity of belief,' in M C Felderhof (ed.), *Religious Education in a Pluralistic Society*, London, Hodder and Stoughton, 1985, pp. 5–17; see also the response by Kevin Nichols in the same volume, pp. 18–22.

6.1 Christian education: a contradiction in terms?
Paul H Hirst

The concept of education

The central thesis of this article[1] is that there has already emerged in our society a view of education, a concept of education, which makes the whole idea of Christian education a kind of nonsense and the search for a Christian approach to, or philosophy of, education a huge mistake. From this point of view the idea that there is a characteristically or distinctively Christian form of education seems just as much a mistake as the idea that there is a distinctively Christian form of mathematics, of engineering or of farming. In mathematics, engineering or farming we have developed activities in which what is right or wrong, or good or bad, of its kind is determined by rational principles which make the activity what it is. Mathematical proofs must be judged right or wrong according to the principles of mathematical reasoning. A bridge to stay up in a force ten gale must be designed according to the principles of engineering. A particular use of land which reduces it to a dust bowl is bad farming judged by the principles of farming. And the principles that govern these matters of mathematics, engineering and farming, are neither Christian nor non-Christian, neither for Christianity nor anti-Christianity. Nor is anything in these areas decided properly by appeal to Christian tradition, the Christian scriptures or anything else of that kind. Once, of course, it was not so. Humanity's view of the physical world and how to cope with it in practical affairs, was once at least in part determined by religious beliefs. It was not thought possible to attain the relevant knowledge on autonomous, independent, rational grounds. But the pursuits I have mentioned have now been recognised as legitimately autonomous and an exactly similar status is, I suggest, quite properly coming to be accorded to education. Here too, we are progressively coming to understand that the issues must be settled independently of any questions of religious beliefs.

Long before I came to this conclusion, that judging what is good or bad in education is nothing to do with whether one is a Christian, a humanist or a Buddhist, I suspected that there was something wrong with the whole idea of Christian education, but could not put my finger on the real cause of my unease. I recognised that what one is offered under this label is often very dubious from

305

both an educational and indeed from a Christian point of view. Much of it is based on very general moral principles, backed by perhaps scripture or Christian tradition, which, having little or no explicit educational content, are applied to educational problems in a highly debatable way. It is not uncommon to hear it argued that Christians, convinced of the value of personal relationships, must clearly object to any school of above five hundred pupils. One is sometimes assured in the name of Christianity, that the comprehensive system is a wicked thing, and that specialisation in the sixth form is equally deplorable. But clearly the general moral principles that people use to back up these beliefs about education do not alone determine any particular, practically relevant educational principles. To get these one must consider equally important matters of psychological and sociological fact, the structure of our social institutions, the availability of money and manpower, and so on. All these and many other considerations must enter into the discussion before one can move from very general principles of a moral kind, to specific educational recommendations, and it is on just these particular considerations that ideas of so-called Christian education are often quite indefensible. The main point to be noted, however, is that none of these considerations has anything to do with Christian beliefs. What is more it seems to me the general principles on which the whole exercise is based are usually not in any sense significantly Christian either, though people might appeal to Christian texts, or Christian tradition in support of them. Working from this end of general moral principles I suggest that one simply cannot produce anything that is in any significant sense a distinctive Christian view of education.

But if one tries to work from the other end, formulating educational principles from what is specifically said in scripture about education, one seems to run into an equally impossible situation. If you take what the bible says about punishment and discipline, and try to compose some general educational principle from this, you will not, I think, get very far. To take ideas of social control out of a biblical, social context, and transfer them directly to an East End school in our twentieth-century industrial society is patently ludicrous. Christians of any intelligence have long since recognised the need to disentangle within biblical teaching the general principles that can be legitimately applied in our own context from the practices justifiable only in the social and cultural circumstances of biblical times. The problem then is how to abstract the principles without entering an inconclusive debate about biblical interpretation. If that hurdle is surmounted is one likely to achieve much that is both educationally significant and distinctively Christian? I think not. And even if one does get so far, how much agreement can there be amongst Christians on particular applications of these principles? Experience suggests very little if any. On these grounds

I concluded long ago, that much as one might like to find a biblical or Christian view of education, it isn't discoverable. Not because I saw anything wrong with the idea in principle, but because in practice it seems to be the case that one just cannot produce anything of substance that deserves to be labelled a Christian view of education.

Such a conclusion is clearly unpalatable to those Christians who are convinced of the total sufficiency of biblical revelation for the conduct of all human affairs in all places and at all times. I suggest, however, that the conclusion is valid, and that the people who hold this view should rethink what they understand by the sufficiency of biblical revelation in these matters. It seems to me that as a matter of fact the bible is insufficient in what it implies for education today and that crudely interpreted and crudely applied its teaching is positively dangerous.

But if I once thought the pursuit of a distinctively Christian form of education in principle satisfactory, I have now come to the conclusion that even that is not so. Let me approach this issue by voicing a possible reaction to what I have already argued. It might be said in reply that surely I have wrecked my case by vastly overstating it. If we cannot get an all embracing view of Christian education that tells us what to do about the comprehensive system, the curriculum, how to teach history, or even whether we ought to have compulsory education, surely there are some things in education on which Christians and, say, humanists would disagree. If so, does it not follow that there is *in part* a distinctively Christian concept of education, one which is distinguishable from other views at least in these particular areas if not maybe in others? If one cannot get everything necessary for educational practice from Christian teaching, surely one can get something, and something distinctive. Well, if so, what? The most likely answer from a Christian is that surely a Christian will want his or her children brought up in the Christian faith, that the humanist will certainly not want that, and that in this respect, their ideas of the content of education will be radically different. At this point, however, a very important shift can occur in the whole discussion, for another Christian may well say that the last thing one should do as part of *education*, is to bring up a child in any faith, even the Christian faith. This second Christian would maintain that communicating our understanding of the Christian faith is a legitimate part of education, and with that many humanists in our society, at any rate, might well agree, whereas bringing a child up in any particular faith is not what *education* is about. What we have here are two quite different views on education. According to the first, it is concerned with passing on to children what we believe, so that they in their turn come to believe it to be true. According to the second view, education should not be determined by what any group simply believes, but by what on publicly acknowledged rational grounds we can claim to know and understand.

The first of these concepts of education I shall call the primitive concept, for it clearly expresses the view of education a primitive tribe might have, when it seeks to pass on to the next generation its rituals, its ways of farming and so on, according to its own customs and beliefs. Whatever is held by the group to be true or valuable, simply because it is held to be true or valuable, is what is passed on so that it comes to be held as true and valuable by others in their turn. On this view, clearly there can be a Christian concept of education, one based on what Christians hold to be true and valuable in education, in which they seek that the next generation shall think likewise. Similarly there can be a humanist or a Buddhist concept, indeed there will be as many concepts of education as there are systems of beliefs and values, concepts overlapping in character in so far as the beliefs and values of the different groups overlap.

The second view of education is much more sophisticated, arising from a recognition that not all the things held to be true or valuable by a group are of the same status. Some of their claims and activities will be rationally defensible on objective grounds, whereas others, perhaps held equally tenaciously, may on objective grounds be highly debatable. Some may in fact be matters of nothing but mere custom and tradition. Once it is fully recognised that the belief that something is true, even if that belief is universal, does not of itself make it true, a new principle emerges for carefully assessing what we pass on to others and how we wish them to regard it. That we hold something to be true or valuable is of itself no reason why anyone else should so regard it. That something can, on the appropriate objective grounds, be shown to be true or reasonable is a very good reason for passing it on to others. But even then what we must surely seek is that they will hold it not because we hold it, but because there are objective grounds. Only then will they be prepared to reconsider, and where necessary revise, their beliefs and practices when new evidence and better argument arise. The second, sophisticated view of education is thus concerned with passing on beliefs and practices according to, and together with, their objective status. It is dominated by a concern for knowledge, for truth, for reasons, distinguishing these clearly from mere belief, conjecture and subjective preference, *even when the latter happen to be justifiable*. On this view, when science is taught, its methods and procedures are seen as important as any contemporary conclusions, for these may in significant respects have to be changed. In history, pupils are introduced to examining evidence so that they come to recognise that claims about what happened must satisfy the canons of historical scholarship. Where there is dispute, debate and divergence of opinion just that is taught. Where in any area there do not seem to be agreed objective principles of judgment, exactly that is what is taught. Of course, mistakes will be made in seeking to follow as closely as possible the ideals of objectivity and reason, but education committed to these ends will be very different from education determined by the particular beliefs and values of a particular group.

On this second view the character of education is not settled by any appeal to Christian, humanist or Buddhist beliefs. Such an appeal is illegitimate, for the basis is logically more fundamental, being found in the canons of objectivity and reason, canons against which Christian, humanist and Buddhist beliefs must, in their turn and in the appropriate way be assessed. When the domain of religious beliefs is so manifestly one in which there are at present no clearly recognisable objective grounds for judging claims, to base education on any such claims would be to forsake the pursuit of objectivity, however firm our commitment might be to any one set of such beliefs. Indeed an education based on a concern for objectivity and reason, far from allying itself with any specific religious claims, must involve teaching the radically controversial character of all such claims. An understanding of religious claims it can perfectly well aim at, but commitment to any one set, in the interests of objectivity it cannot either assume or pursue.

Possible objections

I hope it will not be thought that in the foregoing I have been maintaining something that is necessarily either anti- or un-Christian. I see no reason to think anything I have said is incompatible with any religious position in which truth and objectivity matter, and I am taking it that Christianity at any rate is concerned with asserting truths about what is, in an appropriate sense, objectively the case. If, of course, Christianity is itself held to be in some sense a-rational, irrational or anti-rational then contradictions there certainly are. But then the trouble is, I can see no *reason* why anyone should take such religious claims seriously. Certainly I personally am not prepared to base my life on the glaring contradictions such an approach involves.

It might, however, be objected by some that my whole argument is based on the thesis that there exist vast areas of knowledge and understanding using concepts and canons of thought, objective in character and in no way connected with religious beliefs. This they would deny, insisting that in all areas of knowledge one is necessarily involved in presuppositions of a religious nature. In history, literature or even science one cannot, it is said, escape these elements and certainly in teaching these matters one's commitment necessarily infects all one does. To argue thus is indeed to deny the whole autonomy thesis on which my case rests, but such a denial seems to be so patently false that I find it hard to understand what is being maintained. In what way is mathematics supposed to depend on Christian principles? Its concepts and forms of argument seem to me totally devoid of religious reference. Nor do I understand what is meant by saying that science rests on Christian presuppositions, when the tests for its claims are ultimately matters of sense observation. Scientific terms have meaning and criteria of application which are not connected with religious concepts of any sort. They are in this sense autonomous and scientific understanding is therefore of its nature autonomous. To maintain that it was only in a context of Christian belief that science did in fact arise, even if true, does not affect the nature of the activity of science at all. The pursuit is perfectly compatible with quite other beliefs, as is obvious in the present day, and nothing by way of historical, sociological or psychological analysis can in any way deny the claim that the concepts and principles of science are in no sense logically connected with Christian beliefs. That there is here an autonomous domain of knowledge and understanding seems to me indisputable. And surely this is why what matters in science, as in any other pursuit, is the mastery of its own logical and methodological principles, not holding any particular religious beliefs.

It might be objected that if science is autonomous, historical studies are not, for an understanding of for example the Reformation must be either Catholic or Protestant. Yet surely even this is an unacceptable claim if it is intended to deny the objectivity of contemporary historical scholarship. What matters is truth to the evidence, irrespective of the particular religious beliefs of the *scholar* – indeed these are nowadays recognised as an irelevance, it is the justice to the historical data that counts. The idea of coming to a situation and interpreting it from a set of beliefs to which one subscribes is to reject the demand of historical scholarship. What is true of historical studies is, I suggest, also true of literary and even religious studies. I see no reason why there should not be, and indeed there is already being practised, an objective study of religions in which the particular religious beliefs of students are an irrelevant consideration. To understand beliefs or actions does not necessitate that one either accepts or approves of them and to teach for such an understanding demands acceptance or approval of them by neither teacher nor pupil.

But even if the autonomy thesis is accepted, and it is granted that something called education could be planned and conducted in terms of the second, sophisticated concept that I outlined, it might still be argued that this would be undesirable. If education can be understood in two senses, either in the primitive sense of simply passing on beliefs and practices or in the sophisticated sense of passing on knowledge, understanding and reason, why should we not stick to the first which can take on a distinctively Christian form?

In the first place, I suggest the sophisticated concept is important because it provides a clear and to my mind appropriate demonstration for the educational functions of state run institutions. I personally hold that it is quite improper for state institutions to align themselves with any religious group and in particular to take over any of the affairs that properly belong to the Christian church. The function of the state in religious matters should not, I think, be one of taking any side on issues of so controversial a nature, but the more objective function of preserving freedom and liberty. This is to suggest that there are many areas of life from which the state should keep clear and that in education it should not act outside a domain in which objectivity and reason govern all that is done. This would then leave to the church, the home and other social agencies those matters which might figure in a concept of education in the first or primitive sense, which could not figure in the sophisticated concept. Bringing up a child in a particular faith is thus seen as the proper concern of the home or church but not of the state school. It is seen as an element in education in the first of my two senses but not in the second.

Simply to suggest that education in the second sense is appropriate for state schools does, however, seem to imply that education in the first sense is nevertheless a thoroughly coherent and acceptable concept which can properly be applied in a context wider than or outside the state school. With that conclusion I am, however, far from happy. For, is bringing up children so that they believe what we believe, *education* in any sense that is nowadays acceptable? Indeed I suggest that this pursuit is in fact now increasingly considered immoral, wherever it is conducted. What I want for a child, whether at home, in church or at a state school, is that he or she shall come to believe that there are reasons for believing, accept that there are reasons for accepting and commit him or her self to nothing simply because I say so. Of course, in the early years the child may accept things in this way, but what one is trying to develop in education is an autonomous human being who will be responsible for his or her own judgments as far as possible, certainly on controversial issues of individual importance. It seems incumbent upon me then in home and church as much as in school, to be as objective as I can about all matters. In so far then as education in the first sense goes beyond concern for objectivity and reason, be it conducted in the home or the church, I am against it. I am therefore rejecting the moral acceptability of anything which falls under the first concept of education but not under the second. But in that case, the whole idea of Christian education is one I am rejecting, for I wish to resist the suggestion that it should be conducted anywhere.

But, you might say, that is surely to ask too much. What would be the difference beween the state school and the church and the

home in their educational functions if none of them went beyond
the measured, objective consideration of different religions? In their
educational function there should I think be no difference. Yet the
home and the church do have other functions that do not run counter
to education in the objective sense. Clearly, in areas where there is
radical debate on matters which are of enormous importance for
people's lives, we have by definition issues which cannot be fully
settled simply on objective, rational grounds that are recognisable
as such by all reasonable people. The whole domain of reasoning in
politics, for instance, is one in which rational people disagree, and
we accept that they will in all honesty disagree. There are institutions where political matters can be taught from an objective point
of view, and I trust this is what we do in school. But we also consider
it proper for there to be institutions concerned with promoting and
developing particular political beliefs. What they seek is not in any
sense anti- or ir-rational, but commitment, in that people come to a
decision however difficult, on highly important issues. In a similar
way, in addition to objective education in religious matters, there
is surely a proper area for other religious concerns, concerns that
do not run counter to the interests of education. The significance
of religious commitment, on matters on which equally reasonable
people differ, can be considerable. There is thus a manifold need for
institutions in which people can explore to the full and act together
according to the beliefs they hold, and through which they can also
seek to present and commend to others what they hold to be true.
In the church and the home, children and others are faced with
just these aspects of religious belief and commitment. Provided
they are introduced to them in a way that does not oppose the
development of rational beliefs, there is no need for any conflict
with the interests of education in my second sense. But what we
should call these quite proper activities, in which religious and political groups seek to commend their beliefs and practices to others,
I am not sure. The term education is I suggest inappropriate. My
first sense of that term is so broad that it includes not only these
quite proper activities, but also others which I have argued are
morally indefensible. My second sense of the term is so specific
that it excludes these proper activities. To seek to form a third
concept of education lying between these two, covering both this
category of proper activities and those of education in the second
sense, would, I suggest do us all a dis-service.

Conclusion

At present the concept of education in our society is moving
clearly toward my second sense, a sense so valuable in its central
demarcatory function, that it would seem to me most important
to hang on to this notion. In so far as we do that, there can be

no such thing as Christian education. Not that there is any necessary contradiction between Christian beliefs and education in this sense, provided Christian beliefs form a rationally coherent system. It is rather that the term education is being used to pick out activities that can be characterised independently of any religious reference.

I conclude, then, that we have now reached a stage in the development of our grasp of what education might or might not, ought or ought not to include, that the notion of Christian education is properly regarded as an anachronism. If that is so, Christians working in education would do well to follow the example of those working in engineering or farming, who simply get on with mastering the non-religious principles of their own professional business. And if that seems to be asking for a divorce between one's Christian beliefs and one's professional practice, I can only suggest that any rationally coherent approach to the Christian faith must see it as perfectly consistent with the knowledge and understanding that humanity has amassed on autonomous grounds.

Notes
1. This article was read at a conference organised by the Victoria Institute on 6th February, 1971, and is published here by kind permission of the editor of the Victoria Institute's Journal *Faith and Thought*.

6.2 Christian theology and educational theory: can there be connections?
John M Hull

Introduction

This article is not concerned with religious education in the curriculum but with the nature of the relation between theology and educational theory. All sophisticated religious belief systems have histories of such relations, the literature of Christianity, Judaism and Islam being particularly rich. Theology of education at the present time is an active field of interdisciplinary study. Recent dissertation abstracts indicate the sort of work taking place[1] in an effort to criticise, clarify and give new directions to education in the light of contemporary religious ideas.

It has now been denied that this activity is a legitimate one.

Exposition

In his book *Moral Education in a Secular Society* (University of London Press, 1974) Professor Paul Hirst claims that there can be no useful and coherent relations between theology and educational theory. Hirst argues that 'there has now emerged in our society a concept of education which makes the whole idea of Christian education a kind of nonsense' (p. 77). Just as mathematics, engineering and farming are characterised by intrinsic and autonomous norms, so is education. There can no more be a 'characteristically or distinctively Christian form of education' than there can be a distinctively Christian form of mathematics' (p. 77). The process of secularisation, which has already brought about autonomy in these fields, is now according 'an exactly similar status' to education (p. 68).

Hirst describes two ways in which one might attempt to create a Christian philosophy of education. First, one might start with 'very general moral principles' and seek to draw educational conclusions. But, Hirst remarks, even although these moral principles might be supported from Christian sources, they are 'usually not in any sense significantly Christian' (p. 78). Second, one might begin with what is said in the bible about education and try to apply this to teaching today. Problems such as the cultural remoteness of the

314

Hirst then distinguishes two concepts of education. The first is 'primitive' education, which is the view a 'primitive tribe' might have of education as the uncritical passing on of customs and beliefs.[2] There may be distinctively Christian, humanist or Buddhist concepts of this sort of education 'according to which Christians seek that the next generation shall think likewise' (p. 80). The second concept of education is marked by a concern for objective knowledge, for truth and for reasons, and it will set out for pupils the methods and procedures of the various disciplines according to public criteria. But religious and humanist beliefs, continues the argument, must themselves be assessed by such criteria and so the principles of education are 'logically more fundamental' than those of the particular religious communities. Consequently, 'the character of education is not settled by any appeal to Christian, humanist or Buddhist beliefs' (p. 81).

The autonomy of education is then compared with various other pursuits, such as morality and history; it is concluded that although education may certainly promote an understanding of a faith it may not seek to develop 'a disposition to worship in that faith' (p. 84).

I have no quarrel with this account of the sort of religious education proper to an educational curriculum. It may be worth pointing out that from his 1965 article on religious education[3] through his 1973 article in *Learning for Living*[4] right up to the present book, Hirst has consistently defended the existence of a critical, open study of religion in the schools. Reviewers of *Moral Education in a Secular Society*, confusing a denial that theology of education is proper with a denial that teaching religion is proper, are mistakenly claiming that Hirst is now against any teaching of religion in schools.[5] But Hirst is wrong, in my view, in thinking that in order to protect the independence of secular education against proselytising groups such as Christians it is necessary to deny the possibility of constructing a useful relation between Christian faith and this concept of critical, open education.

Before we consider his discussion in detail, it may be helpful to distinguish five kinds of possible relations between Christian theology and education.

1. Christian theology might be both necessary and sufficient for an understanding of education.
2. Christian theology might provide a necessary but not a sufficient understanding of education. Theology might, in this case, need assistance from philosophy or psychology.
3. Christian theology might provide a sufficient but not a necessary understanding of education. Other belief systems, including non-religious ones, might also be able to offer sufficient accounts of education.

4. Christian theology might provide a possible and legitimate understanding of education, but one which is neither sufficient nor necessary.
5. Christian theology might be impossible and illegitimate as a way of understanding education. It would have no contribution to offer.

It is the last of these positions which Hirst adopts: 'the search for a Christian approach to, or philosophy of, education (is) a huge mistake';[6] 'judging what is good or bad in education is nothing to do with whether one is a Christian, a humanist or a Buddhist'.[7] This, for Hirst, is a matter of principle. 'But if I once thought ... the pursuit of a distinctively Christian form of education in principle satisfactory, I have now come to the conclusion that even that is not so.'[8] Moreover, having relentlessly pressed the attack by showing the insufficiency of the bible for an understanding of education, he will not allow the poor Christian to make a last stand in a tiny corner of the field. 'If one cannot get everything necessary for educational practice from Christian teaching, surely one can get something distinctive' (p. 79). Hirst's reply is that any relation between Christian theology and education will be only with the primitive notion of education. With this area, in which the 'tribe ... seeks to pass on to the next generation its rituals' (p. 80), Christians must be content, and here 'there will be as many concepts of education as there are systems of beliefs and values' (p. 80). This is small comfort indeed, since Hirst goes on to ask whether in this tribal sense the word 'education' should be used at all. 'Indeed I suggest that this pursuit is in fact now increasingly considered immoral.'[9] When it comes to rational, sophisticated education 'dominated by a concern for knowledge, for truth, for reasons' (p. 80) then 'there can be no such thing as Christian education'.[10]

Hirst seems to be reacting against the sort of relations I have set out above as numbers one, two and three. He sometimes uses forensic terminology to describe the improper relations between theology and education. Nothing in education can be 'decided properly by appeal' to Christian sources; 'the issues must be settled independently of any questions of religious belief' (pp. 77f.). He not only undertakes to attack the first three positions and to defend the final one but he seeks to commend this fifth relation to the Christian. He agrees that not all Christians will find his approach acceptable, especially those 'who are convinced of the total sufficiency of biblical revelation for the conduct of all human affairs',[11] but there is no 'necessary contradiction between Christian beliefs and education in this (sophisticated) sense, provided Christian beliefs form a rationally coherent system'.[12] Considerable attention is given to the 'secular Christian', to whom Hirst thinks the fifth position should be acceptable.

Hirst does not appear to envisage the modest *modus vivendi* between theology and education suggested in my fourth kind of relation. Hirst and I are in agreement in rejecting the first three models. In what follows, the various arguments used to support the 'impossible and illegitimate' relation will be examined. We will then estimate Hirst's success in commending this position to the 'secular Christian'.

Criticism

The sociological arguments

The central concept in this opening group of arguments is 'secularisation'. This is described in the opening chapter, applied to morals in following chapters and to the relation between theology and education in chapter five. Secularisation is regarded as 'a decay in the use of religious concepts and beliefs' (p. 1). This means that 'supernatural interpretations of experience have been progressively replaced by others' (p. 2). The status of science, morals, aesthetics and other modes of thought is now such that 'religious considerations can be ignored'. This does not mean that 'all religious beliefs can be shown to be unintelligible or false. It is rather that (they) come to be seen as of no consequence, having nothing to contribute in our efforts to understand ourselves and our world and to determine how we are to live' (p. 2).

It is difficult to ascertain whether Hirst is merely offering a description of certain historical and social processes, or whether he thinks the processes are significant for the logical relations between religion and other modes of thought. Frequently, the former is the impression given, although conclusions tend to be drawn as if the latter had been established. Thus the decay is in the 'use' of religious concepts: 'There was a time when more people were ... involved' in religion, and religious views are now but 'rarely voiced'. So 'religious understanding has ... come to look more and more redundant' and religious beliefs 'come to be seen as of no consequence'. This is the language of mere description. No doubt such a situation exists, and is quite properly bringing about important changes in the relations between the churches and the schools and the way religion is now taught as a subject in schools.[13] But this has little to do with the logical possibility or the intellectual legitimacy of attempting to formulate conceptual links between theology and theories of education.

Basic distinctions about the secularisation processes are ignored. One can usefully distinguish between 'secularisation' as the historical process whereby social and intellectual life has been freed from dominance by theological concepts, and 'secularism', the stronger claim that this has the (logical or psychological) consequence of rendering religious belief (actually or apparently) meaningless and irrelevant. One can also distinguish between ecclesiastical secularisation, which has to do with the relations between institutionalised religion and the rest of society, and theological or conceptual secularisation, which has to do with the coherence and vitality of theology in relations with the secular world. These distinctions between the sociology of religion and the logical relations which theology has with other fields are blurred in general descriptions of 'religion' or 'religious belief'. It could be pointed out, for example, that ecclesiastical secularisation has been followed by the secularisation of theology itself which now exists in a state of secular autonomy similar to that enjoyed by the other intellectual disciplines. Hirst concludes that the autonomy of the secular spheres (he does not reckon theology to be one of them) means that religious considerations 'can be ignored'. Of course they can. Theology is no longer, as it was in the world of the Thomistic *Summa*, both necessary and sufficient for all systematic thought. But must it be ignored? Is the alleged irrelevancy of religious thought a possibility or a necessity? No evidence is offered for believing that the latter is the case, and so Hirst jumps from the first of the five relations between theology and the world of thought to the fourth (or something like it) when considering theology and morals and straight on to the fifth when considering theology and education, without pausing to offer reasons for being required to adopt these later forms of relation.

The second part of Hirst's discussion of secularisation has to do with the 'privatisation' of religion. In interpreting this discussion, it may be helpful to consider an earlier account of privatisation, in which Hirst had suggested that the values upon which the common school must be based should be 'acceptable to all irrespective of any particular religious or non-religious claims'.[14] 'Public values' must be distinguished from these latter 'private values'. The domain of scientific knowledge seems part of the public world but religious beliefs 'which have no generally acceptable public tests of validity'[15] are probably in the private area. Values which 'necessarily rest on particular religious beliefs' are also private, although a citizen may have an education consistent with his or her private religion. In order not to create the impression that the public school is non-religious or anti-religious, it should be understood that the education it offers can be but partial.

Hirst seems to have held that what the private communities of faith do in their schools is genuinely educational, in that it deals with areas of private values with which the public school cannot deal, and in the way such private education is a necessary or at least a legitimate complement to public education. In the later writings we are considering, the distinction between 'primitive' and 'sophisticated' education seems to take the place of the earlier distinction between 'private' and 'public' value education, and the idea of the religious community offering a legitimate complement to public education, a complement arising directly from its own values yet still being educational, becomes less important, if not immoral.

In the public schools, Hirst continues, methods of teaching must also be in terms of public values. 'Are there Christian methods of teaching Boyle's law which differ from atheistic methods?'[16] Hirst however does not deny that a teacher's private values *may* affect his teaching, only that it can never be claimed that his private values *must* affect his teaching. Hirst seems then at this stage to have had in mind something rather like the fourth of our relations between theology and education, in which religious beliefs could provide a possible but not a necessary or sufficient contribution.

The criteria of knowledge, Hirst continues, are public, and the public school can offer education in at least 'established areas of knowledge'.[17] The idea of the 'autonomy' of a 'domain of knowledge' is now introduced in this 1967 essay. Some agreement, Hirst remarks, is mere consensus but some is 'rationally compelled' on the basis of public criteria.[18] At present, we only have consensus agreement in the moral area. But if moral agreement could be won on the basis of public, rational criteria, then we would have an autonomous basis for the common school. In his 1965 article 'Liberal education and the nature of knowledge' the idea of the 'autonomy' of the various forms of knowledge does not appear, but in another article from the same year, 'Morals, religion and the maintained school',[19] the idea of 'autonomy' does emerge when discussing the extent to which morals may be regarded as independent of theology. 'Autonomy' and 'privatisation' both become key concepts in the 1974 book under discussion. The germs of the 1967 article on 'privatisation' are now mature. Morals may at last be justified on independent, rational grounds. Religion however is now severely privatised and the conclusion is drawn that 'When the domain of religious beliefs is so manifestly one in which there are at present no clearly recognisable objective grounds for judging claims, to base education on any such claims would be to forsake the pursuit of objectivity' (p. 81).

So, in a society in which religion has become privatised, 'the widest range of attitudes to religious beliefs is acceptable, provided they are never allowed to determine public issues', and 'it is a mark of the secular society that it is religiously plural, tolerating all forms of religious belief and practice that do not contravene agreed public principles' (p. 3).

One notices the strangely conservative social attitude implied by this approach. Nothing must contravene the public order. We also observe that in discussing society in this way, Hirst is not speaking of the logic or the epistemology of the forms of knowledge, but of convention. The significant 1967 distinction between consensus agreement and rational agreement does not appear. No logical conclusions can be drawn therefore one way or the other about the possibility of relating the conceptual worlds of theology and education on the basis of such an undifferentiated concept of 'privatisation'. We observe finally the stringency of Hirst's conditions. Religion must not be allowed to 'determine' public issues. It must not 'contravene' public principles. But may it not even influence them? (Cf. p. 55.) May it not be allowed to have some legitimate effect? Why, on this argument, *must* it be thought of as having *nothing* to contribute? How can a claim (of whatever strength) that religion must not be allowed to determine public issues such as education lead to the conclusion that there can be no legitimate attempt to construct a Christian philosophy of education in which Christian theology would be but one (influencing but not determining) factor amongst others? What has happened to the private religious values of 1967? A citizen could express these through education provided they did not contravene public values. Must theology now necessarily contravene them? Can Christian faith then never be an ally of the open society?

The logical arguments

Hirst claims that the emerging, secular concept of education makes the possibility of a relation between Christianity and education 'a kind of nonsense' (p. 77).

First argument

Education, like mathematics, engineering and farming, is governed by its own intrinsic principles. What is good of its kind in each of these areas is determined by those inner principles and not by reference to theological factors. Bridges stay or fall down for Christians and atheists alike. God, we may add, sends his rain upon the just and the unjust.

But is there really a parallel of this sort between education and mathematics? Does what appertains in the latter, abstract, self-sufficient form of knowledge in which inescapable conclusions are drawn also apply to a value-laden, practical enterprise like education? Education, it must be remembered, is not one of the forms of knowledge. It does not have a unique and distinctive mode of thought nor a characteristic epistemology, but is, like medicine, an applied field in which various other disciplines, some of which are true forms of knowledge, impinge in order to enable the activity to take place. In the cases of medicine and education, these other disciplines are things like anatomy, chemistry, immunology, philosophy and psychology. Medicine and education do not however lack coherence. They derive it not from the structure of their epistemology but from their concentration upon healing or educating people. Their coherence is such as is demanded by a practical enterprise; it is not the coherence of internally self-sufficient principles and it should not therefore be compared with the logical 'autonomy' of mathematics.

In his 1965 article on 'Liberal education' Hirst described political, legal and educational theory as 'fields where moral knowledge of a developed kind is to be found'.[20] Engineering, in the same article, is described as a 'field' and no doubt this would be true of farming as well. We are thus comparing:

    a.   an indisputable form of knowledge in which moral knowledge of a developed kind is not found (mathematics);
    b.   two fields in which moral knowledge is similarly not well developed (engineering and farming);
    c.   a field in which moral knowledge is well developed (education); and
    d.   a disputable form of knowledge in which moral knowledge is well developed (religion).

It is obvious that (a), (b) and (c) do not exhibit 'exactly similar status' (p. 78) in the kinds and degrees of the autonomy they possess. Their relations both with the moral sphere and the religious sphere will be different in each case. Farming, for example, does not have the self-sufficient logic of mathematics. What is good farming may quite properly be determined by political principles in China, by religious principles in India, and by environmentalist considerations in western Europe. There will be no clash between the principles of good farming and any of these contexts, because the context has a significant part to play in determining what the principles of good farming actually are. There is, of course, a level of unchangeable circumstances, usually based upon cause and effect sequence in the natural world, at which the techniques of farming and education will be autonomous. Even the devil, if he wants tares, has to sow tares. Wheat produces wheat for angels and devils alike. But whether you pluck the tares up or leave them both to grow together until the harvest is a matter of value judgments and long-term considerations involving questions of religion and philosophy which goes far beyond the simple technical level. The objective psychological test will yield the same result for both the Christian and the atheist educational psychologist, and the techniques for the early diagnosis of speech defects are just whatever they are, since speech is just what it is, and defects are defined accordingly. Christians and atheists sharing the same speech conventions will not differ at this level. But to whom the objective test is to be administered, and what use is to be made of the results and why — these problems introduce evaluative questions as well as a wider factual context and at this point the techniques themselves are no longer autonomous. They need the help of sociology, ethics and so on. Secularisation has had considerable effect even at this technical level, since the sensible Christian and the sensible atheist agree in using terms like 'emotional disorder' rather than ones like 'demonic possession', and they agree to use the techniques of medical therapy not those of exorcism. There are other Christians who resist this sort of secularisation, but neither Hirst nor I are concerned with them. The impact of the secularisation process must not be denied, but it must be carefully qualified. Technical autonomy does not bring self-sufficiency to education.

Pedagogy may be described as a conglomerate of technical skills applied in the education of children. Education offers the ideals, the purposes and the values which guide this application. Pedagogy is thus applied education, education is applied philosophical anthropology and it certainly cannot be claimed that philosophical anthropology is determined by principles which are 'neither for nor against' theological anthropology. Even although philosophical anthropology cannot perhaps be 'settled' by 'appeal' to theological anthropology, or to anything else, theology has a legitimate and perhaps a significant contribution to make to its elucidation. When it comes to the question 'What is humanity?' theologians are also human, and if, like philosophers, they are sensible and rational humans, their theological reflections need not be silenced.

Second argument

On this second view (the sophisticated one), the character of education is not settled by any appeal to Christian, humanist or Buddhist beliefs. Such an appeal is illegitimate, for the basis is logically more fundamental, being found in the canons of objectivity and reasons, canons against which Christian, humanist and Buddhist beliefs must, in their turn and in the appropriate way, be assessed' (p. 81). This may be paraphrased as follows. The sophisticated concept of education is governed by rational, objective principles. But these very principles must be used to assess the religious and non-religious belief systems. No such belief system can therefore generate an understanding of such a critical concept of education, because the principles upon which the latter rests are more fundamental than the belief systems themselves.

There are three objections to this.

1. If this is so, education cannot be appraised by anything, since psychology, sociology, and all the rest of the scrutinising disciplines are also, in their turn and in the appropriate way, to be assessed by rational criteria more fundamental than their particular and distinctive techniques of assessment. Even particular

moral criticism is subject to more basic rational moral principles which are used to assess the status of the moral claims being made. This is transcendental autonomy for education with a vengeance.

2. It may be that Hirst is influenced by the thought that theology is in some way a supernatural activity, pretending immunity from rational criticism. If this is in his mind, then it is rather a restricted and perhaps an old-fashioned view of theology. Theology is concerned with the concepts of religion, with their adequacy as expressive of religious experience and with the problems of constructing them into coherent belief systems. It claims validity according to distinctive but not supernatural norms.[21]

3. It may be objected that Hirst does not say 'cannot generate an understanding of' but 'is not settled by any appeal to'. But firstly, Hirst does not distinguish between the adjudicating function of a discipline and its illuminating function. This is a major criticism of his approach. The paraphrase, expressing the milder, illuminatory function, does no injustice to his discernible intentions. Secondly, if however the stronger interpretation is insisted upon, then point (1) above not only still holds good but is strengthened. Disciplines which cannot even illuminate certainly cannot adjudicate.

Third argument
'When the domain of religious belief is so manifestly one in which there are at present no clearly recognisable objective grounds for judging claims, to base education on any such claims would be to forsake the pursuit of objectivity' (p. 81).

1. Such a strongly worded, negative conclusion about the possibility of recognising objective tests of truth in religion appears to be new in Hirst's writings. As recently as 1973, discussing whether religion is a unique form of knowledge in his important article, 'The forms of knowledge revisited', Hirst concluded, 'On the answer to that question few would dare to pronounce categorically. My own view, as in the case of the arts, is that in the present state of affairs we must at least take the claim to knowledge seriously ... Equally, it seems to me unclear that one can coherently claim that there is a logically unique domain of religious *beliefs* such that none of them can be known to be true, all being matters of faith.'[22] It would be interesting to know, since we are not told, what further reflections have enabled Hirst to move from the earlier position where the claim to religious knowledge had at least to be taken seriously to the position in the present book where it is 'so manifest' that religion lacks this status. It is difficult to avoid the impression

that in order to break the links between theology and education Hirst is slightly exaggerating the clarity and the unanimity of the alleged negative verdict upon the logical status of religious claims.

2. But even if we move with Hirst, although he gives us no reason to do so, to the new, severe position, would it follow that there could be no proper or useful relation between theology and education? Although in the 1973 article just mentioned, religion was still being seriously considered for 'form of knowledge' status, history and the social sciences had already been abandoned. 'I now think it best not to refer to history or the social sciences in any statement of the forms of knowledge as such. These pursuits ... may well be concerned with truths of several different logical kinds.'[23] (There is, by the way, a parallel here with religion, since 'Christian theology' is regarded by Hirst as a discipline within religion, and religious studies is cross-disciplinary in several senses.[24]) Indeed, the result of Hirst's 1973 revision of the forms of knowledge argument, which is now cast in more strictly propositional shape, is, as Hirst emphasises, to reduce the forms of the categories of true propositions to only two: 'truths of the physical world' and 'truths of a mental or personal kind'.[25]

   It would appear then that *either* not being a domain of knowledge does not vitiate the capacity of an area of enquiry to relate itself meaningfully to the practical field of education *or* if only domains of knowledge may appraise education, then not only can there be no theology of education, but also no historical appraisal of education, only a dubious aesthetic scrutiny and no psychology or sociology of education.

3. Hirst remarks that the application of the whole theory of the domains of knowledge to education is strictly limited. It may be then that one contribution of theology (if it were to fail to secure 'domain of knowledge' status) might lie in those areas with which the formal epistemological categories do not so easily deal. Hirst mentions several of these.[26]

4. In this argument Hirst again employs the device we find so frequently in the pages we are considering. He sets the most severe conditions, and then allows no place at all in education to a discipline which cannot meet them. So we are required to contemplate the possibility of *basing* education on theology. What does this mean? Does Hirst really anticipate a situation in which Christians would argue that only theists could be educators? This is certainly not what contemporary theology of education seeks to show. Far from insisting that all educators must be theologians, it is only asked that some theologians be allowed to remain educators. Hirst's argument appears then as an unconvincing attempt to establish an excluded middle.

Fourth argument

Hirst claims that 'an education based on a concern for objectivity and reason, far from allying itself with any specific religious claims, must involve teaching the radically controversial character of all such claims. An understanding of religious claims it can perfectly well aim at, but commitment to any one set, in the interests of objectivity, it cannot either assume or pursue' (p. 81).

This claim about the relationship between the 'basis' of education and the need for a critical curriculum raises two questions. First, by what characteristic can a theology generate an understanding of the critical, sophisticated concept of education? Second, what is the relation between the aims of theology of education and the aims of teaching religion as a school subject?

As regards the first question, not all theological systems can avoid the difficulty Hirst mentions. There certainly are forms of theology which can lead only to the 'primitive' concept of education in which, for example, the task would be to ensure that subsequent generations of Christians all thought alike. But just as not all theologies avoid the danger, so also not all of them succumb to it. There are forms of Christian theology in which critical enquiry and controversial examination flow directly and necessarily from the values and beliefs ,to which the theology is committed. It then exhibits these intellectual characteristics not in spite of its commitment but because of it. An alliance (which does not mean an exclusive, unique or necessary derivation of education from this theology) between such theology and such education, far from hindering the critical freedom of education, might do a little to enhance and support it. It is apparent therefore that Hirst does not sufficiently discriminate between the degrees to which different religious belief systems have built into their structures necessary elements of on-going self-criticism.

As for the second question, Hirst and I do not disagree about the aims and limits of religious education as a classroom subject. But whereas he thinks the commitment of the theologian in education inhibits him or her in the carrying out of this critical task, I think it may be of help. I agree too that public educational institutions in a pluralist, secular society ought not to be committed to one religion, and consequently that compulsory, unanimous or official school worship is wrong in principle. Again, the question is whether a Christian philosophy or theology of education precludes or advances that view of religious education and of the stance to be adopted by such institutions.

The methodological arguments

Hirst claims that even if it were a legitimate enterprise, the methodological difficulties are such that no worthwhile work can be done in this area. His discussion has been summarised in the section 'Exposition' above.

Naturally, there are difficulties of method in any interdisciplinary study, and the various fields of practical or applied theology are not exempt. Theology receives no special supernatural aid. There is an extensive modern literature dealing with the relations between Christian theology and, for example, culture, the arts, politics, science and medicine. Many of these studies include detailed consideration of problems of method.[27] In theology of education, the two methods discussed by Hirst are by no means the only ones; indeed, they are, as he points out, rather naïve and inadequate. This is not the place to enter into a discussion of how it might be undertaken, it being sufficient for our present purposes to remark that it is not appropriate to contrast sophisticated educational thinking with a sample of simple and even crude theological methods.

The 'secular Christian'

Hirst suggests that the position he outlines between Christian faith and education is one which ought to commend itself to certain Christians: 'it seems to me it is precisely the concept of education an intelligent Christian must accept' (p. 85).

But this Christian presumably accepts this view of education in so far as he is intelligent and not in so far as he is a Christian *per se*. For if the latter were the case, the secular Christian would have been able to understand the critical concept of education from within the resources of his or her faith and we would then have a Christian theology of secular education which is what Hirst says we cannot have. Nevertheless, Hirst takes some pains to show that the general position in the book is not hostile to Christian faith, and at several points there are quite extended discussions of this matter. It seems to me that in this respect he has failed, and if he had *not* failed, then the position he advocates regarding the impossibility of a Christian understanding of education would have had to undergo revision. In other words, chapters one to four are inconsistent with chapter five, since if Hirst is right in presenting a satisfactory relation between the secular Christian and the secular society with its secularised morals, there remains no reason why he could not also assert a positive relationship between the secularised Christian and secularised education. As it is, he affirms the one and denies the other.

The problems begin in the opening pages. Secular Christians are those 'who seek to go along with the total secularist to the full in all non-religious areas' but continue to maintain that religious beliefs are meaningful. These beliefs 'combine with' or 'complement these other forms of belief in some way' (pp. 2f.). But, we observe, before he can go along with the total secularist to the full, the Christian must come to see that his or her faith has 'nothing to contribute in our efforts to understand ourselves, and our world and to determine how we are to live'. Moreover, if religious beliefs are logically and existentially irrelevant, how can they be intelligibly combined with relevant and intelligible secular concepts? If religious beliefs, on the other hand, are not after all irrelevant, then total secularism is unnecessary. On Hirst's account therefore secular Christians are in an unintelligible position since in seeking to combine intelligible with unintelligible beliefs they are behaving irrationally, or, in insisting that religious belief does have something to contribute, they are refusing to go along with the total secularist.

The discussion of privatisation has serious consequences for the Christian unless, as argued above, it may be thought of as simply a sociological phenomenon. If it is thought to be significant in determining the logical relations between religious beliefs and secular ones, then the privatisation of religion separates the Christian, no matter how secular, from rationality, from the secular reality in and around him or her, from science and (to use the theological word) from creation. No Christian seeking wholeness and truth can accept this account of privatisation. But if only the sociological sense is intended, then there is no logical reason why we should not try to construct relations between theology and secular education. Hirst hopes that his argument will be of interest to those who remain convinced 'even perhaps of the truth of certain central tenets of Christianity' (p. 6). How can one be rationally convinced of the truth of private claims? For 'truth is correspondence with reality' (p. 22).

Hirst outlines two traditional Christian approaches towards morals. The first (pp. 18–21) takes the will of God as ultimate in morals. The second (pp. 21–3) sees morality as based on natural law and therefore supposes a degree of natural autonomy for the moral life. This natural, rational morality is based on God's creation of humanity as free, rational and moral. On this second view the autonomy of science and morals is 'seen as built into Christianity rightly understood' (p. 23). The reader is bound to ask why this argument is not applied to education as well. And then if the autonomy, rationality and secularity of education are similarly built into the structure of Christian faith and can be so elucidated, then the Christian faith does produce a view of education, namely, that it is secular and (in important respects) autonomous. I am not concerned with whether this is a good or bad way to approach the problem; I am merely pointing out a failure in consistency in the argument. Hirst does not seem to see that just as secular Christians like Harvey Cox, whom he quotes, can become advocates of the secular city (an advocacy of which Hirst approves), so they can become advocates of secular education within the secular city,[28] which advocacy Hirst disallows in principle, although it could flow from the very arguments used by him to justify secular morals to the Christian. Whatever secularisation may mean to the secular Christian, it cannot mean that the secular and the autonomous fall outside the scope of Christian appraisal.

This inconsistency can be seen clearly when it is understood that what Hirst proposes in his discussion of the Christian and secular morality is in fact a Christian theological rationale for secular morality; 'a coherent Christian view of morality positively requires it' (p. 52). The teaching of the bible supports this view of natural, rational morals. So the relation between Christian faith and secular morals is that the former leads to the latter, although it is not the only path to it, and the secular morals would still be there even if that particular path to it did not happen to exist. Nevertheless, it remains the case that this is the special kind of morality to which Christian faith actually does lead, and it can be called both the Christian form of ethics and the secular form of ethics. Why then can there not be a Christian form of education which will also be the secular form of education? Hirst thinks that some of 'the most powerful intellectual seeds of secularisation' (p. 23) lie within Christian theology, and are so integral to it that the forging of a theology of the secular is necessary to preserve the rationale integrity of Christian theology itself. 'Christian teaching can never hope to be coherent if it denies the legitimacy of living in secular terms' (p. 27). Why not admit then that some of the seeds of the secularisation of education lie within Christian faith and that the elaboration and further justification of these may constitute a Christian theology of education for today? 'If this emphasises yet again that certain roots of secularisation are to be found in Christianity, let that be recognised' (pp. 26f.).

But even in his justification of secular morals to the Christian, Hirst is less ready to grant the full impact of theological ethics than he should be on his own argument. Moral principles have an 'ultimate status' (pp. 46, 50) and morals have to be 'argued back to the most fundamental principles of all' (p. 27). Religion is often described by Hirst as depending upon appeal to authority (for example, pp. 5, 18f., 53). But Christianity sees morality as having 'its place in some ultimate transcendent scheme of things' (p. 55) and as dealing with 'the ultimate principles of human existence' (p. 55). 'It is in the additional emphasis that religion brings to the development of appropriate moral aspects of the personal life, by seeing them within beliefs, dispositions, and emotions of a wider and metaphysically more ultimate nature, that the religious impact upon morality is centred' (p. 75). Religion thus appears to offer a wider and more coherent pattern of justification for morals. Surely one is morally obliged to accept the most coherent frame of reference provided that frame is not irrational? Although he writes as if privatisation has the effect of isolating religion and depriving theology of applicability, Hirst also speaks of theology as coherent, rational, a systematic whole from which conclusions can be drawn and impetus discovered for other forms of life. Religious morality is concerned with life's 'ultimate metaphysical understanding, its ultimate source and character' (p. 73). Enquiry into theological ethics would appear then to be morally obligatory since it must be a principle of rational morals to seek the widest possible framework and the most ultimate basis. The insistence that what theology contributes to morals is its metaphysical belief system (that is, its religious doctrines) and the repeated denial that religion has anything other than the purely rational (that is not religious doctrines) to offer cannot be easily reconciled in Hirst's discussion. His thought about the relation between theology and secular ethics is ambivalent rather than ambiguous.

Conclusions

I have tried to show that the arguments which Hirst uses to disallow the possibility of connections between Christian theology and educational theory are unconvincing in themselves and inconsistent with his arguments elsewhere in the book about the relation between Christian theology and other spheres such as ethics. I have also tried to show that he does not succeed in commending this approach to the secular Christian, let along the more traditional Christian, because the notion of a secular Christian is, in his account, not intelligible, and because the consequences from that part of his argument which is intelligible would be unacceptable to any Christian in pursuit of rational wholeness. It remains to ask why Hirst should make such genuine efforts to commend his view of ethics to the Christian but remain so adamant about the impossibility of a relation between Christianity and education. I can only assume that an educational philosopher in Britain today, being well aware of the rather unhappy history of some attempts by some churches and of some aspects of theology to control education and to retain it at a 'primitive' level, is particularly sensitive in this area. This is an understandable attitude, but not a philosophical one.

Notes
1. J W Daines, 'A review of unpublished theses in religious education 1968–72,' *Learning for Living*, 12, 4, 1973, pp. 16–21; Derek Webster, 'American research in religious education: a review of selected doctoral theses' *Learning for Living*, 14, 5, 1975, pp. 187–93; David S. Steward, 'Abstracts of doctoral dissertations in religious education 1971–72,' *Religious Education*, 69, 1974, pp. 475ff.
2. Cf. 'the older and undifferentiated concept which refers just to any process of bringing up or rearing.' Paul H Hirst and R S Peters, *The Logic of Education*, London, Routledge and Kegan Paul, 1970, p. 25.
3. Hirst speaks of 'thoroughly open instruction about religious beliefs' and adds a note to the 1974 reprint which reads, 'My view then is that maintained schools should teach "about" religion, provided that it is interpreted to include a direct study of religions, which means entering as fully as possible into an understanding of what they claim to be true.' Paul H Hirst, 'Morals, religion and the maintained school,' *British Journal of Educational Studies*, 14, 1; now in Paul H Hirst, *Knowledge and the Curriculum*, London, Routledge and Kegan Paul, 1974, p. 186f.

4. ' ... there is a proper place in the maintained school for religious studies.' 'Religion, a form of knowledge? A reply,' *Learning for Living*, 12, 4, 1973, p. 10.
5. See the review in *Education for Teaching*, 97, 1975, pp. 88–90.
6. Paul H Hirst, 'Christian education: a contradiction in terms,' *Learning for Living*, 11, 4, 1972, p.6.
7. *Ibid.*
8. *Ibid.*, p. 7.
9. *Ibid.*, p. 10.
10. *Ibid.*, p. 11.
11. *Ibid.*, p. 7.
12. *Ibid.*, p. 11.
13. I have discussed such matters in 'Worship and the secularization of religious education,' chapter four of my *School Worship, an Obituary*, London, SCM Press, 1975, and in 'Religious education in a pluralistic society,' in Monica Taylor (ed.), *Progress and Problems in Moral Education,* Slough, NFER, 1975, pp. 195–205.
14. Paul H Hirst, 'Public and private values and religious educational contents,' in T R Sizer (ed.), *Religion and Public Education*, Boston, Houghton Mifflin Company, 1967, p. 330.
15. *Ibid.*, p. 331.
16. *Ibid.*, p. 332.
17. *Ibid.*, p. 333.
18. *Ibid.*, p. 335.
19. Paul articles are now available in *Knowledge and the Curriculum,* cf. note 3.
20. Paul H Hirst, 'Liberal education and the nature of knowledge,' in R D Archambault (ed.), *Philosophical Analysis and Education,* London, Routledge and Kegan Paul, 1965, p. 131.
21. See for example Bernard Lonergan, *Method in Theology*, London, Darton, Longman and Todd, 1972, Ray L Hart, *Unfinished Man and the Imagination*, New York, Herder and Herder, 1968, and Paul Tillich, *Systematic Theology,* London, Nisbet, 1968, for characteristically modern approaches to theology, and F Schleiermacher, *The Christian Faith*, Edinburgh, T and T Clark, 1928, for a now classical example of theological method from the early nineteenth century in Germany.
22. *Knowledge and the Curriculum, op. cit.,* p. 88.
23. *Ibid.*, p. 87.
24. *Ibid.*, p. 97.
25. *Ibid.*, p. 86.
26. *Ibid.*, p. 96.
27. Illustrations, from theology of culture, of method in modern applied theology are Paul Tillich, *Theology of Culture,* Oxford, Oxford University Press, 1964, Walter J Ong, *The Presence of the Word,* New Haven, Connecticut, Yale University Press, 1967, and, G. Spiegler, *The Eternal Covenant,* San Francisco, Harper and Row, 1967.
28. See the Symposium 'Religious education in the secular city,' by Harvey Cox *et al., Religious Education,* 69, 1966, pp. 83–113.

6.3 Fairness, controversiality and the common school

T H McLaughlin

One of the motives underlying the recently renewed call for separate religious schools is the perception that the common school is, in a number of ways, educationally inadequate in the judgment of parents who are religious believers.

These perceived inadequacies can be of various kinds. For some parents the common school is inadequate because they want their child's schooling to take place in a context in which their religious faith is salient and pervasive, a 'faith-supporting' environment. Such a demand need not be illiberal or indoctrinatory. Whilst some parents seeking separate religious schools may indeed want their religious faith merely inculcated into their children in such a way that it is not open to critical appropriation and challenge, others may share many liberal educational values and merely feel a defensible need for their children's development towards independence and autonomy to proceed from the basis of sustained exposure to a particular norm of belief, practice and value.[1] Regardless of the precise motives of parents seeking separate religious schools, it is clear that what such schools provide cannot be offered in a common school. Because of its very character, the common school in a pluralistic democratic society cannot constitute a 'faith-supporting' environment in any sense requiring the religious beliefs and commitment of the family to be given normative status.

However, common schools are sometimes judged inadequate by standards that such schools themselves espouse. One of the most prominent of these standards is *fairness* in the treatment of value diversity and controversiality. Many religious parents may be happy that their children should attend a common school, and may indeed see such an experience as conferring advantages on the children which are religious as well as educational. Parents of this kind have no unrealistic expectations of the common school as far as the promotion of their religious faith is concerned, but they do expect that it will be *fair* in its handling of religious matters.

What is involved in the common school giving a fair treatment of evaluatively controversial matters, such as religion? In this article, I shall explore some philosophical aspects of this complex question. I shall therefore be concentrating on matters of principle rather than engaging in an investigation into empirical matters about (say) the contingent practical shortcomings of particular schools, programmes or policies.

A full treatment of merely the philosophical aspects of this question requires consideration of a very wide range of issues. I shall focus here on some questions about fairness which arise within a particular interpretation of the basic framework of values which should articulate the work of the common school. For ease of reference, I shall describe this interpretation as involving the notion of 'liberal education', and will attempt below to indicate some of its central features. This interpretation is not only shared by a number of contemporary philosophers of education but is also widely invoked, at least implicitly, by many parents, teachers and others working in, or concerned with, educational matters.

Some religious believers may feel that an adequate treatment of the questions of fairness at issue requires a thoroughgoing critique and rejection of this framework of values. I shall not discuss basic challenges of this kind in this article but will seek to show that *within* liberal educational principles significant questions about fairness in the work of the common school can be identified. One benefit of concentrating upon these questions is that religious believers can pursue them without inviting the response that any concerns they might voice only have force and plausibility if certain religious beliefs or alternative 'frameworks of thought' are accepted.

My discussion, therefore, will illuminate some often neglected implications of liberal educational principles which will help common schools to achieve a greater fairness in their handling of controversial matters and will assist parents and others to make a clearer evaluation of the performance of these schools in this regard.

By 'common school' in this discussion, I mean a school in which all pupils are educated together in one institution regardless of differentiating characteristics such as religious, ethnic or cultural background, gender, social class and so on. Implied in such a notion is a conception of the society in which such a school is located and of the kind of education it should provide. With regard to the conception of society, this is typically the sort of culturally and racially diverse and pluralistic democratic society, with its balance of social and cultural cohesion and diversity, outlined in the Swann Report.[2] With regard to the conception of education, I shall take this to be the one I have described roughly as 'liberal' in character, and which I will outline in more detail shortly.

Controversiality

What is meant by the notion of 'controversiality'? The mere existence of disagreement is, in itself, insufficient to constitute the sort of controversy that is the subject of our concern. Disagreement can be the result of ignorance, misunderstanding or ill-will. A notion of *significant* controversy is at issue here. Dearden attempts to identify this by means of an epistemic criterion. Thus he holds that 'a matter is controversial if contrary views can be held on it without those views being contrary to reason'.[3] As Dearden notes, the category of 'the controversial' in this sense includes a range of several kinds of issue according to the character of the grounds of the disagreement.[4] The precise delineation of the category of the controversial is, of course, itself a controversial matter and I shall return to the implications of this point in due course.

Liberal education

The notion that the pupil should develop critical reflective judgment is at the heart of the liberal conception of education. This is some-times expressed in terms of the achievement of 'autonomy' by the pupil, although this aim needs to be characterised in a careful and nuanced way.[5]

The ideal of liberal education is a complex one. Expressed briefly, it involves:[6]

a. the aim of developing a form of autonomy,
b. an emphasis on fundamental and general knowledge,
c. an aversion to mere instrumentality in determining what is to be learnt, and
d. a concern for the development of critical reason.

There are a number of implications for education in religion arising from this view, which are contained in many familiar contemporary treatments of the subject.[7] Arising from (a) is the claim that children must not have their substantive religious commitment (or lack of it) determined in any way, but must be allowed to make their own judgments on the basis of appropriate reasoning and evaluation. Arising from (b) is a notion that a broad introduction to the religious domain is required, not merely the teaching of one religion, and certainly not as if it were true. Point (c) implies that education must not see itself as having the merely instrumental aim of producing religious persons and (d) gives rise to the insistence that appropriate reasoning be involved in the judgments made by individuals, and that education should develop this capacity.

It is sometimes claimed that liberal education, and the common school in which it is typically embodied, aims at neutrality. This is not true in any straightforward sense. Liberal education, and common schools committed to it, involve a specific and non-neutral commitment to values such as autonomy, rationality, and a range of determinate ethical and political positions.[8] Even in the highly

specific notion of the 'neutral teacher' associated with the Schools
Council Humanities Curriculum Project there is no suggestion that
the teacher can or should be neutral about everything.[9] It is true,
however, that the common school aims at *a certain sort of neutrality* but this needs to be carefully understood.

Liberal education aims at neutrality with respect to substantive
judgments about matters which are controversial in the sense outlined above. With regard to such matters there are no generally
accepted or conclusive answers to the questions at issue. This has
both negative and positive implications for the work of the common
school. On the negative side, the school must avoid insisting upon, or
otherwise transmitting, a definitive view on the disputed questions.
On the positive side, it must promote the pupils' understanding of
the issues and their capacity for personal reflective judgment in
relation to them. Whilst this aim may involve the strategy of 'procedural neutrality', other strategies are available.[10] The scope of the
neutrality of the common school is therefore limited to the stance
taken by the school on substantive conclusions about matters of
a certain kind. This neutrality does not extend beyond this, for
example to the pedagogical implications arising from the stance.
Even 'procedural neutrality' is a pedagogical strategy based on
certain non-neutral commitments.

The role of neutrality in the concept of liberal education may
be illuminated by a brief reference to aspects of the broader philosophy of liberalism with which it is strongly associated.

At the heart of liberalism is a kind of agnosticism, or at least
a lack of certainty, about what the good life, in any substantial
sense, consists in. There exist many competing views, including
religious views, which offer determinate, particular conceptions of
human good or perfection, but there is significant and well grounded
controversy concerning them. In the light of this genuine and fundamental disagreement, liberalism concludes that no one substantial
conception of human good can be shown to be true and imposed
upon others.[11] Therefore Rawls, at any rate in the original version
of this theory in *A Theory of Justice*,[12] invokes a 'thin' theory of
the good, putatively free of significantly controversial assumptions
and judgments, to distribute to individuals in a just way 'primary
goods' (such as liberties and opportunities). These primary goods,
neutral between particular conceptions of the good, enable individuals to pursue, within a framework of justice, many different
ways of, and conceptions of, life. The 'common good' on the liberal
view involves an insistence upon state neutrality on matters which
go beyond justice, in contrast to a common good construed in more
'communitarian' terms, where a particular, 'thick' conception of the
good is presupposed and given general salience.[13] A certain kind of
society and community is demanded by the liberal view, but it is
one which, underpinned by public recognition of the principles of

justice, seeks to sustain a 'culture of freedom' necessary for individuals to pursue their freedom in choice of lives.[14]

This basic position, with its implied distinction between public and private values and domains, is reflected in the notion of the common school. The education offered by such a school, a 'primary good' in the Rawlsian sense, is based on the various publicly agreed values and procedures, seeking to gain not merely understanding but substantive commitment to them. In relation to the diversity which is characteristic of the private domain, the school encourages exploration, understanding, debate and critical reflective decision by individuals.[15]

This general liberal position is, of course, complex and is open to challenge and criticism at a number of points. One major line of criticism, arising from philosophers working in the tradition of 'reformed epistemology', challenges presuppositions in the kinds of reasoning involved, and their alleged neutrality with regard to religious belief.[16] There are a number of other sources of criticism concerning, for example, the clarity and justifiability of the distinction between public and private values, as well as more general critiques emerging from the communitarian critics of liberalism.[17] Such criticisms often constitute a starting point for the development of more holistic conceptions of (say) Christian education which are at odds in various ways with the liberal view.

Religious believers and liberal education

It is not clear, however, that the principles of liberal education, properly understood, are in themselves hostile to (at least certain forms of) religious faith. This is especially true when it is remembered that the liberal theory is pre-eminently one addressing the question of how we should deal with matters of fundamental conflict in a democratic society, and designed to leave open for individual judgment and decision questions about human good in any substantial sense.

Trevor Cooling, in his article 'Evangelicals and modern religious education', identifies three general commitments that such a view of education demands of the religious believer. In his view such a person must accept:[18]

a. 'the fact of religious diversity in the community and acknowledge that equally sincere and genuine people paying equal regard to the evidence available can come to totally different conclusions in matters of religion. There are in the final analysis no universally compelling reasons for adopting any particular religious faith and he (*sic*) must therefore 'respect the right of other people to hold beliefs different from his own';

b.   'that seeking to understand others, even those with whom he disagrees absolutely, is a good thing and that there is always the possibility of learning from them';
c.   'that each pupil is a unique individual and has the right before God to make his own informed and free decision as to the theological stance he will adopt. This means accepting that 'for the Christian teacher the pupil's spiritual and intellectual freedom is at the heart of the truth that has to be conveyed' and that any coercion into belief is denial of that truth'.

These commitments, central to the notion of liberal education and the concept of the common school, are ones which Cooling judges that most evangelicals will have no difficulty in accepting. I judge that this is true also of many other kinds of religious believer.

What has been indicated so far, of course, is merely an acceptance of some basic underlying principles. The acceptability of the liberal educational position in any fuller sense to the religious believer involves detailed consideration of the precise manner in which central concepts such as 'autonomy'[19] and 'critical reason' are being understood. It also depends upon what principled implications are taken to follow from the position for dealing with controversy in the school and classroom.

A commitment to the basic principles of liberal education involves certain constraints of principle concerning the extent to which religious beliefs can influence the educational process in the common school. Thus the school cannot be expected to adopt a unified view of 'Christian education' where all the aspects of the curriculum and life of the school are based explicitly on (say) evangelical biblical principles. To the extent that a writer such as Mark Roques[20] is seeking this, as distinct from wanting the religious point of view to be given fairer treatment, his claims go too far. This is true also of those who see the common school as merely a battleground of conflict between opposing belief systems. Religious believers, however, need also to be cautious about the implicit sort of religious influence that they might seek to bring to bear on the common school. There is a certain ambiguity in the influence which Brian Wakeman[21] considers it appropriate for the Christian teacher to bring to bear upon personal, social and moral education in this context. Some of his claims here are fully compatible with liberal educational principles. Thus he expresses concern about the need to respect autonomy and be alert to the dangers of indoctrination, and outlines how the Christian teacher might not only ensure that Christian perspectives be given a fair hearing but also give an example of a certain sort of behaviour. Elsewhere, however, Wakeman seems to be making claims which are more problematic. This is seen particularly in his claim that 'Mankind's relationship with his (*sic*) maker is the *vital basis'*[22] for work in these areas and in his view that Christianity provides a philosophy of life which should 'undergird' a school's ideals and practices.[23]

Given liberal principles, caution is also needed with regard to the claim that, since we live in a Christian country, Christian values are part of the 'public' rather than the 'private' domain, and therefore that the common school is justified in promoting them alongside other aspects of civic virtue. When a substantial interpretation of 'Christian values' is at issue here, attention needs to be paid to the extent to which there is now significant controversy in our society concerning them. Certainly considerable work needs to be done to show that this kind of argument can support the claim that common schools should teach Christianity as if it were true.[24]

However, given acceptance by the religious believer of the sorts of limitations outlined, a number of critical questions concerning fairness of treatment of controversial questions by the common school comes into focus.

Fairness and controversiality

One way of expressing the task of the common school in these matters is in terms of the achievement of *balance*. However, involved in any application of this notion are evaluative judgments about the elements between which a balance is being sought, and the criteria for what constitutes a balance.[25] Without making these judgments explicit, the notion is little more than a vague statement of an ideal to be aimed at.

What principles emerge from the liberal view concerning such judgments and criteria? At the heart of these principles is the notion that the school must seek, on the basis of the sorts of fundamental and non-negotiable ('public') values sketched earlier, to promote critical reflective judgment and decision on matters which are significantly controversial. These controversial matters are located not merely in the 'private' but also in the 'public' domain. The distinction between 'public' and 'private' values is itself, of course, a matter of controversy. However, I shall employ this rough distinction in my discussion at this point, conscious of the need for a more precise analysis in a fuller account.

'Public' values

The 'public' values implied in liberal education and the work of the common school are particularly important, since they articulate the basic framework for all that takes place. The values are of different kinds, covering inter alia ideals (for example, autonomy), methodological principles (for example, concerning critical reason) and moral and political values (for example, respect for persons and toleration). They are related to the 'culture of freedom' described earlier, and have a broadly procedural feel to them. The possibility of unfairness in the handling of controversial issues can arise in a number of ways relating to these values.

First, the values themselves are complex and capable of variable interpretation. One major implication of this is that they need to be characterised carefully if they are to genuinely facilitate the sort of open discussion and debate in relation to controversy which is at the heart of the liberal position, fully understood. For example, certain rather specific conceptualisations of central concepts such as 'autonomy' and 'critical reason' can illicitly import assumptions antagonistic to religious belief in general or to certain forms of it. This is not a merely theoretical worry, since it can lead at the practical level in schools to various kinds of failure in openness and subtlety of approach to religious matters. It should not be assumed, for example, that only 'liberal' kinds of religious belief are worthy objects of study.[26] Whilst notions such as 'autonomy' and 'critical reason' cannot be subject to complete elasticity of interpretation on the liberal view, alertness is needed concerning unduly restricted conceptions of them.

Second, the proper scope of public values of a moral sort needs to be borne in mind. These delineate only the civic aspects of virtue and should not be presented as covering the whole of the moral life. An example of the sort of concern generated by neglect of this important distinction can be seen in Patricia White's recent discussion of parents' rights in relation to the educational treatment of homosexuality.[27] Liberal educational principles demand that homosexuality not be ignored as an educational issue, and most parent would accept White's case for discussion of it as part of a programme of sex education. The crucial question concerns the values that should govern the process. In her discussion of whether homosexuality is morally wrong, White only considers whether such relationships violate the basic principles which relate to life in a democratic society. Having concluded that they do not, she draws the conclusion that the school not only should present homosexuality as a morally acceptable lifestyle which pupils may adopt but should also contribute to its flourishing. This conclusion, however, runs the risk of underplaying the role that 'private' moral considerations play in judgments of such matters, and of giving an undue salience to 'public' moral considerations. White acknowledges that religious views on the subject should be treated as part of a study of the religions in question. However, these views need to be brought to bear on discussions about the notion of a 'morally acceptable' lifestyle if a full understanding of this is to be developed. This is true also in areas of the curriculum such as personal and social education, where 'public' and 'private' considerations of value are closely interrelated.

The general point here is related to concerns about the promotion by the common school of a secular view of life as a whole. Strictly speaking, if the school is offering an education which is a 'primary good' in the Rawlsian sense it should be seeking to achieve a kind of neutrality about 'substantial conceptions of the good'. It should therefore not seek to support a merely secular conception. Acceptance of the notion that matters of civic virtue should be governed by secular criteria is importantly distinct from promoting a secular view of human good in general. Similar worries arise about the danger that the school may promote relativism. The view that certain matters are in fundamental dispute is importantly distinct from an acceptance of relativism. There may well be practical difficulties facing the common school in avoiding the transmission of general secularist and relativist views. However, liberal educational values confront the common school with a principled obligation to address and resolve them.

Interesting questions arise concerning the ethos of the common school with regard to fairness and controversiality. I cannot, however, pursue them here.[28]

'Private' values

A number of principles for the treatment of 'private' values can be derived from elements of our earlier discussion. Thus a religious perspective, for example, should be approached in a significant way and without illicit preconceptions, should be brought to bear on more general matters of morality and lifestyle, and so on. Implicit in such principles is the need for the common school to devote sufficient resources of time, money and pedagogic expertise to this work.

A number of principles relate to the fact that religious beliefs typically offer a perspective on life as a whole. Common schools have a responsibility to deal with the holistic implications of such beliefs. The need for religious perspectives not to be isolated from discussion of issues of morality and lifestyle has already been mentioned. In addition, the common school must ensure that, although it cannot be expected to teach each subject from a religious perspective, such perspectives are not excluded from them. Another demand of a 'holistic' character arises from the fact that liberal educational principles call for pupils to make a coherent whole of their educational experience in order that they can begin to form their own life ideals. What is required here is an integrative task where the pupils relate the various elements of their educational experience together with their developing wants, motives and the like, so that their autonomous agency in the full sense is constructed. Since the common school cannot impose a determinate life ideal, it must ensure that the child is exposed not merely to possibly disjointed elements of knowledge, but also to the various general 'interpretative attitudes to the world' which lie at the root of different 'world-views'.[29]

Conclusion

In this article I have indicated the scope that exists, within liberal educational principles, for religious believers and others to make significant demands of the common school with regard to its fair handling of controversial questions. The articulation and pursuit of these demands will not only do justice to the demands of religious belief, but will also enhance our grasp and pursuit of liberal educational values themselves.[30]

Notes
1. On this see, for example, T H McLaughlin (1987, 1992).
2. Great Britain Parliament House of Commons (1985, chapter 1).
3. R F Dearden (1984, p. 86).
4. Dearden mentions four kinds of issue: (a) where a matter is in principle one which could be settled by evidence, but that evidence is as yet unavailable; (b) where decision making criteria are agreed but there is disagreement about the weight to be given to different criteria; (c) where no decision making criteria are agreed; (d) where whole frameworks of understanding are in dispute. (R F Dearden, 1984, pp. 86–87).
5. See, for example, G Dworkin (1988); L Haworth (1986); J Raz (1986); J Shortt (1986, 1988); E J Thiessen (1991); K Ward (1983); R Young (1986).
6. For further discussion see, for example, B Ackerman (1980, chapter 5); C Bailey (1984); E Callan (1991); B Crittenden (1982); J Feinberg (1980); A Gutmann (1987); G Haydon (1987); P H Hirst (1974, 1985).
7. Great Britain Parliament House of Commons (1985, chapter 8); P H Hirst, (1974, 1984, 1985); J Hull (1984); Schools Council (1971).
8. See, for example, B Crittenden (1982); P H Hirst (1985).
9. See R F Dearden (1984, chapter 7).
10. On these matters, see, for example, D Bridges (1986); R F Dearden (1984, chapter 7); P Gardner (1989).
11. I shall leave to one side discussions of parents' rights in relation to the upbringing and education of their children. On this matter, see, for example, T H McLaughlin (1984).
12. J Rawls (1971). Compare J Rawls (1985, 1987, 1988).
13. On communitarianism see, for example, A Gutmann (1985); W Kymlicka (1989); A MacIntyre (1981, 1988, 1990); M J Sandel (1982).
14. For an outline of this overall position in more detail see, for example, A Brown (1986, chapter 3); W Kymlicka (1990, chapter 3); S Mendus (1989, chapter 4).
15. See P H Hirst (1974).
16. J Shortt (1991).
17. See note 13. Also E. Callan (1989); B Crittenden (1988); D I Lloyd (1980, 1986).
18. T Cooling (1987, p. 61).
19. See, for example, J Shortt (1986, 1988); E J Thiessen (1991).
20. M Roques (1989).
21. B Wakeman (1984).
22. B Wakeman (1984, p. 42). My italics.
23. B Wakeman (1984, p. 42).
24. Compare Islamic Academy (1990); J Sacks (1991).
25. R F Dearden (1984, chapter 5).
26. T Cooling (1986, 1987).
27. P White (1991).
28. T H McLaughlin (1991).
29. R Barrow (1976, p. 51).
30. I am grateful to participants in the conference 'Towards a Christian theory of education' at Stapleford House Education Centre in January 1992 for their discussion of a paper I presented on themes related to the subject of this article. Versions of some parts of the material in this article were contained in papers

presented to meetings of the Reading and Scottish branches of the Philosophy of Education Society of Great Britain in March 1992. I am grateful to the participants in those discussions for helpful comments.

References

Ackerman, B A (1980) *Social Justice in the Liberal State,* New Haven and London, Yale University Press.

Bailey, C (1984) *Beyond the Present and the Particular: a theory of liberal education,* London, Routledge and Kegan Paul.

Barrow, R (1976) *Common Sense and the Curriculum,* London, George Allen and Unwin.

Bridges, D (1986) 'Dealing with controversy in the school curriculum: a philosophical perspective,' in J J Wellington (ed.) *Controversial Issues in the Curriculum,* Oxford, Basil Blackwell.

Brown, A (1986) *Modern Political Philosophy: theories of the just society,* Harmondsworth, Penguin.

Callan, E (1989) 'Godless moral education and liberal tolerance,' *Journal of Philosophy of Education,* 23, pp. 267–281.

Callan, E (1991) 'Pluralism and civic education,' *Studies in Philosophy and Education,* 11, pp. 65–87.

Cooling, T (1986) 'Evangelicals and modern religious education. Part one: attitudes to evangelical thought within religious education,' *Spectrum*, 18, pp. 123–127.

Cooling, T (1987) 'Evangelists and modern religious education. Part two: the via media – an open approach to religious education,' *Spectrum,* 19, pp. 57–71.

Crittenden, B (1982) *Cultural Pluralism and Common Curriculum*, Victoria, Melbourne University Press.

Crittenden, B (1988) *Parents, the State and the Right to Educate,* Victoria, Melbourne University Press.

Dearden, R F (1984) *Theory and Practice in Education,* London, Routledge and Kegan Paul.

Dworkin, G (1988) *The Theory and Practice of Autonomy,* Cambridge, Cambridge University Press.

Feinberg, J (1980) 'The child's right to an open future,' in W Aiken and H LaFollette (eds).

Gardner, P (1989) 'Neutrality in education,' in R E Goodin and A Reeve (eds) *Liberal Neutrality,* London, Routledge.

Great Britain Parliament House of Commons (1985) *Education for All: the report of the Committee of Inquiry into the Education of Children from Ethnic Minority Groups,* The Swann Report, Cmnd 9453, London, HMSO.

Gutmann, A (1985) 'Communitarian critics of liberalism,' *Philosophy and Public Affairs,* 14, pp. 308–322.

Gutmann, A (1987) *Democratic Education*, Princeton, University Press.

Haydon, G (ed.) (1987) *Education for a Pluralist Society: philosophical perspectives on the Swann Report* (Bedford Way Papers No 30), London, University of London Institute of Education.

Haworth, L (1986) *Autonomy: an essay in philosophical psychology and ethics*, New Haven and London, Yale University Press.

Hirst, P H (1974) *Moral Education in a Secular Society,* London, Hodder and Stoughton.

Hirst, P H (1984) 'Philosophy of Education,' in J M Sutcliffe (ed.) *A Dictionary of Religious Education,* London, SCM pp. 259–261.

Hirst, P H (1985) 'Education and diversity of belief,' in M C Felderhof (ed.) *Religious Education in a Pluralistic Society,* London, Hodder and Stoughton, pp 5–17.

Hull, J M (1984) *Studies in Religion and Education,* London, Falmer Press.

Islamic Academy (1990) *Faith as the Basis of Education in a Multi-Faith Multi-Cultural Country: a discussion document,* Cambridge, The Islamic Academy.

Kymlicka, W (1989) *Liberalism, Community, and Culture,* Oxford, Clarendon Press.

Kymlicka, W (1990) *Contemporary Political Philosophy: an introduction,* Oxford, Clarendon Press.

Lloyd, D I (1980) 'The rational curriculum: a critique,' *Journal of Curriculum Studies,* 12, pp. 331–342.

Lloyd, I (1986) 'Confession and reason,' *British Journal of Religious Education,* 8, pp. 140–145.

MacIntyre, A (1981) *After Virtue: a study in moral theory,* London, Duckworth.

MacIntyre, A (1988) *Whose Justice? Which Rationality?* London, Duckworth.

MacIntyre, A (1990) *Three Rival Versions of Moral Enquiry: encyclopaedia, genealogy and tradition,* London, Duckworth.

McLaughlin, T H (1984) 'Parental rights and the religious upbringing of children,' *Journal of Philosophy of Education,* 18, pp. 75–83.

McLaughlin, T H (1987) 'Education for All, and religious schools,' in G Haydon (ed.) *Education for a Pluralist Society: philosophical perspectives on the Swann Report* (Bedford Way Papers No 30), London, University of London Institute of Education.

McLaughlin, T H (1991) 'Ethos, community and the school,' unpublished paper presented to meeting on Identity, Community and Culture, Centre for Philosophy and Public Affairs, University of St Andrews, December.

McLaughlin, T H (1992) 'The ethics of separate schools,' in M Leicester and M J Taylor (eds) *Ethics, Ethnicity and Education,* London, Kogan Page.

Mendus, S (1989) *Toleration and the Limits of Liberalism,* London, Macmillan.

Rawls, J (1971) *A Theory of Justice,* Oxford, Oxford University Press.

Rawls, J (1985) 'Justice as fairness: political not metaphysical,' *Philosophy and Public Affairs,* 14, pp. 223–251.

Rawls, J (1987) 'The idea of an overlapping consensus,' *Oxford Journal of Legal Studies,* 7, pp. 1–25.

Rawls, J (1988) 'The priority of the right and ideas of the good,' *Philosophy and Public Affairs,* 17, pp. 251–276.

Raz, J (1986) *The Morality of Freedom,* Oxford, Clarendon Press.

Roques, M (1989) *Curriculum Unmasked: towards a Christian understanding of education,* Eastbourne, Monarch.

Sacks, J (1991) *The Persistence of Faith: religion, morality and society in a secular age,* (The Reith Lectures 1990), London, Weidenfeld and Nicolson.

Sandel, M J (1982) *Liberalism and the Limits of Justice,* Cambridge, Cambridge University Press.

Schools Council (1971) *Religious Education in Secondary Schools: working paper 36,* London, Evans/Methuen.

Shortt, J (1986) 'A critical problem for rational autonomy?' *Spectrum,* 18, pp. 107–121.

Shortt, J (1988) 'Faith and autonomy,' *Spectrum,* 20, pp. 39–56.

Shortt, J. (1991) 'Towards a reformed epistemology and its educational significance,' unpublished PhD dissertation, University of London.

Thiessen, E J (1991) 'Christian nurture, indoctrination and liberal education,' *Spectrum,* 23, pp. 105–124.

Wakeman, B (1984) *Personal, Social and Moral Education: a source book,* Tring, Lion.

Ward, K (1983) 'Is autonomy an educational ideal?' *Educational Analysis,* 5, pp. 47–55.

White, P (1991) 'Parents' rights, homosexuality and education,' *British Journal of Educational Studies,* 39, p. 398–408.

Young, R (1986) *Personal Autonomy: beyond negative and positive liberty,* New York, St Martin's Press.

7. Faith and commitment

The related concepts of 'faith' and 'commitment' play important roles both in discussions of the nature of Christian belief, and in considerations of the relationship between education and religion.

In the first article Basil Mitchell, a philosopher of religion who has extended his insights to the practice of religious education, explores the question whether faith and reason are essentially antithetical.[1] The author begins by noting the importance of tenacity, in the sense of a student's persevering 'in the face of his own doubts and the criticisms of (others)', within natural science and (particularly) the human sciences and the humanities. Thus 'the academic normally requires, and characteristically exhibits, a kind of faith; and ... it is reasonable for him to do so'. Such a faith need not be contrary to reason. *Religious* faith goes beyond this only in uniting the elements of comprehensiveness and practicality (offering 'a faith to live by'); but faith *in God,* by contrast, is unconditional trust in a God who is faithful. Yet this 'unconditional trust in God ... cannot be construed as belief that the system itself is unquestionably true'. The article concludes with some reflections on the implications of this discussion for educational debate. Mitchell rejects any forced choice in religious education between the indoctrination of received opinions and education leading to an entirely 'open-ended' critical reflection. He argues instead, following the lead of R S Peters and Gilbert Murray, that 'we have, as educators, to make our pupils heirs to a tradition in such a manner that in due course, they are free to appropriate it, modify it or reject it'. 'Faith and reason: a false antithesis?' was first published in *Religious Studies*, 16, 1980, pp. 131–144.

Brian Hill's study of 'Teacher commitment and the ethics of teaching for commitment,' first published in *Religious Education,* 76, 1981, pp. 322–336, asks whether 'pupils should ever be exposed to the teacher's own ideological stance' in the context of compulsory schooling. Hill first reviews a range of teaching models (the 'positivist', 'rationalist' and 'personalist') and then relates them to the various criteria of indoctrination that have been proposed. The argument uncovers four possible stances of the teacher with regard to her own value position; each stance being related to the different models of teaching. The stances include 'neutral impartiality' (with the teacher as impartial arbitrator) and 'committed impartiality' (in which teachers also 'exhibit their own beliefs as additional data for analysis'). The former stance is criticised for its educationally undesirable consequences, while the latter is defended against the claim that it slides into indoctrination.[2]

Professor Basil Mitchell was formerly Nolloth Professor of the Philosophy of the Christian Religion in the University of Oxford, England. Professor Brian V Hill is Professor of Education in the School of Education of Murdoch University, Murdoch, Western Australia.

Notes
1.   See also Basil Mitchell, *The Justification of Religious Belief*, London, Macmillan, 1973; *Faith and Criticism*, Oxford, Oxford University Press, 1994 and references in the select bibliography.
2.   See also Brian U Hill, *Education and the Endangered Individual*, New York, Teachers College Press, 1973; *The Greening of Christian Education*, Sydney, Lancer, 1985; *That They May Learn,* Exeter, Paternoster; Flemington Markets, Lancer, 1990.

7.1 Faith and reason: a false antithesis?
Basil Mitchell

'I can't believe that,' said Alice.

'Can't you?' the Queen said in a pitying tone. 'Try again: draw a long breath and shut your eyes.'

Alice laughed. 'There's no use trying,' she said. 'One can't believe impossible things.'

'I dare say you haven't had much practice,' said the Queen. 'Why sometimes I've believed as many as six impossible things before breakfast.'

This familiar passage presents a common view of faith, especially religious faith, and no doubt the Revd Charles Lutwidge Dodgson,[1] when he wrote it, was well aware of its theological applications. We tend to think of faith as involving effort, the effort required to believe things that are inherently difficult to believe; and the paradigm case of such faith is religious faith. So it becomes almost part of the definition of faith that it is contrary to reason. For the reasonable man bases his beliefs upon evidence and the degree of conviction he allows himself is strictly in proportion to the strength of the evidence. It 'rises and falls' with the evidence. It follows that there is an inevitable opposition between religion and reason; and, since the rational enterprise *par excellence* is science, this becomes an opposition between religion and science, not − at least primarily − in the sense that the *findings* of religion and science are opposed, but that their methods are. Science is a matter of reason; religion is a matter of faith.

If this way of thinking is correct, it has important implications for education. Scientific education will involve the cultivation of the scientific temper, that is to say, the readiness to approach experience with an entirely open mind and the habit of reaching a conclusion only when the evidence clearly supports it. Since, *ex hypothesi,* religious faith is not based on, and does not appeal to, reason, the only way it could be communicated would be by some form of non-rational persuasion or 'indoctrination'. Religious education ought, therefore, either to be abandoned or to be undertaken in an entirely 'objective' or 'phenomenological' way. Children should not be taught Judaism or Christianity or any other religion but rather taught about them.

Contemporary theologians and educational theorists generally respond to this position in one of two ways. The first is to assimilate Christianity (or any other religion) to the scientific model and to insist that theology should be an entirely 'open-ended' activity. No more than the scientist should the religious believer regard himself as committed to certain beliefs; like the scientist he should rest his convictions upon human experience and be prepared to modify them as and when new evidence requires it. The second is to attempt a counter-attack upon the scientist and to claim that science itself is based upon a kind of faith in that the scientist accepts certain presuppositions about, for example, causality or the uniformity of nature, without which science could not proceed, but which do not require, and cannot be given, any rational justification. So in the end, both science and religion are matters of faith and not reason. And this counter-attack derives some support from the contemporary disenchantment with 'the technocratic society'; for if the entire scientific enterprise represents the effects of a fundamental non-rational decision which modern man took three or so centuries ago, it is open to us now with no sacrifice of integrity to repudiate it in favour of a radically different option.

The question I want to raise is whether the underlying conception of faith and reason as essentially antithetical, a conception common to both parties in the debate, is itself adequate to an understanding of our intellectual life. And I want in the first instance to enquire how far the problem of faith and reason, or something like it, arises in non-religious contexts; and then, and only then, to consider whether there are any peculiar difficulties about the relation between faith and reason in religion.

Let us begin with science itself. The popular picture of science as an entirely open-ended activity and of the scientist as concerned to test a hypothesis and accept or reject it on the basis of the experimental evidence alone, corresponds to what T S Kuhn calls 'normal science'. In the scientist's day to day work there is already in existence and taken entirely for granted by him an accepted theoretical structure and the individual researcher is testing comparatively low-level hypotheses framed in terms of concepts that belong to that structure. Nothing more fundamental than the hypothesis itself hangs upon the experiment, and he is willing to drop that if the experiment is unsuccessful. The experiment would otherwise have no point. The situation, however, is significantly different, and so is the scientist's attitude, if, in the course of his work, he encounters evidence which calls in question the basic theoretical structure itself or some important part of it. It simply is not the case that he is prepared to give up comparatively fundamental laws in the face of recalcitrant observations or, at any rate, to do so without a struggle. Rather than do this he prefers to adopt other devices – to cast doubt on the observations, or to introduce subsidiary hypotheses to explain the discrepancy, or even sometimes to put the observations in cold storage, so to speak, in the hope (or in the faith?) that a suitable explanation conformable to the existing structure will turn up.

Similarly the editor of a scientific journal is by no means entirely open-minded when deciding what to publish; he attaches a good deal of weight to the authority of established scientists, who act as referees, and he is unlikely to publish something by an unknown researcher, which runs strongly counter to the prevailing orthodoxy. To give a specific example, the late Professor Michael Polanyi, in his book *Being and Knowing* describes the vicissitudes of his 'potential theory of adsorption'. He advanced this theory early in his career and was quite unable to get a hearing for it. Although it had good experimental backing, it was out of line with the current direction of that branch of chemistry. Some fifty years later it became generally accepted. Polanyi acknowledges the dangers to which science may be exposed through the suppression of promising new ideas, but then gives it as his considered judgment that the leading scientists of the time were right to dismiss his theory. To have taken it seriously would have involved too great a modification of the accepted structure of chemistry as it was then understood.

Hence scientists need what has been called a 'principle of tenacity' to ensure that they do not generally call in question the fundamental laws of their science as they are currently understood (let alone the entire system). There would, indeed, be no point in their doing so, since there is, *ex hypothesi*, no viable alternative at present in sight, and their ability to go on doing effective scientific work depends upon their trusting the existing framework. Thus the notion that scientific theories 'rise and fall with the evidence' is only partially correct. It is true of a particular scientific hypothesis put forward in the course of research which is being conducted against a background of accepted theory. An expert in the field could no doubt say with reasonable confidence just how it stands at the moment — just how well supported it is. The fundamental scientific law is in a very different case. It is so firmly integrated into the system as a whole that nothing but a large scale Kuhnian revolution could dislodge it.

This is not to say, however, that it cannot be called in question at all — as the second type of response maintains. We have in our own day seen scientists question such apparently basic beliefs as that the speed of light cannot be exceeded or that two events in different places can happen simultaneously or that something cannot just come into existence. Even a comparatively fundamental belief may in the end have to be revised if the time comes when it, or the system of which it is an essential component, can no longer account adequately, or as adequately as some rival theory, for the data of observation.

There are, then, elements of trust and of respect for authority in science which require us to modify to some extent the simple contrast between the open-ended attitude of the scientist and the committed attitude of the person of religious faith. (It is interesting to note, in passing, that another contrast requires also to be modified, *viz* that between the common sense credibility of scientific theories and the incredibility of religious dogma: the scientist also, under the pressure of the demand for simplicity and explanatory power, may be found 'believing six impossible things before breakfast'.)

Nevertheless, even when due allowance has been made for these modifications, they suggest only a rather remote analogy with religious faith. The 'faith' the scientist exhibits is so obvious a requirement of an effective scientific policy that no one would even be tempted to regard faith and reason as antithetical.

Faith and academic study

The sciences that I have been discussing so far are the natural sciences, which are comparatively unified and whose practitioners very largely agree about fundamentals (although I am assured by philosophers of science that this appearance of unity is to some extent deceptive). In the human sciences, and even more obviously in the humanities, there is present not as an occasional phenomenon, but as a regular feature of their operation, a good deal of lively controversy. I need only mention the continuing debate about the relative importance of genetic and environmental factors in the social sciences, conducted often with notable acerbity, and the rival claims of, for example, Skinnerian stimulus-response theory and the various schools of post-Freudian psychodynamics in psychology. That this situation obtains in philosophy or economics is so evident that it scarcely requires illustration. Indeed I think one may generalise and say that the existence of rival 'schools of thought' is, outside the natural sciences, a characteristic feature of academic life, and one which deserves more attention than is usually given it.

In what follows I use the term 'academic' to refer to persons who work in the human sciences or the humanities. If I am right about the prevalence of 'schools of thought' in these areas, the normal situation of the academic is the following.

1. He believes in a certain conception of the way his subject should be treated and has certain views as to what concepts, theories and modes of argument are fundamental to it.
2. In terms of these he believes himself to be in possession of a certain 'body of knowledge' upon which he relies in teaching and research and in making recommendations for practical policy, when called upon to do so.
3. He recognises (or should recognise) that this approach to the subject is not universally accepted and that there exist bodies of scientific and scholarly opinion of a sort that cannot be

entirely discounted, which are to a greater or lesser extent critical of his approach. (I say 'should recognise' because no one acquainted with the facts of academic life can fail to be aware that such recognition is sometimes absent. Far from acknowledging that reasonable men could hold views substantially different from their own, and that some actually do, academics all too often regard their opponents as fools or even knaves.)

4. His way of approaching the subject involves certain judgments, not universally shared, as to what is important and as to what are desirable ends to pursue, and these have implications for practical decision both inside and outside the academic field.

In this typical situation it is evident, I think, that he will need, even more than the natural scientist does, the capacity to persevere in the face of his own doubts and the criticisms of his colleagues. If the subject, as he understands it, is to develop fruitfully, its characteristic theses require to be tested and modified over a reasonable period of time, and this means that he cannot be prepared to abandon the theories and concepts he judges to be central as soon as he is confronted with evidence that calls them in question. He must instead do his best to square them with the new evidence and, as we have seen, he has a number of devices open to him. In the last resort he can simply take the line that 'something will turn up' to vindicate them although he cannot as yet tell what. In the total absence of such a reaction to unfavourable evidence no 'body of knowledge' would ever have time to be built up. The growing child would always be killed by premature antisepsis. Hence the good academic needs to be a determined man, able and willing to persevere in projects and policies he believes in in face of difficulties and uncertainties, as the biographies of eminent scholars and scientists amply testify.

So far I have considered the individual academic as if his problems were purely intellectual ones, but it would be unrealistic to overlook the extent to which even the cloistered scholar is subject to temptations of a non-rational or dubiously rational kind, which relate specifically to his professional work. In particular intellectual fashions are a regular feature – perhaps an unavoidable one – of the academic scene, and it calls for strength of mind to stand out for an approach to his subject which is currently unpopular. The more so because, as Plato recognised, it is often the cleverest people who are the most strongly attracted to such fashions, so that the influence they exert is a psychological force to be reckoned with; and it is one which, in the nature of the case, cannot be treated as merely psychological. The academic may need at one and the same time to resist this force in so far as it threatens his intellectual integrity and independence while yet allowing it due weight in so far as he can see it to have a rational basis.

What I have been saying thus far is open to an obvious objection, *viz* that, although true, it is of merely psychological interest. No one doubts that academics, like other people, are subject to fashions and to prejudices and exposed to temptations to which they often yield or to which they respond inappropriately. They have their share in human weakness; but it palpably *is* human weakness. It is not in principle difficult – and it is in principle necessary – to distinguish between

  a. reasonable policies for the optimum development of a line of enquiry in the long run, and
  b. emotional or attitudinal reactions to the individual's personal predicament which, however understandable, have no rational basis and ought, so far as possible, to be avoided.

In particular, it will be objected, it is neither necessary nor desirable that the academic should *become identified* with a particular school of thought in the way that gives rise to these emotional responses. He need not and should not actually *believe in* his way of viewing the subject, as the putative analogy with religious faith suggests, but rather should remain fundamentally detached from it. He should regard it as offering the best available programme for future investigation, and he should persevere with it for so long and only for so long, as the state of the evidence makes it reasonable to do so. Any sort of personal commitment or emotional involvement is out of place. In the *intellectual* life it is at best a harmless indulgence; whereas it is an essential component of *religious faith*.

By way of reply to this objection it is, I think, legitimate to stress, in the first instance, how rarely this ideal of academic detachment is actually achieved. The way in which academics typically respond to the conditions of academic life is by exhibiting the emotional reactions and the active tendencies which are marks of genuine conviction. I know of one university where the department of social science had to be formally divided on account of an irreconcilable conflict between the proponents of two rival approaches to the subject; and it is my impression that if one is looking for 'odium theologicum' in the contemporary academic scene one is more likely to find it among the social scientists than among the theologians who treat one another's pronouncements with an altogether suspicious tolerance. That such reactions are excessive may readily be granted, but the resemblance to the excesses which have sometimes characterised religious faith is close enough to be suggestive. One thing that it suggests is that it may not normally be possible for a man to sustain the rigours of academic life while remaining entirely detached from the fray. And if he cannot or can only with difficult remain detached ought he to try? May it not, for most temperaments at least, be a condition of success, that the individual internalise, not only the abstract values of impartiality and concern for truth which I take to be the primary academic virtues, but also the attitudes and assumptions characteristic of some particular approach to his subject?

'Success' as so far understood means success in developing a theoretical system; but, as has already been noticed in passing, many academic subjects have practical implications and are engaged in partly for that reason. Many also have – or are believed to have – ideological presuppositions. To the extent that this is so there is a more or less considerable overlap between the positions a man adopts in his academic work and in what may loosely be called his general 'philosophy of life'. And in so far as the former contributes to and is influenced by the latter, it comes to play a part in his personal and social life that is more than merely theoretical. It affects the sort of man he is and helps form his conception of the sort of man he ought to be. A topical illustration of his relationship might be the economics and the politics of Milton Freedman. There is, as comment in the press has emphasised, a fairly close fit between his economic and his political beliefs of such a kind that it is hard to credit that he is committed to the latter, but treats the former with complete intellectual detachment.

Hence I am inclined to suggest that the academic normally requires, and characteristically exhibits, a kind of faith; and moreover that it is reasonable for him to so do. That is to say he adheres to, and believes in, certain schemes of thought of which the following can be said.

1. They are based on evidence and have a rational structure.
2. They are open to criticism and are, as a rule, in fact criticised by those who adopt rival positions.
3. Although one of them may in fact be better based than its rivals, it is not unchallengeably so.
4. They often involve presuppositions of an ideological kind and may have practical implications.
5. They derive from historical traditions of varying ancestries.
6. They are of such complexity that the individual is, as a rule, expert in only part of them and is, therefore, inevitably dependent upon authority to some extent for his understanding of them. He could not provide a clear and articulate justification of his own for all that he accepts from them.
7. They are such that the individual cannot in practice avoid a decision as to whether he accepts them or not, and, in so far as he accepts them, they help to determine the sort of man he is going to be. His 'faith' consists in his determination to adhere to the scheme of thought and allow it to influence his character and conduct, notwithstanding that:

a. there are, and he knows that there are, arguments and evidence that the scheme cannot, so far as he can see, currently accommodate;
b. he cannot personally provide all the credentials of the system on demand;
c. he recognises, or at least ought to recognise, that the scheme could turn out in the end to be in important respects, mistaken (though, of course, he believes it will not).

His faith is constantly being tried in that he is regularly confronted with the arguments of opponents and is not always able to dispose of them. He often has to hang on to his belief, knowing all the time that his opponents could be right and himself and his friends wrong.

In claiming that this represents the characteristic predicament of the academic I do not of course wish to claim that all academic work conforms to the pattern I have outlined. Some subjects and some aspects of all subjects are of so narrowly technical a kind that they do not display some of the features in my list, and there are academics who incline to the view that only questions susceptible of such 'objective' treatment are suitable for serious study. I do not now propose to argue against that view, but am content to note that it is not in practice very widely shared.

Religious faith

Nevertheless, even if it be conceded that the academic does require an attitude akin to faith, there remains at least one important respect in which religious faith is unique. Religious faith unites two features which, in so far as they are found in the academic life, are found there separately. Religious faith is essentially 'a faith to live by'. A man looks to his religion for the meaning of his whole existence and not just of selected bits of it, and he expects from it guidance in the entire conduct of his life. It is, or aims to be, both comprehensive and practical. By contrast most academic disciplines are restricted to certain selected aspects or areas of the world. The natural sciences achieve their characteristic clarity and rigour by a deliberate limitation to certain aspects only of what they study; chiefly those capable of quantitative measurement; and even subjects like sociology or history do not in actuality or intention embrace the whole of human life. On the other hand subjects like metaphysics and theology, which aim at a synoptic vision (and are often suspect on this account) do not have it as their primary function to provide practical guidance. These characteristics of a religious system of belief make it even less manageable than the typical academic discipline – it is even less possible for the individual believer to be reasonably confident that he has mastered all the considerations that are relevant to its truth or falsehood. This need not imply that he can form no reasonable judgment at all – that he can only 'plump' in an entirely non-rational way – but it does mean that any judgment he can make is inevitably far removed from the cool and complete appraisal that an ideally rational being might make if he had all the time in the world and no pressing practical preoccupations. So he is bound to rely to an even larger extent on the authority of others whom he is prepared to trust.

But these characteristics of religious faith are not in themselves uniquely religious. They apply equally to what I earlier called 'philosophies of life' and these, of course, may be entirely secular. In regard to the general conduct of his life a man cannot maintain indefinitely an attitude of academic detachment. He has decisions to make; and the way he makes them will eventually determine the sort of man he becomes. In so far as he endeavours to achieve consistency in his choices and coherence in the reasons he gives for them, he finds himself in fundamentally the same predicament as the man who embraces a religious philosophy of life. The positions he adopts and reasons he relies on will, of course, characteristically be different from those of the religious man, but they will also be to some extent controversial, not only in the sense that they are in fact challenged, but also in the sense that not all the challenges can be discounted as having no rational basis. This is, indeed, the universal human predicament. In everyday life people are constantly required to make decisions in ambiguous situations where, even if they could remain always calm and composed, they would sometimes find it hard to adhere to a consistent policy, situations where they are in fact subject to emotional stresses which are liable to affect their imagination and their judgment. They have no choice but to make and stand by decisions in the face of objective uncertainties and subjective temptations. Even if the academic manages to some extent to avoid this predicament in his specialised work, he becomes exposed to these pressures as soon as he leaves the cloister and joins the others in the general cultural debate, and endeavours to get practical policies adopted that are based upon his theoretical conclusions. It must often happen that unexpected incidents and temporary setbacks tempt him for the time being to doubt the force of arguments which would still seem to him sound if he were in a uniformly cool frame of mind. It is in this characteristically human predicament that faith is needed. A man may, of course, deliberately limit the range and scope of his decisions and live, so far as is practically possible, a thoroughly neutral and uncommitted life. Since most of the issues which engage the attention of his fellows are, in his view, unacceptably controversial he prefers to be a non-voter and a non-participant. The danger is that by refusing to make explicit decisions in these controversial areas he will take over, in effect, the attitudes that prevail, at the time, in his particular milieu. He will not have much in the way of faith; but he is likely to have plenty of prejudices.

But in any case it is not clear that even the most cautious sceptic can avoid the tensions and temptations that I have been describing. His own parsimonious policy is based upon considerations of a broadly philosophical kind which are not shared by many of his colleagues and whose validity he must sometimes feel inclined to question; and he would be less than human if he were not strongly moved on occasions to break out of his narrow perimeter and throw in his lot with one or other of the contending parties beyond it. When assailed by such doubts he too requires the capacity to resist temptation.

My suggestion then is that there is a sense of 'faith' which is common to religious and secular contexts, and that faith in this sense need not be contrary to reason. Of course it can be. There are all too many examples, both secular and religious, of unthinking adherence to systems of belief which have little or no rational basis. And there are, and perhaps inevitably must be, innumerable cases of the comparatively unreflective acceptance of beliefs and attitudes, of whose rational basis those who accept them are largley unaware. The Socratic obligation λογον διδοναι is one which holds for intellectuals, but not everyone is obliged to be an intellectual.

It will, perhaps, be objected that I have assumed throughout, first that a rational choice can, at least in principle, be made between 'philosophies of life' and second that a rational case can be made out for at least some religious 'philosophies of life'; and that both of these assumptions are, at best, controversial. This objection I am bound to admit, nor can I undertake to defend those assumptions within the limits of this article. The most I can do is to insist that they are, at least, controversial.

Faith in God

At this point I must turn to the question which I undertook to discuss at the beginning of my article, namely whether the faith of the religious believer is in all essentials equivalent to that of the adherent, explicit or implicit, of a non-religious philosophy of life who resists temptation to give it up when, in spite of his steady rational conviction in its favour, he encounters arguments and experiences which, logically or psychologically, threaten it. I am inclined to think that there is one important difference – at least where the religion in question is a theistic religion. Faith in God for the Jew, the Christian or the Muslim, is not simply a commitment to a religious philosophy of life; it is a trusting reliance upon God. In this respect it is like faith in a person rather than like faith in some doctrine of human nature. As H H Price has pointed out, if I have faith in my doctor this involves more than my believing that he exists and that he is what he purports to be, a qualified medical practitioner. It means that I rely upon him to care conscientiously for my health, to be honest in his dealings with me, and so on. The sort of faith I have been discussing so far would be analogous to my faith in modern medicine (as distinct from, say, African tribal medicine); and my faith in my doctor, though it presupposes this, is of a different order and goes well beyond it.

There can be no secular equivalent to faith in God in this sense since there is nothing that corresponds, in a secular scheme of things, to a personal God.

However, the existence of religious faith in this additional sense, raises a serious question about the adequacy of my earlier discussion of faith in its religious application. Religious faith, it is commonly agreed, is, of its very nature, unconditional whereas the sort of secular faith I have been discussing must, in the end, be in a certain sense tentative and provisional; it must in principle be open to revision and, in the last resort, rejection. This is involved in my characterisation of 'philosophies of life' as not unchallengeable. For when every allowance has been made for the need to adhere to a philosophy of life with a good deal of determination if it is to undergo adequate testing and provide the individual with 'a faith to live by', there may always come a point when the cumulative case against it becomes so strong that he ought to give it up. If there is no such point, then his faith is no longer based on reason at all but has turned into simply prejudice or sheer fanaticism. Either, then, the conception of religious faith as unconditional has to be rejected, in spite of its centrality in the tradition of the great theistic religions, or the attempt to reconcile faith and reason on the lines indicated earlier has to be abandoned.

One way in which to approach this problem is to stress the distinction between the two senses of faith and to claim that, when this is clearly recognised, the dilemma disappears. The faith that *is* unconditional is the believer's trust in God; it is this which forbids him to despair in the face of doubts and difficulties. This trust is the corollary of God's nature as he believes it to be. The God 'in whom is no variableness and shadow of turning' is a faithful and merciful God who will not abandon his creature. But it does not follow from this that the entire system of belief, including the belief that there is a God and that this God is trustworthy, could not in the end turn out to be false. The unconditional trust in God which is called for within the theistic system cannot be construed as belief that the system itself is unquestionably true.

To this proposed solution it may be objected that, if this is so, the believer's faith is not religiously adequate: it cannot give him the reassurance he needs in face of the 'changes and chances of this transitory life'. As a psychological generalisation about religious believers, this is by no means obviously true. Some may crave logical guarantees of the truth of their beliefs; others may have no need of them. And, even if logical certainty were available, it could not, as a matter of psychology, be relied upon invariably to prevent the dryness of spirit in which even undoubted truths appear empty and unconsoling. If, on the other hand, the objection is not based upon psychology, but the contention is that the believer ought not to be reassured unless there is no possibility of his being proved wrong, it can be pointed out that, as things are, he may have good reasons for believing as he does, and sufficient reasons, along the lines of our previous discussion, for not allowing his beliefs continually to fluctuate.

I confess that I find it difficult to decide whether this reply is adequate or not. I once thought it was, but now I am not so sure. But I am inclined to think that this problem too is not confined to the religious case. There is a parallel in the sphere of personal relations in which certain accounts of the nature of human personality would, if accepted, seem to render irrational certain sorts of response towards people, to which men (or, at any rate, men in our culture) are deeply committed. The obvious example is the account given by B F Skinner, and the practical inferences drawn by him, in *Beyond Freedom and Dignity*. It is hard to see how the unreserved openness and trust which most of us have and believe we ought to have towards our friends and our families could be justified in terms of Skinnerian psychology. How then should we react? Are we entitled to argue *from* our own intuitive conviction of the health and reasonableness of our personal responses *to* the evident falsity of Skinner's account? Must we deny, that is, that this account has any chance of proving true? Or should we conclude that, since Skinner could conceivably be right (though we do not personally believe he is), or some other account of human personality having similar implications could be right, we ought not to be as open and unreserved with those we love as we habitually are? That Skinner's view of human nature does indeed have these implications is, no doubt, open to some question, but it cannot be said to be beyond all reasonable doubt that it does not. In general it would be a bold man who was prepared to claim that there exists today any doctrine of human nature which commands universal assent among all reasonable men, or who was prepared to claim that it was beyond all reasonable doubt that our conception of what human beings are like has no implications for the way we should treat them. If this is so, the man who loves and trust his intimates unreservedly is in a similar case to the one who has unconditional faith in God. Neither can nor should allow his personal responses to be affected by the possibility (which he acknowledges) that he could be wrong in some of his fundamental beliefs.

Educational implications

I said at the beginning of this article that I would end by saying a little about the educational implications of the problem we have been discussing. I noted that in the educational debate, especially in relation to religious education, it is often taken for granted that we have to choose between two alternatives; on the one hand, indoctrination; on the other an entirely open-ended or phenomenological approach. Indoctrination consists in the inculcation of received opinions; the open-ended approach seeks to encourage an attitude that is entirely critical and creative. When presented with these alternatives we have little option but to choose the latter, for 'indoctrination' is evidently not an educational procedure at all. Yet the ideal of an education that aims solely at the development of individuals who are critical and creative seems, on reflection, to be curiously vacuous. To be creative is, so far as it goes, good; but is it of no concern what is created? Criticism is to be encouraged, but upon what is the critical capacity to be exercised? Can the individual learn to be either critical or creative without first having been inducted into a continuing tradition of some kind? As R S Peters (one of the sanest of British education theorists) writes in *Ethics and Education* (p. 104):

> The emphasis on 'critical thinking' was salutary enough, perhaps, when bodies of knowledge were handed on without any attempt being made to hand on also the public procedures by which they had been accumulated, criticised and revised. But it is equally absurd to foster an abstract skill called 'critical thinking' without handing on anything concrete to be critical about.

In talking, as he does here, of something concrete to be handed on Peters seems to be suggesting that there is need for a continuing tradition upon which the individual can draw and to which he can make his own unique contribution. Given such a tradition — so long as it is a reasonable one, and this is an important qualification — there is room for criticism which may result in modifying the tradition or, indeed, rejecting it. Without some such tradition there is, arguably, no possibility of critical or creative thought at all. Nothing is more absurd than to suppose that the individual, however intelligent and industrious he is, can develop the whole of science or any other academic discipline or morality or religion from scratch. He must be prepared to accept authority in all these fields — in fact in respect of everything in which being civilised consists — as a necessary condition of becoming critical and creative in them.

If what I said earlier is correct, about the extent to which controversy is endemic in most academic disciplines and *a fortiori* in all philosophies of life, we cannot expect that any tradition in which, as educators, we stand, will be unchallengeable (although it may be largely unchallenged within a particular culture or intellectual milieu). No doubt there are large areas of factual information and common sense belief which can be taken entirely for granted, but as soon as we penetrate at all deeply beyond these areas into subjects of serious intellectual study, we find ourselves in realms of more or less vigorous controversy. Hence, if anything concrete is to be handed on (to use Peters' words), it is likely to be something that can be controverted. There is a revealing phrase sometimes used by scholars describing their own student days: 'At Oxford (Princeton, Heidelberg) in my day we were *taught to believe* that ... (metaphysics was impossible and that neither Aquinas nor Hegel were worth reading).' This does not generally mean that their teachers inculcated certain doctrines into them in such a way that they were subsequently unable to treat them critically; but rather that their teachers themselves accepted these doctrines, believed themselves to be justified in doing so and, in the way they treated the subject, influenced the students so that they in turn largely accepted them. In this way the students became heirs to a recognisable philosophical tradition. But in so far as the teachers also taught them to be creative and critical (and in our Western universities they generally did), the latter were able to review in course of time what they had thus been 'taught to believe', and so the tradition developed. How to strike the balance between these two elements in the educational process is a practical question of some difficulty, but that a balance needs to be struck, seems to me to be clear.

That this is so is most apparent in the case of the most profoundly critical and creative minds. Much literary and historical research consists in the attempt to uncover the 'influences' which made them what they were and, happily, such research seems always to leave a sheer unexplained leap of originality which it cannot account for. But what does emerge is the extent to which, characteristically, such minds have absorbed the best of the work of their predecessors. Some time ago a friend of mine was engaged in editing the correspondence between Holst and Vaughan Williams and asked me to identify a quotation from Gilbert Murray, which one of them had quoted with approbation to the other. I was somewhat daunted by the prospect of searching through Murray's voluminous writings, but the quotation was about genius and it occurred to me that a possible source, readily available to the general reader, was his little volume on Euripides in the Home University Library. And there, in the introduction, I found what I was looking for. It read:

> Every man who possesses real vitality can be seen as the resultant of two forces. He is first the child of a particular age, society, convention; of what we may call in one word a tradition. He is secondly, in one degree or another, a rebel against that tradition. And the best traditions make the best rebels.

Gilbert Murray, I suggest, gets the balance right. We have, as educators, to make our pupils heirs to a tradition in such a manner that in due course, they are free to appropriate it, modify it, develop it or reject it. If we decline to do this, through fear of exerting undue influence upon them, they will not thereby be enabled to discover some genuinely original alternative of their own; they will simply absorb uncritically the current fashions of the day and make what they can of them. I have argued that a healthy tradition, whether secular or religious, calls for both faith and reason, and that there is an inevitable tension between them. Although in this lecture it is the faith that I have stressed, because, as it seems to me, the need for it is too often overlooked, I hold no brief for unreasoned prejudice. To return to Alice, It will not do to take the White Queen's advice. 'Try again: draw a long breath and shut your eyes.'

Note
1.   Alias Lewis Carroll, *Through the Looking-Glass: and what Alice found there,* London, 1872.

7.2 Teacher commitment and the ethics of teaching for commitment

Brian V Hill

It is unfortunate that most attempts to formulate codes of professional ethics for teachers relapse into either sentimental truisms or industrial bargaining points. The need to develop properly ethical guidelines has become all the more urgent since the close-knit culture of former times in which the teacher's role was well-defined and subordinate broadened into the cultural pluralism of today in which teachers are largely expected to define their own role, without any guarantee of protection from backlash if sectarian elements in the community object to the criteria chosen. Detailed work-value definitions for industrial purposes are seen by many to afford some protection, but they do so only at the cost of eroding the teacher's professional discretion to do what is thought best in the particular situation, and of substituting, in Margaret Mackie's words, 'a tribal ethic' for 'a universal ethic'.[1]

The present article attempts to formulate and to justify ethical guidelines relating to just one aspect of the teacher's role: whether, *prima facie*, pupils should ever be exposed to the teacher's own ideological stance. The problem has its origin in two circumstances: firstly, the plurality of beliefs and value systems in modern society, not all of which may be haughtily dismissed as products of unreason; secondly, an emergent literature on the rights of children in the context of compulsory schooling.[2]

What are teachers to do, given that they have been placed in the position of commending certain learning experiences to their pupils? And specifically, should they allow any of the things they most surely believe and prefer to enter into the educative transaction? I propose to answer this question, firstly, by looking at some of the teaching models currently being advocated; secondly, by relating these to the recent debate on 'indoctrination'; and thirdly, by checking the result against the concepts of 'teacher intentionality' and 'education'. In the light of this analysis, I will then examine four possible stances the teacher may adopt, and conclude with a comment on the bearing that the notion of contractual constraints has on our findings.

Teaching models

The literature and research on teaching reveal great confusion about the characteristics of good teaching. We are, as Shumsky[3] put it, 'in search of a teaching style', and our problem is a shortage not of empirical research findings, but of an agreed normative view of what those findings should add up to. Recommendations that seek to improve on the lacklustre authoritarian instructor of an earlier era tend to move in one of three directions, which I shall call *positivist, rationalist* and *personalist*. The terms will be presented in italics wherever they are used in my stipulative senses, to distinguish them from the variety of other uses they have.

The *positivist* model treats the classroom situation as a set of variables needing to be brought into adjustment in such a way that one variable in particular, learner behaviour, is modified in the desired direction. The teaching act is broken down into component parts such as cueing, sequencing, and reinforcing, in order to estimate more precisely the effect of each on learner behaviour. These and other variables are each assessed and compared using such instruments as control and experimental groups, tests and attitude scales, and statistical analysis. All behaviour is deemed to be open to modification, be it mental or physical, mainly cognitive in origin or mainly affective. On this model, it is otiose to talk about the ethics of teachers revealing their personal values; the point at issue is whether by so doing they will in fact promote the desired learning. If they will, they should. If they will not, they should not. Once we have defined the desired outcome operationally, than the criterion of efficiency identifies the best means.

The *rationalist* model acknowledges the utility of scientific enquiry into teacher behaviour to the extent that it clears the ground for concept development, with the result that the empirical researcher is given freest rein in the years prior to the stage of formal operational thought. But the key to distinctively human learning and behaviour is considered to be autonomous rationality, whereby random learnings are brought under cognised rules, and the reacting organism becomes capable of initiating new responses and choosing between alternative possibilities of action. Potentially, all behaviour is open to critical rational analysis, be it habitual or novel, and for theoretical or practical purposes. On this model, though it is not inappropriate to discuss the ethics of teachers revealing their personal stance, the main point at issue is again empirical: whether by so doing they will help or hinder the student's development towards rational autonomy. Implicit in this model is the belief that the freedom of the rational person is ultimately more significant for education then the determinism implicit in the *positivist* model.

The *personalist* model accepts the *rationalist* concern for human freedom, but rejects the primary emphasis on critical rationality as tending to an over-investment in academic curriculum, and to the neglect of other distinctively human powers such as creativity, dialogue and commitment. It is not without interest in this connection that R S Peters, for example, favours that philosophical tradition that hesitates to apply the concept of 'person' to very young or severely mentally handicapped individuals.[4] Strongly rationalistic, his counterbalancing remarks on 'personal relationships' are thin gruel to *personalists*. The model also rejects the dissection of teaching acts into specific behaviours characteristic of the *positivist* model, on the grounds that this obscures the holistic quality of interpersonal transactions, and reduces the life of feeling to a sterile calculus of affective outcomes. On this view, talk about the ethics of teachers disclosing their personal values is somewhat gauche, because in fact they can do no other; the ethical point that is really at issue is whether one's respect and concern for the pupil's self-development outweighs the temptation to build up one's own ego at the expense of the learner's. The need for a professional ethic is perhaps most clearly acknowledged by the *personalist* model, but this model also runs the greatest risk of substituting emotive slogans for clear guidelines. This point becomes more apparent when we relate our three models to the debate on the concept of indoctrination.

Indoctrination

In recent years this debate has progressed beyond the name-calling stage through the application of the skills of conceptual analysis. As Snook[5] indicates in introducing his useful collection of readings on the topic, analyses of the pejorative use of the term 'indoctrination' disagree on what is the primary defining characteristic of this notion. Some focus on method, others on content, and others on intention.

The case for focusing on method hinges on the possibility of inhibiting the learner's capacity to examine critically what is learned by the use of authoritarian teaching strategies denying access to alternative theories or points of view. The *positivist* model of teaching attracts criticism on these grounds because its deterministic premise invites manipulative strategies. Many of these, indeed, are better described as types of 'conditioning', as in the case of some 'behaviour modification' techniques, since they by-pass the conscious mind altogether, in contrast, as Wilson[6] has pointed out, to indoctrination. The *personalist* model may also be open to the charge of indoctrination *via* method, to the extent that the strength of the teacher-pupil relationship works against the student subjecting the teacher's own stance to critical examination. The *rationalist* model is the one least vulnerable to such criticisms, because it prizes critical rationality so highly. The problem with the *rationalist* approach, however, is how to get it going before the pupil has attained the cognitive stage of formal operations. And this is also the weakness in attempts to define indoctrination in terms of method. It is probable, as Wilson concedes,[7] that some manipulative or authoritarian methods are necessary to the subsequent success of more rational strategies, the crucial variable at the earlier stage being the intention of the teacher, not any particular teaching method as such.

The case for focusing on content derives its plausibility from the obvious linguistic connection between 'doctrine' and 'indoctrination'. The term 'doctrine' customarily connotes beliefs held by some to be true, though they are as yet empirically unconfirmed and believed by others to be false. They are usually contrasted with propositions known to be true.[8] Indoctrination then depends on the teacher representing certain doctrines to students as having the status of truths, irrespective of whether this is done deliberately or inadvertently. Also implied is the exclusion of information about objections and counter-doctrines advanced by other persons. On this criterion, the *positivist* model of teaching is equivocal. On the one hand fealty to the empiricist distinction between verified fact and mere opinion might lead the teacher to adopt a 'stick to the facts' policy which implied that disputed doctrines are best omitted from the syllabus altogether (the 'neutrality gambit'). On the other hand, the teacher's own ideological stance is determinative of content, yet goes unchallenged because the requirements of successful behavioural programming tend to exclude the possibility of students being permitted to call this stance itself into question.

The *personalist* model of teaching would appear to fare well on the criterion of content because, irrespective of the literal content of instruction, a more basic content of self-development and personal relationship would be registering with the learner, in a learning environment allegedly the very opposite of authoritarian. But this view neglects the inevitability of the teacher having to take a stand on the ground rules considered appropriate to human interaction, the possibilities varying from strong paternalism to indulgent libertarianism.[9] At the paternalistic extreme lies the firm inculcation of specific moral doctrines about personal interactions; at the libertarian extreme, advocacy by default of the relativistic doctrine that 'if the parties consent, then all is permitted'. But can the latter reasonably be labelled indoctrination, if it occurs by default as a result of the teacher's striving for total openness'?

The oddity of this move demonstrates the problem of using content as our main criterion, and the problem persists if we use it to appraise the *rationalist* model of teaching. At first, the *rationalist* approach shows up well because it stresses the critical examination of what is taught, and the comparative evaluation of doctrines. But what if we inadvertently represent as truths requiring no further examination, knowledge claims that are subsequently shown to be false? To call this indoctrination in the pejorative sense of the term, given that all our present 'knowledge' is theoretically open to revision, is to banish entirely the alternative concept of 'education'. It is more plausible to suppose that there is something wrong with this way of analysing the concept of indoctrination.

We are brought then to the criterion of intention. I shall say that indoctrination has been attempted if it can be shown that the teacher's intention in teaching P was either to represent as true something known by the teacher to be in dispute amongst intelligent and informed people, or to preclude examination of the evidence for P. This analysis, while stressing intention as a necessary condition, enables us also to identify when criteria of content and method are relevant, and facilitates our critique of teaching models.

The *positivist* model is now the one most vulnerable to the charge of indoctrination, because to the difficulties previously noted is added the fact that the teacher's intention is to cause a determinate outcome. If it is objected that one such intended outcome might well be the enhancement of critical thinking, one is obliged to reply that critical thinking is an open-ended objective, not strictly predictable, hard to assess by scientific methods pre-supposing 'right answers', and hard to promote other than by teachers basing their own teaching strategies on it. The *rationalist* model again fares well, because here the teacher intends above all to enhance the learner's rational autonomy. Nevertheless such a stance is not thereby rendered neutral to ideological values, chief of which is the priority given to the critical, analytic, objective intellect. It is arguable that rationalist approaches have indoctrinated many students to be long on criticism, short on commitment and compassion.

The *personalist* model continues to vacillate. None would question that the teacher's intention is to lead the pupil towards self-realisation, empathy and a commitment to the integrity of other persons. This puts flesh on the bones of the *rationalist* model. But it remains unclear whether such intention stops short of moulding the pupil in the teacher's own image. This is the nub of the question being addressed in this paper, and we must look further into the notion of 'educative intentions'.

Educative intentions

So far I have been concerned to ask how each of the three teaching models stands with respect to the concept of indoctrination. But this question will only be bothersome to those who favour a particular concept of education stressing the development of rational and responsible individuals. For them, indoctrination is a pejorative term antithetical to education. Gatchel's[10] description of how the two concepts have evolved rightly, I think, associates this concept of education with liberal democratic ideology, thereby implying that for those who do not give 'education' this value loading, indoctrination may not necessarily be seen as miseducative. Totalitarian regimes of both past and present illustrate the point in their use of schools to secure the allegiance of the young. Hence it is inevitable that one's concept of education will turn out to be normative, requiring one to admit that certain values are programmed into one's usage; values which require to be justified. The ideological question cannot be avoided by an allegedly neutral analysis.

I suggest that this is the conclusion which has been forced upon R S Peters during his valuable attempts to analyse the concept of education. The beginning of his pilgrimage was an attempt to achieve a normatively neutral analysis. It was then pointed out to him that though he probably had isolated one major concept, there were also others underlying much common usage. He responded by making the modified claim that his 'more differentiated' concept was the one mainly current in 'educational circles'[11] and therefore worth mapping. It was a concept, he said, that 'accorded a central position (to) the development of knowledge and understanding.[12] So does the *rationalist* model of teaching, and it is now proper to suggest that there is another concept of education also current in educational circles which is more *personalist*, and which supplements the development of rational autonomy with the nurture of goodwill towards other persons and a willingness to commit oneself to the feelings and relationships proven, by personal experience as well as by rational reflection, to be enriching and mutual.

Peters rests his case on appeal to widespread usage in educational circles. I believe I can do the same in respect of this more *personalistic* concept, which is much in evidence in current progressivist and free school literature, and in debates about 'open education'. It has always been a part of educational theories built on Judaeo-Christian assumptions, which were given new life in the post-war period in Britain by people like Arnaud Reid and M V C Jeffreys. Given that a good dose of analytic philosophy was needed to pull the visionaries back to earth,[13] we are now able to see that the outcome was not less normatively committed. It is now time, I suggest, to bring the two streams together.

A starting point could well be Jeffreys' emphasis[14] on persons as rational and moral beings, in whose education the deepening of feeling is as important as the sharpening of thinking. Then there is Philip Phenix's criticism[15] that the current conception of rationality tends to exclude 'the life of feeling, conscience, imagination, and other processes that are not rational in the strict sense'.

Responding to such cues, we may then come to see the school as a place for 'tuning up', as it were, the cognitive and affective capacities of learners, so that each may more effectively and sensitively understand his or her environment, and be better placed to exercise autonomous choice in establishing an appropriate and personal life-style. And what of 'commitment' as an educational objective? It is probable that Jeffreys was less accommodating than he should have been of the pluralist character of modern society, and that he cherished an ideal of greater ideological homogeneity in the school than was even then possible or desirable. I think he has been proven right, however, in his insistence that value neutrality is not an option, and that we must therefore negotiate a consensus concerning human values and community purposes which will serve to create a humane climate in the school and provide ethical parameters for teacher behaviour.

It is on the assumption that a view of education embracing these conditions can be formulated, that I affirm the possibility of developing ethical guidelines to monitor teacher intentionality with respect to disclosing one's value-stance to the learner. I propose now to identify four of the possible stances the teacher may adopt, and to assess them in the light of the foregoing analysis.

Exclusive partiality

The first stance I shall call 'exclusive partiality'. By this is meant an intention on the part of teachers to impart their own value stance to the pupils in a manner precluding challenge. Convinced religious believers, for instance, especially if teaching in a church school, may well feel that it is in the students' best interests to implant in them those things that they most surely believe to be true, notwithstanding that there are intelligent and informed people outside who are of contrary opinion. Clearly, in the light of our earlier comments, this is indoctrination, not education, calculated to pre-empt the personal commitments of the learner. From the medieval inquisition to the modern psychiatric prisons of Russia, this attitude reveals a totalitarian intuition that fears or denies the possibility of rational autonomy. Where religious educators have this attitude, what emerges is a heavily paternalistic version of the *personalist* model of teaching. Where religious perspectives are discounted, as in, say, the approach of B F Skinner[16] the result is the *positivist* model at its most brash.

Exclusive neutrality

Paralleling the emergence of the secular democratic state, there was a reaction against the ideologically committed school and the indoctrination that was supposed to occur inevitably within it. So sharp was the acrimony of the nineteenth century debate that some pressed for a teacher stance which I shall represent by the words 'exclusive neutrality'. I am obliged to lay down a stipulation here, because the term 'neutrality' is also used in other ways, sometimes to mean what I shall later term 'impartiality'.[17] I am applying 'exclusive neutrality' to the policy of excluding from the curriculum any subject-matter which contains propositions about beliefs and values that are matters of serious controversy in the community at large.

One motive in the nineteenth century for advocating the total exclusion of such content from the curriculum (and therefore, by implication, from the teacher's self-disclosure) was an exasperated resolve to keep the dogs of strife beyond the school walls. A second motive was to make the curriculum reflect the confident scientific positivism of the time, which asserted that we need only be concerned with that which had been experimentally verified. E J Stormon[18] catches the mood: 'The belief that there is an objective series of facts, etc., which can be fairly satisfactorily delimited, gives rise to the idea that a neutral curriculum of studies can be devised. By restricting oneself to what can be verified or tested, and refraining from affirmations and denials about everything else, one would hope, by this account, to achieve neutrality' He later brands this hope a chimera, but its logical positivist roots have withered faster than its fruits in curriculum design. Both motives influenced developments in my own country of Australia, producing a bleached and patchy educational garment. Similar trends in the USA, particularly in the area of religious studies, were reinforced by the more multi-cultural complexion of its society and a hard-line legal separation of church and state.

In the light of the concept of education commended earlier, the neutralist stance cannot be allowed. The degree of controversy surrounding the excluded doctrines testifies to their significance in the environment which we are pledged to help the child understand. The teacher's silence on such matters tacitly implies that they are unimportant to the business of living, and failure to discuss this as a value claim is indoctrination of a specially pernicious kind, given that consideration of the ends of life as distinct from the means is the area which suffers most from such an embargo. Just such a charge was levied against the American school in Jacques Maritain's telling critique in 1943.[19] Those committed to the *rationalist* model of teaching chafe at the confinement of enquiry; *personalists* lament the neglect of personal values and life-commitments.

Neutral impartiality

Stipulation is again forced upon me when I identify the third possible stance as 'neutral impartiality'.[20] This position, heeding criticisms of the neutrality gambit, requires that the curriculum include examination of all the modes of thought and experience which figure importantly in the life of society. The teacher, however, in situations where disputed beliefs are in question, is charged to function as an impartial arbitrator whose own personal stance is concealed in the interests of avoiding undue psychological pressure on the pupils. One would expect such a stance to fit closely with the *rationalist* model of teacher, and it does.

Criticism comes, of course, from those of *personalist* temper, and relates to both the desirability and the possibility of teachers concealing their own ideological stance. As to desirability, it is claimed that students are presented with a distorted image of humanness in the teacher. *Personalists* insist that teaching is primarily an existential encounter, so that the teacher not only imparts truths and skills by instruction but is, in person, 'a truth for students'.[21] Hence, the attempt to conceal one's personal stance sets at risk our declared curriculum objectives. It may be that the student interprets the teacher's uncommittedness as an endorsement of that fence-sitting spectator stance which looks with critical detachment at the passing show but avoids becoming involved. In the words of Mary Warnock, 'it is hard for pupils, especially if they are quite young, to realise that the neutral teacher is only play-acting'.[22] Alternatively, the impression may be conveyed, particularly in some forms of 'values clarification', that beliefs and values, being ultimately unprovable, are essentially private and to be judged solely by the psychological criterion that they keep the particular believer happy. Alan L Lockwood[23] makes an important point in relation to the 'values clarification' approach which is worth mentioning here. He argues that much of the information solicited in values clarification sessions constitutes a threat to privacy rights.

Since this approach is often hailed as avoiding the perils of teacher partiality, it is the more invidious when no kindred self-disclosure is allowed or required of the teacher. In claiming that what he calls the 'moral development approach' avoids this danger, however, Lockwood exhibits a confidence in the neutral impartiality of the *rationalist* model which is unjustified, and reflects a 'content' view of indoctrination. The only ultimate safeguards against violation of privacy rights are empathy with the feelings of students and a teacher intentionality guided by a professional ethic. Or again, if students press teachers to take a stand on some issue – on which, incidentally, they have all been taking stands – and they decline, despite having advocated rational appraisal, then the very commitment to rationality itself is impugned.[24] Each of these possible consequences of neutral impartiality represents an ideological option, not a neutral position at all. And the dice are loaded towards non-involvement in the common good.

It is not just that neutral impartiality is undesirable because, if successful, it negates important curriculum objectives in the way just described. At a deeper level it is never finally successful. The question may reasonably be asked: can any person, in daily contact with other persons, avoid ideological self-disclosure? Assuredly not. The amount that students are able to infer from unspoken cues and random comments is considerable and often uncomfortably accurate, as I have frequently confirmed by conversation with pupils in Australia's allegedly neutral state systems. The clandestine way in which these data are acquired, however, creates uneasiness about the part beliefs should play in one's public and personal roles, and failure to submit these data, as well as that gathered in class, to rational inspection renders their influence all the more pernicious. And what if they get it wrong? Scrambled messages are dangerous, and a child who admires a teacher may, in the absence of an enquiry into basic motivations, elect to emulate superficial behaviours for the wrong reasons.

Committed impartiality

The fourth possible stance is 'committed impartiality'. In this case, teachers are encouraged both to foster critical analysis and discussion of the grounds for various beliefs and values, and to exhibit their own beliefs as additional data for analysis, provided that their procedures for teaching and assessing remain impartial. Here, it is claimed, the virtues of the neutral impartiality stance are preserved and its defects overcome. Both *rationalist* and *personalist* teachers should be satisfied. Certainly, if the policy can be implemented, then the conditions of the concept of education advocated earlier will be met.

For many thinkers, however, this is the major flaw in the proposal. They doubt that it can be done. It is claimed that precisely because the teacher's influence is as strong as *personalists* say it is, self-disclosure will tip the scales towards indoctrination. This is essentially an empirical claim and, as Kleinig[25] has pointed out, if the reason for advocating what I have called neutral impartiality is fear of 'the excessive authority which the teacher's word possesses', then the solution lies not in adoption of this dubious policy but in an examination of 'those features of the teaching situation, the teacher's methods, and the cultural background, which give rise to such excess'.

Some of the relevant empirical data would include the following. Firstly, the composition of state school staffs is now pluralistic, and students are therefore bound to meet many different value-examplars during their school life. Secondly, given that a policy of neutrality (of either kind) must rely at least as much on conscience as coercion for effective implementation, we may reasonably predict, along games-theory lines, that it will be less effective in muzzling the unethical teacher than the ethical one. Thus, at least in Australia, many teachers with strong moral convictions are standing diffidently by while representatives of radically deviant persuasions unashamedly proselytise in the classroom. I see distinct gains in creating a school climate where teachers can be asked to reveal what views they are representing to children, as contrasted with the hidden ideological agendas of many government schools.

It may occur to the reader that this position is inconsistent with my earlier stand on personal rights to privacy. But we are here talking about teachers, not students, and in view of their responsibility to guide the learning of children and youth, I deem it entirely proper to require them to come clean on the beliefs and values they propose to espouse in front of their students, and to exclude them from the classroom if these can be shown to be improper on grounds of irrelevance to the topic in hand, or imbalance in relation to the representation of alternative views.

Thirdly, recognition of the danger of excessive teacher influence should serve as a warning to take into account factors of human development. Young children are usually more vulnerable to teacher domination than older ones. At all ages, some are more vulnerable than others. And so on. But this is ultimately a challenge to professionalism on the teacher's part, which is compounded jointly of empirical expertise and ethical commitment. The present study has been addressed to the latter.

Assuming, then, that the case for a policy of committed impartiality can be sustained in such ways as these, we may now set out some ethical guidelines, using the following two counter-balancing statements.

1. In respect of important curriculum areas where there is substantial divergence in the beliefs and values of intelligent and informed people in society, the teacher shall encourage critical and compassionate discussion of alternative viewpoints; striving at all times to be impartial in the treatment of the students.
2. It is educationally valuable in such discussions − where relevant, and to the extent allowable in the light of the developmental levels of the students and of such contractual constraints as may be operative in the school − for teachers to reveal their own beliefs and values as committed persons, for consideration as additional data open to examination.

The question of contractual constraints

A postscript is called for in the light of a phrase used in the second of these guidelines which has not been debated in this paper: 'and of such contractual constraints as may be operative in the school'. The argument in this paper has been addressed to educationists, assuming firstly a willingness on their part to concur with a fairly eclectic view of education; and secondly a likelihood that most teachers' personal beliefs and values would fall comfortably within the range of possibilities considered permissible in liberal democratic community. It would, however, be quite ingenuous to expect that the general community would accept both of these assumptions without demur. In respect of the first assumption, many people are quite willing to endorse a mild version of indoctrination, and are conversely somewhat alarmed at the emphasis placed on critical thought. In respect of the second, this article has not been concerned with the nature and ethical legitimacy of constraints laid upon teachers by their conditions of employment and accountability to the community sponsoring the school. These matters call for another enquiry complementary to the present one. Our concern here has been confined to the question of whether, *prima facie*, pupils should ever be exposed to the teacher's own ideological stance.

Notes

1. M Mackie, *Educative Teaching,* Sydney, Angus and Robertson, 1968, p. 63.
2. J I Kleinig, 'Mill, children and rights,' *Educational Philosophy and Theory,* 8, 1976, pp. 1–16.
3. A Shumsky, *In Search of a Teaching Style,* New York, Appleton-Century, 1968.
4. R S Peters, *Ethics and Education,* London, George Allen and Unwin, 1966, pp. 111–112.
5. I A Snook, (ed.), *Concepts of Indoctrination,* London, Routledge and Kegan Paul, 1972.
6. J Wilson, 'Indoctrination and rationality,' in I A Snook, *op. cit.,* p. 20.
7. *Ibid.,* p. 17.
8. The customary connotation in this case is epistemologically misleading. It neglects the post-positivist realisation that most general 'propositions known to be true' are theory-dependent, that is, indebted to views (or doctrines) about the way the world is to be cognised. Once this is conceded, then the potential scope of indoctrinative content is extended well beyond those areas, such as, morals, religion, politics and possibly economics, with which the term 'doctrines' is customarily associated. R Norman illustrates that value-laden nature of *all* school studies in his essay 'The neutral teacher?' in S C Brown (ed.), *Philosophers Discuss Education,* London, MacMillan, 1975, pp. 176f.
9. Compare the disagreements between two theorists as close in spirit as Martin Buber and Carl Rogers, for example on the degree of mutuality between client and therapist (cf. child and teacher). Rogers argues for full mutuality, Buber for recognition that the relation is lop-sided because one person is seeking help and the other is giving it. See M Buber, 'Dialogue between Martin Buber and Carl R Rogers,' in M Buber, *The Knowledge of Man,* London, George Allen and Unwin, 1961.
10. R H Gatchel, 'The evolution of the concept,' in I A Snook, *op. cit..*
11. P H Hirst, and R S Peters, *The Logic of Education,* London, Routledge and Kegan Paul, 1970, p. 24.
12. *Ibid.,* p. ix.
13. Cf. Peters' acerbic comment on Buber's I-Thou, that it 'is sometimes held up as an ideal. But to be near the earth is not altogether unbecoming for those who live on it' (P H Hirst and R S Peters, *op. cit.,* p. 98).
14. M V C Jeffreys, *Personal Values in the Modern World,* Harmondsworth, Penguin 1962.
15. P H Phenix, *Realms of Meaning,* New York, McGraw-Hill, 1964, p. 21.
16. B F Skinner, *Science and Human Behavior,* New York, Free Press and Collier-Macmillan, 1953.
17. Actual uses of the two terms vary widely. Thus I A Snook 'Neutrality and the schools,' *Educational Theory,* 22, 1972, pp. 278–285, uses the term 'neutrality' in a way which reflects my third stance above, whereas D H Munro endorses my usage in his essay 'Pawns against the devil,' in *Melbourne Studies in Education, 1963,* London, Melbourne University Press, 1964.
18. E J Stormon, 'Inadequacies in the concept of neutrality,' in *Melbourne Studies in Education, 1963,* London, Melbourne University Press, 1964.
19. J Maritain, *Education at the Crossroads,* New Haven, Connecticut, Yale University Press, 1943, pp. 1–16.
20. The qualification of 'Impartiality' is made necessary by ambiguities in usage, some admitting of the teacher taking a stand, some not. Thus J I Kleinig, 'Principles of neutrality in education,' *Educational Philosophy and Theory,* 8, 1976, p. 13, suggests that 'a person who is impartial is *not necessarily* one who does not take a stand, but rather one whose stand, if he takes one, is not affected by irrelevant considerations.' I acknowledge the usage, but find Kleinig's sense awkward in the present analysis because it presupposes rational agreement on which considerations are relevant.

21. G S Belkin, 'The teacher as hero,' *Educational Theory,* 22, 1972, pp. 411–419.
22. M Warnock, 'The neutral teacher,' in S C Brown (ed.), *Philosophers Discuss Education,* London, Macmillan, 1975, p. 170.
23. A Lockwood, 'Values education and the right to privacy,' *Journal of Moral Education,* 7, 1978, pp. 17–20.
24. M Warnock, *op. cit.,* pp. 165–168.
25.· J I Kleinig, 'Mill, children and rights,' *op. cit.,* p. 15.

8. Indoctrination and rationality

The vexed issue of indoctrination has already been raised, particularly in section 7. In this section it is explored more fully, with particular reference to formative and critical Christian education.

Elmer Thiessen's article, which focuses on 'Indoctrination and doctrines', was first published in *Journal of Philosophy of Education*, 16, 1982, pp.3 – 17. It argues against the view that teaching doctrines involves indoctrination. The characteristics that have been usually attributed to doctrinal beliefs are surveyed under the headings of their logical status, scope and 'momentous character'. It is claimed both that some of the features listed under these headings do not apply to religious beliefs and that all of them are present, at least to some degree, 'in the paradigm example of non-doctrine, science'. On the basis of this discussion, Thiessen offers a revised analysis of the concept 'doctrine' as used in discussions of indoctrination.[1]

Tasos Kazepides enters the fray as a critic of such attempts to defend the teaching of religious and other beliefs against the charge of indoctrination. His article, published in the Proceedings of the Forty-third Annual Meeting of the Philosophy of Education Society, *Philosophy of Education 1987* (Normal, Illinois), pp. 229 – 240, is entitled 'Indoctrination, doctrines and the foundations of rationality'. Kazepides claims that indoctrination can only be distinguished by its content of doctrinal beliefs (and not, for example, by its method or intention, which are parasitic on the doctrines being inculcated), and that 'there are no such doctrines in science'. Rather, 'the paradigm cases of indoctrination are to be found in religious communities and institutions'. Such (unfalsifiable) doctrines, Kazepides claims, 'do not belong within our rational tradition'. The article concludes by distinguishing these doctrines from the 'river-bed propositions' or assumptions of scientific or common sense believing. These are unavoidable certainties that allow us to think, while doctrines can be doubted and act as 'stoppers that control, limit and channel thought . . . and frustrate critical thinking'.[2]

'Religious upbringing and rational autonomy,' by Ronald S Laura and Michael Leahy, was first published in *Journal of Philosophy of Education*, 23, 1989, pp. 253–265. The authors join those who argue that religious upbringing is compatible with a liberal ideal of rational autonomy, and 'indeed that a respect for that autonomy is a necessary condition of an authentic religious commitment' (see also article 4.1, and section 6). The contribution of this essay to the indoctrination debate centres on the issues of unshakeable beliefs and rival religious beliefs. The 'river-bed propositions' discussed in 8.2 reappear here as 'epistemic primitives' with 'presuppositional', 'constitutive' and 'organisational' functions. The belief that God exists has such a status, and 'a religious upbringing is not necessarily shown to have violated the liberal canon of rational autonomy by the fact that it produces a belief in God that is resistant to falsification', provided that such beliefs are capable of revision — but not by 'a process of evidential assessment'. With reference to the closing of a learner's mind to alternative (religious) positions, the authors offer an account of religious upbringing that involves seeing one's beliefs as revisable and learning the critical apparatus for understanding and appraising the assumptions that lie behind all such beliefs.[3]

The final article in this section is Michael Leahy's 'Indoctrination, evangelisation, catechesis and religious education', first published in *British Journal of Religious Education*, 12, 1990, pp. 137–144. Leahy welcomes the recent revival of discussion on the concept of indoctrination. He begins with a study of the 'standard accounts', that is the intention-, method- and content-accounts (this last with particular reference to the 'falsifiability criterion'), before moving on to articulate Laura's alternative account of indoctrination (see article 8.3) with its concern for teaching the 'critical apparatus' needed for a rational appraisal of taught beliefs. Leahy applies these insights to a distinction between *educational* forms of teaching (which do not 'violate the educational purpose of the classroom') and *religious* forms (which do violate the '"norm" of respect for the autonomy of the school classroom', but do not necessarily violate the '"norms" of respect for freedom and truth'). These latter forms, for example evangelisation and catechesis, are claimed to 'have their place in voluntary settings'.

Dr Elmer J Thiessen teaches philosophy at Medicine Hat College, Alberta, Canada. Dr Tasos Kazepides teaches in the Faculty of Education at Simon Fraser University, Burnaby,

British Columbia, Canada. Professor Ronald S Laura is Professor of Education in the Department of Education of the University of Newcastle, Newcastle, NSW, Australia. Dr Michael Leahy resides in Victoria, Australia.

Notes

1. See also Elmer J Thiessen, *Teaching for Commitment: liberal education, indoctrination and Christian nurture*, Leominster, Gracewing; Montreal, McGill-Queen's University Press, 1993.
2. Cf. article 4.2, and note 1 on p. 170. Other papers by Kazepides are listed in the bibliography.
3. For other articles by Laura see the bibliography.

8.1 Indoctrination and doctrines

Elmer J Thiessen

Although there is still disagreement among philosophers as to what indoctrination means, there is widespread agreement that indoctrination is in some way related to doctrines. This relation between indoctrination and doctrines is primarily understood in two different ways, which are not always clearly distinguished. Many assume an etymological connection between indoctrination and doctrines. R S Peters, for example, argues that 'whatever else indoctrination may mean it obviously has something to do with doctrines'.[1] Antony Flew bluntly states, 'No doctrines, no indoctrination'.[2] This is the way in which the content criterion of indoctrination is generally described. Doctrines are a logically necessary condition of indoctrination.

It is secondly widely maintained that when one is teaching doctrines, there is a high probability that one is indoctrinating. Antony Flew, for example, argues not only that indoctrination is limited to doctrines, but also that the teaching of doctrines very probably involves indoctrination (*Concepts of Indoctrination,* pp. 75ff., 113f.). Even the philosophers who reject the first relation suggesting that doctrinal content is a logically necessary condition of indoctrination, nevertheless still want to maintain that there is a strong contingent connection between indoctrination and doctrines. White and Snook, for example, reject the content criterion of indoctrination, but still argue that the teaching of religious doctrine most often involves indoctrination (*Concepts of Indoctrination,* p. 219).[3]

In this paper I wish to focus primarily on the first claim which suggests that indoctrination is conceptually related to doctrinal content. Despite the widespread acceptance of the content criterion, I want to argue that it is not a necessary condition of indoctrination. Much of the argument used to undermine the first claim will also serve to weaken the second claim. Thus, it will also be suggested that the frequently made assumption concerning the high probability of indoctrination when teaching doctrine is not as strong as is generally maintained. I will further limit my considerations largely to the area of religious beliefs and religious instruction since these are frequently taken as the paradigms of doctrines and indoctrination.

'Doctrines'

It should be obvious that before it is possible to evaluate whether or not indoctrination is limited to the doctrinal sphere it is essential to become clear as to the meaning of the notion 'doctrine', sometimes also identified with or seen as related to ideology.[4]

What is surprising is that despite the widespread acceptance of the content criterion of 'indoctrination' which limits indoctrination to doctrines, very little attention has been focused specifically on the concept 'doctrine' which is presupposed by this criterion. Snook, among others, points to this neglect and then goes on to give, as his 'principal argument' against the content criterion, that the concept 'doctrine' is itself extremely vague (*Indoctrination and Education,* p. 32). But surely this in itself cannot be used as an argument against the content criterion of 'indoctrination'. If a concept is vague, then for the philosopher, this is merely a call for further analysis.

I therefore propose to examine some of the vague descriptions of doctrines as found in the literature on indoctrination. I will limit myself to three authors, Wilson, Flew and Gregory/Woods who make the content criterion primary in their analysis of 'indoctrination', and who therefore have more to say about doctrines than most other writers.[5]

Logical status of doctrinal beliefs

Frequent reference is made, in describing the content criterion of 'indoctrination', to the logical status of those beliefs which are subject to indoctrination (*Aims in Education,* p. 28; *Concepts of Indoctrination,* pp. 107, 172). This phrase is useful in grouping one set of characteristics thought to be essential to doctrines. For Wilson, the essential aspect of the logical status of doctrinal beliefs is that they are uncertain (*Aims in Education,* pp. 27ff.). For Flew, the essential characteristic of a doctrine is that it involves beliefs which are 'either false or not known to be true' (*Concepts of Indoctrination,* pp. 70f., 112f.). Gregory/Woods agree with Flew, except that they do not wish to include false beliefs or 'manifest untruths' as doctrine (*Concepts of Indoctrination,* p. 171). The above summary characterisations of doctrines are, however, highly ambiguous, and thus we need to unpack the various meanings implicit in these descriptions of the logical status of doctrines.

False beliefs: Flew suggests, first of all, that doctrines may involve false beliefs. He interprets Wilson as also defining doctrines in terms of 'the actual falsehood' of beliefs involved (*Concepts of Indoctrination,* pp. 68f.). Wilson, in places, describes beliefs subject to indoctrination as irrational and at times seems to equate these with false beliefs (*Aims in Education,* pp. 35f., 38; *Concepts of Indoctrination,* p. 103). Gregory/Woods, however, explicitly reject this characterisation of doctrines, although one example used at the end of their article would suggest that doctrines do include false beliefs (*Concepts of Indoctrination,* pp. 171, 187).

Beliefs with insufficient or no evidence: we must next consider the frequently recurring phrase 'not known to be true', which, unfortunately, is again highly ambiguous. To say that a doctrine involves a belief not known to be true may mean that there is no evidence for the belief or at least not sufficient evidence. Although these two notions are different, I believe they can be conveniently grouped together. Wilson describes these beliefs as uncertain in the sense 'that we have no logical right to be sure' of them, there is 'no publicly accepted evidence for them' (*Aims in Education,* pp. 27–28). Flew contrasts beliefs which can 'on the best possible evidence, reasonably be said to be known; and those at the opposite extreme for which, whether or not they happen to be true, there is no evidence at all' (*Concepts of Indoctrination,* p. 107). It is the latter which are subject to indoctrination for Flew. Flew approves of Wilson's 'strong emphasis on sufficient and publicly admissible evidence' as a way of avoiding indoctrination (*Concepts of Indoctrination,* p. 82). Gregory/Woods do not explicitly define doctrines in terms of beliefs for which there is no evidence, although they do seem to hint at a lack of scientific evidence for doctrinal beliefs (*Concepts of Indoctrination,* p. 173).

Beliefs with ambiguous evidence: another interpretation of the phrase 'not known to be true or false' is alluded to most clearly by Gregory/Woods. Doctrines on this interpretation include beliefs for which the evidence is ambiguous. 'Doctrines provide, as it were, room for manoeuvre in debate. There is something to be said in support, and something to be said against' (*Concepts of Indoctrination* p. 172). The uncertainty that Wilson and Flew talk about could be attributed to the ambiguity of evidence. Thus, Flew also describes doctrines as involving 'debatable issues' *(Concepts of Indoctrination,* p. 108).

Unfalsifiable beliefs: another important characteristic frequently associated with doctrines is that they cannot be verified or falsified. When Wilson is talking about a deeper level of uncertainty that characterises doctrines such as religious, political and moral beliefs, in contrast to scientific beliefs, he is suggesting that the former are uncertain in the sense that they cannot be verified or falsified. 'We do not know what sort of evidence to look for .... We cannot even be sure that any question of truth, falsehood, or evidence arises at all' with doctrinal beliefs (*Aims in Education,* pp. 29f.). Wilson seems to be alluding to the positivist principle of verification or falsification by which metaphysical, moral and religious beliefs are classified as factually meaningless because there are no criteria by which to settle questions of truth or falsehood.

Flew might be interpreted as alluding to this when he describes indoctrination as 'teaching as known the sort of thing which really is not or *cannot be known'* (*Concepts of Indoctrination,* p. 78 – my emphasis). This would certainly be in line with other articles

Flew has written on religion, where he uses the positivist principle of falsification to show that religious language is factually meaningless (cf. *Concepts of Indoctrination,* p. 116).

Snook and White both interpret Gregory/Woods as also defining doctrines as unverifiable (*Indoctrination and Education,* p. 33; *Concepts of Indoctrination,* pp. 192f.). It would appear that Gregory/Woods do have this interpretation in mind when they characterise an example of a 'pure doctrine' such as religion, in the following way: 'It is logical nonsense to talk, in the sphere of religion of the setting up of hypotheses and of the subsequent attempt to confirm or disconfirm them experimentally' (*Concepts of Indoctrination,* p. 173, cf. p. 168).

Beliefs held incorrigibly: the question of verification or falsification is often confused with what I want to argue is a quite different notion of 'incorrigibility'. Verification or falsification has to do with the logical status of the beliefs involved. But sometimes it is not the beliefs themselves but a certain psychological fact about persons holding these beliefs that makes it impossible to prove these beliefs false to the believer. Thus, doctrines are sometimes described as beliefs which cannot be proved false because *believers* in these doctrines view them as incorrigible.

I believe both Gregory/Woods and Flew have confused the two different notions of incorrigibility and verification/falsification. Gregory/Woods, for example, describe doctrines thus: 'From the standpoint of the believer they have the status of universal, unfalsifiable truths' (*Concepts of Indoctrination,* p. 168). Here we have both a reference to the status of the beliefs themselves, and a reference to the believer. Gregory/Woods clearly move to the notion of incorrigibility when they stress that it is *people* 'who elevate these doctrines to the status of incorrigible truths, who passionately believe in their essential truth', or who hold them as 'absolutely and incorrigibly true' (*Concepts of Indoctrination,* pp. 177, 167f.).

I believe Flew is at times also referring to this psychological characteristic of the way in which people hold on to doctrinal beliefs regardless of the counter evidence. He criticises the traditional Christian church 'which seeks to fix in the minds of children an unshakeable conviction of the truth of its specific doctrines' (*Concepts of Indoctrination,* pp. 114, 76). Thus associated with doctrines is this fact about how they are held with unshakeable conviction. Strictly speaking, this feature of incorrigibility should not be considered under the heading 'logical status of beliefs' at all as it involves a psychological description of the believer. I am treating it here because it is so often associated with the issue of falsification which does involve the question of the logical status of religious beliefs.

Beliefs lacking public agreement: the final interpretation of doctrines as beliefs 'not known to be true or false' involves the lack of public agreement concerning these beliefs. Wilson's description of religious, political and moral beliefs as 'uncertain' clearly turns also on the fact that there is no 'publicly-accepted evidence' for them (*Aims in Education,* p. 28). Even the characterisation of these beliefs as involving a deeper level of uncertainty having to do with the question of whether or not there are any truth criteria involves the problem of lack of agreement. We are agreed, Wilson states, on how to answer scientific questions, but we are not agreed on how to answer metaphysical and moral questions (*Aims in Education,* p. 29). 'These are complex matters, about which philosophers are still not in agreement' (*Aims of Education,* p. 30).

Flew's description of doctrines as 'debatable issues' includes the connotation that these are issues over which there is public disagreement (*Concepts of Indoctrination,* p. 108). Flew chides Wilson for not sufficiently taking into account the fact of 'disagreements about what, or what sort of (thing) is or is not known' (*Concepts of Indoctrination,* p. 78). There is also an implicit reference to public disagreement in Gregory/Woods' statement, 'Doctrines provide, as it were, room for manoeuvre in debate' (*Concepts of Indoctrination,* p. 172).

Scope of doctrinal beliefs

Another important set of characteristics frequently associated with doctrines has to do with their scope. There are two aspects of the scope of doctrinal beliefs that need to be dealt with.

Systems of beliefs: Gregory/Woods make some passing references to 'systems of belief' as another sense of 'doctrine' in the *Oxford English Dictionary:* 'A body or system of principles or tenets; a doctrinal or theoretical system'.

We have already seen how Flew holds that, as a necessary condition, a doctrine is a belief which is either false or at least not known to be true. But this is not sufficient, because as he himself admits, there are many such beliefs which are not classified as doctrines. In order to be classified thus, they must satisfy another condition. They must be 'somehow tied up with something wider and more ideological' (*Concepts of Indoctrination,* p. 71). What Flew means by this is not entirely clear. Part of the meaning seems to be that doctrines involve a wider system of beliefs. This is how White interprets Flew's statement but I believe there is more to it than this (*Concepts of Indoctrination,* pp. 190f., cf. pp. 122f).

Wide scope and generality: I believe the real focus of Flew's description of doctrines as 'somehow tied up with something wider and more ideological', has to do with the wide ranging implications of a doctrinal belief. This is the point stressed by Gregory/Woods. In contrast to other beliefs, doctrines 'have a scope and generality that others do not' (*Concepts of Indoctrination,* p. 168, cf. pp. 174, 185). Often they entail a complete world-view or a comprehensive philosophy of life. This broad scope of doctrine may be due to the fact that they involve a complete system of beliefs. But a single statement involving a fundamental presupposition of a system of beliefs, can itself have a broad scope. Thus I believe Flew does allow for doctrines which are individual statements (for example *Concepts of Indoctrination,* p. 144).

The momentous character of doctrinal beliefs

There is a final set of characteristics of doctrines, stressed by Gregory/ Woods, which are conveniently grouped as involving various aspects of the momentousness of these beliefs.

Importance of beliefs: doctrines, such as we find in religion and politics, involve beliefs that are 'of great moment to mankind involving as they do considerations relating to man's (*sic*) place in the universe and the ways in which societies may best be organised' (*Concepts of Indoctrination,* p. 166, cf. p. 168). The importance of these beliefs derives in part from their scope which we have considered in the previous section. This description is no doubt somewhat vague. But Gregory/Woods are trying to do justice to the fact that generally we would not call unimportant details 'doctrines'.

Self-involving beliefs: Gregory/Woods argue that because doctrines are matters of great moment to mankind, 'acceptance of the doctrinal system of ideology is no mere academic matter — there is commitment to act in particular ways, to profess and act out a particular value and way of life' (*Concepts of Indoctrination,* p. 166, cf. pp. 177f.). Doctrinal beliefs are 'intimately related to action and purposive activity in a way in which many other beliefs are not' (*Concepts of Indoctrination.* p. 168).

Wilson also alludes to this feature of doctrines. He suggests that political and moral beliefs are 'closer to the heart of the individual than other beliefs and skills' (*Aims in Education,* p. 27). Commenting on the content criterion of 'indoctrination', he argues that 'it is not merely contingent that those areas which involve free commitment — preeminently morality, politics and religion — offer model cases for indoctrination' (*Concepts of Indoctrination,* p. 103).

Beliefs promoted with evangelistic zeal: there is also a certain evangelistic zeal which seems to characterise those holding doctrinal beliefs. Gregory/Woods trace this zeal to the fact that such beliefs are considered to be of momentous concern to mankind. The importance of doctrinal beliefs 'leads to a strong urge to convince others, the waverers, the unbelievers, of their essential truth' (*Concepts of Indoctrination,* p. 168, cf. pp. 177f.). This feature is also related to a previous point concerning the actions and attitudes implied by a doctrinal belief (see 'self-involving beliefs'). It would seem that doctrines necessarily entail commitment to evangelism or the persuasion of others to accept these beliefs.

Beliefs backed by a group or an institution: a final aspect of doctrinal beliefs involves their social or institutional character. This feature is again related to the previous points. It is because of the importance of these beliefs, and the need to engage in evangelism, that we find them promoted by a group or an institution. Thus Gregory/Woods and Flew make frequent reference to the Roman Church or the Communist Party as providing the context out of which doctrines arise (*Concepts of Indoctrination,* pp. 166, 187f., 75f., 106, 109).

Religion and science

We are now in a position to evaluate the above characterisations of doctrines as found in the literature on the concept of indoctrination. Before dealing with the major criticism to be made I wish to make a few preliminary comments about past descriptions of doctrines.

It should first of all be noted that there is a criticism implied by the very fact that such a detailed analysis of the past descriptions of doctrines has been required. Given the long-standing and general acceptance of the content criterion, and given the fact that there exists a considerable body of literature dealing with the concept of indoctrination, one would expect that the concept 'doctrine' would already have been clarified. One would further not expect philosophers steeped in the analytic tradition to describe doctrines in vague and ambiguous terms such as the phrase 'not known to be true'. Snook is therefore justified in objecting to the content criterion of 'indoctrination' because of the extreme vagueness of the concept of doctrines (*Indoctrination and Education,* p. 32).

Secondly, I would like to point out that some of the characteristics identified above contradict each other. For example, if it is maintained that doctrines cannot be verified or falsified (see 'unfalsifiable beliefs'), then it cannot also be maintained that doctrines involve those beliefs that are false (see 'false beliefs'). To identify a doctrine as false is to admit the possibility of evidence or counter evidence. But this is precisely what is denied when it is claimed that doctrines cannot be verified or falsified. Further, to talk of 'no evidence' or 'lack of sufficient evidence' (see 'beliefs with insufficient or no evidence'), presupposes that it does make sense to talk of evidence or the lack of it. But to affirm, at the same time, that doctrines cannnot be verified or falsified is to reject the very possibility of talk of evidence, and is therefore again to contradict oneself.

There is a third problem involving the 'logical status' of doctrinal beliefs. If doctrines are defined as false beliefs, or as beliefs with no evidence, insufficient evidence, or even ambiguous evidence a fundamental question arises as to who it is who judges the beliefs to have this status. There are obviously differences of opinion as to whether a belief is false or lacks evidence, and this is problematic for those wishing to define 'doctrines' in terms of these criteria. Although this problem is touched on by some of the writers, I do not think it is adequately dealt with or resolved.

The major criticism I wish to make concerning past descriptions of doctrines is that the characteristics assigned to doctrines do not clearly and unproblematically distinguish paradigm cases of doctrine from paradigm cases of non-doctrine. There is general agreement among those defending the content criterion of 'indoctrination' that religious beliefs are a paradigm of doctrines, and scientific beliefs are a paradigm of non-doctrine. If, therefore, it can be established with some degree of plausibility that the characteristics dealt with in the previous section are present in scientific beliefs, or absent in religious beliefs, then I will have undermined the basic thrust of the content criterion of 'indoctrination', since the whole point of this criterion is to distinguish doctrinal from non-doctrinal beliefs and to limit indoctrination to the former.

I first of all wish to make some general comments about the relation of science and religion which will help to put my specific arguments into context. It must be admitted at the outset that, as Ian Barbour has noted, 'most writers today see science and religion as *strongly contrasting enterprises* which have essentially nothing to do with each other'.[6] However, there are an impressive number of writers, including anthropologists, philosophers, and scientists, who argue that religion and science are similar in aims, methods, and criteria by which to evaluate the fulfilment of these aims. Stewart Guthrie in a recent and important article of this topic argues this position and reviews the writers who also argue for a similarity between science and religion.[7] The issue is by no means settled, but this fact in itself already suggests that the distinction between paradigm cases of doctrine and non-doctrine is at least problematical. In what follows, I will be providing some specific argumentation for the similarity between science and religion. It will be argued that the criteria commonly used to differentiate religion, the paradigm of doctrines, from science, the paradigm of non-doctrine, do not clearly and unproblematically make the distinction they are trying to make.

Logical status of doctrinal beliefs

The first three descriptions of doctrines falling under the logical status of beliefs can be conveniently dealt with as a group. If doctrines are defined in terms of any or all of these criteria, then it should be rather obvious that science too contains doctrines. A review of the history of science would reveal many cases in which false beliefs were adhered to and promulgated. Similar considerations would also suggest that sometimes beliefs are accepted in science which are based on insufficient evidence and even on no evidence at all. Of course the latter phrase raises some additional problems, but these cannot be pursued here.

It can further be argued that there are certain presuppositions or first principles underlying science which various authors have recognised as not being susceptible to proof or evidence. The problem of presuppositions and their status is also related to the problem of verification/falsification, and thus I will postpone consideration of this topic until later.

Finally, it can also be shown that science contains beliefs for which the evidence is ambiguous. Progress in science rests in part on noting anomalies, a process which really involves a recognition of ambiguity in evidence. Various authors have pointed out that no theory ever fits all the relevant observations.[8] If so, it follows that there always remain some observations that seem to mitigate against any particular scientific theory. Thus, the acceptance of a scientific theory always takes place in the context of some ambiguity of evidence.

We have seen that another feature often attributed to doctrines involves their having the status of not being falsifiable or verifiable. It is quite understandable why Wilson, Flew, Gregory/Woods and others would choose the verification/falsification principle as a means of distinguishing doctrine from non-doctrine. One of the main objectives of positivism, which introduced this principle, was to distinguish science from metaphysics and theology, and to rule out the latter as factually meaningless.

It would seem however, that the choice of this principle to distinguish doctrine from non-doctrine is an unhappy one because it was precisely in its attempts to distinguish science from non-science (or nonsense) that positivism encountered most of its difficulties. The verification/falsification principle was revised again and again, largely due to the fact that each version was found, on closer examination, to be inadequate in distinguishing science from metaphysics and theology. Malcolm Diamond, in a recent review of the developments of the positivist movement, comments on the tenacity and even the partisanship that became more and more evident as the positivists pursued their objective.[9]

> There was, after all, something prejudicial and dogmatic about the tortuous efforts of the positivists to achieve a version of the verifiability principle with the right combination of permissiveness ('science-in') and restrictiveness ('metaphysics-out').

It would appear that there is general consensus that the positivists have failed to distinguish science from non-science on the basis of the principle of verification/falsification. Patricia Smart, for example, points to the 'notorious' difficulties of the criterion of verifiability or falsifiability, because a criterion which is stringent enough to exclude metaphysics also excludes propositions of science and a 'criterion which includes scientific statements also includes metaphysics'. Smart concludes that any attempt to define 'doctrines' on the basis of the positivist principle of verification or falsification will only serve to establish that science too contains doctrines.[10] Various writers such as Ronald S Laura and John F Miller have examined the logical status of presuppostions, first-order principles, or epistemic primitives in science and have argued that they are not verifiable or falsifiable.[11] Thus again it would seem that doctrines cannot be distinguished from non-doctrines on the basis of the verification/falsification principle.

We must next consider incorrigibility as a defining feature of 'doctrines'. It must be admitted that religious doctrines are often held in an unshakeable manner. But religious believers do sometimes become agnostics and atheists. There is evolution and change within religious thought. Thus this feature does not invariably accompany so-called doctrines.

It can further be shown that the holding of beliefs in an incorrigible manner is also frequently present in paradigm cases of non-doctrine. A survey of the history of science and other recognised disciplines would reveal many examples of theories stubbornly held on to despite evidence against them. In fact, Flew himself, in another context, gives one such example.[12]

Thomas Kuhn's analysis of the structure of scientific revolutions provides additional support for the claim that the holding of beliefs in an incorrigible manner might also characterise scientists.[13] Incorrigibility occurs both in 'normal science', where the majority of scientists do research under the guidance of a paradigm with its set of presuppositons and techniques which are seldom, if ever, critically examined, as well as in 'extraordinary science' where there is debate among proponents of competing paradigms, but where there are no trans-paradigmatic grounds for evaluating these paradigms. This leads one writer, interestingly, to express concern about the implication that this would make paradigm adoption 'closer to a religious than an intellectual endeavour'.[14]

There is finally some research, referred to by T F Green, which suggests that incorrigibility applies to the holding of beliefs in any areas of thought (*Concepts of Indoctrination,* pp. 29ff.). Thus, it would seem that incorrigibility also cannot be used uniquely to describe religious doctrines.

The final aspect of the logical status of doctrinal beliefs concerns the question as to whether doctrines can be defined in terms of beliefs about which there is public disagreement. This is a very common description and there does seem to be an initial plausibility about it. There does seem to be a tendency to label as doctrinal those areas where debate and disagreement abound. But this description of doctrines is also not without its problems.

There is first of all a problem as to how 'public' is to be defined in the expression 'public agreement'. Is a belief identified as a doctrine so long as less that 100% of the public agrees on it? Or is it only the experts that are consulted? But what if several of the experts disagree with 'established opinion'? Does this make it a doctrine? If public agreement is strictly defined as unanimous agreement by all of the public, then all beliefs are doctrines as it is surely evident that there is no belief that is not disputed by someone. It should also be evident that on this interpretation of 'public agreement', science also contains doctrines as the history of science reveals countless examples of disagreement, not only by the public at large, but also within the scientific community.[15]

If on the other hand, 'public agreement' is defined more loosely so as not to require 100% agreement by all of the public, or even by all the 'experts', then it turns out that religion is no longer doctrinal in nature. Religious beliefs are most often held by a community of people, often by a large community, which even includes many who would otherwise be considered quite rational. I therefore conclude that the notion of public agreement also will not distinguish the paradigm cases of doctrine from those that are non-doctrinal.

Scope of doctrinal beliefs

It has been suggested that doctrines are broad in scope, first of all in the sense that they are tied to a wider system of beliefs. It should be obvious that this feature will not serve to distinguish paradigm cases of doctrine from those that are non-doctrinal, because the sciences surely also involve broad systems of belief (*Indoctrination and Education,* p. 33). Gregory/Woods themselves admit that theories in science function as part of 'a very complex theoretical system' (*Concepts of Indoctrination,* p. 172). Various philosophers have come to see that it is precisely because science too is characterised by 'elaborate systematic conceptual structures' that difficulties arise concerning verification.[16]

It is also evident, as has been argued at length by J P White, that doctrines cannot only refer to 'systems of belief' (*Concepts of Indoctrination,* pp. 122f., 191ff.). We do talk of individual statements as doctrines. We not only speak of 'Catholic doctrine' but also of individual doctrines within Catholicism such as the doctrine of the future life, the doctrine of the infallibility of the Pope. Gregory/Woods themselves give some examples of single propositions which are called doctrines (*Concepts of Indoctrination,* pp. 172, 178, cf. p. 191). If it is argued that an individual statement is a doctrine only if it is tied to a wider doctrinal system of beliefs, as Flew intimates (*Concepts of Indoctrination,* p. 71), then all statements qualify, since all statements evolve in some way from a wider system of beliefs.

If we instead interpret the wide scope of doctrines in terms of the wide-ranging implications of these beliefs, then science again contains doctrines. Surely the principle of causality and determinism is just as broad in scope and generality as many religious claims. In fact many extend this scientific principle to all domains including that of religion. The same could be said for other first-order principles, theories and laws of science. All of them have wide-ranging implications. Broadness of scope, however interpreted, will not therefore distinguish science from the paradigm cases of doctrine.

The momentous character of doctrinal beliefs

This brings us to the final group of criteria, where doctrines are described in various ways as momentous beliefs. We first examined the characterisation of doctrines 'as of great moment to mankind', or 'of momentous concern to mankind'. But according to this, there are many doctrines in science as well. Surely the discovery of nuclear fission is of great moment or of momentous concern to mankind. Surely Darwin's evolutionary theory has been and still is of momentous concern to mankind, inspiring ethical theories, political theories, and perhaps even the horrible atrocities of the Hitler regime, as has been argued by some.[17]

Second Gregory/Woods also suggest that doctrinal beliefs are 'intimately related to action and purposive activity'. They entail commitment to act in accordance with the values inherent in them. There is an initial plausibility to this since the paradigm cases of doctrines, religion, politics and morality are all intimately related to actions and commitments. On the other hand, when one asserts or accepts a scientific theory or observation report, it seems that one can do so without committing oneself to future conduct or without expressing any personal attitude for or against what is asserted.

Before we can critically evaluate this feature of doctrines, we must take note of an ambiguity in the expression 'an intimate tie-up of doctrine and action' (*Concepts of Indoctrination,* p. 167). This expression can first of all be taken to mean that belief in a doctrine necessarily entails a 'commitment to act in particular ways'. Doctrines simply cannot be accepted as 'a mere academic matter' (*Concepts of Indoctrination,* p. 166). To believe is to be committed to certain actions or attitudes. Thus some have suggested that it is impossible to acknowledge the doctrine of God's existence and then not respond to God in worship or obedience. But secondly this phrase can also be interpreted to mean that doctrines are unique in that they entail certain 'action-beliefs'. Here we are not asking, as in the first interpretation, whether doctrines necessarily entail actual commitment. Rather, we are asking whether certain beliefs have as their entailments other beliefs as to what the believer ought to do, and this quite apart from the question as to whether the believer will actually do what he or she ought to do, or act as dictated by beliefs. Gregory/Woods argue, for example, that Catholic doctrine entails that the believer 'is expected to live his life in the sight of God and to strive at all times to see that the quality of that life measures up to the Divine law' (*Concepts of Indoctrination,* p. 167).

There are problems, however, with both interpretations. Surely it is possible for someone to believe that God exists and yet fail to respond in worship or obedience. This may be due to hypocrisy, irrationality, or the wilful refusal to respond as might normally be deemed appropriate. Roger Trigg states, 'It does not seem self-contradictory to imagine someone accepting fully that there is a God and repudiating him completely. This is presumably the position the Devil holds in Christian theology.'[18] This first interpretation of a connection between doctrine and commitment or action is therefore itself an implausible one. We need not therefore ask whether science can be characterised thus, since there are difficulties characterising any beliefs, including religious and political beliefs, as entailing commitment and personal response to action.

Is it secondly the case that all doctrines entail 'action-beliefs'? Gregory/Woods seem to be unaware of the force of a counter-example they themselves raise. They admit that it is 'difficult to see what differences to one's daily life, acceptance or rejection of (Berkeley's metaphysical doctrine) would make' (*Concepts of Indoctrination,* p. 167). Even in the paradigm cases of doctrinal domains, I believe it is possible to identify some beliefs that do not entail action-beliefs. For example, what implications follow from the claim that 'God is eternal spirit', or 'Jesus was crucified'?

A further difficult question can be raised as to whether 'entailment' should be interpreted in a logical sense in the above relation. Surely religious doctrines about what is the case do in some sense have implications for what ought to be done by the believer who accepts these doctrines. But if 'entailment' is interpreted loosely, then science too contains doctrines because many, if not most, scientific statements do 'entail' some action-beliefs. For example, an understanding of the law of gravity 'implies' that one should not jump off a high bridge. The claim, 'H_2SO_4 is an acid', makes chemistry instructors warn students to be careful not to spill any on their hands or clothes. Our 'technological society' and its way of approaching life is surely an 'implication' of the acceptance of the scientific method and the beliefs associated with it. Thus some express concern about science being 'ideological'.

Third, another identifying characteristic of doctrines suggested by Gregory/Woods concerns the evangelistic zeal with which they are promoted. It must be admitted that the holding of religious and political doctrines is often associated with a 'strong urge to convince others'. But is this *necessarily* the case, as it must be, if this feature is part of the analysis of the concept 'doctrine'? We must not let the zeal of a few radicals blind us to the fact that many believers in religious or political doctrines hold their beliefs very dispassionately with little or no attempt to persuade others of what they believe. It is a contingent matter whether doctrines are kept to oneself, shared with others on certain occasions or whether the convincing of others becomes an all-consuming passion.

Evangelistic zeal is also at times present in those holding scientific beliefs. Many would want to give as an example the way in which evolutionary theory is perpetuated in our schools, in print and via the media. They might admit that this does not look exactly like religious evangelism, but this is only due to the fact that evolutionary theory is part of established opinion. If it were a minority view, recourse would have to be taken to special attempts at convincing others, special rallies, paid broadcasts, etc. As it is, these special efforts are unnecessary, since those who accept the evolutionary theory have at their disposal the entire educational system with textbooks and all devoted to their cause. Malcolm Muggeridge speaks to this issue in a more general sense:[19]

> The dogmatism of science has become a new orthodoxy, disseminated by the media and a state educational system with a thoroughness and subtlety far exceeding anything of the kind achieved by the Inquisition.

Fourth, the above argument is also related to the final characteristic attributed to doctrines, namely their being supported by a group of people or an institution. It should be obvious than this feature also will not distinguish paradigm cases of doctrine and non-doctrine. Lest the above quote from Muggeridge be dismissed as obscurantist, let me refer to John Dewey, whose writings have perhaps done more to shape North American education that any other writer. Dewey is very clear in advocating that schools promote science and the use of the scientific method.[20] Thus we have the institution of public education or schools backing and promoting not only science generally, but also specific scientific beliefs. It is simply naive to assume that only religious or political beliefs are backed by an institution.

This concludes a rather detailed evaluation of various features that have been attributed to doctrines in past analyses of 'indoctrination'. I have attempted to show that some of the proposed criteria need not apply to the paradigm cases of doctrine such as religious or political beliefs. However, I was primarily concerned to show that all of the proposed criteria are present, to some degree at least, in the paradigm example of non-doctrine, science. The common assumption that religion and science can be distinguished in terms of possessing or not possessing doctrines is therefore problematic.

It might be objected that there are other criteria which past descriptions of doctrines have somehow overlooked. For example, is not an obvious difference between scientific and religious beliefs that the one refers to the supernatural while the other does not? I would suggest, however, that there are good reasons why this has not been proposed as a distinguishing feature of doctrines. First of all, there is some question as to whether all religions do make reference to the supernatural. Guthrie warns against applying this 'Western folk category' cross-culturally, since some cultures simply do not think in terms of a 'natural-supernatural' distinction. Guthrie further suggests that there may even be some supernatural elements within science![21] Perhaps scientists are merely suppressing the metaphysical assumptions underlying the scientific enterprise. Finally, it would be inadvisable to define 'doctrine' in terms of the supernatural because it is generally believed that indoctrination is not only limited to religious beliefs. Political beliefs are also susceptible to indoctrination and these obviously do not make reference to the supernatural.

There may be other possible criteria of 'doctrines', but until such time as they are proposed, I believe we must conclude that there are problems defining doctrines in such a way as to make religion doctrinal and science non-doctrinal.

The conclusion we have arrived at by way of a detailed critique of various proposed descriptions of doctrines can be further substantiated by an appeal to ordinary usage. We do talk about doctrines in areas other than religion or politics. The *Oxford English Dictionary* assigns three meanings to 'doctrine':

> 1. The action of teaching or instructing; instruction; a piece of instruction, a lesson, precept.
> 2. That which is taught. a. In the most general sense: Instruction, teaching; a body of instruction or teaching ... b. esp. That which is taught or laid down as true concerning a particular subject or department of knowledge, as religion, politics, science, etc.; a belief, theoretical opinion; a dogma, tenet.
> 3. A body or system of principles or tenets; a doctrinal or theoretical system; a theory; a science, or department of knowledge.

We see here that, with all three meanings, there is no restriction of doctrine to the areas of religion or politics. In fact, the last two meanings specifically refer to science as an example of a doctrine.

This is further substantiated by an examination of actual usage of the term 'doctrine'. J S Mill, for example, writes about 'the detailed doctrines of science'.[22] White refers to a recent paper by C P Ormell in which he talks of doctrines in mathematics such as 'the doctrine of Logical Sequence' (*Concepts of Indoctrination,* p. 190). Gregory/Woods themselves give some examples of talk about doctrines in the sciences, but these are dismissed as unusual usages (*Concepts of Indoctrination,* pp. 172ff). The fact remains that these are examples of the term 'doctrine' being used in the sciences, and many more such examples could be provided. Thus, an examination of current actual usage further substantiates the conclusion that any attempt to limit doctrines to areas such as religion or politics is simply due to arbitrary decision.

A proposed analysis of 'doctrine'

Before proceeding to draw some conclusions as to the relation between 'indoctrination' and 'doctrine' it might be well to ask ourselves what can be learned from past descriptions of the term 'doctrine' by way of providing a more adequate analysis of this concept.

It might appear that the conclusion that follows from the arguments of the previous section is that the concept 'doctrine' is simply meaningless. But despite the contradictions, confusions, and fundamental problems concerning the denotation of the concept, which have been found in past descriptions of doctrines, I do not believe the concept is meaningless. Nor should 'doctrine' be equated simply with 'belief', as is suggested by some dictionary definitions. We do not, as Gregory/Woods have argued, 'go around talking about the doctrine that eight pints equal one gallon, or the doctrine that two twos are four' (*Concepts of Indoctrination,* p. 181). I further agree with Patricia Smart that we do not generally speak of observational statements as doctrines.[23]

I suggest the following as a correct analysis of the concept 'doctrine', based in part on past descriptions of this notion, but hopefully avoiding the problems that have been identified in the previous section:

First, 'doctrines' refer to the central beliefs of any belief system, variously identified as 'first-order principles', 'primary beliefs', or 'presuppositions'.[24] Following a model close to that of W V Quine and T F Green, let me propose as a picture of a belief system, a series of concentric circles.[25] At the outer circumference of the belief system are observational statements. The next level involves generalised statements. Further in the interior of the belief system are broader statements still, which may function as first-order principles. I would suggest that these, and the presuppositions at the core of the belief system, are called 'doctrines'. A larger belief system may consist of several smaller belief systems, each of which also has first-order principles, which may also then be identified as 'doctrines'.

Second, doctrines are broad in scope or have wide-ranging implications and this is due to their being central in a belief system. It would seem that the term 'ideology' is at times used to connote this specific sense of 'doctrine'.

Third, doctrines are not verifiable or falsifiable, though this should perhaps be qualified, as there is a sense in which an entire belief system together with its first-order principles can be verified or falsified.

T S Kuhn, for example, speaks of 'scientific revolutions', such as the 'Copernican Revolution', which involved a complete shift in conceptual frameworks. Such a shift is partly a response to problems at the outer periphery of the former belief system, involving observational statements. But various other non-observational criteria are at work in causing major conceptual upheavals, such as internal consistency, simplicity, aesthetic elegance, explanatory power, etc.[26] Thus, there is a sense in which conceptual frameworks and their first-order principles are subject to testing but this is a complex affair. However, if one is speaking of the logical status of statements within a conceptual framework, then first-order principles are unfalsifiable because they 'are used logically as principles in accordance with which evidence is interpreted, and as such logically could not ever be *falsified* if they continued to be used *in this manner*'.[27] Thus, I am defining doctrines as unfalsifiable in this special sense involving their logical status within a belief system.

Fourth, a final characteristic of doctrines involves their importance. This feature is necessarily somewhat vague. It might also seem that the rating of the importance of doctrinal beliefs will be relative to individuals or groups of individuals but I do not believe this involves a serious qualification. Whether individuals agree or disagree with a certain doctrine, both sides would agree that it is an important truth or falsity. This importance of doctrines derives from the fact that they are central and primary beliefs of a belief system and also from their broad scope. Thus I believe Gregory/Woods are correct in suggesting that generally we would not call unimportant details 'doctrines'.

I would tentatively suggest that these four criteria serve to define what is generally understood as a 'doctrine'. Much more could be done by way of expanding and defending the above analysis but this is beyond the scope of the article. It needs to be stressed, however, that this proposed analysis is still in line with the major argument of the previous section where it was concluded that doctrines are found in science as well as religion. Non-falsifiable first-order principles or presuppositions of broad scope and importance are found in all belief systems or forms of knowledge.

Indoctrination and doctrines

We return now to the questions that prompted our enquiry into past descriptions of doctrines. Is indoctrination limited to doctrines? Are doctrines more susceptible to indoctrination than other areas of knowledge and belief?

It is generally assumed that doctrines are only to be found in religion, politics, and morality, and that the danger of indoctrination only exists in these areas. I have argued, however, that 'doctrines' as described by Wilson, Flew, and Gregory/Woods are also found in what is usually taken to be a paradigm of non-doctrine, science. It therefore follows that even if 'indoctrination' is seen as limited to 'doctrines', and if the latter term is understood as it has been in the past, this still does not entail that indoctrination is restricted to the areas of religious, political, and moral beliefs.

This conclusion is further supported by my proposal for a more adequate analysis of the concept 'doctrine'. I have argued that 'doctrines' should be defined in terms of non-falsifiable first-order principles and pre-suppositions of broad scope and importance. But doctrines in this sense are found in science, and indeed in all areas of knowledge. Thus, if the content criterion of 'indoctrination' is accepted, that is, if indoctrination is seen as limited to doctrines, then indoctrination must again be seen as possible in all areas of knowledge and belief.

Thus far we have been assuming that there is a conceptual link between 'indoctrination' and 'doctrines'. I have shown that even if this is assumed, it does not have the usually intended effect of limiting indoctrination to religious, political, and moral beliefs. Another way in which to undermine this limitation of indoctrination to certain areas of belief which are considered suspect is to show that the assumption of a conceptual link between 'indoctrination' and 'doctrines' is itself problematical. This is the strategy of J P White who argues both for a weaker claim, that 'indoctrination' should not be understood as being limited to doctrines at all, and for a stronger claim, about which he is a little less confident, that in-doctrinated beliefs could be of any kind whatever (*Concepts of Indoctrination,* pp. 117ff., 190ff.). Although I am sympathetic with White's arguments, it is not possible to deal with them here. It should be noted, however, that White and I both object to arbitrarily limiting 'indoctrination' to certain spheres or areas of knowledge and belief. Both of us reject the usually accepted denotative defi-nition of 'indoctrination'. Thus our arguments should be seen as complementing each other.

Although the question of a conceptual link between 'indoctri-nation' and 'doctrines' is significant in itself, I would suggest that it is the second question concerning the probability of indoctrinating doctrines that is of greater significance for education. As has already been pointed out, the claim that there is a strong contingent con-nection between indoctrination and doctrines is made both by those who accept the content criterion of 'indoctrination', and by those who reject it. Thus, it is unfortunate that in the literature on indoc-trination, this second question has been treated with even less rigour than the first. It is only possible, here, to make a few comments on this second question based on my critique of past descriptions of doc-trines and my own proposal for a correct analysis of this concept.

It should be noted that in dealing with this second question than the first. It is only possible, here, to make a few comments on this second question based on my critique of past descriptions of doctrines and my own proposal for a correct analysis of this concept.

It should be noted that in dealing with this second question we are assuming that it is possible to define 'indoctrination' in some other way, perhaps the methods criterion.[28] I want to suggest that indoctrination is indeed more likely to occur with regard to doctrine understood in terms of non-falsifiable, first-order principles and presuppositions of broad scope and importance. The reason for this is that it is simply easier to indoctrinate doctrines. It is very difficult to indoctrinate observational statements, or beliefs that are obviously true or false.

It is for this reason that we generally use the word 'indoctrination' in connection with the teaching of doctrines (*Concepts of Indoctrination,* pp. 123, 181). But this is a contingent, not a conceptual matter. The reason why we seldom talk of indoctrinating a 'scientific fact' is that it would be most difficult to obtain. But it is conceivable, and even possible, as White demonstrates (*Concepts of Indoctrination,* pp. 200f.).

Here it is important, however, not to misunderstand what is being said when it is claimed that indoctrination is more likely to occur with regard to doctrines. I have argued that however doctrines are defined, they are to be found in science as well as religion. Thus the suggestion that doctrines are more susceptible to indoctrination *does not mean* that indoctrination is more probable in the areas of religion, politics, and morality, as is generally assumed. Indoctrination may be just as common in the area of science as in the area of religion because there are doctrines in both areas.

Much more would need to be done to establish that indoctrination is indeed just as probable in science as in religion. For example, it would have to be shown that there are just as many doctrines that are non-falsifiable, first-order principles of broad scope and importance, in the area of science as in the area of religion. To show this might be difficult, if not impossible. Thus, we cannot come to any final conclusions concerning the comparative probability of indoctrination in science as against religion.

However, I believe it can be safely maintained that there are doctrines in science, as indeed in all areas of knowledge. I therefore suggest, that the difference in the probability of indoctrination between science and religion is not as great as is generally assumed. I would finally suggest that some of the arguments against religious education, or even against the very possibility of religious education are not as strong as is sometimes assumed.

Notes

1. R S Peters, *Ethics and Education,* London, Allen and Unwin, 1966, p. 41.
2. Antony Flew, 'Indoctrination and religion,' in I A Snook (ed.), *Concepts of Indoctrination,* London, Routledge and Kegan Paul, 1972, p. 114. Hereinafter, cited in the notes as CI.

3. I A Snook, *Indoctrination and Education,* London, Routledge and Kegan Paul, 1972, pp. 56f., 68, 74f. Hereinafter, cited in the notes as IE.

4. For example, Snook, Flew and Green all tend to use 'doctrine' and 'ideology' interchangeably (IE, p. 37; CI, pp. 152, 70f., 81f., 85f., 37f.). Since it is generally assumed that there is an etymological connection between 'indoctrination' and 'doctrines', I will interpret the content criterion in terms of a limitation to doctrinal beliefs, rather than to ideologies. This restriction should not affect the soundness of my critical evaluation of the content criterion. Further, my arguments can easily be extended to include the notion of ideology but such extrapolation will not be undertaken in this paper.

5. John Wilson's essays are contained in T H B Hollins (ed.), *Aims in Education,* Manchester, Manchester University Press, 1964, pp. 24–46. See also John Wilson's essays in Snook's anthology (CI, pp. 17–24, 101–105). The essays by Antony Flew and I M M Gregory and R G Woods are also found in Snook's anthology (CI, pp. 67-92, 106-116, 162-189).

6. Ian Barbour, *Issues in Science and Religion,* New York, Harper and Row, 1971, p. 1.

7. Stewart Guthrie, 'A cognitive theory in religion,' *Current Anthropology,* 21, 1980, pp. 181–203. Hereinafter, S Guthrie.

8. See, for example, Paul Feyerabend, *Against Method: outline of an anarchistic theory of knowledge,* London, New Left Books, 1975, chapter 5.

9. M L Diamond and T V Litzenburg (eds), *The Logic of God: theology and verification,* Indianapolis, The Bobbs-Merrill Co. Inc., 1975 p. 38. Hereinafter, Diamond and Litzenburg.

10. Patricia Smart, 'The concept of indoctrination,' in Glenn Langford (ed.), *New Essays in the Philosophy of Education,* London, Routledge and Kegan Paul, 1973, p. 41f. Hereinafter, P Smart.

11. R S Laura, 'Philosophical foundations of religious education,' *Educational Theory,* 28, 1978, pp. 310–317. Hereinafter, R S Laura. John F Miller, 'Science and religion: their logical similarity,' in M L Diamond and T V Litzenburg, *op. cit.,* pp. 351–380. Hereinafter, J F Miller. See, also T F Green and J P White in CI, pp. 29ff., 193.

12. Flew, in an essay, 'The Jensen uproar,' *Philosophy,* 48, 1973, p. 63, describes the reaction of the scientific community to Arthur Jensen's studies on IQ, and his suggestion 'that genetic factors are strongly implicated in the average Negro-White intelligence difference.... The original publication occasioned an enormous coast to coast brouhaha of protest and denunciation; including tyre-slashing, slogan-painting, telephone abuse and threats, and strident demands to "Fire" or even to "Kill Jensen".' P Smart informs us that the history of non-Euclidean geometry during the early nineteenth century provides us with further examples of incorrigibly held beliefs in science. P Smart, p. 37.

13. See Jon Fennell and Rudy Liverette, 'Kuhn, education and the grounds of rationality,' *Educational Theory,* 29, 1979, pp. 117–127.

14. Quoted by J Fennell and R Liverett, *op. cit.,* p. 118.

15. J S Mill, in commenting on the disagreement that exists over first principles in morality, points out that 'similar discordance exist(s) respecting the first principles of all the sciences, not excepting that which is deemed most certain of them — mathematics' (*Utilitarianism,* chapter 1).

16. J F Miller, *op. cit.,* p. 380; W V Quine and J S Ullian, *Web of Belief,* New York, Random House, 1978, chapter 2.

17. For example, Paul Roubiczek traces Nazi values to Nietsche, who in turn was influenced by Darwin in his book *Existentialism: for and against,* Cambridge, Cambridge University Press, 1966, chapters 1, 2, especially, pp. 20, 34.

18. Roger Trigg, *Reason and Commitment,* Cambridge, Cambridge University Press, 1973, p. 41. It should also be noted that this description of doctrines might be suggested by a certain view of religious language arising out of the positivist challenge. Instead of focusing on the cognitive aspect of religious belief, meaning is here located in the believer's response. However, this view of religious language is by no means accepted by all philosophers and theologians, and it would surely be inadvisable to define 'doctrines' in such a way that it is based on a certain view of religious language which is itself a point of debate.

19. Malcolm Muggeridge, *Jesus: the man who lives,* London, Fontana/Collins, 1975, p. 25.
20. John Dewey, *Democracy and Education,* New York, The Free Press, 1916/1966, chapter 17.
21. S Guthrie, *op. cit.,* pp. 184f.
22. J S Mill, *Utilitarianism, op. cit.,* chapter 1.
23. P Smart, *op. cit.,* p. 40.
24. *Webster's Third New International Dictionary* (1976) hints at this limitation of 'doctrine' when it defines 'indoctrinate' as 'to give instruction especially in fundamentals or rudiments.' Snook also argues that 'the basic assumptions and postulates of an empirical science qualify as doctrines' (IE, p. 35).
25. W V Quine, 'Two dogmas of empiricism,' in *From a Logical Point of View,* Cambridge, Massachusetts, Harvard University Press, 1953, section 6. Green, CI, p. 31.
26. See J F Miller, *op. cit.,* p. 360; S Guthrie, *op. cit.,* pp. 192, 196.
27. J F Miller, p. 360; R S Laura, pp. 312ff.
28. Elsewhere, I have argued that past attempts to define 'indoctrination' in terms of one or more other criteria, including the methods criterion have failed. See E J Thiessen, 'Indoctrination, education and religion: a philosophical analysis,' unpublished PhD dissertation, University of Waterloo, 1980.

8.2 Indoctrination, doctrines and the foundations of rationality
Tasos Kazepides

Although few educational concepts have been subjected to such an extended systematic philosophical scrutiny as has indoctrination, there are still serious disagreements with regard to its exact nature. Consequently, we lack an agreed upon criterion for our educational judgements, deliberations and decisions and our educational policy remains unclear with respect to indoctrination. This is certainly a serious deficiency since, whatever our criterion of it, we all seem to agree that indoctrination is one of the most serious and widespread forms of miseducation.

My view concerning the causes of these disagreements is that they are due largely to the programmatic intentions of some writers on indoctrination and not to the hopeless vagueness and inherent intractability of the concept. Prominent among such writers are the proponents of religious indoctrination who have been reluctant to accept the view that the primary locus of indoctrination is religion. They have maintained, instead, that doctrines are as common in science and other areas and that the criterion of whether a person is indoctrinating is not the doctrinal beliefs that are being inculcated but the miseducative methods or intentions of the teacher.

In this paper I shall argue that indoctrination is but one form of miseducation which must be distinguished from other forms such as propaganda; that it can be explicated only in terms of doctrinal beliefs which are religious or quasi-religious; that there are no such doctrines in science;[1] and that the questionable methods used by the indoctrinator together with his or her intentions are parasitic on the doctrines that are being inculcated.

The context and the problem of indoctrination

When philosophers argue that we ought to examine the various uses of words in their actual contexts, they do not mean that we must consult our dictionaries and enumerate all the various uses of the word we want to clarify.[2] Although such practices may be useful for other purposes they do not settle any philosophical questions; indeed they very often bring forth linguistic skeletons from bygone ages that add further confusions to the subject under examination. What philosophers have in mind is the study and explication of current linguistic usage.[3] If words are tools then we must examine our tools in order to find out what actual work they perform in our language today and for what purposes. It might be worth exploring the reasons why in the Middle Ages the word indoctrination was used interchangeably with teaching, but that enquiry will not clarify our concept of indoctrination today – in fact it presupposes such clarification.

Our concern about indoctrination stems, first, from our commitment to education and the specific epistemological constraints that our concept of education imposes on various activities and institutions. In other words, education implies knowledge and understanding and therefore rules out superstitions, prejudices, doctrines, false beliefs, and the like. Our second reason is that while indoctrinated people are unwilling or incapable of subjecting their doctrinal beliefs to public rational scrutiny, most of them, nonetheless, want their doctrines to function as regulative principles of the way of life of the whole community. It is obvious, then, that indoctrination is a very serious political problem in the modern world.

The paradigm cases of indoctrination are to be found in religious communities and institutions. The ordinary uses of 'indoctrination' suggest that it has to do with the transmission or inculcation of doctrinal beliefs. There is one normative use of 'indoctrination' which does not suggest a specific activity or activities but rather some standards to be met. Just as we educate people *by* teaching them the humanities, the sciences, and the arts, we indoctrinate people *by* teaching them particular doctrines. The difference between education and this sense of indoctrination lies in the nature of the criteria employed. Whereas for education they have to do with worthwhile knowledge and understanding, in the case of indoctrination they are wholly dependent on the nature of the inculcated doctrines. Ayatollahs, evangelists and bishops are not interested in indoctrination-in-general – because there is no such thing – but in the inculcation of specific doctrines that are foundational to their respective ways of life. The prepositional modifiers *into* and *with,* which accompany ordinary uses of the verb 'to indoctrinate' (activity sense), suggest that the doctrinal beliefs must be specific. Thus one indoctrinates the young *into* the doctrines of a particular church or *with* the doctrines of an ideology. In this respect 'indoctrinating *into* or *with*' behaves like 'training *in*': in both cases the prepositions limit the scope of their respective activities and specify their limited contents.

Successful indoctrination results in the acceptance of doctrinal beliefs and commitment to them, whereas successful educational engagements aim at some worthwhile understanding. If a student, after careful consideration, rejects the taught doctrines, the indoctrinator has failed in his or her task. On the other hand, if a student, after critical examination, rejects a scientific claim we do not say that the teacher has failed as an educator – in fact, if the student's rejection is based on clear understanding of what he or she was being taught, we might even conclude that this episode was a paradigm case of educative teaching.

Indoctrination and intentions

Most existing discussions of indoctrination fail to provide a clear demarcation of the concept either because they fail to identify the correct criterion of indoctrination, or when they do, they do not succeed in describing it correctly. In the first category are those who take intention or method to be the criterion, while in the second are those who consider content to be the criterion of indoctrination.

Of the first two criteria, intention is the stronger candidate as it is on the basis of people's intentions that we characterise their actions — not on the basis of some behavioural descriptions of what they do. In most cases where we talk of a teacher indoctrinating students we refer to it as intentional activity. The intention, however, is always parasitic on the doctrines that are being inculcated. In the absence of doctrines there cannot be intention to indoctrinate. Just as 'teaching' implies a triadic relationship between the teacher, the student and what is to be taught, indoctrination implies a similar relationship between the indoctrinator, the student and doctrines. In fact this relationship is stricter in the case of indoctrinating than it is in the case of teaching. In ordinary language we talk about the 'self-taught' person but not about the 'self-indoctrinated' one. In the first case the teacher and the pupil are one and the same person while in the case of indoctrination an external indoctrinator is presupposed. The reason for this discrepancy has to do with the nature of doctrines. Self-taught persons are those who have *discovered* certain truths or new ways of doing things, have developed certain skills or cultivated better tastes, have improved their methods of doing things or discovered new ones. All these things they acquired by trial and error, by following certain rules, by avoiding pitfalls and blind alleys, by correcting their errors and applying new techniques. For all these achievements self-taught persons make use of public criteria, standards, rules, procedures and tests. All these achievements come up to certain public standards. Doctrines, on the other hand, are not the sort of thing that one can be said to have discovered because there are no public, non-sectarian standards they can satisfy. What could it possibly mean to talk of the discovery of the doctrine of the infallibility of the Pope or of the *filioque*?

A second reason for rejecting the intention criterion of indoctrination is that it is of little use for educational planning. A philosophical examination of indoctrination should offer the educational community a clearly demarcated concept that can be used in making important educational decisions regarding, for example, the curriculum of educational institutions. A view of indoctrination, however, that is based exclusively on the intention of the teacher cannot exclude even the most pernicious doctrines from the curriculum. While no educational policy maker can control the intentions of teachers, every responsible educational planner can purify the curriculum by eliminating doctrinal beliefs from it.

My third objection to the intention criterion is that it overlooks the unintended consequences of human actions. Just as we can insult, embarrass, infuriate, or intimidate other people without having the slightest intention of doing so, we can indoctrinate or otherwise miseducate them unintentionally. Surely, educational (or social) planning that disregards the unintended consequences of our actions, programmes, policies, institutional arrangements, etc., must be considered narrow, unrealistic and impoverished. It concentrates exclusively on the elusive intentions of teachers and overlooks the *actual* consequences of our interventions in the lives of the young.

Finally, the proponents of the intention criterion of indoctrination consistently overlook the fact that, like education, indoctrination also has a success or achievement sense. When we consider that aspect of indoctrination intention becomes simply irrelevant. The only criterion that is relevant here is the specific doctrine(s) to which the novices are expected to commit themselves; if there is no commitment to such doctrine(s) we can no longer talk about indoctrination − regardless of the intentions of indoctrinators.

Indoctrination and methods

The last argument against the intention criterion applies as well to the method criterion of indoctrination. The methods used by indoctrinators are irrelevant when we want to ascertain whether a person is indoctrinated. Only content is a necessary and sufficient criterion for such a task.

In order for method to be an adequate criterion of indoctrination there must be methods peculiar to it. It is obvious, however, that there are no such methods. The indoctrinator, because he or she is inculcating doctrines, must resort to some educationally questionable methods such as failing to provide relevant evidence and arguments or misapplying them, misusing his or her authority, etc. These and other such methods, however, can be used for all sorts of educationally illegitimate purposes, not just indoctrination. An account of indoctrination in terms of method alone makes it synonymous with miseducation and thus renders it a useless, blunt tool. The issue is not whether indoctrination is miseducation but what sort of miseducation it is and how it differs from other sorts of miseducation, for example, propaganda. The proponents of the method criterion invariably fail to distinguish between indoctrination and propaganda.

Although propagandists often resort to indoctrination it is not necessary that they do so. In typical cases the indoctrinator believes that his or her doctrines are true or give meaning to life, or that they will bring about peace and justice on earth. In trying to inculcate his doctrines the indoctrinator offers some reasons and some evidence – it is another matter that the reasons and the evidence are based on sectarian, subjective grounds. The indoctrinator is not the pernicious propagandist, however, who conceals or misrepresents facts, appeals to emotions or resorts to threats, hides his real motives, etc., in order to influence the beliefs and attitudes of people for the advancement of self-interest.

Finally, the proponents of the method criterion of indoctrination assume that being rational is simply thinking in a certain manner. As we shall see later, however, being rational is not just a matter of thinking and acting in a certain manner or form but also a matter of thinking certain things.

The nature of doctrines

The most common reason given for abandoning doctrinal content as the necessary and sufficient condition of indoctrination is that the term doctrine is extremely vague.[4] The problem with that claim is that even if true it would still be a non-sequitur. If the word doctrine is vague then that makes 'indoctrination' a vague concept. It does not constitute a good reason for abandoning the criterion.

Very often this claim about vagueness is confused and the real problem is one of ambiguity,[5] not vagueness. Words are *used* ambiguously when it is not clear from the context how they are supposed to be understood. The mere fact that words have variable meaning does not make them ambiguous. We talk, for example, of 'sharp criticism', 'sharp knives' and 'sharp students' without ever getting confused about the meaning of the word sharp in these three contexts. Let us then adopt a similar approach while we look at the uses of the word doctrine in its various contexts.

The word doctrine is sometimes used to mean 'theory' (Einstein's doctrine of relativity), 'principle' or 'policy' (the Monroe Doctrine) and rarely 'rule' (the doctrine of do unto others ...) or 'presupposition' (the doctrine that every event has a cause). In its plural form the word is used to refer to the teachings of wise persons (the doctrines of great educators). To find out whether the word doctrine is used in any of the above senses we must see if we can substitute any of them for the word doctrine; if we cannot, then we can be fairly sure that what is being talked about is a real doctrine. The detection of real doctrines does not require special training and skills; only a very ignorant or retarded person would insist that the doctrine of the infallibility of the Pope or of the Second Coming is actually a theory. We now have a rule of thumb for distinguishing doctrines from non-doctrines, but we have not yet discussed the nature of the doctrines and how they differ from non-doctrines.

The original and proper home of doctrines is religion and the paradigm cases of indoctrination take place in theological schools or seminaries where the study of doctrines is one of their main subjects. In any other department of human enquiry doctrines are like dead rats in epistemological sanctuaries − when they are pointed out by critics they cause great embarrassment to their originators or perpetrators. And there is no canonical repentance available to scientists and others for their mistakes as there might be for religious 'heretics'. The talk about Marx's doctrines, Skinner's doctrines or Darwin's doctrine might be intended as criticism of some of the ideas of these men − unless it is simply casual unguarded talk. In such instances the onus is always on the speaker to demonstrate that some ideas of Marx, Skinner or Darwin are indeed doctrines.[6] There are two views about the nature of doctrines, which I would like to label: the literal *hard* view and the figurative *soft* view. According to the hard view the following conditions apply.

1. Doctrines are in principle unfalsifiable beliefs about the existence of beings, states of affairs or relationships. Clear cases of doctrines are the belief in the triadic nature of the Christian Deity and the belief in the infallibility of the Pope.

2. Doctrines are neither criteria of rationality nor irrationality; they are outside the rational tradition. That is why well-educated persons may accept a doctrine and equally well-educated persons may reject it.

3. Doctrines are not isolated beliefs but form a system of inter-related beliefs that constitutes the foundation of a particular world view, defines human nature, and determines humanity's 'proper' place in the world. This system of doctrines is an all-embracing, totalising view that encompasses every aspect of human life as subsidiary.

4. There is a disparity between the linguistic *form* of a doctrine and its actual *function* within the system. Although all doctrines are descriptive statements (for example, Jesus is the son of God) they have an overriding prescriptive function within their respective contexts. For devout Catholics, for example, the doctrine of the infallibility of the Pope is not meant to be an idle belief − they are expected to obey the infallible Pope. Doctrines, then, are disguised, indirect prescriptions and their violations are not deemed to be normal human errors but punishable sins.

5. Finally, as the last point implies, doctrines presuppose the existence of *authorities* or *institutions* which have the power to uphold them when they are challenged by the critics, the

heretics, or the faithless and to punish the enemies. Without an institution that articulates, orders and defends its doctrines they are in danger of deteriorating into common prejudices, or being abandoned.[7]

Although all doctrines within a doctrinal system meet conditions (1), (2) and (5), not all such doctrines may meet conditions (3) and (4). The reason is that not all doctrines are of equal importance to the system at all times. Some of them may be idle or dead remnants from earlier ways of life and are preserved merely as parts of a tradition.

With the exception of some epistemically primordial beliefs (which I shall discuss later), the only beliefs, outside religious doctrines, that are unfalsifiable are common superstitions, a reason perhaps why some people consider all religious beliefs to be nothing more that superstitions. Superstitions, however, are usually isolated beliefs held by individuals and do not have the broad scope and the overriding prescriptive function of religious beliefs. Moreover, the charge of superstition depends on how one interprets doctrines; they resemble superstitions only if one interprets them to be literal claims, as many people do. But that is not the only way one can interpret doctrines. According to the second, soft view, doctrines, like other religious beliefs, are:[8]

> rules of life dressed up in pictures. And these pictures only serve to *describe* what we are to do, not *justify* it. Because they could provide a justification only if they held good in other respects as well .... Religion says: *Do this! Think like that!* – but it cannot justify this and once it even tries to, it becomes repellent; because for every reason it offers there is a valid counter-reason.

Doctrinal beliefs are not ordinary knowledge claims that can be refuted nor are they hypotheses, opinions, views, conjectures that could be 'possibly', 'perhaps', or 'probably' confirmed or disconfirmed. Anything that we call scientific evidence is, according to Wittgenstein, irrelevant to this interpretation of religious belief. Even the most convincing forecast about the coming of the Day of Judgment would not influence a religious person because 'belief in this happening would not be at all a religious belief ... the best scientific evidence is just nothing'.[9]

Although doctrinal beliefs appear to have a referent they are really about something else: 'The way you use the word "God" does not show *whom* you mean' – but, rather, what you mean.'[10] 'It strikes me,' says Wittgenstein, 'that a religious belief could only be something like a passionate commitment to a system of reference. Hence, although it's *belief,* it's really a way of living, or a way of assessing life.'[11] Confusing religious doctrines with empirical ones is a blunder that reduces all such beliefs to superstition. Wittgenstein repeatedly argued that religious belief 'not only is ... not reasonable, but ... doesn't pretend to be' and that it is 'ludicrous' to make it 'appear to be reasonable'.[12] About those who try to make religious belief appear to be reasonable by appealing to facts and evidence, Wittgenstein says that they are *unreasonable* and that 'if this is religious belief, it's all superstition'.[13]

The distinction between the hard and the soft views of doctrines sketched above is rarely made by religious believers; they usually equivocate by sliding from one into the other. I think it would be reasonable to claim that if we accept the above analysis of doctrines, most of what passes as religion today is superstition. What is of educational interest in this analysis is that however one interprets doctrines they do not belong within our rational tradition, and therefore they should have no place in our educational institutions. Under the first description they are largely superstitions, whereas under the second they are personal perspectives on the world and on human life — and therefore subjective preferences.

Doctrines and the foundations of rationality

It has been argued by several writers that indoctrination is unavoidable in education because it is a prerequisite to the introduction of the young into our rational heritage including science. 'The basic assumptions and postulates of an empirical science,' says Snook, 'qualify as doctrines.'[14] Likewise, Thomas Green maintains that 'Indoctrination ... has a perfectly good and important role to play in education ... Indoctrination may be necessary as a prelude to teaching.'[15] Content, then, according to these writers, cannot be a criterion of indoctrination since the presuppositions of our rational discourse are equally non-rational. But is this all that can be said about the nature of doctrines and the foundations of our rational modes of thinking?

In the remainder of this article I want to show that it is not only what these writers say about doctrines and the epistemic foundations of our thinking, but, more importantly, what they choose to overlook, that reveals their programmatic intentions; that there is a world of difference between doctrines, as I described them earlier, and what Wittgenstein called the 'river-bed',[16] the 'axis',[17] the 'scaffolding',[18] the 'hinges'[19] and the 'unmoving foundations'[20] of all our thoughts, judgments, language and actions. In fact, when I have enumerated the important differences it should become obvious that the similarities between them are superficial and trivial.

It is never made clear by the above writers what they mean by 'assumptions', 'presuppositions', 'postulates', or 'fundamentals' of science. We can identify, however, a great number of propositions that belong to the bed-rock of all our thinking and therefore of science which are not doctrines. Wittgenstein says: 'Propositions of the form of empirical propositions, and not only propositions of logic, form the foundation of all operating with thoughts (with language).'[21] Among these propositions we can distinguish some that are pseudoempirical because they are in fact methodological propositions, that is, rules that are presupposed by any language games we may engage in. They are not propositions that can be doubted, tested, confirmed, or about which one can be mistaken. Examples of such propositions are: 'Physical objects exist' and 'Objects continue in existence when not perceived.' Any attempt to deny such propositions leads to absurdity.

There are, next, empirical propositions about which we 'can hardly be mistaken'.[22] Examples of such propositions are: 'I have two hands', 'I am a human being', 'Automobiles do not grow on trees', and the like. Reasonable people have plenty of doubts, says Wittgenstein, but not about these and a great number of similar propositions. Only 'insane',[23] 'mad',[24] 'demented',[25] or 'idiotic'[26] people would express doubt about such propositions and their doubt would be 'hollow'[27] 'senseless'[28] and 'without consequence'.[29] These and similar river-bed propositions, then, together with propositions of logic and methodological propositions, constitute criteria of rationality about which one cannot be mistaken. A person who insists that his or her head is stuffed with straw is not making a mistake but is mentally disturbed. 'Being reasonable,' says Thomas Morawetz, 'is not just a matter of acting and thinking in a certain manner or form but also a matter of thinking certain *things.*'[30]

Now that we have sketched the nature of doctrines and the nature of the river-bed propositions that lie at the foundations of all our thinking, we can see more clearly the radical differences between them. First, belief or disbelief in doctrines is not a criterion of rationality, whereas the questioning of river-bed propositions is a sign of organic mental disturbance.

Second, there are *alternatives* to particular doctrines but not to the river-bed certainties. One can doubt, question, accept, modify, or abandon doctrinal beliefs but not river-bed propositions.

Third, river-bed propositions are *acquired* or inherited without any thinking, investigation or justification. These ordinary certainties are not matters of knowledge and must be taught as a foundation, substratum or background without evidence and without reasons. 'Knowing only begins at a later level,'[31] says Wittgenstein, when there is 'a possibility of demonstrating the truth'.[32] Doctrines, on the other hand, are *learned.* There is nothing in human experience that requires the doctrine of the infallibility of the Pope or of the *filioque,* whereas everything in human experience presupposes the law of induction or the existence of physical objects.

Fourth, whereas all explanations and justifications come to an end, that end is not doctrines that can be doubted but the river-bed propositions which cannot. Since river-bed propositions are the foundations of all our thought, language and action, they must also be the foundations of all our talk about doctrines. It follows, therefore, that doctrines are not at the same epistemic level as river-bed certainties. The onus, then, is on the proponents of indoctrination to show where doctrines belong since they are not knowledge claims either.

Finally, a word about the functions of the river-bed propositions and of doctrines. While the former enable us to think, the latter act as *stoppers* that control, limit and channel thought, disallow alternative beliefs, and frustrate critical thinking. That is the reason why indoctrination is inherently *authoritarian:* it claims that there are no alternatives whereas, in fact, there are many; it aims at legitimating political authority and power, silencing the opponents and controlling people's lives. The recent actions of the Vatican to uphold and expand the doctrinal beliefs of the church are good examples of what I am talking about.

Notes
1. Even the notorious Trofim Lysenko, who tried to revive Lamarckian views of heredity in the Soviet Union with the help of Stalin and the Central Committee of the Communist Party, was not promoting a doctrine but a defunct theory that happened to agree with the prevailing political ideology in that country — his views were not, in principle, unfalsifiable.
2. P F Strawson, *Individuals,* New York, Doubleday and Co., 1963, p. xiii.
3. John L Austin, *Philosophical Papers,* London, Oxford University Press, 1961, pp. 130–133.
4. I A Snook, *Indoctrination and Education,* London, Routledge and Kegan Paul, 1972, p. 32.
5. J P White makes that claim in 'Indoctrination' in R S Peters (ed.), *The Concept of Education,* London, Routledge and Kegan Paul, 1967, p. 183.
6. For a recent discussion of the alleged tautologies/doctrines contained in Darwin's theory, see Elliott Sober, *The Nature of Selection: evolutionary theory in philosophical focus,* Cambridge, Massachusetts, The MIT University Press, 1984, Chapter 2.
7. Cf. James E McClellan, *Philosophy of Education,* Englewood Cliffs, New Jersey, Prentice-Hall, Inc., 1976, pp. 142–143.
8. Ludwig Wittgenstein, *Culture and Value,* Oxford, Basil Blackwell, 1980, p. 29e.
9. Ludwig Wittgenstein, *Lectures and Conversations on Aesthetics, Psychology and Religious Belief,* Berkeley, University of California Press, 1967, p. 56.
10. L Wittgenstein, *Culture and Value, op. cit.,* p. 50e.
11. *Ibid.,* p. 64e.
12. *Ibid., Lectures and Conversations, op. cit.,* p. 58.
13. *Ibid.,* p. 59.
14. I A Snook, *op. cit.,* p. 35.
15. Thomas F Green, 'Indoctrination and Beliefs,' in I A Snook (ed.), *Concepts of Indoctrination,* London, Routledge and Kegan Paul, 1972, pp. 44–45.
16. Ludwig Wittgenstein, *On Certainty,* New York, Harper and Row, 1969, paragraph 97.
17. *Ibid.,* par. 152.
18. *Ibid.,* par. 211.
19. *Ibid.,* par. 341.
20. *Ibid.,* par. 403.
21. *Ibid.,* par. 401.
22. *Ibid.,* par. 673.
23. *Ibid.,* par. 468.
24. *Ibid.,* par. 281.
25. *Ibid.,* par. 155.

26. *Ibid.,* par. 662.
27. *Ibid.,* par. 257, 312.
28. *Ibid.,* par. 56, 310.
29. *Ibid.,* par. 338.
30. Thomas Morawetz, *Wittgenstein and Knowledge,* Atlantic Highlands, New Jersey, Humanities Press, 1978, p. 75.
31. L Wittgenstein, *On Certainty, op. cit.,* par. 538.
32. *Ibid.,* par. 243.

8.3 Religious upbringing and rational autonomy

Ronald S Laura and Michael Leahy

When the leader of Iran's Islamic Revolution, the Ayatollah Khomeini, condemned Salman Rushdie, the British author of *The Satanic Verses,*[1] to death for the alleged blasphemies contained in that book, booksellers and publishers throughout the liberal democracies of the world were thrown into a dilemma: should they be loyal to their liberal principles and 'publish and be damned', or should they be prudent and avoid the violence that publication and sale of Rushdie's book might provoke? A political crisis like the Rushdie affair highlights, in a far more effective way than can any academic debate, the practical importance to society of the philosophical question at issue: what balance is to be struck in a free society between the right to hold and promote a particular set of 'truths', and the right to freedom of judgment and expression in relation to all truth-claims? Of the areas of social life in which such a balance has to be struck, none is more sensitive that that of the upbringing of children. T H McLaughlin's revival of this debate[2] is, therefore, welcome and timely.

In this article, we shall argue that a particular kind of religious upbringing is compatible with the liberal ideal of rational autonomy, and indeed that a respect for that autonomy is a necessary condition of an authentic religious commitment. We shall also contend that neglect of the claims of religion in our children's upbringing/education – as well as denying their access to what is claimed by some to be a source of 'inexhaustible riches' – is likely to leave them as adults uncomprehending and intolerant of religious claims generally. The possible social consequences of such ignorance and intolerance are evident in the frustrated indignation with which Ayatollah Khomeini's sentence upon Rushdie was greeted throughout the liberal democracies of the world.

In their defence of the liberal position, Callan[3] and Gardner[4] advance two fundamental objections to religious upbringing: first, that such an upbringing is likely to hinder the development of rational autonomy by producing belief(s) which is (are), if not 'unshakeable', at least 'maintained without due regard for relevant evidence and argument';[5] second, that a religious upbringing, by producing acceptance of one belief system as true, logically produces also rejection of its rivals as false, thereby closing the individual's mind where autonomous judgment requires it to be open.

In what follows, our contribution to this debate will consist in demonstrating that these two objections are not insuperable.

Religious upbringing and fixed beliefs

The liberal ideal and 'a coherent primary culture'

'Unshakeable' beliefs are taken by McLaughlin,[6] following J P White,[7] as indoctrinated beliefs. An upbringing which seeks to indoctrinate religious beliefs is unacceptable to liberals, according to McLaughlin, 'since it constitutes an attempt to restrict in a substantial way the child's eventual ability to function autonomously'.[8] However, McLaughlin believes that a religious upbringing is possible which produces less than 'unshakeable' beliefs. Such an upbringing would be one where according to McLaughlin,[9] 'a definite world view *is* (emphasis in original) presented to the child as part of a "coherent primary culture", but where the parent abides by the liberal principles calling for him to allow the child to develop and exercise the freedom to eventually challenge that culture and form his own life ideals'. The resulting beliefs, he says, would not be 'fixed in the sense of "unshakeable" but fixed in the sense of *"stable"'*.[10] Stable beliefs, in this context, are beliefs which are 'open to subsequent challenge and development'.[11]

Prima facie, a child's need for a 'coherent primary culture'[12] would seem to be one which all would acknowledge without qualification. On closer scrutiny, however, we submit that some qualification is required – qualification which exposes a degree of ideological bias in the liberal ideal of neutrality towards competing beliefs. Our contention is that, in certain circumstances, a child's 'primary culture' may be rendered incoherent if that child is taught to adopt a neutral attitude towards all ideologies. Even liberal democracies include amongst their citizens oppressed minorities, for example, aborigines in Australia, blacks in the United States. The dominant feature of the upbringing of such children can frequently be the experience of political, social or economic oppression. The ability of such children to function in their societies may thus be gravely impaired by an upbringing which inculcates in them the belief that the oppressors' view of how society ought to be run is at least as good as theirs. In other words, the liberal and relativist view that every ideology is as much to be respected and tolerated as every other ideology may implicitly legitimate the very positions which any just society ought to challenge. By upholding the canons of *liberalism,* the paradox is that we may be unwittingly violating the canons of *justice.* The adoption of a stance of respectful neutrality towards all ideologies in a pluralist society may thus be a luxury which only the politically and economically dominant groups in such a society can afford. Indeed, the coherence of a child's primary culture in such cases may depend upon the favouring of a particular ideological stance. In some cases, therefore, it may even be a condition of eventual autonomous judgment that a child's upbringing *not* be neutral in relation to all ideologies. Thus, McLaughlin seems to us to be insufficiently critical of the neutrality aspect of the liberal ideal. This criticism applies even more strongly to his treatment of the 'fixed beliefs' criterion of indoctrination.

'Fixed beliefs' as a criterion of indoctrination

McLaughlin accepts, without question, White's claim that at least some beliefs can be fixed 'unshakeably' in a person's mind. Speaking of beliefs which are fixed in the sense that 'nothing can shake them'[13] he writes: 'A child with a set of beliefs "fixed" in this sense possesses the kind of "indoctrinated state of mind" deplored by liberals. It is perfectly true that this state of mind can be developed in a child despite the explicit intention of his parents, and it is important for parents to be alert to this.'[14] It seems to us far from 'perfectly true' that beliefs can be fixed in a child's (or an adult's) mind in such a way 'that nothing can shake them'. This claim is presumably restricted in time to the span of the believer's life. A recantation as late as the hour of death of the relevant belief would thus be sufficient to falsify the unshakeability claim. On the other hand, a persistence in the belief concerned 'unto death' would not verify its unshakeability, owing to the logically unrestricted character of the term 'nothing'. In a person's lifetime, only a finite number of 'things' could be used to weaken his or her belief. Thus, the possibility could never by excluded that one or other of the *untried* strategies of dissuasion might have succeeded with the *ex hypothesi* deceased person. Since demonstration of the possession of unshakeably fixed beliefs in a person is logically impossible, 'unshakeability' cannot function as even a partial criterion of the indoctrination which, according to White, a religious upbringing is likely to produce.

McLaughlin wants to retain the tenacious character of religious belief, but not to close it to rational revision. However, he offers no account of the nature of religious (or other) belief which could show that this was not simply a case of wanting to have his cake and eat it too. His difficulty, in our opinion, is his failure to recognise that resistance to evidential test is not necessarily a sign that the belief concerned has been illegitimately fixed (White's sense of 'indoctrinated') in the child, nor that this belief is closed in principle to the possibility of revision. We believe we can offer an account of the epistemic structure of belief systems which can explain the resistance of some kinds of religious (and other) beliefs to evidential falsification, and show how they may be rationally revised.

Fixed beliefs have been taken by people like White to be irrational because such beliefs resist falsification by relevant evidence.

The assumption implicit in this view, however, is that evidence is a faithful mirror of how things are in the world. The persistence of this naive realist epistemology in the philosophy of education is, to say the least, surprising, given its virtual abandonment among philosophers of science over the last 20 years. T S Kuhn, as long ago as 1969, rejected 'falsificationism' as an account of scientific progress.[15] Kuhn showed that it was characteristic of a particular class of beliefs in science, which he called 'paradigms', to resist attempts at falsification. Because one of the functions of 'paradigms' was to determine what should *count* as evidence of truth or falsity within the areas of science to which they related, 'paradigms' were not themselves subject to falsification by appeal to the evidence licensed by them within those areas. On Kuhn's account of the progress of science, evidence is rooted not in the 'brute facts' of particular areas of the world, but in our *assumptions* about how things are in those areas.

Science as a whole, we submit, like all other belief systems, is based on assumptions about the nature of the world which are even more fundamental to their systems than 'paradigmatic beliefs'. We have called these fundamental assumptions 'epistemic primitives'.[16] The belief in the uniformity of nature, for example, is epistemically primitive in the sense that it defines the nature of scientific reasoning and the tests which serve to characterise it. This being so, the principle of uniformity resists falsification; for it is what has to be believed to falsify anything. It is not something to be tested but rather a condition of test. Appreciation of the logical role played by epistemic primitives will thus put us in a position to provide an epistemic account in which a belief may be recalcitrant to falsification and yet be held perfectly rationally.

Epistemic primitives

The most deeply entrenched beliefs in any conceptual system (apart from our logical primitives which themselves provide the conceptual categories which determine the scope and limits of the patterns of coherent reasoning) are what we call 'epistemic primitives'. Epistemic primitives form a distinct class of beliefs which, together, constitute our epistemic framework for interpreting our entire experience of the world. On this view our chains of reasoning about that experience begin not with some immaculately perceived 'brute facts', but with these epistemically primitive beliefs which express our fundamental suppositions about the nature of our world. These beliefs are primitive in the sense that they have a threefold function in the belief systems which they underpin:

   a.   a presuppositional or foundational function;
   b.   a constitutive function;
   c.   an organisational function.

We turn now to an elucidation of these three functions.

The presuppositional function: Epistemic primitives are the pre-suppositions upon which our belief systems rest. Unlike other beliefs in such systems, they are neither inferences made within the discipline nor conclusions to chains of reasoning. Rather, they are presupposed by all the inferences, and all the chains of reasoning which have meaning within our disciplines. Unless the uniformity of nature is presupposed, the activity of science as we know it cannot be conducted. For science, in whatever branch it is practised, is an attempt to identify and express in laws the regularities supposed to prevail in nature. In other words, physicists do not arrive at their belief that nature behaves in regular ways as a result of repeated observations of such phenomena as apples falling to the ground when detached from their trees. Nor do they feel any more confirmed in this belief following such observations. Their belief in the uniformity of nature is logically prior to such observations in the sense that it is presupposed by them. Indeed, without their belief in the uniformity of nature, they simply could not account for these or any other empirical observations in an intelligible way. For it is their belief in the uniformity of nature which leads them to expect that it is possible to classify the behaviour of apples in any systematic way at all. And if some person should claim to have witnessed an instance of an apple in similar circumstances behaving in some other way, it would be difficult to see how he or she could mean his or her words in the way he or she wants to mean them, since the words themselves violate the principle which gives them their sense.

It is characteristic of 'epistemic primitives' that the enterprise they underpin cannot be engaged in unless they are presupposed. In this sense epistemic primitives are the foundational suppositions of our belief systems. On all empiricist accounts of science, for example, 'proof' of the truth of scientific claims consists in sensory evidence in favour of such claims. The force of the presuppositional function of epistemic primitives against the empiricist view may be expressed thus: '"Proof" presupposes that there are certain beliefs which are not themselves part of what is provable, but which give the concept of provability its sense.'[17] This giving of sense to the concept of provability is the second function of epistemic primitives – their constitutive function.

The constitutive function: To say that epistemic primitives are constitutive of our belief systems is to say that 'the foundational role they play within the belief system determines the nature of the enterprise in which one is engaged'.[18] The primitive belief 'God exists', for example, will characterise the theological enterprise by way of determining the range of acceptable propositions which function as theistic descriptions. Similarly, the belief that diseases have physical causes is constitutive of the science of pathology. Part of what it means to do pathology, in other words, is to seek the physical causes of disease. The belief that diseases have physical causes is not one that is arrived at by doing pathology. It is not a conclusion inferred from some observation or set of observations made in the practice of the discipline. Rather, this belief is the presupposition which gives sense to the making of such observations. The pathologist makes such observations, in other words, because for him or her to do pathology means to seek the causes of diseases by such methods. Unless the pathologist held this belief, the making of such observations would be irrational, at least in the sense that it could not be aimed at discovering causal connections between the phenomena observed and particular diseases. To say that belief in causality is a constitutive belief of pathology, therefore, is to imply that for a pathologist to give up that belief would be equivalent to his or her giving up pathology itself.

An epistemic primitive which underpins a discipline, then, is constitutive of that discipline in the sense that the holding of that belief is part of what it means to engage in that discipline. To give up such a belief, in other words, would be equivalent to giving up the discipline itself.

The organisational function: The third function of epistemic primitives in the belief systems they underpin is their organisational function. They organise their belief systems in the sense that they order the evidential relations that are to prevail in the system. Thus, the pathologist's belief in causality will constitute an organising principle by way of which the data of science is categorised. The pathologist will, accordingly, reject any attempt to account for an illness, for example, in terms of the influence of evil spirits. The ground for rejecting such an account will be that what counts as evidence in pathology is propositions about physical phenomena standing in causal relations to one another. Indeed, the mere presence of certain physical phenomena in cases of a particular disease will not be sufficient to convince the pathologist that he or she has found the cause of the disease. There must also be evidence that such phenomena have a causal relationship to the disease before the pathologist will be satisfied. Thus, the frequent incidence of raised cholesterol levels in the blood of patients suffering heart disease is not in itself sufficient proof that high cholesterol levels are the cause of heart disease. The causal mechanism linking cholesterol levels with the occurrence of heart disease must be identified in order to satisfy the demands of the principle of causality. Epistemic primitives such as this one, therefore, order the evidential relations that prevail within a belief system. At the same time, the position occupied by these primitives in their belief systems is such that they are not testable against the kind of evidence they license as relevant within those systems. Thus, the resistance to falsification offered by the religious belief that God exists can be explained in terms of this characteristic of 'epistemic primitives'.

In the mind of a child, therefore, the fixed character of such primitive beliefs need not, as White's criterion of indoctrination implies, be irrational. From this, it follows that a religious upbringing is not necessarily shown to have violated the liberal canon of rational autonomy by the fact that it produces a belief in God that is resistant to falsification. Rational autonomy would, however, be violated if such beliefs were incapable of revision. Our next task, then, is to show how 'epistemic primitives' in general and religious beliefs like 'God exists' in particular may be revised.

The revisability of epistemic primitives

To say that epistemic primitives cannot be overthrown by contrary evidence is not to say that they cannot be overthrown at all, nor that evidence is irrelevant to their truth or falsity. Rather, it is to say that their invulnerability to evidence derives from the logical role which they play within the system of belief in respect of which they determine what counts as evidence. This being so, the evidence for or against them can be no more secure within the system than they are themselves. On this view, one is no more certain of having a body after than before checking the fact in the mirror. Nor would an individual be prompted to renounce the belief in having only one body solely on the basis of the sight in the mirror of a second embodiment.

Rational arbitration of disputes between competing epistemic primitives does, indeed, take place; but it takes place at the fundamental level in the system, not at the evidential level. The process of overthrowing an epistemic primitive on this view, is one of determining the degree of entrenchment of the relevant primitive in the general body of beliefs about the world formed by our epistemic primitives. All our primitives may, in other words, be doubted, but not all at once. For as Wittgenstein puts it: 'If you tried to doubt everything you would not get as far as doubting anything. The game of doubting itself presupposes certainty.'[19] A doubt about a particular primitive can be held only in virtue of our certainty of another primitive or primitives. For example, a theist may doubt his or her belief in the existence of God, but he or she does so in virtue of the security (at least for the duration of this doubting process) of another primitive; for example, the belief that evil should not seem to be absolutely triumphant over good in the world. An accumulation of evidence to the effect that evil was winning the battle against good might move the theist to seek an alternative belief for ordering that part of his or her experience of the world previously ordered by belief in God. Until and unless a 'better' alternative is found, however, the latter belief will not be given up. For, if nature abhors a vacuum, it could be said that the human craving for understanding abhors any gap in the fundamental beliefs which order its experience of the world. We call this disposition the principle of progressive ordering.

Nor can theists specify in advance the conditions whose fulfilment would lead them to give up their belief in God. For part of what it would mean to specify those conditions would be to specify a different way of organising that area of their experience presently ordered by their belief in God. The recognition of a different and 'better' way of ordering that area of experience would, of course, be tantamount to abandoning one's theism. In this sense, epistemic primitives can be dislodged from their privileged position of priority within the system of belief. Indeed, the abundance of both religious conversions and apostasies throughout history testifies to the fact that such shifts do in fact take place.

Given the foregoing considerations, it is clear that the liberal canon of religious autonomy is not necessarily endangered by a religious upbringing on the ground that the resultant religious beliefs are *in principle* incapable of replacement. It remains to be shown, however, how such revisions may be made possible *in practice* by a religious upbringing.

Indoctrination and critical fallibility

We submit that the 'critical apparatus' necessary to enable a person to appraise the beliefs in which he or she is brought up consists in an understanding of the role played by the interrelationship between the epistemological and the logical underpinnings of the conceptual system and of their contribution to the beliefs which are ordered by them. If the person understands that his or her beliefs about the world are grounded, not in absolutely certain 'brute facts', but in fallible – though not necessarily false – assumptions about the world, he or she will be able to make rational commitments to particular beliefs without denying their corrigibility. Such a person will be able to understand the nature of rational enquiry, and not be misled – as so many students are – into seeing such enquiry as an application of the so-called scientific method for the purpose of establishing the alleged 'brute facts' of the world.

We recognise that such an initiation to the art of rational criticism cannot be accomplished in a single learning session, nor even in an extended series of such sessions. One's mastery of this art will, at best, grow throughout one's life. The foundations of this critical capacity can and should be laid, however, in what Ackerman and McLaughlin refer to as a child's 'primary culture'. The initial steps in this process will consist in alerting the child to the fact that good, sensible people around him or her hold different beliefs on whatever matters are concerned (in our case, religious questions). As the capacity grows in the child to reason about such differences, the process of alerting him or her to the foundations of such reasons in particular ways of seeing the world (or particular aspects of the world) can be taken further. This initiation to the art of rational criticism is unlikely to happen unless the parents or others responsible for the child's upbringing and subsequent education include the achievement of rational autonomy on the child's part amongst their intentions in the conduct of that upbringing and education. However, this *intention* alone will not suffice to ensure the desired result – rational autonomy. Nor, on our view, will the employment in the process of this upbringing/education of so-called rational *methods* alone suffice to achieve this result. Avoidance of emotional or other methods of persuasion not based on reason alone is, of course, desirable in this process; but the prescription of methods based on reason for avoiding indoctrination ignores the ultimate dependence of reasons upon their epistemological underpinnings.

In the case of a religious (theistic) upbringing in particular, neglect of the epistemological foundation of the religious belief system would be neglect of religion's most controversial belief – belief in God. Since the truth of the beliefs of a system is dependent upon what the epistemic primitives of the system concerned determine shall count as truth, the capacity to appraise those truths depends upon an understanding of the system's epistemic primitives and their role in it. This capacity, we submit, can only be developed by coming to grips with whatever issues are involved. In the case of religion, therefore, avoidance of those issues in the course of the child's upbringing only postpones the child's opportunity to develop the capacity to accept or reject religion in the light of critical appraisal. The development of rational autonomy in the person, we submit, is subverted by failure to provide him or her with the critical apparatus necessary for appraisal of whatever beliefs are taught. Since this apparatus can, and should, be provided in the religious upbringing, such an upbringing may not only be consonant with the development of that autonomy, but may also serve to make a positive contribution to its development. It may be helpful to make one further observation before considering the major objection against our epistemic defence of a religious upbringing. This observation is made for the benefit of supporters of such an upbringing. The child's capacity for acceptance of a religious faith grows with his or her capacity to reject it. The capacity for acceptance and for rejection are, in fact, a single capacity. A child's immaturity is often taken by parents and educators as a ground for taking with a grain of salt expressions of religious *scepticism* on the child's part. Consistency demands, however, that immaturity be accepted as a ground for taking the same attitude to the child's expressions of religious *commitment*. Commitment supposes, in other words, a considerable degree of maturity.

The early Christian church implicitly acknowledged this fact in its practice of initiating only adults to membership of the community. The continuing practice of infant baptism in most Christian churches is at odds, in our view, with the belief that the capacity for commitment is dependent upon maturity of the kind acknowledged in the early church. Not being magic, infant baptism does not preclude the possibility of subsequent *critical* initiation to the faith of the kind we have been advocating on the part of parents. However, persistence by the churches in the practice of infant baptism can certainly discourage parents and educators from seeing religious upbringing/education as a critical initiation to the faith concerned. Such discouragement would be inconsistent with the belief widely held amongst Christian churches that an authentic faith is an autonomous faith. One way of summing up our view of the issue between religious upbringing and rational autonomy is to say that rational autonomy is no more undermined by a religious upbringing than is the possibility of an eventual religious commitment by postponement of its institutional expression, for example Christian baptism, until maturity.

Religious vs scientific primitives

There is one major difficulty with our defence of a religious upbringing that remains to be addressed. Religious beliefs, it might be argued, differ from scientific and other beliefs at least in the respect that religious beliefs depend upon the assumption of the existence of a metaphysical reality called 'God'. Scientific and other secular belief systems do not depend, so it might be held, on any such assumption. The foundations of religious belief, it might be concluded, are, therefore, more doubtful than those of science or other secular belief systems. Since part of what 'rational' means when applied to a belief is 'likely to be true', it might be argued that an upbringing in a doubtful belief or set of beliefs such as religious belief(s) offends rationality, and thereby undermines rational autonomy in relation to this belief or set of beliefs. *Prima facie,* this is a formidable objection to the rationality of theism, and therefore to the justifiability of a religious upbringing in a liberal democracy. However, we believe that it is by no means insuperable.

We submit that science and other belief systems are dependent upon assumptions that can be appropriately described as metaphysical. Science, the alleged 'paradigm case' of rational belief,[20] depends upon a number of these assumptions:

a.   that an external world exists;
b.   that nature behaves in a sufficiently uniform way to enable us at least to record its regularities;
c.   that our senses give us a reliable picture of the world;
d.   that every event has an explanation.

We do not form our belief in the existence of an external world as a result of our experience of it. Rather, in order to explain rationally our experience, we need to presuppose the existence of that world. Similarly, our belief in the uniformity of nature is not a conclusion from scientific experiment, but a presupposition which gives sense to our attempts at recording nature's regularities. Our belief in the reliability of our senses cannot be empirically verified, since we have no faculty other than senses with which to test the reliability of sensory data. Finally, belief in the explicability of all events is the *presupposition* which leads us to engage in science, not a *conclusion* arrived at as a result of scientific investigation. All of these assumptions are untestable by empirical means, yet science cannot be engaged in unless they are made. Thus, if the religious belief in God is to be ruled irrational on the ground of its metaphysical character, consistency requires that science too be adjudged irrational on the same ground. Clearly, the interests of neither science nor religion are well served by the application of such a standard. Rational autonomy will be violated as much by an upbringing in 'irrational' scientific foundations as in 'irrational' religious foundations. A more propitious line of enquiry for both enterprises, we suggest, would be one which sought an epistemology capable of accommodating both religion and science. We have attempted that project elsewhere,[21] but space precludes an account of it here.

It should now be clear that the fixed character of religious beliefs may be due to their status as epistemic primitives within the system of religous beliefs. Since resistance to falsification is a feature of the behaviour of the epistemic primitives of all belief systems, the resistance to falsification by religious epistemic primitives is no more irrational than similar resistance offered by the primitives of any other system. Rational autonomy is not endangered, therefore, by the holding of such beliefs, provided that they are capable of revision. Enough has now been said to show that the revision of epistemic primitives is not only possible but does in fact happen. The process of revision is not, however, one of falsification at the evidential level of belief systems, but one of determining the degree of entrenchment which the primitive enjoys within the comprehensive body of our primitive beliefs. Given the foundational role of epistemic primitives within their systems, the conditions of their abandonment can only be specified with hindsight. The revisability of beliefs which are fixed in this sense shows that rational autonomy is not threatened *in principle* by an upbringing in them. *In practice,* however, a religious upbringing must include the provision of the relevant critical apparatus if rational autonomy is to be secured. There is, however, another feature of religious belief which, according to Gardner, undermines rational autonomy by closing such belief to critical scrutiny. This is the force of the second major liberal objection to a religious upbringing that we have discerned in the current debate. We must now consider that objection.

If my religion is true, must yours necessarily be false?

Gardner's objection to a religious upbringing rests on the assumption that a religious upbringing, by producing acceptance of one belief system as true, entails the rejection of its rivals as false, thereby closing the individual's mind where autonomous judgment requires it to be open. Gardner's point is the logical one that assertion of P (some proposition or set of propositions) logically entails denial of not-P. McLaughlin's prescription for reconciling liberal ideals with a religious upbringing, Gardner argues, ignores the force of this logical point. McLaughlin prescribes that children be made aware 'that alternatives (to the religious belief system of their upbringing) do exist'. But genuine alternatives are propositions which are inconsistent with one another. Thus, Gardner asks, 'Can it be thought rational to believe a proposition and to be aware of its negation and to appreciate that what one is aware of conflicts with what one believes, and yet to be open minded about it while continuing to believe what one originally believed? Surely rational thought cannot be reconciled with being open minded about a proposition whilst appreciating that it contradicts or is inconsistent with what one believes.'[22]

It must be conceded at the outset that Gardner's logical point is correct: assertion of P (some proposition or set of propositions) entails the denial of not-P. The question is, however, whether the case of upbringing in a particular religion accompanied by presentation of alternatives is a simple case of encouraging at the same time belief in P, and belief in not-P. Our reply is that in some respects, such is the case, but in other respects, it is not. The question of whether the former concession fatally undermines our account of a liberal religious upbringing is one we shall defer our response to until later. Before addressing ourselves to that major question, we believe it important for purposes of this debate to highlight some of the respects in which the relationship between the religion of one's upbringing and the religions presented as alternatives need not be mutually exclusive belief systems.

Commonality and divergence in religious traditions

First, it is well known that a number of major world religions share a number of fundamental beliefs in common. Christianity, Judaism and Islam, for example, believe in the same god. All three accept at least some sections of the Hebrew bible. Christianity and Judaism accept the Hebrew bible in its entirety, as well as many elements of law, ritual and doctrine. Even the Catholic church which, until Vatican II, was notorious for its claim to be 'the one true church', has now acknowledged the presence of genuine religious values in non-Christian religions. Most Christian churches, of course, acknowledge one revelation which calls them to reunion. In practice, therefore, a religious upbringing could, and from the point of view of a number of these religions should, present other religions with an emphasis on their *common,* rather that their *divergent,* beliefs. Such an emphasis, however, would not resolve the issues of principle raised by the divergent beliefs. Some theoretical basis is needed to show that the possession of divergent beliefs by various religions need not mean that one religious belief system has to be true, and the others false. A brief mention of some of the attempts at establishing such a basis will be helpful here.

Some theologians have posited the theory of a single revelation in which all human-kind can participate.[23] Particular religions, on this view, are manifestations of the apprehension of that revelation by a particular historical community. The divine nature of the revelation means that no apprehension of it will be exhaustive. Thus, divergences in the articulation of its content in terms of doctrine, law, etc. are attributable to the inexhaustible character of the revelation itself, as well as to the frailty of human receptivity. Indeed, one theologian[24] has taken this theory to the point of denying that the theological concept of 'revelation' is to be construed in terms of a message. This leads us to our second reason for saying that the faith of one's upbringing need not be exclusive of 'alternative' faiths.

Religion in the current debate has been equated with systems of beliefs. The existence of other features such as law and ritual have been acknowledged, of course, but the compatibility or incompatibility of rational autonomy and religious upbringing has been argued in terms of the openness, or otherwise, of the beliefs of one's upbringing to rational appraisal. But religion need not be seen primarily as a set of beliefs. Professor Gabriel Moran, for example, has argued that revelation should be seen as an *aesthetic* rather than a *scientific* category.[25] The divine is experienced, on this view, as a discernible presence in human affairs, not as a set of truths to be believed, revealed at some distant point in the past. Of course, formulation of this experience in terms of beliefs is necessary owing to the role of language in human life. Thus, questions of truth and falsity can be raised in relation to the beliefs formulated. Given that the formulations are secondary to the experiences to which they testify, however, a lesser degree of absoluteness may be claimed for them and a correspondingly greater degree of tolerance to other formulations of what is agreed to be revelatory experience is possible. However, even if these two clarifications of the nature of religion qualify to some degree Gardner's point about the mutually exclusive nature of genuine alternatives, they do not remove the difficulty entirely, nor do they deal with the case of non-religious alternatives. It is time now to meet Gardner's point head-on.

Corrigibility and religious commitment

The first point to be made here is that to hold P (some proposition or set of propositions) is not necessarily to hold P *incorrigibly*. Despite the firmness (perhaps justified) with which we may hold P, we do not thereby exclude absolutely the possibility that not-

P may be true, and that we may one day come to hold not-P to be true. A child brought up to hold a particular set of religious beliefs need not, therefore, have been led to hold them incorrigibly. Such a child could hold them firmly, yet not absolutely. Accordingly, the alternatives to this set of religious beliefs may be held to be false, but not incorrigibly so. A religious upbringing need not, therefore, lead to the absolute exclusion of alternatives as serious candidates for truth. But Gardner's standard of open-mindedness is one of neutrality, especially where religious upbringing is concerned: 'To be open minded about atheism requires one to be open minded about theism as well.'[26] The above response is thus unlikely to satisfy him. In order to clinch our case, therefore, we must challenge the standard itself.

The upbringing of children to an attitude of neutrality seems to us to be possible only *in abstracto*. In the concrete situation of most children in liberal democracies – as their parents and other religious educators well know – there is a veritable barrage of belief and value alternatives clamouring for their allegiance in the mass media. We believe that Gardner underestimates considerably the influence of alternative belief/value systems to religious systems during the course of most children's upbringing. He concedes 'that tensions exist between the liberal ideal and atheistic and agnostic upbringing'[27] but argues 'that stronger tensions are more likely to exist when the upbringing is of a strong religious kind'.[28] His reason for this view is that 'a religious position, unlike an atheistic or agnostic one, may well provide a variety of frameworks within which social and moral issues are to be assessed and judged. After all, there is no such thing as an atheistic position on, say, abortion, adultery, sex before marriage, the roles of men and women, the upbringing of children, what is not to be eaten or how one should spend certain days, but many religions provide frameworks within which these and other issues are to be discussed and decided upon.'[29] One might observe in passing that Gardner speaks of atheism and agnosticism in the abstract in this passage, and that some concrete forms of atheism, for example, atheistic communism, scientific humanism, do provide frameworks for assessing many significant beliefs, particularly religious beliefs.

The more important difficulty with Gardner's position, however, is that, in order to facilitate autonomous decision on such issues, he is committed to eliminating the teaching of frameworks for discussing and assessing them. This surely exposes the weakness in the position of neutrality and Gardner's prescription for reaching the liberal goal. Rational discussion of any issue supposes acceptance, at least for the duration of the discussion, of *some* framework of beliefs in virtue of which truth assessments can be made. Elimination of such frameworks from discussions not only cannot ensure autonomous rational assessments of the issues involved, but it actually renders such assessments impossible. If he is to secure his ideal of autonomous rationality, in other words, Gardner cannot escape introducing children to the kinds of frameworks which make such rationality possible. The key to securing rational autonomy in religious and other matters, we submit, lies not in eschewing initiation to such frameworks in a vain effort to maintain neutrality to their alternatives, but in providing the relevant critical apparatus in presenting both the religious frameworks and their alternatives. More needs to be said about Gardner's view of presentation of alternatives as the means of securing the goal of rational autonomy.

The concept of choice implies the existence of alternatives from which to choose. However, the range of alternatives that can be offered to be 'chosen' in any upbringing/education is necessarily limited. If Gardner's prescription for attaining the liberal goal of rational autonomy is to ensure that the child is presented with all religious and non-religious alternatives in the course of his or her upbringing, it is surely absurdly impractical. How many parents or teachers are versed in all the religious alternatives, let alone the non-religious ones, presently accepted in various parts of the world today, not to mention in the past or the future? How many children would be capable of coping with the sheer volume of knowledge involved, even if parents and teachers could provide them with it? We submit that rational autonomy is better secured, once the existence of alternatives is made known to the child, by providing him or her with an understanding of the epistemological bases in which the differences between whatever alternatives he or she may wish to study lie than in the study of an indefinite series of alternatives.

We do not claim that a religious upbringing or later conversion to some religious faith is an indispensable condition of one's being able to appraise such a faith. We have claimed that such an insider's perspective does not preclude the possibility of such an appraisal, and that it can, indeed, facilitate it. One further claim can be added here. Rational appraisal of a world-view, and of its attendant values and attitudes, must surely suppose some attempt at empathising with that view, and those values and attitudes. Empathy falls a long way short of commitment to a faith, but it must come close enough to enable the would-be appraiser to see and feel something of what the believer sees and feels. We find it difficult to see how a neutral approach to the appraisal of religious (and non-religious) positions could result in any greater comprehension of such positions, or tolerance towards them than those evidenced in the reactions of liberal democracies to Ayatollah Khomeini's sentence upon Salman Rushdie.

Concluding remarks

In this article we have argued that a religious upbringing need not violate the ideal of rational autonomy shared by liberal ideology and a number of religious traditions. We have shown that the resistance to falsification offered by beliefs such as the belief in God is a feature of their epistemically primitive character. Persistence in such beliefs in the face of counter evidence is therefore not necessarily irrational. Nor can the charge of irrationality be sustained on the ground that their epistemically primitive character makes such beliefs incapable of revision. Revision of an epistemic primitive, however, given its role as the belief which licenses truth assessments within its system, is not accomplished by a process of evidential assessment. Being one of the assumptions forming our fundamental framework for interpreting all our experience of the world, an epistemic primitive is given up only when it is incompatible with primitives which are more deeply entrenched in that framework, and an alternative primitive for ordering its area of experience is available. In principle, we concluded, epistemic primitives like the theist's belief in God are revisable. Such a revision is also possible in practice provided that the child's upbringing/education in religion includes the provision of an understanding of the interrelationships between the logical and epistemological levels of the system which form the basis of the system's claims to be true. We called the understanding of these interrelationships the 'critical apparatus' of a belief system. To the objection that a religious upbringing results in fixed beliefs, we thus responded by showing that persistence in a certain kind of belief (of which belief in God was one example) need not be irrational, nor exclude the possibility of eventual rational revision.

To the objection that a religious upbringing closed a child's mind to alternatives to which rational autonomy requires the mind to remain open, we argued that critical fallibilism achieves this and demonstrated the limited usefulness of alternatives as means of securing rational autonomy. Firm belief in P (some proposition or set of propositions) does not imply incorrigible preclusion of the possibility that P might be false, and, indeed, that circumstances might arise to make me believe it to be false. It follows that not-P, though firmly believed to be false now, is open to similar revision in the future. A religious upbringing can lead one to see one's beliefs as corrigible, and therefore need not violate rationality by placing them beyond revision. Though provision of some alternatives was necessary to rational autonomy, we argued that the impracticality of providing the full range of religious and non-religious alternatives in an upbringing/education meant such provision could not be the principal means of securing such autonomy. Since the differences between such alternatives lay in their epistemic assumptions, the essential 'critical apparatus' for appraising them consisted in an understanding of the nature of those assumptions, their functions within their own systems and in the overall framework within which we interpret the whole of our experience.

Notes
1. Salman Rushdie, *The Satanic Verses,* New York, Viking, 1988.
2. T H McLaughlin, 'Parental rights and the upbringing of children,' *Journal of Philosophy of Education,* 18, 1984, pp. 75–83. See also T H McLaughlin's second contribution to this debate, 'Religion, upbringing and liberal values,' *Journal of Philosophy of Education,* 19, 1985, pp. 119–127.
3. E Callan, 'McLaughlin on parental rights,' *Journal of Philosophy of Education,* 19, 1985, pp. 111–118.
4. P Gardner, 'Religious upbringing and the liberal ideal of religious autonomy,' *Journal of Philosophy of Education,* 22, 1988, pp. 89–105.
5. E Callan, *op. cit.,* p. 115.
6. T H McLaughlin (1984), *op. cit.,* pp. 77–78.
7. J P White, *The Aims of Education Re-stated,* London, Routledge and Kegan Paul, 1982, cited by T H McLaughlin, 1984, *op. cit.,* p. 77.
8. T H McLaughlin (1984), *op. cit.,* p. 78.
9. *Ibid.*
10. *Ibid.,* p. 80.
11. *Ibid.*
12. A term T H McLaughlin takes from B A Ackerman, *Social Justice in the Liberal State,* New Haven, Yale University Press, 1980, chapter 5.
13. T H McLaughlin (1984), *op. cit.,* p. 80.
14. *Ibid.*
15. T S Kuhn, *The Structure of Scientific Revolutions,* Chicago, University of Chicago Press, 1970, first edition 1969.
16. The first full account of this concept was given in the form of a Presidential Address by R S Laura to *Philosophy of Education Society of Australasia 1980 Conference.* The title of this paper was 'Epistemic relativism: some logical difficulties concerning the rational arbitration of competing conceptual systems.' See also the following works by Laura for applications of this concept to problems in education: 'Philosophical foundations of religious education,' *Educational Theory,* 28, 1978, pp. 310–317: 'The philosophical foundations of science education,' *Educational Philosophy and Theory,* 13, 1981, pp. 1–13: 'To educate or to indoctrinate: that is still the question,' *Educational Philosophy and Theory,* 15, 1983, pp. 43–55; 'The philosophical foundations of medical education,' *Educational Philosophy and Theory,* 17, 1985, pp. 29–43. See also R S Laura and D McCarthy, 'Religious education versus science education: on taking the dogma out of dogmas,' *Educational Research and Perspectives,* 12, 1985, pp. 3–9. P Gardner adverts (pp. 96-97) to the possibility that religious beliefs might be the kinds of beliefs which form the frameworks of 'enquiry and assessment ... and, as a result, they remain immune to, or above, our reflections and decisions.' However, his protest is that such beliefs 'have a tendency to persist even when the spotlight of enquiry focuses on them.' P Gardner appears to assume that such beliefs are subject to evidential assessment 'when the spotlight of enquiry focuses on them.' Our theory of epistemic primitives will show that P Gardner's assumption evidences an incomplete understanding of the epistemic role played by such beliefs, and of the manner in which they may be revised.
17. R S Laura and D McCarthy, *op. cit.,* p. 7.
18. *Ibid.,* p. 8.
19. L Wittgenstein, *On Certainty* (edited by G E M Anscombe and E H Von Wright and translated by D Paul and G E M Anscombe), New York, Harper and Row, 1972, first edition 1969, para. 115.
20. See, for example, the contrast drawn by I M M Gregory and R G Woods between 'the *bona fide* theories ... of the physical sciences' and 'the pure doctrine of religion,' in 'Indoctrination: inculcating doctrines,' in I A Snook (ed.), *Concepts of Indoctrination,* London, Routledge and Kegan Paul, 1972, p. 173.
21. R S Laura and M Leahy, 'The fourth dimension of space: a meeting place of science and religion,' *Journal of Christian Education,* 91, 1988, pp. 5–17. We have collaborated in the production of a fuller account of this epistemology in a book to be titled *Can Religious Education Be Rationally Defended?*

22. P Gardner, *op. cit.,* p. 92.
23. See, for example, G Moran, *The Present Revelation,* New York, Seabury Press, 1972, *passim.* For a critical discussion of current theories of revelation, see A Dulles, *Models of Revelation,* Doubleday, New York, 1983.
24. G Moran, *Interplay,* Winona, St Mary's Press, 1981, p. 54ff.
25. G Moran (1981), *op. cit.,* p. 54.
26. *Op. cit.,* p. 92.
27. *Ibid.,* p. 97.
28. *Ibid.*
29. *Ibid.*

8.4 Indoctrination, evangelisation, catechesis and religious education
Michael Leahy

The recent revival of discussion[1] of the concept of 'indoctrination' is welcome for two reasons. Firstly, it affords me as a philosopher the opportunity to propose some remedies to the defects in the traditional accounts of this key concept of educational theory. Secondly, it offers me as a religious educator the opportunity to defend my teaching against the charge of 'indoctrination', but at the same time to sound a *caveat* to religious educators in relation to their classroom practices.

In this article I wish:

a. to defend a view of 'indoctrination' according to which teachers of the secular subjects of the curriculum run a greater risk of indoctrinating than teachers of religious education; and

b. to show that a defence of such forms of teaching as 'catechesis' and 'evangelisation' against the charge of 'indoctrination' is not a legitimation of the use of such forms in the religious education classroom.

I shall begin by briefly summarising and appraising the three standard accounts of 'indoctrination'. Then I shall set forth the alternative account of 'indoctrination' referred to in (a) above. Finally, I shall propose an account of the distinctions which ought to be recognised between the *church activities* of 'evangelisation' and 'catechesis', and the *school activity* of classroom religious education.

The standard accounts of 'indoctrination'

The concept of 'indoctrination' functions in educational theory as a conceptual tool for distinguishing legitimate from illegitimate forms of teaching. Of the three standard accounts as well as most other accounts of 'indoctrination', legitimate forms of teaching are those which respect what might be called the 'norms' of education. The 'norms' of education implicit in these accounts, on my reading of them, are first respect for *freedom* of the individual in the formation of beliefs, and second respect for *truth*. Indeed, I discern in some of these discussions, particularly in relation to religious education in church schools, a third 'norm' of education. However,

426

since this third 'norm', in my opinion, contrasts 'education' with 'proselytising' rather that with 'indoctrination', I shall complete my discussion of 'indoctrination' before introducing it. The first two 'norms' of education thus lay down my criteria for assessing the standard accounts of 'indoctrination': the ability of those accounts to provide educators with the means of respecting freedom and truth in the teaching of beliefs.

The three accounts of 'indoctrination' which I have called standard are the 'method', 'content' and 'intention' accounts. It will be convenient to begin this discussion with a consideration of the 'intention' account of 'indoctrination'.

Intention accounts

The 'intention' account of 'indoctrination' may be summarised in I A Snook's formula: 'A person indoctrinates P (a proposition or set of propositions) if he teaches with the intention that the pupil believe P regardless of the evidence.'[2] The assumption underlying such accounts is that 'indoctrination' is an *activity* and *activities* are normally specified by intentions:[3]

> At least a minimal necessary condition of something's being indoctrination is that it is an activity; the indoctrinator must be *doing* something. Now, we normally distinguish one activity from another in terms of the agent's intention.

The moral criticism implied in a term like 'indoctrination' is thus inappropriately attributed unless 'indoctrination' is an action distinguished from other actions by its intention. The other assumption implicit in Snook's formula is that provision of *evidence* is what gives us access to *truth*. Since this is the assumption underpinning the 'content' accounts of 'indoctrination' I will postpone criticism of this assumption until I treat those accounts below.

The 'intention' accounts of 'indoctrination', it seems to me, can be criticised on at least two grounds: firstly the relationship they assume between intention and action, and secondly their inability to accommodate 'unintentional indoctrination'.

Firstly, as P J Sheehan points out, 'normally' does not logically entail 'necessarily', and thus actions need not be specified by intentions.[4]

Moreover, it is difficult to see how actions that might be regarded as indoctrinatory could be *specified* by the kinds of intention required by the 'intention' accounts of 'indoctrination'. If we take G E M Anscombe's analysis of 'intention',[5] such actions could not be cases of 'intentional action' because, being accompanied by a multiplicity of intentions, they admit of no *specifying* intention. The alternative to 'intentional action', on Anscombe's analysis, is 'action with the intention that'. But 'action with the intention that' is action of such a particular kind that it is specified by a single intention. Examples of 'action with the intention that' would be 'punching', 'hammering' and 'stitching'. This class of actions is surely too specific in its connotation and too narrow in its scope to accommodate within its denotation the forms of action that are commonly regarded at indoctrinatory. One can 'teach without providing reasons', or 'manipulate student emotions', or 'teach as true beliefs which are not known to be true', to mention but a few examples of actions regarded by some as indoctrinatory, with a multiplicity of intentions. Thus 'indoctrination', it would seem, cannot be reduced to any form of action – on Anscombe's analysis of 'intention', at least – capable of being distinguished by a particular intention in the manner asserted by defenders of the 'intention' account of 'indoctrination'.

The 'intention' account of 'indoctrination' faces the further difficulty of showing that indoctrinatory action is of such a kind that it necessarily conforms with the intention of the performer. One can admit that 'actions with the intention that' are of this kind, but these are of no help here because we have just eliminated such actions as models of indoctrinatory action. Thus defenders of the intention account of 'indoctrination' have to show that indoctrinatory action is of a kind different from 'action with the intention that', and necessarily conforming with the performer's intention.

Secondly, it also seems to me that the 'intention' account does not do justice to the concern held by some for what may be termed 'unintentional indoctrination'.[6] Amongst the referents of this term, I would include teaching which proposes beliefs expressing ideological biases, unrecognised as such by the teachers concerned, such as sexism, racism or class discrimination. The power of such forms of 'hidden curricula' is now universally recognised in curriculum theory. By excluding such undesirable forms of teaching from the class of indoctrinatory teaching, one renounces the prescriptions offered by some accounts of 'indoctrination' as means of combating such forms of teaching.

Although their defenders frequently couch their versions of the 'method' account in terms of prescriptions of various methods of teaching, those versions are, I believe, reducible to a certain prescription. Let me turn now to an appraisal of the 'method' accounts of 'indoctrination'.

The 'method' account

The 'method' account of 'indoctrination' may be defined as 'the teaching of P (some proposition or set of propositions) to students by any method other than providing reasons for P (where P stands for some proposition or set of propositions)'. Thus, the prescription offered by this account for educating rather than indoctrinating is 'teach only by providing reasons for what you teach'. The initial plausibility of this account lies firstly in its agreement with popular usage of the term 'indoctrination' as a synonym for such terms as 'brainwashing' and 'thought control', and secondly in its demand for a rational alternative to such apparently irrational practices. The assumption underpinning the 'method' account of indoctrination is that freedom and truth are safeguarded appropriately in matters of intellectual enquiry by the provision of reasons for the beliefs taught. This assumption, I submit, faces insuperable difficulties.

Logically, the prescription to provide reasons for content taught would permit an *ad infinitum* demand for such reasons from students. Assuming that teachers are supposed to be working within some paradigm of rationality on which truth can be achieved, student access to truth is blocked on the 'method' prescription by its failure to indicate how the quest for reason for P may be rationally terminated. For, unless this quest can be rationally terminated, the student is never going to have the logical ground required for forming a judgment about the truth of P. Thus, in their efforts to protect the *freedom* of students by permitting an unlimited quest for reasons, the holders of the 'method' account of 'indoctrination' unwittingly stultify the students' quest for *truth*. Holders of the 'content' accounts of 'indoctrination', by contrast, see the safeguarding of student access to truth as the sole means of protecting student freedom in matters of intellectual enquiry.

The 'content' account

The 'content' account of 'indoctrination' may be summarised as follows: 'A teacher indoctrinates his/her students by teaching P (some proposition or set of propositions) where P is unfalsifiable'.[7] Holders of this account believe that genuine education consists in the communication of knowledge, and that one of the conditions of a valid knowledge claim is that P be true. Thus, in a public forum like a school classroom, what is taught as true cannot, according to these writers, be just what any individual or group takes to be so. Rather, they argue, what is taught as true must be capable of judgment as such by 'publicly accepted' standards.[8] Such standards turn out, on this account, to be the empirical standards of science. Indeed, holders of the 'content' account often present religious education as the 'paradigm case' of 'indoctrination' and science education as the 'paradigm case' of education.

On this view, the content of religious education is dependent on the truth of such fundamental assumptions as the belief that God exists. This assumption is unfalsifiable, that is, no empirical event can be specified such that its occurrence would be accepted by them as sufficient ground for renouncing this assumption. Scientific beliefs, by contrast, can be falsified, so the argument goes, by empirical tests, and are thus, in principle at least, open to scrutiny by the public at large. Students access to truth, on this account, is thus secured by teaching only empirically falsifiable beliefs, and is blocked by teaching unfalsifiable beliefs. This prescription, I submit, is no more effective at securing student access to truth than the 'intention' or 'method' prescriptions.

Difficulties with the 'falsifiability' criterion

The validity of the 'falsifiability' criterion employed by such holders of the 'content' account as Flew, and Gregory and Woods, depends upon two unsustainable assumptions: firstly, that this criterion can overcome the logical difficulties facing its formulation, and, secondly, that empirical evidence provides us with a theory-independent knowledge of the world (or at least of that aspect of it with which a particular observation or test is concerned).

As regards the first assumption, the difficulty with the 'falsificationist' formulation of the 'content' criterion of 'indoctrination' is that it cannot ensure the falsifiability of existential statements such as 'at least one crow is white'. For no matter how many crows we observed, all of them being black, we could never guarantee that the next one we might observe would not be white. Defenders of this formulation might reply that the unfalsifiability of such restricted generalisations does not matter, because science is concerned only with preserving the falsifiability of unrestricted generalisations like scientific laws and hypotheses. However, R S Laura points out that they do so at the cost of violating a logical principle that he calls 'the principle of propositional or truth-value symmetry'.[9] This principle requires that we distribute symmetrically 'truth-value to statements that are logically equivalent' (*ibid.*, 5–6). Thus the falsification of the unrestricted generalisation 'all crows are black' would be a statement like 'at least one crow is not black'. But the latter is an existential generalisation. This defence of falsificationism is therefore preserving its unrestricted generalisations at the cost of surrendering statements of the very logical kind to which their falsifications belong. Thus the 'falsificationist' formulation of the 'content' criterion of 'indoctrination' is no freer of logical difficulties than its 'verificationist' predecessor.

Even if the logical difficulties associated with the formulation of the 'content' criterion could be overcome, however, a more formidable set of difficulties faces the second of this criterion's underpinning assumptions. This assumption is that, because empirical evidence is ultimately derived from sensory tests of some kind, such evidence will yield the same conclusions about the aspect of the world under investigation to anyone endowed with normal senses and knowledge of how to conduct the relevant tests. This assumption reflects what is sometimes called the 'immaculate perception' theory. According to this theory, states of affairs within the world admit of only one description, and human perceptual and conceptual faculties are capable of apprehending any state of affairs in the world and formulating the appropriate description independent of any influence except the state of affairs itself. This theory has been severely undermined by philosophers of science over the last twenty years or more, so a brief summary of their criticisms will suffice for my purposes here.

Observation, which lies at the basis of empirical research, is now commonly recognised as being observer-dependent in a number of ways. Firstly, observation is selective. No rational set of observations can be conducted without in some way limiting the range of phenomena to be observed. Secondly, even the same retinal image can provide two viewers with different visual experiences. Well-known examples of such experiences are cases where two or more viewers presented with an image of a staircase differ as to whether the image is of the upper of under surface of the staircase. Thirdly, all 'seeing', N R Hanson[10] has shown, is 'seeing as'. Part of the act of 'seeing', in other words, for human beings is seeing the object apprehended in that act as *something:* elephant, plant, etc. Thus, our 'seeing' is theory-dependent at least to the extent that *what* we can see things as is limited by the catalogue of things in the world provided to us in the language we *inherit*. True, the language we inherit can be used to extend that catalogue, but such extensions are themselves theoretical construction of varying levels of sophistication. I conclude, therefore, that states of affairs in the world do not legislate a unique description, as the so-called 'immaculate perception' theory held, and that human apprehension of any state of affairs is dependent upon theory of varying levels of sophistication.

Thus, the 'content' account is no more able than the 'method' and 'intention' accounts of 'indoctrination' to provide students with the secure access to truth required by our second 'norm' of education. I turn now to the task of providing an alternative to these accounts of 'indoctrination'.

An alternative account of 'indoctrination'

Truth was taken in the 'content' account of 'indoctrination' to be a mirror or picture correspondence between states of affairs in the world and what we say about them in our propositions.[11] However, our demonstration that our empirical investigations of the world terminate not in aspects of the world in their 'brute' state, but in *assumptions* about such aspects of the world, rules out such a naive correspondence theory of truth. At the end of our empirical studies, in other words, we are left not with a picture of an aspect of the world as it is in itself, but with a picture of it *as it is taken to be in the particular theoretical frameworks* we have employed in our studies. Widespread recognition of the theory-dependence of scientific research has led to the adoption of different views of the relationship between our theories and the aspects of the world with which our theories are concerned. Rather than adopt the self-refuting position of absolute scepticism, or settle prematurely for a Kuhnian-type relativism,[12] I wish to defend an epistemology of modified scepticism which is based on an ontology of fallibilist realism.

On the latter view, an external world exists independently of what I think or say about it, but I only have access to it, as it were, through my 'thinkings' and 'sayings'. What I say about the world is capable of being true, and indeed I may be justified in firmly believing such propositions to be true, but I am never in a position to assert infallibly that they are true. On this epistemology, then, truth may still be conceived as a correspondence between proposition and fact, but our powers of recognising and encapsulating such correspondence in propositions are fallible. Indeed, such correspondence may be more readily inferred from the coherence of the proposition in which it is expressed with other propositions than from observation and experiment. If such is the nature of truth, a theory of 'indoctrination' which purports to satisfy our second 'norm' of education (the 'norm' of truth) will be one which takes account of this nature. One such account of 'indoctrination' is R S Laura's.[13]

Laura's view of 'indoctrination' may be expressed in the following formula: 'A teacher indoctrinates students in respect of P (some proposition or set of propositions) by teaching students P without at the same time providing them with the "critical apparatus" necessary to enable them rationally to appraise P.' By 'critical apparatus', Laura means an understanding of the logical dependence of the beliefs of a system (such as a subject in the school curriculum) upon those epistemological assumptions in virtue of which those beliefs are held to be true. Laura calls those fundamental assumptions about the nature of the world (or of various aspects of it) in which our empirical enquiries terminate 'epistemic primitives'.

'Epistemic primitives', according to Laura,[14] form a distinct class of beliefs which together constitute our framework for interpreting our entire experience of the world. Every belief system (and thus every subject in the curriculum) thus has its foundations in epistemically primitive beliefs about the nature of the particular aspect of the world with which the system is concerned. To say that a set of beliefs is epistemically primitive to a belief system is to say that they have three functions in the system:

a. they are the *presuppositions* about the nature of the reality with which the system is concerned which provide the foundation for the system's existence;

b. they *constitute* their systems in the sense that they determine what it means to engage in the activity springing from the beliefs of the relevant system, for example, to believe in a transcendent deity is part of what it means to be a Christian; and

c.   they *organise* the system in the sense that they determine the logical relations to prevail within the system, for example, explanations of the problem of evil will ultimately be acceptable to Christians only if such explanations refer to God's purposes rather than to such things as human genetic endowment.

What will count as truth in any belief system, on this theory, will be determined by the 'epistemic primitives' of the relevant system. If student access to truth is to be properly safeguarded, as our second 'norm' of education requires, students will need to be provided, on this theory, not only with an understanding of the content of the subject concerned, but also of the 'epistemic primitives' underpinning that subject. To teach the content of any subject without also providing students with an understanding of that content's dependence on its 'epistemic primitives' would be to *indoctrinate* rather than to *educate.*

Laura's account of 'indoctrination', it seems to me, has two important advantages over the standard accounts. Firstly, it tells what we must do to educate as well as what we are doing if we are indoctrinating. Secondly, Laura's account, by exposing the dependence of all belief systems upon their 'epistemic primitives', alerts us to the danger of indoctrinating in *all* subjects, whereas the standard accounts tend to limit this danger to religion, history and politics.

It would be unfortunate, however, if this demonstration that religion can be taught without indoctrinating were to be taken as justification of all the forms of religion teaching conducted in school classrooms. Indeed, I contend that there is a further 'norm' of education that can be violated by the use of the classroom programme for certain forms of religion teaching. This 'norm' I call the *'norm' of respect for the autonomy of the school classroom.*

Autonomy of the classroom and catechesis/evangelisation

When I speak of the 'autonomy of the classroom', I am asserting that the school classroom has its own peculiar purpose − education. This purpose it to be distinguished from such non-educational purposes as the use of the classroom by governments to promote ideologies such as Nazism or Fascism. Similarly, the use of the classroom by religious groups for the primary purpose of ensuring acceptance or maintenance of their particular religious faiths in students, I take to be a clearly religious rather than educational use of the classroom programme.

The specifying purpose of education as it is carried out in the formal curriculum of a school, college or university is, I submit, to enable students to appraise critically the content of that curriculum. Such institutions may legitimately represent in a variety of ways their commitment to particular sets of beliefs and values. However, they may not, in my view, legitimately substitute *commendation* of such commitments for *critical appraisal* of them as their primary purpose in any part of their classroom curriculum. The classroom programme of any school in any subject, I submit, must hold the truth-claims presented in subjects, as it were, at arm's length for critical appraisal by students. To do otherwise, in my view, is to subvert an educational institution into some other kind of institution such as a forum for ideological propaganda, or a church.

Certain forms of religion teaching, which are sometimes commended for use in Catholic schools but which may also be practised in other schools, are, in my view illegitimate, not because they indoctrinate students, but because they violate the autonomy of the school classroom. Let me be more specific.

The two forms of religion teaching to which I refer are called 'evangelisation' and 'catechesis'. In its fundamental sense, I take the term 'evangelisation' to mean the attempt by a believer or believers in the Christian faith to convert non-believers to that faith. 'Catechesis' I take to mean the dialogue – usually instructional – voluntarily engaged in by believers for the specific purpose of nourishing the faith they share. Both 'evangelisation' and 'catechesis' are bound, I believe, by the nature of faith itself as it is understood in the Christian tradition, to respect the freedom of individuals to form their own judgments as to the truth of the Christian faith. Respect for the 'norms' of freedom and truth, however, is not, in my view, sufficient to qualify such teaching as authentic forms of education.

Forms of teaching which are claimed to be authentic forms of education must always retain as their *primary purpose* the enabling of students to appraise critically the content taught. 'Evangelisation' and 'catechesis', it seems to me, will always *by definition* have 'the conversion of non-believers' in the case of the former, and 'the nourishment of faith' in the case of the latter, as their primary purposes. The enabling of critical appraisal, in other words, can never be more than a secondary purpose of 'evangelisation' or 'catechesis'.[15] The different primary purposes, I submit, are the features which should be taken as distinguishing forms of teaching which are *educational* from forms of teaching belonging to some other category such as *political* or *religious*.

Because they violate the educational purpose of the classroom, therefore, and not because they necessarily violate the 'norms' of respect for freedom and truth, 'evangelisation' and 'catechesis' cannot, in my view, legitimately be done in the formal programme of the school classroom. From their illegitimacy in the formal classroom programme, however, one cannot conclude that 'evangelisation' and 'catechesis' are illegitimate practices in other parts of the school programme. Indeed, it is worth taking a moment to indicate briefly what place these practices might, and perhaps ought, legitimately to occupy in Christian schools.

The place of evangelisation/catechesis in Christian schools

Christian schools are obliged by the explicit mandate of their own tradition to bear witness to the Gospel. They fulfil this mandate in part by including within their formal classroom curriculum a subject called 'religious education'. 'Religious education', I define as *the critical initiation of students into the religious dimension of reality.* To the extent that Christian schools provide students by this means with the opportunity of considering the possibility of such a dimension to reality, they give the study of religion an importance that is generally unrecognised in Australian government schools, most of which include no 'religious education' in their curricula.

Christian schools also have the right and duty to testify to their faith in their human relations practices, especially in their administrative and disciplinary practices. This witness should become more explicit, however, in voluntary activities in the school programme. Prayer groups, social action groups, liturgy groups, retreats, Christian living camps are all examples of voluntary settings in which 'evangelisation' and 'catechesis' would be legitimate.

A Christian school should also bear witness to its faith by providing genuine service to the needy — whether the need be financial or educational. Confinement of its attention to looking after its own domestic needs or, worse still, to the needs of those who can best afford to pay, ought to be seen as self-service, and as such to bear a negative witness to the Gospel.

As others have noted,[16] Christian schools are limited in their own powers to execute the Christian mission of evangelisation. This recognition is, I submit, one sign that we have arrived at a point in the history of religious education from which we are able clearly to distinguish the function of the school from the function of the church itself. In my view, we would do well to recognise that the best witness a Christian school can bear to the Christian faith is to show a readiness to submit that faith to the critical scrutiny of a genuine 'religious education'. By this means, not only are freedom and truth respected, but students are also provided with the religious knowledge necessary to make an informed decision to accept or reject that faith.

Notes
1. Recent publications on 'indoctrination' include R Young, 'Critical teaching and learning,' *Educational Theory,* 38, 1988, pp. 47–59; B Spiecker, 'Indoctrination, intellectual virtues and rational emotions,' *Journal of Philosophy of Education,*

21, 1987, pp. 261–66; B Marthaler, 'Dilemma for religious educators: indoctrination or indifference,' *Religious Education,* 82, 1987, pp. 555–68; W Hare, 'Open-mindedness in moral education,' *Journal of Moral Education,* 16, 1987, pp. 99–107; R Aldrich, 'Learning by faith,' *Education Today,* 36, 1986, pp. 3–14.

2. I A Snook, 'Indoctrination and moral responsibility,' in I A Snook (ed.), *Concepts of Indoctrination,* London, Routledge and Kegan Paul, 1972, p. 154.

3. J P White, 'Indoctrination and intentions,' in I A Snook (ed.), *op. cit.,* p. 121.

4. P J Sheehan, 'Education and indoctrination: some notes,' *Dialogue,* 4, 1970, p. 61.

5. G E M Anscombe, *Intention,* Oxford, Basil Blackwell, 1957.

6. See John Kleinig's useful account of what I have called 'unintentional indoctrination' as a 'perficience' in his *Philosophical Issues in Education,* London, Croom Helm, 1982, p. 29.

7. Holders of the 'content' account of 'indoctrination' include Antony Flew (see his 'Indoctrination and doctrines' and 'indoctrination and religion,' chapters 6 and 9 respectively in I A Snook [ed.], *op. cit.*), I M M Gregory and R W Woods (see their 'Indoctrination: inculcating doctrines,' chapter 14, *ibid.*), and, as a partial criterion, John Wilson. See the latter's 'Education and indoctrination,' in T H B Hollins (ed.), *Aims and Education,* Manchester, Manchester University Press, 1964, chapter 2.

8. John Wilson, *op. cit.,* p. 28.

9. R S Laura, 'The philosophical foundations of science education,' *Educational Philosophy and Theory,* 13, 1981, pp. 1–13.

10. N R Hanson, *Patterns of Discovery,* Cambridge, Cambridge University Press, 1965.

11. Here I am referring to the 'picture' theory of meaning proposed by Ludwig Wittgenstein in his *Tractatus Logicophilosophicus* (1922).

12. T S Kuhn, *The Structure of Scientific Revolutions,* Chicago, University of Chicago Press, 1970, first edition, 1969, postscript.

13. R S Laura, 'To educate or to indoctrinate: that is still the question,' *Educational Philosophy and Theory,* 15, 1983, pp. 43–55.

14. R S Laura, 'Epistemic relativism: some logical difficulties concerning the rational arbitration of competing conceptual systems,' Presidential Address to the Philosophy of Education Society of Australasia, 1980.

15. Kevin Nichols' notion of 'educational catechesis' in his book *Cornerstone,* Middlegreen, St Paul Publications, in my opinion, confuses further the very concepts that need to be clarified. If voluntary participation and existing faith are essential conditions of catechesis, as K Nichols seems to acknowledge ('you cannot catechise a non-believer', p. 15), and indoctrination of religious beliefs is morally wrong (pp. 19–20), it is difficult to see how catechesis can take place in the compulsory religious education classes of Catholic schools in which faith stances range from commitment to avowed unbelief. In my view, K Nichols would do better to distinguish (rather than to conflate) 'religious education' and 'catechesis' according to the different primary purposes I ascribe to them here. It is worth noting that K Nichols dismisses rather than refutes, in his analysis of 'indoctrination' and its bearing on religious education, the challenge to the cognitive status of religious beliefs (pp. 19–20).

16. G Rossiter, 'The need for a "creative divorce" between catechesis and religious education in Catholic schools,' *Religious Education,* 77, 1982, pp. 21–20.

9. Knowledge and understanding

A proper analysis of the status of the cognitive dimension of the Christian religion is foundational to any discussion of the subject-matter content of Christian education, as is a proper understanding of the nature of understanding for any discussion of the purpose and methodology of the practice of Christian education.

D Z Phillips is another philosopher who has been a major influence in the philosophy of religion and has commented on the debate about religion and education.[1] His early article, 'Philosophy and religious education,' was first published in *British Journal of Educational Studies,* 18, 1970, pp. 5–27. He takes Paul Hirst's insistence that there are 'no agreed public tests for truth and falsity' in religion as his starting point (see section 6). Phillip rejects this: 'there are various criteria recognised by religious believers for what can and cannot be said to God and about God' within the religious community, as well as 'tests for what is truly religious'. *Pace* Hirst, then, we may speak of knowledge and truth in religion, and not just about second-best 'beliefs'. Phillips notes Wittgenstein's comments on the nature and role of religious believing, and develops out of this a discussion of the way in which the words 'truth' and 'true' are actually used in religious discourse, and of the irrelevance of 'external checks' in this area. These insights are applied to the debate about the justification of religious education in schools, in which Phillips distinguishes 'between an elucidation of religious beliefs and an advocacy of them', and argues that on philosophical considerations 'it is possible to teach religion in schools'.

Charles Melchert's second article in this reader was published in *Religious Education,* 76, 1981, pp. 178–186. It is entitled '"Understanding" as a purpose of religious education' and plots the range of meaning of talk about understanding in general, and how this relates to discussion concerning education in Christianity and its role in 'fostering understanding'. Melchert notes that 'a variety of methods is necessary to permit the learner to grasp a variety of differing modes of understanding' (that is 'sensori-motor', 'emotional', 'analytic' and 'synthetic'). He comments that uncovering the logic of Christian understanding is essentially the theologian's task, while the educator is primarily concerned with how one comes to that understanding; nevertheless neither can ignore the other's conclusions. The article offers a number of other insights into the fostering of religious understanding as both an activity and a result.

Professor Dewi Z Phillips is Professor of Philosophy in the Department of Philosophy of the University College of Swansea, Wales. Dr Charles F Melchert was formerly Dean and Professor of Education and Religion at the Presbyterian School of Christian Education, Richmond, Virginia, USA. He now resides at Lancaster, Pennsylvania.

Note
1.   See the references to his work in note 5 to the overview of part two. See also Paul H Hirst, 'Philosophy and religious education: a reply to D Z Phillips,' *British Journal of Educational Studies*, 18, 1970, pp. 213–215.

9.1 Philosophy and religious education[1]
D Z Phillips

Here one still believes it is all a matter of Jesuits or Masons, witches or goblins, luck or exorcism, the revolutionary hydra *or the* black wave of reaction, *the miracles of ignorance or those of science. Things are either windmills or giants; we comprehend no middle terms.*

These words were spoken in frustration by Miguel de Unamuno when he saw the reaction to his philosophical work in Spain. Again and again when people considered his views they insisted on forcing them into competing categories. For them, the important question was whether his views were those of a Catholic or a Protestant, a believer or a non-believer, a scholastic or a positivist. The philosophical problems Unamuno wrestled with were by-passed. Their relevance was determined by whether or not they served the interests of a particular cause: things were either windmills or giants. In this context, Unamuno had to battle alone, almost despairing because of the false choice people confronted him with, and because of the lack of middle terms. What did he have in mind when he spoke of this lack? Unamuno wanted to contrast the vision in which everything is seen in terms of a struggle for supremacy, where everything must either be a windmill or a giant, with the neutrality of philosophy. When he accused his contemporaries in Spain of failing to comprehend any middle terms, he was referring directly to their failure to understand the nature of such philosophical enquiry. Of course, no one would deny that Unamuno's philosophical reflections on religion did and do have an influence on people's religious beliefs and on people's opposition to religion. Be that as it may, this is a consequence rather than the point of Unamuno's philosophising. The point of his enquiry was not to show that there is a God or there is no God, but to ask what it means to say that there is a God or that there is no God.[2] These latter questions cut across the polemical confrontation between belief and unbelief. They are part of an activity of conceptual analysis, the aim of which is clarification not victory.

The problem of religious education

Why have I begun this paper by mentioning the troubles which Unamuno faced in Spain? I have done so because very similar troubles beset discussions concerning religous education in schools. Here too, I fear, things are either windmills or giants, with the protagonists comprehending no middle terms. More often than not, the discussion takes the form of a struggle, a battle for the minds of the young. The description of the battle depends on which side provides it. If we look in certain quarters, we find the battle described as the fight by enlightened and progressive parents, movements and authorities, to purge education from indoctrination and to rescue children from the grip of superstition. But if we look in other quarters the description of the battle is very different. Here, it is described as the attempt to defend basic values, and to show that the importance of religion permeates the whole of life. So under the respective banners battle commences. What is often lost sight of, however, is that the disagreement is supposed to be over a matter of education. Just as in the case of the content of Unamuno's philosophical investigations, the issue being discussed is made subordinate to the cause being supported. In the context of the discussion of religious education there is a great need to comprehend middle terms. Because of this, the neutrality of the philosophy of religion has much to offer to the discussion of this vexed question.

Unfortunately, however, the situation is more complex than I have indicated so far. I may well have given the impression that the situation which confronts us is one in which philosophers maintain an admirable neutrality, while religious and anti-religious factions carry out their militant propaganda concerning religion in schools. But that is certainly not the case. The present state of philosophy of religion, to a large extent, also betrays an ignorance of middle terms, and a desire to argue for or against religious beliefs, rather than to elucidate their nature. That being so, it is not surprising to find confusion resulting from the application of such philosophical conceptions to the question of religious education. By considering some aspects of this confusion and contrasting it with the philosophical neutrality I think desirable, I hope to shed a little light on the question of religion in schools.

Let us begin by attempting to summarise a fairly widespread attitude to teaching religion in schools, which is shared by philosophers who are sympathetic to religion and by philosophers who are antagonistic to religion. It amounts to something like this: at the very least there is no case at the moment for teaching religion in schools, since the truths which religion proclaim have, as yet, not been established. This attitude has been expressed by Professor Paul Hirst. He asks, 'What is the status of religious propositions? Is there here a domain of knowledge or simply one of beliefs?'[3] Hirst concludes that all we have is a domain of mere belief, and that therefore there is no justification for state maintained schools to teach religion. He says that 'What knowledge we teach we teach because it comes up to publicly accepted rational tests, convinced that all those prepared to investigate the matter to the appropriate extent will agree on the results.'[4] But according to Hirst, religious beliefs do not come up to the required standard. 'If in fact, as seems to be the case at present, there are no agreed public tests whereby true and false can be distinguished in religious claims, then we can hardly maintain that we have a domain of religious knowledge and truth.'[5] This being so, he argues, there is little justification for the inclusion of religion in an educational syllabus. Hirst does see glimmers of hope in the philosophical activities of the Neo-Thomists which, if realised, would show that religious beliefs have a rational foundation. His final conclusion, however, is not over optimistic, since he describes his hopeful expectations as 'just crystal gazing. In the present state of affairs, whatever other considerations might imply, philosophical considerations would seem to suggest that the 1944 legislation on religious education is unjustifiable.'[6] I shall argue that *philosophical* considerations alone lead to no such conclusion.

The view Hirst is advancing, one which is widespread among philosophers of religion, is that whereas religious beliefs may reflect the private experiences of individual believers, there is no way of knowing whether these experiences reflect what in fact is the case. Hirst asks, 'If I have an experience of encounter how am I to know it is an experience of God and not an hallucination? If the core of the matter is simply commitment or decision, what is there in commitment that guarantees the truth of the beliefs? Private beliefs which lack rational justification may be true, but we cannot know that they are true without there being some public justification. And lacking that, we cannot lay claim to a domain of knowledge.'[7]

The nature of religious belief

But is the account Hirst gives of religious belief a recognisable one? Is it true that there are no public criteria in religion to distinguish between the true and the false, the deep and the shallow, or the genuine and the sham? Is it true that everything is a matter of personal decision, and that religious believers are never quite sure whether they are worshipping or suffering from hallucinations? No agreed public tests; think of the confusion which must reign in religious circles. In order to assess what Hirst is saying we need, following Professor Bouwsma in a similar context, to 'imagine a linguistic cataclysm, something like what happened at the tower of Babel. Perhaps you remember the scripture "Come, let us go down, and then confuse their language that they may not understand one another's speech." Presumably, in this case God took away their definitions, their rules, and their postulates, and the consequence was that the terms of their ordinary — or was it, then, extraordinary? — language, were on that day in May suddenly ambiguous and vague.'[8] Bouwsma was discussing the suggestion made by Feigl and Maxwell, that the terms of ordinary language are notoriously ambiguous and vague. Professor Hirst implies that a similar notoriety is true of religious language: no agreed public tests for truth and falsity. So what Hirst asks us to imagine is not a general linguistic cataclysm such as happened at the Tower of Babel, but a limited linguistic cataclysm confined to religion. What is involved in it? We can be helped to see this by listening to Bouwsma's account of the limited linguistic cataclysm which took place with the Sears-Roebuck mail-order catalogue. Before the event, people know their way about the catalogue: 'People know what they want, they have the money to buy what they want. They study the catalogue, they make out the order, send it off with cheque enclosed, and someone, Mr or Mrs Sears, reads the order, puts the underwear in a box and sends it to the Institute. It gets cold in Minneapolis.'[9] But suddenly all is changed: 'As for what the cataclysm did to the catalogue, what a time they had of it at Sears. All the terms ambiguous and vague! They couldn't fill an order right. A man seemed to want a rake and they gave him socks. It was all guess-work. People were returning articles they never wanted for others they never wanted. No one could say what he wanted and no one else could make out what it was he wasn't saying. It was exasperating. People made hands do what words wouldn't, and got their rakes. But in this case even money couldn't talk. Dollars made no sense. At one o'clock Sears-Roebuck shut up shop, and as at the Tower of Babel, Montgomery-Ward took over the business.'[10] A similar fate befell religious worshippers. Before the cataclysm, they knew what they were doing. They knew the difference between adoration and confession, petition and thanks-giving. But after the cataclysm chaos reigned: people thanked for their sins and asked for more, and their hymns greeted the morning at the end of the day. They asked for things they never wanted, but no one could say what he wanted, and no one else could say what it was she was not saying. Every time people called on God they never knew whether they were mistaken, or whether they were mistaken about their mistakes, or whether their mistaken views about their mistakes were mistakes. People read Tolstoy's story and seemed to understand Sergius's words when he concluded that Pashenka had served God while thinking that she was serving men, while he, thinking he was serving God, had in fact served men. But they only seemed to understand, since no one could be sure whether words meant to Sergius what they meant to him, or indeed, whether words ever meant the same in religion to anyone. As at Sears, it was all guess-work.

So far, we have been trying to see, with Professor Bouwsma's help, what sort of thing Professor Hirst might be asking us to envisage when he tells us that there are no agreed public tests whereby true and false can be distinguished in religious claims. But there is a further complication connected with this attempt. It is not at all certain that a reference to the limited linguistic cataclysm, even with all the difficulties involved in giving a coherent account of such an event, corresponds to what Hirst has in mind. In order to give some kind of account of the cataclysm it was necessary to imagine a 'before' and an 'after'; to imagine what people were doing before the disaster befell them. Before their language became confused religious believers were able to worship, they knew how to use words like 'sinful', 'divine', 'church', etc. etc., but after the cataclysm, as we have seen, they no longer knew their way about. But this is not what Hirst is saying. He is not saying that once upon a time there were agreed public tests for truth and falsity in religion which were lost in a linguistic cataclysm, but that there never have been such tests. In describing the effects of the cataclysm we contrasted them with normality, but for Hirst, what we described as cataclysmic is his description of normality! Hirst is not speculating about what might happen, but about what he claims is in fact the case.

What we have seen, however, is that what he claims about religion is not in fact true. There are various criteria recognised by religious believers for what can and what cannot be said to God and about God. It is not true that there are no tests for what is truly religious. Neither is it true that there are no tests for what is to count as religious as opposed to hallucinatory beliefs. Doctors do not look on church-going or worship as symptoms of religious mania. Furthermore, if a person says he has had a religious vision, it does not follow that he has had one. If a man said that God had told him in a vision to eliminate all coloured people from the face of the earth, this would not be accepted by the Christian community as a vision from God. So it is not all a matter of personal decision or commitment. Professor Hirst's fears about this are born of his failure to give any place to the notion of community in religion. It is little wonder that as a consequence he can find no starting-place to distinguish between what is of God and what is not.[11]

Professor Hirst is also worried by the fact that religious concepts do not come up to a required educational standard, by which he means that there is no guarantee that people will agree about them, no matter how long they discuss them. But if this is to be the test, much else besides religion would have to disappear from the school curriculum, for example, English literature and history. Professor Hirst suffers from a misplaced scepticism. He believes that in order that scepticism might be avoided, agreement must be sought in the sphere of discourse in question. But when historians disagree, they are disagreeing on historical questions. Certain interjections in the dispute would obviously be irrelevant. The fact that this is so shows that there is something being discussed here, and it would not make sense to be sceptical about that. There are disagreements about literary and historical questions, disagreements which, for all we know, may never be resolved. But the mere fact of such disagreement does not lead to general scepticism about history and literature. Unless the disputants had much in common, there would be no possibility of disagreement. Though there are important differences, a similar point can be made about moral disagreement. When people disagree on moral questions, it does not follow that anyone can say what he likes. On the contrary, not any viewpoint could be a moral viewpoint, and within differing viewpoints there are criteria for what can and cannot be said. Professor Hirst seems to think that where there is no agreement in opinions, it is all a matter of personal decision. Clearly, this is not the case.

Professor Hirst might point out, with some justification, that there are important differences between religious beliefs and the examples I have mentioned hitherto. Unlike the previous examples, the dispute about religion which concerns the question of whether it ought to be taught in schools, is not a dispute about a particular question within an accepted realm of discourse, but a dispute about a realm of discourse as such. So that a dispute between a believer and a non-believer over whether religion should be taught in schools is not like a dispute between two historians over a question in their subject. The historians are not disagreeing over whether history is true, whatever that might mean, whereas the truth of religious beliefs is precisely the issue at stake in the other disagreement. So although Hirst puts his point in a confused way when he says that 'What knowledge we teach we teach because it comes up to publicly accepted rational tests, convinced that all those prepared to investigate the matter to the appropriate extent will agree on the results',[12] he probably had in mind the question of the truth of religious beliefs as such, rather than disputed questions within an accepted mode of discourse. We have seen that there are criteria within religious traditions which distinguish between what can and cannot be said, what is true and what is false, what is deep and what is shallow, but this may cut no ice with Hirst. For him, these criteria operate within a class of beliefs which are at best hypothetical. He may want to say that all the distinctions achieve is to distinguish between shrewd guesses and foolish ones, or between the more probable and the less probable. But there are difficulties in this point of view, since unless guesses were sometimes confirmed one could not have a distinction between shrewd and foolish guesses; unless probabilities were sometimes realised, one could not have a distinction between the more and the less probable. But Hirst wants to say that religious guesses or hypotheses are *never* confirmed. That is why we are so unsure of what we have on our hands here; that is why we cannot say whether we have in religion a domain of knowledge which can be taught. There is no escape from the context of conjecture, it seems. Professor Hirst concludes on these grounds that we do not have a domain of knowledge and truth where religious beliefs are concerned, but simply one of beliefs.

What we need here, however, is to compare what Hirst says about religious beliefs with their actual character. If we do this, we shall find, as we have done previously in this paper, that his remarks are extremely misleading.

Clearly, when Hirst refers to religious *beliefs,* he has in mind a contrast with religious *knowledge.* For Hirst, beliefs are a second-best, things we should be cautious and not over-emphatic about. In making this distinction he is, of course, reflecting one common way in which we do speak of beliefs and believing. If I say, 'I believe there is bread in the cupboard', it would make sense for my wife to say, 'You'd better make sure.' Also, when I made my remark, I was indicating my doubt and hesitancy. But if you hear a man testifying and saying, 'I believe in God', you do not take this as an indication of hesitancy on his part. On the contrary, he might well be expressing one of his deepest convictions. By thinking that the word 'belief' where religious beliefs are concerned is synonymous with conjecture or hypothesis, Hirst violates the grammar of the concept in that context.[13] Wittgenstein recognised the importance of noting that 'belief' is used differently in connection with religious beliefs. He says that in religion 'One talks of believing and at the same time one doesn't use "believe" as one does ordinarily. You might say (in the normal use): "You only believe – oh well ..." Here it is used entirely differently; on the other hand it is not used as we generally use the word "'know"'.[14]

Wittgenstein not only wants to separate religious beliefs from the beliefs which are conjectures. He also wants to show that they are different from what we call knowledge. You cannot ask for a verification, an external check, on religion as such. The difference between those who do believe and those who do not is not like the difference between two people with rival hypotheses about the existence of a star. The people in the latter disagreement disagree within a context common to both of them. But the difference between a believer and a non-believer is a difference between someone who does look on this life in a certain way and regulates it accordingly, and someone who has no time for such a response or who sees nothing in it. Wittgenstein says that in religion 'believing obviously plays much more this role: suppose we said that a certain picture might play the role of constantly admonishing me, or I always think of it. Here, an enormous difference would be between those people for whom the picture is constantly in the foreground, and the others who just didn't use it at all.'[15]

The nature of religious truth

What of the question of truth in religion in the light of the foregoing remarks? What follows from them, if they are accepted, is that whereas it makes sense to ask what is truly religious, it makes no sense to ask whether religion as such is true or false, if what one has in mind is an external non-religious or non-moral proof of the truth of religion. One can say that another religion is true or false where this statement is a religious or moral judgment. Professor

Hirst should have recognised that 'truth' as used in connection with empirical statements is different from the notion of truth often used in religion, since he himself uses the word in both ways in his paper. An example of the first way of using 'truth' can be found in asking whether the statement that this road will get me to Swansea is true. Its truth depends on whether or not the road does in fact lead to Swansea. The road might have led me elsewhere. But Hirst also asks whether we have 'a domain of religious knowledge and truth'. Now how is 'truth' being used here? I suggest that it is used in a way akin to that in which it is used when we say, 'There's a lot of truth in that', or the way it was used when Jesus said, 'I am the way, the truth, and the life.' Here there is no question of an external check. If a person says, 'I have come to see the truth of the saying, that it is better to give than to receive', and another person denies this, this is not like a dispute between business partners over whether a proposed venture will in fact materialise in profit. It is a dispute over the worth of generosity. And if someone has come to see the truth of it, that doesn't mean that he has assessed generosity by means of some measure other than generosity. What he has come to see is the beauty of generosity. When he says there is a lot of truth in it, what this comes to in practical terms is that he strives after it and tries to regulate his life accordingly. But while it is correct to say that to actually say that 'It is better to give than to receive' is to commit oneself to this view, it does not follow that this is why one thinks it is true. If someone asked one why one thought it was true, one would start talking, not about oneself or one's commitment, but about generosity.

I am suggesting that the ways in which the words 'truth' and 'true' can be used in connection with generosity is akin to the use of 'truth' in such utterances as 'God is Truth' or 'To love God is to know the truth.' So religious beliefs are not a class of second-best statements, hypotheses awaiting confirmation or conjectures longing to be borne out. They are a body of truths, in the sense I have been talking about, which have played an important part in the history of mankind, and by which many people still regulate or attempt to regulate their lives.

If my arguments are correct I have now removed Hirst's main objections against teaching religion in schools. Hirst argued that religious beliefs are unconfirmed conjectures, matters of personal decision, with no objective standards of validity. On all these points, I have argued, he is mistaken.

Implications for religious education

But what are the implications of what I have said for the teaching of religion? First of all it is quite clear that the questions I have raised in the philosophy of religion *are* raised by quite young children, and persist in more sophisticated forms throughout their school careers. In the sixth form, surely, such questions could be discussed in a philosophical manner. Sudents will be worried about the relations between religious statements and scientific statements, between religious beliefs and factual beliefs, between the notion of empirical truth and truth in religion, and so on. These questions, it seems to me, could and should be discussed, and there are obviously good educational reasons for doing so. These problems are real ones and form as real a part of enquiry as any other subject. I do not know whether one is going to call such discussion religious education or philosophy of religion, but that is not very important. Needless to say, these questions and an adequate discussion of them, presuppose a historical knowledge of the religion in question. It seems that Professor Hirst would not object to this, since he does not think his arguments amount to saying that 'in maintained schools there ought not to be factual instruction about the beliefs that have played and do play so large a part in our history, literature and way of life'.[16] Professor Hirst wants to distinguish between such instruction and advocacy, and I entirely agree with him on this matter. When I say that the notion of truth in religion should be elucidated, that is not the same as saying that it should be advocated. The reactions of children to such elucidation will probably be as varied as that of adults. But there are problems about Hirst's phrase 'factual instruction', since as we have seen, elucidation of the nature of religious beliefs would involve showing the kind of beliefs they are, the role they play in people's lives, and so on. That will involve one inevitably in an elucidation of values and ideals, conceptions of worship and love. If Hirst is including all this within factual instruction, then I agree with him. If he is not, then the factual instruction will not achieve the desired elucidation.

Of course, there are problems about teaching religion to younger children in the earlier classes. They could not indulge in the conceptual comparison and analysis I have said ought to go on in sixth forms. Yet I do not think that this rules out the possibility of the kind of elucidation I have been talking of. The problems made explicit by the sixth-former are present in varied forms in the younger child. The difficulty is that one cannot meet them by the same methods. I think they might be met, however, in the telling of stories. For example, the difference between a regard for generosity and a prudential outlook could be brought out in dramatic form. The child could be brought to see the difference between the two attitudes, how the emphasis differs in each. I see no reason for withholding the term 'elucidation' as a description of this activity. Again, such elucidation can be distinguished from advocacy.

I began this paper with a plea to break down the polemical categories into which discussions of religious education tend to fall. The position I have taken up is in some ways similar to that of Simone Weil when she says 'We perceive more clearly what justice demands in this matter, once the notion of right has been replaced by that of obligation to need. The soul of a child, as it reaches out towards understanding, has need of the treasures accumulated by the human species through the centuries. We do injury to a child if we bring it up in a narrow Christianity which prevents it from ever becoming capable of perceiving that there are treasures of the purest gold to be found in non-Christian civilisations. Lay education does an even greater injury to children. It covers up these treasures, and those of Christianity as well.'[17] Professor Hirst would agree, I think, on the desirability of teaching children something about the truths of other religions, but in answer to his worry that concentration on Christianity smacks of opportunism, Simone Weil would reply that 'as when studying history little French children are told a lot about France, so it is natural that, being in Europe, when you talk about religion you should refer primarily to Christianity'.[18]

Simone Weil says that ordering schoolteachers to talk about God is a joke in extremely bad taste. But it is also foolish to assume a pseudo-neutrality like that of those mentioned in the *Gittins Report* who would say that 'religious education should be postponed until children are mature enough to be presented with the arguments for and against the Christian faith and be able to decide whether they believe it or not'.[19] What are they going to decide about? The attitude expressed pre-supposes that in elucidating the nature of religious beliefs one would be advocating those beliefs, but as we have seen, the elucidation and the advocacy can be distinguished. I find what Simone Weil says about the question of the truth of what is taught far more penetrating. She says that 'One would talk about dogma as something which has played a role of the highest importance in our countries, and in which men of the very greatest eminence have believed wholeheartedly; without hiding the fact either that it has been the pretext for inflicting any number of cruelties. But, above all, one would try to make the children feel all the beauty contained therein. If they ask: "Is it true?", we should answer: "It is so beautiful that it must certainly contain a lot of truth. As for knowing whether it is, or is not, absolutely true, try to become capable of deciding that for yourselves when you grow up." It would be strictly forbidden to add, by way of commentary, anything implying either a negation of dogma or an affirmation of it.'[20] For Simone Weil, the elucidation I talked of is the displaying of a thing of beauty. Whether the child regulates his or her life by this conception of beauty is something he or she will decide in later years. She stresses, however, that the stories are not to be dealt with as things of beauty to delight aesthetes. On the contrary, the study of religious texts, like the study of any texts, should always observe the spirit of the texts, and so stress their connection with the everyday world outside the school.

For example, a rural school should pay particular attention to elucidating the meaning of the pastoral parables. In this way 'thought' and 'work' are no longer looked upon as being in water-tight compartments. Simone Weil makes this point powerfully when she says that 'Naturally, a peasant who is sowing has to be careful to cast the seed properly, and not to be thinking about lessons learnt at school. But the object which engages our attention does not form the whole content of our thoughts. A happy young woman, expecting her first child, and busy sewing a layette, thinks about sewing it properly. But she never forgets for an instant the child she is carrying inside her. At precisely the same moment, somewhere in a prison workshop, a female convict is also sewing, thinking, too, about sewing properly, for she is afraid of being punished. One might imagine both women to be doing the same work at the same time, and having their attention absorbed by the same technical difficulties. And yet a whole gulf of difference lies between one occupation and the other.'[21] These remarks are extremely important as an answer to those who would say that religious beliefs are irrelevant to the wider context of a person's life.

If religious beliefs were elucidated in this way, Simone Weil believes that it would abolish the polemical confrontation between two opposing camps, the secular schoolmaster and the priest. She also thinks that such a presentation of the content of religion 'would imperceptibly imbue the mass of the population with spirituality, if it is still capable of being so imbued'.[22] I do not know whether this latter opinion is true. But my point is that the case for teaching religion in schools stands educationally and independently of this fact. Not only is there a case for teaching religion because of its content and the roles it has played and still plays in human life, but also because of its connections with other educational disciplines, the worth of which are not in dispute. Simone Weil says that 'it is too absurd for words that a French university graduate should have read poetry of the Middle Ages, *Polyeucte, Athalie, Phèdre,* Pascal, Lamartine, philosophical doctrines impregnated with Christianity like those of Descartes and Kant, the *Divine Comedy* or *Paradise Lost,* and never once have opened a bible ... An educational course in which no reference is made to religion is an absurdity.'[23]

Professor Hirst says that religious education must include 'the part played by Christian beliefs in determining our way of life'. It is hard, however, to make Hirst's argument consistent on these matters, since it is clear that he would not endorse the kind of comment I have quoted from the work of Simone Weil. He talks about the legitimacy of talking about an experience of mystery and contingency which may underlie all religion, but he does not want to talk about this in terms of any specific religious beliefs. But this recommendation is unintelligible. As far as a feeling of contingency is concerned, the feeling that we could be crushed at any moment, destroyed as persons, by external circumstances, that in itself is not a religious feeling. Religion enters when there is a certain response to that feeling. But that response need not be forthcoming, and the feeling of contingency may simply paralyse and terrorise a person. So to speak about a feeling of contingency is not necessarily to speak of religious beliefs at all. Secondly, contrast what Hirst says about the notion of mystery with the detailed elucidation of religious beliefs advocated by Simone Weil. I have no idea what an experience of mystery is which is not related to some context or other, for after all, the intelligibility of the notion of experience depends on the context in which it is at work. A context-free concept of mystery would be mysterious indeed. After all, although conceptions of mystery are to be found in various religions, talk about mystery is not meant to be mysterious. Neither are the various criteria for the use of the conceptions in various religious traditions mysterious. So much more is needed than Hirst seems prepared to allow.

But at the close of his article, Hirst's argument takes yet another turn. Hirst sees hope in tendencies to explain religious beliefs as attempts to explain aspects of humanity's natural experience. He says that 'When it comes to tests for the truth of religious statements, the point must be the adequacy of the pictures in making sense of the range and circumstances of the experiences.'[24] This view has a superficial resemblance to the arguments advanced in this article, but there are important differences. Simone Weil stresses the role played by religious beliefs in daily life, but she does not suggest, like Hirst, that the beliefs are to be assessed by the fact in some sense or other. On the contrary, the religious beliefs are said to bring a characteristic emphasis to bear on the facts. The beliefs assess the facts, not the facts the beliefs.

In any case, Professor Hirst only sees these recent attempts to explain religion as the tentative beginnings of future possibilities. He says that 'perhaps this is just crystal gazing', and that in 'the present state of affairs ... philosophical considerations would seem to suggest'[25] that all we ought to have in religious education is the kind of thing he has argued for. I am suggesting, on the other hand, that the crystal in this case is the mistaken philosophical reasoning which has created the problems which Hirst tries to meet in his paper. Philosophical considerations in themselves show that religious education ought to be possible in schools; that there is something there to be elucidated and discussed.

Are we to say, then, that some kind of religious education *ought* to be given in schools? We may or we may not, but it is not a conclusion which *must* follow from the arguments of this article.[26] I have distinguished throughout between an elucidation of religious beliefs and an advocacy of them. The elucidation, nevertheless, calls for a sympathetic relation to religion in the teacher, since, as I said earlier, it involves unpacking the significance of values, ideals, different conceptions of worship and love, and the roles they play in people's lives. This is not a task confined necessarily to religious believers, but it is a task confined to those who take religion seriously, who see something in it, and respect it. This class of teachers could well include someone who had come to the conclusion that religious beliefs were false in that he had a regard in his own life for conflicting beliefs, but thought a great deal needed to be said to appreciate the nature of religious beliefs. Again, this class of teachers might well exclude someone who was a devout believer, but who lacked the ability to elucidate the nature of his or her beliefs. So the ability to teach in this context is not synonymous with the ability to believe; it is synonymous, however, with the ability to respect or to see something in religion. One might compare the case with that of musical education which one equates, with good reason, with musical appreciation. It cannot be put in the hands of the tone deaf.[27] Because of the inseparability of understanding and sympathy where religious education is concerned, many might come to the conclusion that it is simply not possible to find such a condition satisfied sufficiently to feel confident about general provisions for religious education in schools. They might feel that religious education *should* be possible, but that in fact it is not. Compare perhaps: 'People should be able to live in peace, but they don't.'[28] Others, despite the unlikelihood of the conditions for successful teaching of religious education being realised, might still think the risk worth taking, even if they have to supply a corrective themselves. The point to be made is that people may reach *different* conclusions concerning whether religious education ought in fact to be taught, *even when people agree that it should be possible to teach religious education.* Philosophical considerations as such cannot determine the evaluation people make. What such considerations do show is that it is possible to teach religion in schools, and that considerations which suggest the contrary, such as those advanced by Hirst, are based on conceptual confusions.

Notes
1. This article was read to the Philosophy of Education Society of Great Britain at Bristol on 5th October 1968.
2. I was helped to see this with reference to Unamuno by Allen Lacy's stimulating study, *Miguel de Unamuno: the rhetoric of existence,* The Hague, Mouton, 1967. I have reviewed this work in *The Philosophical Quarterly,* 18, 1968.
3. Paul H Hirst, 'Morals, religion and the maintained school,' *British Journal of Educational Studies,* 14, 1965, p. 7.
4. *Ibid.,* p. 12.
5. *Ibid.,* p. 12.
6. *Ibid.,* pp. 17–18.
7. *Ibid.,* p. 17.
8. 'The terms of ordinary language are …,' in *Philosophical Essays,* Nebraska, University of Nebraska Press, 1965, p. 205.
9. *Ibid.,* p. 204.
10. *Ibid.,* p. 206.

11. I have discussed these questions in chapter seven of *The Concept of Prayer,* London, Routledge and Kegan Paul, 1965, 'God's voice and the concept of community.'
12. *Op. cit.,* p. 12.
13. Of course, sometimes religious beliefs are conjectures, for example 'I believe this is the tomb of St Peter,' 'I believe in the authenticity of this holy relic,' etc.
14. Ludwig Wittgenstein, *Lectures and Conversation on Aesthetics, Psychology and Religious Belief,* edited by Cyril Barrett, Oxford, Basil Blackwell, 1966, p. 60.
15. *Ibid.,* p. 56.
16. *Op. cit.,* p.13.
17. Simone Weil, *The Need For Roots,* translated by A F Wills, London, Routledge and Kegan Paul, 1952, pp. 87–88.
18. *Ibid.,* p. 88.
19. *Primary Education in Wales,* Department of Education and Science, Her Majesty's Stationery Office, 1967, pp. 367–8.
20. *Op. cit.,* pp. 88–89.
21. *Ibid.,* pp. 90–91.
22. *Ibid.,* p. 89.
23. *Ibid.,* p. 88.
24. *Ibid.,* p. 17.
25. *Ibid.,* pp. 17–18.
26. I have been helped to see this by some comments made by Professor R F Holland on an earlier version of this paper.
27. Professor R F Holland's example.
28. Professor R F Holland's example.

9.2 'Understanding' as a purpose of religious education

Charles F Melchert

There are many different approaches to religious education currently being espoused, but I suspect that every one of those approaches would agree that one goal of religious education is understanding on the part of the learners. I am usually suspicious of universal agreements. Do we all mean the same thing by 'understanding'? Some favour understanding for it presumes thinking, and education has to do with learning how to think. Some are wary lest too much attention to understanding become another way of returning to exclusively cognitive or rationalistic goals in religious education. Some say one of the dominant dangers of the twentieth century is the 'flight from understanding'. Do all these understand understanding in the same way as I do, when I say the aim of all education is to help others understand?

What is understanding? Does the child who suddenly grasps the significance of the vocable 'Daddy' and the physicist who suddenly sees the destructive potential of nuclear fission engage in the same phenomenon called 'understanding'? What happens when one understands? Is the process of understanding the same for the mathematician, the poet, the philosopher and the mystic?

Meanings of understanding

Let me begin by offering a description of several of the ways we talk about understanding, how we use the language, as a way of giving some sense of the range and complexity of this phenomenon. Then I shall identify four different *modes* of understanding, all of which could be taken as legitimate descriptions of what one is saying when they say 'Ah, now I understand!' Then I shall briefly indicate a few relationships among these, and say a few words about what this might suggest about education in religion.

Understanding 1 (naming): 'I understand that when you say the word 'football' you mean the spherical object with two pointy ends those men are throwing at each other.' Here 'understanding' is the recognition of the naming process so familiar with some kinds of language learning. This kind of learning is basic to many other kinds of understanding, as when one begins to read Piaget and discovers that the necessary first task is to master a whole new vocabulary with its own distinctive meanings.

453

Understanding 2 (meaning): 'I understand that when there is a fiery red sky in the evening, it means there will be rain tomorrow.'[1] 'I understand that if you are silent while I am talking, it means that you do not approve of what I am saying, even though you never say so.' In other words, this is not naming an object with a label, but identifying a pattern which seems consistent enough to call attention to itself and which helps make sense of otherwise inexplicable data or behaviour. Lest these first two types of understanding seem completely discrete, try to identify which kind of understanding would result in language such as 'Tell them I AM sent you.'

Understanding 3 (immediate experience): 'I understand what it means to lose an only son in death, for my son has died.' 'Nobody knows the trouble I've seen . . .' Here is the understanding which is borne of first-hand participatory experience, especially experience which arouses deep, personal or private emotions or attitudes not easily communicated to others.

Understanding 4 (empathetic): 'Now I understand what that mother (above) went through, for though I have never had a son, I have lost a loved one. I can empathise.' This kind of understanding may not be as complete as first-hand experience, but it is a legitimate and authentic form of understanding, especially for those who are both imaginative and emotionally attuned to others.

Understanding 5 (how to): The golfer says, 'I understand that when I feel that muscle in the shoulder tighten, if I start my return swing too soon I will come through with the club-face open and I will slice.' This kind of understanding is not linguistic so much as it is a sensing physical movements which produce a certain result, whether those movements can be articulated in language or not. Indeed, Piaget has shown that children have many understandings which are procedural or behavioural and which cannot be articulated in language, and yet which betray significant understanding of how the world operates.[2] Perhaps it would most accurately be described as a 'know-how' or an understanding 'how to', as in understanding how to drive, yet without consciously thinking about the procedures at all.

Understanding 6 (why): 'Now I understand why Tom dropped out of school, for his father is ill and Tom has to get a job to support the family.' Recognising a person's motives or purposes often enables one to understand behaviour which might well have several possible explanations.

While these examples do not exhaust the linguistic possibilities, they do sample the variety of uses to which the concept 'understanding' might legitimately be put.

Several observations can be made about 'understanding' as revealed in the above forms. First, no matter how sincerely one affirms, 'Now I understand', there is always the possibility of being wrong. Even Understanding 3 with its direct, personal, first-hand experience, can be experienced in ways that are inauthentic or self-deceiving.

Any assertion of understanding is susceptible to a test for truth, no matter how profoundly one may believe that 'Now, at last, I *really* understand.' How often we find that today's profound understandings are tomorrow's misunderstandings or partial understandings.

Second, all 'understanding' is understanding of something – understanding necessarily has an object, even if reflexive. In other words, one of the roots of the experience of understanding is the experience of separateness or distance or differentiation. It is the experience of the unlikeness or nonsense which must be overcome or re-united or brought together into similarity or unity. Is it too much to say that all seeking to understand is a drive to unity, to putting back together what has been rendered asunder? This unity is expressed clearly in another linguistic usage of 'understanding'(7), as when one says, 'I have an understanding with him.' What is implied is that the two have an explicit or implicit agreement, a unified position upon some matter of mutual interest. Third, because all 'understanding' is understanding something, one can attend either to the process or activity of understanding, or to that which is understood. Both are necessary.

Modes of understanding

While these seven linguistic usages of 'understanding' do not exhaust the possibilities, they and, I suspect, other usages, can be reduced to perhaps four *modes* of understanding which are rooted in the constitution of human being.

First there is the bodily or *'sensori-motor understanding'*, as Piaget might call it. Cognitive structures are expressed by active assimilation and accommodation schemas present in physical manipulations of the self and the environment. Many forms of 'understanding how to' are rooted in this sensori-motor mode.

Second there is *emotional understanding,* the 'being understanding' or 'being an understanding person' which is implicit in Understanding 3 and 4. Early in life affective understanding, which is rooted in the limbic region of the human brain, is quite undifferentiated, since in the beginning the infant seems unable to differentiate self from object, and thus would find it impossible to empathise fully with another. Indeed, such may not be truly possible until reversibility is attained. Yet, there does seem to be a 'primitive' understanding, partly emotional and partly physical, which exists in the infant as it relates with the mothering one, almost from the beginning – possibly originating in the pre-birth unity experienced by both mother and father.

Third, there is *analytic understanding,* which is essentially rooted in the increasing ability to discriminate between this and that, to recognise that self and object are distinct. This awareness seems to emerge only gradually, and to extend to refusal to 'own' parts of self. Clearly this analytic understanding is fundamentally the experience of understanding something by taking it apart. It is expressed in the need to label linguistically as well, for though object and name may at first seem to be one, they soon become distinguished as the youngster learns that there may well be several names for the same object, for example, doggie, bow-wow, puppy, pooch, hound, mutt, and Fido. With increasing maturity it becomes apparent that some of those labels are less purely cognitive or descriptive than others, indeed, some names seem to carry with them considerable emotional clout, as when Dad comes in a grouchy mood and yells at the dog, 'Out of my way, mutt!' This analytic understanding has been widely celebrated in recent centuries as the heart of the scientific method, for the ability to take things apart and re-label them has been vital to scientific progress.

Fourth, there is *synthetic understanding,* which like the analytic is a gradually developing mode of understanding. It begins as the reality within which the infant first experiences the world − all in one. As differentiation and separation increase, the drive to find ways to put things back together again finds expression, and the excitement of finding new combinations increases the drive to unite. When things come apart, and self and object becomes relatively distinct, immediately one has the possibility of making all sorts of new combinations of how self and object can relate with each other − possibilities that were not present when self and object were one. Such synthesising possibilities are certainly cognitive in nature, but they are also affective, since the split of self and object also is gradually perceived to include the split between self and mothering one. Indeed, precisely in that relationship are many of the most exciting synthesising possibilities, for the 'object' from which the infant gradually distinguishes itself, turns out to be not another object, but a subject who constantly changes the stimuli physically, cognitively, and effectively.

Synthesising understanding often occurs by means of images or metaphoric devices. The synthetic mode, especially in its more mature forms, presumes the differentiation of the analytic mode of understanding. It often presumes the naming function of Understanding 1, and the two together make possible Understanding 2. Further, it is the fusion of Understanding 1 and Understanding 2, and Understanding 3 or 4 or both which makes possible Understanding 6. Indeed, this last type of linguistic expression, understanding the motives or purposes of oneself or others, makes use of most or all the modes of understanding, analytic, empathetic, synthetic, and often sensori motor.

Fostering understanding

If the above descriptions seem to 'square with reality', there are several observations to be made concerning education in religion, especially Christianity, if, as educators, we are concerned with fostering understanding.

First, different approaches to religious education may agree on the need for understanding, while permitting considerable diversity about what is taken as 'understanding'. Some approaches to religious education seem to prefer fostering understanding in some modes rather than others. Learners can dance an understanding or can do a verbal structural analysis and both can be modes of coming to and expressing understanding.

Second, note that while there are only four modes of coming to understanding, there are no limits to the number of ways one might express an understanding once achieved. Dancing may be a means of reaching some particular understanding, or it may be a means of expressing an understanding achieved in some other mode – or there may be modification of the understanding reached by an analytic mode, for example, as one tries to express it in a bodily way.

This means that the variety of educational methods now urged on teachers are not to be desired simply to prevent boredom among learners, nor even to enable more effective learning by pursuing one mode from several different methodological approaches. A variety of methods is necessary to permit the learner to grasp a variety of differing modes of understanding. I suspect there is no need for me to demonstrate that an incarnational Christianity, in its fullest expressions, requires participation in all four modes of understanding.

Third, understanding can hardly be seen as something that is narrowly the province of rationalistic or intellectualistic concerns. Indeed the danger, it seems to me, is less from rationalism than from teachers who prefer to operate too exclusively in one mode of understanding with learners, and thus sometimes distort the content or subject matter to fit that mode of understanding. In Christian theology, it seems to me that one function of the doctrine of the incarnation is to affirm that empathetic and bodily modes of understanding are appropriate, indeed, indispensable modes of understanding alongside the more usual analytic and synthetic modes. In this matter, attention must be paid to the content of the understanding. What kind of understanding is involved, thus what mode of understanding seems most appropriate if a learner is to come to that understanding?

Fourth, attending to the content or structure or logic of 'an understanding' is properly a theological task, to be done with all the theological tools at one's disposal. The educator, on the other hand, is focally concerned as well with how one comes to that understanding. Yet the educator cannot ignore the substance of 'the understanding', just as the theologian cannot ignore how the understanding comes to be. Using analytic modes of understanding it is difficult or less likely that one will come to empathetic or bodily understandings of some matter. For example, the question facing the educator is not only how we can understand what Moses experienced at the burning bush, but also what did he come to understand of God and his own vocation from that experience? Understanding entails both, and the educator must deal with both. If one treats Moses' experience only analytically, one familiar result could be propositional affirmations about God and God's will. Using only the analytic mode creates or sustains a distance between the content of the understanding and Moses' own existential transformation, a distance which is quite untrue to the experience depicted in the text.

Fifth, many teachers are perhaps more familiar with teaching for knowledge mastery than teaching for understanding, though they often hope understanding will also come. They might well object that it is hard enough to get learners to be concerned for solid knowledge attainment, without throwing in additional concerns about understanding in all four modes. What could possibly provide the additional motivation necessary for that kind of enquiry? Clearly a learner must come to *care,* in order to pursue understanding in the depth and breadth outlined here. First, it should be recognised that there is a latent (at least) caring present in most of us – though often it is buried under layers of other people's expectations of us in educational settings.

Additionally, and it seems so obvious as to sound trite, the teacher must care – must care about understanding. Often the teacher who is passionately committed to coming to grips with the subject, and who cares for getting at the truth of the matter, that teacher will communicate something of that passion to the learners – and it can be infectious.

Finally, there is also a subtle but necessary ingredient that sometimes occurs in the teaching-learning interaction, perhaps especially when understanding emerges. It is a common testimony of those who come to understand something, that often it 'happens to me' as much as I create it. There may well have been considerable hard work leading up to the understanding, yet it comes, whether suddenly or gradually, 'with almost a sense of a gift'. Such a gift, the new understanding, naturally creates considerable excitement and enthusiasm, which enlivens the interaction, but it also can call forth a genuine sense of wonder – wonder that it should happen at all – let alone here and now. Taking 'time out' to savour that wonder (call it a brief moment of worship?) can help energise teacher and learners alike.

Sometimes, it is precisely at such moments the teacher needs to exercise the utmost restraint. We have noted above that understanding emerges, and it seems 'truth-ful' and coherent as it emerges. Often the teacher can see (from previous experience, or a fuller grasp of the subject matter) that the understanding which has just been born, is a very partial understanding, or even wrong. Premature judgment, externally applied, can not only 'set the student right', it can also destroy the legitimate excitement of a hard-won accomplishment, which though partial, may well be a step on the road for the learner. Care must be taken by the teacher to find a time and a way to help the learner come to a fuller understanding and critique of the partial understanding, and see it for what it is, rather than have it 'shot down' on the spot.

Sixth, because understanding implies both activity and result, the educational process can focus on either as well. Education can focus on transmitting the results of past understandings. Obviously such transmission needs to be done, especially with those who are unfamiliar with the past understandings of their community. But much of the purpose of that transmission is that the learner become actively engaged in understanding that content, which implies for the learner a continuous progression, an increase, or deepening, or broadening, or newer understanding or better understanding, and so on. The educator must seek to continue a movement which is intrinsic to a learner's growth process, but which is all too easily stifled in many supposedly educational settings. In growth there is an episodic movement towards synthetic understanding, towards more wholistic understanding, which is more inclusive of more data. This progression is rooted in an interesting dialectic which characterises human development. The infant begins the processes of understanding with an undifferentiated sense of unity (or child-like faith) which is both bodily, empathetic and synthetic. Such undifferentiated unity is appropriate for the infant's understanding of his or her reality. But such understanding will not stand the pressures of maturity and the complex understandings of reality all around. In order to hold on to a child-like faith-understanding as an adult, one must either compartmentalise one's world, or else reduce/maintain one's sense of reality at the same child-like proportions as one's faith-understanding.

To begin to transcend such 'primitive' understandings, the child increasingly differentiates and articulates the world, physically, affectively and cognitively. Such differentiation enables one to cope with increasingly broader ranges of data and more diverse forms of information. The person constantly strives to discover patterns or meanings which bring unity to the diversity of data and experience – and thus provide a more coherent vision of the world. That drive to unity characterises the essence of understanding whether it is the activity of an infant, a dancer, a poet, or a physicist. That drive to unity keeps one moving toward deeper and broader understandings of human reality. Gradually what may begin to emerge is the possibility of affirming a post-critical child-like faith which has about it a sense of primitive wholeness and unity (which some have even called mystical). Such understandings are sometimes called visionary or prophetic, or wishful thinking. But there is about the drive to understand the possibility of emerging with a sense of the whole which in nuanced, flexible and sensitive to subtleties (even aesthetic in quality), yet remains solid, steady, profound and synoptic. Such understandings often profoundly shape the behaviour of the individual and the community.

Such an activity and result, I would propose, is a worthy purpose for religious education in all our faith communities.

Notes
1. May Brodbeck, 'Meaning and Action,' *Philosophy of Science,* 1963, pp. 315–316. M Brodbeck identifies types 1–4 and 6, and provides several of the examples cited here.
2. Jean Piaget, *The Grasp of Consciousness: action and concept in the young,* Cambridge, Massachusetts, Harvard University Press, 1976.

References
Belth, M (1977) *The Process of Thinking,* New York, McKay.
Bringuier, J-C (1980) *Conversations with Jean Piaget,* Chicago, University of Chicago Press.
Brodbeck, M (1963) 'Meaning and action,' *Philosophy of Science,* 30, pp. 309–324.
Brown, S C (ed.) (1975) *Philosophers Discuss Education,* London, Macmillan.
Hamlyn, D W (1978) *Experience and the Growth of Understanding,* London, Routledge and Kegan Paul.
Holmer, P (1978) *The Grammar of Faith,* New York, Harper and Row.
Little, S (1980) 'Religious instruction,' mimeographed manuscript.
Martin, J (1970) *Explaining, Understanding and Teaching,* New York, McGraw-Hill.
Melchert, C F (1978) 'Understanding and religious education,' in I V Cully and K B Cully (eds), *Process and Relationship* (Festschrift for Randolph Crump Miller), Birmingham, Alabama, Religious Education Press, pp. 41–48.
Mischel, T (ed.) (1971) *Cognitive Development and Epistemology,* New York, Academic Press.
Mischel, T (ed.) (1974) *Understanding Other Persons,* Oxford, Blackwell.
Piaget, J (1976) *The Grasp of Consciousness: action and concept in the young child,* Cambridge, Massachusetts, Harvard University Press.
Piaget, J (1978) *Success and Understanding,* Cambridge, Massachusetts, Harvard University Press.
Werner, H (1948) *Comparative Psychology of Mental Development,* New York, Science Editions.
Wittgenstein, L (1958) *Philosophical Investigations* (second edition), Oxford, Blackwell.

10. Relativism and enquiry

The issue of cognitive relativism is one that apparently will not go away in contemporary philosophical and cultural debate.[1] It clearly has profound implications for the work of the Christian educator, as well as for the teacher who seeks to educate others about a variety of religions (see article 3.2).

Alasdair MacIntyre's seminal article, 'Relativism, power and philosophy,' first published in the *Proceedings and Addresses of the American Philosophical Association*, 59, 1985, pp. 5–22, begins by describing relativism as 'one of those doctrines that have by now been refuted a number of times too often'. He presents a perceptive analysis of the origin of the problem: the situation of a bilingual speaker attempting to communicate with her own culture on the one hand and the outside world on the other, who is faced by a choice 'between sets of beliefs so structured that each has internal to it its own standards of truth and justification'. Such a situation, MacIntyre claims, excludes the possibility of appeal to some neutral or independent standard of rational justification and supports a version of relativism that cannot be refuted. It can, however, be *transcended* insofar as one community is critically open enough to recognise 'a possible future defeat of the forms of theory and practice in which it has up till now been taken to be embodied within (its own) tradition, at the hands of some alien and ... as yet largely unintelligible tradition'.

Ian Markham reflects on MacIntyre's position (as expressed in a later book[2]) in an article first published in *Religious Studies*, 27, 1991, pp. 259–267. He summarises MacIntyre's 'contribution to the "faith" and "reason" problem', and argues that it is defective in certain ways: in particular in 'assuming a liberalised account of traditions' and owing 'a greater debt to our post-Enlightenment liberal tradition than he is acknowledging'. Interestingly enough, for the concerns of this reader, Markham opines that the only hope for the success of MacIntyre's liberalised 'tradition-constituted enquiry' lies in *education*. Not only is it education 'which may provoke the sensitivity to

461

the inadequacy' of fundamentalist-type traditions with their 'closed account of disagreement', but it is also education (critical education) 'which alone can provide the context' for the transcending of relativism and for genuine dialogue between traditions. Ian Markham's article is entitled 'Faith and reason: reflections on MacIntyre's "tradition-constituted enquiry".'

Professor Alasdair MacIntyre is McMahon/Hank Professor of Philosophy in the Department of Philosophy at the University of Notre Dame, Indiana, USA. Dr Ian Markham is Lecturer in Theology in the Department of Theology at the University of Exeter, England.

Notes
1. See references in note 19 to the overview of part two.
2. Alasdair MacIntyre, *Whose Justice? Which Rationality?*, Notre Dame, Indiana, University of Notre Dame Press; London, Duckworth, 1988. In this work MacIntyre develops in detail the historical and social contextual character of the principles of theoretical and practical rationality, that is, the 'conception of rational enquiry as embodied in a tradition', and the problem this raises for the possibility of rational debate between traditions — including religious traditions. Such traditions are not limited to an internal justification in the light of their own standards of justification, however, since there is the possibility of an 'epistemological crisis' in which a tradition can change by its adherents' coming to recognise the rational superiority of another tradition's claims (see *ibid.*, chapter 18).

10.1 Relativism, power and philosophy
Alasdair MacIntyre

The debate about relativism

It was Anthony Collins, the friend of John Locke, who remarked that, had it not been for the Boyle Lecturers' annual demonstrations of the existence of God, few people would ever have doubted it.[1] It may have been a similar spirit of argumentative contrariness that led me to begin to appreciate fully both the strength and the importance of the case to be made out in favour of at least one version of relativism only after reading some recent philosophical root and branch dismissals of relativism as such.[2] But of course I ought not to have been such a late-comer to that appreciation. For relativism, like scepticism, is one of those doctrines that have by now been refuted a number of times too often. Nothing is perhaps a surer sign that a doctrine embodies some not to be neglected truth than that in the course of the history of philosophy it should have been refuted again and again. Genuinely refutable doctrines only need to be refuted once.

Philosophical doctrines that are not susceptible of genuine refutation fall into at least two classes. There are some to which, in the light of the rational justification that can be provided for them, we owe simple assent. But there are others to which our assent is or ought to be accorded only with a recognition that what they present is a moment in the development of thought which has to be, if possible, transcended; and this even although we may as yet lack adequate grounds for believing ourselves able to transcend them. Scepticism is one such doctrine; and relativism is another. But no doctrine can be genuinely transcended until we understand what is to be said in its favour. And a first step towards understanding this in the case of relativism must be to show that the purported refutations have largely missed its point and so been misdirected.

It is not that there is nothing to be learned from them. From them we can certainly learn how to formulate relativism in a way that does not gratuitously entangle it with error. So we can learn from Socrates' encounter with the formulations of Protagoras in the *Theatetus*[3] that relativists must be careful not to allow themselves to be trapped into making some type of universal self-referential claim. Such a claim, by denying to all doctrines whatsoever the predicates 'is true' and 'is false', unless these are radically reinterpreted to mean no more than 'seems true to such and such persons' and 'seems false to such and such persons', turns the interesting assertion that relativism is true into the uninteresting assertion that relativism seems true to

463

relativists. And we can learn from Hegel's critique of Kant[4] that relativists must be careful to avoid framing their theses in a way that presupposes the legitimacy of some version of what has come to be called the scheme-content distinction, that is, the distinction between some concept or conceptual scheme on the one hand and on the other an entirely preconceptual world or given waiting to be rescued from in one version blindness, in another nakedness, by being conceptualised.

Yet it is important to be precise about what we have to learn from these refutations of particular formulations of relativism; and it is important therefore not to abstract for formulaic use what we take to be the essence of some refutation from the context in which such as Plato or Hegel embedded it and from which it drew its peculiar force. So we are perhaps entitled to express a certain polite surprise when a contemporary philosopher who has shown both assiduity and ingenuity in trying to make credible the view that 'is true' says no more than is said by 'seems true to such and such persons, namely *us*', asserts that if there were any contemporary relativists, one could use against them some variant of what he calls the 'arguments Socrates used against Protagaras'.[5] The surprise derives from our remembering that the premises from which Plato derived Socrates' refutation of Protagoras' version of relativism also entailed the necessary failure of any reinterpretive reduction of 'is true' to 'seems true to such and such persons'. From these premises the one conclusion is not available without the other.

The same kind of polite surprise is warranted when another distinguished contemporary philosopher, having repeated the substance of Hegel's demonstration of the illegitimacy of any dualism which tears apart conceptual schemes on the one hand and the world on the other, concludes to the necessary incoherence of the very idea of a conceptual scheme.[6] It was after all Hegel who gave its canonical form both to the idea of a conceptual scheme and to that of alternative and incompatible conceptual schemes and he did so without ever violating his own ban on the illegitimate dualist scheme/content and scheme/world distinctions.[7] Nor was Hegel alone in this; the same could be said of his predecessor, Vico,[8] and of his successor, Collingwood.[9]

We need, then, in order to capture the truth in relativism, a formulation of that doctrine which has learnt from both Plato and Hegel: it must avoid Protagorean self-trivialising by giving its due to the Platonic distinction between 'is true' and 'seems true to such and such persons'; and in any appeal that it makes to the idea of alternative conceptual schemes, it must be careful to follow Hegel in leaving no opening for any scheme/content or scheme/world distinction.

The origin of relativism

'Relativism', as I am going to use that expression, names one kind of conclusion to enquiry into a particular class of problems. Those questions arise in the first place for people who live in certain highly specific types of social and cultural situations; but this is not to say that they are not distinctively philosophical questions. They are indeed examples of questions which *both* are inescapable for certain ordinary agents and language-users *and* have the characteristic structure of philosophical problems. It is perhaps unsurprising that they have been overlooked by those recent philosophers who want to make a sharp dichotomy between the realm of philosophical theorising and that of everyday belief because they suppose both that it is philosophers themselves who largely generate philosophical problems by their own misconceptions and that everyday life cannot be apt to suffer from types of disorder which require specifically philosophical diagnosis. This attitude is perhaps a symptom of a certain lack of sociological imagination, of too impoverished a view of the types of social and institutional circumstances which generate philosophical problems. What then are the social and institutional circumstances which generate the cluster of problems to which some version of relativism can be a rational response?

They are the social and institutional circumstances of those who inhabit a certain type of frontier or boundary situation. Consider the predicament of someone who lives in a time and place where he or she is a full member of two linguistic communities, speaking one language, Zuni, say, or Irish, exclusively to the older members of his or her family and village and Spanish or English, say, to those from the world outside, who seek to engage him or her in a way of life in the exclusively Spanish or English speaking world. Economic and social circumstance may enforce on such a person a final choice between inhabiting the one linguistic community and inhabiting the other; and in some times and places this is much more than a choice between two languages, at least in any narrowly conceived sense of 'language'. For a language may be so used, and both Irish and Zuni have in some past periods been so used, that to share in its use is to presuppose one cosmology rather than another, one relationship of local law and custom to cosmic order rather than another, one justification of particular relationships of individual to community and of both to land and to landscape rather than another. In such a language even the proper names may on occasion have such presuppositions.

If, for example, I speak in Irish, even today, let alone three hundred years ago, of Doire Colmcille — of Doire in modern Irish — the presuppositions and implications of my utterance are quite other than if I speak in English of Londonderry. But, it may be asked, are these not simply two names of one and the same place? The answer is first that no proper name of place or person names any place or person *as such;* it names *in the first instance* only *for* those who are members of some particular linguistic and cultural community, by identifying places and persons in terms of the scheme of identification shared by, and perhaps partially constitutive of, that community. The relation of a proper name to its bearer cannot be elucidated without reference to such identifying functions.[10] And secondly that 'Doire Colmcille' names – embodies a communal intention of naming – a place with a continuous identity ever since it became in fact St Columba's oak grove in 546 and that 'Londonderry' names a settlement made only in the seventeenth century and is a name whose use presupposes the legitimacy of that settlement and of the use of the English language to name it. Notice that the name 'Doire Colmcille' is as a name untranslatable; you can translate the Gaelic expression 'Doire Colmcille' by the English expression 'St Columba's oak grove'; but that cannot be the translation of a place name, for it is not itself the name of any place. And what is true of the relationship of 'Doire Colmcille' in Irish to 'Londonderry' in English holds equally of the relationship of the names of the Zuni villages in the sixteenth century, such as 'Itwana', to the Spanish name for them as the Seven Cities of Cibola.[11]

To this the response may be that although there may as a matter of contingent historical fact be certain kinds of association attaching to the use of 'Doire Colmcille' rather than 'Londonderry' or *vice versa,* the use of the name merely *qua* name carries with it no presuppositions concerning political or social legitimacy. And it might be thought that this could be shown by appeal to the fact that some ignorant stranger might use the name 'Londonderry' in order to ask the way and in identifying the place on the map at which he or she wished to arrive would have shown that one *can* use the name for purposes of identification without any such presupposition. But such a stranger is only able now to use a name which has indeed been made available to those outside its primary community of use because the members of the primary community use or used it as they do, and that stranger's secondary use of the name is therefore parasitic upon its uses by the primary community. Moreover such secondary non-presupposition-laden uses do not thereby become names freed from any specific social context of use. They are very specifically names-as-used-by-strangers-or-tourists. Philosophers of logic have sometimes treated the way in which such names are used by strangers or tourists as exemplifying some essential core naming relation, a concept about which I shall have to say something later on in the argument; for the moment I note only that in so doing such philosophers have obscured the difference between the type of natural language in which the standard uses of a variety of expressions commit the user to an expression of a shared, communal belief and the type of natural language in which this is so minimally or not at all.

In the type of frontier or boundary situation which I have been describing, both languages — the Irish of, say, 1700 and the English of the plantation settlements of the same date, or the Zuni Shiwi language of, say, 1540 and the Spanish of the *conquistadores* — are at the former end of this spectrum of natural-languages-in-use. Thus what the bilingual speaker in both members of one of these pairs is going to have to choose between, in deciding to spend his or her life within one linguistic community rather than the other, is also to some substantial degree alternative and incompatible sets of beliefs and ways of life. Moreover each of these sets of beliefs and ways of life will have internal to it its own specific modes of rational justification in key areas and its own correspondingly specific warrants for claims to truth.

It is not that the beliefs of each such community cannot be represented in any way at all in the language of the other; it is rather that the outcome in each case of rendering those beliefs sufficiently intelligible to be evaluated by a member of the other community involves characterising those beliefs in such a way that they are bound to be rejected. What is from the one point of view a just act of war will be from the other theft; what is from the one point of view an original act of acquisition, of what had so far belonged to nobody and therefore of what had remained available to become only now someone's private property, will be from the other point of view the illegitimate seizure of what had so far belonged to nobody because it is what *cannot* ever be made into private property — for example, common land. The Spaniards brought alien concepts of ownership deriving from Roman, feudal and canon law to their transactions with the Indians; the English brought concepts of individual property rights recognised by English common law decisions to Ireland at a time when there was certainly a translation for the Latin 'jus' in Irish, but none for the expression 'a right' (understood as something that attaches not to status, role or function, but to individuals as such).

It will not at this point be helpful to remark either that in both these pairs of linguistic communities a great many other beliefs were of course shared by members of both communities or that in particular no one had ever had any difficulty in translating 'Snow is white' from one language to the other. There are indeed large parts of every language that are translatable into every other; and there are types of routine or routinisable social situations which are reproduced in many — some perhaps even in all — cultures. And the project of matching types of sentence-in-use to types of routinisable situation reproduced in many cultures, and of both to the habits of assenting to or dissenting from the uses of such sentences, will doubtless, if actually carried through rather than merely projected, lay bare the relationship between these facts and the type and range of translatability that hold in consequence of that relationship. But the suspicion which I have gradually come to entertain about this type of project is that what can be expected from it is perhaps not so much an adequate semantics for natural languages or a theory of truth in such languages as a series of excellent Phrase Books for Travellers. For it is precisely those features of languages, mastery of which *cannot* be acquired from such phrase books, which generate untranslatability between languages.

What are those features? They include a power to extrapolate from uses of expressions learned in certain types of situations to the making and understanding of new and newly illuminating uses. The availability of this power to the members of a whole linguistic community of the type which I have been characterising depends in part upon their shared ability to refer and allude to a particular common stock of canonical texts, texts which define the literary and linguistic tradition which members of that community inhabit. For it is by allusion to such texts that linguistic innovation and extrapolation proceed; what those texts provide are both shared exemplars from which to extrapolate and shared exemplars of the activity of extrapolation.

It is characteristically poets and saga reciters who in such societies make and continually remake these at first oral and then written texts; only poetic narrative is memorable in the required way and, as we should have learned from Vico,[12] it is the linguistic capacities and abilities provided by poetry and saga which make later forms of prose possible. Concepts are first acquired and understood in terms of poetic images and the movement of thought from the concreteness and particularity of the imaged to the abstractness of the conceptual never completely leaves that concreteness and particularity behind. Conceptions of courage and of justice, of authority, sovereignty and property, of what understanding is and what failure to understand is, all these will continue to be elaborated from exemplars to be found in the socially recognised canonical texts. And this will still be the case when prose supplements poetry, when law books are added to myth and epic and when dramatic works are added to both. The consequence is that when two such distinct linguistic communities confront one another, each with its own body of canonical texts, its own exemplary images and its own tradition of elaborating concepts in terms of these, but each also lacking a knowledge of, let alone linguistic capacities informed by, the tradition of the other community, each will represent the beliefs of the other within its own discourse in abstraction from the relevant tradition and so in a way that ensures misunderstanding. From each point of view certain of the key concepts and beliefs of the other, just because they are presented apart from that context of inherited texts from which they draw their conceptual life, will necessarily appear contextless and lacking in justification.

Here we confront one more instance of the hermeneutic circle.

The initial inability of the members of each linguistic community to translate certain parts of the language of the other community into their own is a barrier to knowledge of the traditional embodied in the uses of that language; but lack of knowledge of the tradition is itself sufficient to preclude accurate translation of those parts of the alien language. And once again the fact that certain other parts of the two languages may translate quite easily into each other provides no reason at all for scepticism about partial untranslatability. The sentences-in-use which are the untranslatable parts of this type of language-in-use are not in fact capable of being logically derived from, constructed out of, reduced to or otherwise rendered into the sentences-in-use which comprise the translatable part of the same language-in-use. Nor should this surprise us. One of the marks of a genuinely adequate knowledge of two quite different languages by one and the same person is that person's ability to discriminate between those parts of each language which are translatable into the other and those which are not. Some degree of partial untranslatability marks the relationship of every language to every other.

Notice that this recognition of untranslatability never entails an acknowledgment of some necessary limit to understanding. Conversely that we can understand completely what is being said in some language other than our own never entails that we can translate what we understand. And it is this ability both to understand and to recognise the partial untranslatability of what is understood which combines with the specific social, conceptual and linguistic characteristics of the type of boundary situation which I have identified to create the predicament of the bilingual speaker who in that type of situation has to choose between membership in one or other of the two rival linguistic communities.

Remember that the contingent features of that speaker's situation make this not only a choice between languages, but between two mutually incompatible conceptualisations of natural and social reality; and it is not only a choice between two mutually incompatible sets of beliefs, but one between sets of beliefs so structured that each has internal to it its own standards of truth and justification. Moreover, this choice has to be made with only the limited linguistic and conceptual resources afforded by the two languages in question. What constraints do these limits impose?

They exclude the possibility of appeal to some neutral or independent standard of rational justification to justify the choice of one set of beliefs, one way of life, one linguistic community rather than the other. For the only standards of truth and justification made available within the two communities are those between which a choice has to be made. And the only resources afforded for the members of each community to represent the concepts, beliefs and standards of the other ensure that from the point of view of each its own concepts, beliefs and standards will be vindicated and those of its rival found wanting.

Here then two rival conceptual schemes do confront one another. For those culturally and linguistically able to inhabit only one of them no.problem arises. But for our imagined person who has the abilities to understand both, but who must choose to inhabit only one, the nature of the choice is bound, if he or she is adequately reflective, to transform his or her understanding of truth and of rational justification. For he or she will not be able to find application for the concepts of truth and justification which are independent of the standards of one community or the other. There is no access to any subject-matter which is not conceptualised in terms that already presuppose the truth of one set of claims rather than the other. Hegel's proscription of any appeal to an extra-conceptual reality is not being infringed. Each community, using its own criteria of *sameness* and *difference,* recognises that it is one and the same subject-matter about which they are advancing their claim; incommensurability and incompatibility are not incompatible.

The only way to characterise adequately the predicament thus created for our imaginary person is in the idiom which Plato provided. For that person will now have to reinterpret the predicates 'is true' and 'is justified' so that to apply them will in future claim no more than would be claimed by 'seems true to this particular community' or 'seems justified to this particular community'. Rational choice will have transformed our imaginary person into a relativist. But why call this a predicament? Because in so reinterpreting these predicates our imaginary Zuni or Irish persons will have, without in the least intending to, separated him or herself effectively from both contending communities. For no sixteenth or seventeenth century community was able to understand itself relativistically.

To all this the reply may well be: So what? Even it it is conceded that I have provided a defensible version of relativism, and even if it is allowed that our imaginary person did in certain times and places have real counterparts, Irish or Zuni or whatever, what of it? That kind of relativism was imposed by the contingencies of their historical, social and linguistic circumstances, contingencies which deprived our imaginary person and his or her real counterparts of the linguistic and conceptual resources necessary to avoid or refute relativism. But *we,* it may be suggested, do have those resources, so what is the relevance of your philosophical figment to *us?*

Just this is, of course, the question. Is it indeed the case that, if we were to specify the linguistic and conceptual resources that would have to be provided to enable our imaginary person to overcome the particular contingent limitations of his or her situation, we should have shown how relativism can be avoided or refuted? If we succeed in transforming this imaginary person, so that he or she becomes just like us, will the relativisation of the predicates of truth and justification no longer be forced upon him or her, or indeed ourselves? To these questions I therefore turn, but before turning I want to enquire briefly what will be at stake in giving one kind of answer to them rather than another.

The political dimension

The same considerations which ensure that someone compelled to choose between the claims of two rival linguistic communities, in the type of circumstance that I have described, will be unable to appeal to any neutral, independent standard of rational justification by which to judge between their competing claims also ensure that more generally the members of any two such communities will have to conduct their relationship with members of the other community without resort to any such appeal. But where there is no resort to such standards, human relationships are perforce relationships of will and power unmediated by rationality. I do not mean that, where there is no resort to such standards, each of the contending parties in such communal relationships will necessarily act unreasonably, that is unreasonably from its own particular point of view as to what constitutes unreason. But it is just that point of view that in their transactions each community will be trying to impose upon the other. And when it becomes reasonable from the point of view of one of the contending parties to impose their will by force upon the other in the name of their own idiosyncratic conception of reasonableness, that is what they will do.

So it was with the Spanish in their relationships with the Zuni, so it has been with the English in their relationships with the Irish. And one instrument of such force is the imposition of one's own language at the expense of the other's. But can it ever be otherwise? Only if the relativism which emerged as the only rational attitude to the competing claim of two such antagonistic communities turns out not to be the last word on all relationships between rival human communities; only, that is, if linguistic and conceptual resources can indeed by supplied, so that that relativism can be avoided or circumvented. For only in cases where that relativism does not have the last word does the possibility open up of substituting, for a politics in which the exercise of power is unmediated by rationality, a politics in which the exercise of power is both mediated and tempered by appeal to standards of rational justification independent of the particularism of the contending parties.

I am not of course suggesting that the identification and formulation of such nonrelativist standards of truth and justification is ever by itself sufficient to overcome a politics of unmediated will and power, in the conflicts that occur within communities, let alone in the conflicts that occur between communities. And I am not suggesting that force may not on occasion be used to serve the purposes of genuine practical rationality as well as those of idiosyncratic and one-sided reasonableness. I *am* claiming that it is only in those forms of human relationship in which it is possible to .appeal to impersonal standards of judgment, neutral between competing claims and affording the best type of rational justification both relevant and available, that the possibility opens up of unmasking and dethroning arbitrary exercises of power, tyrannical power within communities and imperialist power between communities. Plato was once again right: the argument against the tyrant and the argument against relativised predicates of truth and justification require the same premises.

This would of course be denied by our contemporary post-Nietzschean anti-Platonists. But even they on occasion inadvertently provide support for this thesis. Perhaps the most cogent, because the most systematic, exposition of the view that all attempts to appeal to would-be impersonal standards of truth and rational justification must fail to provide any effective alternative to established distributions of power, just because every such attempt and appeal itself operates according to the laws of some institutionalised distribution of power, is that of Michel Foucault in his earlier writings. So Foucault can write about the politics of truth and the political economy of truth in a way that treats all appeals to truth and to rational justification as themselves particularist forms of power inextricably associated with other forms of imposition and constraint.[13] But Foucault cannot articulate this view either generally or in his detailed institutional studies without presupposing a radical incommensurability thesis, a thesis that indeed only seems to emerge as a conclusion from his studies because it *was* presupposed from the outset. And that thesis is entitled to our assent, if and only if the version of relativism which I have described does have the last word.

So it turns out that how we understand the politics of power depends in crucial part upon the answers that we give to certain philosophical questions. Janice Moulton[14] and Robert Nozick[15] have both recently suggested that philosophy has been damaged by an excessive use of adversarial and antagonistic idioms. We speak too readily, they think, of winning and losing arguments, of others being forced to acknowledge our conclusions and so on; and in so far as such idioms obscure the need for the cooperative virtues in philosophical activity, they are certainly right. Nonetheless the language of antagonism has one important positive function. It signals to us that philosophy, like all other institutionalised human activities, is a milieu of conflict. And the conflicts of philosophy stand in a number of often complex and often indirect relationships to a variety of other conflicts. The complexity, the indirectness and the variety all help to conceal from us that even the more abstract and technical issues of our discipline – issues concerning naming, reference, truth and translatability – may on occasion be as crucial in their political or social implications as are theories of the social contract or of natural right. The former no less than the latter have implications for the nature and limitations of rationality in the arenas of political society. All philosophy, one way or another, is political philosophy.

Sometimes philosophy fares better by our forgetting this, at least temporarily, but we can scarcely avoid bearing it in mind in returning to the question to which the present argument has led: what other resources would our imaginary person in his or her sixteenth- or seventeenth-century boundary situation have had to possess, what resources that he or she lacked would we have to possess, if we are to be able to appeal to standards of judgment in respect of truth and rational justification which do not relativise these predicates to the conceptual scheme of one particular cultural and linguistic community?

The truth in relativism

A necessary first step out of the relativistic predicament would be the learning of some third language, a language of a very different kind from the two available to our imaginary person so far. Such a third language, if it was to provide the needed resources, would have to be a language with two central characteristics. First its everyday use must be such that it does *not* presuppose allegiance to either of the two rival sets of beliefs between which our imaginary person has to choose or indeed, so far as possible, to any other set of beliefs which might compete for allegiance with those two. And secondly it must be able to provide the resources for an accurate representation of the two competing schemes of belief, including that in the tradition of each community which provides that background for its present beliefs, without which they cannot be fully intelligible nor their purported justification adequately understood. What kind of language-in-use would this be?

One central feature that it would have to possess, if it were to satisfy the first of these two conditions, can be illustrated by considering how its use of proper names, for example of place-names, would contrast with that of the languages in terms of which the problem has so far been framed. For in this third language the relationship of a name to what is named will have to be specifiable, so far as possible, independently of any particular scheme of identification embodying the beliefs of some particular community. Names in consequence will have to have become detached from those descriptions which, within some given and presupposed context defined by the beliefs of some particular community, uniquely identify person or place. Particular proper names will have ceased to be equivalent to, and, in virtue of that loss of equivalence will have ceased to have the same sense as, particular definite descriptions. Names of places will have become equally available for any user to employ whatever his or her beliefs. Names having been Fregean will have become by a process of social change Kripkean.[16]

The immediate response of most philosophical logicians will once again be to say that I have in so characterising these changes confused the essential function of naming with its merely contingent accompaniments. But it is just this notion of a single essential naming relationship or function that I reject; just as we have learned that meaning is not a unitary notion, so we ought also to have learned that there are multifarious modes of identifying, picking out, referring to, calling towards, in or up and the like, all of which connect a name and a named, but there is no single core relation of name to named for theories of reference to be theories of. Or rather, if there were to be such a relation, it would be what Russell said it was, and it is notorious that Russell's characterisation of that relation entails that there is indeed a class of proper names, but that none of the expressions which we have hitherto called names is among them.[17]

A second feature of this type of language will be the absence of texts which are canonical for its common use. Allusion and quotation will have become specialised devices and the literate will have been divorced from the literary. For texts, whether oral or written, embody and presuppose beliefs and this type of language is, so far as possible, *qua* language-in-use, neutral between competing systems of beliefs. What it will provide are resources for the representation of an indefinite variety of systems of beliefs, most of them originally at home in very different types of linguistic community by means of a variety of devices which enable those who construct such representations to do so in a way that is quite independent of their own commitments. What kind of devices are these? Where the text is in a foreign language, translation will be supplemented both by paraphrase and by scholarly gloss.[18] Words as common as *'polis'* and *'dikaiosune'* in fifth century Attic Greek cannot be translated in any strict sense into twentieth century English or French or German − examples, it will have been obvious at once, of this type of language − but their use can be quite adequately elucidated. The traditions that appealed to canonical texts can now become matter for successful historical enquiry and the relevant texts embodying those traditions can be established, edited and translated or otherwise elucidated. The belief-system of any and every culture, or of almost any and every culture, can thus be accurately represented within our own. But certain features of the resulting stock of representations need to be taken into account.

One concerns the asymmetry of this representation relation. From the fact that we in modern English or some other modern language, with our academic resources, can accurately represent the belief-system or part of the belief-system of another culture, it does not follow that the corresponding part of our belief-system can be represented in the language-in-use of that other culture. Using modern English Charles H Kahn has shown how the Homeric uses of the verb *eimi* can be accurately and adequately represented.[19] But his explanation of why certain types of translation or paraphrase would be a misrepresentation, namely that, for example, the English verb 'exist' has emerged from a history whose first stage was the transition to classical Greek and which was then informed successively by classical Latin poetic usage, by medieval Latin philosophical usage and finally by some essentially modern preoccupations, so that we just cannot use 'exist' to translate or to explicate the characteristic and varying features of Homeric uses of *eimi,* has as a consequence that it would not have been possible within the Homeric linguistic community to represent accurately the modern English uses of 'exist'. And what is true of the relationship of archaic Greek to modern English would be equally true of the relationship to modern English of seventeenth century Irish or sixteenth century Zuni. But from this fact we might be tempted to draw a mistaken conclusion.

Return to the condition of our imaginary person once poised between sixteenth century Zuni and Spanish or seventeenth century Irish and English, but now, presumably some three hundred years older, considering whether to address his other problems instead in twentieth century English or French or whatever. Since such a person can provide him or herself with such an adequate degree of neutral representation of both systems of belief in a modern language, but cannot represent adequately or neutrally in either of his or her earlier languages either the systems of belief of the rival linguistic communities who spoke those languages or the standpoints afforded by twentieth-century English or French for the provision of such representation, it might seem that the only rational course for such a person is to conduct his or her enquiry from now on in one of the modern languages, thus escaping from some at least of the limit ations imposed on his or her earlier condition, the very limitations which enforced relativist conclusions. But it is just at this point that a second feature of the representations of schemes of belief in specifically modern natural languages presents a crucial difficulty.

The only way in which our frustrated relativist can hope to transcend the limitations which imposed that relativism is by formulating in the language that he or she can now speak, one of the languages of modernity, an impersonal and neutral standard of rational justification in the light of which the claims of the competing belief-systems can be evaluated. But what he or she will in fact learn from acquiring this new language is that it is a central feature of the culture whose language it is that rationally founded agreement as to the nature of the justification required is not to be obtained. Rational justification within the context of such cultures becomes an essentially contested concept and this for a number of distinct, but related types of reason.

One arises from the nature of the historical process which made the language of modernity what it is. A central feature of that process had to be, I have already argued, the detachment of the language-in-use from any particular set of canonical texts; and an early stage in that history was the gradual accumulation in the culture of so many different, heterogeneous and conflicting bodies of canonical texts from so many diverse parts of the cultural past that every one of them had to forgo any exclusive claim to canonical status and thereby, it soon became apparent, any claim to canonical status at all. So the accumulation of Greek, Hebrew and Latin texts at the Renaissance proved only a prologue not only to the annexation of Chinese, Sanskrit, Mayan and Old Irish texts, and to the bestowal of equal status upon texts in European vernacular languages from the thirteenth to the nineteenth centuries, but also to the discovery of a wide range of preliterate cultures, the whole finally to be assembled in that modern liberal arts college museum of academic culture, whose introductory tour is provided by those Great Books courses which run from Gilgamesh to Saul Bellow via Confucius, Dante, Newton, *Tristram Shandy* and Margaret Mead.

What the history that culminates in this kind of educational gallimaufry produced along the way was a large and general awareness of the wide range of varying and conflicting types of justificatory argument used to support various types of contending belief, and also of the wide range of varying and conflicting theoretical accounts of rational justification available to support their use. The consequence was a multiplication of rival standpoints concerning a wide range of subject-matters, none of them able to provide the resources for their own final vindication and the overthrow of their competitors. So within philosophy foundationalists war with coherentists and both with sceptics and perspectivists; while conceptions of truth as empirical adequacy contend against a variety of mutually incompatible realisms and both against truth conceived as disclosure. Within the academic study of literature, controversies over the nature of interpretation and about the justification not only of particular interpretations of particular texts, but even of what it is that such interpretations are interpretations of, parody philosophical debate in both idiom and interminability. And psychology has happily accommodated numbers of mutually incompatible schools of thought, each with its own idiosyncratic account of justification, ever since it became an independent academic discipline.

Where the dominant institutions and modes of thought in our larger political society sanction and even encourage disagreement, as upon theological questions, it is widely accepted that in the debates between contending modes of justification there can be no rational conclusion. But even where those same institutions and modes of thought prescribe a large measure of agreement, as in the natural sciences, not only do non-scientific modes of thought such as astrology (which happens to have its own well-organised and far from unsophisticated standards of justification) continue to flourish alongside the sciences, but it remains impossible to secure agreement on why the key transitions in the past history of our culture from prescientific thought to scientific, and from one mode of scientific thought to another, were or are rationally justified. So incommensurability as a feature of the history of the natural sciences has continually been rediscovered and recharacterised from a variety of justificatory standpoints: by Gaston Bachelard in the context of the French debates of the 1920s; by Michael Polanyi in such a way as to warrant a blend of fideism and realism; by Thomas Kuhn in a way designed to undermine logical empiricism; by Paul Feyerabend in an anarchist mode; and by Ian Hacking in an historical thesis about 'styles of thought'.

The multiplicity of mutually irreconcilable standpoints concerning justification is one that each of us tends to recognise easily and even scornfully in other academic professions. But from within our own profession each of us characteristically views and describes the situation only from the specific point of view of his or her commitments, judging the success and failure of other points of view from the standpoint afforded by standards of justification internal to our own; and by so doing we render our overall cultural situation invisible, at least for most of the time. That this should be the case, that we should tend to be guilty of this kind of onesidedness, is scarcely surprising. It says no more about us than that we are, sociologically at least, normal human beings. The danger of contemporary anti-relativism however is that it suggests that what is in fact a contingent social condition whose limitations it is important for us to overcome is in fact a necessary condition of rational social existence. For antirelativism pictures us first as necessarily inhabiting our own conceptual scheme, our own *weltanschaung* ('*Whose* conceptual scheme, whose *weltanschaung* but our own could we be expected to inhabit?' is the rhetorical question that is sometimes posed) and secondly as necessarily acquiring whatever understanding we may possess of the conceptual schemes and *weltanschaungen* of others by a process of translation so conceived that any intelligible rendering of the concepts and beliefs of the others must represent them as in all central respects similar to our own.

What I have tried to suggest by contrast is that when we learn the languages of certain radically different cultures, it is in the course of discovering what is untranslatable in them, and why, that we not only learn how to occupy alternative viewpoints, but in terms of those viewpoints to frame questions to which under certain conditions a version of relativism is the inescapable answer. And in so doing we are also able to learn how to view our own peculiarly modern stand-point from a vantage point outside itself. For consider now the view of that modern standpoint afforded to our imaginary person who had hoped to remedy the deficiencies of his or her particular type of premodern language by learning to speak one of the languages of modernity.

Where in his or her premodern language he or she was unable to free him or herself from the limitations of the justificatory schemes built into and presupposed by each particular language-in-use, and so was unable to discover a set of neutral and independent standards of rational justification, by appeal to which his or her choice of allegiance to the beliefs and way of life of one community rather than the other could be made, he or she now speaks a language the use of which is free from such commitments. But the culture which is able to make such a language available is so only because it is a culture offering, for the relevant kinds of controversial subject-matter, all too many heterogeneous and incompatible schemes of rational justification. And every attempt to advance sufficient reasons for choosing any one such scheme over its rivals must always turn out to pre-suppose the prior adoption of that scheme itself or of some other. For without such a prior prerational commitment, no reason will count as a good reason.

Hence our imaginary person whose acquisition of one of the natural languages of modernity – twentieth century English or French or whatever – was to rescue him or her from the relativism imposed by his or her previous condition cannot find here any more than there, albeit for very different reasons, any genuinely neutral and independent standard of rational justification. And it remains only to recognise that if our imaginary sixteenth- or seventeenth-century person, knowing both the languages that he or she then knew and subsequently learning our own, would be unable to avoid relativistic conclusions, then we in turn by learning his or her languages, or languages like them, and so learning both to imagine and to understand ourselves from the standpoint of such an external observer, would have to reach the same conclusions. Relativism after all turns out to be so far immune to refutation, even by us.

The transcending of relativism

It does not follow that relativism cannot be transcended. We may be tempted to think so by noticing that the version of relativism which resists refutation is itself a relativised relativism, since what my argu-ments show, if they succeed, are that relativism is inescapable from certain particular points of view – one of which happens to be that which most people in modern societies such as ours take to be their own. And this may seem to provide additional confirmation, if such is still needed, that there is after all no mode of thought, enquiry or practice which is not from some particular point of view, and whose judgments do not therefore take place on the basis of what Edmund Burke called prejudices, prejudgments. But it does not follow, as we might suppose if we did concede the last word to relativism, that we are thereby condemned to or imprisoned within our own particular standpoint, able to controvert that of others only by appealing to standards which already presuppose the standpoint of our own prejudices. Why not?

Begin from a fact which at this stage can be little more than suggestive. It is that those natural languages in which philosophy became a developed form of enquiry, so later generating from itself first the natural and then the social sciences, were in the condition neither on the one hand of sixteenth- and seventeenth-century Zuni and Irish nor in that of the natural languages of modernity. The Attic Greek of the fifth and fourth centuries, the Latin of the twelfth to fourteenth centuries, the English, French, German and Latin of the seventeenth and eighteenth centuries were each of them neither as relatively presuppositionless in respect of key beliefs as the languages of modernity were to become, nor as closely tied in their use to the presuppositions of one single closely knit set of beliefs as some premodern languages are and have been. Consider in this respect the difference between Attic and Homeric Greek or that between mature philosophical Latin after Augustine and Jerome and the Latin that had preceded the discoveries by Lucretius and Cicero that they could only think certain Greek thoughts in Latin if they radically neologised. Such languages-in-use, we may note, have a wide enough range of canonical texts to provide to some degree alternative and rival modes of justification, but a narrow enough range so that the debate between these modes is focused and determinate. What emerges within the conceptual schemes of such languages is a developed problematic, a set of debates concerning a body of often interrelated problems, problems canonical for those inhabiting that particular scheme, by reference to work upon which rational progress, or failure to achieve such progress, is evaluated. Each such problematic is of course internal to some particular conceptual scheme embodied in some particular historical tradition with its own given starting-point, its own prejudices. To become a philosopher always involved learning to inhabit such a tradition, a fact not likely to be obvious to those brought up from infancy within one, but very obvious to those brought up outside any such. It is no accident for example that for Irish speakers to become philosophers, they had first to learn Greek and Latin, like Johannes Scotus Eriugena in the ninth century.

The development of a problematic within a tradition characteristically goes through certain well-marked stages − not necessarily of course the same stages in every tradition − among them periods in which progress, as judged by the standards internal to that particular tradition, falters or fails, attempt after attempt to solve or resolve certain key problems or issues proves fruitless and the tradition appears, again by its own standards, to have degenerated. Characteristically, if not universally, at this stage contradictions appear that cannot be resolved within the particular tradition's own conceptual framework; that is to say, there can be drawn from within the tradition equally well-grounded support for incompatible positions; at the same time enquiries tend to become diverse and particularised and to lose any overall sense of direction; and debates about realism may become fashionable.[20] And what the adherents of such a tradition may have to learn in such a period is that their tradition lacks the resources to explain its own failing condition. They are all the more likely to learn that if they encounter some other standpoint, conceptually richer and more resourceful, which *is* able to provide just such an explanation.

So it was, for example, when Galilean and Newtonian natural philosophy turned out to provide a more adequate explanation by its own standards not only of nature than scholasticism had afforded, but also of why late medieval scholastic enquiries had been only able to proceed so far and no further. Scholasticism's successes and more importantly its frustrations and limitations, judged by scholasticism's own standards of success and failure rather than by any later standards, only became intelligible in the light afforded by Galileo and Newton.

That the theoretical standpoint of Galileo or Newton may have been incommensurable with that of the scholastics is not inconsistent with this recognition of how the later physical tradition transcended the limitations of the earlier. And it is of course not only within the history of natural philosophy that this kind of claim can be identified and sometimes vindicated. Such a claim is implicit in the relationship of some of the medieval theistic Aristotelians to Aristotle in respect of theology and Dante's *Commedia* to the *Aeneid* in respect of poetic imagination.

These examples direct our attention to a central characteristic of theoretical and practical rationality. Rationality, understood within some particular tradition with its own specific conceptual scheme and problematic, as it always has been and will be, nonetheless requires *qua* rationality a recognition that the rational inadequacies of that tradition from its own point of view – and every tradition must from the point of view of its own problematic view itself as to some degree inadequate – may at any time prove to be such that perhaps only the resources provided by some quite alien tradition, far more alien, it may be, than Newton was to the scholastics, will enable us to identify and to understand the limitations of our own tradition; and this provision may require that we transfer our allegiance to that hitherto alien tradition. It is because such rationality requires this recognition that the key concepts embodied in rational theory and practice within any tradition which has a developed problematic, including the concepts of truth and rational justification, cannot be defined exclusively in terms of or collapsed into those conceptions of them that are presently at home within the modes of theory and practice of the particular conceptual scheme of that tradition, or even some idealised version of those conceptions: the Platonic distinction between 'is true' and 'seems true to such and such person' turns out within such traditions to survive the recognition of the truth in relativism.

It is only from the standpoint of a rationality thus characterised, and that is to say from the standpoint of a tradition embodying such a conception of rationality, that a rejoinder can be made to those post-Nietzschean theories according to which rational argument, enquiry and practice always express some interest of power and are indeed the masks worn by some will to power. And in this respect there is a crucial difference between rationality thus understood and the rationality characteristic of the Enlightenment and of its heirs. Ever since the Enlightenment our culture has been far too hospitable to the all too plainly self-interested belief that, whenever we succeed in discovering the rationality of other and alien cultures and traditions, by making their behaviour intelligible and by understanding their languages, what we will also discover is that in essentials they are just like us. Too much in recent and contemporary antirelativism continues to express this Enlightenment point of view and thereby makes more plausible than they ought to be those theories which identify every form of rationality with some form of contending power. What can liberate rationality from this identification is precisely an acknowledgement, only possible from within a certain kind of tradition, that rationality requires a readiness on our part to accept, and indeed to welcome, a possible future defeat of the forms of theory and practice in which it has up till now been taken to be embodied within our own tradition, at the hands of some alien and perhaps even as yet largely unintelligible tradition of thought and practice; and this is an acknowledgement of which the traditions that we inherit have too seldom been capable.[21]

Notes

1. 'An answer to Mr Clarke's third defence of his letter to Mr Dodwell,' in *The Works of Samuel Clarke, DD,* London, 1738, volume 3, p. 883.
2. Most notably by Richard Rorty, 'Pragmatism, relativism, and irrationalism,' *Proceedings and Addresses of the American Philosophical Association,* 53, 1980, pp. 719–738, reprinted in *Consequences of Pragmatism,* Brighton, Harvester Press, 1982, pp. 160–175; and by Donald Davidson, 'On the very idea of a conceptual scheme,' *Proceedings and Addresses of the American Philosophical Association,* 47, 1974, pp. 5–20, reprinted in *Inquiries into Truth and Interpretation,* Oxford, Oxford University Press, 1984, pp. 183–198; and in *Expressing Evaluations,* the 1982 Lindley Lecture at the University of Kansas.
3. *Theatetus* 152a–179b, and especially 170e–171c.
4. See for example in the first part of the *Enzyklopädie der philosophischen Wissenschaften* (1817) translated by William Wallace as *The Logic of Hegel,* Oxford, 1873, section 44, and 'Remark: the thing-in-itself of transcendental

idealism,' appended to chapter I, A(b) of section two of book two of Hegel's *Science of Logic,* London, 1969, which is A V Miller's translation of the *Wissenschaft der Logik* (1812).

5. Richard Rorty, 'Pragmatism, relativism and irrationalism,' in *Consequences of Pragmatism, op. cit.,* p. 167.

6. Donald Davidson argues in 'On the very idea of a conceptual scheme' that the scheme-content distinction involves the notion of a relationship between a language or conceptual scheme on the one hand and on the other 'something neutral and common that lies outside all schemes' (p. 190) and that the only relationships possible between a language or conceptual scheme and such a something are those of the scheme organising, systematising or dividing whatever it is, or of it fitting or accounting for whatever it is. D Davidson then shows that spelling out these relationships involves characterising what was allegedly neutral and common, so that it is neither, but a subject-matter which 'we will have to individuate according to familiar principles,' so that any language which enables us to speak of it 'must be a language very like our own' (p. 192). Hegel argues conversely in the passages cited in note 4 that if we deny to such a something or other those characteristics that it must lack if it is to be genuinely prior to all categorisation, as what is 'neutral and common' (D Davidson's expression) must be, it will turn out to be nothing at all. And in the context of a different discussion, after pointing out that what is alleged to be beyond all conceptualisation by reason of its particularity '*cannot be reached* by language. In the actual attempt to say it, it would therefore crumble away.' *(Phanomenologie des Geistes,* 1807, paragraph 110, A V Miller's translation in *Phenomenology of Spirit,* Oxford, 1977). He points out that in characterising the whatever it is we find ourselves individuating according to familiar principles, anticipating D Davidson very precisely. The page references to D Davidson are to *Inquiries into Truth and Interpretation.*

7. One example of Hegel's treatment of rival conceptual schemes is found in the *Phanomenologie* VI, B, II a 'Der kampf der aufklarung mit dem aberglauben'.

8. For Vico who gave us the first genuinely historical treatment of conceptual schemes, see especially book IV, sections 1-11 of the *Principi di Scienza Nuova* (1744), translated by T G Bergin and H Fisch as *The New Science of Giambattista Vico,* Cornell, 1948.

9. It was of course Collingwood's antirealism, already spelled out in *Speculum Mentis,* Oxford, Oxford University Press, 1924, that committed him to rejection of any version of the scheme-context distinction. For his treatment of alternative conceptual schemes see especially the *Essay on Metaphysics,* Oxford, Oxford University Press, 1940.

10. Paul Zipp in 'About proper names,' *Mind* 86, 1977, draws attention to the importance of attending 'to the relevant anthropological and linguistic date.' An exemplary study is Robin Fox, 'Structure of personal names on Tory Island,' *Man,* 1963, reprinted as 'Personal names,' in *Encounter with Anthropology,* New York, Harcourt Brace Jovanovich, 1973.

11. On the first encounters of the Zuni with the Spaniards see F H Cushing, 'Outlines of Zuni creation myths,' in *13th Annual Report of the Bureau of Ethnology,* Washington, DC, 1896, pp. 326−333, and on the way places are located and the middle place named pp. 367−73.

12. *Principi di Scienza Nuova,* paragraphs 34−36, for example.

13. See for an introduction chapter 5 and chapter 6 (both originally in *Microfisica del Potere,* Turin, 1977) of *Power/Knowledge,* Brighton, Harvester Press, 1980. Chapter 5 is translated by Kate Soper; chapter 6 by Colin Gordon.

14. 'A paradigm of philosophy: the adversary method,' in *Discovering Reality,* Dordrecht, 1983, edited by S Harding and M B Hintikka.

15. *Philosophical Explanations,* Cambridge, Massachusetts, Harvard University Press, 1981, pp. 4−8.

16. What has to be supplied here is an account of how one and the same proper name can be used in a variety of ways which connect it to one and the same bearer.

17. 'The philosophy of logical atomism,' in *Logic and Knowledge,* edited by R C Marsh, London, Allen and Unwin, 1956, pp. 200−203, originally published in *The Monist,* 1918.

18. See John Wallace, 'Translation theories and the decipherment of Linear B,' *Theory and Decision,* 11, 1979.

19. *The Verb 'Be' and its Synonyms,* edited by J W M Verhaar, part 6: *The Verb 'Be' in Ancient Greek* by Charles H Kahn (Foundations of Language Supplement Series, volume 16, Dordrecht, 1973).

20. Neither realism nor antirealism should be thought of as mistakes (or truths) generated by philosophers reflecting upon the sciences from some external standpoint. They are in fact primarily moments in the self interpretation of the sciences. And the growth of debates about realism characteristically is a symptom of the inability of scientists to give a cogent account to themselves of the status of their enquiries.

21. My colleagues John Compton, John Post, Charles Scott and Harry Teloh subjected an earlier version of this address to rigorous and constructive criticism. A different kind of debt is to Brian Friel's play *Translations,* London, Faber and Faber, 1981, and to my former colleague Dennis Tedlock's translations of narrative poetry of the Zuni Indians, *Finding the Centre,* Nebraska, University of Nebraska Press, 1978, which threw a very different light on problems of translation from that afforded by most recent philosophical writing.

10.2 Faith and reason : reflections on MacIntyre's 'tradition-constituted enquiry'
Ian Markham

The problem at the heart of the faith/reason relationship can be set out as follows. Faith implies total commitment whilst reason requires a certain detachment. One cannot be totally committed yet rationally detached at the same time. Therefore faith and reason are two mutually exclusive approaches to religion. Alasdair MacIntyre in *Whose Justice? Which Rationality?* has offered a very interesting perspective on this problem. He has argued, albeit indirectly, that this faith/reason question is a modern problem generated by a certain set of liberal and relativist presuppositions. This paper will summarise MacIntyre's contribution to the discussion, and then point to some of the inadequacies of his account. I will be arguing that commitment to a tradition is largely justified by internal explanations for disagreement. Faith seems to need an intolerant explanation for different traditions. Therefore, MacIntyre is, in fact, handling liberalised forms of the traditions. By tackling MacIntyre's work from the faith/reason angle, I hope to show certain more fundamental problems with his work.

The nature of tradition-constituted enquiry

MacIntyre's discussion of the problem is indirect. His distinctive account of 'faith' and 'reason' arises in connection with his discussion of relativism. The basic error, MacIntyre believes, is the modern liberal conviction that rationality requires detachment. Commitment is incompatible with objectivity. It is here that MacIntyre is providing a distinctive account of the 'faith' and 'reason' problem. He claims it is a modern problem resting on modern liberal presuppositions, which he believes are flawed.

Relativism, argues MacIntyre, arises when people insist that rational evaluation of conflicting traditions is only possible when standing outside these traditions; since this is unobtainable, this then causes relativism to appear as the only option. MacIntyre wants to commend a different approach. It is an approach which is exemplified in *Whose Justice? Which Rationality?* He calls the approach 'tradition-constituted and tradition-constitutive enquiry'[1] (from henceforth referred to as TCE). This approach rejects the *expectations* of the relativist. It does this in two very important ways: first, by not expecting to find a neutral standard; and second by not expecting to arrive at an all-embracing truth which would be an absolute truth. The problem which underpins the objections of the relativist is false expectations. These false expectations have arisen because of the Enlightenment. The Enlightenment project was an unattainable quest for absolute certainty. It is a modern post-Enlightenment problem.

Our current crisis is then compared with the development of certain pre-Enlightenment traditions. Within the histories of these traditions, MacIntyre believes the principles of TCE are expressed. Although Aquinas did not have a neutral vantage point transcending the various conflicting traditions surrounding him, he still managed to make certain 'rational' judgments. In Aquinas there are two conflicting traditions which are engaged in debate and ultimately synthesised. Aquinas harmonises an Aristotelian structure with an Augustinian psychology. MacIntyre's entire book is a study of the principles of engagement between traditions within a historical and cultural framework. How is this possible?

Initially, traditions are founded within a community. A tradition can be said to begin when the beliefs, institutions, and practices are articulated by certain people and/or in certain texts. In such a community authority will be conferred on these texts and voices. In discussing these texts procedures for enquiry will be established. A rationality will develop. Problems for the community arise for any of the following reasons: one, when there are different and incompatible interpretations; two, when incoherences and inadequacies are identified; and three, when there is a confrontation with different systems.[2] When these problems arise, the community faces 'an epistemological crisis'.[3] The term 'epistemological crisis' describes a state where the traditional modes of enquiry are generating problems which the tradition lacks the resources to solve. Such a crisis generates the need for an imaginative conceptual innovation,[4] which gives rise to new beliefs which can be compared and contrasted with the older less adequate beliefs. Such a comparison obviously requires a standard. Here MacIntyre outlines a variation on the correspondence theory of truth.[5] Ultimately, all traditions are trying to explain reality in as comprehensive a way as possible. Truth is ultimately determined when the beliefs correspond with reality.

A tradition is maintained if it can be shown that any proposed modification in belief and outlook can be demonstrated to stand in a continuity with the rest of the tradition. It is possible that during an epistemological crisis, arising as a result of a conflict with another tradition, the adherents may decide that the new tradition is more appropriate than the earlier one. This is crucial. MacIntyre believes that it is possible for one tradition, when engaging another, to find that the other has better conceptual tools to understand human life and activity. A tradition can flounder. Despite the fact that there is no neutral rationality, the adherents find a different tradition's rationality more plausible. A judgment has been made between the two traditions. MacIntyre suggests that the developments in the science of Newton and Galileo might be of this type.[6]

Naturally, this engagement between traditions is not easy. Communication requires a common language, and language presupposes a rationality. MacIntyre believes that the only way for two traditions, with two different languages, to have dialogue, is for the participants to learn a second first-language. This term captures the necessity of learning the language as we did our first language when children. It is not simply a matter of matching sentences from our first language with our second, but of living and thinking with the concepts within the second language. This MacIntyre argues is both possible and necessary.

One notes that his primary objection is to the relativist's belief that one cannot seek truth from within a tradition. One can on MacIntyre's TCE account stand within a tradition and yet still engage other traditions. There is no conflict between rationality and commitment. It is part of the liberal illusion to believe otherwise. The TCE approach is the antithesis of the classical liberal instinct that objectivity requires detachment. And it is when operating with this liberal model that one arrives at the conflict between faith and reason. MacIntyre writes, 'What the Enlightenment made us for the most part blind to and what we now need to recover is ... a conception of rational enquiry as embodied in a tradition'.[7] TCE holds both commitment and rationality together. He is turning the faith/reason difficulty around; one cannot be rational unless one is committed. TCE is fundamentally a rational exercise, and post-Enlightenment liberalism has excluded itself from rational debate.

MacIntyre, in response, is making two points. First, these conditions for detachment and total commitment within any tradition making cognitive claims about the world are, quite literally, unreasonable. It would require a vantage point beyond the historical, cultural contingencies of the human creature. Thus, the problem is involved in the same error as the relativist. One can never be totally certain of any conclusion. Second, in the history of ideas, some of the most committed Christians have also been open to new and fresh ideas. The example pervading *Whose Justice?* is St Thomas Aquinas. He was committed to a tradition, yet in dialogue with other traditions.

Therefore, MacIntyre's contribution to the 'faith' and 'reason' problem can be summarised as follows:[8]

a.   a person is in a tradition and should be committed to that tradition;

b.   there is no neutral vantage point outside all traditions;

c. rationality requires dialogue with different traditions which demands the learning of a second first language, dialogue, and engagement; ultimately, one must concede the possibility that one's tradition could be overwhelmed by epistemological crisis, and a different tradition could have more adequate resources to make sense of the world;

d. so, this commitment to a tradition must not exclude dialogue with other traditions, and must always concede the possibility that one's tradition could be less adequate than other traditions.

The problem of tradition-constituted enquiry

In this section, I will now attempt to show that MacIntyre's account of the faith/reason problem is defective. Although there is much which is perceptive and true in MacIntyre's work, his thoughts on the faith/reason problem contains difficulties, both historical and conceptual. I will attempt to show that certain religious traditions are intrinsically opposed to rational dialogue precisely because they are so all-embracing.[9] This account will concentrate on the major orthodox expressions of the major theistic religions. Commitment to such a tradition is, in practice, generally incompatible with dialogue. My account of the relation between faith and reason will concentrate on certain devices, which for many people serve to enable them to be committed to propositions which are only rationally tentative. The primary purpose of my analysis is to identify a difficulty with MacIntyre's TCE and therefore his inadequate account of the faith and reason relationship.

This alternative account presupposes that no belief, least of all belief in God, can be disentangled from the world-view or, in MacIntyre's terminology, tradition of which it is an important part. Belief in God is part of various traditions attempting to explain and make sense of human life and experience. Commitment is made possible by the all-embracing character of a tradition. A tradition has two explanatory functions. The first concerns the positive features of human life and experience; so, for example, the Christian tradition attempts to explain the apparent purpose, design, and moral obligation we experience. These are positive features of the world in that they are phenomena which can be cited as evidence for the tradition. The second concerns the negative features of human life and experience; for the Christian tradition this would include the fact of evil and, more importantly for my purposes, the existence of different religions. What exactly would be classified as a negative or positive feature would vary from tradition to tradition, but the important point is the fact that each tradition must, if it is going to be successful, provide some sort of explanation for those features which appear to count against itself. One of the most important explanations a tradition must provide will be for the existence of traditions which disagree. In other words, each tradition must supply an explanation of disagreement.

A good illustration of a tradition supplying this internal explanation of the existence of different traditions which disagree is found in the work of St Thomas. Thomism had immense explanatory power and was in many respects very popular and successful. His system of natural theology was intended to show how Christian tradition can explain the positive features of human life and existence. One of the problems for St Thomas is the existence of other religions. The *Summa contra Gentiles* was written as a source book for missionaries involved in converting Moslems and Jews. In his account of unbelief St Thomas shows how his system can explain the existence of other religions. Here St Thomas carefully explains the different sorts of infidelities. There are the Jews who rejected the Old Testament's foreshadowing of the revelation of Christ; there are the Moslems who choose to fight against the revelation; and there are the heretics who rebel against the truth despite growing up with it. The problem in all three cases is simply human sinfulness. This is part of his explanation for these alternative traditions, the other part is the doctrine of predestination. St Thomas writes, 'Some people God rejects. We have seen already that predestination is part of providence, and that its working allows failures in the things in its charge. Since by divine providence human beings are ordained to eternal life, it also belongs to divine providence to allow some to fall short of this goal.'[10] So within the Thomist system there is a two-fold explanation for different traditions − for those who disagree. The first is human sinfulness; and the second is the doctrine of predestination. Moslems are both sinful and not chosen. This internal explanation functions mainly in respect of other traditions in their entirety.

Commitment, in practice, is both made possible and justified by this internal explanation of the negative features of human life and experience. This internal explanation provides the necessary device which entitles one to be committed. Commitment to a tradition is partly shown by the attitude one has to different traditions which disagree. MacIntyre is right to define traditions within communities. And when one appreciates that traditions arise from a historical context within a community one also understands the nature of these internal explanations for different traditions. They are devices which enable a community to retain its identity against other communities. They are the means by which commitment is justified. In declaring the truth of one's own tradition and believing that other people in different traditions are simply being sinful, one is showing one's commitment. True faith requires the capacity to believe despite the opposition; this for most people is only possible when one has a fairly simple internal explanation for those who are opposing.

Clearly, it is possible to think of different models of commitment. And, of course, some traditions are much more open than others. However, for the major theistic traditions in the west, these simple explanations for disagreement justify for most believers their commitment. I suggest that this clarifies the relation between 'faith' and 'reason', for faith tends to be an act of commitment to a tradition with an internal explanation for those who disagree.[11] Commitment is an acceptance of the adequacy of this internal explanation for those disagreeing traditions.

It might be objected that it is wrong to identify St Thomas's account of unbelief with an account of disagreement. After all, Plato and Aristotle were both pagans, but Aquinas considered it important to engage rationally with their work. There are two important remarks I must make in response to this objection. First, Plato (certainly) and Aristotle (slowly) had the special status of Christian pagans. St Thomas was already familiar with the range of Fathers who had interpreted Plato as a man who had foreseen the final revelation of God in Christ. They were not covered by his blanket explanation for pagans. Second, it is true that despite these internal explanations of different traditions, certain influences over a long period from a different tradition can be accommodated. However, from St Thomas's perspective Aristotle was not put under the same heading as the Moslems. It is a misrepresentation to insist that St Thomas Aquinas was primarily a perfect example of a man rationally engaging with two conflicting traditions. The major problem for Aquinas was the existence of completely different religious traditions; it was from that perspective that he managed to synthesise the Augustinian and Aristotelian traditions. After all the Augustinian and medieval Aristotelian traditions are both clearly Christian. Clearly, this is still a remarkable achievement; but, with this internal explanation for these different religions, St Thomas finds it difficult to accommodate these other religious traditions. Although he does want to correct certain Islamic interpretations of Aristotle, the only explanation for the existence of these other religions is to refer on the one hand to human sin, and on the other to predestination. Of course, this explanation makes it impossible for these traditions to be harmonised with Christianity.

There is underpinning this analysis of the faith/reason relation, an important distinction between the psychological and rational explanations for disagreement. The internal explanation for disagreement provides an internal justification for commitment. Elsewhere I have described this internal explanation as a *closed account* for disagreement.[12] For most people the psychological demand for total commitment is made possible by this closed account – this simple all-embracing explanation for disagreement. However, with rational reflection these closed accounts are implausible. There are several difficulties with them. First, they ignore the complexities of traditions in terms of their historical and cultural development. Christianity captured Europe, and Islam captured parts of the Middle East for complicated historical reasons, largely beyond the control of individuals, which makes any claim that one of these religions is being wilfully sinful very implausible. Second, these closed accounts ignore the similarities in terms of argument both for the belief and for each other. It is not simply ironic that two religions agree in attributing the other's disagreement to sinfulness, but reflects on the inadequacy of this account. Any claim to sinfulness depends on identifying deliberate intention to avoid the truth. The fact that they both each believe that they have the truth makes the sinful explanation very unlikely. Third, this closed account collapses when meeting believers from a different religious tradition. The sincerity, integrity, and goodness seen in believers from a wide variety of traditions makes the closed account very unlikely. If goodness comes from God, then goodness in a different religious tradition must come from God.

Rationally, these closed accounts are improbable. This is a discovery which historically must be attributed to our post-Enlightenment liberal tradition. It is partly due to our post-Enlightenment sensitivity to the ease with which evidence can be deduced for different traditions. It is partly due to the post-Enlightenment destruction of the closed accounts which opens up the possibility of tolerance, in the hope of a dialogue leading to truth. However, this points to the central difficulty. Traditions with clear closed accounts, which discourage further reflection, attract many more adherents, than those with tolerant, *open accounts* of disagreement. Tolerant traditions with *open accounts* of disagreement acknowledge the possibility of truth in other traditions. These liberalised traditions acknowledge the complexity of the world and, as a result, appear to lack clarity. They lack a simple message, appear intellectual and complicated, and fail to win much support. It is partly due to this concession − that truth could be found in the traditions with which one, at the moment, disagrees. This attitude to the tradition will makes one's commitment much more tentative. In practice, one will not and cannot be totally committed.

The defects of MacIntyre's TCE should now be apparent. MacIntyre's commitment to a-tradition is limited; it is limited by the demands for rationality. TCE makes two requirements: first, one must always acknowledge the possibility that one's tradition might be overwhelmed; and second, one ought to engage with other traditions by learning a second first-language. TCE denies the internal explanations (that is closed account of disagreement) for the existence of other traditions. TCE denies the power these internal explanations have and the reason why commitment overrides dialogue. In ignoring this internal explanation for disagreement, TCE is conceptually defective. At the same time it is historically defective. The reason, historically, for the rise of tolerance running parallel with the decline in the political power of religious systems is because the internal explanation for disagreement no longer had any power.

Religion, tolerance and education

MacIntyre is assuming a liberalised account of traditions. His traditions have lost their internal explanation for disagreement. They have been exposed to our post-Enlightenment conditions for rational enquiry. Rationality has diluted the commitment. He is still presupposing the supremacy of liberal reason, which places careful limits on one's commitments. It is not really 'Tradition-Constituted Enquiry', but 'Reason-Diluted Commitment.'[13] One stands within a tradition, diluting one's commitment to that tradition by certain rational considerations. MacIntyre rejects any closed account for disagreement, as seen in St Thomas, and advocates an open account without realising that he now stands in a liberalised Thomist tradition. One's rational engagement is made possible by the diluting of one's commitment: one's commitment is diluted by the rejection of any closed account for disagreement.

The tragic case of Salman Rushdie is a good illustration of the inadequacies of TCE. Many Moslems have retained their strong sense of community. Their community is defined by their religion, and their commitment is illustrated by their opposition to those who oppose their religion. For Iranian Moslems, tolerance of error and insult is quite inappropriate. They are certain of the truth of their religion. They are persuaded by the adequacy of the internal explanation for those who believe differently, therefore it would be a denial of their commitment to extend tolerance to Salman Rushdie. It is simply ironic that the Islamic explanation is very similar to the Thomist explanation for disagreement. There is no question of attempting to learn a second first-language to enable one to have dialogue with Salman Rushdie. There is also no question of our Iranian Moslem conceding the conceptual possibility that his tradition is wrong.

MacIntyre has three difficulties. First, it is not true to say that the faith and reason problem is the result of our post-Enlightenment liberal expectations which makes commitment incompatible with rational engagement. Instead, faith is, in practice, made possible by the internal explanation for negative factors, especially the explanation for the different traditions which disagree. Second, TCE has not grappled with the problem of such commitment so grounded within the internal resources of the tradition. MacIntyre is commending a highly sophisticated rational enterprise. But this will not be attractive to anyone completely certain of their own tradition: it would not have attracted much sympathy from the late Ayatollah Khomeini. Third, MacIntyre is unfair to certain forms of liberalism. This point links together the first two points; MacIntyre's proposal is made possible by a liberalising of these traditions. It is only as these traditions are liberalised that his rational dialogue can take place. Basically, MacIntyre has misunderstood the character of commitment, provided a mistaken analysis of a genuine difficulty, and is commending a programme which is influenced by post-Enlightenment liberalism.

The relationship between 'faith' and 'reason' is important for MacIntyre's account. One of the attractions of MacIntyre's TCE is that it appears to offer a committed attitude to a tradition which retains the need for dialogue with other traditions, and therefore tolerance. As a prescriptive claim, commending adherents to traditions to take up his method, then it is not only legitimate but commendable. It is the advocacy of liberalised forms of these traditions. However, as a descriptive claim, he is distorting the history of these traditions. *Whose Justice? Which Rationality?* can appear almost polemical in its setting of liberalism against TCE. However, in fact, MacIntyre is advocating liberalised forms of these traditions, governed by a liberal rationality which he treats as an absolute. He owes a greater debt to our post-Enlightenment liberal tradition than he is acknowledging.

However, that leaves one remaining difficulty. It is here that the faith/reason discussion impinges upon the nature of tolerance. If my account of faith/reason is correct, then the corollary we must face is that the intolerant traditions operating with a closed account of disagreement are always more likely to attract committed adherents. Psychologically, the attraction of a simple, intelligible explanation for those disagreeing with one's tradition is much easier than facing the complexity entailed in an open account of disagreement. The only hope for MacIntyre's liberalised TCE lies in education. It is education which may provoke the sensitivity to the inadequacy of these closed accounts. It is education which alone can provide the context for the learning of second first-language, and genuine dialogue. It is rather ironic that in the end the proposal MacIntyre is making should depend upon the classical liberal vision in which education holds the key. Clearly, MacIntyre is rather more of a liberal than he would dare to admit.[14]

Notes

1. Alasdair MacIntyre, *Whose Justice? Which Rationality?* London, Duckworth, 1988, p. 389.
2. *Ibid.* p. 355.
3. *Ibid.* p. 361.
4. *Ibid.* p. 362.
5. *Ibid.* p. 375ff.
6. *Ibid.* p. 366.
7. A MacIntyre. *Whose Justice?, op. cit.,* p. 7.
8. Some of these arguments can be found in the work of Gadamer. See *Truth and Method,* London, Sheed and Ward, 1975.
9. This concentrates on orthodox religious traditions, although there are some broader political and philosophical applications. Much of the argument is originally developed in my article, 'World perspectives and arguments: disagreements about disagreements,' *The Heythrop Journal,* 30, 1989, pp. 1–12.

10. St Thomas Aquinas, *Summa Theologiae,* volume 32, 2a2ae question 10, article 8. Translated by Thomas Gilby, London, Eyre and Spottiswood, 1975.
11. Commitment, in my judgment, is the major element involved in faith. However, faith will involve many practices, such as worship, which express this commitment and cannot simply be reduced to commitment. This paper, however, is concentrating on the problem of commitment and reason.
12. See my article, 'World perspectives and arguments: disagreements about disagreements,' *The Heythrop Journal,* 30, 1989, pp. 1–12.
13. Professor K Ward suggested this term.
14. I am especially grateful for the criticisms of Professors Ronald Atkinson and Keith Ward, and Canon Brian Hebblethwaite who will disagree with parts of the paper. All my colleagues at Exeter discussed various forms of this paper with me, however, Dr Alastair Logan was especially helpful. This paper was originally delivered at the American Academy of Religion Annual Meeting, Anaheim, California, 1989.

Select bibliography of journal articles on the aims, principles and philosophy of Christian education

* indicates that the piece is reprinted (in whole or part) in this volume.

Aldrich, R (1986) 'Learning by faith,' *Education Today*, 36, pp. 3–14.

Alexander, H A (1986) 'Elliot Eisner's artistic model of education,' *Religious Education*, 81, pp. 45–58.

Allen, R (1973) 'Emotion, religion and education,' *Proceedings of the Philosophy of Education Society of Great Britain*, 7, pp. 181–193 (with a reply by John Wilson, pp.195–203).

Allen, R T (1982) 'Rational autonomy: the destruction of freedom,' *Journal of Philosophy of Education*, 16, pp. 199–207.

Astley, J (1987) 'On learning religion: theological issues in Christian education,' *The Modern Churchman*, 29, pp. 26–34.*

Astley, J (1994) 'The place of understanding in Christian education and education about Christianity,' *British Journal of Religious Education*, 16, pp. 90–101.*

Brummelen, H van (1990) 'Tolerance in public and religiously based schools,' *Ethics in Education*, 9, pp. 8–11.

Callan, E (1985) 'McLaughlin on parental rights,' *Journal of Philosophy of Education*, 19, pp. 111–118.

Chazan, B (1972) '"Indoctrination" and religious education,' *Religious Education*, 67, pp. 243–252.

Cooling, T (1993) 'Professionalism, confessionalism and religious education: an exploration from the British context,' *Spectrum*, 25, pp. 129–145.*

Cox, E (1983) 'Understanding religion and religious understanding,' *British Journal of Religious Education*, 6, pp. 3–7, 13.

Crawford, M and Rossiter, G (1991) 'Teaching wisdom: religious teaching and the moral and spiritual development of young people,' *Journal of Christian Education*, 101, pp. 47–63.

Cully, I V (1967) 'Christian education: instruction or nurture,' *Religious Education*, 62, pp. 225–261.

Durka, G (1981) 'Christian nurture and critical openness: a Roman Catholic view from the United States,' *Lumen Vitae*, 36, pp. 263–286.

Dykstra, C (1981) 'Understanding the place of "understanding",' *Religious Education*, 76, pp. 187–194.

Dykstra, C (1987) 'The formative power of the congregation,' *Religious Education*, 82, pp. 530–546.

Elias, J L (1979) 'Evaluation and the future of religious education,' *Religious Education*, 74, pp. 656–667.

Elias, J L (1982) 'The three publics of religious educators,' *Religious Education*, 77, pp. 615–627.

Finlay, G (1987) 'A "Turangawaewae" for young Catholics: a case for tradition in religious education,' *Catholic School Studies*, 60, pp. 15–19.

Flew, A (1966) 'What is indoctrination?' *Studies in Philosophy and Education*, 4, pp. 281–306.

Francis, L J (1983) 'The logic of education, theology, and the church school,' *Oxford*

Review of Education, 9, pp. 147–162.

Freire, P (1984) 'Education, liberation and the church,' *Religious Education*, 79, pp. 524–545.

Gardner, P (1980) 'Religious education: in defence of non-commitment,' *Journal of Philosophy of Education*, 14, pp. 157–168.*

Gardner, P (1988) 'Religious upbringing and the liberal ideal of religious autonomy,' *Journal of Philosophy of Education*, 22, pp. 89–105.

Gardner, P (1991) 'Personal autonomy and religious upbringing: the problem,' *Journal of Philosophy of Education*, 25, pp. 69–81.

Gardner, P (1993) 'Should we teach children to be open-minded? Or, is the Pope open-minded about the existence of God?' *Journal of Philosophy of Education*, 27, pp. 39–43.

Groome, T H (1976) 'Shared Christian praxis: a possible theory/method of religious education,' *Lumen Vitae*, 31, pp. 186–208.*

Groome, T H (1977) 'The crossroads: a story of Christian education by shared praxis,' *Lumen Vitae*, 32, pp. 45–70.

Groome, T H (1977) 'A task of present dialectical hermeneutics,' *Living Light*, 14, pp. 408–423.

Groome, T H (1988) 'The spirituality of the religious educator,' *Religious Education*, 83, pp. 9–20.

Heywood, D (1988) 'Christian education as enculturation: the life of the community and its place in Christian education in the work of John H Westerhoff III,' *British Journal of Religious Education*, 10, pp. 65–71.

Hill, B V (1981) 'Teacher commitment and the ethics of teaching for commitment,' *Religious Education*, 76, pp. 322–336.*

Hill, B V (1990) 'A time to plant and a time to uproot: values education in the secondary school,' *Journal of Christian Education*, 97, pp. 5–22.

Hill, B V (1990) 'Will and should the religious studies appropriate to schools in a pluralistic society foster religious relativism?' *British Journal of Religious Education*, 12, pp. 126–136.*

Hirst, P H (1965) 'Morals, religion and the maintained school,' *British Journal of Educational Studies*, 14, pp. 5–18.

Hirst, P H (1970) 'Philosophy and religious education: a reply to D Z Phillips,' *British Journal of Educational Studies*, 18, pp. 213–215.

Hirst, P H (1972) 'Christian education: a contradiction in terms?' *Learning for Living*, 11, pp. 6–11.*

Hirst, P H (1981) 'Education, catechesis and the church school,' *British Journal of Religious Education*, 3, pp. 85–93, 101.

Holley, R (1971) 'Learning religion,' *Learning for Living*, 10, 4, pp.14–19.*

Hudson, W D (1982) 'The loneliness of the religious educator,' in J G Priestley (ed.), *Perspectives 9: Religion, Spirituality and Schools*, Exeter, University of Exeter School of Education, pp. 23–36.*

Hudson, W D (1982) 'Educating, socialising and indoctrination: a reply to Tasos Kazepides,' *Journal of Philosophy of Education*, 16, pp. 167–172.

Hull, J M (1972) 'Christian nurture and critical openness,' *Scottish Journal of Theology*, 25, pp. 20–32.

Hull, J M (1976) 'Christian theology and educational theory: can there be connections?' *British Journal of Educational Studies*, 24, pp. 127–143.*

Hull, J et al. (1981) *Understanding Christian Nurture*, London, British Council of Churches.*

Kay, W K and Hughes, F (1985) 'Christian light on education,' *Religious Education*, 80, pp. 51–63.

Kazepides, T (1987) 'Indoctrination, doctrines and the foundations of rationality,' *Philosophy of Education 1987: Proceedings of the Forty-third Annual Meeting of the Philosophy of Education Society,* Normal, Illinois, Philosophy of Education Society, pp. 229–240.*

Kazepides, T (1982) 'Educating, socialising and indoctrinating,' *Journal of Philosophy of Education*, 16, pp. 155–166.

Kazepides, T (1983) 'Is religious education possible? A rejoinder to W D Hudson,' *Journal of Philosophy of Education*, 17, pp. 259–265.

Laura, R S (1978) 'Philosophical foundations of religious education,' *Educational Theory*, 28, pp. 310–317.

Laura, R S (1983) 'To educate or to indoctrinate: that is still the question,' *Educational Philosophy and Theory*, 15, pp. 43–55.

Laura, R S and Leahy, M (1989) 'Religious upbringing and rational autonomy,' *Journal of Philosophy of Education*, 23, pp. 253–265.*

Laura, R S and McCarthy, D (1985) 'Religious education versus science education: on taking the dogma out of dogmas,' *Educational Research and Perspectives*, 12, pp. 3–9.

Leahy, M (1990) 'Indoctrination, evangelisation, catechesis and religious education,' *British Journal of Religious Education*, 12, pp. 137–144.*

MacIntyre, A (1985) 'Relativism, power and philosophy,' *Proceedings and Addresses of the American Philosophical Association*, 59, pp. 5–22.*

Markham, I (1991) 'Faith and reason: reflections on MacIntyre's "tradition-constituted enquiry",' *Religious Studies*, 27, pp. 259–267.*

Marthaler, B L (1987) 'Dilemma for religious educators: indoctrination or indifference,' *Religious Education*, 82, pp. 555–568.

Martin, D M (1987) 'Learning to become a Christian,' *Religious Education*, 82, pp. 94–114.*

McIntyre, J (undated) 'Multi-culture and multi-faith societies: some examinable assumptions,' *Occasional Paper 3*, Oxford, Farmington Institute.

McLaughlin, T H (1984) 'Parental rights and the religious upbringing of children,' *Journal of Philosophy of Education*, 18, pp. 75–83.*

McLaughlin, T H (1985) 'Religious upbringing and liberal values: a rejoinder to Eamonn Callan,' *Journal of Philosophy of Education*, 19, pp. 119–127.

McLaughlin, T H (1992) 'Fairness, controversiality and the common school,' *Spectrum*, 24, pp. 105–118.*

Meakin, D C (1979) 'The justification of religious education,' *British Journal of Religious Education*, 2, pp. 49–55.

Meakin D C (1988) 'The justification of religious education reconsidered,' *British Journal of Religious Education*, 10, pp. 92–96.

Melchert, C F (1974) 'Does the church really want religious education,' *Religious Education*, 69, pp. 12–22.

Melchert, C F (1977) 'What is religious education?' *Living Light*, 14, pp. 339–352.*

Melchert, C F (1978) 'What is the educational ministry of the church?' *Religious Education*, 73, pp. 429–439.

Melchert, C F (1981) '"Understanding" as a purpose of religious education,' *Religious Education*, 76, pp. 178–186.*

Miranda, E O y (1986) 'Some problems with the expression "Christian education",' *British Journal of Religious Education*, 8, pp. 94–102.*

Mitchell, B (1980) 'Faith and reason: a false antithesis,' *Religious Studies*, 16, pp. 131–144.*

Mitchell, B (1980) 'Religious Education,' *Oxford Review of Education*, 6, pp. 133-139.

Mitchell, B (1986) 'Being religiously educated,' in Joanna Yates (ed.), *Faith for the Future*, London, National Society/Church House Publishing, pp. 43–52.

Mitchell, P (1988) 'What is "curriculum"? Alternatives in Western historical perspective,' *Religious Education*, 83, pp. 349–366.

Moore, A J (1987) 'A social theory of religious education,' *Religious Education*, 82, pp. 415–425.

Moran, G (1977) 'Two languages of religious education,' *Living Light*, 14, pp. 7–15.*

Moran, G (1986) 'Interest in philosophy: three themes for religious education,' *Religious Education*, 81, pp. 424–445.

Neiman, A M (1989) 'Indoctrination: a contextualist approach,' *Educational Philosophy and Theory*, 21, pp. 53–61.

Nelson, C E (1972) 'Is church education something particular?' *Religious Education*, 67, pp. 5–16.

Nielsen, K (1984) 'On not being at sea about indoctrination,' *Interchange*, 15, pp. 68–73.

Nipkow, K E (1993) 'Oikumene: the global horizon for Christian and religious education,' *British Journal of Religious Education*, 15, pp. 5–11.

Phillips, D Z (1970) 'Philosophy and religious education,' *British Journal of Educational Studies*, 18, pp. 5–17.*

Ramsey, I T (1962) 'Christian education in the light of contemporary empiricism,' *Religious Education*, 57, pp. 95–96.

Rossiter, G (1982) 'The need for a "creative divorce" between catechesis and religious education in Catholic schools,' *Religious Education*, 77, pp. 21–40.

Rossiter, G (1986) 'The place of faith in classroom religious education,' *Catholic School Studies*, 59, pp. 49–55.

Scott, K (1984) 'Three traditions of religious education,' *Religious Education*, 79, pp. 323–339.*

Sealey, J (1979) 'Education as a second-order form of experience and its relation to religion,' *Journal of Philosophy of Education*, 13, pp. 83–90.*

Sealey, J (1979) 'Teaching "about" and teaching "what is" in religion,' *British Journal of Religious Education*, 2, pp. 56–60.

Slee, N (1989) 'Conflict and reconciliation between competing models of religious education: some reflections on the British scene,' *British Journal of Religious Education*, 11, pp. 126–135.

Snook, I A (1989) 'Contexts and essences: indoctrination revisited,' *Educational Philosophy and Theory*, 21, pp. 62–65.

Spiecker, B (1987) 'Indoctrination, intellectual virtues and rational emotions,' *Journal of Philosophy of Education*, 21, pp. 261–266.

Stannus, M H (1972) 'Knowledge of God: the paradox of Christian education,' *Educational Philosophy and Theory*, 4, pp. 29–46.

Thiessen, E J (1982) 'Indoctrination and doctrines,' *Journal of Philosophy of Education*, 16, pp. 3–17.*

Thiessen, E J (1984) 'Indoctrination and religious education,' *Interchange*, 15, pp. 27–43.

Thiessen, E J (1985) 'Initiation, indoctrination and education,' *Canadian Journal of Education*, 10, pp. 229–249.

Thiessen, E J (1985) 'A defense of a distinctively Christian curriculum,' *Religious Education*, 80, pp. 37–50.

Thiessen, E J (1987) 'Educational pluralism and tolerance,' *Journal of Educational Thought*, 21, pp. 71–87.

Thiessen, E J (1987) 'Two concepts or two phases of liberal education?' *Journal of Philosophy of Education*, 21, pp. 223–234.

Ward, K (1983) 'Is autonomy an educational ideal?' *Educational Analysis*, 5, pp. 47–55.

Warren, M (1987) 'Religious formation in the context of social formation,' *Religious Education*, 82, pp. 515–528.*

Warren, M (1993) 'Religious education and the task of cultural critique,' *Religious Education*, 88, pp. 68–79.

Watson, B (undated) 'Openness and commitment' (with a response by Edward Hulmes), *Occasional Papers 20*, Oxford, Farmington Institute.

Westerhoff, J H (1972) 'A call to catechesis (a response to Charles Melchert),' *Living Light*, 14, pp. 354–356.

Westerhoff, J H (1978) 'A necessary paradox: catechesis and evangelism, nurture and conversion,' *Religious Education*, 73, pp. 409–416.

Westerhoff, J H (1987) 'Formation, education, instruction,' *Religious Education*, 82, 1987, pp. 578–591.*

White, F C (1982) 'Knowledge and relativism I,' *Educational Philosophy and Theory*, 14, 1, pp. 1–13.

White, F C (1982) 'Knowledge and relativism II,' *Educational Philosophy and Theory*, 14, 2, pp. 1–13.

Wilhoit, J (1984) 'The impact of the social sciences on religious education,' *Religious Education*, 79, pp. 367–375.

Wilson, J (undated) *Approach to religious education*, Oxford, Farmington Trust.

Wilson, J (1976) 'Taking religious education seriously,' *Learning for Living*, 16, pp. 18–24.*

Wingeier, D E (1972) 'Christian education as faith translation,' *Living Light*, 14, pp. 393–406.*

Acknowledgements

The publisher and editors would like to acknow·edge the following permissions to reproduce copyright material. All possible attempts have been made to contact copyright holders and to acknowledge their copyright correctly. We are grateful to: *British Journal of Educational Studies*, for D Z Phillips, 'Philosophy and religious education,' 18, 5–17, 1970, for J M Hull, 'Christian theology and educational theory: can there be connections?' 24, 127–143, 1976; *British Journal of Religious Education*, for E Orteza y Miranda, 'Some problems with the expression "Christian education",' 8, 94–102, 1986, for B V Hill, 'Will and should the religious studies appropriate to schools in a pluralistic society foster religious relativism?' 12, 126–136, 1990, for M Leahy, 'Indoctrination, evangelisation, catechesis and religious education,' 12, 137–144, 1990, for J Astley, 'The place of understanding in Christian education and education about Christianity,' 16, 90–101, 1994; *Journal of Philosophy of Education*, for J Sealey, 'Education as a second–order form of experience and its relation to religion,' 13, 83–90, 1979, for P Gardner, 'Religious education: in defence of non-commitment,' 14, 157–167, 1980, for E J Thiessen, 'Indoctrination and doctrines,' 16, 3–17, 1982, for T H McLaughlin, 'Parental rights and the religious upbringing of children,' 18, 75–83, 1984, for R S Laura and M Leahy, 'Religious upbringing and rational autonomy,' 23, 253–265, 1989; *Learning for Living*, for R Holley, 'Learning religion,' 10, 4, 14–19, 1971, for P H Hirst, 'Christian education: a contradiction in terms?' 11, 4, 6–11, 1972, for J Wilson, 'Taking religious education seriously,' 16, 1, 18–24, 1976; *Living Light*, for G Moran, 'Two languages of religious education,' 14, 7-15, 1977, for C F Melchert, 'What is religious education?' 14, 337–352, 1977, for D E Wingeier, 'Christian education as faith translation,' 14, 393–423, 1977; *Lumen Vitae,* for T Groome, 'Shared Christian praxis: a possible theory/method of religious education,' 31, 186–208, 1976; *Panorama*, for T Cooling, 'Professionalism, confessionalism and religious education: an exploration from the British context,' 5, 1, in press; *Perspectives*, for W D Hudson, 'The loneliness of the religious educator,' 9, 23–36, 1982; *Philosophy of Education*, for T Kazepides, 'Indoctrination, doctrines and the foundations of rationality,' from the Proceedings of the forty-third annual meeting of the Philosophy of Education Society, 229-240, 1987; *Proceedings and Addresses of the American Philosophical Association*, for A MacIntyre, 'Relativism, power and philosophy,' 59, 1, 5–22; *Religious Education*, for C F Melchert, '"Understanding" as a purpose of religious education,' 76, 178–186, 1981, for B V Hill, 'Teacher commitment and the ethics of teaching for commitment,' 76, 322–336, 1981, for K Scott, 'Three traditions of religious education,' 79, 323–339, 1984, for D M Martin, 'Learning to become a Christian,' 82, 94–114, 1987, for M Warren, 'Religious formation in the context of social formation,' 82, 515–528, 1987, for J Westerhoff, 'Formation, education, instruction,' 82, 578–591, 1987 (*Religious Education* is published by the Religious Education Association, 409 Prospect Street, New Haven, CT 06511–2177 USA, Membership information available upon request); *Religious Studies*, for B Mitchell, 'Faith and reason: a false antithesis?' 16, 131–144, 1980, for I Markham, 'Faith and reason: reflections on MacIntyre's "tradition-constituted enquiry",' 27, 259–267, 1991; *Spectrum*, for T H McLaughlin, 'Fairness, controversiality and the common school,' 24, 105-118, 1992, for T Cooling, 'Professionalism, confessionalism and religious education: an exploration from the British context,' 25, 129–145, 1993; The Council of Churches for Britain and Ireland, for J M Hull *et al*, 'Critical openness in Christian nurture,' adapted from *Understanding Christian Nurture*, British Council of Churches, 1981, pp. 4–31, and reprinted as part two of *The Child in the Church*, British Council of Churches, 1984.

Index of subjects

Index of names